Houghton
Mifflin
Harcourt

Texas
Environmental
Science

Heithaus • Arms

ABOUT THE COVER

Honeybees (*Apis mellifera*) provide valuable ecosystem services, including crop pollination and honey production. Researchers use a variety of tools to track honeybees, from simple numbered tags to RFID (radio frequency identification) tags.

Photo Credits

Cover, title page: *honeycomb* ©Brian Hagiwara/Foodpix/Getty Images; *bees* ©Old Dog Photography/Flickr/Getty Images; *tree* ©Douglas Waters/The Image Bank/Getty Images.

Cover: *rain forest* ©altrendo nature/Getty Images; *turtles* ©Flickr/Getty Images; *greenhouse* ©Nigel Cattlin/Photo Researchers, Inc.; *arctic* ©Arctic-Images/The Image Bank/Getty Images; *storm chaser* ©Ryan McGinnis/Flickr Select/Getty Images.

Text Credits

Lippincott Williams & Wilkins: Adaptation of "Figure 4: Environmental portion of disease in the major world regions" (retitled "Poor Health by World Region") by Kirk R. Smith from "How Much Global Ill Health Is Attributable to Environmental Factors?" by Kirk R. Smith, Carlos F. Corvalán, and Tord Kjellström from *Epidemiology,* vol. 10, no. 5, September 1999, pp. 573–584. Copyright ©1999 by Epidemiology Resources Inc.

United Nations Population Fund (UNPFA): From "Women and the Environment" from *The State of the World Population 2001,* edited by Alex Marshall. Copyright ©2001 by UNPFA.

AUTHORS

Michael R. Heithaus, Ph.D.
Executive Director, School of Environment, Arts, and Society
Associate Professor, Department of Biological Sciences
  Florida International University
  North Miami, Florida

Mike Heithaus received his Ph.D. in Biological Sciences from Simon Fraser University. He is now the Executive Director of Florida International University's School of Environment, Arts, and Society, which brings together the natural and social sciences and humanities to develop solutions to today's environmental challenges. His research, conducted mainly in Western Australia and south Florida, focuses on predator-prey interactions, including the ecological role of large-bodied predators and herbivores in marine ecosystems. He uses his work to help develop plans for marine conservation. In addition to his research, Dr. Heithaus has worked to bring science and nature to the public through documentary films on the Discovery Channel and the National Geographic Channel, as well as special video projects for the classroom.

Karen Arms, Ph.D., J.D.

Karen Arms received her Ph.D. in molecular biology from Oxford University and a doctor of law from Cornell University. She was an assistant professor of biology at Cornell University, where she taught introductory biology and courses in science and society. She also taught marine biology at the University of Georgia Marine Biology Station and introductory biology at South College in Savannah, Georgia. In addition to *Holt Environmental Science,* Dr. Arms is the author of several college-level biology textbooks. Her interest in and concern for the environment led her to form an ecotourism organization that introduces people to the ecosystems of the southeastern coast.

ACKNOWLEDGMENTS

Contributing Writer

E. Raymond Heithaus
Philip and Sheila Jordan Professor of Environmental Science & Biology
Kenyon College
Gambier, Ohio

Safety Reviewer

Jack Gerlovich, Ph.D.
Associate Professor
School of Education
Drake University
Des Moines, Iowa

Academic Reviewers

Jess F. Adkins, Ph.D.
Assistant Professor of Geochemistry and Global Environmental Science
Division of Geological and Planetary Sciences
California Institute of Technology
Pasadena, California

Foster K. Amey, Ph.D.
Associate Professor of Sociology
Department of Sociology and Anthropology
Middle Tennessee State University
Murfreesboro, Tennessee

Mead Allison, Ph.D.
Associate Professor
Department of Geology and Earth Sciences
Tulane University
New Orleans, Louisiana

David M. Armstrong, Ph.D.
Professor
Environmental, Population, and Organismic Biology
University of Colorado
Boulder, Colorado

Paul D. Asimow, Ph.D.
Associate Professor of Geology and Geochemistry
Division of Geological and Planetary Sciences
California Institute of Technology
Pasadena, California

Nolan B. Aughenbaugh, Ph.D.
Professor
Department of Geology and Geological Engineering
University of Mississippi
University, Mississippi

Janice L. Branson
Assistant Professor
School of Agriculture
Tennessee Technological University
Cookeville, Tennessee

Gary Campbell, Ph.D.
Professor of Mineral Economics
School of Business and Economics
Michigan Technological University
Houghton, Michigan

Laura Chenault, D.V.M.
Bulverde, Texas

Marian R. Chertow, Ph.D.
Assistant Professor of Industrial Environmental Management
Yale School of Forestry and Environmental Studies
Yale University
New Haven, Connecticut

Susan L. Cutter, Ph.D.
Carolina Distinguished Professor
Department of Geography
University of South Carolina
Columbia, South Carolina

Susan B. Dickey, R.N., Ph.D.
Associate Professor
Pediatric Nursing
Temple University
Philadelphia, Pennsylvania

Dale Elifrits, Ph.D.
Professor
Department of Physics and Geology
Northern Kentucky University
Highland Heights, Kentucky

Turgay Ertekin, Ph.D.
George E. Trimble Chair in Earth and Mineral Sciences
Professor of Petroleum and Natural Gas Engineering
Department of Energy and Geo-Environmental Engineering
Pennsylvania State University
University Park, Pennsylvania

Ronald A. Feldman, Ph.D.
Ruth Harris Ottman Centennial Professor for the Advancement of Social Work Education
Director, Center for the Study of Social Work Practice
Columbia University
New York, New York

Linda Gaul, Ph.D.
Epidemiologist
Texas Department of Health
Austin, Texas

Matthew R. Gilligan, Ph.D.
Professor and Program Coordinator, Marine Sciences
Department of Natural Sciences and Mathematics
Savannah State University
Savannah, Georgia

Deborah Jean Gochfeld, Ph.D.
Senior Scientist
National Center for Natural Products Research
University of Mississippi
University, Mississippi

John Goodge, Ph.D.
Associate Professor of Geology
Southern Methodist University
Dallas, Texas

Mary L. Haasch, Ph.D.
NRC Senior Scientist
U.S. Environmental Protection Agency
Duluth, Minnesota

David Haig, Ph.D.
Associate Professor of Biology
Department of Organismic and Evolutionary Biology
Harvard University
Cambridge, Massachusetts

Vicki Hansen, Ph.D.
Professor of Geological Sciences
Department of Geology
Southern Methodist University
Dallas, Texas

Rosalind Harris, Ph.D.
Professor, Rural Agriculture
Department of Sociology
University of Kentucky
Lexington, Kentucky

Richard Hey, Ph.D.
Professor of Geophysics
School of Ocean and Earth Sciences Technology
University of Hawaii
Honolulu, Hawaii

James C. Hower, Ph.D.
Editor-in-Chief
International Journal of Coal Geology
Senior Scientist
Center for Applied Energy Research
University of Kentucky
Lexington, Kentucky

Steven A. Jennings, Ph.D.
Associate Professor of Geography
Department of Geography and
Environmental Studies
University of Colorado
Colorado Springs, Colorado

Elizabeth W. Kleppinger, Ph.D.
Adjunct Professor
Department of Chemistry
Eastern Kentucky University
Richmond, Kentucky

Joel Leventhal, Ph.D.
Emeritus Scientist
U.S. Geological Survey and Diversified
Geochemistry
Lakewood, Colorado

Alex Mills, Ph.D.
University of Toronto
Toronto, Ontario, Canada

Joann Mossa, Ph.D.
Associate Professor
Department of Geography
University of Florida
Gainesville, Florida

Gary Mueller, Ph.D.
Associate Professor of Nuclear Engineering
Department of Engineering
University of Missouri
Rolla, Missouri

Barbara Murck, Ph.D.
Director, Environmental Programs
University of Toronto
Mississauga, Ontario, Canada

Emily Niemeyer, Ph.D.
Assistant Professor of Chemistry
Department of Chemistry
Southwestern University
Georgetown, Texas

Bryan Norton, Ph.D.
Professor
School of Public Policy
Georgia Institute of Technology
Atlanta, Georgia

Eva Oberdörster, Ph.D.
Lecturer
Department of Biological Sciences
Southern Methodist University
Dallas, Texas

Hilary Olson, Ph.D.
Research Scientist
Institute of Geophysics
The University of Texas
Austin, Texas

Ken Peace, C.C.E.
Geology Supervisor
Ark Land Company
St. Louis, Missouri

Per F. Peterson, Ph.D.
Professor and Chair
Department of Nuclear Engineering
University of California
Berkeley, California

David Pimentel, Ph.D.
Professor and Agricultural Ecologist
Department of Entomology,
Systematics and Ecology
Cornell University
Ithaca, New York

Mary M. Poulton, Ph.D.
*Department Head and Associate Professor
of Geological Engineering*
Department of Mining and Geological
Engineering
University of Arizona
Tucson, Arizona

Barron Rector, Ph.D.
*Associate Professor and Extension Range
Specialist*
Texas Agricultural Extension Service
Texas A&M University
College Station, Texas

Steven Richard Reese, Ph.D.
Director, Radiation Center Instructor
Department of Nuclear Engineering
and Radiation Health Physics
Oregon State University
Corvallis, Oregon

Dork Sahagian, Ph.D.
*Research Professor, Stratigraphy and Basin
Analysis, Geodynamics*
Global Analysis, Interpretation, and
Modeling Program
University of New Hampshire
Durham, New Hampshire

Miles Silman, Ph.D.
Associate Professor of Biology
Department of Biology
Wake Forest University
Winston-Salem, North Carolina

Marc Slattery, Ph.D.
*Division Director, NIUST Ocean
Biotechnology Center and Repository*
Department of Pharmacognosy
University of Mississippi
University, Mississippi

Spencer Steinberg, Ph.D.
*Associate Professor, Environmental Organic
Chemistry*
Chemistry Department
University of Nevada
Las Vegas, Nevada

Richard Storey, Ph.D.
Dean of the Faculty and Professor of Biology
Colorado College
Colorado Springs, Colorado

Ramesh Teegavarapu, Ph.D., P.E.
Assistant Professor (Adjunct)
Department of Civil Engineering
Assistant Director
Kentucky Water Resources Research
Institute
University of Kentucky
Lexington, Kentucky

Martin VanDyke, Ph.D.
Professor of Chemistry, Emeritus
Front Range Community College
Westminster, Colorado

Judith Weis, Ph.D.
Professor of Biology
Department of Biological Sciences
Rutgers University
Newark, New Jersey

Elizabeth Wenk, Ph.D.
Adjunct Faculty
Department of Science
Cerro Coso Community College
Bishop, California

Mary Wicksten, Ph.D.
Professor of Biology
Department of Biology
Texas A&M University
College Station, Texas

ACKNOWLEDGMENTS, continued

Teacher Reviewers

Robert Akeson
Science Teacher
Boston Latin School
Boston, Massachusetts

Dan Aude
Magnet Programs Coordinator
Montgomery Public Schools
Montgomery, Alabama

Lowell Bailey
Science Teacher
Bedford North Lawrence High School
Bedford, Indiana

Robert Baronak
Biology Teacher
Donegal High School
Mount Joy, Pennsylvania

Michele Benn
Science Teacher
Beaver Falls High School
Beaver Falls, Pennsylvania

David Blinn
Secondary Sciences Teacher
Wrenshall High School
Wrenshall, Minnesota

Bart Bookman
Science Teacher
Stevenson High School
Bronx, New York

Daniel Bugenhagen
Science Teacher
Yutan Community School
Yutan, Nebraska

Robert Chandler
Science Teacher
Soddy-Daisy High School
Soddy-Daisy, Tennessee

Johanna Chase, C.H.E.S.
Health Educator
California State University
Dominguez Hills, California

Cindy Copolo, Ph.D.
Science Specialist
Summit Solutions
Bahama, North Carolina

Linda Culp
Science Teacher
Thorndale High School
Thorndale, Texas

Katherine Cummings
Science Teacher
Currituck County
Currituck, North Carolina

Alonda Droege
Science Teacher
Evergreen High School
Seattle, Washington

Richard Filson
Science Teacher
Edison High School
Stockton, California

Randa Flinn
Science Teacher
Northeast High School
Fort Lauderdale, Florida

Jane Frailey
Science Coordinator
Hononegah High School
Hononegah, Illinois

Art Goldsmith
Biology and Earth Sciences Teacher
Hallandale High School
Hallandale, Florida

Sharon Harris
Science Teacher
Mother of Mercy High School
Cincinnati, Ohio

Carolyn Hayes
Honors Biology and Environmental Science Teacher
Center Grove High School
Greenwood, Indiana

Stacey Jeffress
Environmental Science Teacher
El Dorado High School
El Dorado, Arkansas

Donald R. Kanner
Physics Instructor
Lane Technical High School
Chicago, Illinois

Edward Keller
Science Teacher
Morgantown High School
Morgantown, West Virginia

Kathy LaRoe
Science Teacher
St. Paul School District
St. Paul, Nebraska

Clifford Lerner
Biology Teacher
Keene High School
Keene, New Hampshire

Stewart Lipsky
Science Teacher
Seward Park High School
New York, New York

Mike Lubich
Science Teacher
Mapletown High School
Greensboro, Pennsylvania

Thomas Manerchia
Environmental Science Teacher, Retired
Archmere Academy
Claymont, Delaware

Tammie Niffenegger
Science Chair and Science Teacher
Port Washington High School
Waldo, Wisconsin

Gabriele DeBear Paye
Science and Environmental Technology Lead Teacher
West Roxbury High School
West Roxbury, Massachusetts

Denice Sandefur
Fire Ecology and Science Teacher
Nucla High School
Nucla, Colorado

Jennifer M. Fritz
Science Teacher
North Springs High School
Atlanta, Georgia

Dyanne Semerjibashian, Ph.D.
Science Teacher
Pflugerville High School
Pflugerville, Texas

Bert Sherwood
Science/Health Specialist
Socorro Independent School District
El Paso, Texas

Dan Trockman
Science Teacher
Hopkins High School
Minnetonka, Minnesota

Jim Watson
Science Teacher
Dalton High School
Dalton, Georgia

Holt McDougal
ENVIRONMENTAL SCIENCE

Yes, it's educational.
No, it's not boring.

Student One Stop

With this convenient DVD, you can carry your textbook in your pocket, along with printable copies of all labs and worksheets.

Online Environmental Science

You'll have access to all program resources at HMDScience.com. In addition to your textbook, you'll find enhanced analysis tools, including the Smart Grapher. Get your hands on Virtual Investigations, Concept Maps, FoldNote animations, and a variety of lab activities.

Textbook

Explore the world around you with pages of colorful photos, helpful illustrations, exciting Case Studies, and hands-on activities using everyday materials. Learn

Look for
ONLINE ENVIRONMENTAL SCIENCE
links throughout the book!

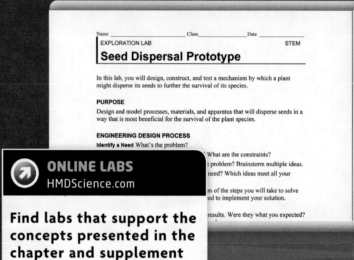

Name _____ Class _____ Date _____
EXPLORATION LAB   STEM
Seed Dispersal Prototype

In this lab, you will design, construct, and test a mechanism by which a plant
might disperse its seeds to further the survival of its species.

PURPOSE

Design and model processes, materials, and apparatus that will disperse seeds in a
way that is most beneficial for the survival of the plant species.

ENGINEERING DESIGN PROCESS

Identify a Need What's the problem?

What are the constraints?
problem? Brainstorm multiple ideas.
need? Which ideas meet all your

of the steps you will take to solve
to implement your solution.

results. Were they what you expected?

ONLINE LABS
HMDScience.com

Find labs that support the concepts presented in the chapter and supplement the labs in your textbook.

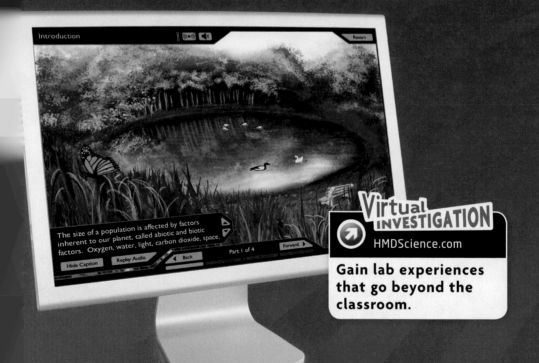

Introduction

The size of a population is affected by factors inherent to our planet, called abiotic and biotic factors. Oxygen, water, light, carbon dioxide, space,

Hide Caption   Replay Audio   Back   Part 1 of 4   Forward

Virtual INVESTIGATION
HMDScience.com

Gain lab experiences that go beyond the classroom.

ECOZINE
HMDScience.com

Stay current with environmental science—related news from around the world. Get the latest updates on all chapter features and share your opinions with other students across the globe!

Look for

LABS ONLINE ↗

↗ HMDScience.com

QuickLab

Complete this easy activity in less than one class period.

Field Activity

Observe and apply a subject in a real-world setting.

STEM Lab

Utilize technology and engineering through hands-on projects.

Exploration Lab

Explore a situation or phenomenon to improve your understanding.

Inquiry Lab

Develop and perform your own procedure, often using a real-life example.

Probeware Lab

Integrate data-collection technology to generate more information and perform deeper analyses.

Other lab types include
- Data Analysis
- Environmental Engineering
- Observation
- Simulation

Exploration Lab
Designing a Hydroponic Garden
RESEARCH

Agricultural land on Earth is decreasing rapidly as the human population puts increased pressures on land. The need to feed an ever-increasing human population has also led to farming practices that promote soil erosion, intensify desertification, and reduce soil fertility. Researchers are investigating new ideas for efficient ways to feed the global population with an increasingly limited growing environment. One way to expand our food resources is to use soil-free farming, or hydroponics. In hydroponics, plants are suspended in a soil-free medium and fed a special solution containing all the nutrients necessary for growth. In this activity, you will have the opportunity to research, design, and build your own hydroponic garden.

OBJECTIVES

Design, build, and **grow** a hydroponic garden.

Observe and describe plant growth in the hydroponic garden.

Evaluate the problems encountered and offer solutions for correcting those problems.

MATERIALS

- aquarium air pump (to provide air for plant roots)
- books and other reference materials on hydroponic gardening
- non-soil growing media (such as vermiculite, perlite, peat moss, or sodium polyacrylate)
- hydroponic nutrient solution or general purpose fertilizer
- mask for breathing protection
- pH indicator paper or solution (such as bromthymol blue)
- pH adjusting solutions (such as pH Plus or pH Minus)
- plant seeds or young seedlings (12)
- plastic plant containers, 8 cm dia. (12)
- plastic plant tray
- self-supporting light fixture

Procedure
PART I—DESIGN PROPOSAL

CONTENTS IN BRIEF

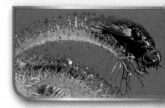

CONTENTS

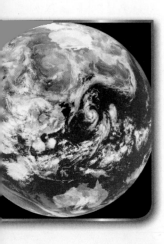

EARTH SCIENCE CONNECTION — This content correlates to common Earth Science standards.

(cr) ©A. Cosmos Blank/Photo Researchers, Inc.; (tr) ©Photodisc/Getty Images

Sunlight

LITTORAL ZONE

BENTHIC ZONE

Decomposers

Phytoplankton and zooplankton

EARTH SCIENCE CONNECTION — This content correlates to common Earth Science standards.

(cl) ©Marty Snyderman/Corbis; (tl) ©Photo Researchers, Inc.; (bc) ©Scimat/Photo Researchers, Inc.; (br) ©M. I. Walker/Photo Researchers, Inc.

UNIT 3 | POPULATIONS

UNIT 4 | WATER, AIR, AND LAND

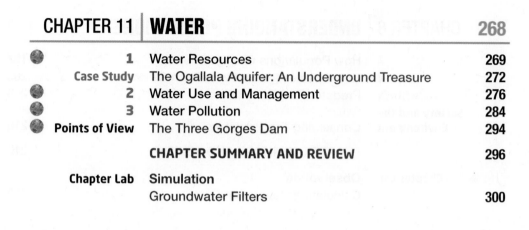

⬤ **EARTH SCIENCE CONNECTION** — This content correlates to common Earth Science standards.

(t) ©Ralph A. Clevenger/Corbis; (b) ©NASA; (c) ©Deborah Davis/Getty Images

UNIT 5 | MINERAL AND ENERGY RESOURCES

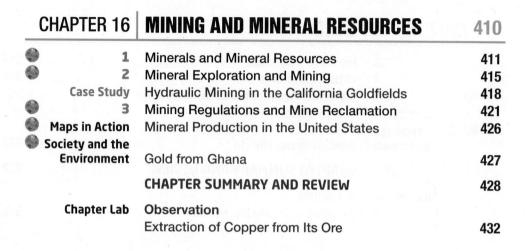

🌐 **EARTH SCIENCE CONNECTION** — This content correlates to common Earth Science standards.

(tl) ©Dale O'Dell/Alamy Images; (cl) ©Accent Alaska.com/Alamy Images; (b) ©Corbis

UNIT 6 | OUR HEALTH AND OUR FUTURE

STUDENT RESOURCES

● **EARTH SCIENCE CONNECTION** — This content correlates to common Earth Science standards.

CHAPTER LABS

EXPLORATIONLABS

INQUIRYLABS

QUICKLABS

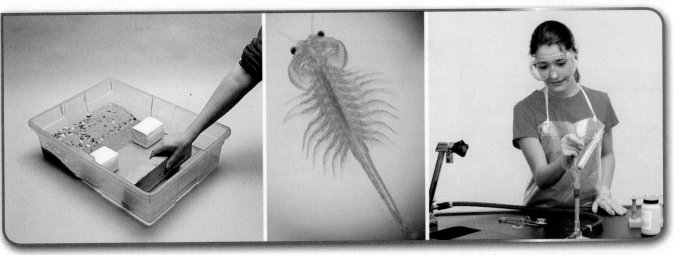

Making a Difference

Maps in Action

Points of View

Society and the Environment

CASE STUDIES

The following safety symbols will appear in this text when you are asked to perform a procedure requiring extra precautions. Once you have familiarized yourself with these safety symbols, turn to Appendix A for safety guidelines to use in all your laboratory work in environmental science.

 EYE PROTECTION

- Wear safety goggles when working around chemicals, acids, bases, flames, or heating devices. Contents under pressure may become projectiles and cause serious injury.
- Never look directly at the sun through any optical device or use direct sunlight to illuminate a microscope.
- Avoid wearing contact lenses in the lab.
- If any substance gets into your eyes, notify your instructor immediately and flush your eyes with running water for at least 15 minutes.

 CLOTHING PROTECTION

- Secure loose clothing and remove dangling jewelry. Do not wear open-toed shoes or sandals in the lab.
- Wear an apron or lab coat to protect your clothing when you are working with chemicals.
- If a spill gets on your clothing, rinse it off immediately with water for at least 5 minutes while notifying your instructor.

 CAUSTIC SUBSTANCES

- If a chemical gets on your skin, on your clothing, or in your eyes, rinse the area immediately and alert your instructor.
- If a chemical is spilled on the floor or lab bench, alert your instructor but do not clean it up yourself unless your instructor directs you to do so.

 CHEMICAL SAFETY

- Always use caution when working with chemicals.
- Always wear appropriate protective equipment. Always wear eye goggles, gloves, and a lab apron or lab coat when you are working with any chemical or chemical solution.
- Never mix chemicals unless your instructor directs you to do so.
- Never taste, touch, or smell chemicals unless your instructor directs you to do so.
- Add an acid or base to water; never add water to an acid or base.
- Never return an unused chemical to its original container.
- Never transfer substances by sucking on a pipet or straw; use a suction bulb.
- Follow instructions for proper disposal.

 ANIMAL SAFETY

- Always obtain permission before bringing any animal to school.
- Handle animals carefully and respectfully.
- Wash your hands thoroughly after handling any animal.

 PLANT SAFETY

- Wear disposable polyethylene gloves when handling any wild plant.
- Do not eat any part of a plant or plant seed used in the lab.
- Wash hands thoroughly after handling any part of a plant.
- When outdoors, do not pick any wild plants unless your instructor directs you to do so.

ELECTRICAL SAFETY

- Do not place electrical cords in walking areas or let cords hang over a table edge in a way that could cause equipment to fall if the cord is accidentally pulled.
- Do not use equipment that has frayed electrical cords or loose plugs.
- Be sure that equipment is in the "off" position before you plug it in.
- Never use an electrical appliance around water or with wet hands or clothing.
- Be sure to turn off and unplug electrical equipment when you are finished using it.

 ## HEATING SAFETY

- Avoid wearing hair spray or hair gel on lab days.
- Whenever possible, use an electric hot plate instead of an open flame as a heat source.
- When heating materials in a test tube, always angle the test tube away from yourself and others.
- Glass containers used for heating should be made of heat-resistant glass.

 ## SHARP OBJECTS

- Use knives and other sharp instruments with extreme care.
- Never cut objects while holding them in your hands. Place objects on a suitable work surface for cutting.
- Never use a double-edged razor in the lab.

 ## HAND SAFETY

- To avoid burns, wear heat-resistant gloves whenever instructed to do so.
- Always wear protective gloves when working with an open flame, chemicals, solutions, or wild or unknown plants.
- If you do not know whether an object is hot, do not touch it.
- Use tongs when heating test tubes. Never hold a test tube in your hand to heat the test tube.

 ## FIRE SAFETY

- Know the location of laboratory fire extinguishers and fire-safety blankets.
- Know your school's fire-evacuation routes.

 ## GAS SAFETY

- Do not inhale any gas or vapor unless your instructor directs you to do so. Do not breathe pure gases.
- Handle materials prone to emit vapors or gases in a well-ventilated area. This work should be done in an approved chemical fume hood.

 ## GLASSWARE SAFETY

- Check the condition of glassware before and after using it. Inform your teacher of any broken, chipped, or cracked glassware, because it should not be used.
- Do not pick up broken glass with your bare hands. Place broken glass in a specially designated disposal container.

 ## WASTE DISPOSAL

- Clean and decontaminate all work surfaces and personal protective equipment as directed by your instructor.
- Dispose of all broken glass, contaminated sharp objects, and other contaminated materials (biological and chemical) in special containers as directed by your instructor.

 ## HYGIENIC CARE/CLEAN HANDS

- Keep your hands away from your face and mouth.
- Always wash your hands thoroughly when you have finished with an experiment.

©blickwinkel/Alamy

Introduction to Environmental Science

Once hatched, these perch will continuously pump water through the mouth and over the gill arches to breathe, which makes them vulnerable to pollutants in their environment. Scientists monitor fish and amphibian species to determine the effects of pollution on the world's ecosystems.

(t) ©Michael Melford/Getty Images; (b) ©Earth Imaging/Stone/Getty Images; (c) ©Charlotte Main/Photo Researchers, Inc.

CHAPTER 1

Section 1
Understanding Our Environment

Section 2
The Environment and Society

Why It Matters

A biologist uses an aerial tramway to survey the rain forest canopy in Costa Rica.

Many plants found in the canopy ecosystem seem better adapted for life in the desert than in the rain forest. Why?

CASESTUDY

Learn more about the delicate balance in an ecosystem and the ways humans can both harm and help an ecosystem in the case study Dam Removal on the Penobscot River on pages 12–13.

ONLINE ENVIRONMENTAL SCIENCE
HMDScience.com

Go online to access additional resources, including labs, worksheets, multimedia, and resources in Spanish.

Science and the Environment

4

©Michael Melford/Getty Images

Understanding Our Environment

When someone mentions the term *environment*, some people think of a beautiful scene, such as a stream flowing through a wilderness area or a rain forest canopy alive with blooming flowers and howling monkeys. You might not think of your backyard or neighborhood as part of the environment. In fact, the environment is everything around us. It includes the natural world as well as things produced by humans. But the environment is also more than what you can see—it is a complex web of relationships that connects us with the world we live in.

What Is Environmental Science?

There is a growing need to understand the environment as a whole, including both its biological and physical features. A wide variety of people contribute to this understanding of the environment, including high school students. In the 1990s, students from Keene High School in **Figure 1.1** studied dwarf wedge mussels in the Ashuelot River of New Hampshire. The mussels, which were once abundant in the river, were in danger of disappearing, and the students wanted to know why. The students tested water samples from different parts of the river, conducted experiments, and asked questions.

The students' efforts were highly praised and widely recognized. More importantly, their work contributed to an ongoing community effort that still works toward the preservation of the endangered dwarf wedge mussel. The students' work is just one example of a field called **environmental science,** the study of the environment that includes the physical, biological, and social sciences.

SECTION 1

Objectives

▶ Define *environmental science*, and compare environmental science with ecology.

▶ List the five major fields of study that contribute to environmental science.

▶ Describe the major environmental effects of hunter-gatherers, the agricultural revolution, and the Industrial Revolution.

▶ Distinguish between renewable and nonrenewable resources.

▶ Classify environmental problems into three major categories.

Key Terms

environmental science
ecology
agriculture
natural resource
pollution
biodiversity

FIGURE 1.1

Student Scientists These students are counting the dwarf wedge mussels in part of the Ashuelot River.

FIGURE 1.2

Environmental Scientists
Scientists from a variety of fields use different methods to study how humans interact with and impact the environment.

Connect to HISTORY

Rachel Carson

Alarmed by the increasing levels of pesticides and other chemicals in the environment, biologist Rachel Carson published *Silent Spring* in 1962. Carson imagined a spring morning that was silent because the birds and frogs were dead after being poisoned by pesticides. Carson's carefully researched book was enthusiastically received by the public and was read by many other scientists, as well as policy makers and politicians. However, many people in the chemical industry saw *Silent Spring* as a threat to their pesticide sales and launched a $250,000 campaign to discredit Carson. Carson's research prevailed, although she died in 1964—unaware that the book she had written was instrumental in the birth of the modern environmental movement.

CHECK FOR UNDERSTANDING

Compare How is ecology related to environmental science?

The Goals of Environmental Science

Environmental scientists have found that the environment is influenced by people and that people are influenced by the environment. A major goal of many environmental scientists is to understand and solve environmental problems. To address this goal, environmental scientists study two main types of interactions between humans and the environment. One area of study focuses on how we use natural resources, such as water and plants. The other area of study focuses on how our actions alter our environment. Environmental scientists must gather and analyze information from many different disciplines. Even though environmental scientists want to solve environmental problems, they are not the same as environmentalists. Scientists study the environment to accurately describe environmental systems and determine how they work. Scientists also can use data and mathematical models to predict how systems might change under different scenarios. It is up to the public, special interest groups, and politicians to make decisions about how to manage the environment. Environmentalism is a social movement that seeks to protect the environment and, because we all depend on the environment, people.

Many Fields of Study

Environmental science is an interdisciplinary science, which means it involves many fields of study. **Ecology** is the study of how living things interact with each other and with their nonliving environment. Chemistry helps us understand how organic matter is transformed and the nature of pollutants. Geology helps us model how water and air move around the globe. Botany and zoology provide information needed to preserve species. Paleontology, the study of fossils, helps us understand how Earth's climate has changed in the past. Using such information about the past can help us predict how future climate changes could affect life on Earth. Often, teams of environmental scientists work together to understand and solve environmental problems.

Studying the environment also involves studying human populations. Environmental scientists may use the social sciences, which include economics, law, politics, and geography. Social sciences can help us answer questions such as How does human migration from rural to urban areas affect the local environment? Or how can economic incentives change people's decisions to protect the environment? **Figure 1.3** lists some of the major fields of study that contribute to the study of environmental science.

FIGURE 1.3

MAJOR FIELDS OF STUDY THAT CONTRIBUTE TO ENVIRONMENTAL SCIENCE

Biology is the study of living organisms.	**Zoology** is the study of animals. **Botany** is the study of plants. **Microbiology** is the study of microorganisms. **Ecology** is the study of how organisms interact with their environment and each other.
Earth science is the study of Earth's nonliving systems and the planet as a whole.	**Geology** is the study of Earth's surface, interior processes, and history. **Paleontology** is the study of fossils and ancient life. **Climatology** is the study of Earth's atmosphere and climate. **Hydrology** is the study of Earth's water resources.
Physics is the study of matter and energy.	**Engineering** is the science by which matter and energy are made useful to humans in structures, machines, and products.
Chemistry is the study of chemicals and their interactions.	**Biochemistry** is the study of the chemistry of living things. **Geochemistry**, a branch of geology, is the study of the chemistry of materials such as rocks, soil, and water.
Social sciences are the study of human populations.	**Geography** is the study of the relationship between human populations and Earth's features. **Anthropology** is the study of the interactions of the biological, cultural, geographical, and historical aspects of humankind. **Sociology** is the study of human population dynamics and statistics.

FIGURE 1.4

Environmental Science and Public Life

Scientists at a conference discuss climate change.

Students study the movements of box turtles.

FIGURE 1.5

Change Three hundred years ago, Manhattan was a very different place. This painting shows an area where Native Americans hunted and fished.

Scientists as Citizens, Citizens as Scientists

Governments, businesses, and communities recognize that studying our environment is vital to maintaining a healthy and productive society. Thus, environmental scientists are often asked to share their research with the world. **Figure 1.4** shows scientists meeting to discuss climate change at a United Nations conference.

Often, the observations of nonscientists are the first step toward addressing an environmental problem. For example, middle-school students first noticed the appearance of deformed frogs in Minnesota lakes. Similarly, the students at Dublin Scioto High School in Ohio, shown in **Figure 1.4**, have studied the habitat of endangered box turtles. A habitat is a place where an organism usually lives. The students wanted to find out how the turtles live and what factors affect their nesting and hibernation sites in their habitat. The students tracked and mapped the turtles' movements, measured atmospheric conditions, and analyzed soil samples. These efforts are important because the box turtle habitat is threatened. The students have presented their findings to city planners, in an effort to protect the most sensitive turtle habitats.

Our Environment Through Time

Wherever humans have hunted, grown food, or settled, they have changed the environment. For example, the land where New York City now stands was once an area where Native Americans hunted game and gathered food, as shown in **Figure 1.5**. The environmental change that has occurred on Manhattan Island over the past 300 years is immense, yet this period of time is just a "blink" in human history.

Hunter-Gatherers

For most of human history, people were *hunter-gatherers,* or people who obtain food by collecting plants and by hunting wild animals or scavenging their remains. Early hunter-gatherer groups were small, and they migrated from place to place as different types of food became available at different times of the year. Even today there are hunter-gatherer societies in the Amazon rain forests of South America and in New Guinea, as shown in **Figure 1.6.**

Hunter-gatherers affected their environment in many ways. For example, some Native American tribes hunted bison that live in grasslands. The tribes set fires to burn the prairies and prevent the growth of trees. This kept the prairies as open grassland where the tribes could hunt bison.

In North America, rapid climate changes and overhunting by hunter-gatherers may have contributed to the disappearance of some species of large mammals. These species include giant sloths, giant bison, mastodons, cave bears, and saber-toothed cats. Large piles of bones have been found where meat was possibly stored during the winter. In Australia and New Zealand, hunter-gatherers caused the extinction of many large species of mammals and birds.

✔ **CHECK FOR UNDERSTANDING**

Identify Name two ways that hunter-gatherers affected their environment.

FIGURE 1.6

Hunter-Gatherers This modern hunter-gatherer group lives in New Guinea, a tropical island off the north coast of Australia.

©David Gillison

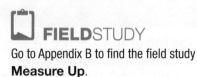

FIELDSTUDY

Go to Appendix B to find the field study
Measure Up.

The Agricultural Revolution

Eventually many hunter-gatherer groups began to collect the seeds of the plants they gathered and to domesticate some of the animals in their environment. **Agriculture** is the practice of growing, breeding, and caring for plants and animals that are used for food, clothing, housing, transportation, and other purposes. The practice of agriculture started in many different parts of the world over 10,000 years ago. This change had such a dramatic impact on human societies and their environment that it is often called the *neolithic agricultural revolution.*

The agricultural revolution allowed human populations to grow at an unprecedented rate. An area of land can support up to 100 times as many people by farming as it can by hunting and gathering. As populations grew, they began to concentrate in smaller areas. These changes placed increased pressure on local environments.

The agricultural revolution also changed the food we eat. The plants we grow and eat today are descended from wild plants. During harvest season, farmers collected seeds from plants that exhibited the qualities they desired. The seeds of plants with large kernels or sweet and nutritious flesh were planted and harvested again. Over the course of many generations, the domesticated plants became very different from their wild ancestors. For example, the grass shown in **Figure 1.7** may be related to the grass from which corn was bred.

As grasslands, forests, and wetlands were replaced with farmland, habitats were destroyed. Slash-and-burn agriculture, shown in **Figure 1.7**, is one of the earliest ways by which land was converted to farmland. Replacing forest with farmland on a large scale caused soil loss, floods, and water shortages. In addition, much of this converted land was farmed poorly and is no longer fertile. The loss of fertile farmland had far-reaching effects. For example, the early civilizations of the Tigris-Euphrates River basin collapsed, in part, because the overworked soil became infertile through salt contamination.

FIGURE 1.7

The Agricultural Revolution

This grass, called Eastern gama grass, is thought to be a relative of the modern corn plant. Native Americans may have selectively bred a grass like this to produce corn.

For thousands of years humans have burned forests to create fields for agriculture. In this photo, a rain forest in Thailand is being cleared for farming.

FIGURE 1.8

Industrial Revolution During much of the Industrial Revolution, few limits were placed on the air pollution caused by burning fossil fuels. Locomotives such as these were powered by burning coal.

Quality of Life The invention of computers has improved the ways that people work, learn, communicate, and entertain themselves.

The Industrial Revolution

For about 2.5 million years the tools of human societies were powered mainly by humans or animals. This pattern changed in the middle of the 1700s with the Industrial Revolution, which involved a shift from energy sources, such as animal muscle and running water, to fossil fuels, such as coal and oil. The increased use of fossil fuels and machines, such as the steam engines shown in **Figure 1.8**, changed society and greatly increased the efficiency of agriculture, industry, and transportation.

During the Industrial Revolution, the large-scale production of goods in factories became less expensive than the local production of goods. Machinery reduced the amount of land and human labor needed for farming. As fewer people grew their own food, populations in urban areas steadily grew. Fossil fuels and motorized vehicles allowed food and other goods to be transported cheaply across great distances.

Improving Quality of Life

The Industrial Revolution introduced many positive changes. Inventions such as the light bulb greatly improved our quality of life. Agricultural productivity increased, and sanitation, nutrition, and medical care vastly improved. Technologies such as the telephone and the portable computer, shown in **Figure 1.8**, enabled people to work and communicate more easily from any location. Yet with all of these advances, the Industrial Revolution introduced many new environmental problems.

In the 1900s, modern societies began to use artificial substances in place of raw animal and plant products. Plastics and many other artificial materials have made life easier. However, we now understand some of the environmental problems they present. Much of environmental science is concerned with the problems associated with the Industrial Revolution.

✔ **CHECK FOR UNDERSTANDING**
Identify Identify three ways that the Industrial Revolution changed society.

FIGURE 1.9

Space This photograph was taken in 1968 by the crew of *Apollo 8*. Photographs such as this helped people realize the uniqueness of the planet we share.

Spaceship Earth

Earth, shown from space in **Figure 1.9**, has been compared to a ship traveling through space, unable to dispose of waste or take on new supplies as it travels. Earth is essentially a *closed system*—the only thing that enters Earth's atmosphere in large amounts is energy from the sun, and the only thing that leaves in large amounts is heat. A closed system has potential problems. Some resources are limited, and as the population grows, the resources will be used. In a closed system there is also the chance that we will produce wastes more quickly than we can dispose of them.

Although Earth can be thought of as a complete system, environmental problems can occur on different scales: local, regional, or global. For example, your community may be discussing where to build a new landfill, or local developers may be arguing with environmentalists about the importance of a rare bird or insect. On a regional level, the drinking water in your area may be affected by a polluted river hundreds of miles away. Other environmental problems are global. For example, carbon dioxide released in one part of the world can contribute to climate change around the globe.

CASESTUDY

Dam Removal on the Penobscot River

Dams on rivers help to produce much-needed electricity without continuously burning fossil fuels. These benefits, however, are accompanied by some environmental, economic, and social costs. The large geographic areas of watersheds (the land area that drains into a river) and the diverse mix of interest groups present challenges to making fair and sustainable decisions about hydropower. How can the right balance be achieved?

The Penobscot River, Maine

The watershed of the Penobscot River is the largest in Maine, and the major streams extend over 8,800 km (about 5,500 miles). Historically, the Penobscot was home to abundant fish and other wildlife. For example, more than 100,000 salmon per year migrated for reproduction from the ocean to this watershed. Salmon and ten other species of migratory fish enriched the watershed and provided food and cultural value for the Wabanaki people, who occupied the area continuously for more than 9,000 years.

European settlement of the area brought construction of many dams to provide power for mills and eventually to produce electricity. In the past few decades all commercial fisheries have been lost and the Penobscot population of salmon was listed under the Endangered Species Act in 2009. Scientists determined that the primary cause of decline is obstruction of fishes' migratory paths by dams.

Dams reduce the environmental benefits of a free-running river in many ways. These benefits include food, recreation, cultural enrichment, and clean water. Varying depths and currents that come with natural flow create diverse habitats that promote diverse wildlife. Periods of fast flow remove silt from gravel beds, which is necessary for many aquatic insects. These insects are food for fish. Many species of fish need sand or gravel to reproduce. Normal river flow helps rivers recover from pollution, and coastal ocean ecosystems are productive because rivers deliver nutrients from land to ocean. These benefits of natural river flow have been revealed by the work of many environmental scientists.

The Penobscot River Restoration Trust

To reconcile the benefits and costs of dams, the Penobscot River Restoration Project brought together a wide variety of groups to develop a plan that is now being implemented.

©NASA

Population Growth: A Local Pressure

One reason many environmental problems are so pressing today is that the agricultural revolution and the Industrial Revolution allowed the human population to grow much faster than it had ever grown before. The development of modern medicine and sanitation also helped increase the human population. As shown in **Figure 1.10**, the human population almost quadrupled during the 20th century. Producing enough food for such a large population has environmental consequences. Many of the environmental problems that affect us today, such as habitat destruction and pesticide pollution, are the result of feeding the world in the 20th century. Other problems, like climate change, are the result of filling the demand for goods and transportation of so many people.

There are many different predictions of population growth for the future. But most scientists think that the human population will almost double in the 21st century before it will begin to stabilize. We can expect that the pressure on the environment will continue to increase as the human population and its need for food and resources grow.

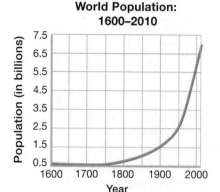

FIGURE 1.10

World Population The size of the human population in 2010 was nearly 14 times larger than it was in 1600.

World Population: 1600–2010

Source: U.S. Census Bureau, International Database

The Penobscot River, Maine

These groups include a hydropower company, the Penobscot Indian Nation (a part of the Wabanaki people), seven conservation groups, and government agencies at the state and federal levels. As part of the plan, hydropower levels will be maintained, but two dams closest to the mouth of the river will be removed, construction of a bypass for migratory fish will occur at a third dam, and passages will be built for fish at four more dams. These actions will be monitored by Maine and Federal agencies. Most importantly, the Penobscot River Restoration Trust was formed to promote continued collaboration and oversight for all the participating groups. Increased access to proper habitat and improved water quality should allow populations of many migratory fishes to grow from no more than 2,000

today to millions of fish! This will revitalize the Penobscot Indian Nation's culture and traditions and will promote sustainable economic development of communities within the watershed.

The story of the Penobscot River is an example of how environmental science and public action work together to solve environmental problems. Good science revealed the causes for decline, needs for ecological restoration, and the engineering solutions to implement large-scale projects. Science will continue to be applied to evaluate the recovery of wildlife, and many groups with different interests working together will ensure the long-term health of the river and local communities.

Critical Thinking

1. **Analyzing Processes** Why was the Penobscot River Restoration Trust formed?

2. **Analyzing Relationships** Describe how environmental science helped the Trust decide that some dams should be removed.

What Are Our Main Environmental Problems?

You may feel as though the world has an unlimited variety of environmental problems. But many environmental problems fall into three categories: resource depletion, pollution, or loss of biodiversity.

Resource Depletion

Any natural material that is used by humans is called a **natural resource.** Natural resources can be classified as renewable or nonrenewable, as shown in **Figure 1.11**. A *renewable resource* is a resource that can be replaced relatively quickly by natural processes. Fresh water, air, soil, trees, and crops are all resources that can be renewed. Energy from the sun is also a renewable resource. A *nonrenewable resource* is a resource that forms at a much slower rate than the rate that it is consumed. The most common nonrenewable resources are minerals and fossil fuels. Once a nonrenewable resource is used up, it may take millions of years to replenish it.

Resources are said to be *depleted* when a large fraction of the resource has been used up. **Figure 1.11** shows a mine where copper, a nonrenewable resource, is removed from the Earth's crust. Some renewable resources can also be depleted. For example, if trees are harvested faster than they can grow naturally in an area, deforestation will result.

Pollution

With the Industrial Revolution, societies began producing wastes faster than the wastes could be disposed of. The wastes accumulate and cause pollution. **Pollution** is an undesired change in air, water, or soil that adversely affects the health, survival, or activities of humans or other organisms. Air pollution levels in Mexico City, as shown in **Figure 1.12**, are dangerously high, mostly because of car exhaust and industrial pollutants.

Biodegradable pollutants can be broken down by natural processes. These pollutants include things such as human sewage and food wastes.

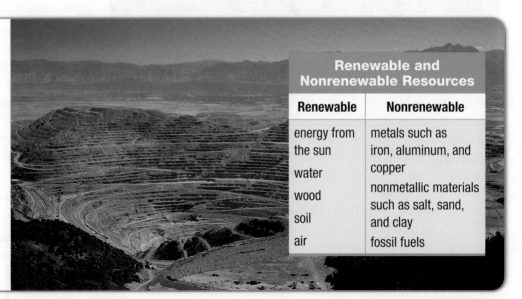

FIGURE 1.11

Resources More than 12 million tons of copper have been mined from the Bingham mine in Utah. Once all of the copper that can be profitably extracted is used up, the copper in this mine will be depleted.

Renewable and Nonrenewable Resources	
Renewable	**Nonrenewable**
energy from the sun	metals such as iron, aluminum, and copper
water	
wood	nonmetallic materials such as salt, sand, and clay
soil	
air	fossil fuels

©Gene Ahrens/Bruce Coleman, Inc./Photoshot

Biodegradable pollutants are a problem when they accumulate faster than they can be broken down. *Nonbiodegradable pollutants,* such as mercury, lead, and some types of plastic, cannot be broken down by natural processes. Because such pollutants do not break down easily, they can build to dangerous levels in the environment.

Because carbon dioxide is generally not harmful to people's health—we breathe it out when we exhale—people often don't think of it as a pollutant. But the huge amounts of CO_2 being released from the burning of fossil fuels are increasing the amount in the atmosphere and changing the climate. Because of this undesirable effect, it may be considered pollution in some forms. Because climate change is a global problem that affects many other environmental problems, many scientists believe that it is the most pressing environmental issue.

Loss of Biodiversity

The term **biodiversity** refers to the number and variety of species that live in an area. Earth has been home to hundreds of millions of species. Only a fraction of those species are alive today. Extinction is a natural process, and several large-scale extinctions, or *mass extinctions*, have occurred through Earth's history. Scientists believe that the pace of extinctions occurring today matches that of mass extinctions in the past. Why should we be concerned about the modern extinction of individual species?

The organisms that share the world with us can be considered natural resources. We depend on other organisms for food, for the oxygen we breathe, and for many other things. A species that is extinct is gone forever, so a species can be considered a nonrenewable resource. Scientists think that if current rates of extinction continue, it may cause problems for human populations in the future because the loss of too many species may cause significant disruption in ecosystems. If this happens, many of the services ecosystems provide to people may be lost. Many people also argue that all species have potential economic, ecological, scientific, aesthetic, and recreational value, so it is important to preserve them.

FIGURE 1.12

Air Pollution The problem of air pollution in Mexico City is compounded because the city is located in a valley that traps air pollutants.

FIGURE 1.13

Loss of Biodiversity The Tasmanian tiger, native to Australia and the island of Tasmania, was declared extinct in 1986.

✓ Section 1 **Formative Assessment**

▶ Reviewing Main Ideas

1. **Describe** the two main types of interactions that environmental scientists study. Give an example of each.

2. **Describe** the major environmental effects of the agricultural revolution and the Industrial Revolution.

3. **Explain** how environmental problems can be local, regional, or global. Give one example of each.

4. **Explain** why environmental science is an interdisciplinary science.

✓ Critical Thinking

5. **Making Comparisons** What is the difference between environmental science and ecology?

6. **Making Inferences** Fossil fuels are said to be nonrenewable resources, yet they are produced by the Earth over millions of years. By what time frame are they considered nonrenewable? Write a paragraph that explains your answer.

- Describe "The Tragedy of the Commons."

- Explain the law of supply and demand.

- List three differences between developed and developing countries.

- Explain what sustainability is, and describe why it is a goal of environmental science.

Key Terms

law of supply and demand
ecological footprint
sustainability

The Environment and Society

When we think about environmental problems and how to solve them, we have to consider human societies, how they act, and why they do what they do. One way to think about society and the environment is to consider how a society uses common resources. A neighborhood park, for example, is a common resource that people share. On a larger scale, the open ocean is not owned by any nation, yet people from many countries use the ocean as a common resource for fishing and for transporting goods. How do societies decide to share common resources? In 1968, ecologist Garrett Hardin published an essay titled "The Tragedy of the Commons," which addressed this question.

"The Tragedy of the Commons"

In his essay, Hardin argued that the main difficulty in solving environmental problems is the conflict between the short-term interests of individuals and the long-term welfare of society. To illustrate his point, Hardin used the example of the commons, as shown in **Figure 2.1.** Commons were areas of land that belonged to a whole village. Anyone could graze cows or sheep on the commons. It was in the best short-term interest of an individual to put as many animals as possible on the commons. Individuals thought, If I don't use this resource, someone else will.

However, if too many animals grazed on the commons, the animals destroyed the grass. Then everyone suffered because no one could raise animals on the commons. Commons were eventually replaced by closed fields owned by individuals. Owners were careful not to put too many animals on their land, because overgrazing meant that fewer animals could be raised the next year. The point of Hardin's essay is that someone or some group has to take responsibility for maintaining a resource. If no one takes that responsibility, the resource can be overused and become depleted.

FIGURE 2.1

"The Tragedy of the Commons"
Hardin observed that when land was held in common (left), individuals tended to graze as many animals as possible. Overgrazing led to the destruction of the land resources. When commons were replaced by enclosed fields owned by individuals (right), people tended to graze only the number of animals that the land could support.

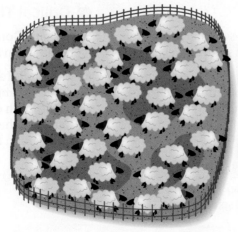

Earth's natural resources are our modern commons. Hardin thought that people would continue to deplete natural resources by acting in their own self-interest to the point of society's collapse. In history there are examples of this occurring, and the Tragedy of the Commons is still occurring for many resources. But humans live in groups and depend on one another. Societies can solve an environmental problem by planning, organizing, considering the scientific evidence, and proposing a solution. The solution may override the interests of some individuals in the short term, but it will improve the environment for everyone in the long term. Environmental science can provide information on how different plans will affect the environment. Society must decide what outcome is desirable.

Economics and the Environment

Economic forces influence how we use resources. Many of the topics you will explore later in this book are affected by economic considerations.

Supply and Demand

One basic rule of economics is the **law of supply and demand,** which states that the greater the demand for a limited supply of something, the more that product is worth. One example of this rule is shown in **Figure 2.2,** which illustrates the relationship between the supply of copper and its price. In recent years, demand for copper has grown beyond the amount that can be supplied in the U.S. This increase in demand and reduction in supply is reflected in the increased price. Many environmental solutions have to take the relationship between supply and demand into account.

Costs and Benefits

The cost of environmental solutions can be high. To determine how much to spend to control air pollution, a community may perform a cost-benefit analysis. A *cost-benefit analysis* balances the cost of the action against the benefit expected from it. The results of a cost-benefit analysis often depend on who is doing the analysis. To an industry, cost of pollution control may outweigh the benefits, but to a nearby community, the benefits may be worth a high price. The cost of environmental regulations is often passed on to the consumer or taxpayer. The consumer can then choose to either pay for the more expensive product that meets environmental regulations or find a cheaper product without the same environmental safeguards.

Risk Assessment

One cost of any action is the risk of an undesirable outcome. Cost-benefit analysis involves *risk assessment,* which is one tool that helps us create cost-effective ways to protect our health and environment. To develop an effective solution to an environmental problem, the public must perceive the risk accurately. This does not always happen. In one study, people were asked to assess the risk from various technologies. The public generally ranked nuclear power as the riskiest technology on the list, whereas experts ranked it 20th—less risky than riding a bicycle.

FIGURE 2.2

Supply and Demand As demand has increased for copper, supply has not been able to keep up. This has led to an increase in the price of copper.

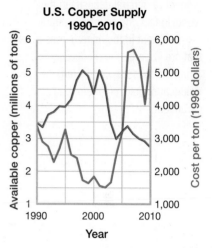

U.S. Copper Supply 1990–2010

Source: U.S. Geological Survey

✔ **CHECK FOR UNDERSTANDING**

Illustrate Use an example to illustrate the law of supply and demand.

Developed and Developing Countries

The decisions and actions of all people in the world affect our environment. But the unequal distribution of wealth and resources around the world influences the environmental problems that a society faces and the choices it can make. The United Nations classifies countries as either developed or developing. *Developed countries* have higher average incomes, slower population growth, diverse industrial economies, and stronger social support systems. They include the United States, Canada, Japan, and the countries of Western Europe. *Developing countries* have lower average incomes, simple and agriculture-based economies, and rapid population growth. Developed and developing countries have different consumption patterns that affect the environment in different ways. In addition, different developing countries are on different paths. Some are experiencing little change in living conditions, while others, like Brazil, China, and India, have emerged as major international economic powers with environmental impacts and challenges similar to those in developed countries.

Population and Consumption

Most environmental problems can be traced back to two root causes. First, the human population in some areas is growing too quickly for the local environment to support it. Second, people are using, wasting, or polluting many natural resources faster than they can be replaced or cleaned up.

FIGURE 2.3

Consumption Trends

A food market in India is shown to the left. The food market above is in the United States. How do these two food markets show differing consumption trends in India and the United States?

(bl) ©Purepix/Alamy Images; (br) ©Photodisc/Getty Images

FIGURE 2.4

INDICATORS OF DEVELOPMENT FOR THE U.S., JAPAN, MEXICO, AND INDONESIA

	Measurement	U.S.	Japan	Mexico	Indonesia
Health	life expectancy in years	78.5	82	76	71
Population growth	per year	0.7%	−0.1%	1.2%	1.0%
Wealth	gross domestic product per person	$47,200	$34,000	$13,900	$4,200
Living space	people per square kilometer	32	339	59	125
Energy use	per person per year (millions of Btu)	330	172	67	25
Pollution	carbon dioxide from fossil fuels per person per year (tons)	17.3	9.5	4.4	1.8
Waste	garbage produced per person per year (kg)	720	400	300	43

Local Population Pressures

When the population in an area grows rapidly, there may not be enough natural resources for everyone in the area to live a healthy, productive life. Often, as people struggle for survival in severely overpopulated regions, forests are stripped bare, topsoil is exhausted, and animals are driven to extinction. Malnutrition, starvation, and disease can be constant threats. Even though there are millions of people starving in developing countries, populations tend to grow most rapidly in these countries. Food production, education, and job creation cannot keep pace with population growth, so each person gets fewer resources as time goes by.

Consumption Trends

For many people in the wealthier part of the world, life is better than ever before. Many environmental problems are being addressed. In addition, the population has stabilized or is growing slowly. But to support this quality of life, developed countries are using much more of Earth's resources than developing countries are. Developed nations use about 75 percent of the world's resources, even though they make up only about 20 percent of the world's population. This rate of consumption creates more waste and pollution per person than in developing countries, as shown in **Figure 2.4.**

Ecological Footprints

One way to express the differences in consumption between nations is as an ecological footprint, as shown in **Figure 2.5.** An **ecological footprint** shows the productive area of Earth needed to support one person in a particular country. It estimates the land used for crops, grazing, forest products, and housing. It also estimates the ocean area used to harvest seafood and the forest area needed to absorb the air pollution caused by fossil fuels. Another footprint is the carbon footprint, or how much carbon dioxide is released into the atmosphere to support a person's lifestyle including goods used and emissions from powering vehicles and houses.

FIGURE 2.5

Ecological Footprints An ecological footprint is a calculation of the amount of land and resources needed to support one person from a particular country. The ecological footprint of a person in a developed country is, on average, four times as large as the footprint of a person in a developing country.

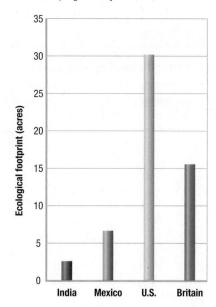

Environmental Science in Context

As you have learned, environmental problems are complex. Simple solutions are rare, and they sometimes cause more damage than the original problem. To complicate matters, the environment has also become a battleground for larger issues that affect human societies. For example, how does society balance the rights of individuals and property owners with the needs of society as a whole? Or, when economic or political refugees emigrate—legally or illegally—what can be done about the devastation they may cause to the local environment? How do human rights relate to the environment?

Critical Thinking and the Environment

People on any side of an environmental issue may feel passionately about their cause, and can consequently distort information and mislead people about the issues. Research done by environmental scientists is often used to make political points or is misrepresented to support controversial viewpoints. In addition to the scientific data, the economic dimensions of an environmental issue can be oversimplified. Even more complication is introduced by the media, which often sensationalizes environmental issues. So, as you make your own decisions about the environment, it is essential that you use your critical-thinking skills.

Learning to think critically about what you see in newspapers, on television, and on the Internet will help you make informed decisions. As you explore environmental science further, you should remember a few things. First, be prepared to listen to many viewpoints. People have many different reasons for the opinions they form. Try to understand what those reasons are before reacting to their ideas. If you want your ideas to be heard, it is important that you listen to the opinions of others, as shown in **Figure 2.6**. Also, identify your own bias. How does it affect the way you interpret the issue?

FIGURE 2.6

Community Involvement Anyone can express an opinion on environmental issues at state and local public hearings.

©Jim West/Alamy Images

Second, investigate the source of the information you encounter. Remember that environmental science is not just somebody's opinion. It is information that has been collected carefully, often by many scientists, and checked for accuracy by other scientists that did not collect or analyze the data. Science is designed to objectively test ideas, not just collect data that support a preconceived bias.

A Sustainable World

Despite the differing points of view on the environment, most people support the goal of achieving sustainability. **Sustainability** is the condition in which human needs are met in such a way that a human population can survive indefinitely at a standard of living similar to the current one. A sustainable world is not an unchanging world; technology advances and human civilizations continue to be productive. But at the present time we live in a world that is far from sustainable. The combination of a large population, the current standard of living in developed countries, and how we produce energy is using resources faster than they can be replaced.

The problems described in this chapter are not insurmountable. Achieving a sustainable world requires everyone's participation. If individual citizens, industries, and governments cooperate, we can move toward sustainability. For example, the Penobscot River is cleaner and healthier now than it was years ago. As another example, bald eagles were once on the brink of extinction. But now they are now making a comeback because of the efforts to preserve their habitat and to reduce pollution from the pesticide DDT.

Nevertheless, our environmental problems are significant and require careful attention and action. The 21st century will be a crucial time in human history. We must find solutions that allow people on all parts of our planet to live in a clean, healthy environment and have the resources they need for a good life.

FIGURE 2.7

Citizens in Action These high school students are taking action to improve their environment. They are cleaning up trash that is clogging an urban creek.

✔ **CHECK FOR UNDERSTANDING**
Explain What is a sustainable world?

✔ Section 2 Formative Assessment

● Reviewing Main Ideas

1. **Describe** three differences between developing and developed nations using the examples in Figure 2.4. Would you classify Mexico as a developing nation? Explain your answer.

2. **Explain** why critical thinking is an important skill in environmental science.

3. **Explain** the law of supply and demand, and give an example of how it relates to the environment.

✔ Critical Thinking

4. **Applying Ideas** The law of supply and demand is a simplification of economic patterns. What other factors might affect the cost of copper?

5. **Evaluating Ideas** Write a description of "The Tragedy of the Commons." Do you think that Hardin's essay is an accurate description of the relationship between individuals, society, and the environment?

Predators of Africa

Hyenas and lions are two of the most recognized predators on the planet. Every year, millions of people go on safari in Africa to see these predators. Millions more see them in documentaries on TV. Most people love lions, but hyenas have a bad reputation.

Since the early 1970s, Dr. Laurence Frank has been studying the predators of Africa in Kenya. By studying the behavior, interactions, and physiology of hyenas, he and other scientists have shown that hyenas don't deserve their reputation. It turns out that hyenas are excellent hunters. Rather than being scavengers and stealing kills from lions, hyenas get almost all of their food by catching their own prey. Also, hyenas are highly social, cooperate with one another, and live in clans where females are the leaders. As top predators, both lions and hyenas are important in Africa. They help keep prey populations in check, including keeping large herbivores from overgrazing plants. But both lions and hyenas are in trouble. Seeing lions and hyenas disappearing from the places he worked caused Dr. Frank to focus his research on finding ways to protect these important predators. He is now the Director of the Living with Lions Project—a group of scientists and Masai warriors working in nonprotected areas of Kenya to protect lions. Not only is it important to protect predators to ensure healthy ecosystems, but "a world without lions would be a very sad place," Dr. Frank has said.

A Lion Guardian takes measurements and attaches a tracking collar to a lion.

Trouble in Africa

Because it is easy to see lions and hyenas in parks and on TV, most people think that they are thriving in Africa. Unfortunately, these predators are disappearing across the continent. Lion numbers in Africa have fallen quickly—from around 200,000 in the 1990s to less than 30,000 in 2011. Lions are no longer found in many rangeland areas that had lions in the early 1990s. Dr. Frank thinks that unless something is done quickly, lions may disappear from Kenya in 10 to 20 years!

There are several reasons that lions and other predators are in trouble. First, their habitat is being destroyed. Predators need to be able to roam huge areas to find enough prey, but much of their natural habitat is being destroyed or is being used for agriculture or raising livestock. In many places, livestock overgraze the plants and there is not enough food to support populations of prey for lions.

Although predators are doing well in some parks and nature reserves, most of these are not big enough to ensure their survival. The small populations of lions that live in these protected areas could easily be wiped out by disease. Also, to find enough prey, predators may have to leave the parks. When predators enter commercial ranches or community grazing lands, they come into conflict with people by killing livestock such as cattle, sheep, and goats.

Both commercial ranchers and traditional herders (the Masai) use the same methods to protect livestock. During the day, the Masai watch over livestock and move them to areas where they can eat and drink. At night, they move the livestock to an enclosure made of thorn bushes (*boma*). The boma is meant to protect cattle from predators and from theft. Some lions, however, will hunt livestock at night by trying to scare them out of the boma.

When a lion kills livestock, the Masai may hunt it down and kill it. Or the Masai may poison the carcass. This will kill the lion when it comes back to finish its meal the next night. But this method also kills entire prides of lions, as well as hyenas, vultures, and other animals that eat the carcass.

Dr. Frank and many other people are trying to find out how to solve the problems that are causing lions to disappear.

Dr. Laurence Frank has studied the predators of Africa for decades, and he is now working to save them through programs such as the Living with Lions Project.

It Takes More Than a Village

Protecting predators isn't easy and it isn't all about science. Important factors include understanding how far predators range, how and why they kill livestock, and how people who have conflicts with lions can be encouraged to help save them.

To do this, the Living with Lions Project is finding ways that the Masai and commercial ranchers can benefit financially from keeping lions around. They are also working to reduce the number of livestock killed by lions and to educate people about the importance of predators and the troubles predators are facing.

One member of the Living with Lions Project is Dr. Leela Hazzah. Dr. Hazzah is the founder of the Lion Guardians. Her idea was to try to convince Masai warriors, who were renowned lion killers, to become lion protectors. Now, Masai warriors have found that lions can be a benefit because they bring tourism. With the help of graduate student and conservation biologist Stephanie Dolrenry, the Lion Guardians have identified every lion in 3500 km^2 and have stopped all lion killing by the Masai. As a result, the population is recovering.

Another example of working with local communities to save predators is Dr. Frank's Laikipia Predator Project. The Project involves commercial ranchers, like Claus Mortensen at Mugie Ranch, and Masai communities working together with scientists. They are using GPS collars on lions to study how lions use the landscape. They need to know how lions respond to movements of livestock, wildlife, and humans. They have found new ways to build bomas that better protect livestock. Also, they have found ways to work together so the money tourists spend when they come to see lions and other wildlife benefits the ranchers and the Masai.

Lions and other predators in Africa are still in trouble. But the work of many people, including Dr. Frank, Dr. Hazzah, the Masai warriors, Stephanie Dolrenry, and Claus Mortensen, is building a blueprint for protecting them. With more hard work and dedicated people, scientists and community members hope these predators will someday thrive again all across Africa.

What Do You Think?

Why is it important that Dr. Frank and Dr. Hazzah work with the Masai and commercial ranchers? If you had money to help protect lions, how would you spend it?

CHAPTER 1 **Summary**

SECTION 1 **Understanding Our Environment**

OBJECTIVES

- Environmental science is an interdisciplinary study of the environment. A goal of many environmental scientists is to understand and solve environmental problems. One important foundation of environmental science is the science of ecology.

- Environmental change has occurred throughout Earth's history.

- Hunter-gatherer societies cleared grassland by setting fires and contributed to the extinction of some large mammals.

- The agricultural revolution caused human population growth, habitat loss, soil erosion, and the domestication of plants and animals.

- The Industrial Revolution caused rapid human population growth and the increased use of fossil fuels. Most modern environmental problems began during the Industrial Revolution.

- The major environmental problems we face today include resource depletion, pollution, and loss of biodiversity.

KEY TERMS

environmental science

ecology

agriculture

natural resource

pollution

biodiversity

SECTION 2 **The Environment and Society**

OBJECTIVES

- "The Tragedy of the Commons" was an influential essay that described the relationship between the short-term interests of the individual and the long-term interests of society.

- The law of supply and demand states that when the demand for a product increases while the supply remains fixed, the cost of the product will increase.

- Environmental problems in developed countries tend to be related to consumption. In developing nations, the major environmental problems are related to population growth.

- Sustainability is the condition in which human needs are met in such a way that a human population can survive indefinitely at a standard of living similar to the current one.

KEY TERMS

law of supply and demand

ecological footprint

sustainability

CHAPTER 1 **Review**

Reviewing Key Terms

Use each of the following terms in a separate sentence.

1. *agriculture*
2. *natural resource*
3. *pollution*
4. *ecological footprint*
5. *sustainability*

Use the correct key term to complete each of the following sentences.

6. The _____ Revolution was characterized by a shift from human and animal power to fossil fuels.

7. Resources that can theoretically last forever are called _____ resources.

8. _____ is a term that describes the number and variety of species that live in an area.

9. Concept Map Use the following terms to create a concept map: *geology, biology, ecology, environmental science, chemistry, geography,* and *social sciences.*

Reviewing Main Ideas

10. An important effect that hunter-gatherer societies may have had on the environment was
    a. soil erosion.
    b. extinction.
    c. air pollution.
    d. All of the above

11. An important effect of the agricultural revolution was
    a. soil erosion.
    b. habitat destruction.
    c. plant and animal domestication.
    d. All of the above

12. Which of the following does *not* describe an effect of the Industrial Revolution?
    a. Fossil fuels became important energy sources.
    b. The amount of land and labor needed to produce food increased.
    c. Artificial substances replaced some animal and plant products.
    d. Machines replaced human muscle and animal power.

13. Pollutants that are not broken down by natural processes are
    a. nonrenewable.
    b. nondegradable.
    c. biodegradable.
    d. Both (a) and (c)

14. All of the following are renewable resources *except*
    a. energy from the sun.
    b. minerals.
    c. crops.
    d. fresh water.

15. In his essay, "The Tragedy of the Commons," one factor that Garrett Hardin failed to consider was
    a. the destruction of natural resources.
    b. human self-interest.
    c. the social nature of humans.
    d. None of the above

16. The term used to describe the productive area of Earth needed to support the lifestyle of one person in a particular country is called
    a. supply and demand.
    b. the ecological footprint.
    c. the consumption crisis.
    d. sustainability.

Short Answer

17. Give an example of how environmental science might involve geology and chemistry.

18. Can biodegradable pollutants cause environmental problems? Explain your answer.

19. In what ways are today's environmental resources like the commons described in the essay "The Tragedy of the Commons"?

20. How could environmental concerns conflict with your desire to improve your standard of living?

21. If you were evaluating the claims made on a Web site that discusses environmental issues, what types of information would you look for?

22. Can species be considered natural resources? Explain your answer.

Interpreting Graphics

The graphs below show the difference in energy consumption and population size in developed and developing countries. Use the graphs to answer questions 23–25.

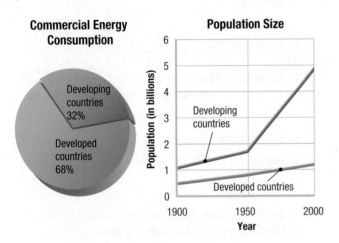

23. Describe the differences in the energy consumption and population growth of developed and developing countries.

24. Do you think that the percentage of commercial energy consumed by developing countries will increase or decrease? Explain your answer.

25. Why is information on energy consumption represented in a pie graph, while population size is shown in a line graph?

Critical Thinking

26. **Analyzing Ideas** Are humans part of the environment? Explain your answer.

27. **Drawing Conclusions** Why do you think that fossil fuels were not widely used until the Industrial Revolution? Write a paragraph that describes your thoughts.

28. **Evaluating Assumptions** Once the sun exhausts its fuel and burns itself out, it cannot be replaced. So why is the sun considered a renewable resource?

29. **Evaluating Assumptions** Read the description of the Industrial Revolution. Were all the effects of the Industrial Revolution negative? Explain your answer.

30. **Demographics** Obtain the 1985 and 2000 census reports for your town or city. Look for changes in demographic characteristics, such as population size, income, and age. Make a bar graph that compares some of the characteristics you chose. How does your city or town compare with national trends? What might be some of the environmental implications of these trends?

31. **Make a Diagram** Many resources can be traced to energy from the sun. For example, plants living in swamps millions of years ago used energy from the sun to grow. Over time, some of these plants became coal deposits. When we burn coal today, we are using energy that radiated from the sun millions of years ago. Choose a resource, and create a diagram that traces the resource back to energy from the sun.

Analyzing Data

Use the table below to answer questions 32–34.

	U.S.	Japan	Indonesia
People per square kilometer	32	339	125
Garbage produced per person per year	720 kg	400 kg	43 kg

32. Analyzing Data Make a bar graph that compares the garbage produced per person per year in each country.

33. Making Calculations Calculate how much garbage is produced each year per square kilometer of each country listed in the table.

34. Evaluating Data Use the information in the table to evaluate the validity of the following statement: In countries where population density is high, more garbage is produced per person.

Making Connections

35. Communicating Main Ideas Briefly describe the relationship between humans and the environment through history.

36. Writing Persuasively Write a persuasive essay explaining the importance of science in a debate about an environmental issue.

37. Outlining Topics Write a one-page outline that describes population and consumption in the developing and developed world.

CASESTUDY

38. The dams on the Penobscot River will be modified to help restore the populations of migratory fish. Describe the three solutions that will be implemented to allow for the migration of fish.

39. When the population of migratory fish decreased because of dams on the Penobscot River, what other populations might have been affected? As the numbers of migratory fish recover, how will those same populations be affected?

Why It Matters

40. Often, researching and effectively addressing environmental concerns requires cooperation from multiple groups, such as corporations, local residents, scientists, and governments. Why is it important to seek agreement among groups with potentially different goals and interests?

STUDYSKILL

Root Words As you study, it may be helpful to learn the meaning of important root words. You can find these roots in most dictionaries. For example, *hydro-* means "water." Once you learn the meaning of this root, you can learn the meanings of words such as *hydrothermal, hydrologist, hydropower,* and *hydrophobic.*

Objectives

Survey an area of land and determine the land's physical features and the types of organisms that live there.

Identify possible relationships between the organisms that live in the area of land you surveyed.

Materials

hand lens

markers or felt-tip pens of several different colors

notebook

pen or pencil

stakes, (4)

string, about 50 m

tape measure or meter stick

optional materials: field guides to insects or plants

What's in an Ecosystem?

How well do you know the environment around your home or school? You may walk through it every day without noticing most of the living things it contains or thinking about how they survive. Ecologists, on the other hand, observe organisms and seek to understand how they interact. In this lab, you will play the role of an ecologist by closely observing part of your environment.

Procedure

1. Use a tape measure or meter stick to measure a 10 m × 10 m site to study. Place one stake at each corner of the site. Loop the string around each stake, and run the string from one stake to the next to form boundaries for the site.

2. Survey the site, and then prepare a site map of the physical features of the area in your science journal or field notes. For example, show the location of streams, sidewalks, trails, or large rocks, and indicate the direction of any noticeable slope.

3. Create a set of symbols to represent the organisms at your site. For example, you might use green triangles to represent trees, blue circles to represent insects, or brown squares to represent animal burrows or nests. At the bottom or side of the site map, make a key for your symbols.

4. Draw your symbols on the map to show the location and relative abundance of each type of organism. If there is not enough space on your map to indicate the specific kinds of plants and animals you observed, record them in your notebook.

5. In your field notes, record any observations of organisms in their environment. For example, note insects feeding on plants or seeking shelter under rocks. Also describe the physical characteristics of your study area. Some characteristics you might consider including are:

    a. **Sunlight Exposure** How much of the area is exposed to sunlight?

    b. **Soil** Is the soil mostly sand, silt, clay, or organic matter?

    c. **Rain** When was the last rain recorded for this area? How much rain was received?

    d. **Maintenance** Is the area maintained? If so, interview the person who maintains it and find out how often the site is watered, fertilized, treated with pesticides, and mowed.

    e. **Water Drainage** Is the area well drained, or does it have pools of water?

    f. **Vegetation Cover** How much of the soil is covered with vegetation? How much of the soil is exposed?

Marking a Site Use stakes and string to mark a site that you will observe in detail.

6. After completing these observations, identify a 2 m × 2 m area that you would like to study in more detail. Stake out this area, and wrap the string around the stakes.

7. Use your hand lens to inspect the area. Be careful not to disturb the soil or the organisms. Then record the types of insects and plants you see.

8. Collect a small sample of soil, and observe it with your hand lens. Record a description of the soil and any organisms that live in it.

Analysis

Organizing Data Use your site map, your classmates' site maps, and your notes to answer the following questions. Write your answers in your science journal.

1. **Identifying Organisms** Use field guides provided by your teacher to identify the organisms you saw. Include both the common and the scientific name for each. Was there more of one particular type of organism in your area?

2. **Analyzing Data** Describe the 2 m × 2 m site you studied. Is this site characteristic of the larger site?

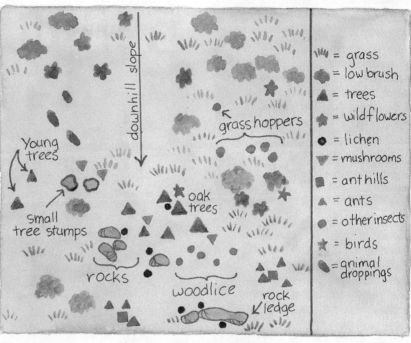

Site Maps Your site map should be as detailed as possible, and it should include a legend.

Conclusions

3. **Interpreting Conclusions** What are the differences between the areas that your classmates studied? Do different plants and animals live in different areas?

4. **Making Predictions** As the seasons change, the types of organisms that live in the area you studied may also change. Predict how your area might change in a different season or if a fire or flood occurred.

Extension

5. **Asking Questions** Based on what you have learned, think of a question that explores how the components of the area you observed interact with each other. For example, you might want to consider the influence of humans on the site; study a particular predator/prey relationship; or explore the effects of physical features, such as water or sunlight, on the growth or behavior of organisms. Write a description of how you would investigate this topic.

CHAPTER 2

Section 1
Scientific Methods

Section 2
Statistics and Models

Section 3
Making Informed Decisions

Why It Matters

Scientists use a variety of techniques to study environmental science topics. In this photo, researchers are monitoring the breeding behaviors of king penguins.

How might the observations made by scientists in the field impact decision-making that affects the environment?

CASESTUDY

Learn about how scientific observations can help solve complex environmental problems in the case study *Saving the Everglades: Making Informed Decisions* on pages 46–47.

Tools of Environmental Science

**ONLINE
ENVIRONMENTAL SCIENCE**
HMDScience.com

Go online to access additional resources, including labs, worksheets, multimedia, and resources in Spanish.

Scientific Methods

Objectives

> List and describe the steps of the experimental method.

> Describe why a good hypothesis is not simply a guess.

> Describe the two essential parts of a good experiment.

> Describe how scientists study subjects in which experiments are not possible.

> Explain the importance of curiosity and imagination in science.

The word *science* comes from the Latin verb *scire*, meaning "to know." Indeed, science is full of amazing facts and ideas about how nature works. But science is not just something you know; it is also something you do. This chapter explores how science is done and examines the tools scientists use.

The Experimental Method

You have probably heard the phrase, "Today scientists discovered…" How do scientists make these discoveries? Scientists make most of their discoveries using the *experimental method*. This method consists of a series of steps that scientists worldwide use to identify and answer questions. The first step is observing.

Observing

Science usually begins with observation. Someone notices, or observes, something and begins to ask questions. An **observation** is a piece of information we gather using our senses—our sight, hearing, smell, and touch. To extend their senses, scientists often use tools such as rulers, microscopes, and even satellites. For example, a ruler provides our eyes with a standard way to compare the lengths of different objects. The scientists in **Figure 1.1** are observing the body length of a tranquilized wolf with the help of a tape measure. Observations can take many forms, including descriptions, drawings, photographs, and measurements.

Students at Keene High School in New Hampshire observed that dwarf wedge mussels were disappearing from the Ashuelot River, which is located near their school. The students also observed that the river is polluted. These observations prompted the students to take the next step in the experimental method—forming hypotheses.

Key Terms

observation
hypothesis
prediction
experiment
variable
experimental group
control group
data
correlation

FIGURE 1.1

Making Measurements These scientists are measuring the body length of a tranquilized wolf for a scientific study.

©Jeff & Alexa Henry

Hypothesizing and Predicting
Procedure
1. Place a plastic or metal tray on a table, with a thin book underneath one end of the tray.
2. Place 50 mL each of potting soil, sand, and schoolyard dirt in separate piles at the high end of the tray.
3. Write a hypothesis that explains which of the three soils will wash away most easily when it rains.
4. Use a toothpick to poke several small holes in the bottom of a paper cup.
5. Pour water into the cup, and slowly sprinkle water over the three piles of soil.

Analysis
1. What happened to the different soils? Explain why.
2. Revise your hypothesis, if necessary, based on your experiment.

Hypothesizing and Predicting

Observations give us answers to questions, but observations almost always lead to more questions. To answer a specific question, a scientist may form a hypothesis. A **hypothesis** (hie PAHTH uh sis) is a testable idea or explanation that leads to a scientific investigation. A hypothesis is more than a guess. A good hypothesis follows from what you already know and can be tested.

The Keene High School students observed two trends: that the number of dwarf wedge mussels on the Ashuelot River was declining over time and that the number of dwarf wedge mussels decreased at sites downstream from the first study site. These trends are illustrated in **Figure 1.2.** Students tested the water in three places and found that the farther downstream they went, the more phosphate the water had. Phosphates are chemicals in many fertilizers.

Armed with their observations, the students might make the following hypothesis: *phosphate fertilizer from a lawn is washing into the river and killing dwarf wedge mussels.* To test their hypothesis, the students make a **prediction,** a logical statement about what will happen if the hypothesis is supported. The students might make the following prediction: *mussels will die when exposed to high levels of phosphate in their water*.

It is important that the students' hypothesis—high levels of phosphate are killing the mussels—can be incorrect. If students successfully raised mussels in water that has high phosphate levels, their hypothesis would not be supported. Every time a hypothesis is not supported, the number of possible explanations for an observation is reduced. By eliminating possible explanations, a scientist can zero in on the best explanation with more confidence.

FIGURE 1.2

Diagramming Trends The diagram below shows the trends observed by the students at Keene High School. Site 1 is upstream. Site 3 is downstream.

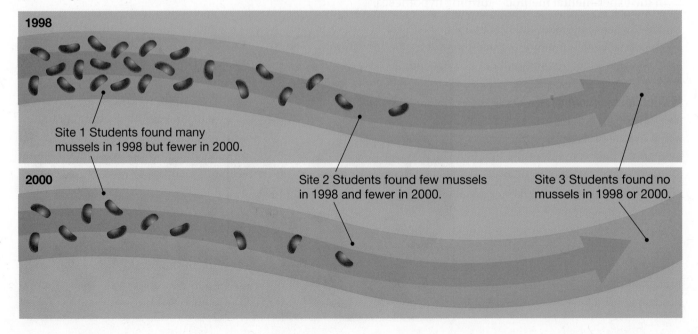

1998

Site 1 Students found many mussels in 1998 but fewer in 2000.

2000

Site 2 Students found few mussels in 1998 and fewer in 2000.

Site 3 Students found no mussels in 1998 or 2000.

Experimenting

The questions that arise from observations often cannot be answered by making more observations. In this situation, scientists usually perform one or more experiments. An **experiment** is a procedure designed to test a hypothesis under controlled conditions.

Experiments should be designed to pinpoint cause-and-effect relationships. For this reason, good experiments have two essential characteristics: a single variable is tested, and a control is used. The **variable** (VER ee uh buhl) is the factor of interest, which, in our example, would be the level of phosphate in the water. To test for one variable, scientists usually study two groups or situations at a time. The variable being studied is the only difference between the groups. The group that receives the experimental treatment is called the **experimental group**. In our example, the experimental group would be those mussels that receive phosphate in their water. The group that does not receive the experimental treatment is called the **control group**. In our example, the control group would be those mussels that do not have phosphate added to their water. If the mussels in the control group thrive while most of those in the experimental group die, the experiment's results support the hypothesis that phosphates from fertilizer are killing the mussels.

The Scientific Process

✓ **CHECK FOR UNDERSTANDING**

Compare What is the difference between an experimental group and a control group?

The Experimental Method in Action at Keene High School

Keene High School students collected mussels (nonendangered relatives of the dwarf wedge mussel) and placed equal numbers of them in two types of aquariums. They ensured that the conditions in the aquariums were identical—same water temperature, food, hours of light, and so on. The students added a measured amount of phosphate to the aquarium of the experimental group. They added nothing to the aquarium of the control group.

A key to the success of an experiment is changing only one variable and having a control group. What would happen if the aquarium in which most of the mussels died had phosphate in the water and was also warmer? The students would not know if the phosphate or the higher temperature killed the mussels.

Another key to experimenting in science is *replication*, or recreating the experimental conditions to make sure the results are consistent. In this case, using ten aquariums—five control and five experimental—would help ensure that the results are not simply due to chance.

Keene High School students conducted an experiment to study the effect of phosphate levels on the growth rates of freshwater mussels.

Critical Thinking

1. **Applying Ideas** Why did the students ensure that the conditions in both aquariums were identical?

2. **Evaluating Hypotheses** How would you change the hypothesis if mussels died in both aquariums?

Courtesy of Cliff Lerner

FIGURE 1.3

Scientific Tools This scientist is analyzing his data with the help of a computer and specialized equipment.

Organizing and Analyzing Data

Keeping careful and accurate records is extremely important in science. A scientist cannot rely on experimental results that are based on sloppy observations or incomplete records. The information that a scientist gathers during an experiment, which is often in numeric form, is called **data**.

Organizing data into tables and graphic illustrations helps scientists analyze the data and explain the data clearly to others. The scientist in **Figure 1.3** is analyzing data on pesticides in food. Graphs are often used by scientists to display relationships or trends in the data. Graphs are especially useful for illustrating conclusions drawn from an experiment.

One common type of graph is called a *bar graph*. Bar graphs are useful for comparing the data for several things in one graph. **Figure 1.4** shows the same data in both table and graph form. Look at the data for Site 3 in the bar graph. The data show that the concentration of phosphates is higher at Site 3 than at Sites 1 and 2, and the concentration of nitrates is lower than at Sites 1 and 2.

Drawing Conclusions

Scientists determine the results of their experiment by analyzing their data and comparing the outcome of their experiment with their prediction. Ideally, this comparison provides scientists with an obvious conclusion. But often the conclusion is not obvious. For example, in the mussel experiment, what if three mussels died in the control tank and five died in the experimental tank? The students could not be certain that phosphate is killing the mussels. Scientists often use mathematical tools, or statistics, to help them determine whether such differences are meaningful or are just a coincidence. Scientists also repeat their experiments.

FIGURE 1.4

Organizing Data The graph and the table above it compare the concentrations of phosphates and nitrates in the Ashuelot River in 2000. Site 1 is upstream of Sites 2 and 3.

POLLUTANT CONCENTRATIONS (MG/L)		
Site	**Nitrates**	**Phosphates**
1	0.3	0.02
2	0.3	0.06
3	0.1	0.07

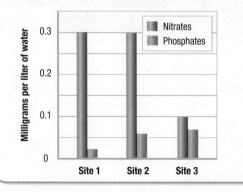

Repeating Experiments

Although the results from a single experiment may seem conclusive, scientists look for a large amount of supporting evidence before they consider a hypothesis to be supported. The more often an experiment can be repeated with the same results, in different places and by different people, the more sure scientists become about the reliability of their results and conclusions.

Communicating Results

Scientists publish their results to share what they have learned with other scientists. When scientists think their results are important, they usually publish their findings as a scientific article in a peer-reviewed journal. This means other scientists have confidence in the quality of their work. A scientific article includes the question the scientist explored, reasons why the question is important, background information, a precise description of how the work was done, the data that were collected, and the scientist's interpretation of the data.

The Correlation Method

Whenever possible, scientists study questions by using experiments. But many questions cannot be studied experimentally. The question "What was Earth's climate like 60 million years ago?" cannot be studied by performing an experiment because the scientists are 60 million years too late. "Does smoking cause lung cancer in humans?" cannot be studied experimentally because doing experiments that might injure people would be unethical.

When using experiments to answer questions is impossible or unethical, scientists test predictions by examining **correlations,** or associations between two or more events. For example, scientists know that the relative width of a ring on a tree trunk is a good indicator of the amount of rainfall the tree received in a given year. Trees produce wide rings in rainy years and narrow rings in dry years. Scientists have used this knowledge to investigate why the first European settlers at Roanoke Island, Virginia (often called the Lost Colony) disappeared and why most of the first settlers at Jamestown, Virginia, died. As shown in **Figure 1.5**, the rings of older trees on the Virginia coast indicate that the Lost Colony and the Jamestown Colony were founded during two of the worst droughts the coast had experienced in centuries. The scientists concluded that the settlers may have starved because the drought made it hard to grow food.

Although correlation studies are useful, correlations do not necessarily prove cause-and-effect relationships between two variables. For example, the correlation between increasing phosphate levels and a declining mussel population on the Ashuelot River does not prove that phosphates harm mussels. Scientists become more sure about their conclusions if they find the same correlation in different places and as they eliminate other possible explanations.

Connect to GEOLOGY

Coral Correlation

Some geologists use an interesting correlation to study records of past climates. Certain species of coral put down layers of skeleton every year and can live for 300 years. Coral skeletons contain the elements strontium, Sr, and calcium, Ca. In some corals, the ratio of these elements in a layer of skeleton correlates with local sea surface temperature at the time that the layer forms. The correlation between the Sr to Ca ratio and the sea temperature provides scientists with one record of how Earth's climate has changed over the centuries.

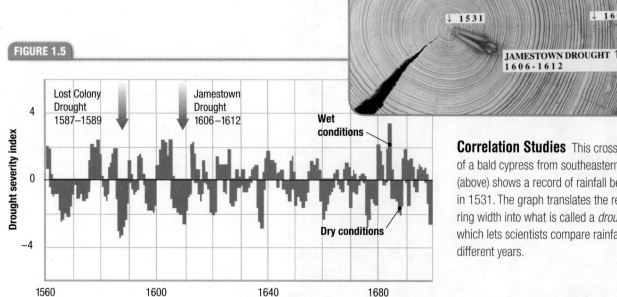

FIGURE 1.5

Courtesy of U of AK Tree-Ring Lab

Source: *Science.*

Correlation Studies This cross section of a bald cypress from southeastern Virginia (above) shows a record of rainfall beginning in 1531. The graph translates the relative tree ring width into what is called a *drought index*, which lets scientists compare rainfall between different years.

Connect to BIOLOGY

Discovering Penicillin

Alexander Fleming discovered penicillin by accident. Someone left a window open near his dishes of bacteria, and the dishes were infected with spores of fungi. Instead of throwing the dishes away, Fleming looked at them closely and saw that the bacteria had died on the side of a dish where a colony of green *Penicillium* mold had started to grow. If he had not been a careful observer, penicillin might not have been discovered. You may find *Penicillium* yourself on moldy bread.

Scientific Habits of Mind

Scientists actually approach questions in many different ways. But scientists tend to share several key habits of mind, or ways of approaching and thinking about things.

Curiosity

Scientists are endlessly curious. Jane Goodall, pictured in **Figure 1.6**, is an inspiring example. She studied a chimpanzee troop in Africa for years. She observed the troop so closely that she came to know the personality and behavior of each member of the troop and greatly contributed to our knowledge of that species.

The Habit of Skepticism

Scientists also tend to be skeptical, which means that they don't believe everything they are told. For example, up until the late 19th century, many people thought that some organisms arose spontaneously from non-living material. A series of scientists, including Francesco Redi in 1668, John Needham in 1745, and Louis Pasteur in 1859, conducted experiments that refuted the possibility of spontaneous generation. Scientists are also skeptical of their own work. They try to think of alternate explanations for their results before publishing them.

Openness to New Ideas

As the example above shows, skepticism can go hand in hand with being open to new ideas. Good scientists keep an open mind about how the world works.

Intellectual Honesty

A scientist may be certain that a hypothesis is correct before it has been fully tested. But when an experiment is repeated, the results may differ from those obtained the first time. A good scientist will consider the possibility that the new results may be accurate, even if this means that the hypothesis might be wrong.

FIGURE 1.6

Curiosity Jane Goodall is famous for her close observations of chimpanzees—observations fueled in part by her endless curiosity.

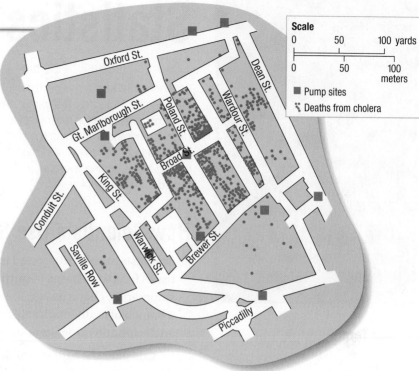

FIGURE 1.7

Creative Problem-Solving John Snow (below) created his famous spot map (right), which let him see a pattern that no one had noticed before.

Imagination and Creativity

Good scientists are not only open to new ideas but able to conceive of new ideas themselves. The ability to see patterns where others do not, or to imagine things that others cannot, allows a good scientist to expand the boundaries of what we know.

An example of an imaginative and creative scientist is John Snow, shown in **Figure 1.7**. Snow was a physician in London during a cholera epidemic in 1854. Cholera, a potentially fatal disease, is caused by a bacterium found in water that is polluted with human waste. Few people had indoor plumbing in 1854. Most people got their water from public pumps; each pump had its own well. To find the polluted water source, Snow made a map showing the homes of everyone who died of cholera. The map also showed the public water pumps. In this example of a correlation study, he found that more deaths occurred around a pump in Broad Street than around other pumps in the area. London authorities ended the cholera epidemic by shutting off the Broad Street pump. Using observation, imagination, and creativity, Snow solved an environmental problem and saved lives.

✔ Section 1 **Formative Assessment**

▶ Reviewing Main Ideas

1. **Describe** the steps of the experimental method.

2. **Name** three scientific habits of mind and explain their importance.

3. **Explain** why a hypothesis is not just a guess.

4. **Explain** how scientists try to answer questions that cannot be tested with experiments.

✔ Critical Thinking

5. **Analyzing Methods** Read the description of experiments. Describe the two essential parts of a good experiment, and explain their importance.

6. **Analyzing Relationships** How can a scientist be both skeptical and open to new ideas at the same time? Write a one-page story that describes such a situation.

- Explain how scientists use statistics.

- Explain why the size of a statistical sample is important.

- Describe three types of models commonly used by scientists.

- Explain the relationship between probability and risk.

- Explain the importance of conceptual and mathematical models.

Key Terms

statistics
mean
distribution
probability
sample
risk
model
conceptual model
mathematical model

Statistics and Models

Environmental science provides a lot of data that need to be organized and interpreted before they are useful. **Statistics** is the collection and classification of data that are in the form of numbers. People commonly use the term statistics to describe numbers, such as the batting record of a baseball player. Sportswriters also use the methods of statistics to translate a player's batting record over many games into a batting average, which allows people to easily compare the batting records of different players.

How Scientists Use Statistics

Scientists are also interested in comparing things, but scientists use statistics for a wide range of purposes. Scientists rely on and use statistics to summarize, characterize, analyze, and compare data. Statistics is actually a branch of mathematics that provides scientists with important tools for analyzing and understanding their data.

Consider the experiment in which students studied mussels to see if the mussels were harmed by fertilizer in their water. Students collected data on mussel length and phosphate levels during this experiment. Some mussels in the control group grew more than some mussels in the experimental group, yet some grew less. How could the students turn this data into meaningful numbers?

Statistics Works with Populations

Scientists use statistics to describe statistical populations. A *statistical population* is a group of similar things that a scientist is interested in learning about. For example, the dwarf wedge mussels shown in **Figure 2.1** are part of the population of all dwarf wedge mussels on the Ashuelot River.

FIGURE 2.1

Statistical Population Students found these dwarf wedge mussel shells in a muskrat den. These mussels are part of the statistical population of all dwarf wedge mussels on the Ashuelot River.

Courtesy of Cliff Lerner

What Is the Average?

Although statistical populations are composed of similar individuals, these individuals often have different characteristics. For example, in the population of students in your classroom, each student has a different height, weight, and so on.

The Keene High School students measured the lengths of dwarf wedge mussels in a population, as shown in **Figure 2.1**. They added the lengths of the mussels and then divided that value by the total number of mussels. This gave the average length of the mussels, which in statistical terms is called the mean. The **mean** is the number obtained by adding the data for a characteristic and dividing this sum by the number of individuals. The mean provides a single measure for a given characteristic of a population. Scientists can compare different populations by comparing their means. The mean length of the mussels in **Figure 2.2** is about 30 mm.

The Distribution

The bar graph in **Figure 2.2** shows the lengths of dwarf wedge mussels in a population. The pattern that the bars create when viewed as a whole is called the *distribution*. A **distribution** is the relative arrangement of the members of a statistical population. In **Figure 2.2**, the lengths of the individuals are arranged between 15 and 50 mm.

The overall shape of the bars, which rise to form a hump in the middle of the graph, is also part of the distribution. The line connecting the tops of the bars in **Figure 2.2** forms the shape of a bell. The graphs of many characteristics of populations, such as the heights of people, form bell-shaped curves. A bell-shaped curve indicates a *normal distribution*. In a normal distribution, the data are grouped symmetrically around the mean.

✔ **CHECK FOR UNDERSTANDING**
Summarize How was the mean length of the dwarf wedge mussel population calculated?

FIGURE 2.2

Size Distribution This bar graph shows the distribution of lengths in a population of dwarf wedge mussels.

✔ **CRITICAL THINKING**
Analyze Data Which shell length was most common in this population of dwarf wedge mussels? Which shell size was least common?

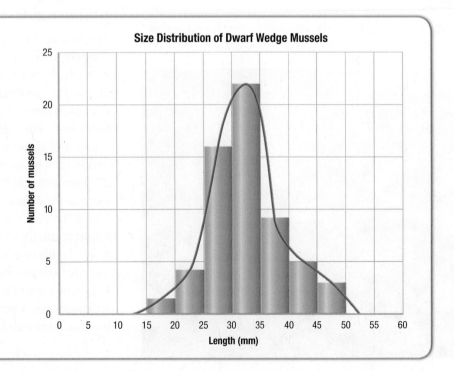

Size Distribution of Dwarf Wedge Mussels

(x-axis: Length (mm), y-axis: Number of mussels)

Probability

Probability is often determined by observing ratios or patterns. For example, imagine that you count 200 pine trees in a forest and notice that 40 of those trees have pine cones. What is the probability that the next pine tree you come across will have pine cones?

What Is the Probability?

The chance that something will happen is called **probability.** For example, if you toss a penny, what is the probability that it will come up heads? Most people would say "half and half," and they would be right. The chance of a tossed penny coming up heads is $\frac{1}{2}$, which can also be expressed as 0.5 or 50%. In fact, probability is usually expressed as a number between 0 and 1 and written as a decimal rather than as a fraction. Suppose the penny comes up heads 7 out of 10 times. Does this result prove that the probability of a penny coming up heads is 0.7? No, it does not. So what is the problem?

The problem is that the *sample size*—the number of objects or events sampled—is too small to yield an accurate result. In statistics, a **sample** is a group of individuals or events selected to represent the population. If you toss a penny 10 times, your sample size is 10. If you continue tossing 1,000 times, you are almost certain to get about 50% heads and 50% tails. In this example, the sample is the number of coin tosses you make, while the population is the total number of coin tosses possible. Scientists try to make sure that the samples they take are large enough to give an accurate estimate for the whole population.

Statistics in Everyday Life

You have probably heard, "There is a 50 percent chance of rain today." **Figure 2.3** shows an example of a natural event that we often associate with probability—a thunderstorm. You encounter statistics often and use them more than you may think. People are constantly trying to determine the chance of something happening. A guess or gut instinct is probably just an unconscious sense of probability.

Probability Most people are familiar with statistics regarding the weather, such as the chance, or probability, that a thunderstorm will occur.

Understanding the News

The news contains statistics every day, even if they are not obvious. For example, a reporter may say, "A study shows that forest fires increased air pollution in the city last year." We could ask many statistical questions about this news item. We might first ask what the average amount of air pollution in the city is. We could gather data on air pollution levels over the past 20 years and graph these data. Then we could calculate the mean, and ask ourselves how different last year's data are from the average. We might graph the data and look at the distribution. Do this year's pollution levels seem unusually high compared to levels in other years? Recognizing and paying attention to statistics will make you a better consumer of information, including information about the environment.

©Kent Wood/Photo Researchers, Inc.

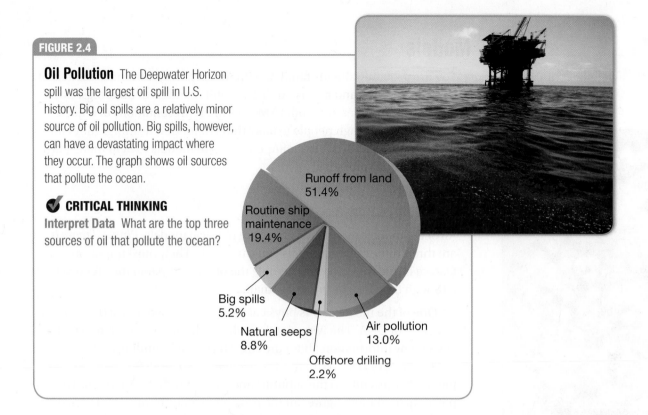

FIGURE 2.4

Oil Pollution The Deepwater Horizon spill was the largest oil spill in U.S. history. Big oil spills are a relatively minor source of oil pollution. Big spills, however, can have a devastating impact where they occur. The graph shows oil sources that pollute the ocean.

✔ **CRITICAL THINKING**

Interpret Data What are the top three sources of oil that pollute the ocean?

Runoff from land
51.4%

Routine ship
maintenance
19.4%

Big spills
5.2%

Natural seeps
8.8%

Offshore drilling
2.2%

Air pollution
13.0%

Thinking About Risk

In scientific terms, **risk** is the probability of an unwanted outcome. For example, if you have no clue about the correct answer on a multiple choice test with four options, you have a 3 in 4 chance of guessing the wrong answer. The risk of guessing incorrectly is $\frac{3}{4}$, or 75 percent. **Figure 2.4** shows a well-publicized environmental problem—an oil spill. As you can see in the circle graph, the risk of pollution from large oil spills is much smaller than the risk of oil pollution from everyday sources.

Individuals intuitively evaluate risk every day and make decisions about what to do or what not to do. For example, deciding whether to cross the street against a red light might get you to school on time, but could have unwanted outcomes, too. General considerations in weighing individual risk include the probability that an event will occur (such as a speeding car entering the intersection), the severity of the outcome if such an event does occur, and whether the exposure to risk is involuntary. People tend to perceive voluntary risk as less likely. Most individual risk analysis includes subjective factors and best guesses about the chances of an event occurring.

Scientists often must calculate risk to large communities of people in order to inform policy decisions in government. These estimates involve data on the history of events, projections for future occurrences, and scientific evidence for adverse outcomes. The challenge for governments is that evaluating adverse outcomes usually involves many citizens. The risk of getting cancer from exposure to a pollutant might just be one in a thousand for each exposed individual, but if a million people are exposed, then 1,000 individuals and their families must deal with the effects of the resulting disease.

Connect to LAW

Oil Tankers

The Oil Pollution Act of 1990 was a response to a huge oil spill from an oil tanker, the *Exxon Valdez*, in Alaska in 1989. The controversial bill had been debated for 14 years; it passed swiftly in the aftermath of the disaster. Under the law, all oil tankers operating in United States waters must be protected with double hulls by 2015.

FIGURE 2.5

Physical Model This plastic model of a DNA molecule is an example of a physical model.

Models

You are probably already familiar with models. Museums have models of ships, dinosaurs, and atoms. Architects build models of buildings. Even crash-test dummies are models. **Models** are representations of objects or systems. Although people usually think of models as things they can touch, scientists use several different types of models to help them learn about our environment.

Physical Models

All of the models mentioned above are physical models. *Physical models* are three-dimensional models you can touch. Their most important feature is that they closely resemble the object or system they represent, although they may be larger or smaller.

One of the most famous physical models was used to discover the structure of DNA. The two scientists who built the structural model of DNA knew information about the size, shape, and bonding qualities of the subunits of DNA. With this knowledge, the scientists created model pieces that resembled the subunits and the bonds between them. These pieces helped them figure out the possible structures of DNA. Discovering the structure of DNA furthered other research that helped scientists understand how DNA replicates in a living cell. **Figure 2.5** shows a modern model of a DNA molecule. The most useful models teach scientists something new and help to further other discoveries.

Graphical Models

Maps and charts are the most common examples of *graphical models*. Showing someone a road map is easier than telling him or her how to get somewhere. An example of a graphical model is the map of the Denver, Colorado, area shown in **Figure 2.6**. Scientists use graphical models to show things such as the positions of the stars, the amount of forest cover in a given area, and the depth of water in a river or along a coast.

FIGURE 2.6

Graphical Model This map of the Denver, Colorado, area is an example of a graphical model.

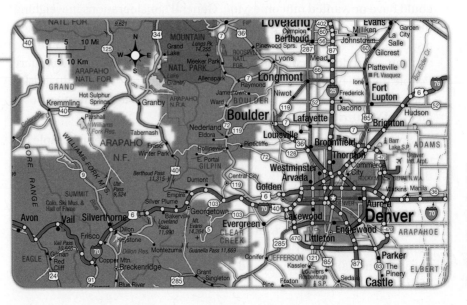

Conceptual Models

A **conceptual model** is a verbal or graphical explanation of how a system works or is organized. A flow-chart diagram is an example of a type of conceptual model. A flow-chart uses boxes linked by arrows to illustrate what a system contains and how those contents are organized.

Consider this example. Suppose that a scientist wants to know how mercury, a poisonous metal, moves through the environment to reach people after the mercury is released from burning coal. The scientist would use an understanding of mercury in the environment to build a conceptual model, as shown in **Figure 2.7**. Scientists often create such diagrams to help them understand how a system works—what components the system contains, how they are arranged, and how they affect one another.

Conceptual models are not always diagrams. They can also be verbal descriptions or even drawings of how something works or is put together. For example, the model of an atom as a large ball circled by smaller balls is a conceptual model of the structure of an atom. As this example shows, an actual model can be more than one type. An atomic model made of plastic balls is both a conceptual model and a physical model.

FIELDSTUDY

Go to Appendix B to find the field study
Organizing Data

✔ **CHECK FOR UNDERSTANDING**

Explain How does building a conceptual model help scientists in their work?

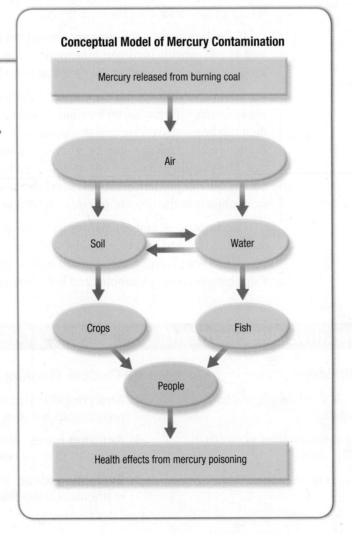

FIGURE 2.7

Conceptual Model This conceptual model shows how mercury released from burning coal could end up reaching people, where it could cause poisoning.

Conceptual Model of Mercury Contamination

Mercury released from burning coal

↓

Air

↓   ↓

Soil ⇄ Water

↓   ↓

Crops   Fish

↘   ↙

People

↓

Health effects from mercury poisoning

FIGURE 2.8

Satellite Image This is a satellite image of the San Francisco Bay Area. Scientists use mathematical models to understand the terrain from the way objects on the surface reflect light. In this image, healthy vegetation is red.

Mathematical Models

A **mathematical model** is one or more equations that represents the way a system or process works. You can represent many common situations using math models. Mathematical models are especially useful in cases with many variables, such as the many things that affect the weather.

Because mathematical models use numbers and equations, people may think the models are always right. But weather models, for example, sometimes predict rain on dry days. In fact, people are the ones who interpret data and write the equations.

If the data or the equations are wrong, the model will not be realistic and so will provide incorrect information. Like all models, mathematical models are only as good as the data that went into building them.

Scientists use the power of computers to model many complex factors. For example, information on location and many wavelengths of reflected light can be used to create amazing images. Look at the image of the San Francisco Bay Area in **Figure 2.8.** This is a "false color" digital satellite image. The satellite measures energy reflected from the Earth's surface. Scientists use mathematical models to relate the amount of energy reflected from objects to the objects' physical condition.

One important tool of environmental science that combines both mathematical and graphical models is Geographic Information Systems (GIS). GIS is a mapping tool that can help scientists understand relationships between many variables and how they affect organisms and people.

✓ Section 2 **Formative Assessment**

▶ Reviewing Main Ideas

1. **Explain** why sample size is important in determining probability.

2. **Explain** what "the mean number of weeds in three plots of land" means.

3. **Describe** three types of models used by scientists.

✔ Critical Thinking

4. **Analyzing Relationships** Explain the relationship between probability and risk.

5. **Applying Ideas** Write a paragraph that uses examples to show how scientists use statistics.

6. **Evaluating Ideas** Why are conceptual and mathematical models especially powerful?

Making Informed Decisions

Objectives

- Describe three values that people consider when making decisions about the environment.

- Describe the four steps in a simple environmental decision-making model.

- Compare the short-term and long-term consequences of two decisions regarding a hypothetical environmental issue.

Scientific research is an essential first step to solve environmental problems. However, many other factors must also be considered. How will the proposed solution affect people's lives? How much will it cost? Is the solution ethical? Questions like these require an examination of **values,** which are principles or standards we consider important. What values should influence decisions that affect the environment? **Figure 3.1** lists some values that often affect environmental decisions. You might think of others as well.

An Environmental Decision-Making Model

Forming an opinion about an environmental issue is often difficult and may seem overwhelming. It helps to have a systematic way of analyzing the issues and deciding what is important. One way to guide yourself through this process is to use a decision-making model. A **decision-making model** is a conceptual model that provides a systematic process for making decisions.

Figure 3.2 shows one possible decision-making model. The first step of the model is to gather information. In addition to watching news reports and reading about environmental issues, you should listen to well-informed people on all sides of an issue. Then consider which values apply to the issue. Explore the consequences of each option. Finally, evaluate all of the information to make a decision.

Key Terms

value
decision-making model

FIGURE 3.1

VALUES THAT AFFECT ENVIRONMENTAL DECISION MAKING

Value	Definition
Aesthetic	what is beautiful or pleasing
Economic	the gain or loss of money or jobs
Educational	the accumulation and sharing of knowledge
Environmental	the protection of natural resources
Ethical/moral	what is right or wrong
Health	the maintenance of human health
Recreational	human leisure activities
Scientific	understanding of the natural world
Social/cultural	the maintenance of human communities and their values and traditions

FIGURE 3.2

Decision-Making Model
This diagram shows a simple decision-making model.

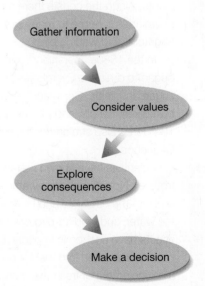

Gather information

Consider values

Explore consequences

Make a decision

FIGURE 3.3

Proposed Nature Preserve
This map shows the proposed nature preserve, which would be home to warblers like the one pictured (right).

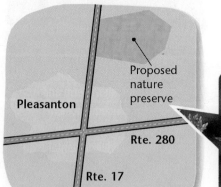

Pleasanton

Proposed nature preserve

Rte. 280

Rte. 17

A Hypothetical Situation

Consider the following hypothetical example. In the town of Pleasanton, in Valley County, biologists from the local college have been studying the golden-cheeked warbler, shown in **Figure 3.3**. The warblers have already disappeared from most areas around the state, and the warbler population is declining in Valley County. The biologists warn county officials that if the officials do not take action, the state fish and wildlife service may list the bird as an endangered species.

Pleasanton is growing rapidly, and much of the new development is occurring outside the city limits. This development is destroying warbler habitat. Valley County already has strict environmental controls on building, but these controls do not prevent the clearing of land.

Saving the Everglades: Making Informed Decisions

The Florida Everglades is an enormous, shallow freshwater marsh. The water in the Everglades slowly flows from Lake Okeechobee to Florida Bay. Much of the marsh is filled with sawgrass and other water-loving plants. Along the coasts there are estuaries with mangrove forests. The Everglades is home to many species of wildlife, such as fish, panthers, alligators, and wading birds.

In the 1880s, marshlands were considered wastelands. So developers began to drain the Everglades and replace marsh with houses and sugarcane fields. Between 1940 and 1971, the Army Corps of Engineers built dikes, canals, and pumping stations that drained even more water. The Corps also straightened the Kissimmee River, which runs into Lake Okeechobee.

Scientists have shown that what remains of the Everglades is in trouble. Not enough freshwater is moving south through the marshes and into the estuaries and Florida Bay. Fertilizer from farms is polluting the water, and wading-bird colonies are much smaller than before. These effects have economic impacts. Because much of the Everglades' water has been diverted into the Atlantic Ocean, the towns of southeast Florida are running out of fresh water and marine life in Florida Bay has declined.

The roseate spoonbill is a colorful resident of the Everglades.

Several groups join together to propose that the county buy several hundred acres of land where the birds are known to breed and save that land as a nature preserve. The groups also propose limiting development on land surrounding the preserve. The group obtains enough signatures on a petition to put the issue to a vote, and the public begins to discuss the proposal.

Some people who own property within the proposed preserve oppose the plan. These property owners have an economic interest in this discussion. They believe that they will lose money if they are forced to sell their land to the county instead of developing it.

Other landowners support the plan. They fear that without the preserve the warbler may be placed on the state's endangered species list. If the bird is listed as endangered, the state will impose a plan to protect the bird that will require even stricter limits on land development. People who have land near the proposed preserve think their land will become more valuable. Many residents of Pleasanton look forward to hiking and camping in the proposed preserve. Other residents do not like the idea of more government regulations on how private property can be used.

The Everglades can be thought of as a shallow, slow-moving river that empties into Florida Bay.

©Matt Bradley/Bruce Coleman, Inc./Photoshot

In the 1990s, a commission reported that the destruction of the Everglades had jeopardized the state's tourism industry, farming, and the economic future of south Florida. The solution was obvious: undo the water-diversion dikes and dams and restore water to the Everglades. Groups that had been fighting over the Everglades for decades met to work on a plan. After five years, environmentalists, politicians, farmers, tourism advocates, and developers agreed on the $7.8 billion Everglades Restoration Plan, which was signed into law in 2000.

No group was fully satisfied with the plan, but all agreed that they were better off with it than without it. As a result of the plan, 7 miles of the Kissimmee River has been restored to its original path. Native plants are absorbing some of the pollution that has killed an estimated $200 million worth of wildlife.

Everglades restoration is ongoing and requires continual research. Scientists continue to study how water flows through the Everglades, how the changing flows from restoration will affect plants and animals, and what levels of nutrients from fertilizer are safe for the ecosystem. With this and other information, the plan can continually be improved.

Critical Thinking

1. **Analyzing Processes** Explain why it was so difficult for people to agree on how to restore the Everglades.

2. **Analyzing Relationships** If your county decided to build a landfill, do you think the decision-making process would resemble the Everglades example?

FIGURE 3.4

Warbler Population

The population of golden-cheeked warblers in the Pleasanton area has declined in recent years.

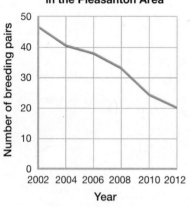

Warbler Population in the Pleasanton Area

How to Use the Decision-Making Model

The hypothetical situation in Pleasanton can be used to illustrate how to use the decision-making model. Michael Price is a voter in Valley County who will vote on whether the county should create a nature preserve to protect the golden-cheeked warbler. The steps Michael took to make his decision about the proposal are outlined below.

Gather Information

Michael studied the warbler issue thoroughly by watching local news reports, reading the newspaper, learning more about golden-cheeked warblers from various Web sites, and attending forums where the issues were discussed. An example of scientific information that Michael considered includes the graph of warbler population decline in **Figure 3.4**. Several of the arguments on both sides made sense to him.

Consider Values

Michael made a table similar to **Figure 3.5** to clarify his thoughts. The values listed are environmental, economic, and recreational. Someone else might have thought other values were more important to consider.

FIGURE 3.5

SHOULD VALLEY COUNTY SET ASIDE A NATURE PRESERVE?			
	Environmental	**Economic**	**Recreational**
Positive short-term consequences	• Habitat destruction in the nature preserve area is slowed or stopped.	• Landowners whose property was bought by the county receive a payment for their land. • Property outside the preserve area can be developed with fewer restrictions.	• Parts of the preserve are made available immediately for hiking and picnicking.
Negative short-term consequences	• Environmental controls are made less strict in parts of the county outside the preserve area.	• Property owners inside the preserve area do not make as much money as if they had developed their land. • Taxpayers must pay higher taxes to buy preserve land.	• Michael could not think of any negative short-term consequences.
Positive long-term consequences	• The population of warblers increases, and the bird does not become endangered. • Other species of organisms are also protected. • An entire habitat is preserved.	• Property near the preserve increases in value because it is near a natural area. • Businesses move to Valley County because of its beauty and recreational opportunities, which results in job growth. • The warbler is not listed as endangered, which avoids stricter controls on land use.	• Large areas of the preserve are available for hiking and picnicking. • Landowners near the preserve may develop campgrounds with bike trails, swimming, and fishing available on land adjacent to the preserve.
Negative long-term consequences	• Other habitat outside the preserve may be damaged by overdevelopment.	• Taxpayers must continue to pay for maintaining the preserve. • Taxpayers lose the tax revenue that this land would have provided if it was developed.	• State officials might restrict some recreational activities on private land within the preserve.

Explore Consequences

Michael decided that in the short term the positive and negative consequences listed in his table were almost equally balanced. He saw that some people would suffer financially from the plan, but others would benefit. Taxpayers would have to pay for the preserve, but all the residents would have access to land that was previously off-limits because it was privately owned. Some parts of the county would have more protection from development, and some would have less.

The long-term consequences of the plan helped Michael make his decision. He realized that environmental values were an important factor. The idea of a bird becoming extinct distressed him. Also, protecting warbler habitat now would cost less than doing it later under a state-imposed plan.

Michael considered that there were long-term benefits to add to the analysis as well. He had read that property values were rising more rapidly in counties with land for recreation. He found that people would pay more to live in counties that have open spaces. Michael had found that Valley County had very little preserved land. He thought that creating the preserve would bring the county long-term economic benefits. He also highly valued the aesthetic and recreational benefits a preserve would offer, such as the running trail in **Figure 3.6**.

Make A Decision

Michael chose to vote for the nature preserve. Other people who looked at the same table of pros and cons might have voted differently. If you lived in Valley County, how would you have voted?

As you learn about issues affecting the environment, both in this course and in the future, use this decision-making model as a starting point to making your decisions. Make sure to consider your values, weigh pros and cons, and keep in mind both the short-term and long-term consequences of your decision.

FIGURE 3.6

Nature Preserve
Land set aside for a nature preserve can benefit people as well as wildlife.

 ## Section 3 **Formative Assessment**

▶ Reviewing Main Ideas

1. **Explain** the importance of each of the four steps in a simple decision-making model.

2. **List** and define three possible values to consider when making environmental decisions.

3. **Describe** in a short paragraph examples of two situations in which environmental values come into conflict with other values.

✔ Critical Thinking

4. **Making Decisions** Pick one of the situations you described in question 3. Make a decision-making table that shows the positive and negative consequences of either of two possible decisions.

5. **Analyzing Information** Suggest how to make the decision-making model presented here more powerful.

A Topographic Map of Keene, New Hampshire

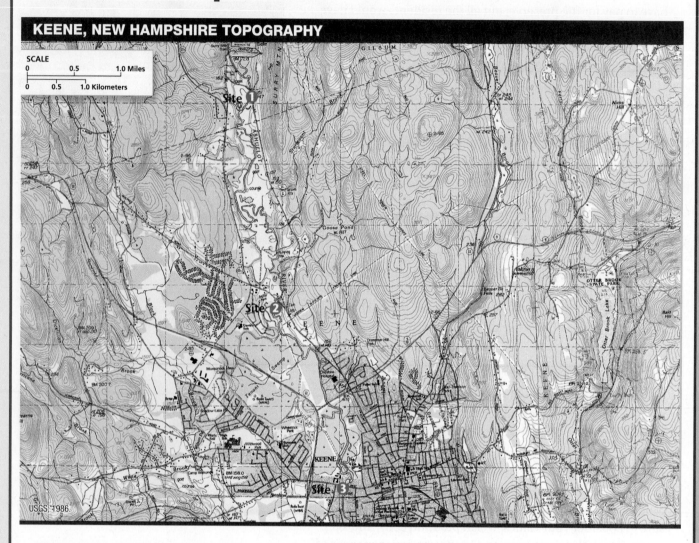

KEENE, NEW HAMPSHIRE TOPOGRAPHY

SCALE

0   0.5   1.0 Miles

0   0.5   1.0 Kilometers

Site 1

Site 2

Site 3

KEENE

USGS, 1986.

Map Skills

Topographic maps use contour lines to indicate areas that share a common elevation. Where the lines are close together, the terrain is steep. Where the lines are far apart, the landscape is flat. In this map, the Ashuelot River flows downhill from Site 1 to Site 3. Use the map to answer the questions below.

1. **Using a Key** Use the scale to calculate the distance between Sites 1 and 2 and between Sites 2 and 3.

2. **Understanding Topography** Are the hills to the east and west of the town of Keene more likely to drain into the river around Site 3 or Site 2? Explain your answer.

3. **Identifying Trends** Which site is more likely to be polluted? Explain your answer.

4. **Analyzing Data** Trace the sections of the Ashuelot River between each site to determine the length of stream between each site.

5. **Interpreting Landforms** A flood plain is an area that floods when a river overflows its banks. Interpret the contour lines to locate the flood plain.

Society and the Environment

ECOZine at HMDScience.com

Go online for the latest environmental science news and updates on all EcoZine articles.

Bats and Bridges

A large colony of Mexican free-tailed bats lives under the Congress Avenue Bridge in Austin, Texas. These bats eat millions of insects a night, so they are welcome neighbors. Communities around the country and around the world have learned of the bats and have asked Austin for help in building bat-friendly bridges. But all that the people of Austin knew was that the bats appeared after the Congress Avenue Bridge was rebuilt in the 1980s. What attracted the bats? The people of Austin had to do a little research.

A Crevice Will Do

In the wild, bats spend the day sleeping in groups in caves or in crevices under the flaking bark of old trees. They come back to the same place every day to roost. Deep crevices in tree bark are rare now that many of our old forests have been cut down, and many bats are in danger of extinction.

In the 1990s, the Texas Department of Transportation and Bat Conservation International, a nonprofit organization based in Austin, set out to discover what made a bridge attractive to bats. They collected data on 600 bridges, including some that had bat colonies and some that did not. They answered the following questions: Where was the bridge located? What was it made of? How was it constructed? Was it over water or land? What was the temperature under the bridge? How was the land around the bridge used?

Some Bridges are Better

Statistical analysis of the data revealed a number of differences between bridges occupied by bats and bridges unoccupied by bats. Which differences were important to the bats and which were not? The researchers returned to the Congress Avenue Bridge in Austin to find out. Crevices under the bridge appeared to be crucial, and the crevices had to be the right size. Free-tailed bats appeared to prefer crevices 1 to 3 cm wide and about 30 cm deep in hidden corners of the bridge, and they preferred bridges made of concrete, not steel.

The scientists looked again at their data on bridges. They discovered that 62 percent of bridges in central and southern Texas that had appropriate crevices were occupied by bats. Now, the Texas Department of Transportation is adding bat houses to existing bridges that do not have crevices. These

Mexican free-tailed bats leave their roost under the Congress Avenue Bridge in Austin, Texas, to hunt for insects.

houses are known as Texas Bat-Abodes, and they can make any bridge friendly to bats.

Bat Conservation International is collecting data on bats and bridges everywhere. Different bat species may have different preferences. A Texas Bat-Abode might not attract bats to a bridge in Minnesota or Maine. If we can figure out what features attract bats to bridges, we can incorporate these features into new bridges and make more bridges into bat-friendly abodes.

What Do You Think?

Many bridges in the United States could provide roosting places for bats. Do you think communities should try to establish colonies of bats under local bridges? How should communities make this decision, and what information would they need to make this decision wisely?

SECTION 1 **Scientific Methods**

OBJECTIVES

- Science is a process by which we learn about the world around us. Science progresses mainly by the experimental method.

- The experimental method involves making observations, forming a hypothesis, performing an experiment, interpreting data, and communicating results.

- In cases in which experiments are impossible, scientists look for correlations between different phenomena.

- Good scientists are curious, creative, honest, skeptical, and open to new ideas.

KEY TERMS

observation
hypothesis
prediction
experiment
variable
experimental group
control group
data
correlation

SECTION 2 **Statistics and Models**

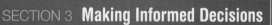

OBJECTIVES

- Scientists use statistics to classify, organize, and interpret data.

- Measures such as means and probabilities are used to describe populations and events.

- Statistics is a powerful tool for evaluating information about the environment.

- Scientists use models, including physical, graphical, conceptual, and mathematical models, to understand the systems they study.

KEY TERMS

statistics
mean
distribution
probability
sample
risk
model
conceptual model
mathematical model

SECTION 3 **Making Informed Decisions**

OBJECTIVES

- Making environmental decisions involves gathering information, considering values, and exploring consequences.

- Decisions about the environment should be made thoughtfully. Using a decision-making model will provide you with a systematic process for making knowledgeable decisions.

- Making a table that lists positive and negative short-term and long-term consequences will help you recognize and weigh your values about an environmental decision.

KEY TERMS

value
decision-making model

CHAPTER 2 **Review**

Reviewing Key Terms

Use each of the following terms in a separate sentence.

1. *experiment*
2. *correlation*
3. *model*
4. *distribution*
5. *values*

For each pair of terms, explain how the meanings of the terms differ.

6. *hypothesis* and *prediction*
7. *risk* and *probability*
8. *distribution* and *population*
9. *sample* and *population*
10. **Concept Map** Use the following terms to create a concept map: *control group, experiment, experimental group, prediction, data, observations, conclusions,* and *hypothesis.*

Reviewing Main Ideas

11. Scientists form _____ hypotheses to answer questions.
    a. accurate
    b. short
    c. mathematical
    d. testable

12. Risk is the _____ of a negative outcome.
    a. sample
    b. statistic
    c. probability
    d. event

13. If the results of your experiment do not support your hypothesis, you should
    a. publish your results anyway.
    b. consider the results abnormal and continue working.
    c. find a way to rationalize your results.
    d. try another method.

14. Models used by scientists include
    a. conceptual models.
    b. variable models.
    c. physical models.
    d. Both (a) and (c)

15. Reading scientific reports is an example of
    a. assessing risk.
    b. considering values.
    c. gathering information.
    d. exploring consequences.

16. A conceptual model represents a way of thinking about
    a. relationships.
    b. variables.
    c. data.
    d. positions.

17. In an experiment, the experimental treatment differs from the control treatment only in the _____ being studied.
    a. experiment
    b. variable
    c. hypothesis
    d. data

18. To fully understand a complex environmental issue, you may need to consider
    a. economics.
    b. values.
    c. scientific information.
    d. All of the above

19. Scientists _____ experiments to make sure the results are meaningful.
    a. perform
    b. repeat
    c. conclude
    d. communicate

Short Answer

20. Explain the statement, "A good scientist is one who asks the right questions."

21. Explain the role of a control group in a scientific experiment.

22. How are statistics helpful for evaluating information about the environment?

23. Explain why environmental scientists use mathematical models.

24. How does making a table help you evaluate the values and concerns you have when making a decision?

Interpreting Graphics

The graph below shows the change in size of a shoreline alligator population over time. Use the graph to answer questions 25–27.

25. Analyzing Data What happened to the density of alligators between 1986 and 1988?

26. Interpreting Data What happened to the trend in the concentration of alligators between 1994 and 1998?

27. Calculate How many times greater was the alligator population in 1986 than it was in 2000?

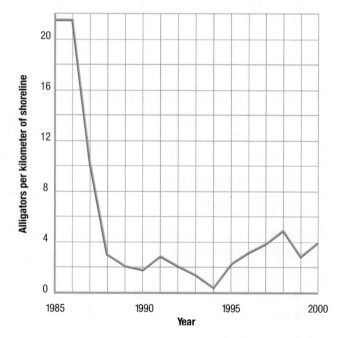

Critical Thinking

28. Draw Conclusions What does a scientist mean by the statement, "There is an 80 percent probability that a tornado will hit this area within the next 10 years?"

29. Infer How does a map of Denver, Colorado allow you to navigate around the city?

30. Evaluate Are complicated models always more accurate? Write a paragraph that uses examples to explain your answer.

31. Interpret Explain what the following statement proves: "We sampled pet owners and found that three out of five surveyed own dogs and two out of five surveyed own cats."

32. Language Arts The word *serendipity,* which means "luck in finding something accidentally," came from a Persian fairy tale called *The Three Princes of Serendip.* In the story, each of the princes discovers something by accident. Research and write a short report on a serendipitous discovery about the environment.

33. Make a Poster Choose an environmental issue in your area. You can choose a real-life problem that you have heard about on the news, such as improving the sewage system or building a new landfill, or you can choose a project that you think should be considered. Research the issue at your school or local library. Prepare a poster listing the groups of people likely to be involved in the decision and the factors that may be taken into consideration, including economic, social, and environmental factors.

Analyzing Data

The table below shows the results of an experiment that tested the hypothesis that butterflies are attracted to some substances but not to others. Twenty-four trays containing four substances were placed in random order on a sandbank to see if butterflies landed on the trays. The number of butterflies that landed on each type of tray and stayed for more than five minutes during a two-hour period was recorded in the table. Use the data in the table below to answer questions 34–35.

BUTTERFLY FEEDING PREFERENCES

	Sugar solution	Nitrogen solution	Water	Salt solution
Number of butterflies attracted	5	87	7	403

34. **Interpret** Do the results in the table show that butterflies are attracted to salt solution but not any other substance? Why or why not? What other data would you like to see to help you evaluate the results of this experiment?

35. **Evaluate** Are there any controls shown in this table? Explain your answer.

Making Connections

36. **Explain** Why is the experimental method an important scientific tool?

37. **Write Persuasively** Write a letter to the editor of your local paper outlining your opinion on a local environmental issue.

CASESTUDY

38. How do scientific activities help to inform decision makers in the Everglades?

39. What is the ecological value of the Everglades?

Why It Matters

40. Explain the importance of observation to environmental science.

STUDYSKILL

Imagining Examples To understand how key terms apply to actual examples, work with a partner and take turns describing an environmental problem and explaining how the key terms relate to the problem.

Risk Assessment

Objectives

Ask questions about possible harm to people or the environment from proximity to a Superfund site.

Design a method of assessing the risk to people and the environment from a Superfund site.

Identify the factors that determine if there is a risk of harm to the environment or human health.

Communicate the possible risks from the Superfund site.

Materials

computer with Internet access

reference books and periodicals

In this lab, you will design a method of assessing the risk from exposure to contaminants from a Superfund hazardous waste site.

Background

The news abounds with stories about oil spills in the ocean, toxic air pollution from chemical plants, and hazardous waste leaks—it seems like we are constantly at risk from some type of ecological disaster. But are we really at that much risk? What exactly is risk and how can we tell if something will affect us?

Risk is the possibility of suffering harm from some sort of hazard. The harm might take the form of an injury, disease, economic loss, or damage to the environment in which we live. In order to determine if something has the possibility to cause harm, scientists often perform a risk assessment. Risk (R) is usually expressed as the probability of exposure (E) to the substance or activity multiplied by the probability of harm (H) occurring due to that exposure. Or, stated mathematically, risk is calculated as $R = E \times H$.

In 1980, the *Comprehensive Environmental Response, Compensation and Liability Act*, or CERCLA, established an environmental program to allow the Environmental Protection Agency (EPA) to clean up abandoned hazardous waste sites in the United States. The long and often complex clean-up process involves identification of the sites, assessment to place them on the National Priorities List (NPL), and the establishment of appropriate plans to remediate them. Any responsible parties must be identified and penalties for damages enforced. Both state and community involvement is desired to ensure long-term protection from harm.

This clean-up process was initially funded by a "polluters tax." This tax penalized polluters who could be identified and used the money to clean up sites where the responsible parties could not be found, could not pay, or refused to pay. However, the tax expired in 1995 and as of 2011, has never been reauthorized by Congress. Approximately 1300 contaminated sites remain on the EPA Superfund list, with 347 cleaned up, and 62 new sites proposed for addition to the list.

Safety Caution

If a local Superfund site is selected, do **NOT** visit the site *under any circumstances.*

Superfund Sites This Superfund site is located in Louisiana.

©Susan Leavines/Photo Researchers/Getty Images

Procedure

1. Using the Internet, select a Superfund site and identify the types of contaminants found in that location.

2. Research details about each contaminant. Material Safety Data Sheets (MSDS) for chemicals may provide useful information. Some sites may have already been treated. In that case, either select another site or base your research on the details of the site prior to remediation.

3. Design a method to assess the risks of harm to people or to the environment from proximity to the Superfund site.

4. Develop a plan to communicate your findings to the class using visual aids on poster board or presentation software that can be projected from a computer.

Procedure Step 1 You can find a list of Superfund sites by searching the Web site of the Environmental Protection Agency.

Analysis

1. **Analyzing Data** In your evaluation, did you consider short-term or long-term consequences to be more important? Why?

2. **Analyzing Results** Which potential consequences had the greatest value according to your ranking? Why?

Conclusions

3. **Evaluating Data** Did the values assigned for each type of risk make a difference in the decision reached on how to remediate the problem? Explain your answer.

Extension

4. **Evaluating Results** Based on the research and discussions in which you have been involved, do you feel the "polluters tax" on oil and chemical companies should be reestablished to provide the funding to clean up the remaining Superfund sites? Explain your answer.

The Dynamic Earth

Why It Matters

Data from NASA satellites enables scientists to determine such things as ecosystem health and air quality and to increase our knowledge of human impact on the planet.

In what ways might satellite observations directly affect your life?

CASESTUDY

Learn about the important services provided by coastal wetlands in the case study The Storm Surge, Tsunamis, and Coastal Wetlands on page 74.

 ONLINE ENVIRONMENTAL SCIENCE
HMDScience.com

Go online to access additional resources, including labs, worksheets, multimedia, and resources in Spanish.

©Earth Imaging/Stone/Getty Images

The Geosphere

Violent eruptions blow the tops off volcanoes, and molten rock from Earth's interior flows across the surface of the planet. Hurricanes batter beaches and change coastlines. Earthquakes shake the ground and topple buildings and freeway overpasses. All of these are the result of the dynamic state of planet Earth. What are the underlying conditions that cause our planet to change constantly?

Earth as a System

Earth consists of rock, air, water, and living things that all interact with each other. Scientists divide this system into four parts. As shown in **Figure 1.1**, the four parts are the geosphere (rock), the atmosphere (air), the hydrosphere (water), and the biosphere (living things).

The solid part of Earth that consists of all rock, as well as the soils and loose rocks on Earth's surface, makes up the **geosphere**. Most of the geosphere is located in Earth's interior. At the equator, the average distance through the center of Earth to the other side is 12,756 km. The atmosphere is the mixture of gases, nearly all of which are found in the first 30 km above Earth's surface. The **hydrosphere** makes up all of the water on or near Earth's surface. Much of this water is in the oceans. Water is also found in the atmosphere, on land, and in the soil. The biosphere is made up of parts of the geosphere, the atmosphere, and the hydrosphere. The biosphere is the part of Earth where life exists. It is a thin layer of living organisms found at Earth's surface and extending from about 9 km above the surface down to the bottom of the ocean.

- Describe the composition and structure of Earth.
- Describe Earth's tectonic plates.
- Explain the main cause of earthquakes and their effects.
- Identify the relationship between volcanic eruptions and climate change.
- Describe how wind and water alter Earth's surface.

Key Terms
geosphere
hydrosphere
crust
mantle
core
lithosphere
asthenosphere
tectonic plate
chemical weathering
erosion

FIGURE 1.1

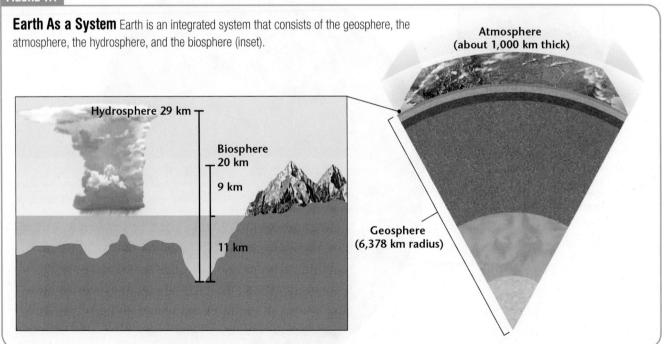

Earth As a System Earth is an integrated system that consists of the geosphere, the atmosphere, the hydrosphere, and the biosphere (inset).

Atmosphere (about 1,000 km thick)

Hydrosphere 29 km

Biosphere 20 km

9 km

11 km

Geosphere (6,378 km radius)

Discovering Earth's Interior

Studying the Earth beneath our feet is not easy. The deepest well that has been drilled into Earth's interior is only about 12 km deep. An alternative method must be used to study the interior of Earth. Scientists can use *seismic waves* to learn about Earth's interior. These waves travel through Earth's interior during an earthquake. If you have ever tapped a melon to see if it is ripe, you know that the state of the melon's interior affects the sound you detect. Similarly, a seismic wave is altered by the nature of the material through which it travels. As shown in **Figure 1.2,** seismologists measure changes in the speed and direction of seismic waves that penetrate the interior of the planet. By doing this, seismologists have learned that Earth is made up of different layers and have inferred from the data what substances make up each layer.

The Composition of the Earth

Scientists divide Earth into three layers—the crust, the mantle, and the core—based on their composition. These layers are composed of progressively denser materials toward the center of the Earth. **Figure 1.3** shows a cross section of Earth. Earth's thin **crust** is composed almost entirely of light elements. The crust makes up less than 1 percent of Earth's mass. The crust is Earth's thinnest layer. It averages about 5 km in thickness beneath the oceans and is 30 km to 35 km thick beneath the continents.

FIGURE 1.2

Seismic Waves Seismologists have measured changes in the speed and direction of seismic waves that travel through Earth's interior. Through this process, they have learned that Earth is made up of different layers.

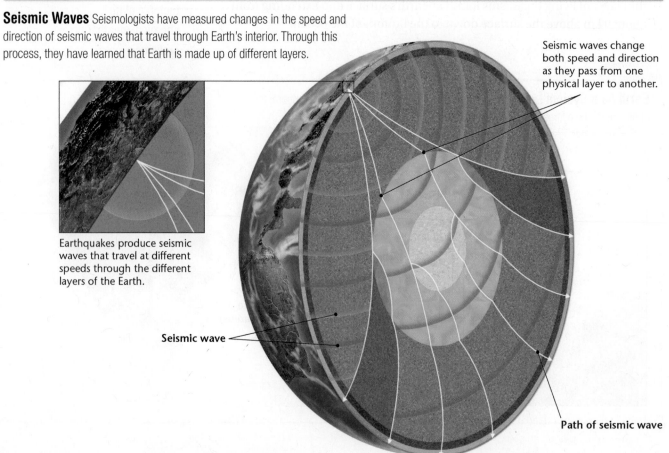

Earthquakes produce seismic waves that travel at different speeds through the different layers of the Earth.

Seismic waves change both speed and direction as they pass from one physical layer to another.

Seismic wave

Path of seismic wave

FIGURE 1.3

Earth's Layers Scientists divide Earth into different layers based on composition and physical properties.

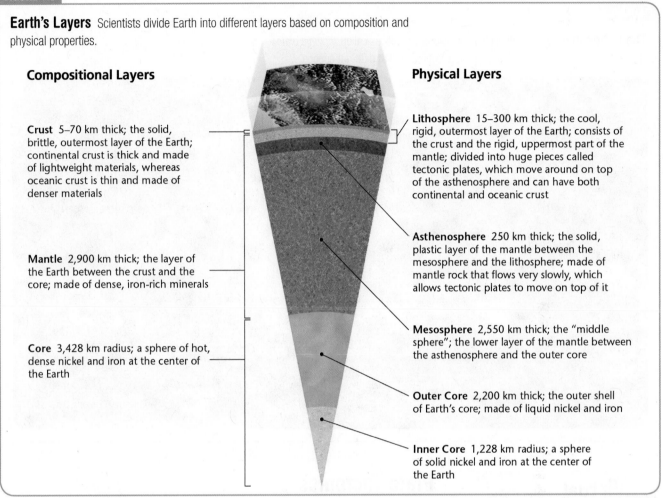

Compositional Layers

Crust 5–70 km thick; the solid, brittle, outermost layer of the Earth; continental crust is thick and made of lightweight materials, whereas oceanic crust is thin and made of denser materials

Mantle 2,900 km thick; the layer of the Earth between the crust and the core; made of dense, iron-rich minerals

Core 3,428 km radius; a sphere of hot, dense nickel and iron at the center of the Earth

Physical Layers

Lithosphere 15–300 km thick; the cool, rigid, outermost layer of the Earth; consists of the crust and the rigid, uppermost part of the mantle; divided into huge pieces called tectonic plates, which move around on top of the asthenosphere and can have both continental and oceanic crust

Asthenosphere 250 km thick; the solid, plastic layer of the mantle between the mesosphere and the lithosphere; made of mantle rock that flows very slowly, which allows tectonic plates to move on top of it

Mesosphere 2,550 km thick; the "middle sphere"; the lower layer of the mantle between the asthenosphere and the outer core

Outer Core 2,200 km thick; the outer shell of Earth's core; made of liquid nickel and iron

Inner Core 1,228 km radius; a sphere of solid nickel and iron at the center of the Earth

The **mantle,** which is the layer beneath the crust, makes up 68 percent of the mass of Earth. The mantle is approximately 2,900 km thick and is made of rocks of medium density. Earth's innermost layer is the **core**. The core, which has a radius of approximately 3,400 km, is composed of the elements having the greatest density.

The Structure of the Earth

If we consider the physical properties of each layer, instead of their chemistry, Earth can be divided into five layers. Earth's outer layer is the **lithosphere.** It is a cool, rigid layer, 15 km to 300 km thick, that includes the crust and uppermost part of the mantle. It is divided into huge pieces called *tectonic plates*. The **asthenosphere** is the layer beneath the lithosphere. The asthenosphere is a pliable, solid layer of the mantle made of rock that flows very slowly and allows tectonic plates to move on top of it. Beneath the asthenosphere is the mesosphere, the lower part of the mantle.

Earth's outer core is a dense liquid layer. The inner core, at the center of the Earth, is dense and solid, made up mostly of the metals iron and nickel. The temperature of the inner core is estimated to be between 4,000°C to 5,400°C. It is solid because it is under enormous pressure. Earth's outer and inner core together make up about one-third of Earth's mass.

✔ **CHECK FOR UNDERSTANDING**

Identify Which of Earth's physical layers is liquid?

FIGURE 1.4

The Lithosphere Earth's lithosphere is divided into pieces called *tectonic plates*. The tectonic plates are moving in different directions and at different speeds.

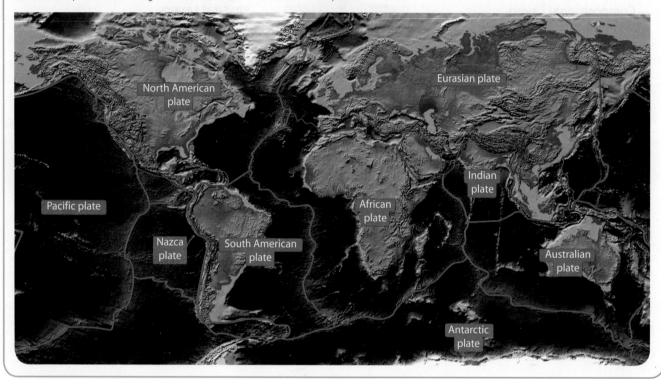

HMDScience.com

Tectonic Plate Boundaries

Plate Tectonics

The lithosphere is divided into pieces called **tectonic plates** that glide across the underlying asthenosphere in much the same way a chunk of ice drifts across a pond. The continents are located on the tectonic plates and slowly, over eons, move around with them. The major plates include the Pacific, North American, South American, African, Eurasian, and Antarctic plates. **Figure 1.4** illustrates the major tectonic plates.

Plate Boundaries

Much of the geologic activity at the surface of Earth takes place at the boundaries between tectonic plates. Plates may move away from one another, collide with one another, or slip past one another. Enormous forces are generated at tectonic plate boundaries, where the crust is pulled apart, is squeezed together, or is slipping. The forces produced at the boundaries of tectonic plates can cause violent changes.

Plate Tectonics and Mountain Building

When tectonic plates collide, the crust becomes thicker, is pushed up, buckles and folds, and eventually forms a mountain range. As shown in **Figure 1.5,** the Himalaya Mountains in south-central Asia began to form when the Eurasian tectonic plate and the Indian tectonic plate began to push into each other about 50 million years ago.

Earthquakes

A *fault* is a break in Earth's crust along which blocks of the crust slide relative to one another. When rocks that are under stress suddenly slip along a fault, a series of vibrations is set off. These vibrations of Earth's crust caused by slippage along a fault are known as *earthquakes*. Earthquakes are occurring all the time, but many are so small that we cannot feel them. Other earthquakes are enormous movements of the Earth's crust that cause widespread damage.

The Richter scale is used by scientists to quantify the amount of energy released by an earthquake. The measure of the energy released by an earthquake is called *magnitude*. The smallest magnitude that can be felt is approximately 2.0, and the largest magnitude that has ever been recorded is 9.5. Each increase of magnitude by one whole number indicates the release of about 30 times more energy than the whole number below it. For example, an earthquake of magnitude 6.0 releases 30 times the energy of an earthquake of magnitude 5.0. Earthquakes that cause widespread damage have magnitudes of 7.0 and greater.

Where Do Earthquakes Occur?

Areas of the world where earthquakes occur are shown on the map in **Figure 1.6**. The majority of earthquakes take place at or near tectonic plate boundaries. Over the past 15 million to 20 million years, many earthquakes have occurred along the San Andreas fault, which runs almost the entire length of California. The San Andreas fault is where parts of the North American plate and the Pacific plate are slipping past one another.

FIGURE 1.5

Plate Collisions The Himalaya Mountains are still growing today because the tectonic plates containing Asia and the tectonic plate containing India continue to collide.

✔ **CHECK FOR UNDERSTANDING**

Explain What is meant by the magnitude of an earthquake?

FIGURE 1.6

Earthquake Zones The largest and most active earthquake zones lie along tectonic plate boundaries.

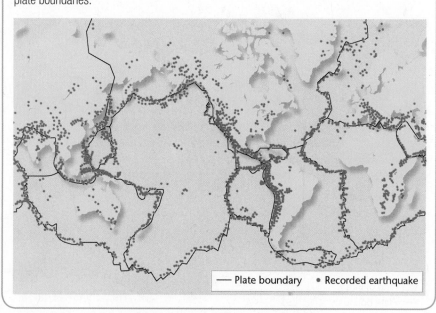

— Plate boundary • Recorded earthquake

©Jock Montgomery/Bruce Coleman, Inc./Photoshotot

Can Animals Predict Earthquakes?

Can animals that live close to the site of an earthquake detect changes in their physical environment prior to an earthquake? Documentation of unusual animal behavior prior to earthquakes can be found as far back as 373 BCE. Examples of this odd behavior include zoo animals refusing to enter shelters at night, snakes and small mammals abandoning their burrows, and wild birds leaving their usual habitats. These behaviors reportedly happened within a few days, hours, or minutes of earthquakes.

Earthquake Hazard

Despite much study, scientists cannot predict when earthquakes will take place. However, information about where they are most likely to occur can help people prepare for them. An area's earthquake-hazard level is determined by past and present seismic activity. The Maps in Action activity located at the end of this chapter shows earthquake-hazard levels for the contiguous United States.

Earthquakes are not restricted to high-risk areas. In 1886, an earthquake shook Charleston, South Carolina, which is considered to be in a medium-risk area. Because the soil beneath the city is sandy, this earthquake caused extensive damage. During shaking from a strong earthquake, sand can act like a liquid and causes buildings to sink. Earthquake-resistant buildings are slightly flexible so that they can sway with the ground motion. This flexibility can greatly reduce damages.

Volcanoes

A *volcano* is a mountain built when magma—melted rock—rises from Earth's interior to its surface. Once the magma reaches the surface, it is known as *lava*. Volcanoes are often located near tectonic plate boundaries where plates are either colliding or separating from one another. Volcanoes may occur on land or under the sea, where they may eventually break the ocean surface as islands. As **Figure 1.7** shows, the majority of the world's active volcanoes on land are located along tectonic plate boundaries that surround the Pacific Ocean.

FIGURE 1.7

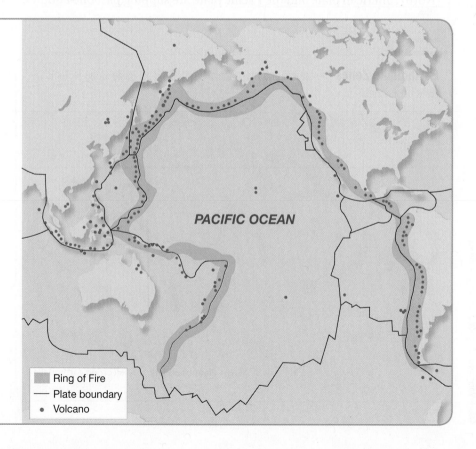

The Ring of Fire Tectonic plate boundaries are places where volcanoes usually form. The Ring of Fire contains nearly 75 percent of the world's active volcanoes that are on land. A large number of people live on or near the Ring of Fire.

✔ **CRITICAL THINKING**

Explain Many of the islands in the central Pacific Ocean are of volcanic origin. Explain how they formed.

PACIFIC OCEAN

Ring of Fire
— Plate boundary
• Volcano

FIGURE 1.8

Mount St. Helens On May 18, 1980, Mount St. Helens in Washington State erupted. Sixty-three people lost their lives, and 596 km² of forest were destroyed in an eruption that blew away the top 410 m of the volcano.

Local Effects of Volcanic Eruptions

A volcano erupts when the pressure of the magma inside becomes so great that it blows open the solid surface of the volcano. Some volcanoes have lava flowing out of them all the time, so the pressure never builds up. Volcanic eruptions can be devastating to local economies and can cause great human loss. Clouds of hot ash, dust, and gases can flow down the slope of a volcano at speeds of up to 160 km/h and sear everything in their path. During an eruption, volcanic ash can mix with water and produce a mudflow. In addition, ash that falls to the ground can cause buildings to collapse under its weight, bury crops, and damage the engines of vehicles. Volcanic ash may also cause breathing difficulties.

Global Effects of Volcanic Eruptions

Major volcanic eruptions, such as the eruption of Mount St. Helens shown in **Figure 1.8,** can change Earth's climate for several years. In large eruptions, clouds of volcanic ash and sulfur-rich gases may reach the upper atmosphere. As the ash and gases spread across the planet, they can reduce the amount of sunlight that reaches Earth's surface. This reduction in sunlight can cause a drop in the average global surface temperature. In the 1991 eruption of Mount Pinatubo in the Philippines, the amount of sunlight that reached Earth's surface was estimated to have decreased by 2 to 4 percent. As a result, the average global temperature dropped by several tenths of a degree Celsius over a period of several years.

Weathering and Erosion

Forces at the boundaries of tectonic plates bring rock to the surface of the Earth. At the Earth's surface, rocks are altered by other forces. The Earth's surface is continually battered by wind and scoured by running water, moving rocks around and changing their appearance. **Chemical weathering** wears down rocks, making them smoother as time passes, and **erosion** transports the materials elsewhere. The older a mountain range is, the longer the forces of weathering and erosion have acted on it. This knowledge helped geologists learn that the rounded Appalachian Mountains in the eastern United States are older than the jagged Rocky Mountains in the west.

Water Erosion

Erosion by both rivers and oceans can produce dramatic changes on Earth's surface. Waves from ocean storms can erode coastlines to give rise to a variety of spectacular landforms. Over time, rivers can carve deep gorges into the landscape, as shown in **Figure 1.9**.

Wind Erosion

Like moving water, wind can also change the landscape of our planet. In places where plants grow, their roots hold soil in place. But in places where there are few plants, wind can blow soil away very quickly. Beaches and deserts, which have loose, sandy soil, are examples of places where few plants grow. Soft rocks, such as sandstone, erode more easily than hard rocks, such as granite, do. In parts of the world, spectacular rock formations are sometimes seen where pinnacles of hard rock stand alone because the softer rock around them has been eroded by wind and/or water.

FIGURE 1.9

Forces of Erosion Over long periods of time, erosion can produce spectacular landforms on Earth's surface.

©Dennis Flaherty/Photo Researchers, Inc.

✓ Section 1 Formative Assessment

▶ Reviewing Main Ideas

1. **Name** and describe the physical and compositional layers into which Earth is divided.

2. **Explain** the main cause of earthquakes and their effects.

3. **Describe** the effects a large-scale volcanic eruption can have on the global climate.

4. **Describe** how wind and water alter Earth's surface.

✓ Critical Thinking

5. **Analyzing Processes** How might the surface of the Earth be different if it were not divided into tectonic plates?

6. **Compare and Contrast** Read about the effects of erosion on mountains on this page. From what you have read, describe the physical features you would associate with a young mountain range and an old mountain range.

The Atmosphere

©NOAA/Department of Commerce/NOAA Central Library U

Earth is surrounded by a mixture of gases known as the **atmosphere**. Nitrogen, oxygen, carbon dioxide, and other gases are all parts of this mixture. Earth's atmosphere changes constantly as these gases are added and removed. For example, animals remove oxygen from the atmosphere when they breathe in and add carbon dioxide when they breathe out. Plants take in carbon dioxide and add oxygen to the atmosphere when they produce food. Gases can be added to and removed from the atmosphere in ways other than through living organisms. A volcanic eruption adds gases. A vehicle both adds and removes gases.

The atmosphere also insulates Earth's surface. This insulation slows the rate at which the Earth's surface loses heat. The atmosphere keeps Earth at temperatures at which living things can survive.

SECTION 2

Objectives

- Describe the composition of Earth's atmosphere.
- Describe the layers of Earth's atmosphere.
- Explain three mechanisms of heat transfer in Earth's atmosphere.
- Explain the greenhouse effect.

Key Terms

atmosphere
troposphere
stratosphere
ozone
radiation
conduction
convection
greenhouse effect

Composition of the Atmosphere

Figure 2.1 shows the percentages of gases that make up Earth's atmosphere. Nitrogen makes up 78 percent of the Earth's atmosphere. It enters the atmosphere when volcanoes erupt and when dead plants and animals decay. Oxygen, the second most abundant gas in Earth's atmosphere, is primarily produced by plants and algae. Other gases, including argon, carbon dioxide, methane, and water vapor, make up the rest of the atmosphere.

In addition to gases, the atmosphere contains many types of tiny, solid particles, or atmospheric dust. Atmospheric dust is mainly soil but includes salt, ash from fires, volcanic ash, particulate matter from combustion, skin, hair, bits of clothing, pollen, bacteria and viruses, and microscopic particles and liquid droplets called *aerosols*.

Air Pressure

The atmosphere is pulled toward Earth's surface by gravity. As a result of the pull of gravity, the atmosphere is denser near Earth's surface. Most of the mass of Earth's atmospheric gases is located within 30 km of our planet's surface. Because gravity pulls the molecules of air downwards, the amount of air decreases at higher altitudes. The air also becomes less dense as elevation increases, so breathing at higher elevations is more difficult.

FIGURE 2.1

Physical and Chemical Composition of the Atmosphere

❶ Scientists on board a research plane from the National Oceanic and Atmospheric Administration (NOAA) are making measurements of temperature; humidity, barometric pressure, and wind speed.

❷ Nitrogen and oxygen make up 99 percent of the composition of the atmosphere.

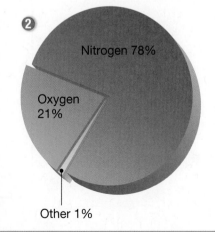

Nitrogen 78%

Oxygen 21%

Other 1%

Layers of the Atmosphere

The atmosphere is divided into four layers based on temperature changes that occur at different distances above the Earth's surface. **Figure 2.2** shows the four layers of Earth's atmosphere.

The Troposphere

The atmospheric layer nearest Earth's surface is the troposphere. The **troposphere** extends to about 18 km above Earth's surface. Almost all of the weather occurs in this layer. The troposphere is Earth's densest atmospheric layer. Temperature decreases as altitude increases in the troposphere, as shown in **Figure 2.2**.

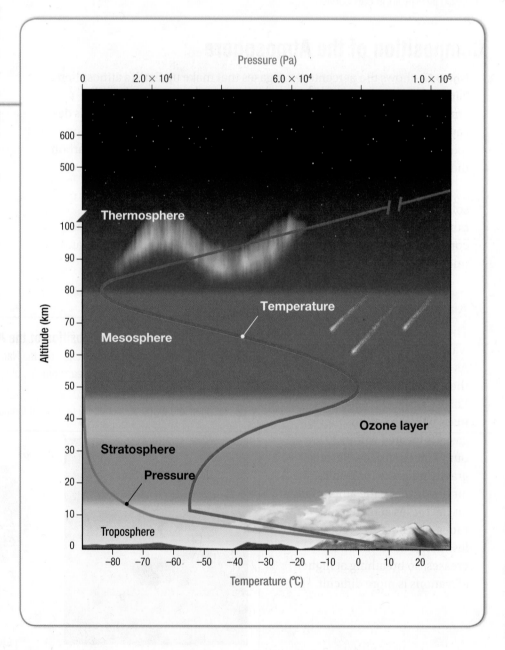

FIGURE 2.2

Atmospheric Layers The layers of the atmosphere differ in temperature and pressure.

(tl) ©NASA; (tr) SPL/Photo Researchers, Inc.

The Tropopause This sunrise scene that was taken from space captures the tropopause, the transitional zone that separates the troposphere (yellow layer) from the stratosphere (white layer). The tropopause is the illuminated brown layer.

Auroras The *aurora borealis*, or Northern Lights, can be seen in the skies around Earth's North Pole.

The Stratosphere

Above the troposphere is the stratosphere. The **stratosphere**, separated from the troposphere by the *tropopause*, shown in **Figure 2.3**, extends from about 18 km to an altitude of about 50 km. Temperatures rise as altitude increases because ozone in the stratosphere absorbs the sun's ultraviolet (UV) energy and warms the air. **Ozone,** O_3, is a molecule made up of three oxygen atoms. Almost all the ozone in the atmosphere is concentrated in the ozone layer in the stratosphere. Ozone reduces the amount of harmful UV radiation that reaches Earth.

The Mesosphere

The layer above the stratosphere is the *mesosphere*. This layer extends to an altitude of about 80 km. The mesosphere is the coldest layer of the atmosphere. Its temperatures have been measured as low as -93°C.

The Thermosphere

Farthest from Earth's surface is the thermosphere. In the *thermosphere*, nitrogen and oxygen absorb solar radiation, resulting in temperatures above 2,000°C. Despite these high temperatures, the thermosphere would not feel hot to us. Air particles that strike one another transfer heat. The air in the thermosphere is so thin that air particles rarely collide, so little heat is transferred.

Nitrogen and oxygen atoms in the lower region of the thermosphere (about 80 km to 550 km above Earth's surface) absorb harmful solar radiation, such as x-rays and gamma rays. This absorption causes atoms to become electrically charged. Electrically charged atoms are called ions. The lower thermosphere is called the *ionosphere*. Sometimes ions radiate energy as light. This light often glows in spectacular colors in the night skies near the Earth's North and South Poles, as shown in **Figure 2.4**.

ECOFACT

The Mesosphere
In geology, the term *mesosphere*, which means "middle sphere," refers to the 2,550 km thick physical layer of the Earth that lies below the asthenosphere. The mesosphere is also the name of the atmospheric layer that extends from 50 to 80 km above Earth's surface.

✔ **CHECK FOR UNDERSTANDING**
Infer How does ozone in the stratosphere affect life on the Earth's surface?

Energy in the Atmosphere

As shown in **Figure 2.5**, energy from the sun is transferred in Earth's atmosphere by three mechanisms: radiation, convection, and conduction. **Radiation** is the transfer of energy as electromagnetic waves. When you stand before a fire or a bed of coals, the warmth you feel has reached you by radiation. **Conduction** is the transfer of energy in the form of heat from a warmer object to a colder object when the objects are placed in direct physical contact. **Convection** is the transfer of energy that takes place when variations in temperature move the matter making up air. For example, if you live in a colder climate, the heating vents in your home are probably on or near the floor, so that the house will warm as the air rises upwards.

Warming of the Atmosphere

Solar energy reaches Earth as electromagnetic radiation, which includes visible light, infrared radiation, and ultraviolet light. Our planet only receives about two-billionths of this energy. However, this seemingly small amount of radiation contains a tremendous amount of energy. As shown in **Figure 2.5**, about half of the solar energy that enters the atmosphere passes through and is absorbed by Earth's surface. The rest is absorbed or reflected in the atmosphere by clouds, gases, and dust, or it is reflected by Earth's surface. On a sunny day, rocks may become too hot to touch. If Earth's surface continually absorbed energy, it would get hotter and hotter. This does not happen, because the oceans and the land radiate some of the energy they have absorbed back into the atmosphere.

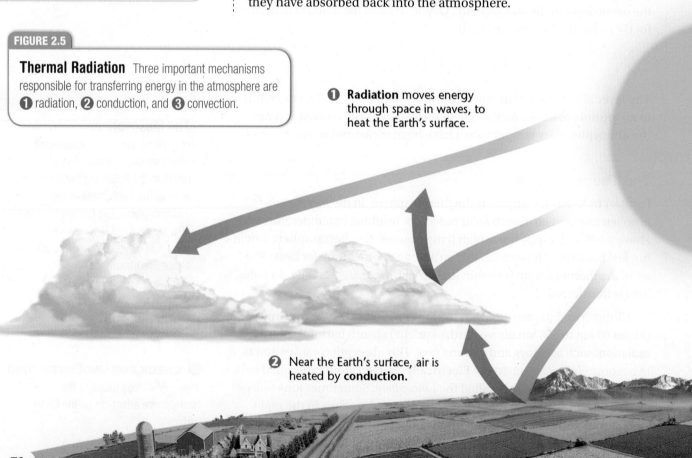

FIGURE 2.5

Thermal Radiation Three important mechanisms responsible for transferring energy in the atmosphere are ❶ radiation, ❷ conduction, and ❸ convection.

❶ **Radiation** moves energy through space in waves, to heat the Earth's surface.

❷ Near the Earth's surface, air is heated by **conduction**.

You may have noticed that dark-colored objects become much hotter in the sun than light-colored objects. Dark-colored objects absorb more solar radiation than light-colored objects, so dark-colored objects have more energy to release as heat. Because of the dark color of street and parking lot surfaces, the temperature in cities is higher than the temperature in the surrounding countryside.

The Movement of Energy in the Atmosphere

Air that is constantly moving upward, downward, or sideways causes Earth's weather. In the troposphere, currents of less dense air, warmed by the Earth's surface, rise into the atmosphere, and currents of denser cold air sink toward the ground. As a current of air rises into the atmosphere, it begins to cool and condense. The air current sinks instead of continuing to rise. So, the air current moves back toward Earth's surface until it is warmed, becomes less dense, and begins to rise again. This continual process, called a *convection current,* moves the air in a circular pattern. A convection current can be seen in **Figure 2.5.**

✔ **CHECK FOR UNDERSTANDING**
Explain Why does cool air sink and warm air rise in the atmosphere?

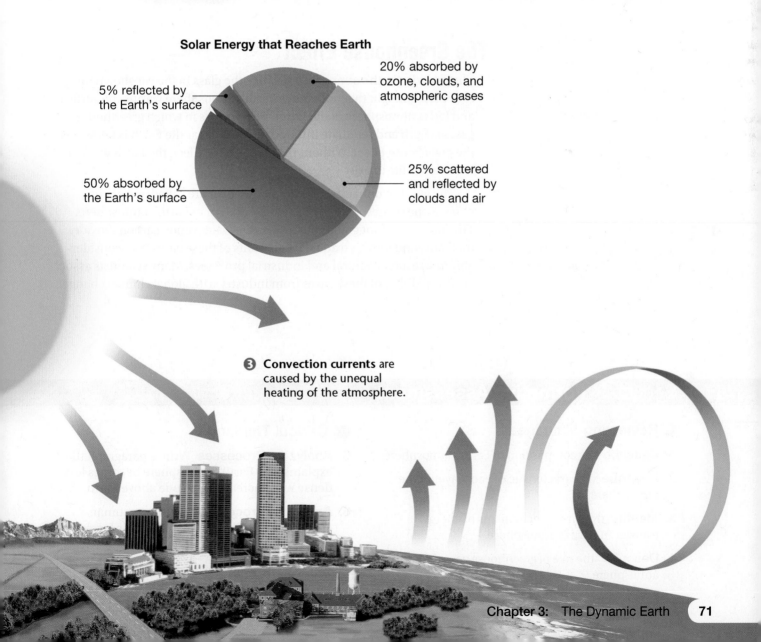

Solar Energy that Reaches Earth

5% reflected by the Earth's surface

20% absorbed by ozone, clouds, and atmospheric gases

50% absorbed by the Earth's surface

25% scattered and reflected by clouds and air

❸ **Convection currents** are caused by the unequal heating of the atmosphere.

FIGURE 2.6

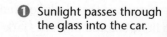

The Greenhouse Effect The gases in the atmosphere act like a layer of glass. Both allow solar energy to pass through. But glass and some of the gases in the atmosphere absorb energy and stop it from escaping into space.

① Sunlight passes through the glass into the car.

② The interior absorbs radiant energy.

✔ **CRITICAL THINKING**

Explain What is the relationship between the greenhouse effect and global climate change?

③ The glass in the car stops most of the radiant energy from escaping, increasing the temperature inside the car.

The Greenhouse Effect

The gases in Earth's atmosphere act like the glass in the car shown in **Figure 2.6.** Sunlight that penetrates Earth's atmosphere warms the surface and lower atmosphere of the Earth. The process in which greenhouse gases absorb and reradiate infrared radiation near the Earth is known as the **greenhouse effect.** Without the greenhouse effect, the Earth would be too cold for life to exist.

The gases in our atmosphere that trap heat are called *greenhouse gases*. None of these have a high concentration in Earth's atmosphere. The most abundant greenhouse gases are water vapor, carbon dioxide, methane, and nitrous oxide. The amounts of these gases vary considerably as a result of natural and industrial processes. Many scientists associate the addition of these gases from industry with global climate change.

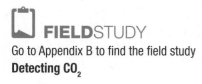

FIELDSTUDY

Go to Appendix B to find the field study **Detecting CO₂**

✔ Section 2 **Formative Assessment**

▶ Reviewing Main Ideas

1. **Describe** the composition of Earth's atmosphere.
2. **Describe** a characteristic of each layer of the atmosphere.
3. **Identify** the three mechanisms of energy transfer in Earth's atmosphere.
4. **Describe** the role of greenhouse gases in Earth's atmosphere.

✔ **Critical Thinking**

5. **Analyzing Processes** Write a paragraph that explains why Earth's atmosphere becomes less dense with increasing altitude above Earth.
6. **Analyzing Processes** How does human activity change some greenhouse-gas levels?

The Hydrosphere and Biosphere

Life on Earth is restricted to a very narrow layer around Earth's surface. In this layer, called the *biosphere*, everything that organisms need to survive can be found. One of the requirements of all living things is liquid water.

The Hydrosphere and Water Cycle

The hydrosphere includes all of the water on or near Earth's surface, such as the water in the oceans, lakes, rivers, wetlands, polar icecaps, soil, rock layers beneath Earth's surface, and clouds.

The continuous movement of water into the air, onto land, and then back to water sources is known as the **water cycle**, which is shown in **Figure 3.1**. **Evaporation** is the process by which liquid water is heated by the sun and then rises into the atmosphere as water vapor. Water continually evaporates from Earth's oceans, lakes, streams, and soil, but the majority of the water evaporates from the oceans. In the process of **condensation**, water vapor forms water droplets on dust particles. These water droplets form clouds, in which the droplets collide, stick together, and create larger, heavier droplets. These larger droplets fall from clouds as rain in a process called **precipitation**. Precipitation may also take the form of snow, sleet, or hail.

SECTION 3

Objectives

▶ Name the three major processes in the water cycle.

▶ Describe the properties of ocean water.

▶ Describe the two types of ocean currents.

▶ Explain how the ocean regulates Earth's temperature.

▶ Discuss the factors that confine life to the biosphere.

▶ Explain the difference between open and closed systems.

Key Terms

water cycle
evaporation
condensation
precipitation
salinity
fresh water
biosphere

FIGURE 3.1

The Water Cycle The major processes of the water cycle include ❶ evaporation, ❷ condensation, and ❸ precipitation.

❷ CONDENSATION

❶ EVAPORATION

❸ PRECIPITATION

©Peter Wey/Fotolia

Submarine Volcanoes

Geologists estimate that approximately 80 percent of the volcanic activity on Earth takes place on the ocean floor. Most of this activity occurs as magma slowly flows onto the ocean floor where tectonic plates pull away from each other. But enormous undersea volcanoes are also common. Off the coast of Hawaii, a submarine volcano called the *Loihi Seamount* rises 5,185 m from the ocean floor. Loihi is just 915 m below the ocean's surface, and in several thousand years, this volcano may become the next Hawaiian Island.

Earth's Oceans

We talk about the Atlantic Ocean, the Pacific Ocean, the Arctic Ocean, the Southern Ocean, and the Indian Ocean. However, if you look at **Figure 3.2**, you see that these oceans are all joined. This single, large, interconnected body of water is called the *world ocean*. Its waters cover a little over 70 percent of the Earth's surface. As we will see, the world ocean plays many important roles in regulating our planet's environment.

The largest ocean on Earth is the Pacific Ocean. It covers a surface area of approximately 155,557,000 km^2 and has an average depth of 4,280 m. The deepest point on the ocean floor is in the Pacific Ocean. This point is called the Challenger Deep and is located east of the Philippine Islands at the bottom of the Mariana Trench and is deeper than Mount Everest is tall.

The second-largest ocean on Earth is the Atlantic Ocean. It covers a surface area of 76,630,000 km^2, which is about half the area of the Pacific Ocean. Like the Pacific Ocean, the Atlantic Ocean can be divided into a north half and a south half based on the directions of surface current flow north and south of the equator.

CASESTUDY

Storm Surge, Tsunamis, and Coastal Wetlands

Coastal wetlands include mangrove forests and salt marshes. These ecosystems filter the water, are a home for many species, prevent erosion, and provide recreational and commercial opportunities for people. Coastal wetlands are worth billions of dollars to the economy every year, but in many areas of the world they have been removed for human development.

In the last several years major natural disasters have shown how vulnerable coastal areas can be. Hurricane Katrina along the Gulf of Mexico and tsunamis in Japan and southeast Asia killed thousands of people and resulted in billions of dollars of damage. In these areas, many coastal wetlands had been removed. Could mangrove forests or coastal marshes have reduced the damage?

The plants of coastal wetlands can reduce the height of waves, so the surge of water moving inland from

Saltmarsh cordgrass, shown in a salt marsh at the New River Inlet, North Carolina, helps to anchor shorelines.

hurricanes or a tsunami may not travel as far. It also may not be as powerful. Another way that wetlands provide protection from disasters is by building up sediment and holding it together. By creating more land and stable shorelines, the wetlands will reduce damage from waves even more.

Multiple studies have found that the loss of human lives and livestock as well as the economic damage inflicted on an area by hurricanes are less when they are protected by coastal wetlands. We know less about how wetlands protect coastal communities from tsunamis, but one study found that having coastal trees reduced the loss of human life by 5%.

©Norm Thomas/Photo Researchers, Inc.

The Indian Ocean covers a surface area of 73,762,000 km² and is the third-largest ocean on Earth. It has an average depth of 3,890 m.

In 2000, the waters that completely surround the continent of Antarctica were designated as the Southern Ocean. Although it has no land mass to separate it from the others, it can be distinguished by the rapid movement of its waters around Antarctica, known as the Antarctic Circumpolar Current. It encompasses an area of approximately 20,327,000 km².

The smallest ocean is the Arctic Ocean, which covers 14,560,000 km². The Arctic Ocean is unique because much of its surface is covered by floating ice. This ice, which is called *pack ice*, forms when either waves or wind drive together frozen seawater, known as sea ice, into a large mass.

©Vincent Laforet, POOL/AP Images

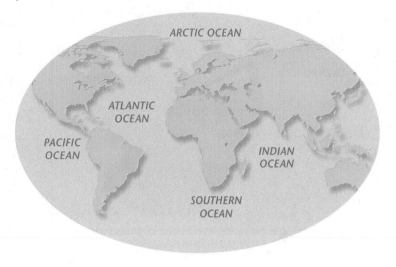

FIGURE 3.2

World Ocean The Pacific, Atlantic, Indian, Southern, and Arctic Oceans are interconnected into a single body of water, the world ocean, which covers 70 percent of Earth's surface.

Over 80% of New Orleans was submerged by floodwater when Hurricane Katrina struck in August, 2005.

Not all types of coastal wetland will provide the same amount of protection. For example, dense mangrove forests are better than those with fewer trees. Also, it is important that wetlands are relatively large. The tsunami in the Indian Ocean in 2004 and the oil from the Deepwater Horizon spill in 2010 killed large areas of wetlands, but only in a strip along the coast. The mangrove forests and marshes further inland mostly survived and allowed the wetlands to remain largely intact.

Even though coastal wetlands are a benefit during natural disasters, they are not a substitute for other methods of protection, like early warning systems. Because wetlands provide many benefits other than reducing the impacts of natural disasters, it is important to preserve them.

Many communities have decided that protecting remaining coastal wetlands is not enough. They are working to restore degraded wetlands or create new wetlands where they have been destroyed. Scientists are working to find out the best ways to restore wetlands to provide many benefits including increasing tourism, increasing fish populations, and protecting coastal communities.

Critical Thinking

Explain A local city commission is trying to decide what should be done with a large vacant area along the coast. Provide an argument why it might be a good idea to create a coastal wetland.

FIGURE 3.3

Dissolved Solids This pie graph shows the percentages by weight of dissolved solids found in ocean water. Sodium and chlorine, the two elements that form salt, are the most important dissolved solids in ocean water.

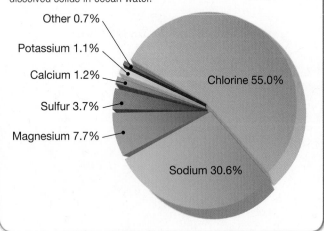

Other 0.7%
Potassium 1.1%
Calcium 1.2%
Sulfur 3.7%
Magnesium 7.7%
Chlorine 55.0%
Sodium 30.6%

Virtual INVESTIGATION
HMDScience.com

Understanding Ocean Currents

Ocean Water

The difference between ocean water and fresh water is that ocean water contains more salts. These salts have dissolved out of rocks on land and have been carried down rivers into the ocean over millions of years. Underwater volcanic eruptions also add salts to the ocean.

Most of the salt in the ocean is sodium chloride, which is made up of the elements sodium and chlorine. **Figure 3.3** shows the concentration of these and other elements in ocean water. The **salinity** of ocean water is the concentration of all the dissolved salts it contains. The average salt content of ocean water is 3.5 percent by weight. The salinity of ocean water is lower in places that get a lot of rain or in places where fresh water flows into the sea. Salinity is higher where water evaporates rapidly and leaves the salts behind.

Temperature Zones

Figure 3.4 shows the temperature zones of the ocean. The surface of the ocean is warmed by the sun. In contrast, the depths of the ocean, where sunlight never reaches, have temperatures only slightly above freezing. Surface waters are stirred up by waves and currents, so the warm *surface zone* may be as much as 350 m deep. Below the surface zone is the *thermocline*, which is a layer about 300 to 700 m deep where the temperature falls rapidly with depth. From the bottom of the thermocline, down to the bottom of the ocean, lies the cold, dark *deep zone*.

FIGURE 3.4

Ocean Zones Water in the ocean can be divided into three zones based on temperature.

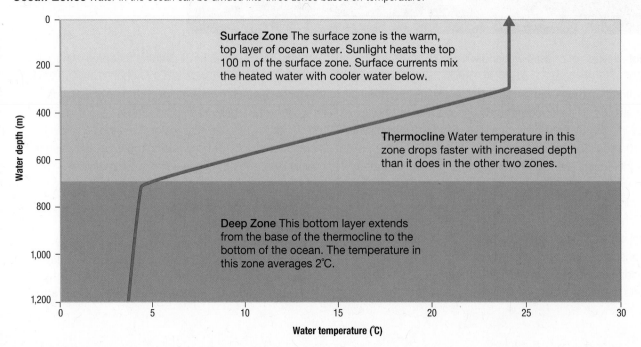

Surface Zone The surface zone is the warm, top layer of ocean water. Sunlight heats the top 100 m of the surface zone. Surface currents mix the heated water with cooler water below.

Thermocline Water temperature in this zone drops faster with increased depth than it does in the other two zones.

Deep Zone This bottom layer extends from the base of the thermocline to the bottom of the ocean. The temperature in this zone averages 2°C.

Water depth (m)

Water temperature (°C)

A Global Temperature Regulator

One of the most important functions of the world ocean is to absorb and store energy from sunlight. This capacity of the ocean to absorb and store energy from sunlight regulates temperatures in Earth's atmosphere.

The world ocean absorbs over half the solar radiation that reaches the planet's surface. The ocean both absorbs and releases heat more slowly than land does. As a consequence, the temperature of the atmosphere changes much more slowly than it would if there were no ocean on Earth. If the ocean did not regulate atmospheric and surface temperatures, the temperature would be too extreme for life on Earth to exist.

Local temperatures in different areas of the planet are also regulated by the world ocean. Currents that circulate warm water cause the land areas they flow past to have a more moderate climate. For example, the British Isles are warmed by the Gulf Stream, which moves warm waters from lower latitudes toward higher latitudes, as shown in **Figure 3.5**.

✔ **CHECK FOR UNDERSTANDING**

Compare How does the absorption and release of heat by the ocean differ from the absorption and release of heat by land?

FIGURE 3.5

The Gulf Stream In this infrared satellite image, the Gulf Stream is moving warm water (shown in red, orange, and yellow) from lower latitudes into higher latitudes. The British Isles are warmed by the waters of the Gulf Stream.

✔ **CRITICAL THINKING**

Predict If cold water from melting polar ice were to shut down the Gulf Stream, what would happen to the climate of the British Isles?

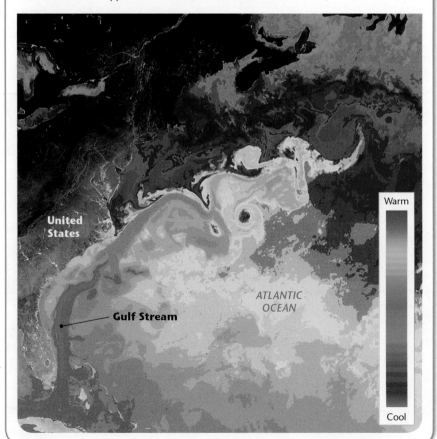

United States

ATLANTIC OCEAN

Gulf Stream

Warm

Cool

Connect to MATH

The Influence of the Gulf Stream

The temperature of the British Isles is moderated by the Gulf Stream. Plymouth, England, and Winnipeg, Canada, are located at approximately 50° north latitude. Plymouth, which is located in the southwest of England near the Atlantic Ocean, has average low temperatures of 4°C in December, 3°C in January, and 3°C in February. Winnipeg, which is located in the interior of North America, has average low temperatures of −18°C in December, −23°C in January, and −20°C in February. What is the difference in average low temperatures in degrees Celsius between Plymouth and Winnipeg?

Deep Ocean Currents
Procedure
1. Fill a large glass container or aquarium with hot water.
2. Next, fill a 100 mL beaker with very cold water, adding several drops of dark food coloring.
3. Hypothesize an explanation for what might happen when the cold water is added to the hot water.
4. Holding the beaker above the larger container, carefully pour the icy water into the hot water.

Analysis
1. What did you observe when the cold water was poured into the hot water?
2. Explain why this occurred and how it relates to ocean currents.

Ocean Currents

Streamlike movements of water that occur at or near the surface of the ocean are called *surface currents*. Surface currents are wind driven and result from global wind patterns. **Figure 3.6** shows the major surface currents of the world ocean. Surface currents may be warm-water currents or cold-water currents. Currents of warm water and currents of cold water do not readily mix with one another. Therefore, a warm-water current like the Gulf Stream can flow for hundreds of kilometers through cold water without mixing and losing its heat.

Surface currents can influence the climates of land areas they flow past. As we have seen, the Gulf Stream moderates the climate in the British Isles. The Scilly Isles in England are as far north as Newfoundland in northeast Canada. However, palm trees grow on the Scilly Isles, where it never freezes, whereas Newfoundland has long winters of frost and snow.

Deep currents are streamlike movements of water that flow very slowly along the ocean floor. Deep currents form when the cold, dense water from the poles sinks below warmer, less dense ocean water and flows toward the equator. The densest and coldest ocean water is located off the coast of Antarctica. This cold water sinks to the bottom of the ocean and flows very slowly northward to produce a deep current called the Antarctic Bottom Water. The Antarctic Bottom Water creeps along the ocean floor for thousands of kilometers and reaches a northernmost point of approximately 40° north latitude. It takes several hundred years for water in this deep current to make this trip northward.

FIGURE 3.6

Surface Currents The oceans' surface currents circulate in different directions in each hemisphere.

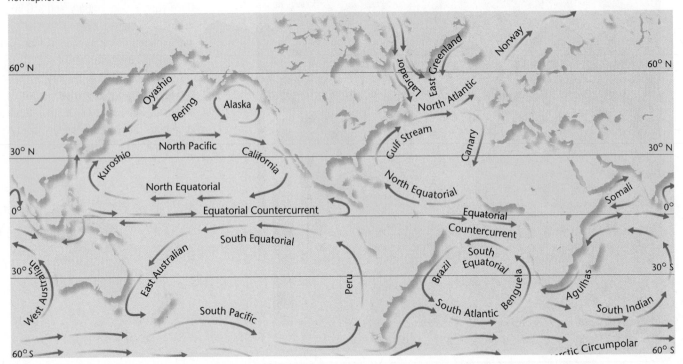

Fresh Water

Most of the water on Earth is salt water in the ocean. A little more than 3 percent of all the water on Earth is **fresh water**. Most of the fresh water is locked up in icecaps and glaciers that are so large they are hard to imagine. For instance, the ice sheet that covers Antarctica is as large as the United States and is up to 3 km thick. The rest of Earth's fresh water is found in lakes, rivers, wetlands, the soil, rock layers below the surface, and in the atmosphere.

River Systems

A river system is a network of streams that drains an area of land. A river system contains all of the land drained by a river, including the main river and all its tributaries. As shown in **Figure 3.7**, *tributaries* are smaller streams or rivers that flow into larger ones. Some river systems are enormous. For example, most of the precipitation that falls between the Rocky Mountains in the west and the Appalachian Mountains in the east eventually drains into the Mississippi River. The Mississippi River system covers about 40 percent of the contiguous United States.

Groundwater

Rain and melting snow sink into the ground and run off the land. Some of this water ends up in streams and rivers, but most of it trickles down through the ground and collects as *groundwater*. Groundwater fulfills the human need for fresh drinking water and supplies water for many agricultural and industrial uses. But groundwater accounts for less than 1 percent of all the water on Earth.

Aquifers

A rock layer that stores and allows the flow of ground-water is called an *aquifer*. The surface of the land where water enters an aquifer is called a *recharge zone*. **Figure 3.8** shows the location of aquifers in the contiguous United States.

FIGURE 3.7

River System This photo shows a network of tributaries flowing into a river in the wetlands of southern Louisiana.

✓ **CRITICAL THINKING**

Infer Looking at the photograph, why would pesticides sprayed on crops near the head of the main river be of concern to people near the coast?

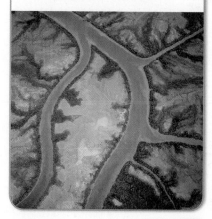

FIGURE 3.8

Aquifers Aquifers underlie much of the United States. The brown areas are rocks that contain relatively little stored water.

Aquifers

The Biosphere

If the Earth were an apple, the biosphere would be its skin. This comparison illustrates how small the layer of Earth that can support life is in relation to the size of the planet. The **biosphere** is the narrow layer around Earth's surface in which life can exist. The biosphere is made up of the uppermost part of the geosphere, most of the hydrosphere, and the lower part of the atmosphere. The biosphere extends about 12 km into the ocean and about 9 km into the atmosphere.

Life exists on Earth because of several important factors. Most life requires liquid water, moderate temperatures, and a source of energy. The materials that organisms require must continually be cycled. Gravity allows a planet to maintain an atmosphere and to cycle materials. Suitable combinations of the things that organisms need to survive are found only in the biosphere.

The biosphere is located near Earth's surface because most of the sunlight is available near the surface. Plants on land and in the ocean are shown in **Figure 3.9**. Plants need sunlight to produce their food, and almost every other organism gets its food from plants and algae. Most of the algae float at the surface of the ocean. These tiny, free-floating, marine algae are known as *phytoplankton*. Except for bacteria that live at hydrothermal vents, most of the organisms that live deep in the ocean feed on dead plants, animals, and protists that drift down from the surface.

✔ **CHECK FOR UNDERSTANDING**

Explain What makes life possible in the biosphere?

FIGURE 3.9

The Biosphere This illustration of the biosphere shows the concentration of plant life on land and in the ocean. The colors represent different concentrations of plant life in different regions.

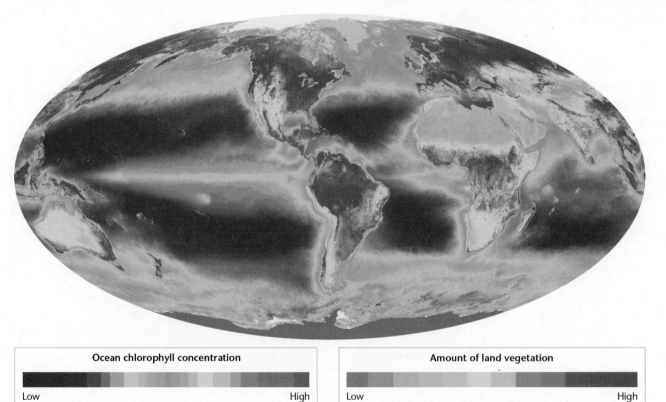

Ocean chlorophyll concentration	
Low	High

Amount of land vegetation	
Low	High

Energy Flow in the Biosphere

When an organism in the biosphere dies, its body is broken down and the matter in its body becomes available to other organisms. This matter is continually recycled. Energy, however, must be supplied constantly. The Eden Project, shown in **Figure 3.10**, is a closed system that models this flow of matter and energy.

In a *closed system*, energy enters and leaves the system, but matter does not. Earth is a closed system because the only thing that enters in significant amounts is energy from the sun, and the only thing that leaves in significant amounts is heat. Energy from the sun is used by plants in the biosphere to make their food. When an animal eats a plant, the energy stored in the plant is transferred to the animal. The animal, in turn, may be eaten by another animal. At each stage in the food chain, some of the energy is lost to the environment as heat, which is eventually lost into space.

In an *open system*, both matter and energy are exchanged between a system and the surrounding environment. Earth was once an open system. Matter was added to the early Earth as it was hit by comets and meteorites. Now, however, little matter reaches Earth this way.

FIGURE 3.10

Closed System The Eden Project is an attempt to model the biosphere. In this project, plants from all over the world live in a closed system. The Eden Project is housed within a series of domes that were constructed in an old clay pit in England.

Section 3 Formative Assessment

▶ Reviewing Main Ideas

1. **Name** and describe each of the three major processes in the water cycle.

2. **Describe** the properties of ocean water.

3. **Describe** the two types of ocean currents.

4. **Name** two factors that confine living things to the biosphere.

✔ Critical Thinking

5. **Analyzing Processes** Read about the ocean's role in regulating temperature under the heading "A Global Temperature Regulator." How might Earth's climate change if the land area on Earth were greater than the area of the world ocean?

6. **Analyzing Relationships** Why is the human body considered an open system?

Earthquake Hazard Map of the Contiguous United States

EARTHQUAKE HAZARD LEVELS

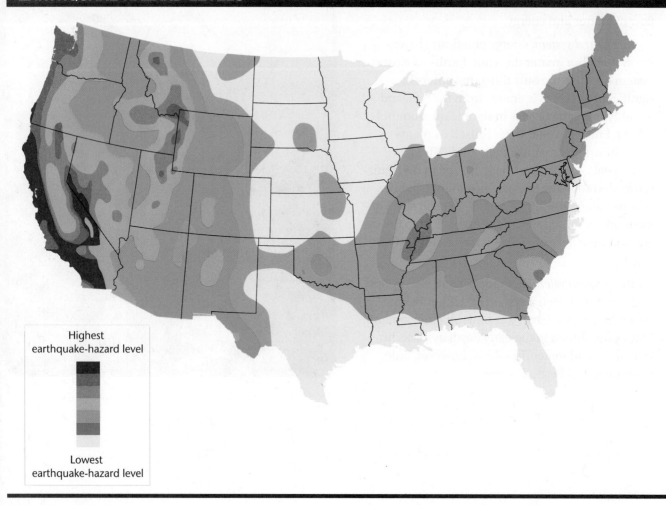

Highest
earthquake-hazard level

Lowest
earthquake-hazard level

Map Skills

Use the earthquake-hazard map of the contiguous United States to answer the questions below.

1. **Using a Key** Which area of the contiguous United States has a very high earthquake-hazard level?

2. **Using a Key** Determine which areas of the contiguous United States have very low earthquake-hazard levels.

3. **Analyzing Relationships** In which areas of the contiguous United States would scientists most likely set up earthquake-sensing devices?

4. **Inferring Relationships** Most earthquakes take place near tectonic plate boundaries. Based on the hazard levels, where do you think a boundary between two tectonic plates is located in the United States?

5. **Forming a Hypothesis** The New Madrid earthquake zone passes through southeastern Missouri and western Tennessee and has experienced some of the most widely felt earthquakes in U.S. history. Yet this earthquake zone lies far from any tectonic plate boundary. Propose a hypothesis that would explain these earthquakes.

Ocean Currents

Ocean currents are important in transporting heat, water, nutrients, pollutants, and organisms around the world. Even though they are important, ocean currents have been hard to study. Scientists used to drop labeled bottles in the oceans in different places and then record where they were picked up. Now, oceanographers attach transmitters to drifters. These transmitters send their position to satellites overhead, providing scientists with information that is helpful in a variety of ways, from protecting endangered species to making important decisions with far-reaching effects.

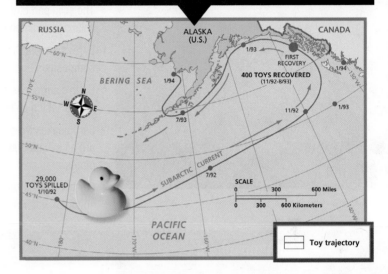

This map shows the possible trajectory of the toys and their estimated locations on certain dates as they floated across the Pacific Ocean from the point of the spill to recovery points in Alaska.

Watch Out for Debris!

The Hawaiian monk seal is one of the most endangered marine mammals in the world, with a population around 1,200 individuals. Monk seals live in the remote Northwest Hawaiian Islands (NWHI), hundreds of kilometers from the nearest human populations. Unfortunately, many seals have still been killed when they were entangled in discarded fishing gear that was dumped into the ocean hundreds or thousands of kilometers away. This is because the currents of the Pacific Ocean carry the debris to the areas where the seals feed, rest, and have their pups. Since 1996, around 500 metric tons of debris have been removed from the beaches of the NWHI! This has helped keep monk seals safer, but the currents keep bringing more debris to Hawaii, so these efforts must continue.

Oil Drilling

In order to meet the energy demands of the world, it is necessary to drill oil wells in deep ocean waters. During the summer of 2010, the Deepwater Horizon oil platform exploded and sank, releasing about five million barrels of oil into the Gulf of Mexico. Understanding currents was critical to responding appropriately to the spill. The Loop Current could have taken oil from off of Louisiana to the Florida Keys and even up the East Coast of the U.S. Luckily, the loop current

did not form in a way to take oil south. Instead, the oil stayed relatively close to the spill. In fact, the currents kept the oil in a place where bacteria could help to break it down, possibly reducing the impact of the spill.

Toys Ahoy!!

Despite more advanced methods, data that help us understand ocean currents sometimes come from the most unusual sources! In 1992, a container ship traveling northwest of Hawaii ran into a storm. One of the containers that washed overboard held 29,000 plastic toys. Over the next few years, the toys began washing up along the Alaskan coast from Sitka to the Bering Sea. Comparing data from the toys with other data, the researchers concluded that, although the current across the northeast Pacific Ocean changes little from year to year, in 1990 and 1992 the current was unusually far north.

What Do You Think?

Oil fields off the north coast of Cuba are now being opened for oil drilling. People in the Florida Keys and southeast Florida are concerned about this drilling. Use the map of currents in **Figure 3.6** as a reference to explain why. How should the U.S. respond to this drilling?

SECTION 1 **The Geosphere**

OBJECTIVES

- The solid part of the Earth that consists of all rock, and the soils and sediments on Earth's surface, is the geosphere.
- Earth's interior is divided into layers based on composition and structure.
- Earth's surface is broken into pieces called *tectonic plates*, which collide, separate, or slip past one another.
- Earthquakes, volcanic eruptions, and mountain building are all events that occur at the boundaries of tectonic plates.
- Earth's surface features are continually altered by the action of water and wind.

KEY TERMS

geosphere
hydrosphere
crust
mantle
core
lithosphere
asthenosphere
tectonic plate
chemical
weathering
erosion

SECTION 2 **The Atmosphere**

OBJECTIVES

- The mixture of gases that surrounds the Earth is called the *atmosphere*.
- The atmosphere is composed almost entirely of nitrogen and oxygen.
- Earth's atmosphere is divided into four layers based on changes in temperature that take place at different altitudes.
- Heat is transferred in the atmosphere by radiation, conduction, and convection.
- Some of the gases in Earth's atmosphere slow the escape of heat from Earth's surface in what is known as the greenhouse effect.

KEY TERMS

atmosphere
troposphere
stratosphere
ozone
radiation
conduction
convection
greenhouse effect

SECTION 3 **The Hydrosphere and Biosphere**

OBJECTIVES

- The hydrosphere includes all of the water at or near Earth's surface.
- Water in the ocean can be divided into three zones—the surface zone, the thermocline, and the deep zone—based on temperature.
- The ocean absorbs and stores energy from sunlight, regulating temperatures in the atmosphere.
- Surface currents in the ocean affect the climate of the land they flow near.
- The biosphere is the narrow layer at the surface of the Earth where life can exist.
- Earth is a closed system because energy enters and leaves Earth, but matter does not.

KEY TERMS

water cycle
evaporation
condensation
precipitation
salinity
fresh water
biosphere

Reviewing Key Terms

Use each of the following terms in a separate sentence.

1. *tectonic plate*
2. *erosion*
3. *radiation*
4. *ozone*
5. *salinity*

For each pair of terms, explain how the meanings of the terms differ.

6. *lithosphere* and *asthenosphere*
7. *conduction* and *convection*
8. *crust* and *mantle*
9. *evaporation* and *condensation*
10. **Concept Map** Use the following terms to create a concept map: *geosphere, crust, mantle, core, lithosphere, asthenosphere,* and *tectonic plate.*

Reviewing Main Ideas

11. The thin layer at Earth's surface where life exists is called the
    a. geosphere.
    b. atmosphere.
    c. hydrosphere.
    d. biosphere.

12. The thin layer of the Earth upon which tectonic plates move around is called the
    a. mantle.
    b. asthenosphere.
    c. lithosphere.
    d. outer core.

13. Seventy-eight percent of Earth's atmosphere is made up of
    a. oxygen.
    b. hydrogen.
    c. nitrogen.
    d. carbon dioxide.

14. The ozone layer is located in the
    a. stratosphere.
    b. mesosphere.
    c. thermosphere.
    d. troposphere.

15. Convection is defined as the
    a. transfer of energy across space.
    b. direct transfer of energy.
    c. trapping of heat near the Earth by gases.
    d. transfer of heat by currents.

16. Which of the following gases is *not* a greenhouse gas?
    a. water vapor
    b. nitrogen
    c. methane
    d. carbon dioxide

17. Liquid water turns into gaseous water vapor in a process called
    a. precipitation.
    b. convection.
    c. evaporation.
    d. condensation.

18. Currents at the surface of the ocean are moved mostly by
    a. heat.
    b. wind.
    c. salinity.
    d. the mixing of warm and cold water.

19. Which of the following statements about the biosphere is *not* true?
    a. The biosphere is a system closed to matter.
    b. Energy enters the biosphere in the form of sunlight.
    c. Nutrients in the biosphere must be continuously recycled.
    d. Matter is constantly added to the biosphere.

Short Answer

20. How do seismic waves give scientists information about Earth's interior?

21. Explain the effect of gravity on Earth's atmosphere.

22. Explain how convection currents transport heat in the atmosphere.

23. Why does land that is near the ocean change temperature less rapidly than land that is located farther inland?

24. Why is life on Earth confined to such a narrow layer near the Earth's surface?

Interpreting Graphics

The map below shows the different amounts of chlorophyll in the ocean. Chlorophyll is the pigment that makes plants and algae green. Chlorophyll identifies the presence of marine algae. The red and orange colors on the map show the highest amounts of chlorophyll; the blue and purple colors on the map show the smallest amounts of chlorophyll. Use the map to answer questions 25–26.

25. **Infer** Is there a greater concentration of marine algae at location A or at location B?

26. **Conclude** What conclusion can you reach about conditions in the parts of the ocean where marine algae may prefer to live?

Chlorophyll Content

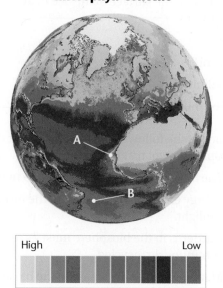

Critical Thinking

27. **Making Predictions** The eruption of Mount Pinatubo in 1991 reduced global temperature by several tenths of a Celsius degree for several years. Write a paragraph predicting what might happen to Earth's climate if several large-scale eruptions took place at the same time.

28. **Analyzing Processes** Read about the heating of Earth's surface and the absorption of incoming solar radiation under the heading "Warming of the Atmosphere." How might the Earth be different if the Earth's surface absorbed greater or lesser percentages of radiation?

29. **Analyzing Processes** Surface currents are deflected by continental landmasses. How might the pattern of Earth's surface currents change if the Earth had no landmasses? Where on the world ocean might the majority of warm surface currents be located? Where would the cold surface currents be located?

30. **History** Scientists believe that some human migration between distant landmasses may have taken place on rafts powered only by the wind and ocean currents. Look at Figure 3.6, which shows the Earth's surface currents. Hypothesize potential migratory routes these early seafarers may have followed.

31. **Plotting Seismic Activity** Most earthquakes take place near tectonic plate boundaries. Using the encyclopedia, the Internet, or another source, find at least 20 locations where major earthquakes took place during the 20th century. Plot these locations on a map of the world that shows Earth's tectonic plates. Did the majority of earthquakes occur at or near tectonic plate boundaries?

Analyzing Data

Use the graph below to answer questions 32–33.

32. Analyzing Data Rearrange the oceans in order of highest depth-to-area ratio to lowest depth-to-area ratio.

33. Making Calculations On the graph, you are given the average depths of the four oceans. From these data, calculate the average depth of the world ocean.

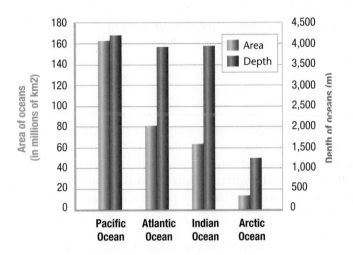

Making Connections

34. Communicating Main Ideas Describe the three important ways in which the movement of energy takes place in Earth's atmosphere.

35. Writing Persuasively Write a persuasive essay that explains why the Earth today should be regarded as a closed system for matter rather than an open system.

36. Outlining Topics Write a one-page outline that describes some of the important interactions that take place in the Earth system.

CASESTUDY

37. According to the passage, what purpose do coastal wetlands perform to reduce the damage from a storm surge?

38. According to the passage, what two factors increased the effectiveness of wetlands in reducing damage from tsunamis?

Why It Matters

39. Explain how using satellites to monitor weather conditions benefits people globally.

STUDYSKILL

The Importance of Nouns Most multiple-choice questions center around the definitions of nouns. When you study, pay attention to the definitions of nouns that appear to be important in the text. These nouns will often be boldfaced key terms or italicized secondary terms.

Beaches

Objectives

Examine models that show how the forces generated by wave action build, shape, and erode beaches.

Hypothesize ways in which beaches can be preserved from the erosive forces of wave activity.

Materials

metric ruler

milk cartons, empty, small (2)

pebbles

plaster of Paris

plastic container (large) or long wooden box lined with plastic

rocks, small

sand, 5 to 10 lb

wooden block, large

Almost one-fourth of all the structures that have been built within 150 m of the U.S. coastline, including the Great Lakes, will be lost to beach erosion over the next 60 years, according to a June 2000 report released by the Federal Emergency Management Agency (FEMA). The supply of sand for most beaches has been cut off by dams built on rivers and streams that would otherwise carry sand to the sea. Waves generated by storms also erode beaches. Longshore currents, which are generated by waves that break at an angle to a shoreline, transport sediment continuously and change the shape of a shoreline.

You will now use a series of models to help you understand how beaches can be both washed away and protected from the effects of waves and longshore currents.

Procedure

1. At least one day before you begin the investigation, make two plaster blocks. Mix a small amount of water with plaster of Paris until the mixture is smooth. Add five or six small rocks to the mixture for added weight. Pour the plaster mixture into the milk cartons. Let the plaster harden overnight. Carefully peel the milk cartons away from the plaster.

2. Prepare a wooden box lined with plastic or another similar large, shallow container. Make a model of a beach by placing a mixture of sand and small pebbles at one end of the container. The beach should occupy about one-fourth the length of the container. See step 2. In the area in front of the sand, add water to a depth of 2 to 3 cm. Use the large wooden block to generate several waves by moving the block up and down in the water at the end of the container opposite the beach. Continue this wave action until about half the beach has moved. Record your observations.

3. Remove the water, and rebuild the beach. In some places, breakwaters have been built offshore in an attempt to protect beaches from washing away. Build a breakwater by placing two plaster blocks across the middle of the container. Using the metric ruler, leave a 4 cm space between the blocks. See step 3. Use a wooden block to generate waves. Describe the results.

4. Drain the water, and make a new beach along one side of the container for about half its length. See step 4. Using the wooden block, generate a series of waves from the same end of the container as the end of the beach. Record your observations.

Step 2 Use a wooden block to generate waves at the end of the container opposite the beach.

5. Rebuild the beach along the same side of the container. *Jetties* or *breakwaters* are structures that can be built out into the ocean to intercept and break up a longshore current. Make a jetty by placing one of the small plaster blocks in the sand. See step 5. As you did in the previous steps, use the wooden block to generate waves. Describe the results.

6. Remove the wet sand, and put it in a container. Dispose of the water. (Note: Follow your teacher's instructions for disposal of the sand and water. Never pour water containing sand into a sink.)

Step 3 Build a breakwater by placing two plastic blocks across the middle of the container.

Analysis

1. **Describing Events** In step 2 of the procedure, what happened to the beach when water was first poured into the container? What happened to the particles of fine sand? Predict what would happen to the beach if it had no source of additional sand.

2. **Analyzing Results** In step 3 of the procedure, did the breakwater help protect the beach from washing away?

3. **Describing Events** What happened to the beach that you made in step 4 of the procedure? What happened to the shape of the waves along the beach?

4. **Analyzing Results** What effect did the jetty have on the beach that you made in step 5 of the procedure?

Step 4 Make a beach lengthwise along one side of the container. The length of the beach should equal one-half the length of the container.

Conclusions

5. **Drawing Conclusions** What can be done to preserve a beach area from being washed away as a result of wave action and longshore currents?

6. **Drawing Conclusions** What can be done to preserve a beach area that has been changed as a result of excessive use by people?

Extension

7. **Building Models** Make a beach that would be in danger of being washed away by a longshore current. Based on what you have learned, build a model in which the beach would be preserved by a breakwater or jetties. Explain how your model illustrates ways in which longshore currents can be intercepted and broken up.

Step 5 Place one of the small plaster blocks in the sand to make a jetty.

Ecology

This Australian plant called the Alice sundew gets the nutrients that it needs to survive by dissolving insects that get stuck on its sticky tips.

CHAPTER 4

Why It Matters

In a coral reef ecosystem, reef-building coral combine with algae to produce a colony that gathers energy from the sun, and creates shelter for many organisms.

Identify some of the possible interactions between organisms in the coral reef ecosystem in this photo.

CASESTUDY

Learn about how organisms adapt to environmental changes in the case study Darwin's Finches on page 98.

The Organization of Life

ONLINE ENVIRONMENTAL SCIENCE
HMDScience.com

Go online to access additional resources, including labs, worksheets, multimedia, and resources in Spanish.

©Photodisc/Getty Images

Ecosystems: Everything Is Connected

SECTION 1

Objectives

▶ Distinguish between the biotic and abiotic factors in an ecosystem.

▶ Describe how a population differs from a species.

▶ Explain how habitats are important for organisms.

Key Terms

ecosystem
biotic factor
abiotic factor
organism
species
population
community
habitat

You may have heard the concept that in nature everything is connected. What does this mean? Consider the following example. In 1995, scientists interested in controlling gypsy moths, which kill oak trees, performed an experiment. The scientists removed most mice, which eat young gypsy moths, from selected plots of oak forest. The number of gypsy moth eggs and young increased dramatically. The scientists then added acorns to the plots. Mice eat acorns. The number of mice soon increased, and the number of gypsy moths declined as the mice ate them as well.

This result showed that large acorn crops can suppress gypsy moth outbreaks. Interestingly, the acorns also attracted deer, which carry parasitic insects called ticks. Young ticks soon infested the mice. Wild mice carry the organism that causes Lyme disease. Ticks can pick up the organism when they bite mice. Then the ticks can bite and infect humans. This example shows that in nature, things that we would never think are connected—mice, acorns, ticks, and a human disease—can be linked to each other in a complex web.

Defining an Ecosystem

The mice, moths, oak trees, deer, and ticks in the previous example are all part of the same ecosystem. An **ecosystem** (EE koh sis tuhm) is all of the organisms living in an area together with their physical environment. An oak forest is an ecosystem. A coral reef is an ecosystem. Even a vacant lot, as shown in **Figure 1.1**, is an ecosystem.

FIGURE 1.1

Vacant Lot Ecosystem This vacant lot is actually a small ecosystem. It includes various organisms, such as plants and insects, as well as soil, air, and sunlight.

©Brian Nolan/iStock

FIGURE 1.3

Cold Ecosystem This caribou is a biotic factor in Denali National Park, Alaska.

✔ **CRITICAL THINKING**

Identify List the abiotic and biotic factors you see in the ecosystem shown here.

FIGURE 1.2

Coastal Ecosystem Like all ecosystems, this coastal region includes basic components such as rock, air, and plants.

Ecosystems Are Connected

People often think of ecosystems as isolated from each other, but ecosystems do not have clear boundaries. Things move from one ecosystem into another. Soil washes from a mountain into a lake, birds migrate from across hundreds of miles, and pollen blows from a forest into a field.

The Components of an Ecosystem

In order to survive, ecosystems need certain basic components. These are energy, mineral nutrients, carbon dioxide, water, oxygen, and living organisms. As shown in **Figure 1.2**, plants and soil are two of the obvious components of most land ecosystems. The energy in most ecosystems comes from the sun.

To appreciate how all of the things in an ecosystem are connected, think about how a car works. The engine alone is made up of hundreds of parts that all work together. If even one part breaks, the car might not run. Likewise, if one part of an ecosystem is destroyed or changes, the entire system may be affected.

Biotic and Abiotic Factors

An ecosystem is made up of both living and nonliving things. All of the organisms, including animals, fungi, bacteria, and plants are called **biotic factors**. Biotic factors include dead organisms, dead parts of organisms, such as leaves, or an organism's waste products. **Abiotic** (ay bie AHT ik) **factors** are the nonliving parts of the ecosystem, including air, water, rocks, sand, light, and temperature. **Figure 1.3** shows several biotic and abiotic factors in an Alaskan ecosystem.

©BIOS

FIGURE 1.4

Organization in an Ecosystem An individual organism is part of a population, a community, an ecosystem, and the biosphere.

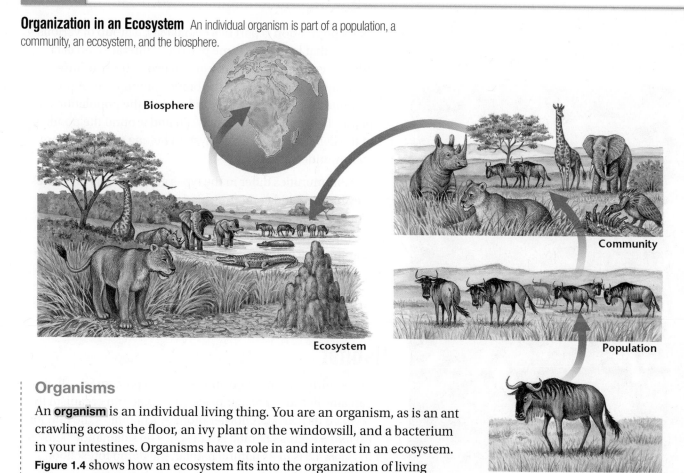

Biosphere

Community

Population

Ecosystem

Organism

Organisms

An **organism** is an individual living thing. You are an organism, as is an ant crawling across the floor, an ivy plant on the windowsill, and a bacterium in your intestines. Organisms have a role in and interact in an ecosystem. **Figure 1.4** shows how an ecosystem fits into the organization of living things. A **species** is a group of organisms that can mate to produce fertile offspring. All humans, for example, are members of the species *Homo sapiens.* All black widow spiders are members of the species *Latrodectus mactans.* Every organism is classified as a member of a species.

Populations

Members of a species may not all live in the same place. Field mice in Maine and field mice in Florida will never interact even though they are members of the same species. An organism lives as part of a population. A **population** is a group of the same species that live in the same place. For example, all the field mice in a corn field make up one population of field mice. An important characteristic of a population is that its members usually breed with one another rather than with members of other populations. The bison in **Figure 1.5** will usually mate with another member of the same herd, just as the wildflowers will usually be pollinated by other flowers in the same field.

FIGURE 1.5

Populations Two of the populations shown here are a population of pink Australian strawflowers (left) and a herd of bison (right).

(bl) ©Corbis; (br) ©Joe Austin Photography/Alamy Images

FIGURE 1.6

Habitat Salamanders, such as this European fire salamander, live in habitats that are moist and shaded.

✔ **CHECK FOR UNDERSTANDING**

Explain Why is an organism's habitat important for that organism?

Communities

Every population is part of a **community,** a group of various species that live in the same place and interact with each other. A community differs from an ecosystem because a community includes only the biotic components. A pond community, for example, includes all of the populations of plants, fish, and insects that live in and around the pond. All of the living things in an ecosystem belong to one or more communities.

Communities differ in the types and numbers of species they have. A land community is often characterized by the types of plants that are dominant. These plants determine the other organisms that can live in this community. For example, the dominant plant in a Colorado forest might be its ponderosa pine trees. This pine tree community will have animals, such as squirrels, that live in and feed on these trees.

Habitat

The squirrels mentioned above live in a pine forest. All organisms live in particular places. The place an organism lives is called its **habitat.** A howler monkey's habitat is the rain forest and a cactus's habitat is a desert. The salamander shown in **Figure 1.6** is in its natural habitat, the damp forest floor.

Every habitat has specific biotic and abiotic factors that the organisms living there need to survive. A coral reef contains sea water, coral, sunlight, and a wide variety of other organisms. If any of these factors change, then the habitat changes.

Organisms tend to be very well suited to their natural habitats. Indeed, animals and plants cannot usually survive for long periods of time away from their natural habitats. For example, a fish that lives in the crevices of a coral reef will die if the coral reef is destroyed.

✔ Section 1 **Formative Assessment**

▶ Reviewing Main Ideas

1. **Describe** a population not mentioned in this section.

2. **Describe** which factors of an ecosystem are not part of a community.

3. **Explain** the difference between a population and a species.

✔ Critical Thinking

4. **Recognize Relationships** Write your own definition of the term *community,* using the terms *biotic factors* and *abiotic factors.*

5. **Inferring Conclusions** Why might a scientist say that an animal is becoming rare because of habitat destruction?

Evolution

Organisms tend to be well suited to where they live and what they do. **Figure 2.1** shows a chameleon (kuh MEEL ee uhn) capturing an insect. Insects are not easy to catch, so how does the chameleon do it? Chameleons can change the color and pattern of their skin, and then blend into their backgrounds. Their eyes are raised on little, mobile turrets that enable the lizards to look around without moving. An insect is unlikely to notice such an animal sitting motionless on a branch. When the insect moves within range, the chameleon shoots out an amazingly long tongue to grab the insect.

Evolution by Natural Selection

In 1859, English naturalist Charles Darwin observed that organisms in a population differ slightly from each other in form, function, and behavior. Some of these differences are *hereditary* (huh RED i ter ee)—that is, passed from parent to offspring. For more than 150 years, scientists have shown that the environment exerts a strong influence over which individuals survive to produce offspring. The environment also influences how many offspring individuals have. Some individuals, because of certain traits, are more likely to survive and reproduce than other individuals. This is called **natural selection**–the process by which individuals that are better adapted to their environment survive and reproduce with more success than less well adapted individuals do.

Over many generations natural selection causes the characteristics of populations to change. A change in the genetic characteristics of a population from one generation to the next is known as **evolution.**

SECTION 2

Objectives

▶ Explain the process of evolution by natural selection.

▶ Explain the concept of adaptation.

▶ Describe the steps by which a population of insects becomes resistant to a pesticide.

Key Terms

natural selection
evolution
adaptation
artificial selection
resistance

✔ **CHECK FOR UNDERSTANDING**
Relate How is natural selection related to the process of evolution?

FIGURE 2.1

Adaptations for Catching Prey A chameleon catches an unsuspecting insect that has strayed within range of the lizard's long and fast-moving tongue.

©Picture Press/Alamy Images

Connect to GEOLOGY

Darwin and Fossils
In the 1800s, fossil hunting was a popular hobby. The many fossils that people found started arguments about where fossils come from. Darwin's theory of evolution proposed that fossils are the remains of extinct species from which modern species evolved. When his book on the theory of evolution was first published in 1859, it became an immediate bestseller.

Nature Selects

Darwin thought that nature selects for certain traits, such as sharper claws or lighter feathers, because organisms with these traits are more likely to survive and reproduce. For example, lions that have the trait of sharper claws can kill their prey more easily than lions with duller claws. Thus, lions with sharper claws are more likely to survive and reproduce. Over time, the lion population includes a greater and greater proportion of lions with sharper claws. As the populations of a given species change, so does the species. **Figure 2.2** summarizes the premises of the theory of evolution by natural selection. Darwin proposed this theory after drawing a conclusion based on these premises.

FIGURE 2.2

EVOLUTION BY NATURAL SELECTION

Premises	Conclusion
1. Individuals in a population vary in each generation.	Based on these four premises, individuals with genetic traits that make them more likely to grow up and reproduce in the existing environment will become more common in the population from one generation to the next.
2. Some of these variations are genetic, or inherited.	
3. More individuals are produced than live to grow up and reproduce.	
4. Individuals with some genes are more likely to survive and reproduce than individuals with other genes.	

CASESTUDY

Darwin's Finches

Charles Darwin and Alfred Wallace independently discovered that natural selection is a mechanism leading to evolutionary change. Organisms that live on oceanic islands inspired both scientists. Both saw that plants and animals on islands were often unusual species found nowhere else. Darwin was impressed by the mockingbirds in the Galápagos Islands, an isolated group of volcanic islands in the Pacific Ocean west of Ecuador. There are four species of mockingbirds with even more distinctive forms among them, each differing in subtle ways, and each island having only one form.

Other scientists discovered that the Galápagos Islands also contain 14 unique species of finch-like birds, which have become known as Darwin's finches. All the species look generally similar, but different species have differently specialized beaks adapted to eating different types of food. Some species have large, parrot-like beaks adapted to

Notice the beaks in the two species of Darwin's finches. What do you think these finches eat?

cracking big seeds, some species have slim beaks that are used to sip nectar from flowers, and some species have become insect eaters. Recent genetic analysis indicates

(cr) ©Ryan M. Bolton/Alamy Images; (tl) ©Auscape International

FIGURE 2.3

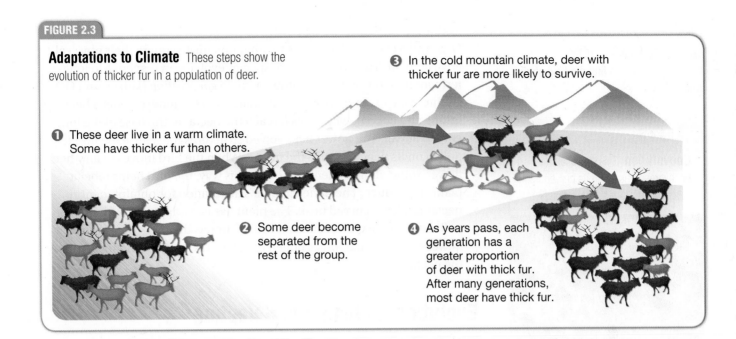

Adaptations to Climate These steps show the evolution of thicker fur in a population of deer.

❶ These deer live in a warm climate. Some have thicker fur than others.

❷ Some deer become separated from the rest of the group.

❸ In the cold mountain climate, deer with thicker fur are more likely to survive.

❹ As years pass, each generation has a greater proportion of deer with thick fur. After many generations, most deer have thick fur.

Figure 2.3 shows an example of evolution in which a population of deer become isolated in a cold area. Many die, but some have genes for thicker, warmer fur. These deer are more likely to survive, and their young with thick fur are also more likely to survive to reproduce. The deer's thick fur is an **adaptation,** an inherited trait that increases an organism's chance of survival and reproduction in a certain environment.

that all the Galápagos finches evolved from a single species of seed-eating finch that came from the South American mainland. As populations of the finches became established on the various islands, the successful finches were those able to eat what they found on their island.

Princeton University scientists Peter and Rosemary Grant have spent 40 years studying Darwin's finches on one of the Galápagos Islands. Here, one species, the medium ground finch, has a short, stubby beak and eats seeds as well as a few insects. The Grants found that the main factor that determined whether a finch lived or died was how much food was available. During a long drought in 1977, many plants died and the small seeds that the finches eat became scarce. Finches that had large beaks were much more likely to have survived. Large beaks allowed them to eat larger seeds from the larger plants that had survived the drought.

The finches that survived the drought passed their genes for larger beaks to their offspring. Two years later, the Grants found that the beaks of medium ground finches

on Daphne Major were larger, on average, than they had been before the drought. The Grants had observed evolution occurring in birds over a short period of time. The studies of finches have documented many details about how one species responds to selection.

Scientists have found other cases where organisms respond rapidly to selection. For example, bacteria acquire resistance to antibiotics and agricultural pests develop tolerance to pesticides. Fish found in ponds with predators have different body shapes than the same species in ponds without predators. On a South Pacific island, a population of butterflies developed resistance to a deadly bacteria in one year!

Critical Thinking

Analyzing Relationships Could the finches that evolved bigger beaks in this study evolve smaller beaks some day?

FIELDSTUDY

Go to Appendix B to find the field study **Coevolution.**

FIGURE 2.4

Coevolution This Hawaiian honeycreeper is using its curved beak to sip nectar from a lobelia flower.

Connect to MATH

Plumper Pumpkins

Each year a farmer saves and plants only the seeds from his largest pumpkins. Suppose that he starts with pumpkins that average 5 kg and each year grows pumpkins that are 3 percent more massive, on average, than those he grew the year before. What will be the average mass of his pumpkins after 10 years?

Coevolution

Organisms evolve adaptations to other organisms and to their physical environment. The process of two species evolving in response to long-term interactions with each other is called *coevolution* (koh ev uh LOO shuhn). One example is shown in **Figure 2.4**. The honeycreeper's beak is long and curved, which lets it reach the nectar at the base of the long, curved flower. The flower has evolved structures that cause the bird to get pollen on its head as it sips the nectar. When the bird moves to another flower, some of the pollen rubs off. In this way, the bird helps lobelia plants reproduce. The honeycreeper's adaptation for obtaining more nectar is a long, curved beak. The plant has two adaptations for greater pollination. One is sweet nectar, which attracts the birds. The other is a flower structure that forces pollen onto a bird's head when the bird sips the nectar.

Evolution by Artificial Selection

Many populations of plants and animals do not live in the wild but are cared for by humans. People control how these organisms reproduce and therefore how they evolve. The two species in **Figure 2.5** are closely related. Over thousands of years, humans bred the ancestors of today's wolves to produce the variety of dog breeds. The selective breeding of organisms by humans for specific characteristics is called **artificial selection.**

The fruits, grains, and vegetables we eat were also produced by artificial selection. By selecting for traits such as size and sweetness, farmers directed the evolution of crop plants. As a result, crops produce fruits, grains, and roots that are larger, sweeter, and easier to harvest than their wild relatives. Native Americans cultivated the ancestor of today's corn from a grasslike plant in the mountains of Mexico. Modern corn is very different from the wild plant that was its ancestor.

FIGURE 2.5

Artificial Selection As a result of artificial selection, the Chihuahua on the right looks very different from its wolf ancestor on the left.

(bl) ©Lisa Dearing/Alamy Images; (tl) ©P. La Tourrette/VIREO; (br) ©BIOS

FIGURE 2.6

Example of the Evolution of Resistance

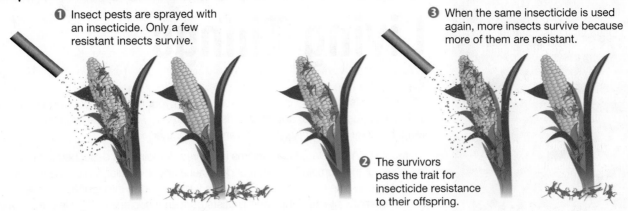

1 Insect pests are sprayed with an insecticide. Only a few resistant insects survive.

3 When the same insecticide is used again, more insects survive because more of them are resistant.

2 The survivors pass the trait for insecticide resistance to their offspring.

Evolution of Resistance

Sometimes humans cause populations of organisms to evolve unwanted adaptations. You may have heard about insect pests that are resistant to pesticides and about bacteria that are resistant to antibiotics. What is resistance, and what does it have to do with evolution?

Resistance is the ability of one or more organisms to tolerate a particular chemical designed to kill it. An organism may be resistant to a chemical when it contains a gene that allows it to break the chemical down into harmless substances. By trying to control pests and bacteria with chemicals, humans promote the evolution of resistant populations.

Pesticide Resistance

Consider the evolution of pesticide resistance among corn pests, as shown in **Figure 2.6.** A pesticide is sprayed on corn to kill grasshoppers. Most of the grasshoppers die, but a few survive. The survivors happen to have a version of a gene that protects them from the pesticide. The surviving insects pass on the gene to their offspring. Each time the corn is sprayed, insects that are resistant to the pesticide will have a greater chance of survival and reproduction. As a result, the insect population will evolve to include more and more resistant members.

✔ **CHECK FOR UNDERSTANDING**

Identify Name two different organisms that have evolved resistance?

✔ Section 2 **Formative Assessment**

▶ Reviewing Main Ideas

1. **Explain** what an adaptation is, and provide three examples.

2. **Explain** the process of evolution by natural selection.

3. **Describe** one way in which artificial selection can benefit humans.

4. **Explain** how a population of insects could become resistant to a pesticide.

✔ Critical Thinking

5. **Relating Concepts** Read the description of evolution by natural selection in this section and describe the role that the environment plays in the theory.

6. **Recognizing Relationships** A population of rabbits evolves thicker fur in response to a colder climate. What is this an example of? Explain your answer.

Objectives

▶ Name the three domains and the four kingdoms of organisms and list characteristics of each.

▶ Explain the importance of bacteria and fungi in the environment.

▶ Describe the role of protists in the ocean environment.

▶ Describe how organisms interact and depend on each other for survival.

Key Terms

archaea
bacteria
fungus
protist
gymnosperm
angiosperm
invertebrate
vertebrate

The Diversity of Living Things

Life on Earth is incredibly diverse. Take a walk in your neighborhood, and you might see trees, birds, insects, and maybe fish in a stream. All of these organisms are living, but they are all very different from one another.

Most scientists classify organisms into three domains, as described in Figure 3.1. Members of the domains Archaea and Bacteria are unicellular, which means they consist of only one cell. Domain Eukarya is further divided into four kingdoms. The cells of animals, plants, fungi, and protists contain a *nucleus* (NOO klee uhs), which consists of a membrane that surrounds a cell's genetic material. Bacteria, fungi, and plants all have *cell walls*, structures that surround their cells and provide them with support.

Archaea and Bacteria

Archaea and bacteria have several features in common, even though they are not closely related. They are microscopic, unicellar organisms that usually have cell walls and reproduce by dividing in half. Unlike members of the domain Eukarya, they lack nuclei. **Archaea** are often found in extreme places, such as hot springs. They differ from bacteria in their genetics and the makeup of their cell wall. **Bacteria** are very common and can be found in many places, including soil and animal bodies.

FIGURE 3.1

LEVELS OF CLASSIFICATION		
	Characteristics	**Examples**
Domain Archaea	unicellular; cells lack nuclei; reproduce by dividing in half; often found in harsh environments	methanogens (live in swamps and produce methane gas) and extreme thermophiles (live in hot springs)
Domain Bacteria	unicellular; cells lack nuclei; reproduce by dividing in half; incredibly common	proteobacteria (common in soils and in animal intestines) and cyanobacteria (also called *blue-green algae*)
Domain Eukarya	unicellular and multicellular; cells contain nuclei; reproduce asexually and sexually	fungi, protists, plants, and animals
Kingdom Fungi	absorb their food through their body surface; have cell walls; most live on land	yeasts, mushrooms, molds, mildews, and rusts
Kingdom Protista	most are unicellular but some are multicellular; most live in water	diatoms, dinoflagellates, amoebas, trypanosomes, paramecia, algae, and *Euglena*
Kingdom Plantae	multicellular; make their own food by photosynthesis; have cell walls	ferns, mosses, trees, herbs, and grasses
Kingdom Animalia	multicellular; no cell walls; ingest their food; live on land and in water	corals, sponges, worms, insects, fish, reptiles, birds, and mammals

Bacteria and the Environment

Bacteria play many important roles in the environment. Some kinds of bacteria break down the remains and wastes of other organisms and return nutrients to the soil. Others recycle mineral nutrients, such as nitrogen and phosphorus. For example, certain kinds of bacteria play a very important role by converting nitrogen in the air into a form that plants can use. Nitrogen is important because it is a main component of proteins and genetic material.

Bacteria also allow many organisms, including humans, to extract certain nutrients from their food. The bacteria in **Figure 3.2** are *Escherichia coli*, or *E. coli,* a bacterium found in the intestines of humans and other animals. *E. coli* helps digest food and release vitamins that humans need. A different strain, or form, of *E. coli* can cause severe food poisoning.

Fungi

A **fungus** (plural, *fungi*) is an organism whose cells have nuclei and cell walls. A mushroom is the reproductive structure of a fungus. The rest of the fungus is an underground network of fibers. These fibers absorb food from decaying organisms in the soil.

Fungi get their food by releasing chemicals that help break down organic matter, and then absorbing the nutrients. The bodies of most fungi are a huge network of threads that grow through the soil, dead wood, or other material on which the fungi are feeding. Like bacteria, fungi play an important role in the environment by breaking down the bodies and body parts of dead organisms.

Some fungi cause diseases, such as athlete's foot. Other fungi add flavor to food. The fungus in blue cheese, shown in **Figure 3.3**, gives the cheese its strong flavor. And fungi called *yeasts* produce the gas that makes bread rise.

(tr) ©SPL/Photo Researchers, Inc.; (bl) ©Arco Images GmbH/Alamy Images; (br) ©Igor Kisselev/Alamy Images

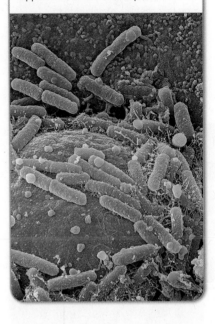

FIGURE 3.2

Bacteria These long, orange objects are *E. coli* bacteria as they appear under a microscope.

✔ **CHECK FOR UNDERSTANDING**

Compare Name one way that bacteria and fungi are similar and one way that they are different.

FIGURE 3.3

Fungi A mushroom (left) is the reproductive structure of a fungus that lives in the soil. The cheese (right) gets its taste and its blue color from a fungus.

FIGURE 3.4

Protists

Most people have some idea what bacteria and fungi are, but few could define a protist. **Protists** are a diverse group of both unicellular and multicellular organisms. Some, such as amoebas, are animal-like. Others, such as the kelp and diatoms in **Figure 3.4,** are plantlike. Still others are more like fungi. Most protists are unicellular microscopic organisms, including amoebas and *diatoms* (DIE uh tahms). Diatoms float on the ocean surface. The most infamous protist is *Plasmodium*, the unicellular organism that causes the disease malaria. From an environmental standpoint, the most important protists are probably algae. Algae are plantlike protists that can make their own food using the sun's energy for photosynthesis. Green pond "scum" and seaweed are examples of algae. Algae range in size from the giant kelp to the unicellular *phytoplankton*, which are the initial source of food in most ocean and freshwater ecosystems.

Plants

Plants are multicellular organisms that have cell walls and make their own food using energy from the sun. Most plants live on land, where the resources a plant needs are separated between the air and the soil. Sunlight, oxygen, and carbon dioxide are in the air, and minerals and water are in the soil. Plants have roots that access water and nutrients in the soil and leaves that collect light and gases in the air. Leaves and roots are connected by *vascular tissue*, conducting tissue that transports water and food. Vascular tissue has thick cell walls, so a wheat plant or a tree is like a building supported by its plumbing.

Plants with no vascular tissue are called *nonvascular* plants. Because nonvascular plants lack specialized conducting tissues as well as true roots, stems, and leaves, water must move from the environment and throughout the plant. As a result, nonvascular plants, such as mosses, live in damp places, as shown in **Figure 3.5.**

Protists Microscopic, unicellular diatoms (left) live in the plankton. Kelp (right) are large, multicellular protists that live attached to the ocean floor.

✔ **CRITICAL THINKING**

Recognize What do the protists in these photos have in common?

VirtuaL INVESTIGATION

HMDScience.com

Protists

FIGURE 3.5

Nonvascular Plants Mosses live in damp places because they need water to reproduce.

Gymnosperms

Pine trees and other evergreens with needle-like leaves are gymnosperms (JIM noh spuhrmz). **Gymnosperms** are woody plants that produce seeds, but their seeds are not enclosed in fruits. Gymnosperms such as pine trees are also called *conifers* because their seeds are inside cones, as shown in **Figure 3.6**.

Gymnosperms have several adaptations that allow them to live in drier conditions than lower plants can. Gymnosperms produce *pollen,* which protects and moves sperm between plants. These plants also produce *seeds,* which protect developing plants from drying out. And a conifer's needle-like leaves lose little water. Much of our lumber and paper comes from gymnosperms.

Angiosperms

Most land plants today are **angiosperms** (AN jee oh spuhrmz), flowering plants that produce seeds in fruit. All of the plants in **Figure 3.7** are angiosperms. The flower is the reproductive structure of the plant. Some angiosperms, such as grasses, have small flowers that produce pollen that is carried by the wind. Other angiosperms have large flowers that attract insects or birds to carry their pollen to other plants. Many flowering plants depend on animals to disperse their seeds and carry their pollen. For example, a bird that eats a fruit will drop the seeds elsewhere, where they may grow into new plants.

Most land animals could not survive without flowering plants. Most of the food humans eat, such as wheat, rice, beans, oranges, and lettuce, comes from flowering plants. Building materials and fibers, such as oak and cotton, also come from flowering plants.

FIGURE 3.6

Gymnosperms This gymnosperm has male and female reproductive structures called *cones*.

✔ **CHECK FOR UNDERSTANDING**

Relate How do angiosperms depend on animals, and how do animals depend on angiosperms?

FIGURE 3.7

Angiosperms This meadow contains a wide array of angiosperms, including grasses, trees, and wildflowers.

QUICKLAB

Pollen and Flower Diversity
Procedure
1. Use a cotton swab to collect pollen from a common flowering plant.
2. Tap the cotton swab on a microscope slide and cover the slide with a cover slip.
3. Examine the slide under a microscope, and draw the pollen grains in your science journal.
4. Repeat this exercise with a grass plant in bloom.

Analysis
1. Based on the structure of the flower and pollen grains, explain which plant is pollinated by insects and which is pollinated by wind.

Animals

Animals cannot make their own food like plants can. They have to take in food from their environment. In addition, animal cells have no cell walls, so animals' bodies are soft and flexible. Some animals have evolved hard skeletons against which their muscles can pull to move their bodies. As a result, animals are much more mobile than plants, and all animals move around in their environments during at least one stage in their lives.

Invertebrates

Animals that lack backbones are **invertebrates** (in VUHR tuh brits). Many invertebrates live attached to hard surfaces in the ocean and filter their food out of the water. These organisms move around only when they are larvae (juveniles). At this early stage of life, they are part of the ocean's floating plankton. Filter feeders include corals, various worms, and mollusks such as clams and oysters. **Figure 3.8** shows a variety of invertebrates. Other invertebrates, including squid in the ocean and insects on land, move around actively in search of food.

More insects exist on Earth than any other type of animal. Insects have a waterproof external skeleton that keeps them from losing water in dry environments. Insects move quickly and they reproduce quickly. Also, most insects can fly. Their small size allows them to live on little food and to hide from enemies in small spaces, such as a seed or in the hair of a mammal.

Many insects and plants have evolved together and depend on each other to survive. Insects carry pollen from male parts of flowers to female parts of flowers to fertilize a plant's egg, which develops into a fruit. Without insect pollinators, we would not have tomatoes, cucumbers, apples, and many other crops. Insects also eat other insects that we consider to be pests. But, humans and insects are often enemies. Bloodsucking insects transmit human diseases, such as malaria, sleeping sickness, and West Nile virus. Insects probably do more damage indirectly, however, by eating crops.

FIGURE 3.8

Invertebrates Examples of invertebrates include the banana slug (left), the leaf-footed bug (middle), and the cuttlefish (right).

FIGURE 3.9

Vertebrates Examples of vertebrates include the toco toucan (left), the blue-spotted stingray (middle), and the snow leopard (right).

Vertebrates

Animals that have backbones are called **vertebrates.** Members of three vertebrate groups are shown in **Figure 3.9.** The first vertebrates were fish, but today many vertebrates live on land. Amphibians, which include toads, frogs, and salamanders, are partially aquatic. Nearly all amphibians must return to water to lay their eggs.

The first vertebrates to complete their entire life cycle on land were the reptiles, which today include turtles, lizards, snakes, and crocodiles. These animals have an almost waterproof egg, which allows the egg to hatch on land.

Birds are warm-blooded vertebrates with feathers. Bird eggs have hard shells. Adult birds keep their eggs and young warm until they develop insulating layers of fat and feathers. *Mammals* are warm-blooded vertebrates that have fur and feed their young milk. The ability to maintain a high body temperature allows birds and mammals to live in cold areas, where many other land vertebrates cannot survive.

ECOFACT

Conserving Water

Arthropods and vertebrates are the only two groups of animals that have adaptations that prevent dehydration so effectively that some of them can move about freely on land on a dry, sunny day.

✔ Section 3 **Formative Assessment**

✔ Reviewing Main Ideas

1. **Describe** how animals and angiosperms depend on each other. Write a short paragraph to explain your answer.

2. **Describe** the importance of protists in the ocean.

3. **Name** the four kingdoms of Eukarya, and give two characteristics of each.

4. **Explain** the importance of bacteria and fungi in the environment.

✔ Critical Thinking

5. **Recognize Relationships** Explain how the large number and wide distribution of angiosperm species is related to the success of insects.

6. **Comparing Structures** Write a short paragraph that compares the reproductive structures of gymnosperms and angiosperms.

Butterfly Ecologist

Imagine millions of butterflies swirling through the air like autumn leaves, clinging in tightly packed masses to tree trunks and branches, and covering low-lying forest vegetation like a luxurious, moving carpet. According to Alfonso Alonso, this is quite a sight to see.

For many winters Alonso would climb up to the few remote sites in central Mexico where anywhere from 23 million to over 170 million monarch butterflies spend the winter depending on the site. His interest in monarchs came from a desire to help preserve their habitat and the butterflies themselves. His work helped him earn a Ph.D. in zoology from the University of Florida.

Monarchs are famous for their long-distance migration. The butterflies that eventually find their way to Mexico come from as far away as the northeastern United States and southern Canada. Some of them travel up to 4,828 km before reaching central Mexico.

Wintering Habitat at Risk

Unfortunately, the habitat that the monarchs travel long distances to reach is increasingly threatened by illegal logging and other human activities. Logging reduced the size of the wintering region by approximately 44 percent between 1971 to 1999. Mexico has set aside several of the known butterfly sites as sanctuaries, but even these are endangered by people who cut down fir trees for fuel or money.

Alonso's work and the work of other ecologists after him has helped Mexican conservationists better understand and protect monarch butterflies. Especially important is Alonso's discovery that the monarchs depend on bushlike vegetation, called *understory vegetation*, that grows beneath the fir trees.

A Sea of Orange At their overwintering sites in Mexico, millions of monarchs cover trees and bushes in a fluttering carpet of orange and black.

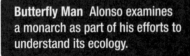

Butterfly Man Alonso examines a monarch as part of his efforts to understand its ecology.

UNITED STATES

MEXICO

Gulf of California

Gulf of Mexico

Monarch Butterfly Sanctuaries

PACIFIC OCEAN

✪ Mexico City

BELIZE

HONDURAS

GUATEMALA

Monarch Sanctuaries Monarch butterflies spend the winter at forested sites just above Mexico City.

Keeping Warm

Alonso's research showed that when the temperature falls below freezing, as it often does in the mountains where the monarchs winter, understory vegetation can mean the difference between life and death for some monarchs. These conditions are life threatening to the monarchs because low temperatures (−1°C to 4°C, or 30°F to 40°F) limit their movement. In fact, the butterflies are not able to fly at such low temperatures. They can only crawl. At even colder temperatures (−7°C to −1°C, or 20°F to 30°F), monarchs resting on the forest floor may freeze to death. But if the forest has understory vegetation, the monarchs can slowly climb the vegetation until they are at least 10 cm above the ground, where it is warmer. This tiny difference in elevation can provide a microclimate that is warm enough to ensure the monarchs' survival.

The importance of understory vegetation was not known before Alonso did his research. Now, thanks to his work, Mexican conservationists will better protect the understory vegetation. And the Mexican government has passed a new decree that protects monarchs in areas the butterflies are known to use.

The Need for Conservation

Although the monarchs continue to enjoy the forests where they overwinter, those forests are still threatened. There is little forest left in this area, and the need for wood increases each year. Alonso hopes his efforts will help protect the monarch both now and in the future.

Now that he has completed his Ph.D., Alonso is devoting himself to preserving monarchs and other organisms. He works as assistant director for conservation and development for the Smithsonian Institution's Monitoring and Assessment of Biodiversity (MAB) program. He is developing several new projects in collaboration with others including a forest conservation project in Madagascar, and conservation projects in Panama and Mexico that combine cultural values with natural values to preserve threatened areas.

Information...

If you are interested in learning more about monarchs, including their spectacular migration, visit the Web site for Monarch Watch. Monarch Watch is an organization based at the University of Kansas that is dedicated to educating people about the monarch and promoting its conservation.

What Do You Think?

As a migrating species, monarchs spend part of their lives in the United States and part in Mexico. Should the U.S. and Mexico cooperate in their efforts to understand and manage the monarch? Should nations set up panels to manage other migrating species, such as many songbirds?

©Lincoln Brower

SECTION 1 Ecosystems: Everything Is Connected

OBJECTIVES

- Ecosystems are composed of many interconnected parts that often interact in complex ways.
- An ecosystem is all the different organisms living in an area as well as the physical environment.
- Organisms live as populations of one species in communities with other species. Each species has its own habitat, or type of place that it lives.

KEY TERMS

ecosystem
biotic factor
abiotic factor
organism
species
population
community
habitat

SECTION 2 Evolution

OBJECTIVES

- Natural selection is the process by which organisms with particular traits are better adapted to their environment to survive and reproduce more successfully.
- Natural selection is responsible for evolution—a change in the genetic characteristics of a population from one generation to the next.
- By selecting which domesticated animals and plants breed, humans cause evolution by artificial selection.
- We have unintentionally selected for pests that are resistant to pesticides and for bacteria that are resistant to antibiotics.

KEY TERMS

natural selection
evolution
adaptation
artificial selection
resistance

SECTION 3 The Diversity of Living Things

OBJECTIVES

- Organisms can be divided into three domains and four kingdoms, which are distinguished by the types of cells they possess and how they obtain their food.
- Bacteria and fungi play the important environmental roles of breaking down dead organisms and recycling nutrients.
- Gymnosperms, which include the conifers, are the earliest plants with seeds. Angiosperms are flowering plants.
- Insects, invertebrates that are the most successful animals on Earth, affect humans in both positive and negative ways.
- Vertebrates, or animals with backbones, include fish, amphibians, reptiles, birds, and mammals.

KEY TERMS

archaea
bacteria
fungus
protist
gymnosperm
angiosperm
invertebrate
vertebrate

Reviewing Key Terms

Use each of the following terms in a separate sentence.

1. *adaptation*
2. *invertebrate*
3. *abiotic factor*
4. *habitat*
5. *species*

For each pair of terms, explain how the meanings of the terms differ.

6. *community* and *population*
7. *evolution* and *natural selection*
8. *gymnosperm* and *angiosperm*
9. *bacteria* and *protists*
10. Concept Map Use the following terms to create a concept map: *ecosystem, abiotic factor, biotic factor, population, species, community,* and *habitat*.

Reviewing Main Ideas

11. Which of the following pairs of organisms belong to the same population?
    a. a dog and a cat
    b. a marigold and a geranium
    c. a human mother and her child
    d. a spider and a cockroach

12. Which of these phrases does *not* describe part of the process of evolution by natural selection?
    a. the environment contains limited resources
    b. organisms produce more offspring than will survive to reproduce
    c. communities include populations of several species
    d. organisms in a population differ in their traits

13. Which of the following components of an ecosystem are *not* abiotic factors?
    a. wind
    b. small rocks
    c. sunlight
    d. tree branches

14. Some snakes produce a powerful poison that paralyzes their prey. This poison is an example of
    a. resistance.
    b. an adaptation.
    c. a reptile.
    d. an abiotic factor.

15. Angiosperms called roses come in a variety of shapes and colors as a result of
    a. natural selection.
    b. coevolution.
    c. different ecosystems.
    d. artificial selection.

16. Unicellular organisms that live in swamps and produce methane gas are
    a. protists.
    b. archaea.
    c. fungi.
    d. bacteria.

17. Which of the following statements about protists is *not* true?
    a. Most of them live in water.
    b. Some of them cause diseases in humans.
    c. They contain genetic material.
    d. Their cells have no nucleus.

18. Which of the following statements about plants is *not* true?
    a. They make their food from oxygen and water through photosynthesis.
    b. Land plants have cell walls that help hold their stems upright.
    c. They have adaptations that help prevent water loss.
    d. Plants absorb nutrients through their roots.

Short Answer

19. List five components that an ecosystem must contain to survive.

20. What is the difference between biotic and abiotic factors in an ecosystem?

21. What is the difference between adaptation and evolution?

22. Describe the three steps by which a population of insects becomes resistant to a pesticide.

23. List the four kingdoms of organisms in the Domain Eukarya and the characteristics of each kingdom.

Interpreting Graphics

Below is a graph that shows the number of aphids on a rose bush during one summer. The roses were sprayed with a pesticide three times, as shown. Use the graph to answer questions 24 and 25.

24. What evidence is there that the pesticide killed aphids?

25. Aphids have a generation time of about 10 days. Is there any evidence that the aphids evolved resistance to the pesticide during the summer? Explain your answer.

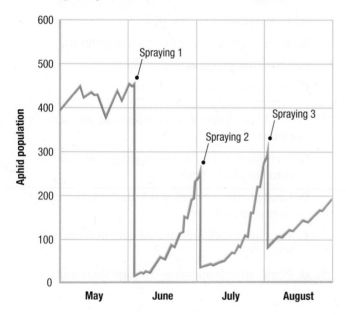

Critical Thinking

26. Analyzing Ideas Can a person evolve? Read the description of evolution in this chapter and explain why or why not.

27. Making Inferences A scientist applies a strong fungicide, a chemical that kills fungi, to an area of forest soil every week during October and November. How might this area look different from the surrounding ground at the end of the experiment?

28. Drawing Conclusions In what building in your community do you think bacteria are evolving resistance to antibiotics most rapidly? Explain your answer.

29. Evaluating Viewpoints Many people assume that the human population is no longer evolving. Do you think these people are right? Explain your answer.

30. Analyzing Information Find out how the isolation of populations on islands has affected their evolution. Research a well-known example, such as the animals and plants of Madagascar, the Galápagos Islands, or the Hawaiian Islands. Write a short report on your findings.

31. Observe Observe an ecosystem near you, such as a pond or a field. Identify biotic and abiotic factors and as many populations of organisms as you can. Do not try to identify the organisms precisely. Just list them, for example, as spiders, ants, grass, not as a specific type. Make a poster showing the different populations. Put the organisms into columns to show which of the kingdoms they belong to.

Analyzing Data

Use the graph below to answer questions 32–33.

32. Analyzing Data The graph below shows the mass of different types of organisms found in a meadow. How much greater is the mass of the plants than that of the animals?

33. Analyzing Data What is the ratio of the mass of the bacteria to the mass of the fungi?

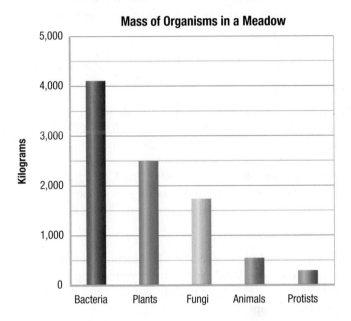

Mass of Organisms in a Meadow

Making Connections

34. Communicating Main Ideas Why is evolution considered to be such an important idea in biology?

35. Outlining Topics Outline the essential steps in the evolution of pesticide resistance in insects.

©Photodisc/Getty Images

36. How does environmental change affect the survival of a species?

37. What is the relationship between natural selection and adaptation?

Why It Matters

38. What might happen to a population of fish if a predator moved to the coral reef?

STUDYSKILL

Make an Outline After reading each section, summarize the main ideas into a short outline, leaving space between each entry. Then write the key terms under the subsection in which they are introduced, followed by a short definition for each.

S.T.E.M.

How Do Brine Shrimp Select a Habitat?

Objectives

Observe the behavior of brine shrimp.

Identify a variable, and design an experiment to test the effect of the variable on habitat selection by brine shrimp.

Materials

aluminum foil

brine shrimp culture

corks sized to fit tubing

Detain™ or methyl cellulose

fluorescent lamp or grow light

funnel

graduated cylinder or beaker

hot-water bag

ice bag

magnifying glass or dissecting microscope

metric ruler

Petri dish

pipet

plastic tubing, 40 cm × 1 cm, clear, flexible

screen, pieces

screw clamps

tape

test-tube rack

test tubes with stoppers

Different organisms are adapted for life in different habitats. For example, brine shrimp are small crustaceans that live in saltwater lakes. Organisms select habitats that provide the conditions, such as a specific temperature range and amount of light, to which they are best adapted. In this investigation, you will construct a chamber to explore habitat selection by brine shrimp and determine which environmental conditions they prefer.

Procedure

Establish a Control Group

1. To make a test chamber and establish a control group, divide a piece of plastic tubing into four sections by making a mark at 10 cm, 20 cm, and 30 cm from one end. Label the sections "1," "2," "3," and "4."

2. Place a cork in one end of the tubing. Then transfer 50 mL of brine shrimp culture to the tubing. Place a cork in the other end of the tubing. Set the tube aside, and let the brine shrimp move about the tube for 30 min.

3. After 30 min, divide the tubing into four sections by placing a screw clamp at each mark on the tubing. While someone in your group holds the corks firmly in place, tighten the middle clamp at 20 cm and then tighten the other two clamps.

4. Remove the cork from the end of section 1 and pour the contents of section 1 into a test tube labeled "1." Repeat this step for the other sections by loosening the screw clamps and pouring the contents of each section into their corresponding test tubes.

5. To get an accurate count for the number of brine shrimp in each test tube, place a stopper on test tube 1, and invert the tube gently to distribute the shrimp. Use a pipet to transfer a 1 mL sample of the culture to a Petri dish. Add a few drops of Detain™ to the sample so that the brine shrimp move slower. Count and record the number of brine shrimp in the Petri dish. Place the Petri dish under a dissecting microscope or use a magnifying glass for better observation.

Making a Test Chamber Use a screw clamp to divide one section of tubing from another.

6. Empty the Petri dish, and take two more 1 mL samples of brine shrimp from test tube 1. Calculate the average of the three samples recorded for test tube 1.

7. Repeat steps 5 and 6 for each of the remaining test tubes to count the number of brine shrimp in each section of tubing.

Ask a Question

8. Write a question you would like to explore about brine shrimp habitat selection. For example, you can explore how temperature or light affects brine shrimp. To explore the question, design an experiment that uses the materials listed for this lab.

9. Write a procedure and a list of safety precautions for your group's experiment. Have your teacher approve your procedure and pre-cautions before you begin the experiment.

10. Set up and conduct your group's experiment.

Analysis

1. **Constructing Graphs** Make a bar graph of your data. Plot the environmental variable on the x-axis and the number of brine shrimp on the y-axis.

2. **Evaluating Results** How did the brine shrimp react to changes in the environment?

3. **Evaluating Methods** Why did you need a control in your experiment?

4. **Evaluating Methods** Why did you record the average of three samples to count the number of brine shrimp in each test tube in steps 6 and 7?

Conclusions

5. **Drawing Conclusions** What can you conclude from your results about the types of habitat that brine shrimp prefer?

Extension

6. **Formulating Hypotheses** Now that you have observed brine shrimp, write a hypothesis about how brine shrimp select a habitat that could be explored with another experiment, other than the one you performed in this lab. Formulate a prediction based on your hypothesis.

Brine Shrimp These crustaceans have specific habitat preferences.

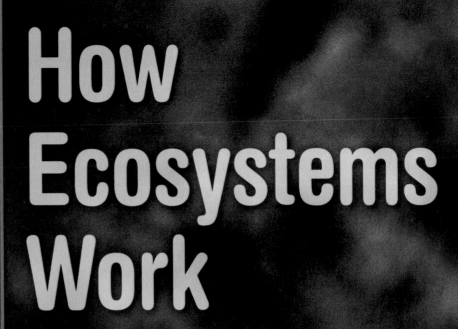

Chapter 5

Why It Matters

This frog gets the energy it needs to survive by eating other organisms, such as damselflies. Frogs and damselflies are both consumers in an aquatic food chain.

How does energy continue to be transferred in this food chain?

CASE STUDY

Learn how pollutants, like the pesticide DDT, are transferred through a food chain in the case study DDT in an Aquatic Food Chain on page 120.

How Ecosystems Work

ONLINE
ENVIRONMENTAL SCIENCE
HMDScience.com

Go online to access additional resources, including labs, worksheets, multimedia, and resources in Spanish.

©A. Cosmos Blank/Photo Researchers, Inc.

Energy Flow in Ecosystems

Organisms need energy to survive, grow, and reproduce. Different organisms get energy from different sources, but the ultimate source of energy for almost all organisms on Earth is the sun.

Life Depends on the Sun

Energy from the sun enters an ecosystem when organisms use sunlight to make sugar in a process called **photosynthesis**. During photosynthesis, plants, algae, and some bacteria capture light energy from the sun and use it to convert carbon dioxide and water into sugar and oxygen, as shown in **Figure 1.1**. The result of photosynthesis is the production of sugar molecules known as *carbohydrates*. Carbohydrates are energy-rich molecules that organisms use to move, grow, and reproduce. As organisms consume other plants or animals, energy is transfered from one organism to another.

Plants, such as sunflowers, produce carbohydrates in their leaves. When an animal eats a plant, or the fruit or seeds of a plant, some energy is transferred from the plant to the animal. When animals are consumed by other organisms, energy is again transferred.

SECTION 1

Objectives

▶ Describe how energy is transferred from the sun to producers and then to consumers.

▶ Describe one way in which consumers depend on producers.

▶ Identify two types of consumers.

▶ Explain how energy transfer in a food web is more complex than energy transfer in a food chain.

▶ Explain why an energy pyramid is a representation of trophic levels.

Key Terms

photosynthesis
producer
consumer
decomposer
cellular respiration
food chain
food web
trophic level

FIGURE 1.1

Photosynthesis During photosynthesis, plants use light energy from the sun to make carbohydrates. The chloroplasts in the leaves and stems of these sunflowers contain a green chemical called *chlorophyll*. Chlorophyll absorbs the light energy needed for photosynthesis.

$$6CO_2 + 6H_2O + \text{solar energy} \rightarrow C_6H_{12}O_6 + 6O_2$$

FIGURE 1.2

Transfer of Energy Almost all organisms depend on the sun for energy. Plants like the clover shown above get energy from the sun. Animals such as the rabbit and coyote get their energy by eating other organisms.

From Producers to Consumers

When a rabbit eats a clover plant, the rabbit gets energy from the carbohydrates produced in the plant through photosynthesis. If a coyote eats the rabbit, some of the energy is transferred from the rabbit to the coyote. As shown in **Figure 1.2**, the clover, rabbit, and coyote ultimately get their energy from the sun. The clover is a **producer**, an organism that makes its own food. Producers are also called *autotrophs*, or self-feeders. The rabbit and the coyote are **consumers**, organisms that get their energy by eating other organisms. Consumers are also called *heterotrophs*, or other-feeders. Producers, such as plants, most algae, and some bacteria, absorb light energy directly from the sun. Consumers get energy indirectly from the sun by eating producers or other consumers.

✔ **CHECK FOR UNDERSTANDING**

Relate How do producers and consumers get energy from the sun?

FIGURE 1.3

Deep-Ocean Ecosystem These tube worms depend on bacteria that live inside them to survive. The bacteria (right) use energy from hydrogen sulfide to make their own food.

An Exception: Deep-Ocean Ecosystems

In the depths of the ocean where there is no sunlight, you might not expect to find much life. But scientists have found large communities of worms, clams, crabs, mussels, and barnacles living near thermal vents in the ocean floor. These deep-ocean communities exist in total darkness, where photosynthesis cannot occur. So where do these organisms get their energy? One source of energy comes from organic matter that drifts down from above as organisms die. Another source comes from bacteria, such as those pictured in **Figure 1.3**, that live in some of these organisms. These bacteria use hydrogen sulfide to make their own food. Hydrogen sulfide is present in the hot water that escapes from the thermal vents. These sulfur-metabolizing bacteria produce carbohydrates using energy obtained from the chemical hydrogen sulfide in a process called *chemosynthesis*. The bacteria are eaten by other underwater organisms and thus support a thriving ecosystem.

What Eats What

Organisms can be classified by the source of their energy, as shown in **Figure 1.4**. Consumers that eat only plants are called *herbivores*. Rabbits are herbivores as are cows, sheep, deer, grasshoppers, and many other animals. Consumers, such as lions and hawks, that eat only other animals are called *carnivores*. You already know that humans are consumers, but what kind of consumers are we? Because humans can eat both plants and animals, we are called *omnivores*. Bears, pigs, and cockroaches are other examples of omnivores.

Consumers that get their food by breaking down organic matter from dead organisms are called **decomposers**. Some bacteria and fungi are decomposers. The decomposers allow the nutrients in the rotting material to return to the soil, water, and air.

Connect to MATH

A Meal Fit for a Grizzly Bear

Grizzly bears are omnivores that can eat up to 15 percent of their body weight per day when eating salmon and up to 33 percent of their body weight when eating fruits and other vegetation. How many pounds of salmon can a 200 lb grizzly bear eat in one day? How many pounds of fruits and other vegetation can the same bear eat in one day?

FIGURE 1.4

WHAT EATS WHAT IN AN ECOSYSTEM		
	Energy source	**Examples**
Producer	makes its own food using light energy (photosynthesis) or chemical sources (chemosynthesis)	grasses, ferns, cactuses, flowering plants, trees, algae, and some bacteria
Consumer	gets energy by eating producers or other consumers	mice, starfish, elephants, turtles, humans, and ants

TYPES OF CONSUMERS IN AN ECOSYSTEM		
	Energy source	**Examples**
Herbivore	producers	cows, sheep, deer, and grasshoppers
Carnivore	other consumers	lions, hawks, snakes, spiders, sharks, and whales
Omnivore	both producers and consumers	bears, pigs, gorillas, rats, raccoons, cockroaches, some insects, and humans
Decomposer	breaks down organic matter from dead organisms	fungi and bacteria

Consumers Bears, such as this grizzly bear, are omnivores. Grizzly bears eat other consumers, such as salmon, but they also eat various plants.

Cellular Respiration: Burning the Fuel

So far, you have learned how organisms get energy. But how do they use the energy they get? To understand the process, use yourself as an example. Suppose you have just eaten a large meal. The food you ate contains a lot of energy. Your body gets the energy out of the food by using the oxygen you breathe to break down the food. By breaking down the food, your body obtains the energy stored in the food.

The process of breaking down carbohydrates to yield energy is called **cellular respiration**, which occurs inside the cells of organisms. This process is different from breathing, another form of *respiration*. During cellular respiration, cells absorb oxygen and use it to release energy from food. As you can see in **Figure 1.5,** the chemical equation for cellular respiration is essentially the reverse of the equation for photosynthesis. During cellular respiration, sugar molecules are broken down in the presence of oxygen, yielding energy. Water and carbon dioxide are waste products.

FIGURE 1.5

Cellular Respiration Through cellular respiration, cells use sugar and oxygen to produce carbon dioxide, water, and energy.

$$C_6H_{12}O_6 + 6O_2 \longrightarrow 6CO_2 + 6H_2O + \text{energy}$$

CASESTUDY

DDT in an Aquatic Food Chain

In the 1950s and 1960s, something strange was happening in the estuaries near Long Island Sound, near New York and Connecticut. Birds of prey, such as ospreys and eagles, that fed on fish in the estuaries had high concentrations of the pesticide DDT in their bodies. But when the water in the estuaries was tested, it had low concentrations of DDT.

What accounted for the high levels of DDT in the birds? Poisons that dissolve in fat, such as DDT, can become more concentrated as they move up a food chain in a process called *biological magnification*. When the pesticide enters the water, algae and bacteria take in the poison. When fish eat the algae and bacteria, the poison dissolves into the fat of the fish rather than diffusing back into the water. Most of the poison remains in an animal's body once it is eaten. Each time a bird feeds on a fish, the bird accumulates more DDT in its fatty tissues. In some estuaries on Long Island Sound, DDT concentrations in fatty tissues of organisms were magnified almost 10 million times from the bottom to the top of the food chain.

Large concentrations of DDT may kill an organism, weaken its immune system, cause deformities, or impair its ability to reproduce.

A high concentration of DDT decreases the thickness and the strength of eggshells of many birds of prey.

©Harry Engels/Photo Researchers, Inc.

You use a part of the energy you obtain through cellular respiration to carry out your daily activities. Every time you walk, breathe, sleep, think, or play a sport, you use energy. The energy you obtain is also used to make more body tissues and to fight diseases so that you grow and stay healthy. Excess energy you obtain is stored as fat or sugar. All living things use cellular respiration to get the energy they need from food molecules. Even organisms that make their own food through photosynthesis use cellular respiration to obtain energy from the carbohydrates they produce.

Energy Transfer

Each time one organism eats another organism, a transfer of energy occurs. In order to understand and manage ecosystems, environmental scientists must be able to trace the flow of energy through ecosystems. They also need to know how much energy flows to different parts of the ecosystem. By knowing how energy flows within an ecosystem and how much energy different species use, scientists can find out how organisms depend on one another to survive.

Poisons such as DDT have the greatest effect on organisms at the top of food chains. For example, the osprey shown here would have a greater concentration of DDT in its body than the perch it's about to eat.

©Fritz Polking/Bruce Coleman, Inc./Photoshot

DDT can also weaken the shells of bird eggs. When eggs break too soon, bird embryos die. Therefore, the effects of these chemicals cause a huge drop in the population of carnivorous bird species.

The U.S. government recognized DDT as an environmental contaminant and in 1972 banned its sale except in emergencies. The aquatic food chains immediately started to recover, and the populations of ospreys and eagles started to grow.

Food chains are still not free of DDT. DDT is still legal in some countries where, for example, it is sometimes used in large quantities to eliminate mosquitoes that carry the disease malaria.

Critical Thinking

1. **Analyzing Processes** DDT does not dissolve readily in water. If it did, how would the accumulation of the pesticide in organisms be affected?

2. **Evaluate** Even though DDT is harmful to the environment, why is it still used in some countries?

FIGURE 1.6

Food Chain Energy is transferred from one organism to another in a food chain. Algae are the producers in this ocean food chain.

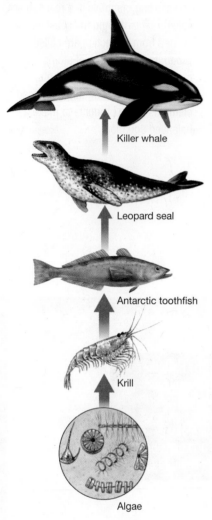

Killer whale

Leopard seal

Antarctic toothfish

Krill

Algae

Food Chains and Food Webs

A **food chain** is the path in which energy is transferred from one organism to the next as each organism eats another organism. **Figure 1.6** shows a typical food chain in an ocean ecosystem. Algae are eaten by krill, which are eaten by fish, such as the Antarctic toothfish. These fish, in turn, are eaten by leopard seals, which are eaten by killer whales.

In natural ecosystems, energy does not flow in simple chains. Most organisms eat more than one kind of food, and many species are eaten by more than one predator. A food web, such as the one shown in **Figure 1.7,** is a better depiction of energy flow in ecosystems. A **food web** includes more organisms and shows the feeding relationships between organisms that are possible in an ecosystem.

Trophic Levels

Each step through which energy is transferred in a food chain is known as a **trophic level.** In **Figure 1.6,** the algae are in the bottom trophic level (trophic level 1), the krill are in the next level (trophic level 2), and so on. Each time energy is transferred from one organism to another, less energy is available to organisms at the next trophic level. Some of the energy is lost as heat. Organisms use much of the remaining energy to carry out life functions, such as cellular respiration and moving.

FIGURE 1.7

Food Web This food web shows how the largest organisms depend on the smallest organisms in an ocean ecosystem.

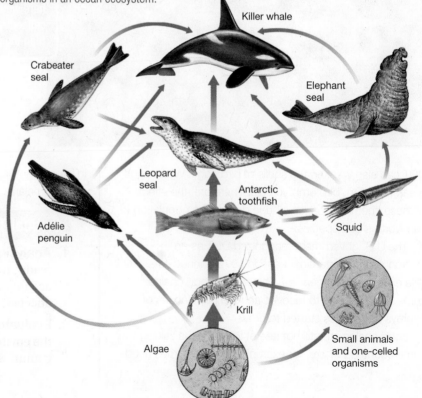

Killer whale

Crabeater seal

Elephant seal

Leopard seal

Antarctic toothfish

Squid

Adélie penguin

Krill

Algae

Small animals and one-celled organisms

Because organisms require energy for all of their life functions, only about 10 percent of the energy from one trophic level is stored in the bodies of organisms at the next level. This 10 percent that is stored is all that is available to the next trophic level when one organism consumes another organism.

Energy Pyramids

One way to visualize the loss of energy from one trophic level to the next is to draw an energy pyramid like the one shown in **Figure 1.8**. Each level in the energy pyramid represents one trophic level. Producers form the base of the pyramid, the lowest trophic level, which contains the most energy. Herbivores make up the second level. Carnivores that feed on herbivores form the next level, and carnivores that feed on other carnivores make up the top level. The higher the trophic level, the less stored energy there is to be passed on.

How Energy Loss Affects an Ecosystem

The decreased amount of energy at each trophic level affects the organization of an ecosystem. First, because so much energy is lost at each level, there are fewer organisms at the higher trophic levels. For example, zebras and other herbivores vastly outnumber lions and other predators on the African savanna. In this example, there simply are not enough herbivores to support more carnivores.

Second, the loss of energy between trophic levels limits the number of trophic levels in an ecosystem. Ecosystems rarely have more than four or five trophic levels because the ecosystem does not have enough energy left to support higher levels. For example, a lion typically needs up to 250 km² of land to hunt for food. Killer whales may have to move across hundreds or thousands of kilometers during their foraging. The organisms that feed on organisms at the top trophic level are usually small, such as parasitic worms and fleas that require a very small amount of energy.

FIGURE 1.8

Energy Pyramid This energy pyramid shows how energy is lost from one trophic level to the next. The grass at the bottom level stores 1,000 times more energy than the hawk at the top level.

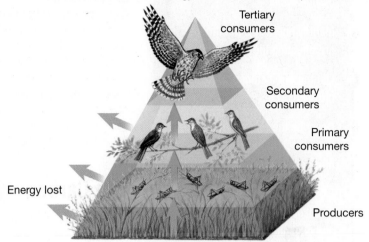

Tertiary consumers

Secondary consumers

Primary consumers

Energy lost

Producers

Virtual INVESTIGATION
HMDScience.com
Ecosystems and Energy Pyramids

Section 1 Formative Assessment

◗ Reviewing Main Ideas

1. **Describe** how energy is transferred from one organism to another.

2. **Describe** the role of producers in an ecosystem.

3. **Explain** the difference between an herbivore and an omnivore.

4. **Compare** energy transfer in a food chain to energy transfer in a food web.

✔ Critical Thinking

5. **Interpreting Graphics** Explain the feeding relationships of the crabeater seal in Figure 1.7.

6. **Inferring Relationships** Could more people be supported by 20 acres of land if they ate only plants instead of both plants and animals? Explain your answer.

- Describe the short-term and long-term process of the carbon cycle.

- Identify one way that humans are affecting the carbon cycle.

- List the three stages of the nitrogen cycle.

- Describe the role that nitrogen-fixing bacteria play in the nitrogen cycle.

- Explain how the excess use of fertilizer can affect the nitrogen and phosphorus cycles.

Key Terms

carbon cycle
nitrogen-fixing bacteria
nitrogen cycle
phosphorus cycle

The Cycling of Matter

Everything is made of matter. *Matter* is anything that has mass and takes up space. Organisms need both energy and matter to live, grow, and reproduce. Energy and matter are constantly moving through ecosystems. The *law of conservation of energy* states that energy cannot be created or destroyed. Energy changes forms. For example, producers change light energy to chemical energy in sugars. The *law of conservation of matter* states that matter cannot be created or destroyed. Instead, matter moves through the environment in different forms. Ecosystems do not have clear boundaries, so some energy and matter can leave them. In this section, you will read about three cycles by which matter and energy are reused—the carbon cycle, the nitrogen cycle, and the phosphorus cycle.

The Carbon Cycle

Carbon is an essential component of proteins, fats, and carbohydrates, which make up all organisms. The **carbon cycle** is a process by which carbon is cycled between the atmosphere, land, water, and organisms. As shown in **Figure 2.1**, carbon enters a short-term cycle in an ecosystem when producers, such as plants, convert carbon dioxide in the atmosphere into carbohydrates during photosynthesis. When consumers eat producers, the consumers obtain carbon from the carbohydrates. As the consumers break down food during cellular respiration, some of the carbon is released back into the atmosphere as carbon dioxide. Producers also release carbon dioxide during cellular respiration.

Some carbon enters a long-term cycle. For example, carbon may be converted into *carbonates*, which make up the hard parts of bones and shells. Bones and shells do not break down easily. So, over millions of years, carbonate deposits have produced huge formations of limestone rocks. Limestone is one of the largest *carbon sinks*, or carbon reservoirs, on Earth.

FIGURE 2.1

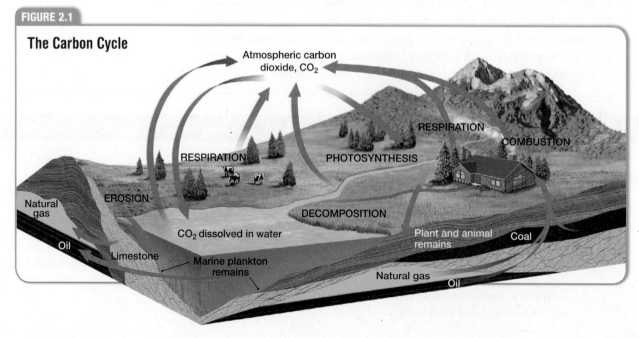

The Carbon Cycle

Some carbohydrates in organisms are converted into fats, oils, and other molecules that store energy. The carbon in these molecules may be released into the soil or air after an organism dies. These molecules can form deposits of coal, oil, and natural gas underground. The deposits are known as *fossil fuels*. Fossil fuels are made up of carbon compounds from the bodies of organisms that died millions of years ago.

How Humans Affect the Carbon Cycle

When we burn fossil fuels, carbon is released into the atmosphere as carbon dioxide. Cars, factories, and power plants rely on fossil fuels to operate. In the year 2009, vehicles, such as the truck in **Figure 2.2**, were the source of just over one-third of all carbon dioxide emitted in the United States. Each year, about 8.4 billion metric tons of carbon dioxide are released into the atmosphere by the burning, or combustion, of fossil fuels and the natural burning of wood in forest fires. About half of this carbon dioxide remains in the atmosphere. As a result, the amount of carbon dioxide in the atmosphere has steadily increased.

Increased levels of carbon dioxide in the atmosphere are the major contributor to climate change. Carbon dioxide is a greenhouse gas. *Greenhouse gases*, including water vapor and other gases, absorb and re-radiate infrared energy, warming Earth. Plants absorb some of the carbon dioxide, but scientists estimate that, each year, over a billion metric tons of carbon dioxide dissolves into the ocean, a carbon sink. The increase in carbon dioxide can lower the pH, which can impact marine organisms.

FIGURE 2.2

Carbon Emissions This truck releases carbon into the atmosphere when it burns fuel to operate.

✓ **CRITICAL THINKING**

Relate Explain how the carbon emission from this truck enters and exits producers, such as the trees shown in this photo.

QUICKLAB

Make Every Breath Count
Procedure

1. Pour 100 mL of water from a graduated cylinder into a 250 mL beaker. Add several drops of bromthymol blue to the beaker of water. Make sure you add enough to make the solution a dark blue color.
2. Exhale through a straw into the solution until the solution turns yellow. (CAUTION: Be sure not to inhale or ingest the solution.)
3. Pour the yellow solution into a large test tube that contains a sprig of Elodea.
4. Stopper the test tube, and place it in a sunny location.
5. Observe the solution in the test tube after 15 minutes.

Analysis

1. What do you think happened to the carbon dioxide that you exhaled into the solution?
2. What effect do plants, such as the *Elodea*, have on the carbon cycle?

FIGURE 2.3

The Nitrogen Cycle

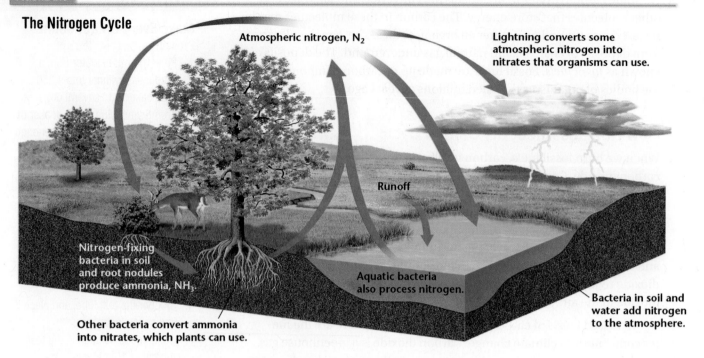

Atmospheric nitrogen, N_2

Lightning converts some atmospheric nitrogen into nitrates that organisms can use.

Runoff

Nitrogen-fixing bacteria in soil and root nodules produce ammonia, NH_3.

Aquatic bacteria also process nitrogen.

Bacteria in soil and water add nitrogen to the atmosphere.

Other bacteria convert ammonia into nitrates, which plants can use.

FIGURE 2.4

Nitrogen-Fixing Bacteria The swellings on the roots of this soybean plant are called *nodules*. Nitrogen-fixing bacteria, shown magnified at the top right, live inside the nodules of some plants.

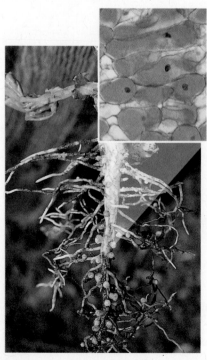

The Nitrogen Cycle

All organisms need nitrogen to build *proteins*, which are used to build new cells. Nitrogen makes up 78 percent of the gases in the atmosphere. However, most organisms cannot use atmospheric nitrogen. It must be altered, or fixed, before organisms can use it. Only a few species of bacteria, called **nitrogen-fixing bacteria,** can fix atmospheric nitrogen into a useful form called ammonia. All other organisms depend upon these bacteria to supply nitrogen. As shown in **Figure 2.3**, nitrogen-fixing bacteria are a crucial part of the **nitrogen cycle,** a process in which nitrogen is cycled between the atmosphere, soil, and organisms. Some nitrogen enters the soil through fixation by lightning. Energy in lightning breaks apart nitrogen molecules in the air, which recombine with oxygen molecules to form nitrogen oxide. Rainwater combines with nitrogen oxide to form nitrates that enter the soil.

Nitrogen-fixing bacteria, shown in **Figure 2.4**, live in nodules on the roots of plants called *legumes*. Legumes include beans, peas, and clover. The bacteria use sugars provided by the legumes to produce nitrogen-containing compounds such as nitrates. The excess nitrogen fixed by the bacteria is released into the soil. Some nitrogen-fixing bacteria live in the soil. Plants that do not have nitrogen-fixing bacteria in their roots get nitrogen from the soil. Animals get nitrogen by eating plants or other animals, both of which are sources of usable nitrogen.

Decomposers and the Nitrogen Cycle

In the nitrogen cycle, nitrogen moves between the atmosphere and living things. Some of the nitrogen that cycles from the atmosphere to living things is released to the soil with the help of bacteria. These decomposers are essential to the nitrogen cycle because they break down

(inset) ©Garry DeLong/Photo Researchers, Inc.; (bl) ©G.R. Roberts Photo Library wastes, such as urine, dung, leaves, and decaying plants and animals and return the nitrogen from these wastes to the soil. If decomposers did not exist, much of the nitrogen in ecosystems would be stored forever in wastes, corpses, and other parts of organisms. After decomposers return the nitrogen to the soil, bacteria transform a small amount of the nitrogen into nitrogen gas, which then returns to the atmosphere. So, most of the nitrogen that enters an ecosystem stays within the ecosystem. It cycles between organisms and the soil, and is constantly reused.

The Phosphorus Cycle

The element phosphorus is part of many molecules that make up the cells of living organisms. For example, phosphorus is needed to form bones and teeth in animals. Plants get the phosphorus they need from soil and water, while animals get their phosphorus by eating plants or other animals that have eaten plants. The **phosphorus cycle** is the movement of phosphorus from the environment to organisms and then back to the environment. This cycle does not include the atmosphere because phosphorus rarely occurs as a gas.

Phosphorus enters soil and water in many ways, as shown in **Figure 2.5.** When rocks erode by weathering, some phosphorus dissolves as phosphate in soil, water, and groundwater. Plants absorb phosphates in the soil through their roots. Phosphorus also leaches into soil and water when phosphate is excreted in waste from organisms and when organisms die and decompose. Some phosphorus also washes off the land and ends up in bodies of water. Many phosphates are not soluble in water, so they sink to the bottom of water bodies, and accumulate as sediment. Over many thousands of years, the sediments become rock.

FIGURE 2.5

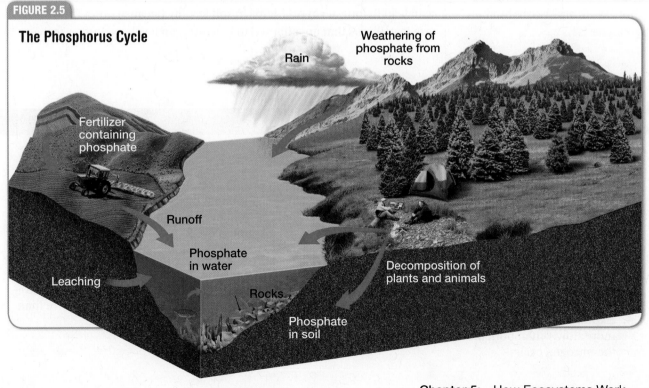

The Phosphorus Cycle

Rain

Weathering of phosphate from rocks

Fertilizer containing phosphate

Runoff

Phosphate in water

Leaching

Rocks

Decomposition of plants and animals

Phosphate in soil

FIGURE 2.6

Fertilizers and Algal Blooms More than 30 percent of fertilizer may flow with runoff from farmland into nearby waterways. Large amounts of fertilizer in water can cause an excessive growth of algae (right).

Fertilizers and the Nitrogen and Phosphorus Cycles

People often apply fertilizers to stimulate and maximize plant growth. Fertilizers contain both nitrogen and phosphorus. If excessive amounts of fertilizer are used, the fertilizer can enter terrestrial and aquatic ecosystems through runoff. Excess nitrogen and phosphorus in an aquatic ecosystem or nearby waterway can cause rapid and overabundant growth of algae, which results in an *algal bloom*. An algal bloom, as shown in **Figure 2.6**, is a dense, visible patch of algae that occurs near the surface of water. Algal blooms, along with other plants and the bacteria that break down dead algae, can deplete an aquatic ecosystem of important nutrients such as oxygen. Fish and other aquatic organisms need oxygen to survive.

Humans add so much nitrogen to the environment, that we have doubled the amount of fixed nitrogen entering ecosystems on land. This can lead to long-term problems in soil fertility because other nutrients are lost. Plants that are adapted to low nitrogen levels no longer thrive.

☑️ **CHECK FOR UNDERSTANDING**

Recognize How do algal blooms harm aquatic ecosystems?

(l) ©Nigel Cattlin/Photo Researchers, Inc.; (r) ©G.R. Roberts Photo Library

---

✓ Section 2 Formative Assessment

▶ Reviewing Main Ideas

1. **Describe** the two processes of the carbon cycle.

2. **Describe** how the burning of fossil fuels affects the carbon cycle.

3. **Explain** how the excessive use of fertilizer affects the nitrogen cycle and the phosphorus cycle.

4. **Explain** why the phosphorus cycle occurs more slowly than both the carbon cycle and the nitrogen cycle.

✓ Critical Thinking

5. **Making Comparisons** Write a short paragraph that describes the importance of bacteria in the carbon, nitrogen, and phosphorus cycles. What role do bacteria play in each cycle?

6. **Applying Ideas** What is one way that a person can help to reduce the level of carbon dioxide in the atmosphere? Can you think of more than one way?

How Ecosystems Change

Ecosystems are constantly changing. A forest hundreds of years old may have been a shallow lake a thousand years ago. A dead tree falls and lets sunlight reach the forest floor. The sunlight allows dormant or new seeds to germinate, and soon wildflowers and shrubs cover the forest floor. Mosses, shrubs, and small trees cover the concrete of a demolished city building. These are all examples of an environmental change called ecological succession.

Ecological Succession

Ecological succession is a gradual process of change and replacement of some or all of the species in a community. Ecological succession may take hundreds or thousands of years. Each new community that arises makes it harder for the previous community to survive. If given enough time, communities may stop changing for long periods of time. Small changes will continue to happen, but eventually a community can become stable. American beech trees, shown in **Figure 3.1,** are a species found in a stable community.

Succession can occur in areas that previously did not support life, such as on rocks or sand dunes. This type of succession is called **primary succession**. A more common type of succession, called **secondary succession,** occurs in areas where an ecosystem has previously existed. For example, ecosystems that have been disturbed or disrupted by humans or animals, or by natural processes such as storms, floods, and earthquakes can regrow through secondary succession.

Key Terms
ecological succession
primary succession
secondary succession
pioneer species
climax community

✔ **CHECK FOR UNDERSTANDING**
Compare How is secondary succession different from primary succession?

FIGURE 3.1

Ecological Succession American beech trees are a stable community species, establishing themselves in a given region.

©Hans Reinhard/Bruce Coleman, Inc./Photoshot

FIGURE 3.2

Pioneer Species Over a long period of time, lichens can break down rock into soil.

Primary Succession

Primary succession can occur on new islands created by volcanic eruptions, in areas exposed when a glacier retreats, or on any other surface that has not previously supported life. Primary succession is much slower than secondary succession because primary succession begins where there is no soil. It can take several hundred to several thousand years to produce fertile soil naturally. Imagine that a glacier melts and exposes an area of bare rock. The first species to colonize the bare rock will most likely be bacteria and lichens, which can live without soil. A species that colonizes an uninhabited area and begins the process of ecological succession is called a **pioneer species.** Lichens, shown in **Figure 3.2**, are important pioneer species in primary succession. They are the colorful, flaky patches that you see on trees and rocks. A lichen is a producer that is actually composed of two different species, a fungus and green algae or cyanobacteria. The algae or the cyanobacteria photosynthesize, while the fungus absorbs nutrients from rocks and holds water. Together, they begin to break down the rock.

CASESTUDY

Communities Maintained by Fire

Fireweed is one type of plant that colonizes land after the land has been burned by fire.

Fires set by lightning or human activities occasionally sweep through large areas. Burned areas undergo secondary succession. In the forests of the Rocky Mountains, for example, burned areas are rapidly colonized by fireweed, which clothes the slopes with purple flowers. In some places, fire determines the nature of the climax community. In the United States, ecological communities that are maintained by fire include the chaparral of California, the temperate grassland of the Midwest, and many southern and western pine forests.

Plants native to these communities are adapted to living with fire. A wildfire that is not unusually hot may not harm fire-adapted pine trees, but it can kill deciduous trees— those trees that lose their leaves in winter. Seeds of some species will not germinate until exposed to temperatures of several hundred degrees. When a fire sweeps through a forest, the fire kills plants on the ground and stimulates the seeds to germinate.

Longleaf pines have a strange growth pattern. When they are young, they have long needles that reach down to the ground. The trees remain only about a half of a meter high for many years, while they store nutrients. If a fire occurs, it sweeps through the tops of the tall trees that survived the last fire. The young longleaf pines near the ground may escape the fire. Then, the young pines use their stored food to grow very rapidly. A young pine can grow as much as 2 m each year. Soon the young pines are tall enough so that a fire near the ground would not harm them.

If regular fires are prevented in a fire-adapted community, deciduous trees may invade the area. These

As the growth of the lichen breaks down the rock, water may freeze and thaw in cracks, which further breaks up the rock. Soil slowly accumulates as dust particles in the air are trapped in cracks in the rock.

Dead remains of lichens and bacteria add to the soil in the cracks. Mosses may increase in number and break up the rock even more. When the mosses die, they decay and add nutrients to the growing pile of soil. Thus, fertile soil forms from the broken rock, decayed organisms, water, and air. Primary succession can also be seen in any city street, as shown in **Figure 3.3**. Mosses, lichens, and weeds can establish themselves in cracks in a sidewalk or building. As well, fungi and mosses can invade a roof that needs repair. Even a big city, such as New York City, would eventually turn into a cement-filled woodland if it were not constantly maintained.

FIGURE 3.3

Primary Succession in Urban Areas Plants that grow through cracks in city sidewalks can also be described as pioneers of primary succession.

These young lodgepole pine trees have started growing after a devastating forest fire.

This firefighter is helping to maintain a controlled fire in South Dakota.

trees form a thick barrier near the ground. In addition, their dead leaves and branches pile up on the ground and form extra fuel for fires. When a fire does occur, it is hotter and more severe than usual. The fire destroys not only the deciduous trees but also the pines. It may end up as a devastating wildfire.

Although it may seem odd, frequent burning is essential to preserve many plant communities and the animals that depend on them. This is the reason the U.S. National Park Service adopted the policy of letting fires in national parks burn if they do not endanger human life or property.

This policy caused a public outcry when fires burned Yellowstone National Park in 1988, because people did not understand the ecology of fire-adapted communities. The fires later became an opportunity for visitors to learn about the changes in an ecosystem after a fire.

Critical Thinking

1. **Understanding Processes** Explain how a longleaf pine tree might be more likely to survive a forest fire than a deciduous tree, such as a maple or oak tree.

2. **Understanding Concepts** Why must controlled fires be set in some ecosystems? What are the advantages? What are the disadvantages?

FIGURE 3.4

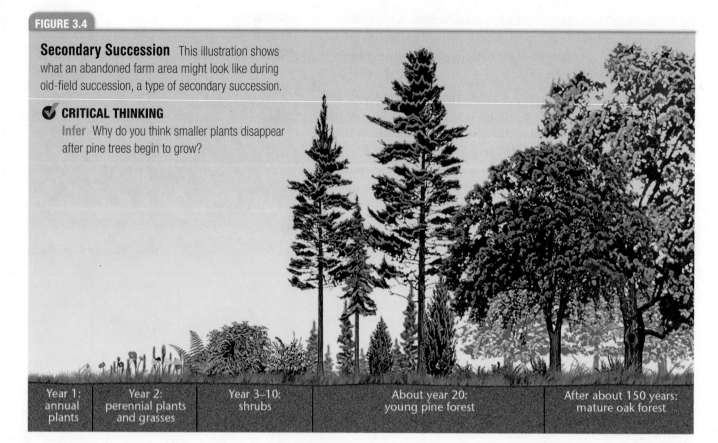

Secondary Succession This illustration shows what an abandoned farm area might look like during old-field succession, a type of secondary succession.

✓ **CRITICAL THINKING**

Infer Why do you think smaller plants disappear after pine trees begin to grow?

| Year 1: annual plants | Year 2: perennial plants and grasses | Year 3–10: shrubs | About year 20: young pine forest | After about 150 years: mature oak forest |

FIELDSTUDY

Go to Appendix B to find the field study **Investigating Succession**.

Secondary Succession

When a community is partially or completely destroyed by a natural or a human-caused disaster, another community eventually takes its place. For example, when fire destroys a forest, new communities begin to grow in place of the old ones. Pioneer species colonize the area first and, over time, more stable species become established. A **climax community** is a final and stable community. Even though a climax community continues to change in small ways, this type of community may remain the same through time if it is not disturbed.

Old-field Succession

When farmland is abandoned, a type of secondary succession called *old-field succession* occurs. When a field is no longer cultivated, pioneer species such as grasses and weeds quickly grow and cover the abandoned land. The grasses and weeds produce many seeds to cover large areas. Over time, taller plants grow in the area and shade the ground, keeping light from the shorter plants. The long roots of the taller plants also absorb most of the water in the soil. The pioneer plants soon die from lack of sunlight and water. As succession continues, growing trees deprive the taller plants of light and water. Finally, slower-growing trees, such as oaks, hickories, beeches, and maples, take over the area and block sunlight to the smaller trees. As shown in **Figure 3.4**, the area can eventually establish a climax community dominated by a mature oak forest. The field in **Figure 3.5** was once used as farm land, but has since been abandoned.

FIGURE 3.5

Old-Field Succession This field was once plowed, but has since been abandoned for one or more growing seasons. It is slowly becoming forested land.

©Stephen Collins/Photo Researchers, Inc.

Fire and Secondary Succession

Fires caused by lightning are a natural cause of secondary succession in some communities, as discussed in the Case Study. Some species of trees, such as the Jack pine, can release their seeds only after they have been exposed to the intense heat of a fire. Minor forest fires remove accumulations of brush and deadwood that would otherwise contribute to major fires that burn out of control. Fire is important in helping forests return nutrients to the soil. Secondary succession uses these nutrients to grow. After a fire, heavy growth of small plants near the ground often occurs and new trees flourish. Some animal species also depend on occasional fires because they feed on the vegetation that sprouts after a fire has cleared the land. Therefore, foresters sometimes allow natural fires to burn unless the fires are a threat to human life or property.

Virtual INVESTIGATION
HMDScience.com

Protecting Natural Resources

✓ **CHECK FOR UNDERSTANDING**
Identify List two ways that fire can be beneficial to a forest community.

Section 3 Formative Assessment

▶ Reviewing Main Ideas

1. **Compare** primary and secondary succession.

2. **Describe** what role a pioneer species plays during the process of ecological succession.

3. **Explain** why putting out forest fires may be damaging in the long run.

4. **Describe** the role lichens play in primary succession. Write a short paragraph to explain your answer.

✓ Critical Thinking

5. **Analyzing Processes** Over a period of 1,000 years, a lake becomes a maple forest. Is this process primary or secondary succession? Explain your answer.

6. **Analyzing Relationships** How are lichens similar to the pioneer species that colonize abandoned farm areas? How are they different?

Tracking Bats and Insects in Texas

These images of bat and insect concentration in Central Texas were created using Doppler radar on the evening of May 19, 2002. Doppler radar can track the movement of objects in the air by bouncing electromagnetic energy off of them.

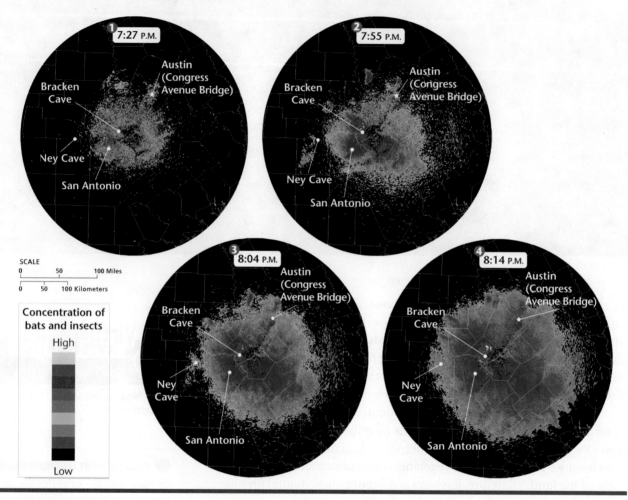

Map Skills

Doppler radar can track the movment of objects in the air by bouncing electromagnetic energy off of them. Use these Doppler radar images from May 19, 2002 of bats and insects in Central Texas to answer the questions below.

1. **Analyzing Data** At what time was the bat and insect concentration the lowest? At what time was the bat and insect concentration the highest?

2. **Interpreting Graphics** Use the concentration key to determine which area of Central Texas has the highest concentration of bats and insects at 8:14 p.m.

3. **Analyzing Data** Approximately how many kilometers wide is the concentration of bats and insects at 7:27 p.m.? at 8:14 p.m.?

4. **Inferring Relationships** Bracken Cave is home to 20 million bats that eat millions of pounds of insects nightly. Approximately how far is Bracken Cave from the city of San Antonio? If the bat population in the cave drastically decreased, what effect would this decrease have on the people living in San Antonio?

5. **Predicting Patterns** These Doppler radar images of bats and insects were taken in the beginning of the summer season. How might these four images look in the month of December?

Society and the Environment

ECOZine at HMDScience.com

Go online for the latest environmental science news and updates on all EcoZine articles.

Changing Seas

Most of the food we eat comes from agriculture and farming, but we also rely on the fishing industry. About 15% of the animal protein consumed in the world comes from fish and other marine and aquatic organisms. But many fish species have been overharvested. The swordfish and cod fisheries of the North Atlantic and the salmon fishery off the northwestern coast of the United States are examples of depleted fisheries. In many parts of the world, sharks are disappearing rapidly because of the demand for shark fin soup. Some fisheries now contain so few fish that harvesting them is not economical. And the size of some of the harvested fish that remain are now smaller because they don't survive long enough to grow.

Fishing Down the Food Chain

Fish such as sharks, tuna, and cod are top carnivores in ocean food chains and food webs. As populations of these fish have declined, species from lower trophic levels that were once swept back into the sea have become more common in fish markets. Organisms from lower trophic levels such as mullet, squid, and herring, which often are used as bait, now appear on restaurant menus. Also, the high prices for large fish have encouraged fisheries to catch these predators. In 2012, one bluefin tuna weighing almost 273 kg sold for over

Despite the challenges of catching large fish, the demand outweighs the cost.

$700,000! At prices that high, it is economical to keep fishing even after populations are scarce.

Scientists are working to determine what species are most at risk of overfishing and what will happen to ecosystems if overfishing continues. If the food webs of ocean ecosystems are altered too much, the commercial fishing industry will be in trouble so it makes economic sense for fishers to protect the oceans.

Creating Sustainable Fisheries

One aim of environmental science is to determine how fisheries can be managed so that they are sustainable or capable of supplying the same number of fish to be harvested each year. One solution is to establish "no-take" zones. These are areas of the sea where no fishing is permitted. Fish populations grow rapidly in these zones. When a population grows in a "no-take zone," some organisms leave the zone and become available to fishers. "No-take" zones help populations recover and allow food chains and food webs to remain intact.

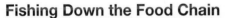

Overfishing from higher trophic levels means commercial fishers must harvest from lower trophic levels to meet demand .

What Do You Think?

The next time you go to a fish market or seafood restaurant, take note of the different types of species for sale. Write down the names of the species, and try to assign each species to a trophic level. How many of the species for sale belong to lower trophic levels? How many belong to higher trophic levels? How do prices differ between the species for sale?

SECTION 1 **Energy Flow in Ecosystems**

OBJECTIVES

- Most organisms depend on the sun for energy. Producers harness the sun's energy directly through photosynthesis, while consumers use the sun's energy indirectly by eating producers or other consumers.
- The paths of energy transfer can be followed through food chains, food webs, and trophic levels.
- Only about 10 percent of the energy that an organism contains is transferred to the next trophic level when the organism is eaten.

KEY TERMS

photosynthesis
producer
consumer
decomposer
cellular respiration
food chain
food web
trophic level

SECTION 2 **The Cycling of Matter**

OBJECTIVES

- Materials in ecosystems are recycled and reused by natural processes.
- Carbon, nitrogen, and phosphorus are essential for life. Each of these elements follows a cycle.
- Humans can affect the cycling of materials in an ecosystem through activities such as burning fossil fuels and applying fertilizer to soil.

KEY TERMS

carbon cycle
nitrogen-fixing
  bacteria
nitrogen cycle
phosphorus cycle

SECTION 3 **How Ecosystems Change**

OBJECTIVES

- After a disturbance, organisms in an environment follow a pattern of change over time, known as ecological succession.
- Primary succession occurs on a surface where no ecosystem existed before. Secondary succession occurs on a surface where an ecosystem existed before.
- Climax communities are made up of organisms that take over an ecosystem and remain until the ecosystem is disturbed again.

KEY TERMS

ecological
  succession
primary
  succession
secondary
  succession
pioneer species
climax
  community

Reviewing Key Terms

Use each of the following terms in a separate sentence.

1. *photosynthesis*
2. *trophic level*
3. *carbon cycle*
4. *nitrogen-fixing bacteria*
5. *decomposers*

For each pair of terms, explain how the meanings of the terms differ.

6. *producer* and *consumer*
7. *primary succession* and *secondary succession*
8. *nitrogen cycle* and *phosphorus cycle*
9. *food chain* and *food web*
10. **Concept Map** Use the following terms to create a concept map: *algae, humans, solar energy, carnivores, consumers, producers, directly, herbivores, indirectly,* and *omnivores.*

Reviewing Main Ideas

11. Which of the following statements is *not* true of consumers?
    a. They get energy indirectly from the sun.
    b. They are also called *heterotrophs.*
    c. They make their own food.
    d. They sometimes eat other consumers.

12. Which of the following is correctly arranged from the lowest trophic level to the highest trophic level?
    a. bacteria, frog, eagle, raccoon
    b. algae, deer, wolf, hawk
    c. grass, mouse, snake, eagle
    d. grass, bass, minnow, snake

13. Communities of bacteria have been found living thousands of feet underwater. Which of the following statements is a proper conclusion to draw about these bacteria?
    a. Somehow they are conducting photosynthesis.
    b. They are living on borrowed time.
    c. They were somehow introduced by human activities.
    d. They use an energy source other than sunlight.

14. Which of the following pairs of organisms probably belong to the same trophic level?
    a. humans and bears
    b. bears and deer
    c. humans and cows
    d. both (a) and (c)

15. The energy lost between trophic levels
    a. can be captured only by parasitic organisms.
    b. cools the surrounding environment.
    c. is used in the course of normal living.
    d. evaporates in the atmosphere.

16. From producer to secondary consumer, about what percentage of energy is lost?
    a. 10 percent
    b. 90 percent
    c. 99 percent
    d. 100 percent

17. Which of the following statements about the nitrogen cycle is *not* true?
    a. Animals get nitrogen by eating plants or other animals.
    b. Plants generate nitrogen in their roots.
    c. Nitrogen moves back and forth between the atmosphere and living things.
    d. Decomposers break down waste to yield ammonia.

18. Which of the following are most likely to be the pioneer organisms on an area of bare rock?
    a. trees
    b. shrubs
    c. lichens
    d. perennial grasses

19. Excessive use of fertilizer that contains nitrogen and phosphorus
    a. affects the carbon cycle.
    b. may cause algal blooms in waterways.
    c. causes soil erosion.
    d. contributes to primary succession.

Short Answer

20. Explain the relationship between cellular respiration and photosynthesis.

21. Why is the number of trophic levels that can exist limited?

22. Why are decomposers an essential part of an ecosystem?

23. Write a short paragraph that explains why the phosphorus cycle occurs slower than the carbon and nitrogen cycles.

24. Describe what happens to carbon dioxide in the carbon cycle.

Interpreting Graphics

Use the diagram to answer questions 25–27.

25. How many organisms depend on the squid as a source of food?

26. If the population of Adélie penguins decreased drastically, what effect would this have on elephant seals?

27. What role do algae play in this food web?

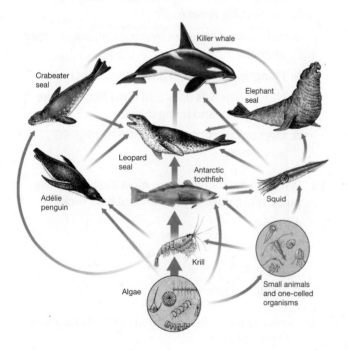

Critical Thinking

28. **Comparing Functions** How are producers and decomposers opposites of each other?

29. **Inferring Relationships** Abandoned fields in the southwestern part of the United States are often taken over by mesquite trees, which can grow in nutrient-poor soil. If the land is later cleared of mesquite, the soil is often found to be enriched with nitrogen and is more suitable for crops. What might be the reason for this phenomenon?

30. **Understanding Concepts** Read the description under the head "What Eats What" in this chapter, and explain why decomposers are considered to be consumers.

31. **Drawing Conclusions** Suppose that a plague eliminates all the primary consumers in an ecosystem. What will most likely happen to organisms in other trophic levels in this ecosystem?

32. **Interpreting Data** If a lake contains 600,000 kg of plankton and the top consumers are a population of 40 pike, which each weigh an average of 15 kg, how many trophic levels does the lake contain? Make a graph or pyramid that illustrates the trophic levels.

33. **Compare and Contrast** Do a special project on succession. Find areas in your community that have been cleared of vegetation and left unattended at different times in the past. Ideally, you should find several areas that were cleared at different times, including recently and decades ago. Photograph each area, and arrange the pictures to show how succession takes place in your geographic region.

Analyzing Data

Use the data in the table below to answer questions 34–35.

PERCENTAGE OF FERTILIZER USE PER YEAR	
Region of the World	**Percentage**
North America	17
Asia	48
Africa	2
Europe	14
Latin America and the Caribbean	18
Oceania	1

34. Making Calculations If 137.25 million metric tons of fertilizer is used worldwide per year, how many million metric tons does Asia use?

35. Graphing Data Make a bar graph that compares the percentage of fertilizer use in different regions worldwide per year.

Making Connections

36. Communicating Main Ideas Describe the importance of the carbon, nitrogen, and phosphorus cycles to humans.

37. Writing from Research Research information on how countries regulate carbon dioxide emissions. Write an essay that describes the laws regulating carbon dioxide emissions and the solutions some countries have devised to decrease the amount of carbon dioxide emitted.

CASESTUDY

38. Compare energy transfer in a food chain and a food web with the transfer of pollutants in a food chain and a food web.

39. How can a change in an ecosystem impact the biogeochemical cycles, for example the carbon cycle?

Why It Matters

40. How does a change in a food web relate to energy flow within an ecosystem?

STUDYSKILL

Taking Multiple-Choice Tests When you take multiple-choice tests, be sure to read all of the choices before you pick the correct answer. Be patient, and eliminate choices that are obviously incorrect.

Factors that Influence Ecosystems

Objectives

Hypothesize how precipitation and altitude affect the types of vegetation in an ecosystem.

Graph and **analyze** ecosystem data to confirm or refute your hypothesis.

Materials

colored pencils

metric ruler

Ecosystems are communities of plants, animals, and other organisms that live and interact with each other and with nonliving environmental factors. The nonliving factors, or conditions, include temperature, precipitation, altitude, and latitude, among others. These factors play an important role in determining what types of vegetation can live in an ecosystem.

Latitude, for example, has a strong influence on an area's temperature, resulting in climates such as polar, tropical, and temperate. These climates determine different natural biomes that have characteristic species of plants. However, a careful look at a map reveals that ecosystems existing at the same latitude often have different climates. Why? In this laboratory activity, you will hypothesize how other nonliving factors influence the characteristics of ecosystems within the same latitude range. Then you will analyze and graph data from different areas of the United States to test your hypotheses.

Procedure

1. Form two hypotheses—one that relates differences in ecosystem vegetation to rainfall and another that relates differences in ecosystem vegetation to altitude. Complete the following sentences to form your two hypotheses.

  a. Ecosystem distribution is related to precipitation; regions that receive large amounts of precipitation are wet and therefore _____.

  b. Ecosystem distribution is related to altitude; regions at high elevations are cold and therefore _____.

2. Look at the data table. The table lists major U.S. cities and weather stations between 36° and 41° north latitude. It also lists the altitude, average annual precipitation, and ecosystem for each location. Construct a graph with two y-axes to plot the data in the table. Plot altitude on the left-hand y-axis and annual rainfall on the right-hand y-axis. Plot distance on the x-axis. Use one of your colored pencils to connect the data points for altitude. Use another color to connect the data points for annual rainfall. You may also find it useful to label the location names on the grid above your data points. Your completed line graph will help you interpret any relation among rainfall, altitude, and biome type.

CHARACTERISTICS OF LOCATIONS ACROSS THE U.S.

Location	Distance from San Francisco (miles)	Altitude above sea level (feet)	Average rainfall (in/yr)	Biome or ecosystem
San Francisco, CA	0	250	23	redwood forest
Sacramento, CA	100	26	19	grassland
Donner Pass, CA	200	7,000	69	coniferous forest
Reno, NV	250	4,400	8	cool desert
Salt Lake City, UT	650	4,200	16	cool desert
Loveland Pass, CO	900	11,000	38	coniferous forest
Denver, CO	950	5,325	12	short grass prairie
Topeka, KS	1,450	925	34	tall grass prairie
St. Louis, MO	1,750	567	37	broadleaf forest
Cincinnati, OH	2,100	488	40	broadleaf forest
Washington, D.C.	2,500	9	39	broadleaf forest

Analysis

1. **Identifying Patterns** Which types of ecosystems occur in areas of high and low precipitation?

2. **Examining Data** Is there a trend in the amount of precipitation from Denver to San Francisco or from Denver to Washington, D.C.?

3. **Analyzing Results** How do mountain ranges affect precipitation? Give an example that supports your answer.

Conclusions

4. **Evaluating Data** Which is the more important factor in determining an area's ecosystem, the amount of precipitation or altitude? Is there an interaction between these two factors?

5. **Defending Conclusions** Does the data support or refute your hypotheses about the effects of precipitation and altitude on an ecosystems type?

Chapter 6

Biomes

Why It Matters

The sloth is just one of the many organisms found in the tropical rain forest, which contains more plant and animal species than any other biome.

Why might it be important to study such a diverse biome?

CASESTUDY

Learn about the connection between deforestation and floods in the case study Deforestation, Climate, and Floods on pages 150–151.

ONLINE
ENVIRONMENTAL SCIENCE
HMDScience.com

Go online to access additional resources, including labs, worksheets, multimedia, and resources in Spanish.

©Photo Researchers, Inc.

What Is a Biome?

Earth is covered by many types of ecosystems. Ecologists group these ecosystems into larger areas known as biomes. A **biome** is a large region characterized by a specific type of climate and certain types of plants and animal communities. The map in **Figure 1.1** shows the locations of the world's major land, or terrestrial, biomes. In this chapter, you will take a tour through these terrestrial biomes—from lush rain forests to water-starved deserts and the frozen tundra. When you read about each biome, notice the adaptations the species that live there have to survive in each biome's very different environments.

Biomes and Vegetation

Biomes are described by their vegetation because the plants that grow in a certain region are the most noticeable characteristics of that region. The plants, in turn, determine the other organisms that can live there. For example, mahogany trees grow in tropical rain forests because they cannot survive cold, dry weather. Organisms that depend on mahogany trees live where these trees grow.

Plants in a particular biome have adaptations that let them survive there. These adaptations include size, shape, and how they manage water. For example, plants that grow in the tundra tend to be short because they cannot obtain enough water to grow larger. They also have a short summer growing season. Desert plants, such as cactuses, have modified leaves. These specialized structures enable cactuses to conserve and retain water.

SECTION 1

Objectives

- Describe why vegetation is used to describe a biome.

- Explain how temperature and precipitation determine which plants grow in an area.

- Explain how latitude and altitude affect which plants grow in an area.

Key Terms

biome
climate
latitude
altitude

✔ **CHECK FOR UNDERSTANDING**

Explain How are ecosystems related to biomes?

FIGURE 1.1

Biome Map The ecosystems of the world can be grouped into regions called biomes. These biomes, shown below, are named for the vegetation that grows there.

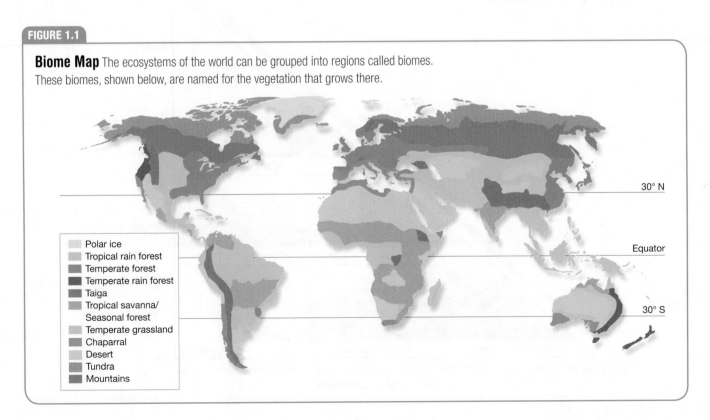

- Polar ice
- Tropical rain forest
- Temperate forest
- Temperate rain forest
- Taiga
- Tropical savanna/ Seasonal forest
- Temperate grassland
- Chaparral
- Desert
- Tundra
- Mountains

30° N

Equator

30° S

FIGURE 1.2

Growing Season Soil in the tundra is frozen most of the year. Small plants such as these have about two months in summer to grow and reproduce before temperatures become too cold again.

Biomes and Climate

Biomes are defined by their plant life, but what factors determine which plants can grow in a certain area? The main factor is climate. **Climate** refers to the weather conditions, such as temperature, precipitation, humidity, and winds, that occur in an area over a long period of time. Temperature and precipitation are the two most important factors that determine a region's climate.

Temperature and Precipitation

Most organisms are adapted to live within a certain range of temperatures and will not survive at temperatures too far outside of that range. The length of the growing season, or the period when temperatures are high enough for plants to grow, also affects plants, as shown in **Figure 1.2**.

Precipitation is another factor that limits the organisms that are found in a biome. All organisms need water. The larger an organism is, the more water it needs. For example, biomes that do not receive enough rainfall to support large trees support communities dominated by small trees, shrubs, and grasses. In biomes where rainfall is not frequent, the vegetation is mostly made up of cactuses and desert shrubs. In extreme cases, lack of rainfall results in no plants, no matter what the temperature is. As shown in **Figure 1.3**, the higher the temperature and precipitation are, the taller and denser the vegetation is. Notice how much more vegetation exists in a hot, wet tropical rain forest than in a dry desert.

FIGURE 1.3

Temperature and Precipitation As temperature and precipitation decrease, the climate of an area becomes drier and vegetation becomes sparser.

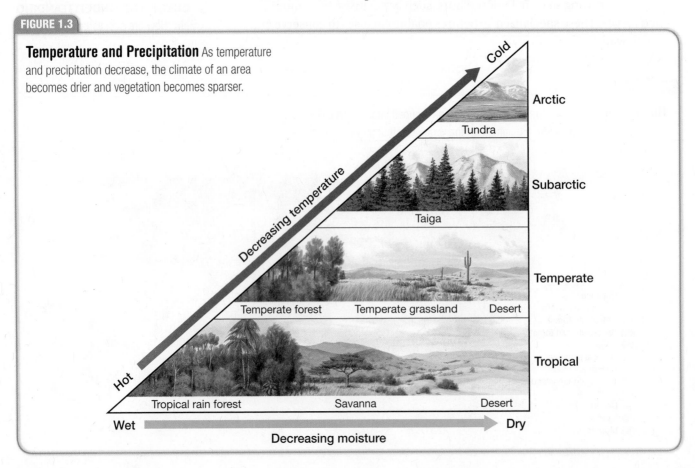

©Chris Fragassi/Alamy Images

FIGURE 1.4

Latitude and Altitude As latitude and altitude increase, biomes and vegetation change.

Mountains
(ice and
snow)

Tundra (herbs,
lichens, and
mosses)

Taiga
(coniferous
forests)

Temperate
deciduous
forests

Tropical
rain forests

Altitude

Tropical
rain forests

Temperate
deciduous forests

Taiga

Tundra

Polar ice

Latitude

Latitude and Altitude

Climate varies with both latitude and altitude, and so do biomes. **Latitude** is the distance north or south of the equator and is measured in degrees, with the equator equal to 0°. **Altitude** is the height of an object above sea level. Climate gets colder as either latitude or altitude increase. This explains why biomes at high altitudes are similar to those at high latitudes.

Figure 1.4 shows that as latitude and altitude increase, biomes and vegetation change. For example, the trees of tropical rain forests usually grow closer to the equator at low altitudes, while the mosses and lichens of the tundra usually grow closer to the poles. The land located in the temperate region, between about 30° and 60° north latitudes and 30° and 60° south latitudes, includes biomes such as temperate forests and grasslands, which usually have the moderate temperatures and fertile soil that are ideal for agriculture.

 ## Section 1 **Formative Assessment**

▶ Reviewing Main Ideas

1. **Describe** how plants determine the description of a biome.

2. **Explain** how temperature affects which plants grow in an area.

3. **Explain** how precipitation affects which plants grow in an area.

4. **Define** *latitude* and *altitude*. How is latitude different from altitude? How do these factors affect the organisms that live in a biome?

✔ Critical Thinking

5. **Making Inferences** The equator passes through the country of Ecuador. But the climate in Ecuador can range from hot and humid to cool and dry. Write a short paragraph that explains what might cause this range in climate.

6. **Analyzing Relationships** Look at **Figure 1.1**, and locate the equator and 30° north latitude. Which biomes are located between these two lines?

▶ List three characteristics of tropical rain forests.

▶ Name and describe the main layers of a tropical rain forest.

▶ Describe one plant in a temperate deciduous forest and an adaptation that helps the plant survive.

▶ Describe one adaptation that may help an animal survive in the taiga.

▶ Name two threats to the world's forest biomes.

Key Terms

tropical rain forest
emergent layer
canopy
epiphyte
understory
temperate rain forest
temperate deciduous forest
taiga

Forest Biomes

The air is hot and heavy with humidity. You walk through the shade of the tropical rain forest, step carefully over tangles of roots and vines, and brush past enormous leaves. Life is all around you, but you see little vegetation on the forest floor. Birds call, and monkeys chatter from far above.

Tropical Rain Forests

Of all the biomes in the world, forest biomes are the most widespread and are home to the greatest diversity of plants, animals, and other organisms. Trees need a lot of water, so forests exist where precipitation is plentiful. Tropical forests, temperate forests, and taiga are the main types of forest biomes.

Tropical rain forests are always humid and warm and get about 200 to 450 cm of rain a year. They help regulate world climate and play vital roles in the nitrogen, oxygen, and carbon cycles. The tropical climate is ideal for a wide variety of plants and animals, as shown in **Figure 2.1**. The warm, wet conditions also nourish more species of plants than does any other biome. While one hectare (10,000 m²) of temperate forest usually contains two dozen species of trees, the same area of tropical rain forest may contain more than 250 species of trees. Tropical rain forests are located in a belt around Earth near the equator, as shown in **Figure 2.2**. Because they are near the equator, tropical rain forests receive strong sunlight and maintain a relatively constant temperature year-round.

FIGURE 2.1

Species Diversity Tropical rain forests contain a larger number of species than any other biome.

Tropical rain forests receive large amounts of precipitation all year long.

Glasswing butterflies live in the rain forests of Costa Rica.

The *Rafflessia keithii* flower grows in the rain forests of Borneo.

FIGURE 2.2

Tropical Rain Forest The world's tropical rain forests have heavy rainfall during much of the year and fairly constant, high temperatures.

Limon, Costa Rica

Tropical rain forest

30°

Equa

30

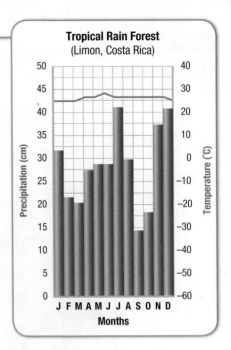

Tropical Rain Forest
(Limon, Costa Rica)

Precipitation (cm)

Temperature (°C)

J F M A M J J A S O N D
Months

Nutrients in Tropical Rain Forests

You might think that the diverse plant life in a tropical rain forest grows on rich soil, but it does not. Most nutrients are found within the tropical plants, and not within the soil. Organic matter decays quickly in hot, wet conditions. Decomposers on the rain-forest floor break down organic matter and return the nutrients to the soil, but plants quickly absorb the nutrients. Some trees in a tropical rain forest support fungi that feed on dead organic matter on the rain-forest floor. In this relationship, the fungi transfer the nutrients from the dead organic matter directly to the tree.

The nutrients are removed so efficiently from the soil in a tropical rain forest that water running out of the soil may be as clear as distilled water. Many of the trees form above-ground roots, or lateral supports called buttresses, that grow sideways from the trees and provide the trees with extra support in the thin soil.

Red-and-green macaws live in the trees of the Amazon rain forest.

Mountain gorillas live in the rain forests of Rwanda.

FIGURE 2.3

Rain Forest Layers The plants in tropical rain forests form distinct layers. The plants in each layer are adapted to a particular level of light. The taller trees absorb the most light, while the plants near the forest floor are adapted to growing in the shade.

Emergent layer
Upper canopy
Lower canopy
Understory

Bright light
Filtered light
Dense shade

Layers of the Rain Forest

In tropical rain forests, different types of plants grow in different layers, as shown in **Figure 2.3**. The four main layers above the forest floor are the emergent layer, the upper canopy, the lower canopy, and the understory. The top layer is the **emergent layer**. It consists of the tallest trees, which reach heights of 60 to 70 m. Trees in the emergent layer grow above the tops of most other trees in the forest.

The next layer, considered the primary layer of the rain forest, is called the **canopy**. Trees in the canopy can grow more than 30 m tall. The tall trees form a dense layer that absorbs up to 95 percent of the sunlight. The canopy can be split into an upper canopy and a lower canopy. The lower canopy receives less light than does the upper canopy. Plants called **epiphytes**, such as the orchid in **Figure 2.4**, use the entire surface of a tree as a place to live. Epiphytes grow on trees instead of on the ground. Some grow high in the canopy, where their leaves can reach the sunlight needed for photosynthesis. Growing on tall trees also allows them to absorb the water and nutrients that run down the tree after it rains. Most animals that live in the rain forest live in the canopy because they depend on the abundant flowers and fruits that grow there.

Below the canopy, very little light reaches the next layer, called the **understory**. Trees, shrubs, and other plants that are adapted to shade grow here. Most plants in the understory do not grow more than 3.5 m tall. Herbs with large, flat leaves grow on the forest floor. These plants capture the small amount of sunlight that penetrates the understory. Most of our house plants are native to tropical rain-forest floors. Because they are adapted to low levels of light, they are able to grow indoors.

Connect to CHEMISTRY

Medicines from Plants

Many of the medicines we use come from plants native to tropical rain forests. Chemists extract and test chemicals found in plants to determine if the chemicals can cure or fight diseases. Rosy periwinkle, a plant that grows in the tropical rain forests of Madagascar, is the source of two medicines, vinblastine and vincristine. Vinblastine is used to treat Hodgkin's disease, a type of cancer, and vincristine is used to treat childhood leukemia.

Species Diversity in Rain Forests

The tropical rain forest is the biome with the largest number of species. The species diversity of rain forest vegetation has led to the evolution of a diverse community of animals. Most rain-forest animals are specialists that use specific resources in particular ways. Some rain forest animals have amazing adaptations for capturing prey, and other animals have adaptations that they use to escape predators. For example, the giant anteater in **Figure 2.4** uses its long tongue to reach insects in small cracks and holes where other animals cannot reach. The great hornbill (shown below) uses its strong, curved beak to crack open nutshells. Insects, such as the Costa Rican hooded praying mantis in **Figure 2.4**, use camouflage to avoid predators. These insects may be shaped like leaves or twigs.

FIGURE 2.4

Adaptations Plant and animal adaptations in the tropical rain forest include ❶ the long tongue of a giant anteater, ❷ the strong, curved beak of a great hornbill, ❸ the shape of a Costa Rican hooded praying mantis, and ❹ an orchid attached to a tall tree.

Threats to Rain Forests

Tropical rain forests once covered about 20 percent of Earth's land area. Today, they cover less than 7 percent. Every 60 seconds, nearly 150 acres of tropical rain forest are cleared for logging operations, agriculture, cattle ranching, or oil exploration. *Habitat destruction* occurs when land inhabited by an organism is destroyed or altered. This destruction is the usual reason for a species becoming extinct. Warming temperatures and changes in precipitation from climate change also threaten rain forests.

An estimated 50 million people live in tropical rain forests. These people are also threatened by habitat destruction. Their food, building materials, culture, and traditions come from and are uniquely connected to the rain forest. Habitat loss also destroys their way of life.

Plants and animals that live in rain forests are also threatened by trading. Many plant species found only in tropical rain forests are valuable and marketable to industries. Animals are threatened by exotic-pet trading. Some exotic-pet traders illegally trap animals, such as parrots, and sell them in pet stores at high prices.

✔️ **CHECK FOR UNDERSTANDING**
Identify What are two main threats to the organisms that live in tropical rain forests?

Deforestation, Climate, and Floods

A plant absorbs water from the soil through its roots and transports the water to its stems and leaves. Water then evaporates from pores in plant leaves into the atmosphere through a process called *transpiration*. A large tree may transpire as much as five tons of water on a hot day. Water absorbs heat when it evaporates. Therefore, the temperature is much cooler under a tree on a hot day than under a wood or brick shelter.

When rain falls on a forest, much of the rain is absorbed by plant roots and transpired into the air as water vapor. Water vapor forms rain clouds. Much of this water will fall as rain downwind from the forest. Because of the role trees play in transpiration, *deforestation*, the clearing of trees, can change the climate. If a forest is cut down or replaced by smaller plants, much of the rainfall is not absorbed by plants. Instead, the rain runs off the soil and causes flooding as well as soil erosion. The climate downwind from the forest becomes drier.

Deforestation led to the disastrous flooding of the Yangtze River in China in 1998. More than 2,000 people died in the floods, and at least 13 million people had to leave their homes. When the Yangtze River

A man makes his way past flooded buildings in his street on a makeshift raft after the Yangtze River reached record-high levels in July 1998.

flooded, the water poured into a flood plain where over 400 million people lived. Serious flooding occurred again in 2010 and 2011. It is estimated that 85 percent of the forest in the Yangtze River basin has been cut down. The millions of tons of water that these trees once absorbed now flow freely down the river and spread across fields and into towns during the seasonal monsoon rains. In response to data from environmental scientists, the Chinese government is now instituting massive reforestation efforts.

Deforestation has also caused major floods in places such as Bangladesh. The Ganges River starts high in the Himalaya Mountains and flows through Bangladesh. Deforestation of the Himalaya Mountains left few trees to stop the water from flowing down the mountain. Therefore, most of the water flows into the river when it rains. Heavy

Temperate Rain Forests

Temperate rain forest occurs in North America, Australia, and New Zealand. Temperate rain forests have large amounts of precipitation, high humidity, and moderate temperatures. The Pacific Northwest houses North America's only temperate rain forest, shown in **Figure 2.5**. There, tree branches are draped with mosses and tree trunks are covered in lichens. The forest floor is blanketed with lush ferns. Evergreen trees that are 90 m tall, such as the Sitka spruce and the Douglas fir, dominate the forest. Other large trees, such as western hemlock, Pacific silver fir, and redwood, can also be found in temperate rain forests.

Even though some temperate rain forests are located at high latitudes, they still maintain moderate temperatures year-round because nearby ocean waters blow cool ocean wind over the forest. As ocean winds meet coastal mountains, a large amount of rainfall is produced. Rainfall and ocean breezes keep temperatures cool in the summer, but warmer than might be expected in the winter. These wet and warm conditions mean that trees have long growing seasons and plenty of water to grow very tall.

FIGURE 2.5

Pacific Northwest The only temperate rain forest in North America is located in the Pacific Northwest, such as the one shown below in Olympic National Park.

Deforestation reduces the amount of water that is absorbed by plants after it rains. The more trees that are cleared from a forest, the more likely a flood will occur in that area.

rains have eroded and carried away so much soil from the slopes of the mountains that the soil has formed a new island in the Bay of Bengal.

People are beginning to understand the connection between deforestation and floods. People held protests in northern Italy in 2000 after floods covered a town that had never been flooded before. The townspeople claimed that authorities had permitted developers to cover the hills with homes. These developers cut down most of the trees and covered much of the land with asphalt. After heavy rains, the water was no longer absorbed by trees and soil, so the water flowed down the hills and flooded the town.

Critical Thinking

1. **Identifying Relationships** How might deforestation in China and other countries affect the overall climate of Earth?

2. **Analyzing a Viewpoint** Imagine that you are a city council member and must vote on whether to clear a forest so that a mall can be built. List the pros and cons of each viewpoint. After reviewing your list, how would you vote? Explain your answer.

FIGURE 2.6

Temperate Deciduous Forest The difference between summer and winter temperatures in temperate deciduous forests is extreme.

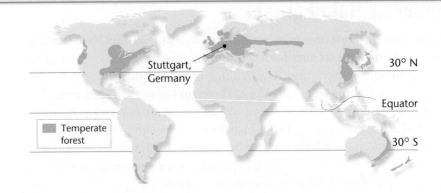

Stuttgart, Germany

30° N

Equator

30° S

Temperate forest

Temperate Deciduous Forests

If you walk through a North American deciduous forest in the fall, you will be awash in color. Leaves in every shade of orange, red, and yellow crackle beneath your feet. Most birds have flown south. The forest is quieter than it was in the summer. You see mostly chipmunks and squirrels gathering and storing the food they will need during the long, cold winter.

In **temperate deciduous forests**, trees drop their broad, flat leaves each fall. These forests once dominated vast regions of Earth, including parts of North America, Europe, and Asia. Today, temperate deciduous forests are generally located between 30° and 50° north latitudes, as shown in **Figure 2.6**. The range of temperatures in a temperate deciduous forest can be extreme, and the growing season lasts for only four to six months. Summer temperatures can soar to 35°C. Winter temperatures often fall below freezing, so little water is available for plants and growing seasons tend to be shorter than in the temperate rain forests. Just as temperatures change with the seasons, so does the vegetation, as shown in **Figure 2.7**. Although there is enough moisture for decomposition, temperatures are low during the winter. As a result, organic matter decomposes fairly slowly. This means that the soil contains more organic matter and nutrients than the soil in a tropical rain forest.

FIGURE 2.7

Distinct Seasons The change of seasons in a temperate deciduous forest is shown here.

Plants of Temperate Deciduous Forests

Like the plants of tropical rain forests, the plants in deciduous forests grow in layers. Tall trees, such as maple, oak, and birch, dominate the forest canopy. Small trees and shrubs cover the understory. Because the floor of a deciduous forest gets more light than does the floor of a rain forest, more plants such as ferns, herbs, and mosses grow in a deciduous forest.

Temperate-forest plants are adapted to survive seasonal changes. In the fall, most deciduous trees begin to drop their leaves. In the winter, soil moisture changes to ice, which causes the remaining leaves to fall to the ground.

©Kathy Collins/Photographer's Choice/Getty Images

Herb seeds, bulbs, and rhizomes (underground stems) become dormant in the ground and are insulated by the soil, leaf litter, and snow. In the spring, when the sunlight increases and the temperature rises, trees grow new leaves, seeds germinate, and rhizomes and roots grow new shoots and stems.

Animals of Temperate Deciduous Forests

The animals of temperate deciduous forests are adapted to use the forest plants for food and shelter. Squirrels eat the nuts, seeds, and fruits in the treetops. Bears feast on insects and the tubers and berries of the forest plants. Grasshoppers eat almost all types of vegetation found throughout the forest. Deer, such as the one shown in **Figure 2.8**, and other herbivores nibble leaves from trees and shrubs.

Many birds nest in the relative safety of the canopy. Most of these birds are migratory. Because many birds cannot survive harsh winters, each fall they fly south to find warmer weather and more food. Each spring, they return north to nest and feed. Animals that do not migrate use various strategies for surviving the winter. For example, some mammals reduce their activity during the cold winter months so that they do not need as much food for energy.

(tr) ©William Leaman/Alamy Images; (inset) ©Don Johnston/All Canada Photos/Corbis

FIGURE 2.8

Deciduous Forest Animals Woodpeckers and deer are among the many animals that live in the temperate deciduous forest.

Taiga

The **taiga** is the northern coniferous forest that stretches in a broad band across the Northern Hemisphere just below the Arctic Circle. As shown in **Figure 2.9**, winters in the taiga are long (6 to 10 months) and have average temperatures that are below freezing and often fall to –20°C. Many trees seem like straight, dead shafts of bark and wood—until you look up and see their green tops. Plant growth is most abundant during the summer months because of nearly constant daylight and larger amounts of precipitation.

FIGURE 2.9

Taiga The taiga has long, cold winters and small amounts of precipitation, as shown in the climatogram at right.

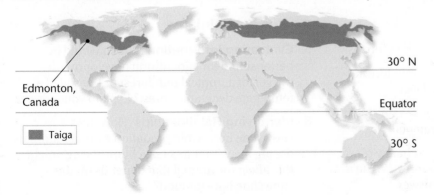

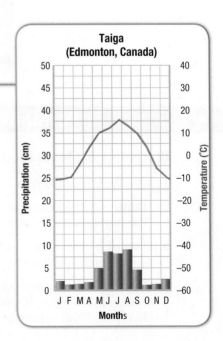

FIGURE 2.10

Taiga Plant Adaptations The seeds of conifers are protected inside tough cones like the one below. Also, the narrow shape and waxy coating of conifer needles help the tree retain water.

Plants of the Taiga

A conifer is a tree with needle-like leaves and seeds that develop in cones. The shape of the leaves and their waxy coating prevent the tree from losing too much water. This is especially important when the ground is frozen and the roots cannot replace lost water by absorbing more from the soil. As **Figure 2.10** shows, many conifers are shaped like a large cone. The cone-like shape helps to prevent snow from building up on the branches and causing the branches to break under the weight.

Conifer needles contain substances that make the soil acidic when the needles fall to the ground. Most plants cannot grow in acidic soil, which is one reason the forest floor of the taiga has few plants. In addition, soil forms slowly in the taiga because the climate and acidity of the fallen needles slow decomposition.

Animals of the Taiga

The taiga has many lakes and swamps that in summer attract birds that feed on aquatic organisms. Many birds migrate south to avoid winter in the taiga. Because food is scarce during the winter, some year-round residents, such as jumping mice, burrow underground to hibernate. As shown in **Figure 2.11**, some animals, such as snowshoe hares, have adapted to reduce the risk of predation by lynxes, wolves, and foxes by shedding their brown summer fur and growing white fur that camouflages them in the winter snow.

FIGURE 2.11

Taiga Animal Adaptations In the taiga, a snowshoe hare's fur changes color according to the seasons to help camouflage the animal from predators.

(tl) ©Walter H. Hodge; (inset) ©Stuart Cobley/Alamy Images; (bl) ©Paul E Tessier/Photodisc/Getty Images

Section 2 Formative Assessment

▶ Reviewing Main Ideas

1. **List** three characteristics of tropical rain forests.

2. **Name** the main layers of a tropical rain forest. What kinds of plants grow in each layer?

3. **Describe** two ways in which tropical rain forests of the world are being threatened.

4. **Describe** how a plant survives the change of seasons in a temperate deciduous forest. Write a short paragraph to explain your answer.

✓ Critical Thinking

5. **Evaluating Information** Which would be better suited for agricultural development: the soil of a tropical rain forest or the soil of a temperate deciduous forest? Explain your answer.

6. **Identifying Relationships** How does a snowshoe hare avoid predation by other animals during the winter in a taiga biome? How might this affect the animal that depends on the snowshoe hare for food?

Grassland, Desert, and Tundra Biomes

In areas with too little precipitation or too many fires for large trees or shrubs to survive, smaller plants dominate biomes. Where there is almost no rainfall at all, few plants can grow and we find desert. Thus, warm areas with little precipitation are characterized by savanna and desert biomes. Temperate areas have grassland, chaparral, and desert biomes. Fire can play an important role in determining what biome is found in warm regions. Cold areas have tundra and desert biomes.

Savannas and Tropical Seasonal Forests

Parts of Africa, India, Australia, and South America are covered by grasslands called savanna. A **savanna** is a tropical biome dominated by grasses, shrubs, and small trees. *Tropical seasonal forests* have larger growths of trees. Compared to savannas, tropical seasonal forests have slightly wetter conditions and less frequent fires. As **Figure 3.1** shows, rain falls mainly during the wet season, which lasts for only a few months of the year. This is the only time that plants can grow. African savannas support an amazing variety of herbivores, such as antelopes, giraffes, and elephants, as well as the predators that hunt them, such as cheetahs, lions, and hyenas.

Plants of the Savanna and Tropical Seasonal Forests

Because most of the rain falls during the wet season, plants must be able to survive long periods of time without water. In the dry season, plants lose their leaves or die back. When the rain returns, they start to grow again. Many plants have large, horizontal root systems so they can draw water from as large an area as possible. The coarse savanna grasses have vertical leaves that expose less of their surface area to the hot sun to further help the grasses conserve water. Trees and shrubs often have thorns or sharp leaves that keep hungry herbivores away.

- Describe the difference between tropical and temperate grasslands.

- Describe the climate in a chaparral biome.

- Describe two desert animals and the adaptations that help them survive.

- Describe one threat to the tundra biome.

Key Terms

savanna
temperate grassland
chaparral
desert
tundra
permafrost

FIGURE 3.1

Tropical Savanna and Seasonal Forests Wet and dry seasons characterize this biome.

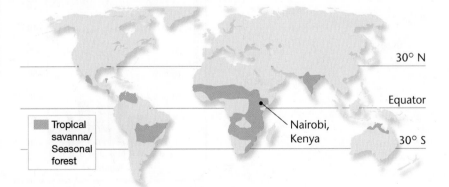

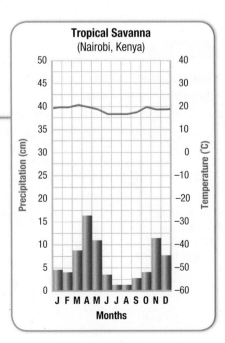

Tropical Savanna (Nairobi, Kenya)

FIGURE 3.2

Migratory Animals Herbivores of the savanna, such as the elephants shown here, range widely in search of food.

Animals of the Savanna

Grazing herbivores, such as the elephants shown in **Figure 3.2**, have adopted a migratory way of life. They follow the rains to areas of newly sprouted grass and watering holes. Some predators follow and stalk migratory animals for food. Many savanna animals give birth only during the rainy season, when food is most abundant and the young are more likely to survive. Also, some species of herbivores eat vegetation at different heights than do other species. For example, small gazelles graze on grasses, black rhinos browse on shrubs, and giraffes feed on tree leaves.

Temperate Grasslands

Temperate grassland covers large areas of the interior of continents, where there is moderate rainfall but trees and shrubs cannot be established because there is not enough rain or fires are too frequent. The prairies in North America, the steppes in Asia, the veldt in South Africa, and the pampas in South America are temperate grasslands. Their locations are shown in **Figure 3.3**.

FIGURE 3.3

Temperate Grassland Small amounts of rainfall, periodic droughts, and high temperatures in the summer characterize this biome.

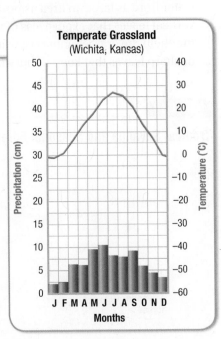

©Tim Davis/Photo Researchers, Inc.

Mountains often play a crucial role in maintaining grasslands. For example, in North America, rain clouds moving from the west release most of their moisture as they pass over the Rocky Mountains. As a result, the shortgrass prairie just east of the Rockies receives so little rain that it looks almost like a desert. The amount of rain increases as you move east, which lets taller grasses and some shrubs grow. Grassland plants dry out in the summer, so lightning strikes often start fires. **Figure 3.4** shows two examples of temperate grasslands.

Plants of Temperate Grasslands

Temperate grassland vegetation consists of grasses and wildflowers. Although there is only a single layer of vegetation, many species may be present. Shrubs and trees grow only where the soil contains extra water, usually on the banks of streams.

Periodic fires are an important part of temperate grassland ecosystems. In fact, some plants have adapted to fire by producing fire-resistant seeds that need the fire's heat to begin the process of germination. The root systems of grassland plants form dense layers that survive drought and fire. **Figure 3.5** shows how the heights of grasses and the depths of their roots vary.

Grasslands are highly productive because of their fertile soil. The summer is hot and the winter is cold, so the plants die back to their roots in the winter. Low temperatures in the winter slow decomposition. As a result, the rate at which dead plants decay is slower than the rate at which new vegetation is added each year. Over time, organic matter accumulates in the soil. This means that grasslands have the most fertile soil in the world. Most grasslands have been converted to farmland for growing crops such as wheat and corn.

FIGURE 3.4

Grasses The steppes in Asia (top) and the pampas in South America (bottom) are dominated by grasses and other plants that are adapted to temperate grasslands.

FIGURE 3.5

Grass Height and Root Depth The height of grassland plants and the depth of their roots depend on the amount of rainfall that the grasslands receive.

✔ CRITICAL THINKING

Apply What would you expect the root length to be for a plant that grows in a prairie that receives 20 cm of precipitation annually?

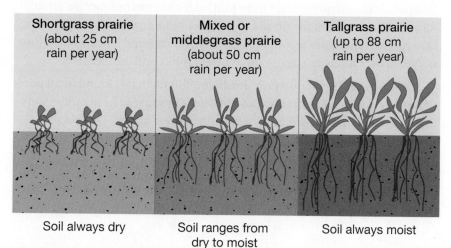

Shortgrass prairie (about 25 cm rain per year)	Mixed or middlegrass prairie (about 50 cm rain per year)	Tallgrass prairie (up to 88 cm rain per year)
Soil always dry	Soil ranges from dry to moist	Soil always moist

FIGURE 3.6

Underground Burrows Prairie dogs, such as the one shown here, live in temperate grasslands. Prairie dogs live in colonies and burrow in the ground to build mounds, holes, and tunnels.

QUICKLAB

Plant Adaptations
Procedure
1. Working in a small group, use a hand lens or binocular microscope to closely examine the leaves, stems, and roots of various plants provided by your teacher.
2. Based on the characteristics of the plants and the descriptions of the biomes given in the text, predict what type of biome each plant comes from.
3. Construct a data table where you can record each plant name, a description of its physical characteristics, and your biome predictions for each.

Analysis
1. What common characteristic did you observe in the plants from dry climates and those from cold climates? Why do you think the plants from two very different climates share this characteristic?
2. Choose a characteristic you observed in one particular plant and explain how that adaptation might help the plant to better survive in its biome.

Animals of Temperate Grasslands

Grazing animals, such as pronghorn and bison, have large, flat back teeth for chewing the coarse prairie grasses. Other grassland animals, such as badgers, prairie dogs, and burrowing owls, live protected in underground burrows as shown in **Figure 3.6.** The burrows shield the animals from fire and weather and protect them from predators.

Threats to Temperate Grasslands

Farming and overgrazing have changed the grasslands. Grain crops cannot hold the soil in place as well as native grasses can because the roots of crops are shallow and the soil is ploughed regularly, so soil erosion eventually occurs. Erosion is also caused by overgrazing. When grasses are constantly eaten and trampled, the grasses cannot regenerate or hold the soil. This constant use can change fruitful grasslands into less productive, desertlike biomes. The Dust Bowl era, which affected the Great Plains in the 1930s, is a dramatic example of what can happen when temperate grasslands are converted to agricultural land and improperly managed.

Chaparral

Temperate woodland biomes have fairly dry climates but receive enough rainfall, or mists from the ocean, to support more plants than do deserts. One type of temperate woodlands consists of scattered tree communities made up of coniferous trees such as piñon pines and junipers.

The **chaparral** is a temperate shrubland biome that is found in all parts of the world with a Mediterranean climate. These areas have moderately dry, coastal climates, with little or no rain in the summer. Look at the famous white letters that spell Hollywood across the California hills in **Figure 3.7.** Now imagine the scrub-covered settings common in old westerns. Both of these landscapes are part of the chaparral biome. As shown in **Figure 3.8,** chaparral is located in the middle latitudes, about 30° north and south of the equator.

FIGURE 3.7

Chaparral Plants The chaparral in the Hollywood hills is home to plants such as the manzanita, which is shown at right.

Plants of the Chaparral

Most chaparral plants are low-lying evergreen shrubs and small trees that tend to grow in dense patches. Common chaparral plants include chamise, manzanita, scrub oak, olive trees, and herbs, such as bay laurel. These plants have small, leathery leaves that retain water. The leaves also contain oils that promote burning, which is an advantage because natural fires destroy trees that might compete with chaparral plants for light and space. Chaparral plants are so well adapted to fire that they can resprout from small bits of surviving plant tissue.

Animals of the Chaparral

A common adaptation of chaparral animals is camouflage, which is shape or coloring that allows an animal to blend into its environment. Animals such as quail, lizards, chipmunks, and mule deer have a brownish-gray coloring that lets them move through the brush without being noticed.

Threats to the Chaparral

Worldwide, the greatest threat to chaparral is human development. Because chaparral biomes get a lot of sun, are near the oceans, and have a mild climate year-round, humans tend to develop the land for commercial and residential use.

FIGURE 3.8

Chaparral A Mediterranean climate characterizes this biome.

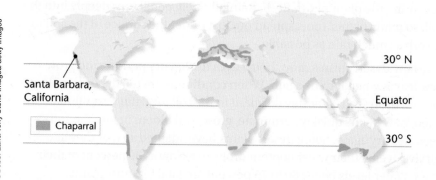

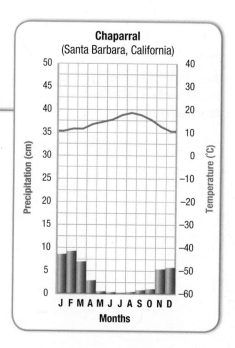

©Bobbi Lane/Tony Stone Images/Getty Images

FIGURE 3.9

Desert A lack of precipitation characterizes this biome. Deserts typically receive less than 25 cm of precipitation a year.

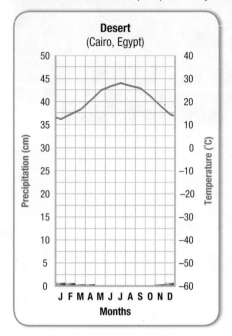

Desert
(Cairo, Egypt)

Desert

Cairo, Egypt

30° N

Equator

30° S

FIELDSTUDY

Go to Appendix B to find the field study **Xeriscaping.**

Deserts

When some people think of a desert, they think of the hot sand that surrounds the Egyptian pyramids. Other people picture the Sonoran Desert and its mighty saguaro cactuses, or the magnificent rock formations of Monument Valley in Arizona and Utah. Many kinds of deserts are located throughout the world, but one characteristic that they share is that they are among the driest places on Earth.

Deserts are areas that have widely scattered vegetation and receive very little rain. In extreme cases, it never rains and there is no vegetation. The distribution of Earth's deserts is shown in **Figure 3.9.** Even in hot deserts near the equator, there is so little insulating moisture in the air that the temperature changes rapidly during a 24-hour period. The temperature may go from 40°C (104°F) during the day to near-freezing at night. Deserts are often located near mountain ranges, which block the passage of rain clouds.

Plants of the Desert

All desert plants have adaptations for obtaining and conserving water, which allow the plants to live in dry, desert conditions. Plants called *succulents,* such as cactuses, have thick, fleshy stems and modified leaves called spines that store water. Their spines also have a waxy coating that prevents water loss. Sharp spines on cactuses keep thirsty animals from devouring the plant's juicy flesh. Rainfall rarely penetrates deeply into the soil, so many plants' roots spread out just under the surface of the soil to absorb as much rain as possible.

Many desert shrubs drop their leaves during dry periods and grow new leaves when it rains again. When conditions are too dry, some plants die and drop seeds that stay dormant in the soil until the next rainfall. Then, new plants quickly germinate, grow, and bloom before the soil becomes dry again. Some desert plants have adapted so that they can survive even if their water content drops to as low as 30 percent of their mass. Water levels below 50 to 75 percent are fatal for most plants.

FIGURE 3.10

Desert Adaptations Desert plants survive harsh conditions by having specialized structures that limit the loss of water. Desert animals bury themselves underground or burrow in cactuses to avoid extreme temperatures and predators.

Elf owls burrow in cactuses to avoid hot temperatures during the day.

The Sonoran Desert in Arizona appears lush with plant life just after the winter rains.

The flapnecked chameleon lives in the deserts of Namibia.

This sidewinder has a unique way of moving so that only small portions of its body are in contact with the hot sands at any one time.

Animals of the Desert

Reptiles, such as Gila monsters and rattlesnakes, have thick, scaly skin that prevents water loss. Amphibians, such as the spadefoot toad, survive scorching desert summers by *estivating*—burying themselves in the ground and sleeping through the dry season. Some animals, such as the elf owl shown in **Figure 3.10**, nest in cactuses to avoid predators. Desert insects and spiders are covered with body armor that helps them retain water. In addition, most desert animals are nocturnal, which means they are active mainly at night or at dusk, when the air is cooler.

FIGURE 3.11

Tundra The precipitation that the tundra biome receives remains frozen much of the year.

Tundra

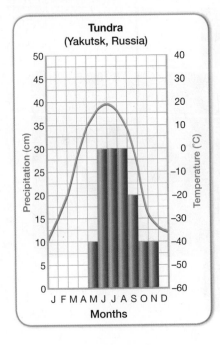

Tundra
(Yakutsk, Russia)

Tundra

The **tundra** biome is located in northern arctic regions, as shown in **Figure 3.11**. The winter is too cold and dry to permit the growth of trees in this biome. In many areas of the tundra, the deeper layers of soil, called **permafrost**, are permanently frozen throughout the year. As a result, the topsoil is very thin. In the summer, when the thin topsoil layer thaws, the tundra landscape becomes quite moist and spongy and is dotted with bogs. These wet areas are ideal breeding grounds for enormous numbers of swarming insects, such as mosquitoes and black flies, and for the many birds that feed on the insects.

Vegetation of the Tundra

Over 400 species of wildflowers, such as the fireweed shown in **Figure 3.12**, grow in the tundra during the summer. Mosses and lichens, which can grow without soil, cover vast areas of rocks in this biome. The soil is thin, so plants have wide, shallow roots to help anchor them against the icy winds. Most flowering plants of the tundra, such as campion and gentian, are short. Growing close to the ground keeps the plants out of the wind and helps them absorb heat from the sunlit soil during the brief summer. Woody plants and perennials such as willow and birch have evolved dwarf forms and grow flat or grow along the ground.

FIGURE 3.12

Short Growing Season During its brief summer, the Alaskan tundra is covered by flowering plants and lichens.

©WorldFoto/Alamy Images

FIGURE 3.13

Breeding Grounds Many migratory animals, such as snow geese (left) and caribou (right), return to the tundra each year to breed.

Animals of the Tundra

Millions of migratory birds fly to the tundra to breed in the summer. Food is abundant in the form of plants, mollusks, worms, and especially insects. Caribou, shown in **Figure 3.13**, migrate throughout the tundra in search of food and water. Wolves roam the tundra and prey on caribou, moose, and smaller animals, such as lemmings, mice, and hares. These animals burrow underground during the winter but they are still active. Many animals that live in the tundra year-round, such as arctic foxes, lose their brown fur and grow white fur that camouflages them with the winter snow. These animals are also extremely well insulated.

Threats to the Tundra

The tundra is one of the most fragile biomes on the planet. Its food webs are relatively simple, so they are easily disrupted. Because conditions are so extreme, the land is easily damaged and slow to recover. Until recently, the tundra was undisturbed by humans. But oil has been located in some tundra regions, such as in northern Alaska. Oil exploration, extraction, and transport can disrupt the habitats of the plants and animals in many parts of the tundra. Global climate change is the most widespread threat to tundra, partly because the largest warming trends are in the arctic region. Warming lowers the level of permafrost, promoting the growth of shrubs and small trees.

Connect to MATH

U.S. Oil Production
On average, the United States produces an estimated 8.1 million barrels of oil per day. How many millions of barrels of oil does the United States produce in 1 year? If all of the oil-producing countries of the world produce an estimated 74.13 million barrels of oil per day, what percentage of worldwide oil does the United States produce?

✔ Section 3 **Formative Assessment**

▶ Reviewing Main Ideas

1. **Describe** two desert animals and the adaptations that help them survive.

2. **Describe** how savannas differ from temperate grasslands.

3. **Compare** the plants that live in deserts with the plants that live in the tundra biome.

4. **Describe** one threat to the tundra biome.

✔ Critical Thinking

5. **Making Inferences** Former grasslands are among the most productive farming regions. Read the description of temperate grasslands in this section and explain why this statement is true.

6. **Analyzing Relationships** Explain why elephants and caribou, which live in very different biomes, both migrate.

A Little Piece of Cajun Prairie

Cajun prairie is a distinct grassland, named for the settlers who lived there. It once covered more than 2.5 million acres of southwest Louisiana. Today, only about 100 acres of Cajun prairie remain. If the work of two biologists and many volunteers pays off, however, a little piece of Cajun prairie will always exist in Louisiana.

"I think that saving Cajun prairie is important because once it is gone, you cannot bring it back," says Charles Allen, a retired professor from the University of Louisiana and the botanist for Louisiana's Fort Polk. "There are plants and animals there that have never been tested for uses by humans. We could be losing a plant that would cure cancer, or provide food or fiber," he says.

Allen and biologist Malcolm Vidrine, a professor of biology at Louisiana State University in Eunice, have been working for almost two decades to restore Cajun prairie.

Although Cajun prairie and the tallgrass prairies of the Midwest both belong to the temperate grassland biome, Cajun prairie soil has unique characteristics. It is made of tight, heavy clays that formed as a result of coastal flooding and rains. This soil, combined with frequent lightning fires, makes it difficult for trees to grow but easy for prairie plants to flourish.

Settling on the Prairie

In the mid-1700s, many French Acadians, later known as Cajuns, arrived in Louisiana from Nova Scotia, Canada. They sustained themselves for over 100 years by fishing, hunting, and some farming. They also sustained their environment because their lifestyle caused little damage to the prairie.

The establishment of the railroad in the late 1800s brought new settlers to farm the rich land. These settlers brought with them new, more intensive agricultural practices and established herds of cattle that overgrazed the vegetation. By the early 20th century, most of the Cajun prairie had disappeared.

Today, the Cajun prairie ecosystem is labelled as "imperiled globally" by the Nature Conservancy, an organization dedicated to preserving natural communities. There are now fewer than 100 acres of Cajun prairie left in Louisiana. The railroad led to the near disappearance of the prairie, but it has also played an important role in saving the last remaining

Charles Allen is shown here collecting seeds from a compass plant at a Cajun prairie remnant. The leaves of the compass plant face east to catch the sun.

Cajun prairie, preserved on this 10-acre site, once covered nearly 10 percent of Louisiana.

ECOZine at HMDScience.com

Go online for the latest environmental science news and updates on all EcoZine articles.

Volunteers such as these students used seeds and sod gathered from remnants to create a new Cajun prairie habitat in Eunice, Louisiana.

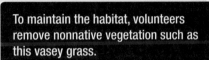

To maintain the habitat, volunteers remove nonnative vegetation such as this vasey grass.

pieces of prairie. The remaining prairie is mostly in remnants of small, narrow strips along railroad right-of-ways. Because the railroad owned these pieces of land, they were never farmed.

The Eunice Cajun Prairie Restoration Project

In the late 1980s, Allen and Vidrine located as many remnant strips as they could. They chose 10 of the strips and studied them carefully. They found almost 600 species of plants in the 10 strips.

The Eunice Cajun Prairie Restoration Project began in the summer of 1988. Its goal was to restore and preserve a small Cajun prairie in the city of Eunice, Louisiana.

A 10-acre site in Eunice was mowed, and herbicide was used to destroy the nonnative vegetation. Volunteers from local elementary and high schools collected bags of seeds from Cajun prairie plants growing in the remnant strips. That winter, controlled burns were used to prepare the site. On a designated

planting day, the students spread the seeds they had collected. The site was then lightly tilled. Sod was removed from the remnant strips and replanted at the Eunice site during the next three seasons.

Restoration is an ongoing effort. Yearly controlled burns maintain the habitat. The fires destroy shrubs and trees, but do not kill most of the prairie plants. Spot herbicides are used on the more pervasive nonnative species, such as the Chinese tallow tree, the most threatening nonnative species for the prairie. The seeds of this tree are easily spread when birds eat the seeds and deposit them in droppings.

Today, nearly 300 native Cajun prairie species, including little bluestem, Eastern gama grass, blazing stars, and hairy sunflower, have been reestablished at the site. As well, the rare wild coco orchid *(Pteroglossaspis ecristata)* has been found at the site. This is a very positive sign because few of these orchids have been found in the remnant strips or in Louisiana. Much of the Eunice site is now almost completely Cajun prairie.

What Do You Think?

Are there threatened habitats in your area? What factors do you think led to the loss of these habitats? Is it possible for people to settle in a habitat without having a negative impact? How were the Cajuns able to sustain themselves on the prairie without destroying the habitat?

©Dr. Charles Allen

SECTION 1 **What Is a Biome?**

OBJECTIVES

- Scientists classify the ecosystems of the world into large areas called *biomes*.
- Biomes are described by their plant life because specific climate conditions support the growth of specific types of vegetation.
- Climate determines which plants can grow in an area. Latitude and altitude affect climate in similar ways.

KEY TERMS

biome
climate
latitude
altitude

SECTION 2 **Forest Biomes**

OBJECTIVES

- Major forest biomes include tropical rain forest, temperate rain forest, temperate deciduous forest, and taiga.
- Tropical rain forests have high rainfall and high temperatures throughout the year. They contain the most species diversity of all biomes.
- Temperate forests experience seasonal variations in precipitation and temperature. Their vegetation is adapted to surviving these changes.
- Forest biomes are threatened by deforestation through logging, ranching, and farming.

KEY TERMS

tropical rain forest
emergent layer
canopy
epiphyte
understory
temperate rain forest
temperate deciduous forest
taiga

SECTION 3 **Grassland, Desert, and Tundra Biomes**

OBJECTIVES

- Savannas are located north and south of tropical rain forests and have distinct wet seasons.
- Temperate grasslands get too little rainfall to support trees. Grasslands are dominated mostly by different types of grasses and flowering plants.
- Deserts are the driest biomes on Earth.
- Plant and animal species found in each biome adapt to the environment in which they live.

KEY TERMS

savanna
temperate grassland
chaparral
desert
tundra
permafrost

Reviewing Key Terms

Use each of the following terms in a separate sentence.

1. *biome*
2. *climate*
3. *epiphyte*
4. *tundra*
5. *permafrost*

For each pair of terms, explain how the meanings of the terms differ.

6. *understory* and *canopy*
7. *latitude* and *altitude*
8. *chaparral* and *desert*
9. *tropical rain forest* and *temperate deciduous forest*
10. Concept Map Use the following terms to create a concept map: *threats to an ecosystem, erosion, overgrazing, logging, grasslands, rain forests, tundra, deserts, oil extraction,* and *irrigation.*

Reviewing Main Ideas

11. Approximately what percentage of the Earth's species do tropical rain forests contain?

    a. 7 percent
    b. 20 percent
    c. 40 percent
    d. 50 percent

12. Animal species of the tropical rain forest

    a. compete more for available resources than species native to other biomes do.
    b. have adaptations that minimize competition.
    c. have adaptations to cope with extreme variations in climate.
    d. are never camouflaged.

13. Migration of animals in the savanna is mostly a response to

    a. predation.
    b. altitude.
    c. rainfall.
    d. temperature.

14. Spadefoot toads survive the dry conditions of the desert by

    a. migrating to seasonal watering holes.
    b. finding underground springs.
    c. burying themselves in the ground.
    d. drinking cactus juice.

15. The tundra is most suitable to a vertebrate that

    a. requires nesting sites in tall trees.
    b. is ectothermic.
    c. has a green outer skin for camouflage.
    d. can migrate hundreds of kilometers each summer.

16. A biome that has a large amount of rainfall, high temperatures, and poor soil is a

    a. temperate woodland.
    b. temperate rain forest.
    c. tropical rain forest.
    d. savanna.

17. The two main factors that determine where organisms live are

    a. soil type and precipitation.
    b. temperature and precipitation.
    c. altitude and precipitation.
    d. temperature and latitude.

18. Which of the following biomes contains large trees?

    a. savanna
    b. temperate rain forest
    c. chaparral
    d. desert

19. The most common types of plants in the taiga biome are

    a. deciduous trees.
    b. short shrubs.
    c. coniferous trees.
    d. grasses.

Short Answer

20. Unlike the jungles you see in movies, the floor of an undisturbed tropical rain forest usually has little vegetation. Explain why it lacks vegetation.

21. What is the relationship between root systems and erosion in a grassland ecosystem?

22. How might a mountain affect where particular types of biomes are located?

23. Well-preserved mammoths have been found buried in the tundra. Explain why the tundra preserves animal remains well.

24. In what ways does deforestation contribute to a change in climate and increase the chance of floods in a biome?

Interpreting Graphics

Use the diagram below to answer questions 25–27.

25. **Determine** Why are tall trees found in the taiga but not in the tundra?

26. **Analyze** As moisture decreases, what happens to the amount of vegetation in an area?

27. **Analyze** What does the diagram tell you about the temperature of and precipitation in temperate grasslands?

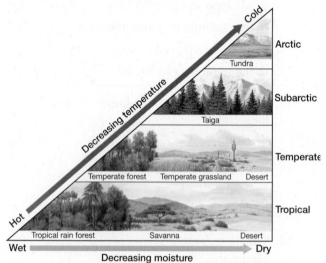

Critical Thinking

28. **Comparing Processes** American prairies and Asian steppes contain different plant species but are dominated by grasses. Write a short paragraph that explains why the two grasslands contain different species but the same types of plants.

29. **Classifying Information** Read the description of tropical rain forests in this chapter, and list two factors that are responsible for the biodiversity of this biome. Describe two reasons for the decline of tropical rain forests.

30. **Analyzing Relationships** If you took a population of squirrels from the southeastern United States and introduced them into a Central American rain forest, they would probably not survive. Why do you think the squirrels would not survive even though they are naturally adapted to life in a forest?

31. **Making Inferences** How might prairie fires set from natural and human causes have affected the evolution of fire resistance in prairie grasses?

32. **Geography** Use a world map to find locations of the various biomes. Then, make a poster that contains photos or illustrations of plants and animals native to each biome.

33. **Food Webs In Your Biome** Do a special project on the ecosystems in your biome. Use field guides to find out what plants and animals live in your biome. Then, draw a food web that shows how organisms in each ecosystem could be related.

Analyzing Data

Use the table below to answer questions 34–35.

AMOUNT OF TROPICAL RAINFOREST		
Country	Amount of tropical rain forest (km²)	Amount of annual deforestation (km²/y)
A	1,800,000	50,000
B	55,000	3,300
C	22,000	6,000
D	530,000	12,000
E	80,000	700

34. Calculate What percentage of tropical rain forest is being destroyed each year in country A? What percentage of tropical rain forest is being destroyed in country D?

35. Interpreting Data According to the table, which country's tropical rain forest will be completely destroyed first? Which country's rain forest will be completely destroyed last?

Making Connections

36. Communicating Main Ideas Describe the importance of conserving the biomes of the world. What can you do to help conserve the world's biomes?

37. Writing From Research Choose one biome and research the threats that exist against it. Write a short essay that describes the threats and any actions that are being taken to help save the biome.

CASESTUDY

38. Why does deforestation often result in flooding?

39. How does deforestation affect the climate?

Why It Matters

40. How does the presence of the rain forest affect your life?

STUDYSKILL

Concept Maps Remembering words and understanding concepts are easier when information is organized in a way that you recognize. For example, you can use key terms and key concepts to create a concept map that links them together in a pattern you will understand and remember.

Identify Your Local Biome

Objectives

Collect information from international, national, and local resources about the biome in which you live.

Perform field observations to identify the name of the biome in which you live.

Materials

binoculars (optional)

field guide to local flora and fauna

globe or atlas

graph paper (optional)

notebook

pencil or pen

ruler

In what biome do you live? Do you live in a temperate deciduous forest, a desert, or a temperate grassland, such as a prairie or savanna? In this lab, you will explore certain characteristics of the biome in which you live. With the information you gather, you will be able to identify which biome it is.

Procedure

1. Use a globe or atlas to determine the latitude at which you live. Record this information.

2. Consider the topography of the place where you live. Study the contour lines on a map or surface variations on a globe. What clues do you find that might help identify your biome? For example, is your area located near a mountain or an ocean? Record your findings.

3. Prepare a climatogram of your area. A climatogram is a graph that shows average monthly values for two factors: temperature and precipitation. Temperature is expressed in degrees Celsius and is plotted as a smooth curve. Precipitation values are given in centimeters and are plotted as a histogram.

To make a climatogram, obtain monthly averages of precipitation and temperature for one year from an online resource such as the National Weather Service (NWS). Make a data table, and record these values. Next, draw the vertical and horizontal axes of your climatogram in your notebook or on graph paper. Then, show the temperature scale along the vertical axis on the right side of the graph and the precipitation scale along the vertical axis on the left side of the graph. Show months of the year along the horizontal axis. Finally, plot your data.

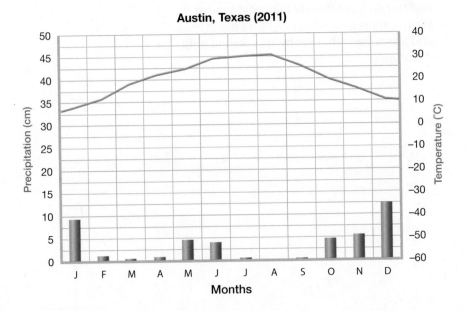

Climatograms The temperature and precipitation for Austin, Texas is shown in this climatogram.

4. Go outside to observe the plants growing in your area. Bring a field guide, and respond to the following items in your notebook.

   a. Sketch or describe as many plants that are common in your area as you can. Use your field guide to identify each of these species.

   b. Describe three or more adaptations of each plant to the local climate.

   c. Which of the plants that you observed are native to your area? Which have been introduced by humans? Which of the introduced plants can survive on their own in local conditions? Which of the introduced plants require extensive care by humans to remain alive?

   d. Look for evidence that animals have left behind—footprints, nests, dens or burrows, hair or feathers, scratches, or urine markings. Sketch or describe as many different animal species as possible. Identify each species by using your field guide.

   e. Describe three or more adaptations that each animal has developed in order to survive in local climatic conditions.

Analysis

1. **Analyzing Data** Compare your local climatogram to the biome climatograms shown in this chapter. Which biome has a climatogram most similar to the data you graphed?

2. **Analyzing Results** Consider your latitude, topographical findings, and observations of local plants and animals. Combine this information with your climatogram, and determine which biome best matches the area in which you live.

Different Biomes These two cities are located in two different biomes. East Orange Village, Vermont (top) is located in a temperate deciduous forest, and Tucson, Arizona (bottom) is located in a desert.

Conclusions

3. **Evaluating Results** Does your climatogram match any of the seven major terrestrial climatograms shown in the chapter? Describe any differences between your biome and the biome it best matches. Why do these differences occur?

4. **Applying Conclusions** Species are adapted to the climate of the biome in which they live. What might happen to these species if climate conditions change?

Extension

5. **Classifying Information** Name the three plant adaptations and the three animal adaptations that you observed. Explain in detail how each of these adaptations meets the conditions of your biome.

Chapter 7

Section 1
Freshwater Ecosystems

Section 2
Marine Ecosystems

Why It Matters

Gentle, slow-moving manatees are often called sea cows because they spend their days lazily grazing on aquatic vegetation. In North America, most manatees are found in the estuaries, bays, and coastal ecosystems of places like Florida. Manatees are 3–4 m in length, weigh 360 to 545 kg, and can live up to 60 years. Unfortunately, even though the slow-moving manatees have few natural enemies, they are often hit and killed or injured by boats.

How might boaters help to protect the manatee?

CASESTUDY

Learn more about how the restoration of Chesapeake Bay is helping the plants and wildlife that are dependent on its ecosystem in the case study Restoration of Chesapeake Bay on page 180.

Aquatic Ecosystems

ONLINE ENVIRONMENTAL SCIENCE
HMDScience.com

Go online to access additional resources, including labs, worksheets, multimedia, and resources in Spanish.

©Marty Snyderman/Corbis

Freshwater Ecosystems

SECTION 1

Objectives

▶ Describe the factors that determine where an organism lives in an aquatic ecosystem.

▶ Describe the littoral zone and the benthic zone that make up a lake or pond.

▶ Describe two environmental functions of wetlands.

▶ Describe one threat against river ecosystems.

The types of organisms in an aquatic ecosystem are mainly determined by the water's *salinity*—the amount of dissolved salts the water contains. As a result, aquatic ecosystems are divided into freshwater ecosystems and marine ecosystems.

Freshwater ecosystems include the sluggish waters of lakes and ponds, such as the lake shown in **Figure 1.1**, and the moving waters of rivers and streams. They also include areas where land, known as a **wetland**, is periodically under water. Marine ecosystems include the diverse coastal areas of marshes, bays, and coral reefs as well as the deep, vast oceans.

Characteristics of Aquatic Ecosystems

Factors such as temperature, sunlight, oxygen, nutrients, and the nature of the bottom determine which organisms live in which areas of the water. For instance, sunlight reaches only a certain distance below the surface of the water, so most photosynthetic organisms live on or near the surface.

Aquatic organisms are grouped by location and by their adaptations. There are three groups of aquatic organisms. **Plankton** are organisms that cannot swim against currents, so they are drifters. Drifting algae, called *phytoplankton*, are the food base for most aquatic ecosystems. Most phytoplankton are microscopic. Drifting animals, which may be microscopic or as large as a jellyfish, are called *zooplankton*. **Nekton** are free-swimming organisms, such as fish and whales. **Benthos** are bottom-dwellers, such as mussels, worms, and barnacles. Many benthic organisms live attached to hard surfaces or burrow into softer sediments. Decomposers, which break down dead organisms, also live in aquatic ecosystems.

Key Terms

wetland
plankton
nekton
benthos
littoral zone
benthic zone
eutrophication

FIGURE 1.1

Freshwater Ecosystems Lake Louise in Alberta, Canada, is an example of a freshwater ecosystem.

©Jan-Peter Lahall/Peter Arnold, Inc./Getty Images

FIGURE 1. 2

Pond Dwellers Amphibians, such as this bullfrog, live in or near lakes and ponds.

FIGURE 1.3

Surface Life In a pond or lake ecosystem, the most diverse and abundant life occurs near the shore, where sunlight and nutrients are plentiful. In the open water, sunlight at and near the surface supports drifting phytoplankton.

Lakes and Ponds

Lakes, ponds, wetlands, rivers, and streams make up the various types of freshwater ecosystems. Lakes, ponds, and wetlands can form naturally where groundwater reaches the Earth's surface. As well, beavers can create ponds by damming up streams. Humans intentionally create artificial lakes by damming flowing rivers and streams to use them for power, irrigation, water storage, and recreation.

Life in a Lake

Lakes and ponds can be structured into horizontal and vertical zones. In the nutrient-rich **littoral zone** near the shore, aquatic life is diverse and abundant. Plants, such as cattails and reeds, are rooted in the mud underwater, and their upper leaves and stems emerge above the water. Plants that have floating leaves, such as water lilies, are rooted here also. Farther from the shore, in the open water *limnetic zone*, there are no rooted plants. Here, phytoplankton make their own food by *photosynthesis*. As shown in **Figure 1.3**, nutrients and sunlight influence the location and types of organisms in a pond or lake ecosystem.

Some bodies of fresh water have areas so deep that there is too little light for photosynthesis. In these deep areas, bacteria and other decomposers live on dead plants and animals that drift down from above. Fish adapted to cooler water also live there. Eventually, dead and decaying organisms reach the **benthic zone**, the bottom of a pond or lake, which is inhabited by decomposers, insect larvae, and clams.

Some animals that live in lakes and ponds have interesting adaptations that help them obtain what they need to survive. Water beetles use the hairs under their bodies to trap surface air so that they can breathe during their dives for food. Barbels help catfish sense food as they swim over dark lake bottoms. In regions where lakes partially freeze in winter, amphibians (**Figure 1.2**) burrow partway into the mud to hibernate.

Sunlight

LITTORAL ZONE

Decomposers

BENTHIC ZONE

Phytoplankton and zooplankton

How Nutrients Affect Lakes

Nutrients in aquatic ecosystems determine the amount of plant and algal growth. **Eutrophication** is an increase in the amount of nutrients. Lakes with large amounts of algae and plant growth from excessive nutrients are *eutrophic lakes* (**Figure 1.4**). As the plants and algae multiply, the number of bacteria feeding on the decaying organisms also grows. These bacteria use the oxygen dissolved in the lake water. Eventually, the reduced amount of oxygen kills oxygen-loving organisms. Lakes naturally become eutrophic over time, but the process can be accelerated by runoff. *Runoff* is precipitation that can carry pollutants like fertilizers from land into bodies of water.

FIGURE 1.4

Eutrophication A eutrophic lake, like the one below, contains large amounts of plants as a result of high levels of nutrients.

Freshwater Wetlands

Freshwater wetlands are areas of land, with special soils and plants, that are covered with fresh water for at least part of the year. The two main types are marshes and swamps. *Marshes* contain nonwoody plants, such as cattails, while *swamps* are dominated by woody plants, such as flood-tolerant trees and shrubs.

Wetlands perform several important environmental functions (**Figure 1.5**). Wetlands act as filters or sponges because they absorb and remove pollutants from the water that flows through them. Therefore, wetlands improve the water quality of lakes, rivers, and reservoirs downstream. Wetlands also control flooding by absorbing extra water when rivers overflow, which protects farms and urban and residential areas from damage. Many of the freshwater game fish caught in the United States each year use the wetlands for feeding and spawning. In addition, wetlands provide a home for native and migratory wildlife, including ducks and blue herons (**Figure 1.6**). Wetland vegetation also traps carbon that would otherwise be released as carbon dioxide, which has been linked to rising atmospheric temperatures.

✔ **CHECK FOR UNDERSTANDING**

Explain How can wetlands reduce damage that is caused by flooding?

FIGURE 1.6

Wetland Dwellers Wetlands provide habitat for many plants and animals, including the great blue herons shown below.

FIGURE 1.5

ENVIRONMENTAL FUNCTIONS OF WETLANDS
trapping and filtering sediments, nutrients, and pollutants, which keep these materials from entering lakes, reservoirs, and oceans
reducing the likelihood of a flood, protecting agriculture, roads, buildings, and human health and safety
buffering shorelines against erosion
providing spawning grounds and habitat for commercially important fish and shellfish
providing habitat for rare, threatened, and endangered species
providing recreational areas for activities such as fishing, birdwatching, hiking, canoeing, photography, and painting

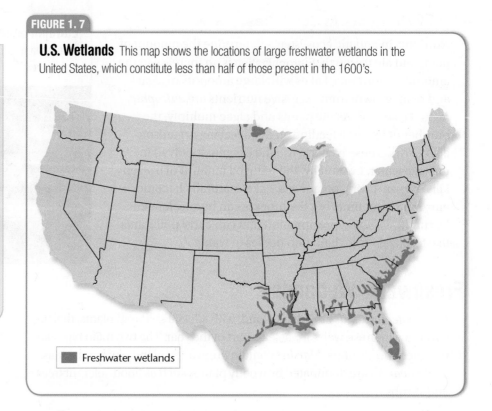

Connect to HISTORY

The Florida Everglades

Because of the work of many writers, conservationists, and naturalists, former U.S. President Truman dedicated the Everglades National Park in 1947. The park was established to protect the wildlife and habitat of the Florida Everglades. The Florida Everglades is one of only three sites on Earth declared an International Biosphere Reserve, a World Heritage Site, and a Wetland of International Importance. The other two sites are located in Tunisia and Bulgaria.

FIGURE 1. 7

U.S. Wetlands This map shows the locations of large freshwater wetlands in the United States, which constitute less than half of those present in the 1600's.

Freshwater wetlands

Marshes

As shown in **Figure 1.7**, most large freshwater wetlands in the United States are located in the Southeast. The Florida Everglades is the largest freshwater wetland in the United States. Freshwater marshes tend to occur on low, flat lands and have few, if any, woody trees or plants. In shallow waters, plants such as reeds, rushes, and cattails root themselves in the rich bottom sediments. As shown in **Figure 1.8**, the leaves of these and other plants stick out above the surface of the water year-round.

The benthic zones of marshes are nutrient-rich and contain plants, algae, many types of decomposers, and scavengers. Waterfowl, such as grebes and ducks, have flat beaks adapted for sifting through the water for fish and insects. Water birds have spear-like beaks that they use to grasp small fish and to probe for frogs buried in the mud. Marshes are also home to migratory birds from temperate and tropical habitats.

The salinity of marshes varies. Some marshes have fresh water, some have slightly salty (brackish) water. Salt marshes have water that is as salty as ocean water. The organisms that live in and around a marsh are generally adapted to the specific range of salinities of the marsh's water.

FIGURE 1.8

Marsh A marsh is a type of wetland that contains nonwoody plants.

✔ **CRITICAL THINKING**

Compare How is a swamp different from a marsh?

Swamps

Swamps occur on flat, poorly drained, wooded land, often near streams. The species of trees and shrubs in a swamp depend on the salinity of the water and the climate of the area. Freshwater swamps include acidic *bogs,* filled with sphagnum or peat moss, which are found in colder climates, and cypress swamps, which are found in warmer areas. These, along with alkaline *fens,* are the ideal habitat for many amphibians, such as frogs, because of the continuously moist environment. Swamps also attract birds, such as wood ducks that nest in hollow trees near or over the water. Reptiles, like the American alligator in **Figure 1.9**, are the major predators of swamps and will eat almost any organism that crosses their path.

FIGURE 1.9

Swamp The American alligator is a common reptile that lives in marshes and swamps.

Human Impact on Wetlands

Wetlands were previously considered to be wastelands that provided breeding grounds for disease-carrying insects. Many have been drained, filled, and cleared for farms or residential and commercial development, as shown in **Figure 1.10**. For example, the Florida Everglades once covered 8 million acres of south Florida, but now covers less than 2 million acres. The important role of wetlands as purifiers of wastewater and in flood prevention is now recognized. Wetlands are vital habitats for wildlife. The federal government, as well as international treaties, protect many wetlands, and most U.S. states now prohibit the destruction of certain wetlands.

Connect to MATH

Wetland Conversion
From 1982 to 1992, approximately 1.6 million acres of wetlands on nonfederal lands in the United States were converted for other uses. Fifty-seven percent of the wetlands were converted into land for development. Twenty percent of the wetlands were converted into land for agriculture. How many acres of land were converted into land for development? How many acres of land were converted into land for agriculture?

FIGURE 1.10

Wetland The wetland on the right has been drained for agricultural purposes. Wetlands such as this typically serve as breeding areas for ducks. The oil rig on the left is located in a marsh along the coast of Louisiana.

FIGURE 1.11

Water Flow A river changes dramatically as it flows from a mountaintop to flat land.

 ©Michal Sleczek/Flickr/Getty Images; (t) ©Design Pics/Bilderbuch/Getty Images

✔ **CHECK FOR UNDERSTANDING**

Predict What effect can runoff have on the health of organisms that live in and around a river?

Rivers

Rivers can originate from underground springs, snow melt in mountains, or where smaller streams merge together. At its headwaters, a river is usually cold and full of oxygen and runs swiftly through a shallow riverbed. Further along, it becomes warmer, wider, and slower, containing more vegetation and less oxygen. **Figure 1.11** compares the water flow of two sections of two different rivers. A river changes with the land and the climate through which it flows. Runoff, for example, may wash nutrients and sediment from the surrounding land into a river, which eventually drains into the ocean. These materials affect the growth and health of the organisms in the river.

Life in a River

Near the headwaters, mosses anchor themselves to rocks by using rootlike *rhizoids*. Trout and minnows are also adapted to the cold, oxygen-rich waters. Trout are powerful swimmers and have streamlined bodies that present little resistance to the strong current. Downstream, in the calmer waters, plants such as the crowfoot set roots in the river's rich sediment. Fish such as catfish and carp thrive where the water slows and deepens.

Rivers in Danger

Communities and industries affect the health of rivers. People draw water from rivers to use in homes and manufacturing. People also use rivers to dispose of their sewage and garbage. These practices have polluted rivers with toxins. The toxins have killed river organisms and have made river fish unsuitable for eating. Today, runoff from the land deposits pesticides and other poisons into rivers and coats riverbeds with toxic sediments. In addition, dams alter the ecosystems in and around a river.

✔ Section 1 **Formative Assessment**

▶ **Reviewing Main Ideas**

1. **List** two factors that determine where an organism lives in an aquatic ecosystem.

2. **Compare** the littoral zone of a lake with the benthic zone of a lake.

3. **List** two environmental functions that wetlands provide. How do these functions affect you?

4. **Describe** one threat against river ecosystems.

✔ **Critical Thinking**

5. **Identifying Relationships** A piece of garbage that is thrown into a stream may end up in a river or an ocean. What effects might one piece of garbage have on an aquatic ecosystem? What effects might 100 pieces of garbage have on an aquatic ecosystem?

6. **Analyzing Processes** Write a short paragraph that explains how fertilizing your yard and applying pesticides can affect the health of a river ecosystem.

Marine Ecosystems

Marine ecosystems are ecosystems that contain salt water. Such ecosystems are found in and around the world's oceans. In the open water, the amount of sunlight and available nutrients vary from one part of an ocean to another. In coastal areas, the water level and salinity usually change during the day.

Coastal Wetlands

Coastal land areas that are covered by salt water for all or part of the time are known as *coastal wetlands*. Coastal wetlands provide habitat and nesting areas for many fish and wildlife. Coastal wetlands also filter out pollutants and sediments, protect shorelines from erosion, and provide recreational areas for boating, fishing, and hunting. Wetlands absorb excess rain, which protects areas from flooding: a crucial ecological service.

Estuaries

Many coastal wetlands form in estuaries. An **estuary** is an area in which fresh water from a river mixes with salt water from the ocean. As the two bodies of water meet, currents form and cause mineral-rich mud and dissolved nutrients to fall to the bottom. **Figure 2.1** illustrates how the waters mix in such a way that the estuary becomes a nutrient trap. These nutrients then become available to producers, and in some shallow areas, marsh grass will grow in the mud. Estuaries tend to be very productive ecosystems because they constantly receive fresh nutrients from the river. The surrounding land, such as the mainland or a peninsula, protects estuaries from the harsh force of ocean waves.

SECTION 2

Objectives

▸ Explain why an estuary is a very productive ecosystem.

▸ Compare salt marshes and mangrove swamps.

▸ Describe two threats to coral reefs.

▸ Describe two threats to ocean organisms.

Key Terms

estuary
salt marsh
mangrove swamp
barrier island
coral reef

FIGURE 2.1

Estuary The mixing of fresh water and salt water at the mouth of a river creates a nutrient-rich estuary.

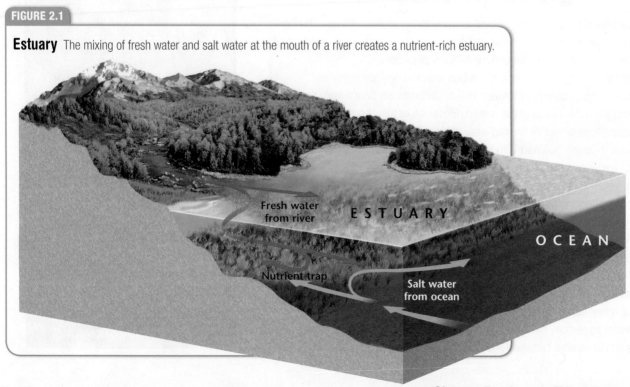

Fresh water from river

ESTUARY

OCEAN

Nutrient trap

Salt water from ocean

QUICKLAB

Estuaries
Procedure
1. Fill a clean fish bowl two-thirds full with tap water.
2. Pour 200 mL of ocean saline solution into a 250 mL beaker and add 5 drops of red food coloring.
3. Slowly pour the saline solution into the water in the bowl.
4. Record your observations.
5. Repeat using the estuary solution.

Analysis
1. What do your observations tell you about how fresh water and sea water interact in an estuary?
2. Why is this interaction so important to species that live in the estuary?

Plants and Animals of Estuaries

For a week each spring, horseshoe crabs, shown in **Figure 2.2**, crawl out of the ocean and onto the beaches of Delaware Bay. In the shallow areas along the shore, the crabs mate and lay billions of eggs. Many migrating shorebirds depend on these eggs for food.

Estuaries support many marine organisms because estuaries receive plenty of light for photosynthesis and abundant nutrients for plants and animals. Rivers supply nutrients that have been washed from the land, and because the water is shallow, sunlight can reach all the way to the bottom of the estuary. The light and nutrients support large populations of rooted plants as well as plankton. The plankton in turn provide food for larger animals, such as fish. Dolphins, manatees, otters, and other mammals often feed on fish and plants in estuaries. Oysters, barnacles, and clams live anchored to marsh grass or rocks and feed by filtering plankton out of the water. Organisms that live in estuaries are able to tolerate variations in salinity because the salt content of the water varies as fresh water and salt water mix when tides go in and out.

CASESTUDY

Restoration of the Chesapeake Bay

The Chesapeake Bay is the largest estuary in the United States. The bay produces large amounts of seafood each year, supports many species of wildlife, and provides recreation for millions of people.

However, the ecosystems of the bay are threatened by several environmental problems. Pollution builds up because only a very narrow opening joins the bay and the ocean. Because of this the small tide flushes pollutants out of the bay very slowly. By 1980, the Chesapeake Bay was severely polluted with toxic industrial chemicals. Pesticides as well as excess nutrients ran into the bay from housing developments, farms, and wastewater (including sewage). Marsh grasses and plankton were dying, and fish, oysters, and crabs were disappearing. Birds of prey, such as bald eagles, had almost vanished. Therefore, environmentalists and residents became alarmed and launched campaigns to save the bay.

Restoring Chesapeake Bay habitats and water quality is not easy. Maryland and Virginia, the main bordering states of the bay, have different environmental laws. Also, the bay's watershed covers parts of four other states. Interested groups would have to work together if they were to restore the bay. The Chesapeake Bay Program was set up as a partnership between the Environmental Protection Agency, the

The Chesapeake Bay forms where the Potomac, Rappahannock, and other rivers meet the Atlantic Ocean.

Estuaries provide protected harbors, access to the ocean, and connection to a river. As a result, many of the world's major ports are built on estuaries. Of the 10 largest urban areas in the world, 6 were built on estuaries. These 6 cities are Tokyo, New York, Shanghai, Buenos Aires, Rio de Janeiro, and Mumbai.

Threats to Estuaries

Estuaries in populated areas were often used as solid waste landfills. The landfills were then developed and used as building sites. This practice occurred widely in California, which now has plans to restore some of its estuary wetlands. The pollutants that damage estuaries are the same pollutants that damage other aquatic ecosystems: sewage, industrial waste, and runoff from agricultural, domestic, and urban sources. Most of these pollutants eventually break down over time, but estuaries cannot cope with the excessive amounts produced by dense human populations.

(b) ©Bill Garrett/America 24-7/Getty Images; (t) ©Paul Sutherland/National Geographic Society/Corbis

FIGURE 2.2

Estuary Life Horseshoe crabs go to the Delaware Bay, an estuary between New Jersey and Delaware, to lay their eggs.

This great egret lives in one of the estuaries that borders the Chesapeake Bay.

District of Columbia, Maryland, Pennsylvania, Virginia, and citizen advisory groups. Goals included reducing chemical pollution, removing dams that prevented fish from migrating, and reforesting river banks to reduce soil erosion.

Remarkable progress has been made in the last 30 years. As of 2010, around twenty-eight percent of the tidal waters that were analyzed showed no impairment from chemical contaminants. Blue crabs, for which the bay is famous, have rebounded from an average of 192 million in 1990 to 315 million in 2010. Planting trees has restored forested buffers to about 60 percent of the watershed, and populations of fish, such as striped bass, are increasing.

However, the number of people in the bay area is increasing and development is reducing forests at the rate of 100 acres per day. Also because of development, forested areas are becoming fragmented, reducing their ability to improve water quality and provide habitat for wildlife.

Concerned citizens have formed the Chesapeake Bay Program to study, preserve, and restore the bay's ecosystems. Many other parts of the United States have developed similar stewardship programs to protect their waterways.

Learn more about the watershed where you live and what you can do to help protect it. Participate in river, creek, and beach clean-ups and promote sustainable development in your community that will improve the future quality of life for people and the environment.

Critical Thinking

1. **Predicting Consequences** If the Chesapeake Bay Program had never been founded, what might have happened to the Chesapeake Bay? Select one organism and explain how it might have been affected.

2. **Identifying Relationships** How may the use of less fertilizer on plants and lawns help the Chesapeake Bay and other estuaries?

Mangroves Mangrove swamps are found along warm, tropical coasts and are dominated by salt-tolerant mangrove trees.

Mangrove Swamps

Mangroves cover 180 billion square meters of tropical coastlines around the world. The largest single mangrove swamp is 5.7 billion square meters, located in the Sundarbans of Bangladesh. This single mangrove swamp provides habitat for the Bengal tiger and helps supply approximately 300,000 people with food, fuel, building materials, and medicines.

✔ **CHECK FOR UNDERSTANDING**
Name two things that a salt marsh has in common with a mangrove swamp.

Salt Marshes

In estuaries, where rivers deposit their load of mineral-rich mud, **salt marshes** form. Here, thousands of acres of salt marsh support a community of clams, fish, and birds. The marsh also acts as a nursery in which many species of shrimps, crabs, and fishes find protection when they are small. As they grow to maturity and migrate to the sea, they are eaten by larger fish or caught by commercial fisheries. Salt marshes, like other wetlands, absorb pollutants and protect inland areas.

Mangrove Swamps

Mangroves, such as those shown in **Figure 2.3**, are several species of small trees adapted for growing in shallow salt water. Most mangroves have wide, above-ground root systems for support. Dense growths of mangrove trees in swampy areas called **mangrove swamps** are found in tropical and subtropical zones. Mangrove swamps help to protect the coastline from erosion and reduce the damage from storms. They provide habitat for about 2,000 animal species. Like salt marshes, mangrove swamps have been filled with waste or used for development projects in many parts of the world.

Rocky and Sandy Shores

Rocky shores have many more plant and animal species than sandy shores do. The rocks anchor seaweed and the many animals that live on it, such as sea anemones, mussels, and sponges. Life on sandy shores, although less diverse, is abundant in the water and in the sand and sediments. In the water and on land, animals are adapted to the effects of drying and exposure at low tide. At low tide, birds poke and prod about for animals that have not attached themselves firmly enough or buried themselves deeply enough to escape the tidal pull. **Barrier islands**, such as the one in **Figure 2.4**, often run parallel to sandy shores. These islands help to protect the mainland and the coastal wetlands from storms and ocean waves and often provide habitat for wildlife.

Barrier Islands This barrier island is located off the coast of Long Island, New York. Barrier islands are separated from the mainland and help protect the shore of the mainland from erosion.

✔ **CRITICAL THINKING**
Explain How do barrier islands protect the main shoreline from erosion?

FIGURE 2.5

Coral Reefs Coral reefs are found in warm, shallow waters, where there is enough light for photosynthesis. Coral reefs support a great diversity of species.

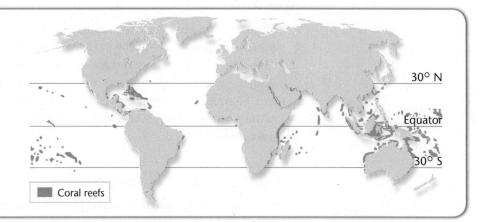

30° N

Equator

30° S

■ Coral reefs

Coral Reefs

Coral reefs are limestone ridges built by tiny coral animals called *coral polyps* and the algae that live inside them. Coral polyps secrete skeletons of limestone (calcium carbonate), which slowly accumulate and form coral reefs. Thousands of species of plants and animals live in the cracks of coral reefs, which makes coral reefs, like Australia's 1600-mile-long Great Barrier Reef, among the most diverse ecosystems on Earth.

Because reef-building corals live only in warm salt water where there is enough light for photosynthesis, coral reefs are found in shallow, clear tropical seas. **Figure 2.5** shows the locations of coral reefs. Only the outer layer of a reef contains living corals, which build their rock homes with the help of the photosynthetic algae that live within them. Some coral reefs have been building for hundreds of thousands of years. Corals, such as those shown in **Figure 2.6**, are predators that never chase their prey. Their stinging polyps capture small animals that float or swim close to the reef. Because of their convoluted shape, coral reefs provide a habitat for a magnificent variety of fish, snails, clams, sponges, anemones, and many other types of marine organisms.

Coral Reefs in Danger

Coral reefs are fragile ecosystems. If the surrounding water is too hot or cold for too long, or if it is too muddy, polluted, or high in nutrients, the algae that live in the corals will leave or die. As a result, the corals turn white, a condition called *coral bleaching*. If coral bleaching occurs often or long enough, coral animals and the reefs they build will die.

Since the twentieth century, bleaching events have been occurring more frequently, mainly due to human activities. About 50 percent of the world's coral reefs are now in danger of destruction. In addition, climate change, oil spills, and polluting runoff have been linked to the destruction of coral reefs. Overfishing also upsets the balance of a reef ecosystem by devastating fish populations. Because coral reefs grow slowly, a reef may not be able to repair itself when parts of it are stressed or destroyed.

FIGURE 2.6

Polyps Coral reefs (bottom) are built by tiny coral animals called coral polyps. The stinging polyps of fire coral (top) capture animals by poisoning them.

Oceans

Because water absorbs light, sunlight that plants can use for photosynthesis penetrates only about 100 m (330 ft) into the ocean. As a result, much of the ocean's life is concentrated in the shallow, coastal waters. Here, sunlight penetrates to the bottom and rivers wash nutrients from the land. Seaweed and algae grow anchored to rocks, and phytoplankton drift on the surface. Invertebrates and fish that feed on these plants are also concentrated near the shore.

Plants and Animals of Oceans

In the open ocean, phytoplankton grow only in areas where there is enough light and nutrients. As a result, the open ocean is one of the least productive of all ecosystems. Phytoplankton have buoyancy devices, such as oil bubbles, that prevent them from sinking into deep water, which is too dark for photosynthesis. The sea's smallest herbivores are the zooplankton, which live near the surface with the phytoplankton they eat. The zooplankton include jellyfish, tiny shrimp, and the larvae of fish and bottom-dwelling animals, such as oysters and lobsters. Fish feed on the plankton as do marine mammals such as whales.

The depths of the ocean are perpetually dark, so most food at the ocean floor consists of dead organisms that fall from the surface. Decomposers, filter feeders, and the organisms that eat them live in the deep areas of the ocean, along with *chemosynthetic* organisms that derive nutrients from chemicals in the water or substrate. **Figure 2.7**

FIELDSTUDY
Go to Appendix B to find the field study
Once Upon a Time.

FIGURE 2.7

Layers of the Ocean The amount of sunlight available determines which organisms can live in each layer of the ocean.

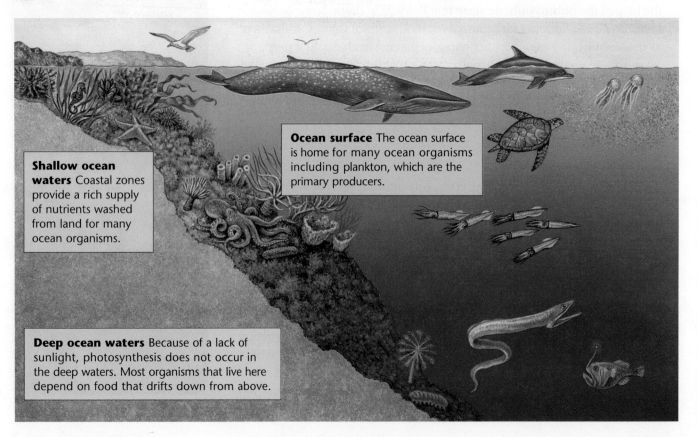

Shallow ocean waters Coastal zones provide a rich supply of nutrients washed from land for many ocean organisms.

Ocean surface The ocean surface is home for many ocean organisms including plankton, which are the primary producers.

Deep ocean waters Because of a lack of sunlight, photosynthesis does not occur in the deep waters. Most organisms that live here depend on food that drifts down from above.

illustrates the types of organisms that may be found in the layers of the ocean at various depths, depending on available sunlight.

Threats to the Oceans

Although oceans are huge, they are steadily becoming more polluted. Most ocean pollution arises from activities on land. For example, runoff from fertilized fields, golf courses, or suburban lawns may cause algal blooms, some of which are poisonous. Waste from cities and industries, fertilizers, and sewage running off the land are the main sources of coastal pollution in the United States.

Overfishing and certain fishing methods are also destroying some fish populations. Immense trawl nets can entangle organisms that are larger than the holes in the nets. Marine mammals such as dolphins, and animals like sea turtles, which must breathe air, can drown in the nets if the nets are not equipped with escape mechanisms. Some ships illegally discard fishing lines into the ocean, where they can strangle and kill animals such as the sea lion in **Figure 2.8.**

Arctic and Antarctic Ecosystems

The arctic ecosystems at the North and South Poles are marine ecosystems because nearly all the food comes from the ocean and seas.

The Arctic Ocean is rich in nutrients from the surrounding land masses. It supports large populations of plankton, which feed a rich diversity of fish in the open water and under the ice. The fish are food for ocean birds, whales, and seals. Beluga whales, shown in **Figure 2.9**, feed on nearly 100 different arctic organisms. Fish and seals also provide food for polar bears and people on land.

The Antarctic is the only continent never colonized by humans. Even during the summer, only a few plants grow at the rocky edges of the continent. As in the Arctic, plankton form the basis of the Antarctic food web. They nourish large numbers of fish, whales, and birds such as penguins, which cannot fly because their wings have evolved for swimming.

FIGURE 2.8

Wildlife Threats This sea lion was strangled by a fishing net off the coast of California.

✔ **CHECK FOR UNDERSTANDING**
What are two threats to organisms that live in the ocean?

FIGURE 2.9

Arctic Dweller Beluga whales inhabit the Arctic Ocean.

(cr) ©Image Life/Corbis; (t) ©Photo Researchers/Photo Researchers/Getty Images

Section 2 Formative Assessment

▶ Reviewing Main Ideas

1. **Explain** why estuaries are very productive ecosystems. Why are estuaries vulnerable to the effects of pollution?

2. **Compare** salt marshes with mangrove swamps.

3. **Describe** two factors that can damage coral reefs.

4. **List** two ways in which animals of the oceans are threatened.

✔ Critical Thinking

5. **Predicting Consequences** Suppose that the sea level suddenly rose by 100 m. What would happen to the world's coral reefs? Explain.

6. **Analyzing Processes** Read the description of estuaries in this section, and explain why cities are often built on estuaries. How would building a city on an estuary affect the plants and animals living in the estuary?

Viewing Wetlands Historically

WETLANDS IN THE UNITED STATES, 1780S VS. 1980S

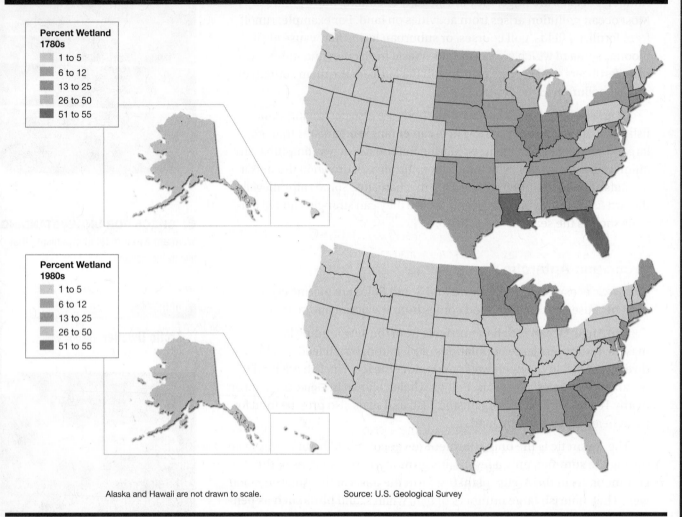

Percent Wetland 1780s
- 1 to 5
- 6 to 12
- 13 to 25
- 26 to 50
- 51 to 55

Percent Wetland 1980s
- 1 to 5
- 6 to 12
- 13 to 25
- 26 to 50
- 51 to 55

Alaska and Hawaii are not drawn to scale.   Source: U.S. Geological Survey

MAP SKILLS

Use the maps of wetland loss in the United States to answer the questions below.

1. **Using a Key** Use the key to determine how many states had a decrease in wetland distribution from 6 to 12 percent to 1 to 5 percent.

2. **Analyzing Data** Is there any state on the map of wetland distribution in the 1980s that has the same percentage of wetland distribution as it did in the 1780s? If so, how many?

3. **Interpreting Data** Are these maps an accurate indicator of wetland distribution change? Explain.

4. **Making Inferences** What might have caused Florida's and Louisiana's wetlands to decrease in distribution?

5. **Using a Key** Use the key to determine how many states had a decrease in wetland distribution from 26 to 50 percent to 13 to 25 percent.

6. **Identifying Trends** If these trends of wetland loss continued as shown, what would a map of United States wetland distribution look like today?

Society and the Environment

ECOZine at HMDScience.com

Go online for the latest environmental science news and updates on all EcoZine articles.

Hurricane Katrina and New Orleans

The city of New Orleans was built on the Mississippi River Delta, about 160 kilometers upriver from the Gulf of Mexico. This city is vulnerable to flooding from the Mississippi River, Lake Pontchartrain to the north, and heavy rainfall from tropical storms. In addition, hurricanes that pass over the coast can create storm surges—waves up to 9 meters.

To help protect New Orleans from flooding, engineers and city planners built levees and flood walls along the river banks and lakeshore. They constructed pumps to move floodwater from lower-lying areas through canals into Lake Pontchartrain. Despite these measures, Hurricane Katrina overwhelmed the city in late August, 2005. Why was the damage so severe?

Analyses of the catastrophe concluded that human-made changes in the natural environment were partly responsible for the damage.

Over 80 percent of New Orleans was submerged by floodwater when Hurricane Katrina struck in August, 2005.

Protection from the Sea

The Mississippi River Delta formed from sediment carried down the river over several thousand years. It consists of saltwater and freshwater marshes, mud flats, and creeks, collectively known as coastal wetlands. Winds and currents move loose sediment to build up barrier islands. These islands shelter the coastal wetlands and mainland from the ocean. Plants growing in the wetlands trap sediment and help to stabilize the land. The Louisiana coast has about 40 percent of all the coastal marshes in the continental United States. These coastal wetlands are an important habitat for crustaceans, mollusks, fish, and birds. As well, they filter out pollutants from the river, absorb floodwater, and help to supply fresh water to aquifers.

Eroding the Barrier Islands

As levees were constructed to confine the flow of the Mississippi River, sediment carried by the river was flushed farther out into the Gulf of Mexico. The sediment was no longer deposited to build up more land.

Canals that were built through the barrier islands to handle river traffic increased the erosion of the coastal wetlands. Soil dug from the canals was piled on the banks, smothering

vegetation that had helped to hold the banks in place. The increased speed and volume of the water in the canals washed away more soil from the barrier islands. As the barrier islands eroded, the marshes and land behind them were left exposed and were washed away.

The Impact of Katrina

Most of the damage from Hurricane Katrina was caused by rising water that overflowed or broke through the levees.

A wide shipping canal funneled a 4.6 meters storm surge from the ocean into the city. The storm surge broke through the banks of the canal. Other canals, built to drain water into Lake Pontchartrain, had their flow reversed as the water level in the lake rose. Eventually, the city's drainage system failed when most of the pumping stations were submerged.

As a result of these factors, an estimated 300,000 homes were destroyed or damaged beyond repair. More than 1300 people, 70 percent of whom were elderly, died.

What Do You Think?

Many engineers and environmental scientists had predicted that the risk of flooding in New Orleans had been increased by poorly designed levees and canals, and by massive erosion. Should a city have been built in an environment known to be so unstable?

SECTION 1 **Freshwater Ecosystems**

OBJECTIVES

- Aquatic ecosystems can be classified as freshwater ecosystems or marine ecosystems. The plants and animals in aquatic ecosystems are adapted to specific environmental conditions.

- Freshwater ecosystems include lakes, ponds, freshwater wetlands, rivers, and streams. The types of freshwater ecosystems are classified by the depth of the water, the speed of the water flow, and the availability of minerals, sunlight, and oxygen.

- Freshwater wetlands serve many functions within ecosystems. They trap and filter sediments and pollutants; reduce the likelihood of a flood; and buffer shorelines against erosion.

KEY TERMS

wetland
plankton
nekton
benthos
littoral zone
benthic zone
eutrophication

SECTION 2 **Marine Ecosystems**

OBJECTIVES

- Marine ecosystems are identified by the presence of salt water and include coastal wetlands, coral reefs, oceans, and polar ecosystems.

- Estuaries are among the most productive of ecosystems because they constantly receive fresh nutrients from a river and from an ocean. Estuaries provide habitat for a multitude of plants and animals.

- Coral reefs are susceptible to destruction because they must remain at tropical temperatures and they must receive a large amount of sunlight. Coral reefs provide habitat for approximately one-fourth of all marine species.

- Almost every person has an impact on aquatic ecosystems. Through understanding how we affect aquatic ecosystems, we can reduce the negative effects we have on them.

KEY TERMS

estuary
salt marsh
mangrove swamp
barrier island
coral reef

Reviewing Key Terms

Use each of the following terms in a separate sentence.

1. *wetland*
2. *mangrove swamp*
3. *estuary*
4. *eutrophication*
5. *benthos*

For each pair of terms, explain how the meanings of the terms differ.

6. *littoral zone* and *benthic zone*
7. *plankton* and *nekton*
8. *salt marsh* and *barrier island*
9. *wetland* and *coral reef*
10. **Concept Map** Use the following terms to create a concept map: *lakes, estuaries, aquatic ecosystems, coral reefs, freshwater wetlands, freshwater ecosystems, rivers, oceans, marshes, marine ecosystems, swamps, coastal ecosystems,* and *mangrove swamps.*

Reviewing Main Ideas

11. Wetlands are most important to fisheries in the United States because
    a. wetlands are the easiest place to catch fish.
    b. wetlands are the breeding grounds for insects that are eaten by fish.
    c. wetlands provide the most desirable species of fish.
    d. many of the fish caught each year use wetlands for feeding and spawning.

12. Animals that live in estuaries
    a. tend to produce few offspring.
    b. are usually found in unpolluted environments.
    c. must be adapted to varying levels of salinity.
    d. are adapted to cold-water conditions.

13. Bacteria can kill organisms in eutrophic lakes by
    a. feeding on decaying plants and animals.
    b. reducing oxygen dissolved in the water.
    c. Both (a) and (b)
    d. Neither (a) nor (b)

14. Arctic ecosystems are considered marine ecosystems because
    a. arctic ecosystems contain an enormous amount of frozen sea water.
    b. arctic ecosystems are inhabited by few organisms.
    c. sunlight is limited.
    d. phytoplankton form the basis of arctic food webs.

15. Which of the following statements does *not* describe a function of wetlands?
    a. Wetlands buffer shorelines against erosion.
    b. Wetlands provide spawning grounds for commercially important fish and shellfish.
    c. Wetlands filter pollutants.
    d. Wetlands make good hazardous waste dumpsites.

16. Tiny animals, called *coral polyps*, that secrete limestone create
    a. barrier islands.
    b. coral reefs.
    c. swamps.
    d. salt marshes.

17. Mangrove trees grow
    a. along riverbanks.
    b. in freshwater wetlands.
    c. in tropical areas and in subtropical areas.
    d. in the benthic zones of lakes.

18. The Florida Everglades
    a. is the largest freshwater marsh in the United States.
    b. protects threatened and endangered wildlife.
    c. provides habitat for migratory birds.
    d. All of the above

19. Which of the following actions is an example of how humans affect wetlands?
    a. draining a wetland to create farmland
    b. clearing a wetland to build a housing development
    c. using a wetland as a landfill
    d. All of the above

Short Answer

20. How does the phrase "the best of both worlds" relate to an estuary?

21. Explain the difference between the types of organisms that make up these classes: plankton, nekton, and benthos.

22. List three functions of wetlands.

23. Describe what happens when a lake is considered to be eutrophic.

24. What type of vegetation dominates mangrove swamps?

Interpreting Graphics

The pie graph below shows the percentage of coral reefs at risk in the world. Use the pie graph to answer questions 25–27.

25. Compute What percentage of coral reefs are still living?

26. Calculate If there is a total of 255,300 km² of coral reefs in the world, how many square kilometers of coral reefs are at a high risk of being destroyed?

27. Determine How many square kilometers of coral reefs are at a medium risk of being destroyed? Assume there is a total of 255,300 km² coral reefs in the world.

Status of the World's Coral Reefs

high risk 24%
destroyed 20%
medium risk 26%
low risk 30%

Source: Global Coral Reef Monitoring Network

Critical Thinking

28. Analyzing Relationships Write a short paragraph that explains the relationship between the speed of a river and the oxygen content of a river.

29. Determining Cause and Effect Explain what may happen if the use of fertilizer on farms and lawns around an estuary is not controlled.

30. Making Comparisons Read the paragraph under the heading "Threats to Estuaries" in this chapter. How do these threats compare with those described under the heading "Threats to the Oceans?"

31. Analyzing Relationships Explain why planting trees along a riverbank might benefit a river ecosystem.

32. Demography Six out of 10 of the largest urban areas were built on estuaries. Three of these cities are Tokyo, New York, and Rio de Janeiro. Research the population of each of these cities, and predict what may happen if population numbers continue to increase.

33 Research a Local Aquatic Ecosystem Observe an aquatic ecosystem near your school or home. This ecosystem can be as simple as a pond or stream or as complex as a lake or estuary. Observe the color of the water and the types of plants and animals. Record any interactions among the organisms that you observe. When you have recorded all of your data and observations, write a one-page report on the aquatic ecosystem.

Analyzing Data

Use the graph below to answer questions 34–35.

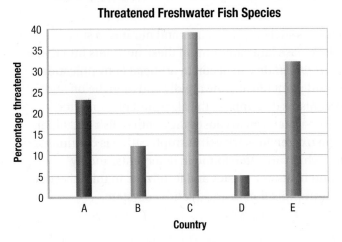

Threatened Freshwater Fish Species

34. **Analyzing Data** The graph above illustrates the percentage of freshwater fish species that are threatened in specific countries. What percentage of freshwater fish species are threatened in country B? in country D?

35. **Evaluating Data** If the number of freshwater fish species in country C totals 599 different species, how many of these species are threatened?

Making Connections

36. **Communicating Main Ideas** What effect does overfishing have on estuaries? What effect does overfishing have on oceans?

37. **Writing from Research** Research endangered marine mammals of ocean and polar ecosystems. Write a one-page report on the factors that have caused these mammals to become endangered.

CASESTUDY

38. After reading the passage, explain how estuaries show characteristics and wildlife of both freshwater and marine ecosystems.

39. Describe two environmental conditions that threaten the existence of aquatic organisms.

Why It Matters

40. Describe the ways in which humans impact aquatic ecosystems.

STUDYSKILL

Graph Skills Taking the following steps when reading a graph will help you correctly interpret the information. Be sure to read the title so that you understand what the graph represents. If the graph has axes, read the titles of both the x- and the y-axis. Examine the range of values on both the x- and the y-axis. Finally, examine the data on the graph, reading them from left to right, and put into words what you think the graph represents.

Eutrophication: Too Much of a Good Thing?

Objectives

Observe the effects of nitrates and phosphates on an aquatic ecosystem.

Compare the growth of organisms in different levels of nutrients.

Predict possible effects nitrates and phosphates would have on an aquatic ecosystem in your area.

Materials

distilled water

eyedropper

fertilizer, household use

fluorescent lamp

graduated cylinder

guide to pond life identification

jars or plastic soda bottles, 1 L (3)

microscope

microscope slides with coverslips

permanent marker

plastic wrap

pond water that contains viable organisms

stirring rod

Plants depend on nutrients such as phosphates and nitrates to survive. However, when people release large amounts of these nutrients into rivers and lakes, *artificial eutrophication* can occur. In artificial eutrophication, nutrients cause algae and plant life to grow rapidly and then die off and decay. When microorganisms decompose the algae and plant matter, they use up oxygen in the water, which causes the death of fish and other animals that depend on oxygen for survival. Eutrophication is commonly caused by phosphates, which are often found in detergents, and by nitrates, which are found in animal wastes and fertilizers. In this lab, you will observe artificial eutrophication in an aquatic ecosystem.

Procedure

1. Working with your team, use a marker to label one of your three bottles (or jars) as your "Control," a second bottle "Fertilizer," and a third bottle "Excess fertilizer."

2. Put 750 mL of distilled water in each of the three bottles. Read the label on the fertilizer container to determine the recommended dilution of fertilizer for watering plants. To the "Fertilizer" bottle, add the amount of fertilizer recommended for a quart of water. To the "Excess fertilizer" bottle, add 10 times this amount of fertilizer. Stir the contents of each bottle thoroughly to dissolve the fertilizer.

3. Obtain a sample of pond water. Stir it gently but thoroughly to ensure that the organisms in it are evenly distributed. Measure 100 mL of pond water into each of the three bottles.

4. Cover each bottle loosely with plastic wrap. Place all three bottles about 20 cm from a fluorescent lamp. (Do not place the bottles in direct sunlight, as this may cause them to heat up too much.)

5. Observe a drop of pond water from your sample, under the microscope. On a sheet of paper, draw at least four different organisms that you see. Determine whether the organisms are algae (usually green) or consumers (usually able to move). Describe the total number and type of organisms that you see.

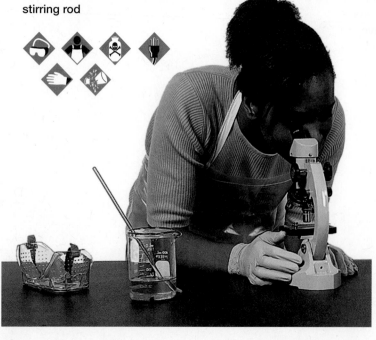

Step 5 Observe a drop of pond water under the microscope.

6. Based on what you have learned about eutrophication, make a prediction about how the pond organisms will grow in each of the three bottles.

7. Observe the bottles when you first set them up and at least once every three days for the next 3 weeks. Make a data table to record the date, color, odor, and any other observations you make for each bottle.

8. When life-forms begin to be visible in the bottles (probably after a week), use an eyedropper to remove a sample of organisms from each bottle and observe the sample under the microscope. Record your observations.

9. At the end of your 3-week observation period, again remove a sample from each bottle and observe it under the microscope. Draw at least four of the most abundant organisms that you see, and describe how the number and type of organisms have changed.

Step 7 Record your observations of the bottles every 3 days for 3 weeks.

Analysis

1. **Describing Events** After three weeks, which bottle shows the most abundant growth of algae? What may have caused this growth?

2. **Analyzing Data** Did you observe any effects on organisms other than algae in the bottle that had the most abundant algae growth? Explain.

Conclusions

3. **Applying Conclusions** Did your observations match your predictions? Explain.

4. **Drawing Conclusions** How can artificial eutrophication be prevented in natural water bodies?

Extension

5. **Designing Experiments** Modify the experiment by using household dishwashing detergent instead of household fertilizer. Are the results different?

6. **Research and Communications** Research the watersheds that are located close to your area. How might activities such as farming and building affect watersheds?

ECOZINE
HMDScience.com

Go online for more information about
these feature articles in the unit:

©Prisma/SuperStock

Populations

This school of young striped eel catfish gathers into a huge, writhing ball to defend against predators. Forming a ball makes the fish look like one large organism, and the fish's stripes may make it hard for a predator to see individual fish.

Chapter 8

Understanding Populations

Section 1
How Populations Change in Size

Section 2
How Species Interact with Each Other

Why It Matters

Killer whales hunt and eat sea lions. Would a change in the numbers of sea lions have an effect on the killer whales?

CASESTUDY

Learn more about the relationships between predators and their prey in the case study Predator-Prey Adaptations on pages 206–207.

ONLINE ENVIRONMENTAL SCIENCE
HMDScience.com

Go online to access additional resources, including labs, worksheets, multimedia, and resources in Spanish.

©Still Pictures

How Populations Change in Size

Two hundred years ago, no quagga mussels inhabited Lake Michigan, and blue whales numbered 275,000 in our oceans. Today, nearly a billion quagga mussels disrupt the ecology of Lake Michigan, and blue whale numbers are barely recovering from a low of 2,000 individuals reached under the pressure of whaling. These are opposite extremes of environmental problems expressed at the level of populations, where the balance between births and deaths can lead either to stability or major changes.

▶ Describe the three main properties of a population.

▶ Describe exponential population growth.

▶ Describe how the reproductive behavior of individuals can affect the growth rate of their population.

▶ Explain how population sizes in nature are regulated.

What Is a Population?

A **population** is the set of individuals within a species living in the same place at the same time. All the bass in an Iowa lake make up one population. **Figure 1.1** shows other examples of a population and part of a population. The adults within a population form a reproductive group because, by definition, organisms breed with members of their own population. For example, bass in one lake will breed with each other and will not breed with bass from other lakes.

Key Terms
population
density
dispersion
growth rate
reproductive potential
exponential growth
carrying capacity

FIGURE 1.1

Populations All the palm trees on an island is a population, and a school of fish in a body of water is part of a population.

(r) ©Paul & Paveena Mckenzie/Oxford Scientific/Getty Images; (l) ©Sylvain Sonnet/Photographer's Choice/Getty Images

FIGURE 1.2

Population Density Populations may have very different sizes, densities, and dispersions. Flamingos (right) are usually found in huge, dense flocks, whereas most snakes (left) are solitary and are dispersed randomly.

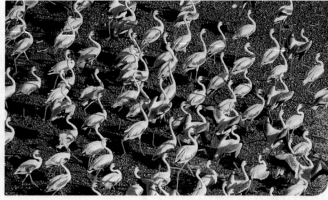

Properties of Populations

Populations may be described in terms of size, density, and dispersion, as shown in **Figure 1.2**. Population size is the total number of individuals, whereas **density** is the number of individuals per unit area or volume, such as the number of bass per cubic meter of water in a lake. A population's **dispersion** describes the arrangement of its individuals in space. A population's dispersion may be *even, clumped,* or *random*.

How Does a Population Grow?

A population gains individuals with each new offspring or birth and loses them with each death. The resulting population change over time can be represented by the equation below. The percentage change in the size of a population over a given period of time is that population's **growth rate.** The growth rate is the *birth rate* minus the *death rate*.

Over time, the growth rate of a population changes because birth rates and death rates increase or decrease. "Growth" rates can be positive, negative, or zero. For a population's growth rate to be zero, the average number of births must equal the average number of deaths. A population would remain the same size if each pair of adults produced exactly two offspring, and each of those offspring survived to reproduce. If the adults in a population are not replaced by new births, the growth rate will be negative and the population will decrease.

(tr) ©Norman Tomalin/Bruce Coleman, Inc./Photoshot; (l) ©Design Pics/Jack Goldfarb/Getty Images

---

How Fast Can a Population Grow?

A female sea turtle may lay 2,000 eggs in her lifetime. **Figure 1.3** shows newly hatched sea turtles leaving their nests for the ocean. If all of them survived, the turtle population would grow rapidly. But many young turtles are eaten by crabs or fish, and others starve. All populations experience deaths, but death rates can differ among species and populations. To understand the fastest hypothetical growth rate, scientists first consider what might happen when death rates are very low.

Reproductive Potential

A species' *biotic potential* is the fastest rate at which its populations can grow. This rate is limited by the maximum number of offspring that each member of the population can produce, which is called its **reproductive potential.** Some species have much higher reproductive potentials than others. A bacterium can produce 19 million descendants in a few days or weeks. A pair of bowhead whales would take hundreds of years to leave that many descendants!

Reproductive potential is higher when individuals produce more offspring at one time, reproduce more often, and reproduce earlier in life. Reproducing earlier in life has the greatest effect on reproductive potential. Reproducing early shortens the *generation time,* the average time it takes a member of the population to reach the age when it reproduces.

Small organisms, such as bacteria, have short generation times. Some bacteria can reproduce when they are only twenty minutes old. As a result, their populations can grow quickly. In contrast, large organisms, such as elephants and humans, become sexually mature only after a number of years. The human generation time is about 20 years, so humans have a much lower reproductive potential than bacteria.

Exponential Growth

Populations sometimes undergo **exponential growth,** which means they grow faster and faster. For example, if a pair of dogs gives birth to 6 puppies, there will be 6 dogs in one generation. If each dog in that generation mates and has a litter of 6 puppies, there will be 36 dogs in the next generation. The following generation will contain 216 dogs, and so on. If the number of dogs is plotted on a graph versus time, the graph will have the shape shown in **Figure 1.4.**

Exponential growth occurs in nature only when populations have plenty of food and space, and have little or no competition or predators. For example, populations of quagga mussels imported into the United States initially underwent exponential growth. Similar population explosions occur when bacteria or mold grow on a new source of food.

FIGURE 1.3

Reproductive Potential Most organisms have a reproductive potential that far exceeds the number of their offspring that will survive. Very few of these baby sea turtles will survive long enough to breed.

FIGURE 1.4

Population Growth Population growth is graphed by plotting population size over a period of time. Exponential population growth will look like the curve shown here.

✔ **CRITICAL THINKING**

Explain Under what conditions does exponential population growth take place?

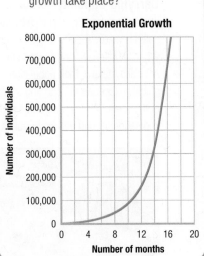

Carrying Capacity of Islands

Islands are good places to study carrying capacity because islands have clear boundaries. The Pribilof Islands off the coast of Alaska were the site of a well-studied population explosion and crash. In 1911, 25 reindeer were introduced on one of the islands. By 1938, the herd had grown to 2,000 animals. The reindeer ate mostly lichens, which grow back very slowly. By 1950, there were only 8 reindeer alive on the island.

What Limits Population Growth?

Because natural conditions are neither ideal nor constant, populations cannot grow forever and rarely grow at their reproductive potential. Eventually, resources are used up or the environment changes, and deaths increase or births decrease. Under the forces of natural selection in a given environment, only some members of any population will survive and reproduce. Thus, the properties of a population tend to change over time.

Carrying Capacity

The blue line in **Figure 1.5** represents a population that seems to approach a particular size over time. This theoretical limit, the dashed yellow line, is called carrying capacity. At high densities, populations move toward lower birth rates or higher death rates (this is called *density dependence*). **Carrying capacity** is the population size where birth rates and death rates are equal. Another definition of carrying capacity for a particular species is the maximum population that its ecosystem can support indefinitely.

A population may increase beyond its carrying capacity, but it cannot stay at an increased size for long. If a population is larger than the carrying capacity, it may use up its resources, and fewer individuals will survive to reproduce. Carrying capacity is difficult to predict or calculate. However, it can be estimated by looking at average population sizes or by observing a population crash after a certain size has been exceeded.

The history of rabbits in Australia demonstrates both exponential growth and carrying capacity. Originally, there were no rabbits in the native ecosystems of Australia. When rabbits were introduced there in 1859, their numbers increased rapidly because they had plenty of vegetation to eat, no competition, and no predators. But eventually, disease and starvation caused the rabbit population to crash. Over time, the vegetation recovered, and the rabbit population increased again.

FIGURE 1.5

Carrying Capacity An example of carrying capacity is shown by the dashed yellow line in the graph (right). When rabbits were introduced into Australia (below), their population quickly exceeded the carrying capacity of the area. Rabbits have eaten all the vegetation around this water hole.

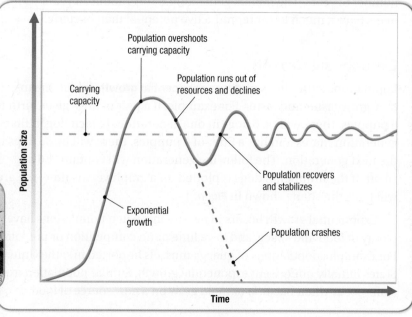

Population overshoots carrying capacity

Population runs out of resources and declines

Carrying capacity

Population size

Population recovers and stabilizes

Exponential growth

Population crashes

Time

©Bettmann/Corbis

FIGURE 1.6

Competition Members of a population often compete with each other. These plants (below) are growing over each other as they compete for light. These wolves (right) are competing for food and for social dominance.

Resource Limits

A species reaches its carrying capacity when it consumes a particular natural resource at the same rate at which the ecosystem produces the resource. That natural resource is then called a *limiting resource* for the species in that area. For example, plant growth is limited by supplies of water, sunlight, and mineral nutrients. The supply of the most severely limited resources determines the carrying capacity of an environment for a particular species at a particular time.

Competition Within a Population

The members of a population tend to use the same resources in the same ways, so they will eventually compete with one another as the population approaches its carrying capacity. An example is mealworm larvae in a sack of flour. Adults of this beetle will lay their eggs in a sack of flour, and leave. Most of the first larvae to hatch will have plenty of flour to eat and will grow to adulthood. However, the sack has a limited amount of food, and mealworms from eggs that were laid later may not have enough food to survive to adulthood.

Instead of competing directly for a limiting resource, members of a species may compete indirectly for a resource by competing for social dominance or for a territory. A *territory* is an area defended by one or more individuals against other individuals. The territory is of value not only for the space but also for the shelter, food, or breeding sites it contains. Many organisms expend a large amount of time and energy competing with members of the same species. Some examples of competition within species are shown in **Figure 1.6.**

Connect to MATH

Growth Rate

A growth rate is a change in a population's size over a specific period of time.

$$\text{growth rate} = \frac{\text{change in population}}{\text{time}}$$

Imagine a starting population of 100 individuals. If there were 10 births and 5 deaths in a given year, what was the population's growth rate for the year? In the next year, if there were 20 births and 10 deaths, what would the new growth rate be? If births increased by 10 and deaths increased by 5 for each of the next 5 years, how would you describe the growth of this population?

✓ CHECK FOR UNDERSTANDING

Describe Describe one example of competition among members of a population.

FIGURE 1.7

Density-Dependent Change
The way a disease spreads through a population is affected by the population's density. These pine trees have been infected by a disease carried by the southern pine beetle. This disease has spread rapidly through timber forests in the United States.

FIGURE 1.8

Density-Independent Change
Weather events usually affect every individual in a similar way, so such events are considered density-independent regulation.

Patterns of Population Change

Rates of birth or death in a population may be *density dependent* or *density independent*. Density-dependent deaths occur more quickly in a crowded population than in a sparse population. Limited resources, predation, and disease often result in higher rates of death in dense populations than in sparse populations. The pine trees in **Figure 1.7** are infected with a disease that is spreading in a density-dependent pattern. Many of the same kind of pine tree are growing close to each other, so a disease-carrying beetle easily spreads the disease from one tree to another.

When a cause of death is density independent, a certain proportion of a population dies regardless of the population's density. This type of regulation affects all members of a population in a general or uniform way. Severe weather and natural disasters are often density-independent causes of death. The winter storm shown in **Figure 1.8** froze crops and fruiting trees regardless of the density of plants in the area. Populations can show alternating periods of exponential growth and population crashes with density-independent death rates. Many species of animals in unpredictable environments show this pattern of population change.

 Section 1 **Formative Assessment**

▶ Reviewing Main Ideas

1. **Compare** two populations in terms of size, density, and dispersion. Choose any populations you know of.

2. **Describe** exponential population growth.

3. **Describe** three methods by which the reproductive behavior of individuals can affect the growth rate of a population.

4. **Explain** how population sizes in nature are regulated.

✓ Critical Thinking

5. **Making Predictions** How accurately do you think the future size of a population can be predicted? What information might be needed to make a prediction?

6. **Compare and Contrast** Read the description of the populations of rabbits in Australia and reindeer in the Pribilof Islands. List the similarities and differences between these two histories.

How Species Interact with Each Other

Objectives

- Explain the difference between niche and habitat.

- Give examples of parts of a niche.

- Describe the five major types of interactions between species.

- Explain the difference between parasitism and predation.

- Explain how symbiotic relationships may evolve.

Organisms in the wild interact with many different species. For example, in the African savanna, lions hunt zebras, fight with hyenas, and are fed upon by fleas and ticks. Negative interactions between species, like competition and predation, aren't the only type of interactions. Sometimes different species help each other. For example, cleaner fish remove parasites from fish living on coral reefs.

An Organism's Niche

Many ecologists are interested in understanding species' role in ecosystems and requirements for survival. To do this they measure a species' niche. There are several ways to define a niche. A **niche** (NICH) can be the range of conditions in which a species can survive. For example, a plant may only be able to survive in a particular range of temperatures, with a certain amount of rainfall, and with access to enough nutrients.

Other scientists are interested in the ecological role of a species. These scientists define a species' niche by the resources they use, or the species they feed on. For example, zebras are large herbivores on African grasslands. Kangaroos occupy a similar niche in Australia. Herbivores often interact with carnivores, like lions, if they both exist in the same habitat. Some parts of a lion's niche are shown in **Figure 2.1**. A niche is different from a *habitat*. An organism's habitat is a location. However, an organism's pattern of use of its habitat is part of its niche.

Key Terms

niche
competition
predation
parasitism
mutualism
commensalism
symbiosis

FIGURE 2.1

A Lion's Niche Parts of a lion's niche are shown here. Can you think of other parts?

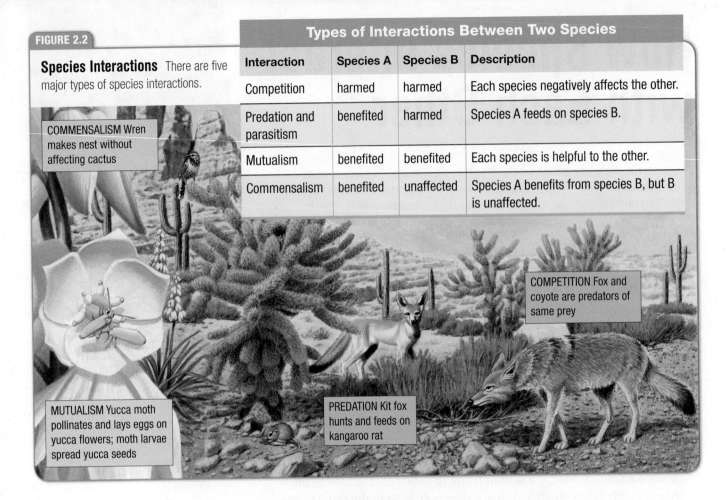

FIGURE 2.2

Species Interactions There are five major types of species interactions.

Types of Interactions Between Two Species

Interaction	Species A	Species B	Description
Competition	harmed	harmed	Each species negatively affects the other.
Predation and parasitism	benefited	harmed	Species A feeds on species B.
Mutualism	benefited	benefited	Each species is helpful to the other.
Commensalism	benefited	unaffected	Species A benefits from species B, but B is unaffected.

COMMENSALISM Wren makes nest without affecting cactus

COMPETITION Fox and coyote are predators of same prey

MUTUALISM Yucca moth pollinates and lays eggs on yucca flowers; moth larvae spread yucca seeds

PREDATION Kit fox hunts and feeds on kangaroo rat

✓ CHECK FOR UNDERSTANDING

Identify What determines how a species interaction is categorized?

FIELDSTUDY

Go to Appendix B to find the field study **Observing Competition**.

Ways in Which Species Interact

The five major types of species interactions, summarized in **Figure 2.2,** are competition, predation, parasitism, mutualism, and commensalism. These categories are based on whether each species causes benefit or harm to the other species in a given relationship. Not all interactions occur directly. For example, a tiger shark may cause sea turtles to not use certain areas. Seagrasses in these areas are not grazed as heavily. Tiger sharks have a positive indirect interaction with the seagrass!

Competition

For most organisms, competition is part of daily life. Seed-eating birds compete with each other for seeds under a bush, and the bush competes with the tree next to it for nutrients in the soil. **Competition** is a relationship in which different individuals or populations attempt to use the same limited resource. Each individual has less access to the resource and is harmed by the competition.

Competition can occur both within and between species. Members of the same species compete with each other because they require the same resources—they occupy the same niche. When members of different species have niches that *overlap* they may compete for some resources. If two species have requirements that are too similar, one species may eliminate the other from a habitat. This is called *competitive exclusion*.

Types of Competition

Species may compete in different ways. Sometimes, individuals try to get as many resources as they can but do not fight over resources or get in each other's way. In this type of scramble competition, the winner is the individual or species that gets the most resources the fastest. Some examples of scramble competition are fish feeding on plankton or sea turtles and sea cows feeding on seagrass. In interference competition, individuals fight over resources or get in each others' way when feeding. For example, lions will steal kills from wild dogs and hyenas.

Adaptations to Competition

If two species have identical resource needs in the same ecosystem, the more successful species might drive out the less successful species. The individuals that do best and leave the most offspring will be those that either feed on slightly different resources or use resources in different ways.

One way competition can be reduced between species is by dividing up the niche. *Niche restriction* occurs when each species uses less of the niche than it is capable of using. Niche restriction is observed in closely related species that use the same limited resources within a habitat. For example, two similar barnacle species compete for space in the intertidal zone of rocky shorelines. One of the species, *Chthamalus stellatus*, is found only in the upper level of the zone when the other species is present. But when the other species is removed from the area, *C. stellatus* is found at deeper levels, as shown in **Figure 2.3.** In the presence of competition, the actual niche used by a species may be smaller than the potential niche. Ecologists have observed various other ways of dividing up a niche among groups of similar species.

Virtual INVESTIGATION
HMDScience.com

Populations and Communities

FIGURE 2.3

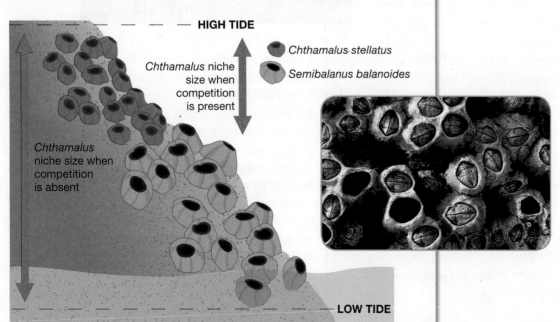

Niche Restriction The barnacle species *Chthamalus stellatus* uses less of its potential niche when competing for space with a similar barnacle species, *Semibalanus balanoides.*

HIGH TIDE

Chthamalus niche size when competition is present

● *Chthamalus stellatus*
◒ *Semibalanus balanoides*

Chthamalus niche size when competition is absent

LOW TIDE

FIGURE 2.4

Predation This predatory bird had to outrun its prey. Many organisms are adapted to avoid predation.

Predation

An organism that feeds on another organism is called a *predator*, and the organism that is fed upon is the *prey*. This kind of interaction is called **predation.** Examples of predation include sharks eating fish, bats eating insects, or wolves eating deer. **Figure 2.4** shows a predatory bird with its captured prey.

Predators come in many shapes and sizes. Tiny spiders, lizards, lions, and blue whales are all predators. Some predators eat only specific types of prey. For example, the Canadian lynx feeds mostly on snowshoe hares during the winter. In this kind of close relationship, the sizes of each population tend to increase and decrease in linked patterns, as shown in **Figure 2.5.** Other predators will feed on many types of prey or switch between different types of prey.

Most predators are themselves prey of other predators. For example, lizards are predators of insects, but are prey of hawks. Because almost all species (including blue whales) have predators, most organisms have evolved some mechanisms to avoid or defend against predators.

CASESTUDY

Predator-Prey Adaptations

Understanding predator-prey interactions is very important for predicting how ecosystems will respond to human activities or environmental changes. Most organisms, including blue whales, are at risk from predators. That means there is strong selective pressure for adaptations that help them stay safe. Some adaptations are physical features of prey. Some are behaviors that help them avoid running into predators or get away when they have been spotted. But predators also have physical features and behaviors that help them catch their prey.

Many animals are camouflaged—disguised so that they are hard to see. An animal's camouflage usually disguises its recognizable features. Most camouflage helps the animal blend into its surroundings. Many predators are camouflaged too. Wobbegong sharks look like a piece of coral and lunge off the bottom at fish that don't recognize them. Lions blend into the grasslands where they hunt so they can sneak up on their prey.

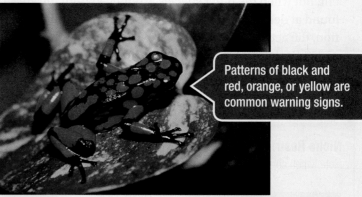

Patterns of black and red, orange, or yellow are common warning signs.

Some prey animals contain toxic chemicals that harm or deter predators. Many animals that have chemical defenses have a striking coloration. This warning coloration alerts potential predators to stay away. Patterns with black stripes and red, orange, or yellow are common in many species of bees, wasps, skunks, snakes, and poisonous frogs. Warning coloration works well against predators that can learn and that have good vision.

During the course of evolution, members of several well-protected species have come to resemble each other. For example, both bees and wasps often have black and yellow stripes. This is an example of mimicry of one species by another. The advantage of mimicry is that the more individual organisms that have the same pattern, the less

FIGURE 2.5

Predator-Prey Populations

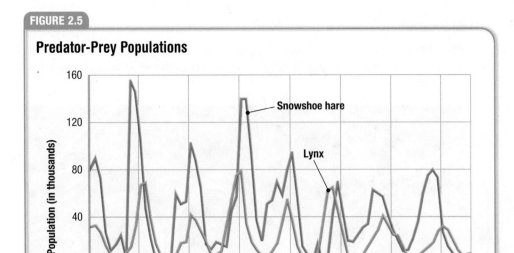

Populations of predators depend on populations of prey, so changes in one of these populations may be linked to changes in the other. This graph shows population estimates over time for Canadian lynx and their favorite food, snowshoe hares.

Both predators and prey may exhibit an adaptation such as camouflage or mimicry. The wobbegong (left) sits in wait for its prey. The protective quills of this porcupine (right) are a simple but effective way to repel predators.

chance any one individual has of being killed. Predators learn to avoid all animals that have similar warning patterns.

Occasionally, a harmless species is a mimic of a species that has chemical protection. You have probably tried to get away from insects that you thought were wasps or bees. In fact, some of them were probably flies. Several species of harmless insects have evolved to mimic wasps and bees. On the other hand, sometimes a predator may look like another, less threatening species. Some species of spiders may be mistaken for ants or other types of insects.

Other prey defenses include protective coverings. The quills of a porcupine, the spines of a cactus, and the shell of a turtle are all examples of protective covering. Some defenses, including spines of stingrays and horns of buffalo, are very dangerous for predators.

Anti-predator behaviors are an important way animals stay safe. Prey may form large groups, move away from dangerous habitats, use impressive escape behavior when attacked, or even attack a predator! To counter prey defenses, predators may work together to catch prey, carefully attack dangerous prey, or change how they hunt to be more successful.

Critical Thinking

1. **Making Comparisons** For each of these types of adaptations, give an additional example.
2. **Determining Cause and Effect** Write a paragraph to explain how one of these adaptations might have evolved.

(tr) ©SPL/Photo Researchers, Inc.; (tl) ©John Shaw/Bruce Coleman, Inc./Photoshot; (b) ©Carol Farneti-Foster/Oxford Scientific/Getty Images

FIGURE 2.6

Parasitism   Parasites such as ticks (left) and intestinal worms (right) could be harmful to you. People try to avoid these parasites, almost as if they were predators. In what ways are parasites like predators?

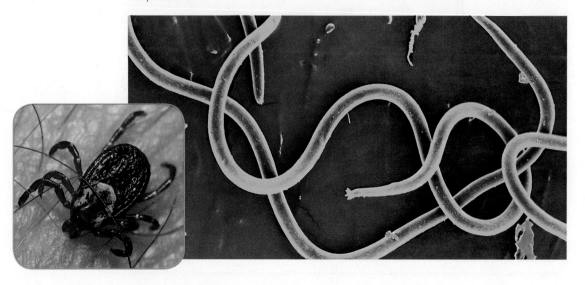

Parasitism

An organism that lives in or on another organism and feeds on it is a *parasite*. The organism the parasite takes its nourishment from is known as the host. The relationship between the parasite and its host is called **parasitism.** Examples of parasites are ticks, fleas, tapeworms, bloodsucking leeches, and mistletoe. Some photos of parasites are shown in **Figure 2.6.**

Unlike predators, parasites usually do not kill their hosts. Therefore, some people consider vampire bats to be parasites. In fact, a parasite can have an evolutionary advantage if it allows its host to live longer. However, the host is often weakened or exposed to disease by the parasite.

Mutualism

Many species depend on another species for survival. In some cases, neither organism can survive alone. A close relationship between two species in which each species provides a benefit to the other is called **mutualism.** Certain species of bacteria in your intestines form a mutualistic relationship with you. These bacteria help break down food that you could not otherwise digest or produce vitamins that your body cannot make. In return, you give the bacteria a warm, food-rich habitat.

Another case of mutualism happens in the bull-thorn acacia trees of Central America. Most acacia trees have spines that protect them against plant-eating animals, but the bull-thorn acacias have an additional protection—an ant species that lives only on these trees. The trees provide these ants shelter within hollow thorns. The trees also supply sugary nectar glands, shown in **Figure 2.7**, and nutrient-rich leaf tips. In turn, the ants defend the tree against herbivores.

FIGURE 2.7

Mutualism   These acacia trees in Central America have a mutualistic relationship with these ants. The trees provide food and shelter to the ants, and the ants defend the tree from herbivores.

✔ **CRITICAL THINKING**

Describe   Why is the relationship between ants and acacia trees categorized as mutualistic?

FIGURE 2.8

Commensalism Some orchids have a commensal relationship with certain species of trees. The orchid benefits from growing on the tree, because the orchid is exposed to more rain and sunlight than if it grew on the ground. The tree is not harmed or helped by the orchid.

Commensalism

A relationship in which one species benefits and the other species is neither harmed nor helped is called **commensalism.** An example is the relationship between certain orchids and trees, shown in **Figure 2.8**. The orchid grows around the tree's branches without harming the tree. The height exposes the orchid to rain and sunlight. Another example of commensalism is pilot fish swimming in front of a shark or sea turtle. The small fish get protection and access to food. The shark is not affected by the fish, and they are too small to bother eating.

Symbiosis and Coevolution

A relationship in which two species live in close association is called **symbiosis.** Many types of species interactions are considered symbiotic. In some cases a symbiotic relationship is parasitic. In some cases, it is commensalism or mutualism. For example, the symbiotic mutualism between corals and the small algae living inside them that make food for corals allows huge reefs to form!

Over time, species in close relationships may coevolve. These species may evolve adaptations in response to one another. For example, coevolution can be seen in the relationships of flowering plants and their pollinators. Many types of flowers seem to match the feeding habits of certain species of insects or other animals that spread pollen. Predators and prey also can coevolve, with prey evolving better ways to escape and predators evolving to be better hunters.

Connect to BIOLOGY

An Ecosystem in Your Body
Our health is affected by our relationships with microorganisms in our digestive system, skin, and other parts of our body. For example, live-culture yogurt is considered a healthy food because the kinds of bacteria it contains are beneficial to us. The bacteria assist our digestion of dairy products and also compete with other microorganisms, such as yeast, that might cause infections.

✔ Section 2 **Formative Assessment**

▶ Reviewing Main Ideas

1. **List** as many parts as you can of the niche of an organism of your choice.

2. **Give examples** of species that have the same habitat but not the same niche that a lion has.

3. **Describe** the five types of species interactions.

✔ Critical Thinking

4. **Making Comparisons** Read the definition of parasites and predators, and then explain how parasites differ from predators.

5. **Analyzing Relationships** Choose an example of mutualism, and then describe the long process by which the relationship could have evolved.

Conserving Top Predators

Successful reintroduction of wild wolves in the American West has led to significant changes in the ecosystem.

Return of Wolves

By the early 1900s wolves had been virtually eliminated from most of their native range in the United States. They were hunted vigorously because they killed livestock. In Yellowstone National Park, wolves were hunted to extinction.

When the wolves disappeared, populations of elk—a favorite food of wolves—began to increase. As early as the 1930s, environmental scientists were worried that elk overgrazing was harming the park.

In 1995, the first wolves were reintroduced into Yellowstone, and their populations have been increasing in the park and other areas of the American West. In Yellowstone, wolf populations grew to over 170 animals, but subsequently declined to around 100. The population decline appears to be partially due to decreases in populations of elk—the favorite food of wolves. Elk also changed their behavior to stay safer from wolves.

The return of wolves to Yellowstone has triggered other changes in the ecosystem. Plant communities changed in response to less grazing from elk. For example, willow trees near rivers have increased. Willow is a tree beavers need to survive the winter, so populations of beavers have increased. The beavers have changed streams and ponds, creating habitat for many other species.

Changes in ecosystems after the reintroduction of wolves have been so large that some scientists have suggested that predators should be reintroduced to more areas to improve ecosystem health.

Ocean Predators

While wolves are making a comeback on land, large predators in the ocean are in trouble. One example of ocean predators in trouble is sharks. Sharks are being overfished around the world, mainly to fill demand for shark fin soup. In many places,

The impact of tiger sharks on ocean ecosystems is a subject of study for the Shark Bay Ecosystem Research Project in Australia.

valuable fins are removed from the shark, and the rest of the body is thrown back into the sea. Tens of millions of sharks are killed each year. Unlike other fish, sharks take years before they can reproduce and they only have a few young each year. That means that they cannot survive heavy fishing. It is estimated that populations of sharks may have declined by more than 90% in some cases!

Should we worry about the disappearance of sharks? Recent studies say yes! Work in Western Australia by the Florida International University–led Shark Bay Ecosystem Research Project has shown that tiger sharks may be as important to ocean ecosystems as wolves are on land. By changing where and how marine herbivores like turtles and sea cows feed, tiger sharks protect seagrass. This seagrass is food and habitat for many species of fish and invertebrates, including many species people eat. Scientists also have found that having healthy shark populations is associated with healthy ecosystems in other parts of the world.

People also have found out that living sharks are more valuable than dead sharks. Not only do living sharks help keep ecosystems healthy, but scuba divers will travel from all over the world to see them in their natural habitat. If there are enough sharks, each one may be worth more than $1 million in tourism over its lifetime!

Some environmental scientists and conservation groups are now trying to convince governments that sharks should be protected and efforts be made to help their populations increase where they have been overfished. Good science and economics have caused some governments to listen.

In some places, trade in shark fins is now illegal. In others, including the USA, sharks must be brought to shore with their fins attached. That means that fewer sharks can be caught on a single fishing trip. Also, species that are most in trouble are now protected in many areas.

In other areas, shark sanctuaries have been created. Inside these sanctuaries, no sharks can be caught and killed. Palau created the first shark sanctuary in 2009. Since then, Honduras, The Bahamas, the Maldives, Tokelau, and the Republic of the Marshall Islands have set aside huge areas of ocean as shark sanctuaries.

Environmental scientists are now studying how ocean ecosystems respond to the protection of sharks. Perhaps the same benefits seen on land with the return of wolves will occur in the oceans.

This graph depicts the early-winter population of wolves in Yellowstone Park since reintroduction. The population has been impacted by many factors, including disease and decreases in the populations of elk (a favorite food).

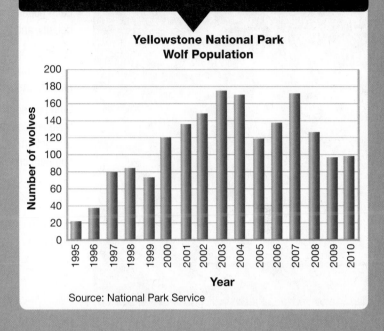

Source: National Park Service

Ongoing Challenges

Even though things are looking up for wolves in North America and sharks in some places of the world, there are still major challenges. Throughout most of the world, predators on land are still in trouble. They are being killed because they eat livestock and their habitat is being destroyed. In the oceans, species of large sharks and other marine predators that may be among the most important to ecosystems can swim for thousands of miles. That means they often leave even large sanctuaries and can be caught in fisheries. Environmental scientists are working hard to understand these challenges and to find solutions that balance having healthy populations and ecosystems with people's needs.

What Do You Think?

Some people argued that wolves should not be reintroduced to Yellowstone National Park. Although wolves were endangered in most of the United States, there were still many wolves in Alaska and in Canada. They also thought that wolves would kill livestock if their populations grew large. Do you think reintroducing wolves was a good idea? Why or why not?

SECTION 1 **How Populations Change in Size**

OBJECTIVES

- Each population has specific properties, including size, density, and pattern of dispersion.

- When a population has few limits on its growth, it may undergo exponential growth. This is the fastest possible growth rate of the population.

- When a population has few limits to its growth, it may have an exponential growth rate. Usually, population growth is limited by factors such as disease and competition.

- Carrying capacity is the maximum population a habitat can support over a long period of time.

- Populations may be subject to density-dependent regulation.

KEY TERMS

population
density
dispersion
growth rate
reproductive potential
exponential growth
carrying capacity

SECTION 2 **How Species Interact with Each Other**

OBJECTIVES

- The niche of an organism is its requirements for survival and/or its feeding relationships.

- Interactions between species are categorized based on the relative benefit or harm that one species causes the other. The categories are competition, predation, parasitism, mutualism, and commensalism.

- Competition between species occurs when their niches overlap. The competition may be direct or indirect.

- Pairs of species that have close relationships often evolve adaptations in response to one another.

KEY TERMS

niche
competition
predation
parasitism
mutualism
commensalism
symbiosis

Reviewing Key Terms

Use each of the following terms in a separate sentence.

1. *reproductive potential*
2. *carrying capacity*
3. *competition*
4. *symbiosis*

For each pair of terms, explain how the meanings of the terms differ.

5. *niche* and *habitat*
6. *predator* and *prey*
7. *predation* and *parasitism*
8. *mutualism* and *commensalism*
9. Use the following terms to create a concept map: *symbiosis, predation, predator, prey, parasitism, parasite, host, mutualism,* and *commensalism.*

Reviewing Main Ideas

10. In which of the following pairs do both organisms belong to the same population?
    a. a rose and a carnation
    b. a zebra and a horse
    c. two residents of New York City
    d. two similar species of monkeys

11. A population of some species is most likely to grow exponentially
    a. if the species is already very common in the area.
    b. when the species moves into a new area of suitable habitat.
    c. when it uses the same habitat as a similar species.
    d. if the population size is already large.

12. A population will most likely deplete the resources of its environment if the population
    a. grows beyond carrying capacity.
    b. must share resources with many other species.
    c. moves frequently from one habitat to another.
    d. has a low reproductive potential.

13. The growth rate of a population of geese will probably increase within a year if
    a. more birds die than are hatched.
    b. several females begin laying eggs at younger ages than their mothers did.
    c. most females lay two eggs instead of three during a nesting season.
    d. some birds get lost during migration.

14. Which of the following is an example of competition between species?
    a. two species of insects feeding on the same rare plant
    b. a bobcat hunting a mouse
    c. a lichen, which is an alga, and a fungus living as a single organism
    d. a tick living on a dog

15. Which of the following statements about parasitism is true?
    a. The presence of a parasite does not affect the host.
    b. Parasitism is a cooperative relationship between two species.
    c. Parasites always kill their hosts.
    d. Parasites benefit while their hosts are harmed.

16. Ants and acacia trees have a mutualistic relationship because
    a. they are both adapted to a humid climate.
    b. they are part of the same ecosystem.
    c. they benefit each other.
    d. the ants eat parts of the acacia tree.

17. Which of the following is an example of coevolution?
    a. flowers that can be pollinated by only one species of insect and insects adapted to use only that flower
    b. rabbits that invade a new habitat
    c. wolves that compete with each other for territory
    d. bacteria that suddenly mutate in a lab

Short Answer

18. A tapeworm lives in the intestines of a cow and feeds by absorbing food that the cow is digesting. What kind of relationship is this? Explain your answer.

19. Explain how two species can compete for the same resource even if they never come in contact with each other.

20. Snail kites are predatory birds that feed only on snails. The kites use their hooked, needlelike beaks to pull snails from their shells. Explain how these specialized beaks might have evolved in these birds.

21. What would happen to the population of snail kites mentioned in question 20 if the snails' habitat was destroyed? Explain your answer.

Interpreting Graphics

The graph below shows the population of some reindeer that were introduced to an Alaskan island in 1910. Use the graph to answer questions 22–24.

22. Describe this population's changes over time.

23. What might have happened in 1937?

24. Is it possible to estimate the island's carrying capacity for reindeer? Explain your answer.

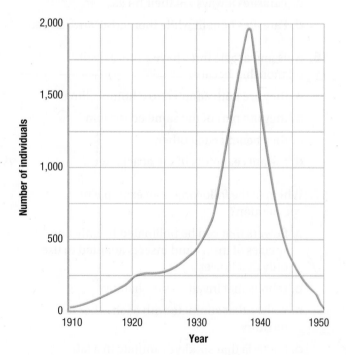

Critical Thinking

25. **Analyzing Relationships** Read the explanations of competition and predation. If one species becomes extinct, and then soon after, another species becomes extinct, was their relationship most likely competition or predation? Explain your answer.

26. **Evaluating Hypotheses** Scientists do not all agree on the specific carrying capacity of Earth for humans. Why might this carrying capacity be difficult to determine?

27. **Evaluating Conclusions** A scientist finds no evidence that any of the species in a particular community are competing and concludes that competition never played a role in the development of this community. Could this conclusion be valid? Write a paragraph to explain your answer.

28. **Health** Viruses are the cause of many infectious diseases, such as common colds, flu, and chickenpox. Viruses can be passed from one person to another in many different ways. Under what conditions do you think viral diseases will spread most rapidly between humans? What can be done to slow the spread of these viruses?

29. **Create a Habitat and Interaction Map** Create a visual representation of the habitat and interactions of an organism of your choice. Research the organism's habitat, behaviors, and interactions with other species. If possible, observe the organism (without disturbing it) for a day or more. Create a piece of art to show all of the interactions that this organism has with its environment.

Analyzing Data

Use the equation below to answer questions 30–31.

Change in population size = Births − Deaths

30. **Extending an Equation** The equation gives the change in a population over a given amount of time (for example, an increase of 100 individuals in one year). Use the two parts on the right side of the equation to write an inequality that would be true if the population were increasing. Rewrite the inequality for a decreasing population.

31. **Analyzing an Equation** Suppose you are studying the small town of Hill City, which had a population of 100 people in the first year of your study. One year later, 10 people have died, and only 9 mothers have given birth. Yet the population has increased to 101. How could this increase happen?

Making Connections

32. **Communicating Main Ideas** Why do population sizes not grow indefinitely?

33. **Creative Writing** Write a science fiction story about life without competition.

34. **Writing from Research** Find information in encyclopedias or natural history references about different kinds of mutualism. Summarize the similarities and differences between the various relationships. Focus on the ways in which each species benefits from the other species.

CASESTUDY

35. Both predators and prey use camouflage. Describe how they each use a similar adaptation in different ways.

36. Some adaptations of both predators and prey involve group behaviors. Describe an example of a prey animal using a group behavior. Also, describe an example of predators working together.

Why It Matters

37. Killer whales hunt and eat a variety of prey, not just sea lions. Research and describe three adaptations that make killer whales effective predators.

STUDYSKILL

Review with a Partner To review the main ideas of the text, try summarizing with a partner. Take turns reading a passage, and then try to summarize aloud what you have read. Try not to look back at the text. Then, discuss and review the text with your partner to check your understanding.

Calculating Generation Rate

Objectives

Experiment on organism competition.

Predict the effects of competition on number differences between competing populations.

Design an experiment to test the effects of competition on changing an environmental condition.

Materials

distilled water, boiled and cooled (stock)

microorganisms, *Blepharisma* (stock in glass bowl)

microorganisms, *Euplotes* (stock in glass bowl)

microscope, stereoscopic dissecting

micropipettes, Pasteur, glass, fine-tipped, fitted with rubber bulbs

plastic well plate, six-well with cover (3)

paper, graph (2)

water, bottled spring (stock)

wheat germ kernel

Organisms compete for resources as they interact with their environment. Resources include foods, open spaces, and hiding places. When organisms compete for resources, populations may be limited.

Many studies of competing organisms, including microorganisms, were performed. The studies' results were summarized into what is known as the *competitive exclusion principle.* This principle states that two species cannot coexist indefinitely on the same limited resource. Organisms that are more adaptive tend to grow and displace those that do not adapt as well to changing conditions.

The *generation rate,* or *generation number,* is the number of generations of an organism that have been produced during a specified amount of time. This can be calculated using the equation:

$$\text{Generation number (g)} = \frac{(\log B - \log A)}{\log 2}$$

Procedure

1. Label each well of a plastic well plate with the numbers 1 through 6. Fill each of the wells with 5 mL of bottled spring water. Add 0.5 mL of wheat germ kernel to each well.

2. Place one *Blepharisma* in each well. Place covers on each of the six wells and label the well plate "*Blepharisma* Only."

3. Repeat step 1 using a separate well plate. Place one *Euplotes* in each well. Place covers on each of the six wells and label this plate "*Euplotes* Only." Before beginning the experiment, make and record a hypothesis.

4. Count the number of cells per well daily for five days. Perform the count using a stereoscopic dissecting microscope. With some practice, you should be able to estimate the number of cells for each genus by scanning the contents of each well. Slow-moving ciliates such as *Blepharisma* are easy to count by eye. You can also use the micropipettes to do manual counts. Remove each organism as it is counted to another container while viewing through the stereoscopic dissecting microscope. When finished counting a well, be sure to return all organisms to the same well from which you removed them.

5. Record the results of the counts of step 4 in a table.

6. Repeat step 1 using a separate well plate. Place one individual cell of each of the two genera into each of wells 1 through 4.

7. Place two cells of the *Blepharisma* in well 5. This is a control population for the *Blepharisma.*

8. Place two cells of the *Euplotes* in well 6. This is the control population for the *Euplotes*.

9. Place covers on each of the six wells and label this culture dish "Mixed/Control."

10. Count the number of cells per well daily for five days. Follow the instructions of step 4 on how to perform a count. Construct data tables for each of the three plates. Each data table should record the counts for each well for five days. Record the results each day.

Analysis

1. Constructing Graphs Use a separate sheet of graph paper to plot growth curves for the *Blepharisma* populations. Place the title "*Blepharisma* Populations" at the top of the graph paper. Using data from your tables, plot the average number of *Blepharisma* you observe each day on the *y*-axis and the number of days on the *x*-axis. Label the curve "No competition." On this same graph, use the data from your tables to plot a curve of the average number of *Blepharisma* you observe each day in the mixed environments. Label this curve "Competition." On this same graph, use the data from your tables to plot a curve of the number of *Blepharisma* you observe each day in the control environment. Label this curve "Control." Use the data in your tables and another piece of graph paper to plot growth curves for *Euplotes* populations. All averages are to be calculated by adding the counts in each well for a given day and dividing by the number of wells.

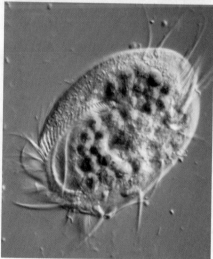

2. Organizing Data Calculate a generation rate for each of the six curves on your graphs. Show all calculations.

Conclusions

3. Drawing Conclusions Draw conclusions as to which organism will outcompete the other in the mixed environment. What do the generation rates for each of the six population curves suggest about this competition? How does this compare to your hypothesis?

Light microspcopy of *Blepharisma* (top) and *Euplotes* (bottom)

4. Making Predictions Imagine that you created a mixed environment starting with five times more of the organism with the lower generation rate. Do you think this would change the results of a competition? Explain.

Extension

5. Designing Experiments Design an experiment (objective, materials, and procedure) that tests the effect of a change in environmental conditions on the two microorganisms. Decide which condition you will change compared to the experiment you already performed. Make sure that you include unmixed, mixed, and control populations in your experiment.

Chapter 9

Section 1
Studying Human Populations

Section 2
Changing Population Trends

Why It Matters

China, with one of the world's largest populations, had a 70 percent increase in energy use from 2000–2005. This resulted in a corresponding rise in air pollution. During the same five-year period, 54 percent of the seven major rivers in China contained water unfit for human consumption.

How do population issues in China affect people elsewhere in the world?

CASESTUDY

Learn more about what Thailand is doing to solve their population issues in the case study Thailand's Population Challenges on page 228.

The Human Population

ONLINE ENVIRONMENTAL SCIENCE
HMDScience.com

Go online to access additional resources, including labs, worksheets, multimedia, and resources in Spanish.

©Syndicated Features Limited/The Image Works

Studying Human Populations

The human population of Earth grew faster in the 20th century than it ever has before. This rapid growth has led to environmental problems around the globe. We therefore must try to understand and predict changes in human populations.

Demography is the study of populations. For human populations, demographers study the processes that influence the populations of countries to make comparisons and predictions. These include human behavior, economics, and social structure. Countries have been grouped by demographers into two general categories, which define the ends of a continuum in patterns of development. *Developed* countries have higher average incomes, slower population growth, and diverse industrial economies. *Developing* countries have lower average incomes, simple agriculture-based economies, and rapid population growth.

The Human Population Over Time

After growing slowly for thousands of years, the industrial and scientific revolutions in the 1800s brought a period of *exponential growth*, meaning that population growth rates increased during each decade (**Figure 1.1**). This growth was mostly due to increases in food production and improvements in hygiene. However, it is unlikely that Earth can sustain this growth for much longer. Some scientists believe that we cannot indefinitely sustain the current world population at today's standards of living.

SECTION 1

Objectives

> Describe how the size and growth rate of the human population has changed in the last 200 years.

> Define four properties that scientists use to predict population sizes.

> Make predictions about population trends based on age structure.

> Describe the four stages of the demographic transition.

> Explain why different countries may be at different stages of the demographic transition.

Key Terms

demography
age structure
survivorship
fertility rate
migration
life expectancy
demographic transition

FIGURE 1.1

Exponential Growth Curve After growing slowly for thousands of years, the human population began to grow rapidly in the 1800s.

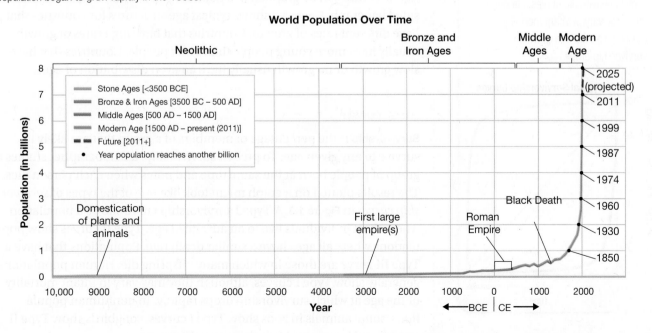

World Population Over Time

Legend:
- Stone Ages [<3500 BCE]
- Bronze & Iron Ages [3500 BC – 500 AD]
- Middle Ages [500 AD – 1500 AD]
- Modern Age [1500 AD – present (2011)]
- Future [2011+]
- Year population reaches another billion

FIGURE 1.2

Age-Structure Diagrams These graphs allow demographers to compare the distribution of ages and sexes in a population. Each graph shows a typical shape for a population with a particular rate of growth.

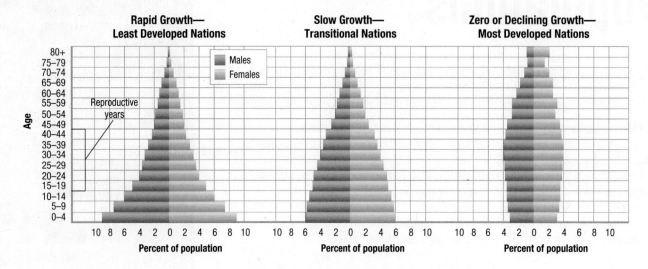

Forecasting Population Size

How will your community change in the next 20 years? Will it need more schools or more retirement centers? Will more people move in and create demand for more roads and utility services? Demographers look at many properties of populations to predict such changes.

Age Structure

Demographers can make many predictions based on **age structure**—the distribution of ages in a specific population at a certain time. For example, if a population has more young people than older people, the population size will likely increase as the young people grow up and have children. Age structure can be graphed in a *population pyramid*, a type of double-sided bar graph. **Figure 1.2** shows typical age structures for countries that have different rates of growth. Countries that have high rates of growth usually have more young people than older people. Countries that have slow growth or no growth usually have an even distribution of ages.

Survivorship

Survivorship is the percentage of members of a group that are likely to survive to any given age. To predict survivorship, a demographer studies a group of people born at the same time and notes when each person dies. The results plotted on a graph might look like one of the types of *survivorship curves* in **Figure 1.3**. A Type I survivorship curve shows a population where most individuals live to an advanced age. Type II curves show populations where all ages have a similar death rate. Populations that have a Type III curve are those in which many offspring die. Human populations generally show Type I curves, although they may vary in infant mortality or the age at which survivorship drops rapidly. In nonhuman populations, some animals in zoos show Type I curves, songbirds show Type II curves, and insects and fish show Type III curves.

FIGURE 1.3

Survivorship Curve Human populations in general tend to show Type I survivorship curves, although they may vary in infant mortality or the advanced age at which survivorship drops rapidly.

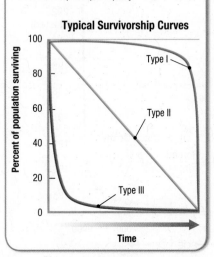

FIGURE 1.4

Fertility Rate The total fertility rate in the United States went through many changes from 1900 to 2000. The *baby boom* was a period of high fertility rates, and the *baby bust* was a period of decreasing fertility.

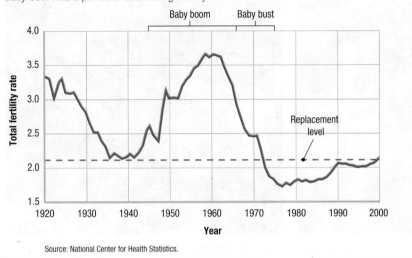

Source: National Center for Health Statistics.

Connect to MATH

Extending the Equation for Population Change

The following equation is a simple way to calculate the change in a population over a period of time:

$$\frac{change\ in}{population} = (births - deaths)$$

However, this equation does not account for changes due to migration. Rewrite the equation to include *immigration* and *emigration*.

Next, create an example word problem that would require the use of this new equation. Trade problems with a classmate, and try to solve the classmate's new word problem.

Fertility Rates

The number of babies born each year per 1,000 people in a population is called the *birthrate*. Demographers also calculate the **fertility rate**, or the average number of children a woman gives birth to in her lifetime.

A graph of historical fertility rates for the United States is shown in **Figure 1.4**. In 1972, the fertility rate dropped below replacement level for the first time in U.S. history. *Replacement level* is the average number of children two parents must have in order to "replace" themselves in the population. This number is about 2.1, or slightly more than 2, because not all children born will survive and reproduce.

Fertility rates in the United States remained below replacement level for most of the 1990s. However, due to births and immigration, the population continued to grow (**Figure 1.5.**) Fertility in the U.S. since 2000 has increased to around 2.06.

Migration

The movement of individuals from one area to another is **migration.** Movement into an area is *immigration* and movement out of an area is *emigration*. Migration between and within countries is a significant part of population change. If not for immigration, the populations of many developed countries might be decreasing.

✔ CHECK FOR UNDERSTANDING

Predict How can a population pyramid help demographers predict changes in a population over time?

FIGURE 1.5

U.S. Population Growth The population of the United States has continued to grow in the last half-century because of births as well as immigration.

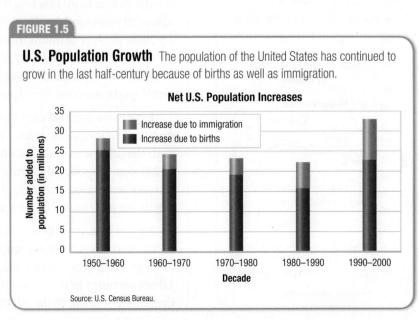

Source: U.S. Census Bureau.

FIGURE 1.6

Increasing Life Expectancy Preventive medicine, sanitation, and better nutrition have increased life expectancy in many parts of the world.

Declining Death Rates

The dramatic increase in Earth's human population in the last 200 years has happened because death rates have declined more rapidly than birth rates. Death rates have declined mainly because more people now have access to adequate food, clean water, and safe sewage disposal. The discovery of vaccines in the 18th century also contributed to declining death rates, especially among infants and children. These factors are illustrated in the images shown in **Figure 1.6**.

Life Expectancy

The average number of years members of a population are likely to live is their **life expectancy.** Life expectancy is most affected by *infant mortality*, the death rate of infants less than a year old. In 1900, life expectancy was about 30 years worldwide, and the infant mortality rate was very high. By 2000, the rate of infant mortality was less than one-third of the rate in 1900. The graph in **Figure 1.7** illustrates that average life expectancy has increased to more than 67 years worldwide. For people in a number of developed countries, life expectancy is 80 years or more.

Expensive medical care is not necessarily helpful in preventing infant deaths. The infant mortality rate differs greatly among countries. In fact, with the highest average income in the world, the U.S. ranks only 48 out of 221 countries for infant mortality. Infant health is affected more by the parents' access to education, food, fuel, and clean water. If these basic needs are met, most children will have a good chance of surviving.

Meanwhile, new threats to life expectancy arise as populations become more dense. Contagious diseases such as AIDS and tuberculosis are a growing concern in a world where such diseases can spread quickly. Life expectancy in many south African countries has decreased in recent decades as a result of the AIDS epidemic.

FIGURE 1.7

Average Life Expectancy Since 1900, average life expectancy has increased worldwide (red line), although it remains lower in less developed countries (blue and purple lines).

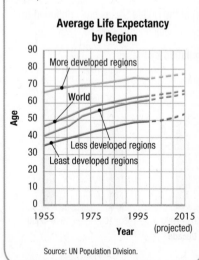

Average Life Expectancy by Region

More developed regions

World

Less developed regions

Least developed regions

Age

1955   1975   1995   2015 (projected)

Year

Source: UN Population Division.

The Demographic Transition

Populations in most developed countries are growing at fairly low rates. How can populations quadruple in one century, then stop growing or shrink in the next century? The **demographic transition** is a model that describes how economic and social changes affect population growth rates. The model is based on observations of the histories of developed countries. The graph in **Figure 1.8** compares trends in birth rates, death rates, and population sizes during the four stages of the transition.

Stages of the Transition

In the first stage of the demographic transition, a society is in a preindustrial condition. The birth rate and the death rate are both at high levels and the population size is stable. Most of the world was in this condition until about 1700, when the scientific and industrial revolutions began.

In the second stage, death rates decline as hygiene, nutrition, and education improve. But birth rates remain high, so the population grows very fast. In this stage, the population can double in less than 30 years.

In the third stage of the demographic transition, population growth slows because the birth rate decreases. As the birth rates and death rates grow closer, the population size stabilizes at a point that is higher than before the demographic transition. In most countries that have passed through the transition, the population quadrupled during the 1900s.

In the fourth stage, the birth rate drops below replacement level, so the size of the population begins to decrease. It has taken from one to three generations for the demographic transition to occur in most developed countries. Recent studies suggest that more stages may occur where birth rates rebound.

✔ **CHECK FOR UNDERSTANDING**
Interpret Which stage of the demographic transition is characterized by a high birth rate and a declining death rate?

FIGURE 1.8

Demographic Transition The four stages of the demographic transition are shown here from left to right. Note the changes in population size with changing birth and death rates. Do you think that all countries will fit this pattern?

✔ **CRITICAL THINKING**
Predict Do you think that all countries will fit this pattern?

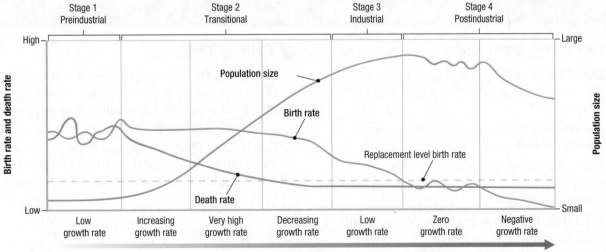

Connect to BIOLOGY

Female Influence

Females have the primary influence over reproductive rates in most species of animals, because they invest more energy in reproduction than males do. Females usually produce and lay eggs or carry the fetus and give birth, and care for the offspring. The time and resources a female invests in each successful offspring is usually greater than the energy a male must invest.

Women and Fertility

The factors most clearly related to a decline in birth rates are increasing education and economic independence for women. In the demographic transition model, the lower death rate of the second stage is usually the result of increased levels of education. Educated women find that they do not need to bear as many children to ensure that some will survive. Also, the women may learn family planning techniques. They are able to contribute to their family's increasing prosperity by working, while spending less energy bearing and caring for children. Some countries that want to reduce birth rates have placed a priority on the education of females, as shown in **Figure 1.9**.

Large families are valuable in communities in which children work or take care of older family members. But as countries modernize, parents are more likely to work away from home. If parents must pay for child care, children may become a financial burden rather than an asset. The elderly will not need the support of their children if pensions are available. All of these reasons contribute to lower birth rates. Today, the total fertility rate in developed countries is about 1.85 children per woman, while in developing countries, the rate is about 4.2 children per woman.

FIGURE 1.9

Educating Women These women in Bolivia are learning to read. Many countries include the education of women in development efforts.

©Sean Sprague/The Image Works

✔ **CRITICAL THINKING**

Explain why some countries might be reluctant to educate women, even though it might improve the overall quality of living for a country.

Section 1 **Formative Assessment**

▶ Reviewing Main Ideas

1. **Describe** how the size and growth rate of the human population has changed in the last 200 years.

2. **Define** four properties that scientists use to predict population sizes.

3. **Explain** what we can predict about a population's likely growth rates based on its current age structure.

4. **Describe** the four stages of the demographic transition.

✔ Critical Thinking

5. **Analyzing Relationships** Read the description of life expectancy in this section. Explain why the oldest people in a population may be much older than the average life expectancy.

6. **Evaluating Theories** Do you think that all countries will follow the pattern of the demographic transition? Explain your answer.

Changing Population Trends

Some countries have followed the model of the demographic transition—they have reached large and stable population sizes and have increased life expectancies. But in many parts of the world, populations continue to have high rates of growth, which creates environmental problems. A rapidly growing population uses resources at an increased rate and can overwhelm the infrastructure of a community. **Infrastructure** is the basic facilities and services that support a community, such as public water supplies, sewer lines, power plants, roads, schools, and hospitals. The symptoms of overwhelming population growth include suburban sprawl, overcrowded schools, polluted rivers, barren land, and inadequate housing, as shown in **Figure 2.1**.

Problems of Rapid Growth

People cannot live without sources of clean water, fuel, and land that can be used to acquire and produce food. A rapidly growing population can use resources faster than the environment can renew them, unless resources come from elsewhere. Standards of living decline in an area when wood is removed from local forests faster than it can grow back, or when wastes overwhelm local water sources. Vegetation, water, and land are the resources most critically affected by rapid population growth.

- Describe three problems caused by rapid human population growth.

- Compare population growth problems in more-developed countries and less-developed countries.

- Analyze strategies countries may use to reduce their population growth.

- Describe worldwide population projections into the next century.

Key Terms
infrastructure
arable land
urbanization
least developed countries

FIGURE 2.1

Resource Depletion Rapid population growth can put pressure on water sources, land, and materials used for fuel or shelter. The makeshift housing shown here is one consequence of unmanaged growth.

©Adrian Murrell/Stone/Getty Images

ECOFACT

Land Area per Person
If each person alive on Earth in the year 2000 was given an equal portion of existing surface land, each person would get about 0.025 km² (7.3 acres, or about four football fields), In the year 2050, each person might get 0.017 km² of land (4.2 acres, or about three football fields).

FIGURE 2.2

Fuelwood Gathering fuel is part of daily survival in many developing countries. If there is not enough wood to use for fuel, people may have to burn crop residue. This can lead to soil erosion and lower agricultural productivity.

A Shortage of Fuelwood

Women in Myanmar gathering firewood are shown in **Figure 2.2**. In many of the poorest countries, wood is the main fuel source. When populations are low, people can use fallen tree limbs for fuel, which does not harm the trees. When populations grow rapidly, deadwood does not accumulate fast enough to provide enough fuel. People begin to cut down living trees. Parts of Africa, Asia, and India have been cleared of vegetation by people collecting fuelwood.

A supply of fuel ensures that a person can boil water and cook food. In many parts of the world, water taken directly from wells or public supplies is not safe to drink because it carries parasites or diseases. The water can be sterilized by boiling it, but fuel is needed to do so. Also, food is often unsafe or harder to digest unless it is cooked. Without enough fuelwood, many people suffer from disease and malnutrition.

Unsafe Water

In places that lack infrastructure, the local water supply may be used not only for drinking and washing but also for sewage disposal. As a result, the water supply becomes a breeding ground for organisms that cause diseases such as dysentery, typhoid, and cholera.

Many cities have populations that are doubling every 15 years, and water systems cannot be expanded fast enough to keep up with this growth. In 2001, over 1 billion people worldwide lacked safe drinking water and more than 3 million died of diseases that were spread through water. The Rio Grande, shown in **Figure 2.3**, is one example of an unsafe water source used by many people.

FIGURE 2.3

Unsafe Water This woman is washing clothes in the Rio Grande on the U.S.-Mexico border. In areas that have no sewage or water treatment systems, people may use the same water supply for drinking, bathing, washing, and sewage disposal.

Lima, Peru, is another example of an area with unsafe water. More than half of the population of Lima is housed in slums or shantytowns that have no plumbing. The bacteria that cause cholera thrived in Lima's unmanaged water sources in 1991. In that year, Lima's population suffered the first cholera epidemic that had occurred in the Western Hemisphere in 75 years.

Impacts on Land

People prefer to live where they have easy access to resources. Growing populations may have a shortage of **arable land**, which is land that can be used to grow crops. Growing populations also make trade-offs between competing uses for land such as agriculture, housing, or natural habitats.

For example, Egypt's population of approximately 83 million is growing at 1.92 percent per year. For food and exportable products, Egypt depends on farming within the Nile River valley, shown in **Figure 2.4**. Most of the country is desert, and less than 4 percent of Egypt's land is arable. However, the Nile River valley is also where most Egyptians live. Egyptians continue to build housing on what was once farmland, which reduces the amount of land Egypt has available for agricultural purposes.

Much of the world's population is undergoing **urbanization**, the movement of people from rural areas to cities. In the United States, many people work in the cities but move into suburban areas around the cities. This *suburban sprawl* leads to traffic jams, inadequate infrastructure, and the reduction of land for farms and wildlife habitat. Meanwhile, housing within cities becomes more costly, more dense, and in shorter supply.

FIELDSTUDY
Go to Appendix B to find the field study
Population Issues.

✓ CHECK FOR UNDERSTANDING
Infer How has rapid population growth affected arable land in Egypt?

FIGURE 2.4

Urbanization A large proportion of the United States is arable land, but suburban sprawl (left) creates many problems. Most of Egypt's population is crowded into the narrow Nile River valley.

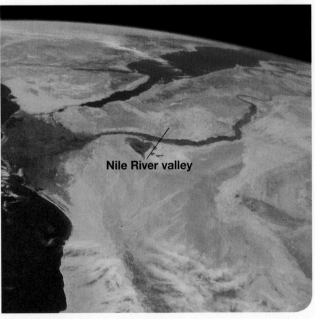

Nile River valley

(l) ©Kevin Fleming/Corbis; (br) ©Johnson Space Center/NASA

A Demographically Diverse World

As you have seen, demographers may categorize countries as either developed or developing. However, some demographers may prefer the terms *more developed* and *less developed* to describe countries or regions, because the reality of development is complex and politically sensitive.

Not every country in the world is progressing through each stage of the demographic transition according to the model. Some countries now have modern industries, but incomes remain low. A few countries have achieved stable and educated populations with very little industrialization. Some countries seem to remain in the second stage of the model. These countries have rapid population growth but are unable to make enough educational and economic gains to reduce the birth rate and move into the third stage.

In recent years, the global community has begun to focus on the **least developed countries**. These countries show few signs of development and in some cases have increasing death rates while birth rates remain high. Least developed countries are officially identified by the United Nations using three criteria: low income, weak human assets, and economic vulnerability. The low income criterion is based on a three-year average of gross national income per person of less than $750. Human assets that are considered include nutrition, health, education, and adult literacy.

CASESTUDY

Thailand's Population Challenges

Population growth is a major concern for many developing countries. But the options are limited for a country that has a poor economy and growing demands for limited resources. Thailand is one country that has effectively and purposefully slowed its population growth.

Around 1970, Thailand's population was growing at a rate of more than 3 percent per year, and the average Thai family had 6.3 children. The country had increasing environmental problems, including air pollution in major cities and unsafe water supplies. Thailand's emissions of carbon dioxide from burning fossil fuels almost doubled between 1990 and 1997. In Thailand's capital, Bangkok, one-ninth of residents have respiratory problems, and many people die of waterborne diseases each year.

In 1971, Thailand's government adopted a policy to reduce Thailand's population growth. The policy included increased education for women, greater access to health care and

Bangkok, Thailand, is one of the most crowded and polluted cities in the world. However, population growth is slowing in Thailand, and some environmental problems are starting to be solved.

©Jodi Cobb/Getty Images

The third criterion, economic vulnerability, is based on such indicators as the instability of agricultural production and the export of goods and services. Some of these least developed countries that have been identified by the United Nations include Haiti, Madagascar, Malawi, Somalia, Samoa, Afghanistan, Bangladesh, and the Sudan. These countries may be given priority for foreign aid and development programs to address both their population problems and environmental issues.

Growth rates for different parts of the world are shown in **Figure 2.5**. Populations are relatively stable in Europe, the United States, Canada, Russia, South Korea, Thailand, China, Japan, Australia, and New Zealand. In contrast, populations are still growing rapidly in less developed regions. Most of the world's population is now within Asia.

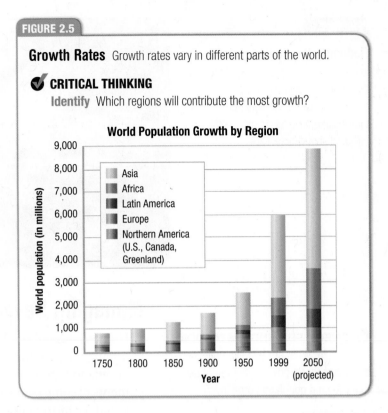

FIGURE 2.5

Growth Rates Growth rates vary in different parts of the world.

✔ **CRITICAL THINKING**

Identify Which regions will contribute the most growth?

World Population Growth by Region

- Asia
- Africa
- Latin America
- Europe
- Northern America (U.S., Canada, Greenland)

THAILAND'S POPULATION STRATEGIES
improved health care for mothers and children
openness of the people, government, and community leaders to changing social traditions
cooperation of private and nonprofit organizations with the government
increases in women's rights and ability to earn income
economic incentives such as building loans for families who participated in family planning programs
creative family planning programs promoted by popular government leaders
high literacy rates of women (80 percent in 1980 and 94 percent in 2000)

contraceptives, and economic incentives to parents who have fewer children. Fifteen years later, the country's population growth rate had been cut to about 1.6 percent. By 2012, the growth rate had fallen to 0.54 percent and the average Thai family had 1.7 children. The infant mortality rate had also declined by 2012.

How did Thailand make such major changes with limited resources? Demographers believe the changes are due to the combination of strategies shown in the table above.

Critical Thinking

1. **Applying Ideas** For what reasons could Thailand be described as a developing country in the 1970s? In what ways was it able to change?

2. **Expressing Viewpoints** Do you approve of all of the strategies that the government of Thailand employed in order to reduce their population growth? Do the goals justify the strategies they used? Write a persuasive paragraph to defend your opinion.

FIGURE 2.6

Reducing Population China has implemented a long campaign to reduce birth rates. Strategies have included economic rewards for single-child families and advertising such as the billboard shown here.

Managing Development and Population Growth

Humans throughout history have witnessed the negative effects of population growth. Today, less-developed countries know that continued population growth can limit their economic development. The governments of some countries, such as China, Thailand, and India, have tried to reduce birth rates using public advertising, as shown in **Figure 2.6**, family planning programs, economic incentives, or legal punishments.

In 1994, the United Nations held the International Conference on Population and Development (ICPD). This conference involved debates relating population, development, and the environment. Achievement of the *Millenium Development Goals* (MDG), as seen in **Figure 2.7**, that resulted from the ICPD is targeted for 2015. Many countries favor stabilizing population growth, especially through improvements in women's status. In fact, worldwide fertility rates are dropping, as shown in **Figure 2.8**.

✔ **CHECK FOR UNDERSTANDING**

Recognize What are two examples of strategies that a government might use to try to limit population growth?

FIGURE 2.7

MDG BY 2015

Provide universal access to a full range of safe and reliable family-planning methods and related reproductive health services.

Reduce infant mortality rates to below 35 infant deaths per 1,000 live births and mortality rates of children under five years old to below 45 deaths per 1,000 live births.

Close the gap in maternal mortality between developing and developed countries. Achieve a maternal mortality rate below 60 deaths per 100,000 live births.

Increase life expectancy at birth to more than 75 years. In countries with the highest mortality, increase life expectancy at birth to more than 70 years.

Increase universal access to and completion of primary education, and redress gender imbalances at higher levels of education.

Source: UN Population Fund.

FIGURE 2.8

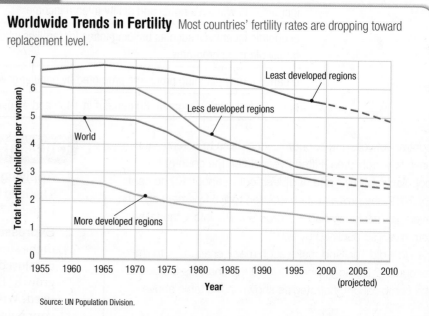

Worldwide Trends in Fertility Most countries' fertility rates are dropping toward replacement level.

Source: UN Population Division.

©Louise Gubb/The Image Works

Growth Is Slowing

The human population of the world is now more than 7 billion and is still increasing. The worldwide population growth rate peaked at about 87 million people per year between 1985 and 1990. In contrast, the population grew by 81 million people per year from 1990 to 1995.

Fertility rates have declined since about 1970 in developed and less-developed regions. However, rates are still much higher in less-developed regions. Demographers predict that this trend will continue and that global population growth will be slower in this century than in the last century. If current trends continue, most countries will have replacement level fertility rates by 2050. If so, world population growth would eventually stop. However, ways must be found to make fewer resources stretch much further, in order for Earth to sustain its human population.

Projections to 2050

Figure 2.9 shows United Nations projections of population growth to 2050. The medium-growth line, predicted by most demographers, assumes that global fertility rates will decline to replacement level by 2050. The high- and low-growth lines would result from higher or lower fertility rates.

FIGURE 2.9

Projections Current fertility trends will result in a world population of about 9 billion in 2050 (middle line). Economic or political changes could lead to higher or lower numbers.

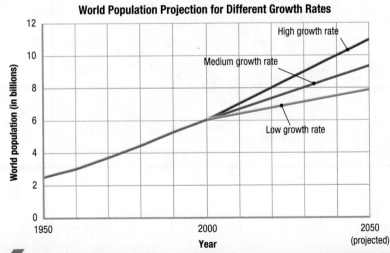

World Population Projection for Different Growth Rates

Section 2 **Formative Assessment**

▶ Reviewing Main Ideas

1. **Describe** three problems caused by rapid human population growth.

2. **Compare** population growth in more-developed countries to population growth in less-developed countries.

3. **Describe** worldwide population projections for the next 50 years.

✓ Critical Thinking

4. **Analyzing a Viewpoint** Write a comparison of the pros and cons of the strategies nations have used to reduce population growth.

5. **Analyzing Relationships** Do you think that changing birth rates will by themselves cause a nation to undergo further development?

Fertility Rates and Female Literacy in Africa

FEMALE LITERACY VS FERTILITY RATES

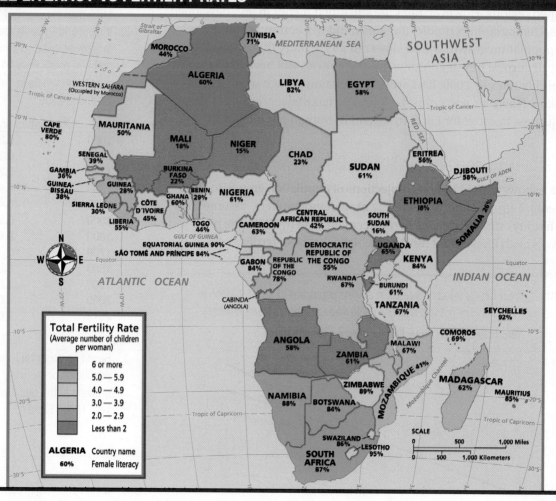

MAP SKILLS

Use the map of Africa to answer the questions below.

1. **Describing Locations** Which regions of Africa have the highest female literacy (percentage of females who can read and write)? the lowest female literacy? Which regions have the highest fertility rates? the lowest fertility rates?

2. **Analyzing Data** Choose 20 countries and make a graph comparing the total fertility rates and female literacy of each country.

3. **Comparing Data** Worldwide, the average total fertility rate is about 2.8 children per woman, and the average female literacy is 74 percent. How does Africa compare with the rest of the world in both aspects?

Lost Populations: What Happened?

At various points in human history, entire populations have disappeared and left mysterious remains such as the Egyptian pyramids and the Anasazi pueblos in the southwestern United States. Why did these people and their civilizations disappear? Archeologists sometimes find evidence that environmental destruction was one of the reasons the populations disappeared.

Rapa Nui (Easter Island)

On the island of Rapa Nui, in the Pacific Ocean, the first European visitors were amazed to find huge stone heads that were kilometers from the quarries where the heads had been made. It seemed impossible that the islanders could have moved the heads. There were no horses, oxen, or carts on the island and there were also no trees, that could have been used as rollers to move the heads. The islanders were using grass and reeds to make fires because the island was barren grassland.

A Changed Environment

Researchers have now shown that Rapa Nui was very different when it was first colonized by Polynesians around 1200 CE. In the oldest garbage heaps on the island, archaeologists have found that one-third of the bones came from dolphins. To hunt dolphins, the islanders must have had strong canoes made of wood from tall trees. Pollen grains,

These large stone figures found on Easter Island were made by a civilization that has disappeared.

which are used to identify plants, show that the island was once covered by a forest that contained many species found nowhere else in the world.

But by 1600 CE trees were rare and the Easter Island palm tree was extinct. The palm seeds were probably eaten by rats that the Polynesians had brought to the island. With the destruction of the forest, every species of native land bird also became extinct. With the added stress of disease carried by the European visitors, the local human population crashed.

The people of Easter Island destroyed their environment by overusing its natural resources and introducing new species such as chickens and rats. The people were reduced from a complex civilization to a primitive lifestyle. Easter Island is a small-scale example of what ecologists worry could happen to Earth's entire human population.

These ruins in New Mexico were built by the Chaco Anasazi civilization around 900 CE. Environmental changes are thought to have affected this population.

What Do You Think?

Industrialized countries have started to invest in environmental improvements, such as replanting forests that have been destroyed and protecting endangered species. Do you think this makes these countries safe from the kind of environmental disasters that destroyed the Easter Island civilization?

(b) ©Walter Rawlings/Robert Harding World Imagery/Getty Images; (t) ©Getty Images

SECTION 1 **Studying Human Populations**

OBJECTIVES

- Human population growth has accelerated in the last few centuries. The main reasons for this growth were improvements in hygiene and increases in food production, which accompanied the industrial and scientific revolutions.

- Demographers try to predict population trends using data such as age structure, survivorship, fertility rates, migration, and life expectancy.

- In the demographic transition model, countries progress through four stages of change in birth rates, death rates, and population size. Not all countries closely follow this model, so it is important to examine each region individually.

KEY TERMS

demography

age structure

survivorship

fertility rate

migration

life expectancy

demographic transition

SECTION 2 **Changing Population Trends**

OBJECTIVES

- When a growing population uses resources faster than they can be renewed, the resources most critically affected are fuelwood, water, and arable land.

- In this century, countries may be labeled more developed or less developed. Not all countries are going through the demographic transition in the same way that the more-developed countries did.

- Some countries attempt to reduce birth rates directly through public advertising, family planning programs, economic incentives, or legal punishments for their citizens.

KEY TERMS

infrastructure

arable land

urbanization

least developed countries

Reviewing Key Terms

Use each of the following terms in a separate sentence.

1. *demography*
2. *demographic transition*
3. *infrastructure*
4. *least developed countries*

For each pair of terms, explain how the meanings of the terms differ.

5. *age structure* and *survivorship*
6. *infant mortality* and *life expectancy*
7. *death rate* and *fertility rate*
8. *urbanization* and *migration*
9. **Concept Map** Use the following terms to create a concept map: *rapid human population growth, demographic transition, survivorship, fertility rate, fuelwood, water,* and *land.*

Reviewing Main Ideas

10. Age structure data include all of the following *except*
    a. the number of members of a population who are between 5 and 11 years old.
    b. the ratio of males to females in a population.
    c. the amount of population change due to immigration or emigration.
    d. the ratio of older people to younger people in a population.

11. Human population growth accelerated in recent centuries mostly because of
    a. the bubonic plague.
    b. better hygiene and food.
    c. the discovery of electricity.
    d. improved efficiency of fuel use.

12. Which countries have Type I survivorship?
    a. the most developed countries
    b. the least developed countries
    c. countries in the second stage of the demographic transition
    d. countries in the first stage of the demographic transition

13. The demographic transition is a(n)
    a. untested hypothesis.
    b. natural law.
    c. model based on observed patterns.
    d. international law.

14. A country in the second stage of the demographic transition may have all of the following *except*
    a. increasing agricultural production.
    b. improving healthcare and education.
    c. decreasing population size.
    d. decreasing death rates.

15. Which of the following resources is likely to be impacted the most by a rapidly growing population?
    a. clothing
    b. food
    c. housing
    d. water

16. Which of the following diseases is often spread through unsafe public water sources?
    a. dysentery
    b. flu
    c. chickenpox
    d. AIDS

17. Which of the following uses of wood is the most important for basic human needs?
    a. heating the home
    b. boiling water
    c. making tools
    d. building shelter

18. In this century, the world population is likely to
    a. remain the same.
    b. continue to grow exponentially.
    c. decline rapidly because fertility rates are already below replacement level.
    d. stabilize after fertility rates fall below replacement level.

Short Answer

19. What are the main reasons that life expectancy has increased worldwide?

20. How does the age structure of a population help predict future population growth?

21. What is the relationship between education and fertility rates in a human population?

22. Which properties of a population change during the demographic transition?

23. Which key resources are impacted the most by rapidly growing populations?

24. Which regions of the world are generally more developed? less developed?

Interpreting Graphics

The graph below shows each region's contribution to world population growth. Use the graph to answer questions 25–27.

25. Determine Which region(s) are projected to increase in population size?

26. Predict Which region(s) are projected to decline in population size?

27. Explain Can you assume that all the countries within each region have the same growth patterns? Explain your answer.

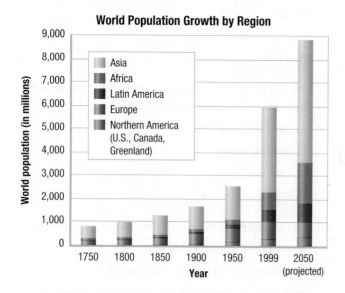

Critical Thinking

28. Analyzing Predictions Why are human population trends difficult to predict? Describe an example of an event that would change most demographic predictions.

29. Analyzing Methods In what ways does the study of human populations differ from the study of wildlife ecology?

30. Identifying Relationships What other factors, besides those already mentioned, might have an effect on fertility rates in a given population?

31. Evaluating Models Write an evaluation of the demographic transition model of how populations will develop. How useful is the demographic transition model in predicting the future? What assumptions are made by the model? What criticisms could be made of the model?

32. Careers Demographers are employed by many kinds of organizations including governments, health organizations, and insurance companies. How can their skills be useful to each of these organizations?

33. Social Studies Find out the demographic history, for the last 100 years, of a developing country of your choice. Explain how closely this country's pattern of development follows the demographic transition model.

34. Research Demographic Trends Look up population statistics for your local city, county, or state. Read and take notes about recent demographic trends and predictions for the next few decades. Make a summary of your findings.

Analyzing Data

Use the graph below to answer questions 35–37.

35. Analyzing Data At which times did the fertility rate change most drastically in the United States?

36. Graphing Data Sketch a copy of the graph below. Smooth the bumps to give an idea of general trends.

37. Drawing Conclusions On your new graph, draw a second line to show the changes in population size that you would predict to result from the given fertility rates over time.

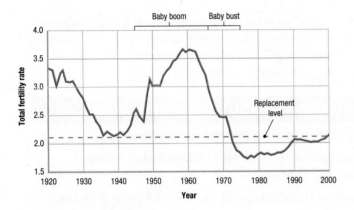

Making Connections

38. Writing Persuasively Write an opinion article for a newspaper or magazine. Argue either for or against a policy related to immigration or family planning.

39. Writing Using Research Look up recent census data from your city, county, or state. Write a paragraph that describes the major demographic trends of the last few years.

40. According to the article, for what reasons did Thailand decide to reduce the size of its population?

41. After reviewing the case study, explain the relationship it indicates between reducing population size and improving the lives of women.

Why It Matters

42. Why should people in the United States be concerned about population size in other countries?

STUDY SKILL

Quantitative Terms Look for key terms in the graphs in this chapter. In your science journal, copy the graphs and write brief descriptions of how key terms may relate to the graphs and to other key terms. For example, copy Figure 3, and write "Low infant mortality corresponds to high life expectancy in a Type I survivorship curve."

Objectives

Predict which variable has a greater effect on population growth rates.

Calculate changes for a given population over a 50-year period.

Graph the resulting population's age structure by creating a population pyramid.

Compare the effects of fertility variables on population growth rates.

- - - - - - - - - - - - - - - - - - -

Materials

calculator or computer

colored pencils or markers

graph paper

notebook

pen or pencil

ruler

How Will Our Population Grow?

If you were a demographer, you might be asked to determine how a population is likely to change in the future. You have learned that the rate of population growth is affected by both the number of children per family and the age at which people have children. But which factor has a greater effect? To explore this question, you will use age-structure diagrams—also called population pyramids—such as the one shown below.

Procedure

1. In this lab you will calculate future population trends for an imaginary city. To compare how fertility variables may affect population growth, each group of students will test the effects of different assumptions. Assume the following about the population of this city:

ASSUMPTIONS ABOUT THE POPULATION
• Half the population is male and half is female.
• Every woman will have all of her children during a given five-year period of her life.
• Everyone who is born will live to the age of 85 and then die.
• No one will move into or out of the city.

2. Your teacher will divide the class into four groups. Each group will project population growth using the following assumptions:

ASSUMPTIONS ABOUT THE WOMEN IN THE POPULATION		
Group	Each Woman Gives Birth to	While in the Age Range of
A	5 children	15–19
B	5 children	25–29
C	2 children	15–19
D	2 children	25–29

3. Predict which of the four groups will have the greatest population growth in 50 years. Write down the order you would predict for the relative size of the groups from largest population to smallest population.

4. The table at right shows the population of our imaginary city for the year 2000. Use the data in the table to make an age-structure diagram (population pyramid) for the city. Use the example diagram at left to help you.

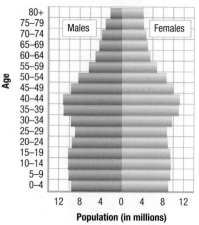

Age Structure You will make an age-structure diagram, such as this graph of the U.S. population in 2000.

5. Make a table similar to the one shown at right. Add columns for the years 2005, 2010, and for every fifth year until the year 2050.

6. Calculate the number of 0- to 4-year-olds in the year 2005. To do this, first determine how many women will have children between 2000 and 2005. Remember that half of the population in each age group is female, and that members of the population will reproduce at specific ages. Multiply the number of childbearing women by the number of children that each woman will have. For example, Group A will have 12,500 new births by 2005.

7. Fill in the columns for the years 2005 and 2010. Determine the number of people in each age group by "shifting" each group from 2000. For example, the number of 5- to 9-year-olds in 2005 will equal the number of 0- to 4-year-olds in 2000.

8. Calculate the total population for each five-year period.

9. Repeat the process described in steps 3–8 for each column to complete the table through the year 2050.

Analysis

1. **Constructing Graphs** Plot the growth of the population on a line graph. You may want to use a computer to graph the results.

2. **Constructing Graphs** Make a population pyramid for the population in 2050.

Conclusions

3. **Evaluating Data** Compare your graphs with the graphs of the other three groups. Were your predictions correct?

4. **Drawing Conclusions** Which variable had a greater effect on population growth—the number of children each woman had or the age at which each woman had children?

5. **Interpreting Information** Did any of the groups show no growth in the population? Explain these results.

Extension

6. From the age-structure diagram on the previous page, what would you predict to happen to the U.S. population in the next 20 years? in the next 50 years? What parts of the age structure are most important to these predictions?

POPULATION IN EACH AGE GROUP, 2000–2050

Age	2000	2005	2010
80+	100		
75–79	500		
70–74	600		
65–69	700		
60–64	800		
55–59	900		
50–54	1,000		
45–49	1,250		
40–44	1,500		
35–39	2,000		
30–34	2,500		
25–29	3,000		
20–24	4,000		
15–19	5,000		
10–14	6,500		
5–9	8,000	10,000	
0–4	10,000	12,500	
Total	48,350		
Females that give birth	2,500		
New births	12,500		

Sample Population Data Use this table as an example to calculate the age structure for each generation of your imaginary population. Add columns for five-year periods up to 2050. Examples of some of Group A's results are shown in red.

Chapter 10

Biodiversity

Section 1
What Is Biodiversity?

Section 2
Biodiversity at Risk

Section 3
The Future of Biodiversity

Why It Matters

Ecosystems around the world are home to unique communities of species. Scientists discover new species every year, and some species go extinct before they are known to science.

Why is it important to maintain biodiversity in an ecosystem?

CASESTUDY

Learn about scientists' quests to discover new species in the Amazonian rain forest in the case study A Genetic Gold Rush in the Rain Forests on pages 248–249.

©John Shaw/Bruce Coleman, Inc.

What Is Biodiversity?

SECTION 1

Objectives

- Describe the diversity of species on Earth, and relate the difference between known numbers and estimated numbers of species.

- List and describe three levels of biodiversity.

- Explain four ways in which biodiversity is important to ecosystems and humans.

- Analyze the potential value of a single species.

Every day, somewhere on Earth, several unique species of organisms become *extinct* as the last members of the species die—often because of human actions. Scientists are not sure how many species are becoming extinct or even how many species there are on Earth. How much extinction is natural? Can we—or should we—prevent extinctions? The study of biodiversity helps us think about these questions, but does not give us all the answers.

A World Rich in Biodiversity

The term **biodiversity**, which is short for "biological diversity," usually refers to the number of different species in a given area. Certain areas of the planet, such as tropical rain forests, contain an extraordinary variety of species. The complex relationships between so many species are hard to study, but humans may need to understand and preserve biodiversity for our own survival.

Unknown Diversity

The study of biodiversity starts with the unfinished task of cataloging all the species that exist on Earth. As shown in **Figure 1.1**, the number of species known to science is about 1.9 million, most of which are insects. However, the actual number of species on Earth is unknown. Scientists agree that we have not studied Earth's species adequately. Recently, it was estimated that there are around 9 million species of eukaryotes, which includes protists, animals, and plants. New species are considered *known* when they are collected and described scientifically. Unknown species may exist in remote wildernesses, deep in the oceans, and even in cities.

Key Terms

biodiversity
gene
keystone species
ecotourism

FIGURE 1.1

Number of Species on Earth

About 1.9 million species on Earth are known to science. Many more species are *estimated* to exist, especially species of smaller organisms. Scientists continue to revise these estimates.

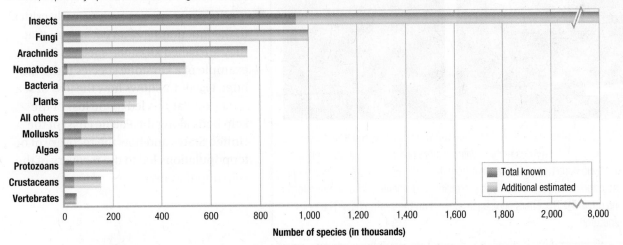

Source: World Conservation Monitoring Center.

Levels of Diversity

Biodiversity can be studied and described at three levels. *Species diversity* refers to the number of different species in an area. This kind of diversity has received the most attention and is most often what is meant by *biodiversity*. *Ecosystem diversity* refers to the variety of habitats, communities, and ecological processes within and between ecosystems. *Genetic diversity* refers to all the different *genes* contained within all members of a population. A **gene** is a piece of DNA that codes for a specific trait that can be inherited by an organism's offspring.

Benefits of Biodiversity

Biodiversity can affect the stability of ecosystems and the sustainability of populations. In addition, there are many ways that humans clearly use and benefit from the variety of life forms on Earth. Biodiversity may be more important than we realize.

FIGURE 1.2

Keystone Species The sea otters of North America are an example of a keystone species, upon which a whole ecosystem depends.

In the 1800s, sea otters were hunted for their fur. They disappeared from the Pacific coast of the U.S. ❶ Sea urchins, with no more predators, multiplied and ate the kelp. The kelp beds began to disappear from the area. ❷ In 1937, a small group of surviving otters was discovered. With protection and scientific efforts, the otter populations grew. ❸ The otters once again preyed on the sea urchins. The kelp beds regenerated.

Species Are Connected to Ecosystems

We depend on healthy ecosystems to ensure a healthy biosphere that has balanced cycles of energy and nutrients. Species are part of these cycles. Many species play important roles in ecosystems. Every species is probably either dependent on or depended upon by at least one other species in ways that are not always obvious. When one species disappears from an ecosystem, a strand in a food web is removed. How many threads can be pulled from the web before it collapses? We often do not know the answer until it is too late. In general, the more species there are, the more stable an ecosystem is.

But some species are so clearly critical to the functioning of an ecosystem that they are called **keystone species**. One example of a keystone species is the sea otter. **Figure 1.2** shows how the loss of sea otter populations led to the loss of the kelp beds along the Pacific coast of the United States and how the recovery of otter populations led to the recovery of the kelp populations.

Species and Population Survival

Genetic diversity within populations is important to species survival. If there is high genetic diversity, it is more likely that some individuals will be adapted to survive new diseases or environmental changes. When a population shrinks, its genetic diversity decreases as though it is passing through a bottleneck, as shown in **Figure 1.3**. Even if the population can increase again, its genetic diversity will be reduced, putting it at risk. Then, members of the population may become more likely to inherit genetic diseases.

Medical, Industrial, and Agricultural Uses

People throughout history have used the variety of organisms on Earth for food, clothing, shelter, and medicine. Of the top 150 prescription drugs used in the United States, 74 percent are derived from plants. Almost all antibiotics are derived from chemicals found in fungi. **Figure 1.4** lists some plants from which medicines are derived.

For some industries, undiscovered and poorly studied species represent a source of potential products. New chemicals and industrial materials may be developed from chemicals discovered in all kinds of species. The scientific community continues to find new uses for biological material and genetic diversity.

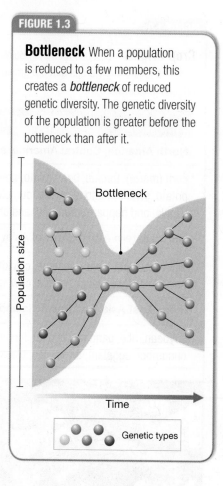

FIGURE 1.3

Bottleneck When a population is reduced to a few members, this creates a *bottleneck* of reduced genetic diversity. The genetic diversity of the population is greater before the bottleneck than after it.

Population size

Bottleneck

Time

Genetic types

FIGURE 1.4

COMMON MEDICINES DERIVED FROM PLANTS		
Medicine	Origin	Use
Neostigmine	calabar bean (Africa)	treatment of glaucoma and basis for synthetic insecticides
Turbocurarine	curare vine (South America)	surgical muscle relaxant; treatment of muscle disorders; and poison for arrow tips
Vincristine, vinblastine	rosy periwinkle (Madagascar)	treatment of pediatric leukemia and Hodgkin's disease
Bromelain	pineapple (South America)	treatment to control tissue inflammation
Taxol	Pacific yew (North America)	anticancer agent
Novacaine, cocaine	coca plant (South America)	local anesthetic and basis for many other anesthetics
Cortisone	wild yam (Central America)	hormone used in many drugs
L-dopa (levodopa)	velvet bean (tropical Asia)	treatment of Parkinson's disease
Reserpine	Indian snakeroot (Malaysia)	treatment to reduce high blood pressure

✔ **CHECK FOR UNDERSTANDING**

Explain Why is genetic diversity important for the survival of a species?

FIGURE 1.5

Crop Origins A produce market in Bolivia shows a diversity of native foods. Many crops that are grown in the United States originated elsewhere.

FOOD ORIGINS

North America, Central America, and South America

corn (maize), tomato, bean (pinto, green, and lima), peanut, potato, sweet potato, avocado, pumpkin, pineapple, cocoa, vanilla, and pepper (green, red, and chile)

Northeastern Africa, Central Asia, and Near East

wheat (several types), sesame, chickpea, fig, lentil, carrot, pea, okra, date, walnut, coffee, cow, goat, pig, and sheep

India, East Asia, and Pacific Islands

soybean, rice, banana, coconut, lemon, lime, orange, cucumber, eggplant, turnip, tea, black pepper, and chicken

Humans benefit from biodiversity every time they eat. Most of the crops produced around the world originated from a few areas of high biodiversity. Some examples of crop origins are shown in **Figure 1.5**. Most new crop varieties are *hybrids*, or crops developed by combining genetic material from more than one population. Depending on too few plant varieties for food is risky. For example, famines have resulted when an important crop was wiped out by disease. But some crops have been saved from diseases by being crossbred with wild plant relatives. In the future, new crop varieties may come from species not yet discovered.

Ethics, Aesthetics, and Recreation

Some people believe that we should preserve biodiversity for ethical reasons. They believe that species and ecosystems have a right to exist whether or not they have any other value. To people of some cultures and religions, each organism on Earth is a gift with a higher purpose.

People also value biodiversity for aesthetic or personal enjoyment—keeping pets, camping, photographing wildflowers, or watching wildlife. Some regions earn the majority of their income from **ecotourism**, which is a form of tourism that supports the conservation and sustainable development of ecologically unique areas.

Section 1 **Formative Assessment**

▶ Reviewing Main Ideas

1. **Describe** the general diversity of species on Earth in terms of relative numbers and types of organisms. Compare known numbers of species to current estimates.

2. **Describe** three levels of biodiversity. Which level is most commonly meant by *biodiversity*?

3. **Explain** how biodiversity is important to ecosystems, and give examples of how it is important to humans.

✔ Critical Thinking

4. **Analyzing a Viewpoint** Is it possible to put a price on a single species? Explain your answer.

5. **Predicting Consequences** What is your favorite type of organism? If this organism were to go extinct, how would you feel? What would you be willing to do to try to save it from extinction? Write a short essay describing your reaction.

Biodiversity at Risk

Objectives

- Define and give examples of *endangered* and *threatened* species.

- Describe several ways that species are threatened with extinction globally.

- Explain which types of threats are having the largest impact on biodiversity.

- List areas of the world that have high levels of biodiversity and many threats to species.

- Compare the amount of biodiversity in the United States to that of the rest of the world.

About 65 million years ago, about half the species on Earth—including dinosaurs (with the exception of birds)—disappeared. The extinction of many species in a relatively short period of time is called a *mass extinction*. Earth has experienced several mass extinctions, as shown in **Figure 2.1**. It takes millions of years for biodiversity to rebound after a mass extinction.

Current Extinctions

Scientists warn that we are in the midst of another mass extinction. The rate of extinction is estimated to have increased by a multiple of 50 since 1800. Between 1800 and 2000, up to 25 percent of all species on Earth may have become extinct. The current mass extinction is different from those of the past because humans are the primary cause of the extinctions.

Species Prone to Extinction

Cockroaches and rats are not likely to become extinct because they have large populations that adapt easily to many habitats. But species with small populations in limited areas can easily become extinct. Species that are especially at risk of extinction include those that migrate, those that need large or special habitats, and those that are exploited by humans.

An **endangered species** is a species that is likely to become extinct if protective measures are not taken immediately. A **threatened species** is a species that has a declining population and that is likely to become endangered if it is not protected. Additional categories of risk exist for certain legal and biological purposes.

Key Terms

endangered species
threatened species
exotic species
poaching
endemic species

FIGURE 2.1

Extinction Events

When extinction rate is plotted against time, mass extinctions appear as periodic peaks rising above background extinction levels.

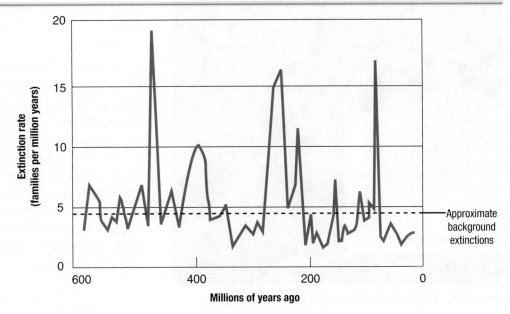

Source: University of California Berkeley.

FIGURE 2.2

SPECIES KNOWN TO BE THREATENED OR EXTINCT WORLDWIDE

Type of Species	Number Threatened (all categories of risk)	Number Extinct (since ~1800)	Percent of Species that May be Threatened
Mammals	1,130	87	26
Birds	1,183	131	12
Reptiles	296	22	3.3
Amphibians	146	5	3.1
Fishes	752	92	3.7
Insects	555	73	0.054
Other crustaceans	408	9	1.03
Mollusks and worms	938	303	1.3
Plants	30,827	400	20

Source: UN Environment Programme.

How Do Humans Cause Extinctions?

In the past two centuries, human population growth has accelerated and so has the rate of extinctions. The numbers of worldwide species known to be threatened, endangered, or recently extinct are listed in **Figure 2.2**. The major human causes of extinction today are the destruction of habitats, the introduction of nonnative species, pollution, and the overharvesting of species.

Habitat Destruction and Fragmentation

As human populations grow, we use more land to construct buildings and harvest resources. In the process, we destroy and fragment the habitats of other species. It is estimated that habitat loss causes almost 75 percent of the extinctions that are now occurring.

Due to habitat loss, the Florida panther is one of the most endangered animals in North America. The panther and its historical range are shown in **Figure 2.3**. Two hundred years ago, cougars—a species that includes panthers and mountain lions—ranged from Alaska to South America. Cougars require expansive ranges of forest habitat and large amounts of prey. Today, much of the cougars' habitat has been destroyed or broken up by roads, canals, and fences. In 2011, only about 150 Florida panthers made up the only remaining wild cougar population east of the Mississippi River.

FIGURE 2.3

Florida Panther Range The purple area on the map shows the range of the Florida panther when settlers first arrived in the southeastern United States.

Range at about 1500 CE

Current range

Source: Florida Fish and Wildlife Conservation Commission

©Thomas Kitchin & Victoria Hurst/Corbis

Invasive Exotic Species

An **exotic species** is a species that is not native to a particular region. Even such familiar organisms as cats and rats are considered to be exotic species when they are brought to regions where they never lived before. Exotic species can threaten native species that have no natural defenses against them. The invasive fire ants in **Figure 2.4** threaten livestock, people, and native species throughout the southeastern United States.

Harvesting, Hunting, and Poaching

Excessive hunting and harvesting of species can also lead to extinction. In the United States in the 1800s and 1900s, two billion passenger pigeons were hunted to extinction and bison were hunted nearly to extinction. Thousands of rare species worldwide are harvested and sold for use as pets, houseplants, wood, food, or herbal medicine.

Many countries now have laws to regulate hunting, fishing, harvesting, and trade of wildlife. However, these activities continue illegally, a crime known as **poaching**. In poor countries especially, local species are an obvious source of food, medicine, or income. In addition, not all threatened species are legally protected.

Pollution

Pesticides, cleaning agents, drugs, and other chemicals used by humans are making their way into food webs around the globe. The long-term effects of chemicals may not be clear until after many years of use. The bald eagle is a well-known example of a species that was endangered because of a pesticide known as DDT. Although DDT is now illegal to use in the United States, it is still manufactured here and used around the world.

©M. Timothy O'Keefe/Bruce Coleman, Inc./Photoshot

Connect to ECOLOGY

Extinction and Global Change

Scientists have worried for some time that environmental pollutants might cause drastic changes in our atmosphere and biosphere. However, it is difficult to draw a direct link from global changes to specific extinctions.

In recent decades, scientists have observed a worldwide decline in amphibian species. Unlike most cases of habitat loss or overhunting, there is no single clear cause for these extinctions, which are occurring more than 100 times faster than the average extinction rate. Pollution of water sources with hormone-like chemicals, increased UV radiation exposure, climate change, and fungal disease are all likely culprits.

FIGURE 2.4

Invasive Species Mounds made by fire ants cover many fields in the southeastern United States. As with other invasive exotic species, these ants had no natural predators and little competition from native species when they were first brought into the country by accident.

Areas of Critical Biodiversity

Some parts of the world contain a greater diversity of species than others. An important feature of such areas is that they have a large portion of **endemic species**, which are species that are native to and found only within a limited area. Ecologists often use the numbers of endemic species of plants as an indicator of overall biodiversity, because plants form the basis of ecosystems on land. Ecologists increasingly point out the importance of biodiversity in oceans, and have identified particular areas where biodiversity is greatest and also at risk, such as the coral reefs of Indonesia and the Philippines.

Tropical Rain Forests

The remaining tropical rain forests cover less than 7 percent of the Earth's land surface. Yet biologists estimate that over half of the world's species live in these forests. Most of these species have never been described. Unknown numbers of species are disappearing as tropical rain forests are cleared for farming or cattle grazing. Meanwhile, tropical forests are among the few places where some native people maintain traditional lifestyles and an intimate knowledge of their forest homes. The case study below explains the increasing value of such knowledge in the global marketplace.

CASESTUDY

A Genetic Gold Rush in the Rain Forests

Environmental scientists have found that societies benefit from the services that are provided by ecosystems, such as cleaning water and air and reducing flooding. People also can learn how to take advantage of the diverse characteristics of the species that form ecosystems. This aspect has been especially true in the tropics, which contain two-thirds of the world's species of plants.

The diversity of tropical plants and animals is important to local people for food, shelter, and medicine. Because native peoples of the tropics have depended on their local environment for thousands of years, they have an incredible knowledge of the uses of organisms that live there. In the Amazon, the Yanomamö are still living a lifestyle of intimate connection to their forest home. The Yanomamö make use of thousands of plants, fungi, and animals for food, drugs, weapons, and art. Amazonian natives such as the Yanomamö are probably best known for their use of poison dart frog skin excretions for hunting.

Over the past several decades, scientists have been exploring the tropics to learn more about the potential uses of tropical plants and animals. The application of biological science to create new products such as drugs is part of the modern biotechnology industry.

This botanist is researching the uses of rain forest plants and other species with the help of this local person.

©Alison Wright/Photo Researchers, Inc.

Coral Reefs and Coastal Ecosystems

Coral reefs occupy a small fraction of the marine environment yet contain the majority of the biodiversity there. Reefs provide millions of people with food and tourism revenue. They protect coasts from waves and flooding and are sources of new chemicals. But reefs are poorly studied and are not well protected by laws. Nearly 60 percent of Earth's coral reefs are threatened by human activities such as overfishing and pollution. Similar threats affect coastal ecosystems, such as swamps, marshes, shores, and kelp beds. Coastal areas are travel routes for many migrating species as well as links to ecosystems on land.

Islands

When an island rises from the sea, it is colonized by a limited number of species from the mainland. These colonizing species may then evolve into several new species. Thus, islands often hold a very distinct but limited set of species. For example, the Hawaiian Islands have 28 species of an endemic family of birds called *honeycreepers*. Honeycreepers and many other island species are endangered by competition from exotic species.

✔ **CHECK FOR UNDERSTANDING**

Explain Why is the biodiversity of coral reefs and coastal ecosystems threatened?

This industry applies what they learn from Earth's biodiversity—especially in terms of the chemicals in their bodies and their genetic material—to research and development. Governments of tropical countries have taken notice of the increased international interest in their biological assets. For example, the government of Brazil has claimed the right to tax or patent any genetic material that is harvested from within its borders.

Researchers work with native people, especially those who work as healers, to identify species that may be useful as medicines. Biochemists study the structure and uses of chemicals found within these species. They have been amazed by the complex combinations of new chemicals they have discovered in many rain-forest species. Some of these chemicals are already being used in medicines today.

The biodiversity of the tropics is at risk and forests are disappearing rapidly. Many scientists are concerned that we are losing species that could have been important crops or could have provided life-saving medicines. When we protect rain forests, we are not only protecting important ecosystems, but also species that may help to make the lives of millions—or even billions—of people better.

The Yanomamö are among the few native peoples of the tropical rain forests who still live traditional lifestyles and use their knowledge of the forests to meet all of their needs.

Critical Thinking

1. **Expressing Viewpoints** To whom do you think the genetic material of the rain forests should belong? What are some ways this benefit of biodiversity might be shared with the whole world?

©Still Pictures/Peter Arnold, Inc.

Biodiversity Hotspots

The most threatened areas of high species diversity on Earth have been labeled *biodiversity hotspots*. Thirty-five of these areas, shown in **Figure 2.5**, have been identified by international conservationists. The hotspot label was developed by ecologists in the late 1980s to identify areas that have high numbers of endemic species but that are also threatened by human activities. Most of these hotspots have lost at least 70 percent of their original natural vegetation. The hotspots include mostly tropical rain forests, coastal areas, and islands. In Madagascar, for example, only 18 percent of the original forests remain. More than 80 percent of Madagascar's 10,000 flowering plant species are endemic, as are 91 percent of its 300 reptile species. All 33 species of lemur, which make up a tenth of the world's primate species, are found only in Madagascar.

FIGURE 2.5

Hotspots Conservationists have identified these 35 *biodiversity hotspots* (green). Examples of endangered species from some areas are shown.

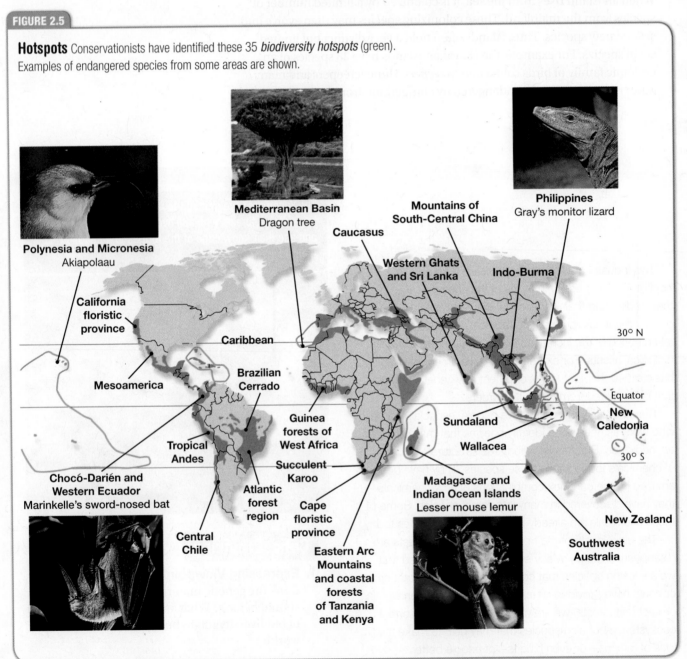

Polynesia and Micronesia
Akiapolaau

Mediterranean Basin
Dragon tree

Mountains of
South-Central China

Caucasus

Philippines
Gray's monitor lizard

Western Ghats
and Sri Lanka

Indo-Burma

California
floristic
province

Caribbean

30° N

Mesoamerica

Brazilian
Cerrado

Sundaland

Equator

New
Caledonia

Tropical
Andes

Guinea
forests of
West Africa

Wallacea

30° S

Chocó-Darién and
Western Ecuador
Marinkelle's sword-nosed bat

Succulent
Karoo

Madagascar and
Indian Ocean Islands
Lesser mouse lemur

New Zealand

Atlantic
forest
region

Central
Chile

Cape
floristic
province

Southwest
Australia

Eastern Arc
Mountains
and coastal
forests
of Tanzania
and Kenya

FIGURE 2.6

At-Risk Species Examples of at-risk species and populations in the United States include **1** the cecropia moth, (declining populations), **2** the tulip poplar tree (limited distribution), **3** the desert pupfish (endangered), and **4** the northern spotted owl (threatened).

Biodiversity in the United States

You may notice that three of the biodiversity hotspots in **Figure 2.5** are partly within U.S. borders. The United States includes a wide variety of unique ecosystems, including the Florida Everglades, the California coastal region, Hawaii, the Great Plains prairies, and the forests of the Pacific Northwest. The United States holds unusually high numbers of species of freshwater fishes, mussels, snails, and crayfish. Species diversity in the United States is also high among groups of land plants such as pine trees and sunflowers. Some examples of the many species and populations that are at risk of being lost are shown in **Figure 2.6**.

The California Floristic Province, a biodiversity hotspot, is home to 3,488 native plant species. Of these species, 2,124 are endemic and 565 are threatened or endangered. The threats to this area include the use of land for agriculture and housing, dam construction, overuse of water, destructive recreation, and mining—all stemming from local human population growth.

Section 2 Formative Assessment

▶ Reviewing Main Ideas

1. **Describe** four ways that species are being threatened with extinction globally.

2. **Define** and give examples of *endangered species* and *threatened species*.

3. **List** areas of the Earth that have high levels of biodiversity and many threats to species.

4. **Compare** the amount of biodiversity in the United States to that of the rest of the world.

✔ Critical Thinking

5. **Interpreting Graphics** The biodiversity hotspots shown in **Figure 2.5** share several characteristics besides a great number of species. Look at the map, and name as many shared characteristics as you can.

6. **Expressing Opinions** Which of the various threats to biodiversity do you think will be most difficult to stop? Which are hardest to justify? Write a paragraph to explain your opinion.

- ▶ List and describe four types of efforts to save individual species.

- ▶ Explain the advantages of protecting entire ecosystems rather than individual species.

- ▶ Describe the main provisions of the Endangered Species Act.

- ▶ Discuss ways in which efforts to protect endangered species can lead to controversy.

- ▶ Describe three examples of worldwide cooperative efforts to prevent extinctions.

Key Terms

germ plasm
Endangered Species Act
habitat conservation plan
Biodiversity Treaty

The Future of Biodiversity

Slowing the loss of species is possible, but to do so we must develop new approaches to conservation and sensitivity to human needs around the globe. In this section, you will read about efforts to save individual species and to protect entire ecosystems.

Saving Species One at a Time

When a species is clearly on the verge of extinction, concerned people sometimes make extraordinary efforts to save the last few individuals. These people hope that a stable population may be restored someday.

Captive-Breeding Programs

Sometimes, wildlife experts may attempt to restore the population of a species through *captive-breeding* programs. These programs involve breeding species in captivity, with the hope of reintroducing populations to their natural habitats. One example of a captive-breeding program involves the California condor, shown in **Figure 3.1**.

Condors are scavengers. They typically soar over vast areas in search of dead animals to eat. Habitat loss, poaching, and lead poisoning brought the species near extinction. In 1986, the nine remaining wild California condors were captured by wildlife experts to protect the birds and to begin a breeding program. Birds bred in captivity were released into the wild in the hope that they would breed there. By 2011, there were 210 condors in the wild, several of them juveniles that had hatched from eggs laid in the wild. But, the survival of this species remains doubtful.

FIGURE 3.1

Captive Breeding The California condor (left) nearly became extinct in the 1980s. A captive-breeding program (right) is returning some condors to the wild.

©David Clenenden/U.S. Fish and Wildlife Service

Preserving Genetic Material

One way to save the essence of a species is by preserving its genetic material. **Germ plasm** is any form of genetic material, such as that contained within the reproductive, or germ, cells of animals and plants. Germ-plasm banks store germ plasm for future use in research or species-recovery efforts. Material may be stored as seeds, sperm, eggs, or pure DNA. Millions of seeds are being preserved in the Millennium Seed Bank in West Sussex, England. These seeds are stored in special controlled environments, as shown in **Figure 3.2**, to keep the genetic material intact for many years. Farmers and gardeners also preserve germ plasm when they save and share seeds.

Zoos, Aquariums, Parks, and Gardens

The original idea of zoos was to put exotic animals on display. However, in some cases, zoos now house the few remaining members of a species and are perhaps the species' last hope for survival. Zoos, wildlife parks, aquariums, and botanical gardens are living museums of the world's biodiversity. Botanical gardens, such as the one shown in **Figure 3.3**, house about 90,000 species of plants worldwide. Even so, these kinds of facilities rarely have enough resources to preserve more than a fraction of the world's rare and threatened species.

More Study Needed

Ultimately, saving a few individuals does little to preserve a species. Captive species may not reproduce or survive again in the wild. Also, small populations are vulnerable to infectious diseases and genetic disorders caused by inbreeding. Conservationists hope that these strategies are only used as a last resort to save species.

FIGURE 3.2

Seed Banks Seeds are stored in controlled conditions. The samples may be able to reproduce organisms many years from now.

FIGURE 3.3

Botanical Gardens This botanical garden is contained within a clear dome in Queen Elizabeth Park in Vancouver, Canada. The dome houses over 500 species of plants from all over the world as well as over 100 species of tropical birds.

(b) ©Cameramann International; (t) ©James King-Holmes/Photo Researchers, Inc.

✔ **CHECK FOR UNDERSTANDING**

Summarize Why does protecting the habitat of threatened and endangered species involve large areas?

FIGURE 3.4

Sustainable Land Use Another conservation strategy is to promote more creative and sustainable land uses. This coffee crop is grown in the shade of native tropical trees. This practice is restoring habitat for many migrating songbirds.

Preserving Habitats and Ecosystems

The most effective way to save species is to protect their habitats. But a species confined to a small area could be wiped out by a single natural disaster. Some species require a large range to find food, a suitable mate, and rear their young. Therefore, protecting the habitats of endangered and threatened species often means preserving or managing large areas.

Conservation Strategies

Most conservationists now give priority to protecting entire ecosystems rather than individual species. By protecting entire ecosystems, we may be able to save most of the species in an ecosystem instead of only the ones that have been identified as endangered. The public has begun to understand that Earth's biosphere depends on all its connected ecosystems.

To protect biodiversity worldwide, conservationists focus on the hot-spots described in the previous section. However, protecting hotspots is not enough. One strategy is to identify areas of native habitat that can be preserved, restored, and linked into large networks. Another promising strategy is to promote products that have been harvested with sustainable practices, such as the shade-grown coffee shown in **Figure 3.4**.

More Study Needed

Conservationists emphasize the need for more detailed studies of eco-systems. Only in recent decades has there been research into such basic questions as, How large does a protected preserve have to be to maintain a certain number of species? How much fragmentation can a particular ecosystem tolerate? What are the key species needed to maintain ecosystem functions? Important progress has been made to answer these questions that allows informed decisions affecting biodiversity to continue to be made while further studies are conducted.

©Andy Nelson/Christian Science Monitor/Getty Images

Legal Protections for Species

Many nations have laws and regulations designed to prevent the extinction of species, and those in the United States are among the strongest. Even so, there is controversy about how to enforce such laws and about how effective they are.

U.S. Laws

In 1973, the U.S. Congress passed the **Endangered Species Act** and has amended it several times since. This law, summarized in **Figure 3.5**, is designed to protect plant and animal species in danger of extinction. Under the first provision, the U.S. Fish and Wildlife Service (USFWS) must compile a list of all endangered and threatened species in the United States. As of 2012, 1,383 species of plants and animals were listed as endangered or threatened. Dozens more are considered for the list each year. The second main provision of the act protects listed species from human harm. Anyone who harms, buys, or sells any part of these species is subject to a fine. The third provision prevents the federal government from carrying out any project that jeopardizes a listed species.

Recovery and Habitat Conservation Plans

Under the fourth main provision of the Endangered Species Act, the USFWS must prepare a *species recovery plan* for each listed species. These plans often propose to protect or restore habitat for each species. However, attempts to restrict human uses of land can be controversial. Real estate developers may be prohibited from building on their own land because it contains critical habitat for a species. People may lose income when land uses are restricted and may object when their interests are placed below those of another species.

Although battles between developers and environmentalists are widely publicized, in most cases compromises are eventually worked out. One form of compromise is a **habitat conservation plan**—a plan that attempts to protect one or more species across large areas of land through trade-offs or cooperative agreements. The region of California shown in **Figure 3.6** is part of a habitat conservation plan.

FIGURE 3.5

MAJOR PROVISIONS OF THE ENDANGERED SPECIES ACT

The U.S. Fish and Wildlife Service must compile a list of all endangered and threatened species in the United States.

Endangered and threatened animal species may not be caught or killed. Endangered and threatened plants on federal land may not be uprooted. No part of an endangered and threatened species may be sold or traded.

The federal government may not carry out any project that jeopardizes endangered species.

The U.S. Fish and Wildlife Service must prepare a species recovery plan for each endangered and threatened species.

FIGURE 3.6

This region of San Diego, California, is home to several endangered species. A habitat conservation plan attempts to protect these species by managing a large group of lands in the area.

FIGURE 3.7

Poaching Scenes like this one of elephant tusk poaching were common before the worldwide ban on the sale of ivory as part of CITES.

International Cooperation

At the global level, the International Union for the Conservation of Nature and Natural Resources (IUCN) facilitates efforts to protect species and habitats. This organization is a collaboration of almost 200 government agencies and over 700 private conservation organizations. The IUCN publishes *Red Lists* of species in danger of extinction around the world. The IUCN also advises governments on ways to manage their natural resources, and works with groups such as the World Wildlife Fund to sponsor conservation projects.

International Trade and Poaching

One product of the IUCN has been an international treaty called *CITES* (the Convention on International Trade in Endangered Species). The CITES treaty was the first effective effort to stop the slaughter of African elephants. Elephants were being killed by poachers who would sell the ivory tusks. Efforts during the 1970s and 1980s to limit the sale of ivory did little to stop the poaching. Then in 1989, the members of CITES proposed a worldwide ban on all trade in ivory, hoping to prevent scenes like those shown in **Figure 3.7**.

Some people worried that making ivory illegal might increase the rate of poaching instead of decrease it. They argued that illegal ivory, like illegal drugs, might sell for a higher price. But after the ban was enacted, the price of ivory dropped, and elephant poaching declined dramatically.

The Biodiversity Treaty

One of the most ambitious efforts to tackle environmental issues on a worldwide scale was the United Nations Conference on Environment and Development, also known as the first *Earth Summit*. More than 100 world leaders and 30,000 other participants met in 1992 in Rio de Janeiro, Brazil.

Connect to MATH

Measuring Risk

There are many ways to categorize a species' degree of risk of extinction. The IUCN and the Nature Conservancy have multiple ranks for species of concern, ranging from "presumed extinct" to "secure." According to one study of 20,500 species in the United States, 1,400 of those species were at some risk. Calculate this number of species at risk as a percentage. Use this percentage to estimate how many species may be at risk around the world.

An important result of the Earth Summit was an international agreement called the **Biodiversity Treaty**. The treaty's goal is to preserve biodiversity and ensure the sustainable and fair use of genetic resources in all countries. However, the treaty took many years to be adopted into law by the U.S. government. Some political groups objected to the Treaty, especially to the suggestion that economic and trade agreements should take into account any impacts on biodiversity that might result from the agreements. The international community will thus continue to have debates like those that have surrounded the Endangered Species Act in the United States.

Private Conservation Efforts

Many private nonprofit organizations work to protect species worldwide, often more effectively than government agencies. The World Wildlife Fund encourages the sustainable use of resources and supports wildlife protection. The Nature Conservancy has helped purchase millions of hectares of habitat preserves in more than 30 countries. Conservation International helps identify biodiversity hotspots and develop ecosystem conservation projects in partnership with other organizations and local people. Greenpeace International organizes direct and sometimes confrontational actions, such as the one shown in **Figure 3.8**, to counter environmental threats.

FIGURE 3.8

Activism These Greenpeace activists are blocking the path of a nuclear submarine.

✔ CRITICAL THINKING
Decide Do you think this is an effective way to protect species? Explain.

Balancing Human Needs

Attempts to protect species often come into conflict with the interests of the world's human inhabitants. Sometimes, an endangered species represents a source of food or income. In other cases, a given species may not seem valuable to those who do not understand the species' role in an ecosystem. Many conservationists feel that an important part of protecting species is making the value of biodiversity understood by more people.

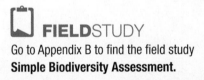

FIELDSTUDY
Go to Appendix B to find the field study
Simple Biodiversity Assessment.

✔ Section 3 **Formative Assessment**

▶ Reviewing Main Ideas

1. **Describe** four types of efforts to save individual species.

2. **Explain** the advantages of protecting entire ecosystems rather than individual species.

3. **Describe** the main provisions of the Endangered Species Act.

4. **Give** examples of worldwide cooperative efforts to prevent extinctions.

✔ Critical Thinking

5. **Analyzing Methods** Read the headings in this section. Which type of effort to preserve species do you think is most worthwhile?

6. **Comparing Viewpoints** Discuss ways in which efforts to protect species can lead to controversy.

7. **Inferring Relationships** Why was a complete ban of ivory sales more effective than a limited ban?

Dr. E. O. Wilson: Champion of Biodiversity

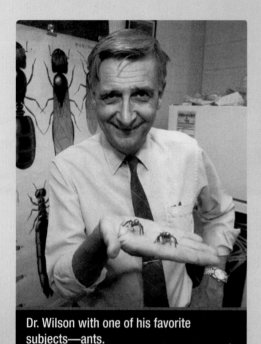

Dr. Wilson with one of his favorite subjects—ants.

Dr. Edward Osborne Wilson deserves some of the credit for the fact that this book includes a chapter called "Biodiversity." Just a few decades ago, the word *biodiversity* was used by few scientists and wasn't found in many dictionaries. Dr. Wilson has helped make the concept and value of biodiversity widely recognized, through his extensive research, publishing, organizing, and social advocacy.

Since his early career as a pioneer in the fields of entomology and sociobiology, Dr. Wilson has gained recognition for many additional accomplishments. He has written two Pulitzer Prize-winning nonfiction books and has received the National Medal of Science and dozens of other scientific awards and honors. Wilson is widely recognized as one of the most influential scientists and citizens of our time.

It All Started with Bugs

Even before his scientific career, Wilson developed a fascination with insects and the natural world. He always had high expectations of himself but made the best of circumstances. Although his parents were divorced and his father's government career required frequent moves, Wilson found companionship in the woods of the southern United States or the museums of Washington, D.C. After injuries damaged his vision and hearing, Wilson focused his scientific skills on the smaller forms of life.

By the time he earned his master's degree at the University of Alabama at the age of 20, Wilson was well known as a promising *entomologist*— an expert on the insect world. His specialty is the study of ants and their complex social behaviors. So it makes sense that Wilson next went to study at Harvard University, home to the world's largest ant collection. While at Harvard, he earned his Ph.D., conducted field research around the world, collected more than 100 previously undescribed species, and wrote several books on insect physiology and social organization. He eventually became curator of the Museum of Entomology at Harvard.

Clearly, Wilson has a passion for insects. "There is a very special pleasure in looking in a microscope and saying I am the first person to see a species that may be millions of years old," he says. Some of Wilson's research has focused on the social behavior of ants. Among other important scientific findings, Wilson was the first to demonstrate that ant behavior and communication is based mostly on chemical signals.

ECOZine at HMDScience.com — Go online for the latest environmental science news and updates on all EcoZine articles.

From Insects to Humans

In 1971, Wilson published *The Insect Societies,* which surveyed the evolution of social organization among wasps, ants, bees, and termites. Wilson began to extend his attempts to understand the relationship of biology and social behavior to other animals, including humans. In 1975, Wilson published a controversial book exploring these new ideas, called *Sociobiology.* Now an accepted branch of science, sociobiology is the study of the biological basis of social behavior in animals, including humans.

During Wilson's studies of the behavior of ants and other social insects, he became interested in the insects' role in the ecosystems where he studied them. Some of his research involved camping for months at a time in a remote wilderness such as the Amazon basin, carefully studying the activities of certain species. His writings include amazing tales of watching huge colonies of "driver" ants swarm out over an area, capturing and killing a great many other species in their path.

In 1990, Wilson received his second Pulitzer Prize for co-authoring *The Ants,* an enormous encyclopedia of the ant world. In addition to describing 8,800 known species of ants, the book details the great variations among ant species in terms of anatomy, biochemistry, complex social behaviors, and especially their critical role in many ecosystems. Wilson reminds us that ants "are some of the most abundant and diverse of the Earth's 1.4 million species. They're among the little creatures that run the Earth. If ants and other small animals were to disappear, the Earth would rot. Fish, reptiles, birds—and humans—would crash to extinction."

Onward to Biodiversity

As with many great scientists, each thing Dr. Wilson studies leads him to new questions and new ideas. During his research, Wilson spent time reflecting and writing on the nature of ecosystems, the importance of biodiversity, and the role of humans in relation to these. In 1992, he put many of these ideas into another popular book called *The Diversity of Life.* This book combined Wilson's engaging writing style and personal expertise with the latest ecological research. The book showed both how such incredible biodiversity has evolved on Earth and how this asset is being lost because of current human activities. The book clearly explained for the general public many of the problems and potential solutions regarding biodiversity that we have studied in this chapter.

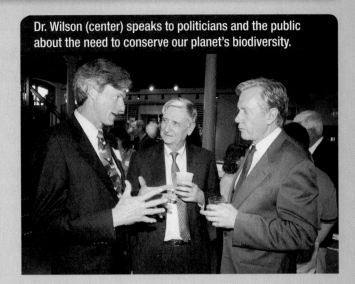

Dr. Wilson (center) speaks to politicians and the public about the need to conserve our planet's biodiversity.

Urgent Work

Despite his fame, Wilson is a soft-spoken fellow who would prefer to live a quiet life with his research and with his family in their home in the woods of Massachusetts. But the urgent problem of species loss makes Wilson willing to face the public. "Humanity is entering a bottleneck of overpopulation and environmental degradation unique in history. We need to carry every species through the bottleneck . . . Along with culture itself, they will be the most precious gift we can give future generations."

In the early 2000s, Dr. Wilson began promoting the need for a global biodiversity survey. This project would involve an international scientific effort on par with the Human Genome Project.

This vision for a global biodiversity survey led to the Encyclopedia of Life (EOL) project. The EOL is a free, online collaborative encyclopedia with the goal of providing information about all 1.9 million species that have been described. Wilson states that "to describe and classify all of the species of the world deserves to be one of the great scientific goals of the new century." As of September 2011, hundreds of partners have added more than 700,000 species to EOL and Wilson's vision is moving toward being fulfilled.

What Do You Think?

Do you find insects interesting? Could you imagine yourself as an entomologist? Do you think that Dr. Wilson made a goal early in his life to be an internationally famous conservationist? What has led him to take on this role?

SECTION 1 What Is Biodiversity?

OBJECTIVES

- Biodiversity usually refers to the number of different species in a given area.
- The study of biodiversity starts with the unfinished task of identifying and cataloging all species on Earth. Although scientists disagree about the probable number of species on Earth, they do agree that we need to study biodiversity more thoroughly.
- Humanity benefits from biodiversity in several ways and perhaps in some unknown ways.

KEY TERMS

biodiversity
gene
keystone species
ecotourism

SECTION 2 Biodiversity at Risk

OBJECTIVES

- Many scientists are now concerned that loss of biodiversity is the most challenging environmental issue we face.
- The most common cause of extinction today is the destruction of habitats by humans. Unregulated hunting and the introduction of nonnative species also contribute to extinctions.
- Certain areas of the world contain a greater diversity of species than other areas. An important feature of such areas is that they have a large portion of endemic species.
- The United States has a very important role in preserving biodiversity through laws and regulations.

KEY TERMS

endangered species
threatened species
exotic species
poaching
endemic species

SECTION 3 The Future of Biodiversity

OBJECTIVES

- Most major conservation efforts concentrate on protecting entire ecosystems rather than individual species.
- The Endangered Species Act establishes protections for endangered and threatened species in the United States. The act has generated some controversy and has been amended several times.
- International cooperation has led to increased recognition and protection of biodiversity worldwide.
- The desire to protect biodiversity often conflicts with other human interests.

KEY TERMS

germ plasm
Endangered Species Act
habitat conservation plan
Biodiversity Treaty

(t) ©David Courtenay/Oxford Scientific/Getty Images; © ©Millard H. Sharp/Photo Researchers, Inc.; (b) ©Chuck Place/Alamy Images

CHAPTER 10 Review

Reviewing Key Terms

Use each of the following terms in a separate sentence.

1. *keystone species*
2. *ecotourism*

For each pair of terms, explain how the meanings of the terms differ.

3. *hunting* and *poaching*
4. *endemic species* and *exotic species*
5. *endangered species* and *threatened species*
6. *gene* and *germ plasm*
7. *CITES* and *Biodiversity Treaty*
8. **Concept Map** Use the following terms to create a concept map: *biodiversity, species, gene, ecosystem, habitat loss, poaching, exotic species, germ plasm, captive breeding programs,* and *habitat preservation.*

Reviewing Main Ideas

9. The term *biodiversity* refers to
   a. the variety of species on Earth.
   b. the extinction of the dinosaurs.
   c. habitat destruction, invasive exotic species, and poaching.
   d. the fact that 40 percent of prescription drugs come from living things.

10. Most of the living species known to science
    a. are large mammals.
    b. live in deserts.
    c. live in the richer countries of the world.
    d. are insects.

11. Some species are so important to the functioning of an ecosystem that they are called
    a. threatened species.
    b. keystone species.
    c. endangered species.
    d. extinct species.

12. When sea otters disappeared from the Pacific coast of North America,
    a. the area became overrun with kelp.
    b. the number of fish in the kelp beds increased.
    c. the number of sea urchins in the kelp beds increased.
    d. the area became overrun with brown seaweed.

13. Which of the following statements about the Endangered Species Act is *not* true?
    a. Parts of an endangered animal, such as feathers or fur, may be traded or sold but only if the animal is not killed.
    b. A species is considered endangered if it is expected to become extinct in the near future.
    c. The federal government cannot carry out a project that may jeopardize an endangered plant.
    d. A recovery plan is prepared for all animals that are listed as endangered.

14. Because of efforts by the Convention on International Trade in Endangered Species (CITES),
    a. the poaching of elephants increased.
    b. the cost of ivory worldwide increased.
    c. the international trade of ivory was banned worldwide.
    d. a captive-breeding program for elephants was established.

15. Emphasizing the preservation of entire ecosystems will
    a. cause the economic needs of farmers to suffer in order to save a single species.
    b. decrease biodiversity, especially in tropical rain forests, coral reefs, and islands.
    c. throw the food webs of many ecosystems out of balance.
    d. save many unknown species from extinction.

Short Answer

16. When was hunting a major cause of extinctions in the United States?

17. What are exotic species, and how do they endanger other species?

18. Why do biologists favor using an ecosystem approach to preserve biodiversity?

19. Describe three ways that preserving biodiversity can come into conflict with human interests.

Interpreting Graphics

The graph below shows the numbers of various types of species that are officially listed as endangered or threatened in the United States and internationally. Use the graph to answer questions 20–23.

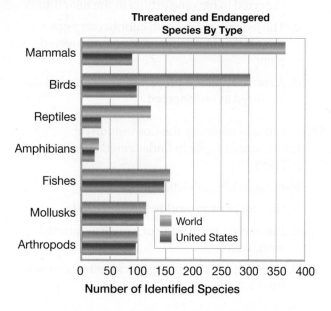

Threatened and Endangered Species By Type

Mammals
Birds
Reptiles
Amphibians
Fishes
Mollusks
Arthropods

World
United States

0   50   100 150 200 250 300 350 400
Number of Identified Species

20. Critique Do these numbers necessarily reflect *all* species that may be in danger? Explain your answer.

21. Assess Which types of species might be underrepresented in the graph?

22. Analyze Compare the United States and world listings. What trends do you see in the types of species listed in the graph?

23. Evaluate Given this information, which types of species might need further research worldwide?

Critical Thinking

24. Comparing Processes Read the passage in this chapter that describes current extinctions. How are the extinctions that are occurring currently different from most extinctions in the past?

25. Analyzing Methods With unlimited funding, could zoos and captive-breeding programs restore most endangered animal populations? Explain your answers.

26. Determining Cause and Effect How might the loss of huge tracts of tropical rain forests have an effect on other parts of the world?

27. Literature Try to remember or find some children's stories that include wild animals that are currently endangered, threatened, or extinct. Write a description of how these animals are portrayed in the stories. In your description, compare the animals in the stories to what you know about the real animals.

28. Geography Obtain a list of the plants and animals that are endangered in your state. Find out where these species live, and mark the locations on a map of your state. Research the effects of habitat loss on species in your county or in surrounding areas.

29. Analyzing Limits In 2010 the United Nations reported that governments were largely ignoring the Biodiversity Treaty, allowing the extinction of species to continue at an alarming rate. What does this fact reveal about the limitations of international treaties?

Analyzing Data

Use the table below to answer questions 30–31.

ESTIMATES OF KNOWLEDGE OF EARTH'S SPECIES

Type of Species	Number of Species Described	Described Species as % of Total	Number Threatened or Extinct	Accuracy of Estimates
Bacteria	4,000	0.40	(unknown)	very poor
Vertebrates	52,000	94.55	3,843	good
Crustaceans	40,000	26.67	628	moderate
Plants	270,000	84.38	31,277	good

30. Analyzing Data Which of the types of species in the table are most accurately described? What do the numbers indicate about how well various species are studied?

31. Applying Quantities Which of the types of species may represent the greatest unknown loss of biodiversity? Which type of species is probably least important for further research into biodiversity?

Making Connections

32. Writing Persuasively Write a letter to the editor of a publication or to an elected representative in which you express your opinion regarding protections of endangered species that might affect your local area.

33. Outlining Topics Outline the major strategies for protecting biodiversity that have been described in this chapter. List pros and cons of each strategy.

CASESTUDY

34. Why might scientists want to consult with indigenous cultures when searching an area for new species?

35. Describe the controversy regarding who should profit from the discovery of new species. Who do you think should profit from such discoveries? Explain your answer.

Why It Matters

36. Why should we strive to maintain biodiversity?

37. Why is it of particular importance to protect hotspots?

STUDYSKILL

Use a Map As you review the chapter, refer to an atlas, to the maps in the Appendix, or to previous chapters about biomes to compare information. Draw your own map or make a list of the locations of some of the interesting species and ecosystems that you learn about.

Differences in Diversity

Objectives

Observe and measure differences in species diversity between two locations.

Graph and analyze data collected to reflect differences in species diversity.

Evaluate the possible reasons for observed differences in biodiversity.

Infer other human activities that may influence local biodiversity.

Materials

graph paper

hand lens

meterstick or tape measure

pen or pencil

string or chalk line

optional materials: local-area field guides for plants, animals, and soil organisms; shovel or trowel

Procedure Step 2 Measure and mark off sample areas for your observation and counts of species diversity.

Biodiversity is most obvious and dramatic in tropical rain forest and coral reef ecosystems, but you do not have to travel that far to observe differences in species diversity or to see the effects that humans can have on biodiversity.

Recall that biodiversity is most often defined as the number of different species that are present in a given area. This measure can be estimated by making a sample count of species within a representative area. It is often easiest and most effective to collect or observe small organisms, such as insects and soil dwellers, or stationary organisms, such as plants and trees. In this activity, you will investigate the differences in species diversity in two areas that are close to each other, but that are affected differently by humans. You may work in teams or groups.

Procedure

1. Choose two sites for your analysis. Site 1 should be an area that has been greatly affected by humans, such as your school building and the surrounding sidewalks, parking area, or groomed lawns. Site 2 should be an area within view of site 1 but that is less affected by humans, such as a wooded area or a vacant lot overgrown with weeds. If directed by your teacher, you may choose more than two sites. Also ask your teacher about your sample square size.

2. At each site, measure a 5 m × 5 m square area using the meterstick or tape measure. You might use the edge of a building as a side of your square, or you might use trees as the corners. Mark the measurement of the area with string or a chalk line, as shown in the photograph.

3. Observe each site carefully, and record a detailed description of each site. Include as many features as possible, such as location, soil condition, ways the area is used, amount of sun or rain exposure, and other factors that might affect the organisms that exist there.

4. For each site, create a table similar to the one shown below.

SPECIES COUNTS PER SITE		
Species Type	Site Number ___	Site Number ___
Animals		
Plants		
Fungi and other soil organisms		

5. Using your hand lens, find as many different species as possible within the site. Record each new species by placing a slash or tick mark in the column for each different species identified in each general category. You do not need to identify every organism by scientific name, but using a set of field guides may help you have an idea of what you are finding. You may also make more specific categories (such as birds, insects, grasses, and trees) if you are able. Be careful not to disturb the area unnecessarily.

6. Repeat steps 2–5 for each site. If directed by your teacher, compare your data with those of other groups.

7. After you have made and recorded all of your observations, put away your materials and restore anything you disturbed at the sites.

Analysis

1. Constructing Graphs Create a bar graph of the number of species counted at each site. As directed by your teacher, you may combine all species counts into one total per site or graph each category of organisms separately.

2. Analyzing Results Based on your observations of the organisms found at the sites, which area reflected a higher level of biodiversity?

3. Interpreting Results What factors may have contributed to the differences in biodiversity at the sites?

Conclusions

4. Drawing Conclusions What can you conclude about the effect of human activities on biodiversity?

5. Applying Conclusions What other human activities, besides those you observed directly, could have affected the biodiversity present at your sites?

6. Evaluating Methods Do you feel that the method used in this lab was an effective way to identify biodiversity in an area? Why or why not? How could it have been improved?

Extension

7. Research and Communications If you were able to use local field guides, what can you generalize about the organisms that you were able to identify? Pay attention to aspects such as how easily recognizable each organism is, how common it is in your local area, where it is found outside of your area, or what other unique facts are known about the biology or habitat needs of the organism.

Procedure Step 5 Observe and record how many different types of organisms you find within each sample area.

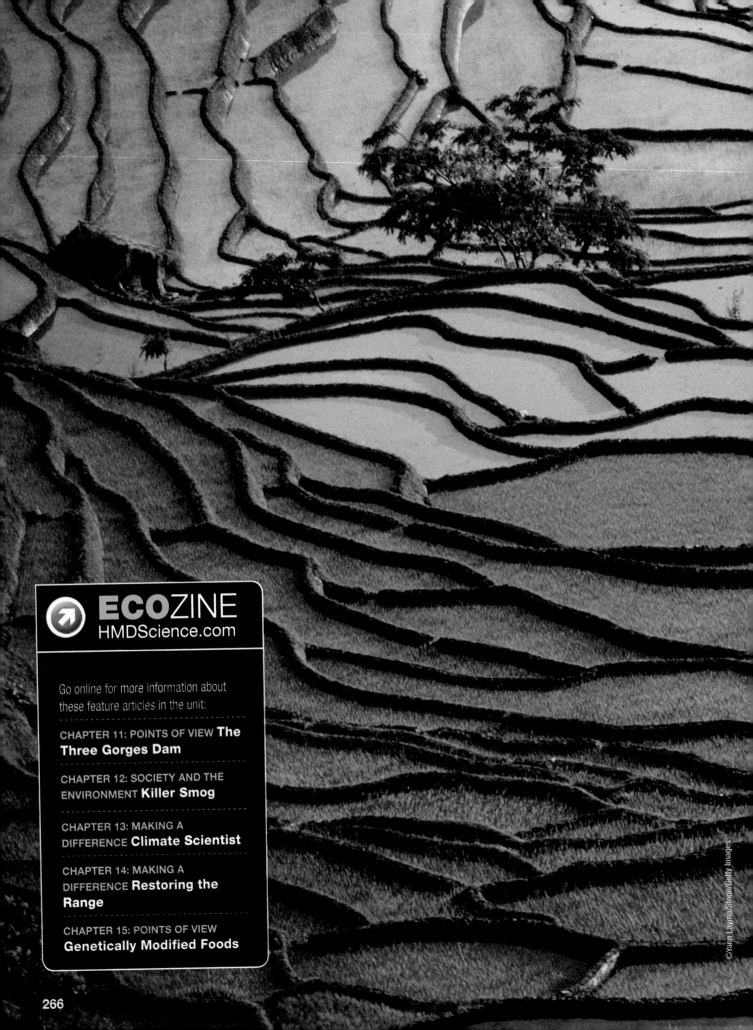

©Yann Layma/Stone/Getty Images

Water, Air, and Land

For thousands of years, humans have altered the environment to grow food. These rice paddies in China are built to trap water from the monsoon rains.

(l) ©Ralph A. Clevenger/Corbis; (tc) ©Deborah Davis/Getty Images; (c) ©NASA; (b) ©David R. Frazier Photolibrary, Inc./Alamy; (bc) ©Jim Wark/Airphoto

Chapter 11

Water

Section 1
Water Resources

Section 2
Water Use and Management

Section 3
Water Pollution

Why It Matters

Approximately 800 million people across the world do not have access to safe drinking water. This access is directly related to poverty and some 6000 children die every day. These deaths are mostly from disease associated with lack of clean drinking water, poor sanitation, and poor hygiene.

What could be done to help alleviate these problems?

CASESTUDY

Learn more about one of the world's largest known aquifers in the case study The Ogallala Aquifer: An Underground Treasure on page 272.

ONLINE ENVIRONMENTAL SCIENCE
HMDScience.com

Go online to access additional resources, including labs, worksheets, multimedia, and resources in Spanish.

Water Resources

SECTION 1

Objectives

▸ Describe the distribution of Earth's water resources.

▸ Explain why fresh water is one of Earth's limited resources.

▸ Describe the distribution of Earth's surface water.

▸ Describe the relationship between groundwater and surface water in a watershed.

The next time you drink a glass of water, think about where the water came from. Did you know that some of the water in your glass may have been part of a rainstorm that pounded Earth long before life existed? Or that the water you washed your car with may have been part of a dinosaur that lived millions of years ago? The water we use today has been around since water first formed on Earth billions of years ago. Water is essential to life on Earth. Humans can survive for more than a month without food, but we can live for only a few days without water.

Two kinds of water are found on Earth. Fresh water—the water that people can drink—contains little salt. Salt water—the water in oceans—contains a higher concentration of dissolved salts and minerals. Most human uses for water, such as drinking and agriculture, require fresh water.

Key Terms
surface water
river system
watershed
groundwater
aquifer
porosity
permeability
recharge zone

The Water Cycle

Earth is often called "the Water Planet" because it has an abundance of water in all forms: solid, liquid, and gas. Water is a renewable resource because it is circulated in the water cycle, as shown in **Figure 1.1**. In the water cycle, water molecules travel between Earth's surface and the atmosphere. Water evaporates at the surface and leaves behind salts and other compounds. As the water vapor rises through the atmosphere, the gas cools and condenses into drops of liquid water that form clouds. Eventually the water in clouds falls back to Earth and replenishes Earth's sources of water. The oceans are an important part of the water cycle because they contain almost all of the planet's water.

FIGURE 1.1

Water Cycle The water cycle is the continuous movement of water between Earth and its atmosphere.

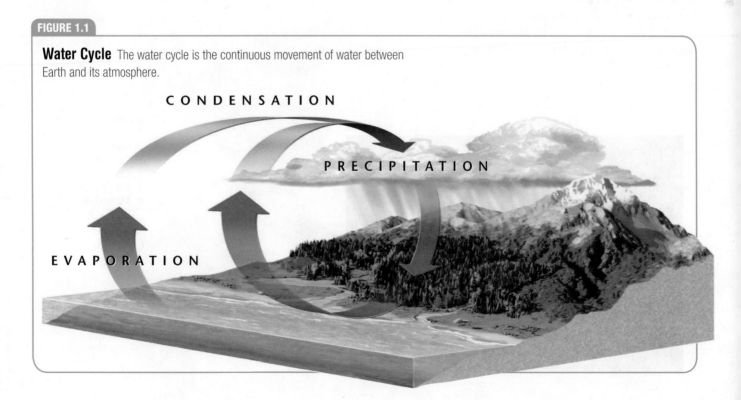

CONDENSATION

PRECIPITATION

EVAPORATION

FIGURE 1.2

Global Water This pie graph shows the distribution of water on Earth. What percentage of Earth's fresh water is in a form that humans can use?

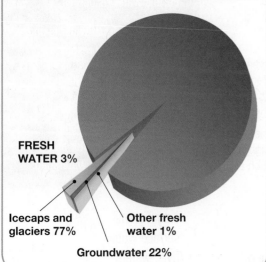

FRESH WATER 3%

Icecaps and glaciers 77%

Other fresh water 1%

Groundwater 22%

✔ **CHECK FOR UNDERSTANDING**

Explain What are some things most large cities use surface water for?

Global Water Distribution

To understand why fresh water is such a limited resource, you have to understand how little fresh water is found on Earth. Although 71 percent of the Earth's surface is covered with water, nearly 97 percent of Earth's water is salt water in oceans and seas. **Figure 1.2** illustrates this relationship. Of the fresh water on Earth, about 77 percent is frozen in glaciers and polar icecaps. Only a small percentage of the water on Earth is liquid fresh water that humans can use. The fresh water we use comes mainly from lakes and rivers and from a relatively narrow zone beneath Earth's surface.

Surface Water

Surface water is fresh water on Earth's land surface. Surface water is found in lakes, rivers, streams, and wetlands. Throughout history, people have built cities, towns, and farms near reliable sources of surface water. Some of the oldest cities in the world were built near rivers. Today, most large cities depend on surface water for their water supplies. Rivers, lakes, man-made reservoirs, aquifers, and streams provide drinking water, water to grow crops, food such as fish and shellfish, power for industry, and a means of transportation by boat.

FIGURE 1.3

Watersheds of the World This map shows the Earth's major watersheds. The highlighted area of the satellite image below shows that the Mississippi River watershed covers almost half of the United States.

Missouri R.

Mississippi R.

Ohio R.

Arkansas R.

Tennessee R.

Red R.

North America
1. Yukon
2. Mackenzie
3. Columbia
4. Colorado
5. Rio Grande
6. Mississippi

South America
7. Orinoco
8. Amazon
9. Paraná

©E.R.I.M./Stone/Getty Images

River Systems

Have you ever wondered where all the water in a river comes from? Most streams form as water from falling rain and melting snow drains from mountains, hills, plateaus, and plains. Others form from ground-water moving to the surface. As streams flow downhill, they combine with other streams and form rivers. The more streams that run into a river, the larger the river becomes. As streams and rivers move across the land, they form a flowing network of water called a **river system**. If a river system is viewed from above, it can look like the roots of a tree that are feeding into a trunk. The Mississippi, the Amazon, and the Nile are enormous river systems because they collect the water that flows from vast areas of land. The Amazon River system is the largest river system in the world—it drains an area of land that is nearly the size of Europe.

Watersheds

The area of land that is drained by a river is known as a **watershed**. The watershed of the Mississippi River is shown in the satellite image in **Figure 1.3**. The amount of water that enters a watershed varies throughout the year. Melting snow, as well as rains can dramatically increase the amount of water in a watershed. Other times of the year, the river system that drains a watershed may be reduced to a trickle. Pollution anywhere in a watershed may end up polluting all of the water downstream. Communities dependent on rivers can be severely affected by natural and man-made changes to the river system.

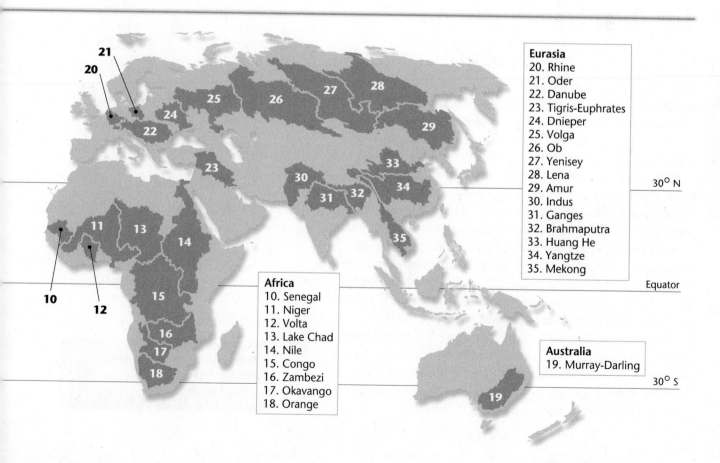

Eurasia
20. Rhine
21. Oder
22. Danube
23. Tigris-Euphrates
24. Dnieper
25. Volga
26. Ob
27. Yenisey
28. Lena
29. Amur
30. Indus
31. Ganges
32. Brahmaputra
33. Huang He
34. Yangtze
35. Mekong

Africa
10. Senegal
11. Niger
12. Volta
13. Lake Chad
14. Nile
15. Congo
16. Zambezi
17. Okavango
18. Orange

Australia
19. Murray-Darling

30° N

Equator

30° S

Groundwater

Most of the fresh water that is available for human use cannot be seen—it exists underground. When it rains, some of the water that falls onto the land flows into lakes and streams. But much of the water percolates through the soil and down into the rocks beneath. Water that is found beneath Earth's surface in the spaces in sediment and rock formations is called **groundwater**.

As water travels beneath Earth's surface, it eventually reaches a level where the rocks and soil are saturated with water. This level is known as the *water table*. In wet regions, the water table may be at Earth's surface, and a spring of fresh water may flow out onto the ground. But in deserts, the water table may be hundreds of meters beneath Earth's surface. The water table is actually not as level as its name implies. The water table has peaks and valleys that match the shape of the land above it. Just as surface water flows downhill, groundwater tends to flow slowly from the peaks of the water table to the valleys. As groundwater slowly percolates downward, some impurities may be filtered out. However, it may also accumulate minerals from the materials through which it passes.

CASESTUDY

The Ogallala Aquifer: An Underground Treasure

Anyone who has eaten food produced in the United States has probably enjoyed the benefits of the Ogallala Aquifer. This enormous underground water system formed from glaciers that melted at the end of the last Ice Age, 12,000 years ago. Today, the Ogallala Aquifer supplies about one-third of the groundwater used in the United States.

People began to use the Ogallala Aquifer extensively for irrigation in the 1940s. With help from this ancient water source, the Great Plains became one of the most productive farming regions in the world. Farmers seemed to enjoy a limitless supply of fresh water. But in recent years, the Ogallala Aquifer has started to show its limits. Water is being withdrawn from the aquifer 10 to 40 times faster than it is being replaced. In some places, the water table has dropped more than 30 m (100 ft) since pumping began. Continuing drought conditions have increased its rate of depletion.

Humans are not the only living things that depend on the Ogallala Aquifer. In some areas, the aquifer flows onto the surface and creates wetlands, which are a vital habitat for many organisms, especially birds. These wetlands are often the first habitats to disappear when the aquifer doesn't recharge and the water table falls.

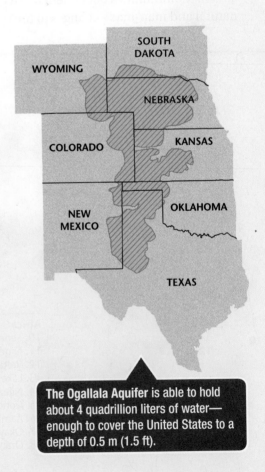

The Ogallala Aquifer is able to hold about 4 quadrillion liters of water—enough to cover the United States to a depth of 0.5 m (1.5 ft).

Aquifers

An underground formation that contains groundwater is called an **aquifer**. The water table forms the upper boundary of an aquifer. Most aquifers consist of materials such as rock, sand, and gravel that have a lot of spaces where water can accumulate. As well, groundwater can dissolve rock formations, such as those made of limestone, and fill vast caves with water, which creates underground lakes. Aquifers are an important water source for many cities and for agriculture.

Porosity and Permeability

Although most rocks appear solid, many kinds of rocks contain small holes, or pore spaces. **Porosity** is the percentage of the total volume of a rock that has spaces (pores). Water in an aquifer is stored in the pore spaces and flows from one pore space to another. The more porous a rock is, the more water it can hold. The ability of rock or soil to allow water to flow through it is called **permeability**. Materials such as gravel that allow the flow of water are *permeable*. Materials such as clay or granite that do not allow the flow of water are *impermeable*. The most productive aquifers usually form in permeable materials, such as sandstone, limestone, or layers of sand and gravel.

✔ **CHECK FOR UNDERSTANDING**
Compare How does the level of the water table in wet regions differ from ihe level in deserts?

Sandhill cranes are among the many kinds of birds that rely on water from the Ogallala Aquifer.

Many people are working together to try to conserve the Ogallala Aquifer. For example, some farmers have begun to limit irrigation during bird migrations in order to allow surface-water levels to rise. Other farmers have adopted water-saving irrigation systems and are planting crops such as wheat or grain sorghum, which require less water than corn or cotton.

Farmers and other residents of the Great Plains recognize the value of the Ogallala Aquifer and are pressuring politicians to replace policies that encourage wasting water with policies that promote water conservation. These efforts may help save this underground treasure.

Critical Thinking

1. **Applying Ideas** Most of the water in the Ogallala Aquifer came from glaciers that melted thousands of years ago. What is the aquifer's primary water source today?

2. **Expressing Viewpoints** Do you think residents of the Great Plains are the only people who have an interest in conserving the Ogallala Aquifer? Write an editorial that expresses your viewpoint.

©Superstock/Alamy Images

FIGURE 1.4

Anatomy of an Aquifer Aquifers are underground formations that hold water. Impermeable rock can be porous or nonporous, but only permeable rock allows water to pass through it.

✔ **CRITICAL THINKING**

Explain In addition to pollution, what factors are causing many aquifers to be threatened?

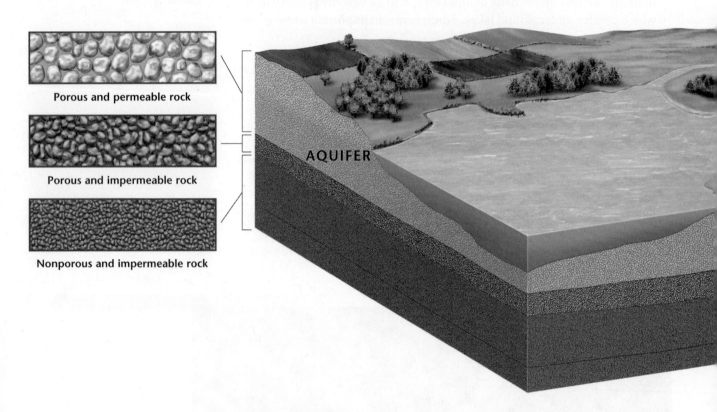

Porous and permeable rock

Porous and impermeable rock

Nonporous and impermeable rock

AQUIFER

The Recharge Zone

To reach an aquifer, surface water must travel down through permeable layers of soil and rock. Notice the permeable layers above the aquifer in **Figure 1.4**. An area of Earth's surface from which water percolates down into an aquifer is called a **recharge zone**. Recharge zones are environmentally sensitive areas because any pollution in a recharge zone can also enter the aquifer.

The size of an aquifer's recharge zone is affected by the permeability of the surface above the aquifer. Structures such as buildings and parking lots can act as impermeable layers to reduce the amount of water entering an aquifer and concentrate runoff pollution. Communities should carefully manage recharge zones, because surface water can take a very long time to refill an aquifer. In fact, aquifers can take tens of thousands of years to recharge.

Wells

If you go nearly anywhere on Earth and dig a hole deep enough, you will eventually find water. A hole that is dug or drilled to reach groundwater is called a *well*. For thousands of years, humans have dug wells in order to reach groundwater for drinking and agricultural purposes.

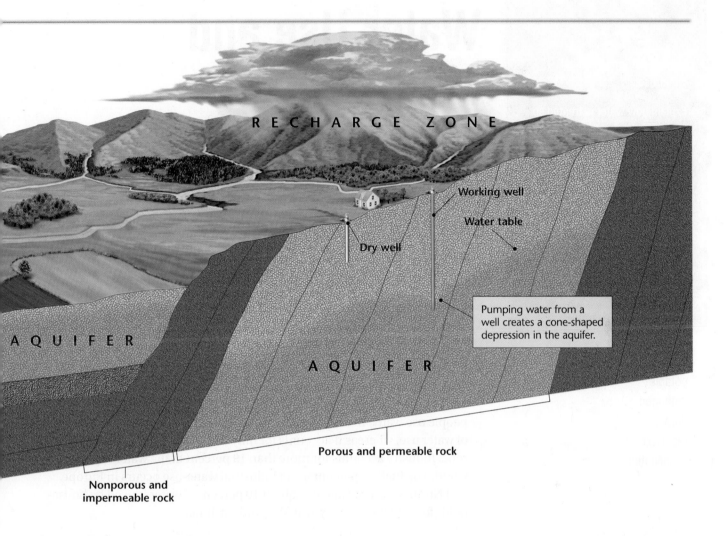

RECHARGE ZONE

Working well

Water table

Dry well

Pumping water from a well creates a cone-shaped depression in the aquifer.

AQUIFER

AQUIFER

Porous and permeable rock

Nonporous and impermeable rock

Groundwater may be a more reliable source of water than surface water in some areas because some contaminants are filtered out as the water travels underground. The height of the water table changes, so wells are drilled to extend below the water table. If the water table falls below the bottom of the well, the well will dry up. In addition, if groundwater is removed faster than it is recharged, the water table may fall below a well. To continue supplying water, the well must be drilled deeper.

Section 1 Formative Assessment

▶ Reviewing Main Ideas

1. **Describe** the distribution of water on Earth. Where is most of the fresh water located?

2. **Explain** why fresh water is considered a limited resource.

3. **Explain** why pollution in a watershed poses a potential threat to the river system that flows through it.

4. **Describe** how water travels through rock.

✔ Critical Thinking

5. **Making Comparisons** Read the description of aquifers. Why is an underground lake an aquifer?

6. **Analyzing Relationships** Describe the relationship between groundwater and surface water in a watershed. What human activities in a recharge zone can affect the groundwater?

- Identify patterns of global water use.

- Explain how water is treated so that it can be used for drinking.

- Identify how water is used in homes, in industry, and in agriculture.

- Describe how dams and water diversion projects are used to manage freshwater resources.

- Identify five ways that water can be conserved.

Key Terms

potable
pathogen
dam
reservoir
desalination

Water Use and Management

When a water supply is polluted or overused, everyone living downstream can be affected. The number of people who rely on Earth's limited fresh water reserves is increasing every day. In fact, a shortage of clean, fresh water is one of the world's most pressing environmental problems. According to the World Health Organization, more than 800 million people lack access to a clean, reliable source of fresh water.

Global Water Use

To understand the factors that affect the world's supply of fresh water, we must first explore how people use water. **Figure 2.2** shows the three major uses for water—residential use, agricultural use, and industrial use.

Most of the fresh water used worldwide is used to irrigate crops. Patterns of water use are not the same everywhere, however. The availability of fresh water, population sizes, and economic conditions affect how people use water. In Asia, agriculture accounts for more than 80 percent of water use, whereas it accounts for only 34 percent of water use in Europe. Industry accounts for more than 19 percent of the water used in the world. The highest percentage of industrial water use occurs in Europe and North America. Globally, about 10 percent of water is used by households for activities such as drinking and washing.

Residential Water Use

There are striking differences in residential water use throughout the world. For example, the average person in the United States uses about 300 L (80 gal) of water every day. But in India, the average person uses only 41 L of water every day.

FIGURE 2.1

Drinking-Water Treatment

❶ **First Filtration** The source water supply is filtered to remove large organisms and trash.

❷ **Coagulation** Alum is rapidly mixed into the water and forms sticky globs called *flocs*. Bacteria and other impurities cling to the flocs, which settle to the bottom of a tank.

❸ **Second Filtration** Layers of sand, gravel, and hard coal filter the remaining impurities.

FIGURE 2.2

Global Water Use Europe is the only continent that uses more water for industry than for agriculture.

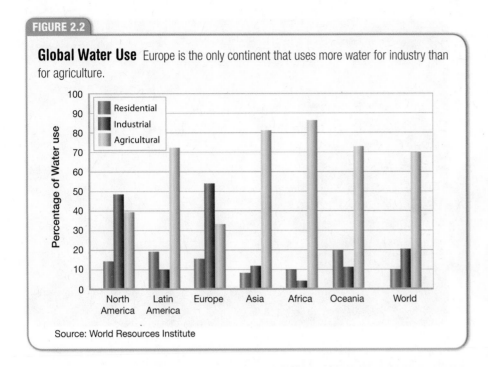

Source: World Resources Institute

FIGURE 2.3

DAILY WATER USE IN THE UNITED STATES (PER PERSON)

Use	Water (in liters)
Showers	43.9
Clothes washer	56.8
Dishwashers	3.8
Toilets	70.0
Baths	4.5
Leaks	36.0
Faucets	41.3
Other domestic	6.1
Outdoor total	381.6
Indoor total	262.3
Total use	650.3

Source: U.S. Environmental Protection Agency.

In the United States, only about half of residential water use is for activities inside the home, such as drinking, cooking, washing, and toilet flushing. The remainder of the water used residentially is used outside the home for activities such as watering lawns and washing cars as shown in **Figure 2.3**. In many parts of the country, water is in short supply and there may be water restrictions for outside usage.

Water Treatment

Most water must be treated to make it **potable**, or safe to drink. Water treatment removes elements such as mercury, arsenic, and lead, which are poisonous to humans even in low concentrations. These elements are found in polluted water, but they can also occur naturally in groundwater. Water treatment also removes **pathogens**, which are organisms that cause illness or disease. Bacteria, viruses, protozoa, and parasitic worms are common pathogens. Pathogens are found in water contaminated by sewage or animal feces. There are several methods of treating water to make it potable. **Figure 2.1** shows a common drinking-water treatment method that includes both physical and chemical treatment.

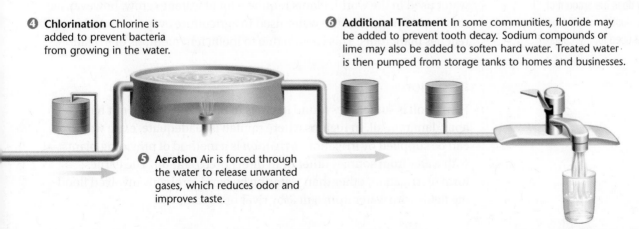

④ **Chlorination** Chlorine is added to prevent bacteria from growing in the water.

⑤ **Aeration** Air is forced through the water to release unwanted gases, which reduces odor and improves taste.

⑥ **Additional Treatment** In some communities, fluoride may be added to prevent tooth decay. Sodium compounds or lime may also be added to soften hard water. Treated water is then pumped from storage tanks to homes and businesses.

FIGURE 2.4

Industry Water is a very important industrial resource. These nuclear power plant cooling towers release the steam produced from water used to cool a nuclear reactor.

Industrial water use (world) 19%

Other water use (world) 81%

Industrial Water Use

Industry accounts for more than 19 percent of water used in the world. Water is used to manufacture goods, to dispose of waste, and to generate power. The amount of water needed to manufacture everyday items can be astounding. For instance, nearly 1,000 L of water are needed to produce 1 kg of aluminum, and almost 500,000 L of water are needed to manufacture an automobile.

Most of the water that is used in industry is used to cool power plants, as shown in **Figure 2.4**. Power-plant cooling systems usually pump water from a surface water source such as a river or lake, carry the water through pipes in a cooling tower, and then pump the water back into the source. The returned water is usually warmer than the source, but it is generally clean and can be reused.

Agricultural Water Use

Did you know that it can take nearly 300 L (80 gal) of water to produce one ear of corn? That's as much water as an average person in the United States uses in a day! Agriculture accounts for about 67 percent of the water used in the world. Plants require a lot of water to grow, however, as much as 80 percent of the water used in agriculture evaporates and never reaches plant roots. This is often due to inefficient methods of irrigation.

Irrigation

Fertile soil is sometimes found in areas of the world that do not have abundant rainfall. In regions where rainfall is inadequate, extra water can be supplied by irrigation. *Irrigation* is a method of providing plants with water from sources other than direct precipitation. The earliest form of irrigation, other than watering by hand, probably involved flooding fields with water from a nearby river or stream.

✓ **CHECK FOR UNDERSTANDING**

Compare How does the amount of water used for industry compare with the amount of water used for agriculture?

©Jim Zuckerman/Corbis

FIGURE 2.5

Agriculture High-pressure overhead sprinklers (left) are inefficient because a lot of water is lost to evaporation. Water-filled ditches (right) irrigate cotton seedlings.

Other water use (world) 33%

Agricultural water use (world) 67%

Many different irrigation techniques are used today. For example, some crops, such as cotton, are irrigated by shallow, water-filled ditches, as shown in **Figure 2.5**. In the United States, high-pressure overhead sprinklers are the most common form of irrigation. This method of irrigation is inefficient because nearly half the water evaporates and never reaches the plant roots. Irrigation systems that use water more efficiently are becoming more common. This has become even more important because some slowly recharged aquifers are becoming depleted.

Water Management Projects

For thousands of years, humans have altered streams and rivers to make them more useful. Around two thousand years ago, the Romans built *aqueducts*, like the one shown in **Figure 2.6**, which are systems of pipes and tunnels that brought water from the mountains to the dry areas of Italy, France, and Spain. Some Roman aqueducts are still in use. Today's water projects are more complex and show a greater understanding of human and ecological needs.

Water management projects, like dams and canals, are designed to meet the needs of people with inadequate water supplies. These projects can have various goals, such as bringing in water to make a dry area habitable, creating a reservoir for recreation or drinking water, or generating electric power. Such water management projects have proved that if water can be piped in, people can live and grow crops in desert areas. However, extensive water projects like these tend to have both financial and ecological costs.

FIGURE 2.6

Aqueduct This aqueduct in Spain was built almost two thousand years ago by the Romans.

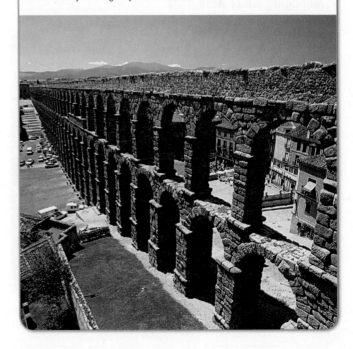

Water Diversion Projects

All or part of a river can be diverted into canals that carry water across great distances. The canal in **Figure 2.7 ❶** diverts the Owens River in California to provide drinking water for Los Angeles. Another river, the Colorado River, is diverted to provide water for states such as Arizona, Utah, and California. The river begins as a stream in the Rocky Mountains and quickly grows larger as other streams feed into it. As the Colorado flows south, however, so much of the river's water is diverted for irrigation and drinking water that the river often runs dry. It only reaches the Gulf of California, in Mexico, in the wettest years. In Florida, people are working to remove levees and canals that were used to drain the Everglades. The goal of this is to provide both adequate water for a growing population and sufficient water flow through the ecologically-important Everglades.

Dams and Reservoirs

Dams are built across rivers to control the river's flow. When a river is dammed, an artificial lake, or **reservoir**, is formed behind the dam. Reservoirs can be used for flood control, drinking water, irrigation, recreation, and industry. Hydroelectric dams use the power of flowing water to turn a turbine to generate electrical energy. About 20 percent of the world's electrical energy is generated by hydroelectric dams (**Figure 2.7 ❷**).

Although dams provide many benefits, interrupting a river's flow can also have far-reaching consequences. When the land behind a dam is flooded, people are often displaced and entire ecosystems can be destroyed. It is estimated that 50 million people around the world have been displaced by dam projects. Dams also affect the land below them.

FIGURE 2.7

Managing Water Resources

This canal carries water more than 300 km across mountains and deserts to supply drinking water to Los Angeles, California.

Dams, such as this one in Zimbabwe, are built to manage freshwater resources.

As a river enters a reservoir, it slows down and deposits some of the sediment it carries. This fertile sediment builds up behind a dam instead of enriching the land farther down the river. As a result, the farmland below a dam may become less productive. Dam failure can be another problem. If a dam bursts, people living along the river below the dam can be killed. In the United States, the era of large dam construction is over. Some dams are even being removed. But in developing countries, such as Brazil, India, and China, the construction of large dams continues.

Water Conservation

As water sources become depleted, water becomes more expensive. Wells must be dug deeper, water must be piped greater distances, and polluted water must be cleaned up before it can be used. Ecosystems may also be disrupted and some types of agriculture may become impossible to sustain. All of these issues make water conservation extremely important.

Water Conservation in Agriculture

Most of the water loss in agriculture comes from evaporation, seepage, and runoff, so technologies that reduce these problems help to conserve water. *Drip irrigation systems* offer a promising step toward conservation. Shown in **Figure 2.8,** drip irrigation systems deliver small amounts of water directly to plant roots by using perforated tubing. Water is released to plants as needed and at a controlled rate. These systems are sometimes managed by computer programs that coordinate watering times by using satellite data. A well-designed drip irrigation system loses little water.

Water Conservation in Industry

Many industries have developed water conservation plans. Some industries are using salt water instead of fresh water, but the most widely used water conservation plans involve the recycling of cooling water and wastewater. Instead of discharging used water into a nearby river, businesses often recycle water. Thus, the production of 1 kg of paper now uses less than 30 percent of the water it required 50 years ago. Small businesses are also helping conserve water. Denver, Colorado, was one of the first cities to realize the value of conserving water in business. The city of Denver pays small businesses to conserve water. This saves money for the city and businesses and makes more water available for other uses.

Connect to MATH

Israeli Agriculture
From 1950 to 1980, Israel reduced the amount of water loss in agriculture from 83 percent to 5 percent, mainly by switching from overhead sprinklers to water-saving methods such as drip irrigation. If a small farm uses 10,000 L of water a day for overhead sprinkler irrigation, how much water would be saved in one year by using a drip irrigation system that consumes 75 percent less water?

FIGURE 2.8

Drip Irrigation Drip irrigation systems use perforated tubing to deliver water directly to plant roots.

✔ **CHECK FOR UNDERSTANDING**
Describe What are two ways in which water is conserved in industry?

FIGURE 2.9

WHAT YOU CAN DO TO CONSERVE WATER

Take shorter showers, and avoid taking baths unless you keep the water level low.
Install a low-flow shower head in your shower.
Install inexpensive, low-flow aerators in your water faucets at home.
Purchase a modern, low-flow toilet, install a water-saving device in your toilet, or simply place a water-filled bottle inside your toilet tank to reduce the water used for each flush.
Do not let the water run while you are brushing your teeth.
Fill up the sink basin rather than letting the water run when you are shaving, washing your hands or face, or washing dishes.
Wash only full loads in your dishwasher and washing machine.
Water your lawn sparingly.

Xeriscaping This xeriscaped yard in Arizona features plants that are native to the state. What kinds of plants are native to your region?

Water Conservation at Home

Although households use much less water than agriculture or industry, a few changes to residential water use will make a significant contribution to water conservation. People can conserve water by changing a few everyday habits and by using only the water that they need. Some of these conservation methods are listed in **Figure 2.9**.

Water-saving technology, such as low-flow toilets and shower heads, can also help reduce household water use. These devices are required in some new buildings. As well, many cities pay residents to install water-saving equipment in older buildings.

About one-third of the water used by the average household in the United States is used for landscaping. To conserve water, many people water their lawns at night to reduce the amount of water lost to evaporation. Another way people save water used outside their home is a technique called *xeriscaping* (ZIR i skay ping). Xeriscaping involves designing a landscape that requires minimal water use. The image in **Figure 2.9** shows one example of xeriscaping in Arizona.

Can one person make a difference? When you multiply one by the millions of people who are trying to conserve water—in industry, on farms, and at home—you can make a big difference.

Solutions for the Future

Ensuring adequate supplies of fresh water will continue to be a global challenge in the future, particularly in the developing nations. Major factors to consider will include increasing temperatures and changing precipitation patterns resulting from global climate change.

It is critical that long-term solutions to balance the needs of people and ecosystems be put into place. Work is underway to develop new water resources, such as desalination, transporting fresh water, and developing new technologies.

Desalination

Some coastal communities rely on the oceans to provide fresh water. **Desalination** (DEE SAL uh NAY shuhn) is the process of removing salt from salt water. Some countries in drier parts of the world, have built desalination plants to provide fresh water. Most desalination plants heat salt water and collect the fresh water that evaporates. **Figure 2.10** shows one such plant in Kuwait. Because desalination consumes a lot of energy, the process is too expensive for many nations to consider.

Transporting Water

In some areas of the world where freshwater resources are not adequate, water can be transported from other regions. For example, some Greek islands in the Mediterranean Sea have ships travel regularly from the mainland towing enormous plastic bags full of fresh water. The ships anchor in port, and the fresh water is pumped onto the islands.

Low-Cost Solutions

In many arid regions, there is ground water that cannot be reached without great effort and expense. One low cost approach being used in some developing nations is to provide inexpensive technologies to construct wells and pumps for economically-disadvantaged communities.

FIGURE 2.10

Desalination Most desalination plants, such as this one in Kuwait, use evaporation to separate salt from ocean water.

©Steve Rayme/National Geographic Image Collection

✓ Section 2 Formative Assessment

▶ Reviewing Main Ideas

1. **Describe** the patterns of global water use for each continent shown in the bar graph in **Figure 2.2.**

2. **Describe** the drinking water treatment process in your own words.

3. **Describe** the benefits and costs of dams and water diversion projects.

4. **List** at least three things you can do to help conserve the world's water supply.

✓ Critical Thinking

5. **Making Comparisons** Write a description of the evaporative method of desalination using terms from the water cycle.

6. **Identifying Alternatives** Describe three ways that communities can conserve their freshwater resources.

Water Pollution

Objectives

▶ Compare point-source pollution and nonpoint-source pollution.

▶ Classify water pollutants by five types.

▶ Explain why groundwater pollution is difficult to clean up.

▶ Describe the major sources of ocean pollution, and explain the effects of pollution on ecosystems.

▶ Describe six major laws designed to improve water quality in the United States.

Key Terms

water pollution
point-source pollution
nonpoint-source pollution
wastewater
artificial eutrophication
thermal pollution
biomagnification

You might think that you can tell if a body of water is polluted by the way that the water looks or smells, but sometimes you can't. There are many different forms of water pollution. **Water pollution** is the introduction of chemical, physical, or biological agents into water that degrade water quality and harm the organisms that depend on the water. Almost all of the ways that we use water contribute to water pollution. However, the two underlying causes of water pollution are industrialization and rapid human population growth.

In the last 30 years, developed countries have made great strides in cleaning up many polluted water supplies. Despite this progress, some water is still dangerously polluted in the United States and in other countries. In developing parts of the world, water pollution is a big problem. Industry is usually not the major cause of water pollution in developing countries. Often, the only water available for drinking in these countries is polluted with sewage and agricultural runoff, which can spread waterborne diseases. To prevent water pollution, people must understand where pollutants come from and have access to adequate sanitation facilities. Water pollution comes from two types of sources: point and nonpoint sources.

Point-Source Pollution

When you think of water pollution, you probably think of a single source, such as a factory, a wastewater treatment plant, or a leaking oil tanker. These are all examples of **point-source pollution,** which is pollution discharged from a single source. **Figure 3.1** lists some additional examples of point-source pollution. Point-source pollution can often be identified and traced to a source. But even when the source of the pollution is known, enforcing cleanup may be difficult.

FIGURE 3.1

POINT-SOURCE POLLUTION

leaking septic-tank systems
leaking storage lagoons for polluted waste
unlined landfills
leaking underground storage tanks that contain chemicals or fuels such as gasoline
polluted water from abandoned and active mines
water discharged by industries
public and industrial wastewater treatment plants

Point-Source Pollution Point-source pollution comes from a single, easily identifiable source. In this photo, the waste from an iron mine is being stored in a pond.

©Thomas Del Brase/Photodisc/Getty Images

Nonpoint-Source Pollution

Nonpoint-source pollution, also known as runoff pollution, comes from many different sources that are often difficult to identify. **Figure 3.2** shows common sources of nonpoint pollutants. Other sources might include road salt in northern climates, soil eroded from cleared land, or acid drainage from mine tailings. If any land surface in a watershed is polluted, runoff from a rainstorm can carry the pollution into a nearby river, stream, or lake. **Figure 3.3** illustrates some sources of nonpoint pollution.

Because nonpoint pollutants can enter bodies of water in many different ways, they are extremely difficult to regulate and control. The accumulation of small amounts of water pollution from many sources is a major issue—according to the EPA, nonpoint sources remain the largest source of water quality problems in the United States. Controlling nonpoint sources of pollution depends to a great extent on public awareness of the effects of activities such as spraying lawn chemicals and using storm drains to dispose of used motor oil.

FIGURE 3.2
NONPOINT SOURCES OF POLLUTION

chemicals added to road surfaces (salt and other de-icing agents)
water runoff from city and suburban streets that may contain oil, gasoline, animal feces, and litter
pesticides, herbicides, and fertilizer from residential lawns, golf courses, and farmland
feces and agricultural chemicals from livestock feedlots
precipitation containing air pollutants
soil runoff from farms and construction sites
oil and gasoline from personal watercraft

FIGURE 3.3

Nonpoint-Source Pollution

Examples of nonpoint-source pollution include ❶ livestock polluting water holes that can flow into streams and reservoirs, ❷ oil on a street, which can wash into storm sewers and then drain into waterways, and ❸ thousands of watercraft, which can leak gasoline and oil.

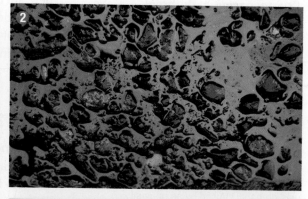

FIGURE 3.4

POLLUTANT TYPES AND SOURCES

Type of pollutant	Agent	Major sources
Pathogens	disease-causing organisms, such as bacteria, viruses, protozoa, and parasitic worms	mostly nonpoint sources: sewage or animal feces, livestock feedlots, and poultry farms; sewage from overburdened wastewater treatment plants
Organic matter	animal and plant matter remains, feces, food waste, and debris from food-processing plants	mostly nonpoint sources
Organic chemicals	pesticides, fertilizers, plastics, detergents, gasoline and oil, and other materials made from petroleum	mostly nonpoint sources: farms, lawns, golf courses, roads, wastewater, unlined landfills, and leaking underground storage tanks
Inorganic chemicals	acids, bases, salts, and industrial chemicals	point sources and nonpoint sources: industrial waste, road surfaces, wastewater, and polluted precipitation
Heavy metals	lead, mercury, cadmium, and arsenic	point sources and nonpoint sources: industrial discharge, unlined landfills, some household chemicals, and mining processes; heavy metals also occur naturally in some groundwater
Physical agents	heat and suspended solids	point sources and nonpoint sources: heat from industrial processes and suspended solids from soil erosion

FIELDSTUDY

Go to Appendix B to find the field study
Sources of Water Pollution

Principal Water Pollutants

There are many different kinds of water pollutants, both natural and man-made. **Figure 3.4** lists some common pollutants and some of the sources of each. Agriculture, forestry, grazing, septic systems, recreational boating, industry, urban runoff, construction, physical changes to stream channels, and habitat degradation can all be sources of pollution.

Wastewater

Do you know where water goes after it flows down the drain in a sink? In urban areas, the water usually flows through a series of sewage pipes that carry it—and all the other wastewater in your community—to a wastewater treatment plant. **Wastewater** is water that contains waste from homes or industry. There, water is filtered and treated to make the water clean enough to return to a river, lake, or the oceans. In many rural areas, homes may have individual septic systems, or in some countries, no treatment at all.

Treating Wastewater

Figure 3.5 illustrates a typical municipal wastewater treatment process. Most wastewater from homes contains biodegradable material, like paper, soap, or body wastes that can be broken down by living organisms.

But wastewater treatment plants may not remove all of the harmful substances in water. Some household and industrial wastewater and some storm-water runoff contain toxic substances that cannot be removed by standard methods of treatment.

Sewage Sludge

The solid material that remains after wastewater treatment is *sewage sludge*. When sludge contains dangerous concentrations of toxic chemicals, it must be disposed of as hazardous waste. The sludge is often incinerated, and then the ash is buried in a secure landfill.

If the toxicity of sludge can be reduced to safe levels, sludge can be used as a fertilizer or combined with clay to make bricks for buildings.

✓ **CHECK FOR UNDERSTANDING**
Explain Why is it so expensive to dispose of sewage sludge?

FIGURE 3.5

Wastewater Treatment Process

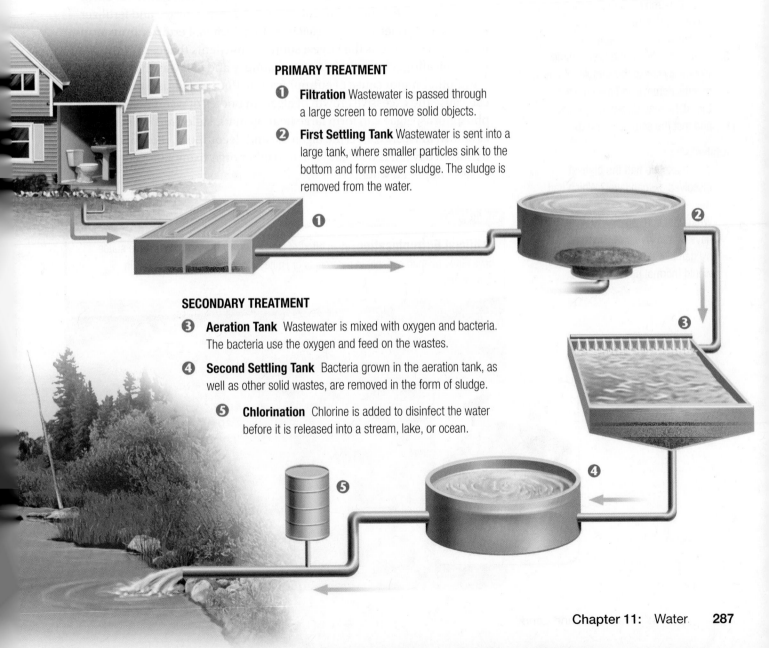

PRIMARY TREATMENT

❶ **Filtration** Wastewater is passed through a large screen to remove solid objects.

❷ **First Settling Tank** Wastewater is sent into a large tank, where smaller particles sink to the bottom and form sewer sludge. The sludge is removed from the water.

SECONDARY TREATMENT

❸ **Aeration Tank** Wastewater is mixed with oxygen and bacteria. The bacteria use the oxygen and feed on the wastes.

❹ **Second Settling Tank** Bacteria grown in the aeration tank, as well as other solid wastes, are removed in the form of sludge.

❺ **Chlorination** Chlorine is added to disinfect the water before it is released into a stream, lake, or ocean.

1. Start with three water samples. One water sample should be tap water from a faucet without an aerator. Leave some air space at the top of the bottle. One sample should be collected by submersing the container completely underwater in a larger container, allowing all air to escape from the bottle. Put the lid on the container while it is still underwater. The third sample should be water that has been boiled and allowed to cool.

2. Using a dissolved-oxygen (DO) test kit or electronic DO probe, test the second and third water samples. Record your measurements.

3. Tighten the lid on the first sample. Vigorously shake the sample for one minute. Remove and then replace the lid. Repeat. Uncap the jar quickly and test the sample. Record.

Analysis

1. Which sample had the highest dissolved oxygen level? Which had the lowest level?

2. What effect do rapids and waterfalls have on the levels of dissolved oxygen in a stream? What effect would thermal pollution have?

Artificial Eutrophication

Most natural nutrients in water come from organic matter, such as leaves and animal waste. They are broken down into mineral nutrients by decomposers such as bacteria and fungi. These nutrients flow downstream or settle to the bottom in a process called *sedimentation*. Nutrients are an essential part of any aquatic ecosystem; too many nutrients can disrupt an ecosystem. When lakes and slow-moving streams contain an abundance of nutrients, they are *eutrophic* (yoo TROH fik).

Eutrophication can be a natural process. When organic matter builds up in a body of water, it will begin to decay and decompose. The process of decomposition uses up oxygen. As oxygen levels decrease, the types of organisms that live in the water change over time. For example, as a body of water becomes eutrophic, plants take root in the nutrient-rich sediment at the bottom. As more plants grow, the shallow waters begin to fill in. Eventually, the body of water becomes a swamp or marsh.

Eutrophication is accelerated when inorganic plant nutrients, such as phosphorus and nitrogen, enter the water from sewage and fertilizer runoff. This is referred to as **artificial eutrophication**. Fertilizer from farms, lawns, and gardens is the largest source of nutrients that cause artificial eutrophication. Phosphates in some laundry and dishwashing detergents are another major cause of eutrophication. Phosphorus is a nutrient that can cause the excessive growth of algae. In bodies of water polluted by phosphorus, algae can form large floating mats, called *algal blooms*, as shown in **Figure 3.6**. As the algae die and decompose, most of the dissolved oxygen is used and fish and other organisms suffocate in the oxygen-depleted water.

FIGURE 3.6

Artificial Eutrophication In an effort to limit artificial eutrophication, some states have either banned phosphate detergents or limited the amount of phosphates in detergents.

(inset) ©Getty Images; (br) ©Nick Hawkes/Ecoscene/Corbis

FIGURE 3.7

Thermal Pollution Fish kills, such as this one in Brazil, can result from thermal pollution.

Thermal Pollution

If you look at **Figure 3.7**, you might assume that a toxic chemical caused the massive fish kill in the photo. But the fish were not killed by a chemical spill—they died because of thermal pollution. When the temperature of a body of water, such as a lake or stream, increases, thermal pollution can result. **Thermal pollution** can occur when power plants and other industries use water in their cooling systems and then discharge the warm water into a lake or river.

Thermal pollution can cause large fish kills if the discharged water is too warm for the fish to survive. But most thermal pollution is more subtle. If the temperature of a body of water rises even a few degrees, the amount of dissolved oxygen (DO) in the water decreases significantly. As oxygen levels drop, aquatic organisms may suffocate and die. If the flow of warm water into a lake or stream is constant, it may cause the total disruption of an aquatic ecosystem.

Groundwater Pollution

Pollutants usually enter groundwater when polluted surface water percolates down from the Earth's surface. Any pollution of the surface water in an area can affect the groundwater. Pesticides, herbicides, chemical fertilizers, and petroleum products are common groundwater pollutants. Leaking underground storage tanks are another major source of groundwater pollution. It is estimated that there are millions of underground storage tanks in the United States. Most of the storage tanks—located beneath gas stations, farms, and homes—hold petroleum products, such as gasoline and heating fuel. As these underground storage tanks age, they may develop leaks, which allow pollutants to seep into the soil and groundwater.

Connect to CHEMISTRY

Dissolved Oxygen
Sufficient levels of dissolved oxygen are critical to the health of aquatic communities. Gaseous oxygen enters water by diffusion from the surrounding air, as a byproduct of photosynthesis, and as a result of the rapid movement (aeration) of water. The amount of oxygen that water can hold is determined by the water's temperature, pressure, and salinity. Slow-moving water tends to have low levels of dissolved oxygen, while rapidly flowing streams have higher levels. Artificial eutrophication and thermal pollution also reduce levels of dissolved oxygen. When dissolved oxygen levels remain below 2 mg/L for several hours, many fish and other organisms suffocate, and massive fish kills can result.

The location of aging underground storage tanks is not always known, so the tanks often cannot be repaired or replaced until after they have leaked enough pollutants to be located. Modern underground storage tanks are contained in concrete and have many features to prevent leaks. Other sources of groundwater pollution include septic tanks, unlined landfills, and industrial wastewater lagoons, as shown in **Figure 3.8**.

Cleaning Up Groundwater Pollution

Groundwater pollution is one of the most challenging environmental problems that the world faces. As you have learned, groundwater recharges very slowly. The process for some aquifers to recycle water and purge contaminants can take hundreds or thousands of years. Groundwater is also difficult to decontaminate because the water is dispersed throughout large areas of rock and sand. Pollution can cling to the rock and soil, so, even if all of the water in an aquifer were pumped out and replaced with clean water, it would become recontaminated. In 2011, the U.S. government stopped construction of a major oil pipeline because of concerns about polluting the giant Ogallala aquifer.

FIGURE 3.8

Sources of Groundwater Pollution This diagram shows some of the major sources of groundwater pollution. Runoff and percolation transport contaminants to the groundwater.

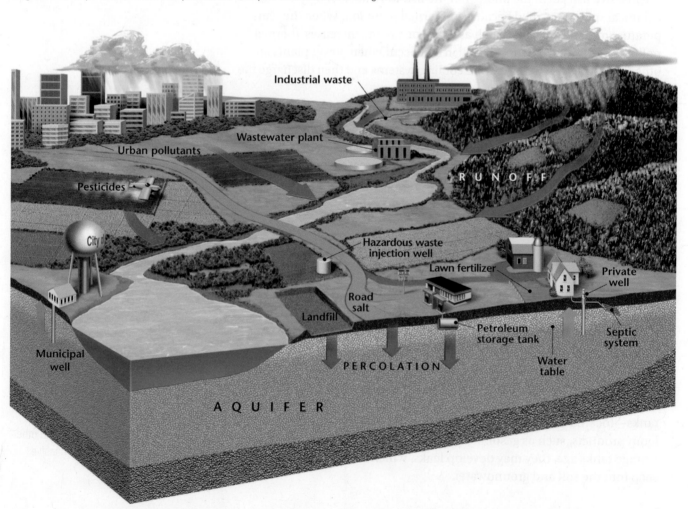

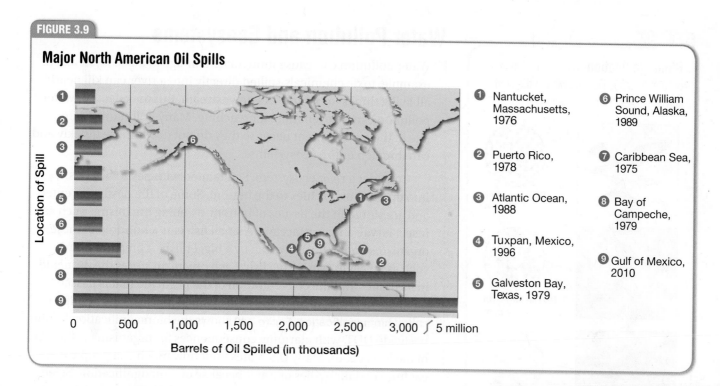

FIGURE 3.9

Major North American Oil Spills

Location of Spill

Barrels of Oil Spilled (in thousands)

0   500   1,000   1,500   2,000   2,500   3,000 ⌠ 5 million

1. Nantucket, Massachusetts, 1976
2. Puerto Rico, 1978
3. Atlantic Ocean, 1988
4. Tuxpan, Mexico, 1996
5. Galveston Bay, Texas, 1979
6. Prince William Sound, Alaska, 1989
7. Caribbean Sea, 1975
8. Bay of Campeche, 1979
9. Gulf of Mexico, 2010

Ocean Pollution

Pollutants are often dumped directly into the oceans. For example, ships can legally dump wastewater and garbage overboard in some parts of the ocean. But at least 85 percent of ocean pollution—including pollutants such as oil, toxic wastes, and medical wastes—comes from activities on land. If polluted runoff enters rivers, the rivers may carry it to the ocean. Most activities that pollute oceans occur near the coasts, where much of the world's human population lives. Sensitive coastal ecosystems, such as coral reefs, estuaries, and coastal marshes, are the most affected by pollution. In many coastal areas, *dead zones* exist, where excess nutrients from runoff have caused low oxygen levels.

Oil Spills

Oil spills can occur on land or in water, but are most infamous in oceans. Disasters such as the 1989 *Exxon Valdez* oil spill in Alaska and the 2010 *Deepwater Horizon* spill, illustrated in **Figure 3.9** make front-page news around the world. Each year, approximately 37 million gallons of oil from tanker accidents are spilled into the oceans. The *Deepwater Horizon* disaster was notable because of the amount of oil spilled, the great depth at which the spill occurred, and the use of dispersants to keep oil from reaching the coasts.

Oil spills can have dramatic ecological effects, but are not the only source of oil pollution in the oceans. Most of the oil that pollutes the oceans comes from nonpoint sources on land. Every year, almost 10 times the amount of oil spilled by tankers enters the ocean from land. Avoiding and responding to all sources of oil pollution are important for protecting ocean ecosystems.

✔ CHECK FOR UNDERSTANDING

Explain How can limiting nonpoint sources of oil pollution help to keep the oceans clean?

Water Pollution and Ecosystems

Water pollution can cause immediate damage to an ecosystem. For example, toxic chemicals spilled directly into a river can kill nearly all living things for kilometers downstream. But the effects of water pollution can be even more far reaching. Many pollutants accumulate in the environment because they do not decompose quickly and can threaten entire ecosystems.

Consider a river ecosystem. Soil tainted with pesticides washes into the river and settles to the bottom. Some of the pesticides enter and are stored in the tissues of bottom-dwelling organisms, such as insect larvae and crustaceans. A small fish eats a hundred of these organisms and in turn, is eaten by a bigger fish. A predatory bird, such as an eagle, eats 10 big fish. Each organism stores the pesticide in its tissues and the concentration of the pesticide that is passed on to the next organism in the food chain increases. This buildup is called **biomagnification**. **Figure 3.10** shows the biomagnification for the pesticide DDT, with alarming consequences for organisms at the top of the food chain. Many U.S. states limit how much fish people can eat from certain bodies of water because of biomagnification. Scientific evidence also indicates that some chemicals that we might not think of as pollutants, like caffeine and human medications, can enter ecosystems and cause health issues for aquatic animals.

Cleaning Up Water Pollution

In 1969, the Cuyahoga River in Cleveland, Ohio, was so polluted that the river caught on fire as shown in **Figure 3.11**. This event was a major factor in the passage of the Clean Water Act of 1972. The stated purpose of the act was to "restore and maintain the chemical, physical, and biological integrity of the nation's waters." The goal of the act was to make all surface water clean enough for fishing and swimming by 1983. This goal was not achieved, however, much progress has been made since the act was passed. The percentage of lakes and rivers that are fit for swimming and fishing has increased by about 30 percent, and many states have passed stricter water-quality standards. Many toxic metals are now removed from wastewater before the water is discharged.

The Clean Water Act opened the door for other water-quality legislation, some of which is described in **Figure 3.12**.

The Federal Water Pollution Act of 1972, which was amended in 2002, was aimed at restoring and maintaining the quality of all U.S. waters. Legislation has improved water quality in the United States, but the cooperation of individuals, businesses, and the government will be essential to maintaining a clean water supply in the future.

FIGURE 3.10

Biomagnification The accumulation of pollutants at successive levels of the food chain is called biomagnification.

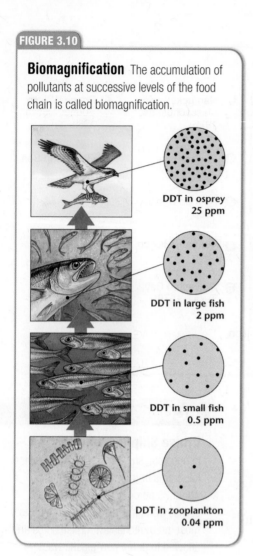

DDT in osprey
25 ppm

DDT in large fish
2 ppm

DDT in small fish
0.5 ppm

DDT in zooplankton
0.04 ppm

FIGURE 3.11

Burning River The Cuyahoga River was so polluted with petroleum and petroleum byproducts that it caught on fire and burned in 1969.

©Bettmann/Corbis

FIGURE 3.12

FEDERAL LAWS DESIGNED TO IMPROVE WATER QUALITY IN THE UNITED STATES

1972 Clean Water Act (CWA) The CWA set a national goal of making all natural surface water fit for fishing and swimming by 1983 and banned pollutant discharge into surface water after 1985. The act also required that metals be removed from wastewater.

1972 Federal Water Pollution Control Act, amended 2002 The objective of this act was to restore and maintain the chemical, physical, and biological integrity of U.S. waters.

1975 Safe Drinking Water Act (SDWA), amended 1996 This act introduced programs to protect groundwater and surface water from pollution. The act emphasized sound science and risk-based standards for water quality. The act also empowered communities in the protection of source water, strengthened public right-to-know laws, and provided water system infrastructure assistance.

1980 Comprehensive Environmental Response Compensation and Liability Act (CERCLA) This act is also known as the Superfund Act. The act made owners, operators, and customers of hazardous waste sites responsible for the cleanup of the sites. The act has reduced the pollution of groundwater by toxic substances leached from hazardous waste dumps.

1987 Water Quality Act This act was written to support state and local efforts to clean polluted runoff. It also established loan funds to pay for new wastewater treatment plants and created programs to protect major estuaries.

2000 Oceans Act This act created the U.S. Commission on Ocean Policy to develop recommendations for a new coordinated and comprehensive national ocean policy.

 ## Section 3 **Formative Assessment**

▶ Reviewing Main Ideas

1. **Explain** why point-source pollution is easier to control than nonpoint-source pollution.

2. **Identify** the major types of water pollutants. Suggest ways to reduce the levels of each type of pollutant in a water supply.

3. **Describe** the unique problems of cleaning up groundwater pollution.

4. **Describe** the source of most ocean pollution. Is it point-source or nonpoint-source pollution?

✔ Critical Thinking

5. **Interpreting Graphics** Read the description of biomagnification. Draw a diagram that shows the biomagnification of a pollutant in an ecosystem.

6. **Applying Ideas** What can individuals do to decrease ocean pollution? Write and illustrate a guide that gives at least three examples.

The Three Gorges Dam

China's Yangtze River is the third longest river in the world after the Nile and the Amazon. The Yangtze River flows through the Three Gorges region of central China, which is famous for its natural beauty and historical sites. For thousands of years, the area's sheer cliffs have inspired paintings and poems. This idyllic region seems like the sort of place that would be protected as a park or reserve. But in fact, it is the site for the Three Gorges Dam—the largest hydroelectric dam project in the world. Now that the dam is fully operational, the Yangtze River forms a reservoir that is 595 km (370 mi) long—as long as Lake Superior. In other words, the reservoir is about as long as the distance between Los Angeles and San Francisco!

Advantages

The dam has several purposes. It controls the water level of the Yangtze River to reduce downstream flooding. About 1 million people died in the last century from flooding along the river. The damage caused by a severe flood in 1998 is estimated to have cost as much as the entire dam project. During dry times, release of water from the dam increases freshwater for agriculture and people downstream.

The dam provides millions of people with hydroelectric power. China now burns air-polluting coal to meet about two-thirds of the country's energy needs. With all its turbines operational, the dam will provide enough electrical energy to power a city that is 10 times the size of Los Angeles. With the Yangtze's flow controlled, the river is deep enough for large ships to navigate on it, so the dam will also increase trade nearly ten-fold in a relatively poor region of China.

Disadvantages

The project has many drawbacks, however. The reservoir behind the dam has flooded an enormous area. Almost 1.5 million people living in the affected areas were relocated—there were 13 cities and hundreds of villages in the area of the reservoir. As the reservoir's waters rose, they destroyed fragile ecosystems and valuable archeological sites.

Pollution in the Yangtze River above the dam has increased much more than anticipated by engineers. Slower water flow fails to flush away sewage and other pollution. Flooded urban and industrial areas contribute a mixture of other pollutants.

This aerial view shows the reservoir that formed behind the Three Gorges Dam.

The Three Gorges Dam is named for the beautiful canyons that were flooded after its construction.

(bg) ©Flemming Sœgaard Jensen/Flickr/Getty Images; (bl) ©DigitalGlobe/Getty Images

ECOZine
at HMDScience.com

Go online for the latest environmental science news and updates on all EcoZine articles.

Long-Term Concerns

Before construction, some people raised concerns about geological instability that might result from so much added weight. Experience is justifying those concerns. The dam was built over a fault line. In late 2011, Chinese government officials acknowledged that regular landslides and earthquakes were increasing dangers for local people. Another concern is that the reservoir may quickly fill with sediment. The Yangtze picks up enormous amounts of yellowish soil and sediment as it flows across China. With the river slowed by the dam, much of the silt is deposited in the reservoir. As sediment builds up behind the dam, the deposited sediment will reduce the size of the reservoir, limiting the flood prevention and power generating capacities of the dam. In addition, productive farming regions below the dam will be deprived of the fertile sediment that is deposited every year when the river floods, and river banks may become more eroded because the river carries less replacement sediment from upstream.

The completed dam helps to reduce downstream flooding, and provide electricity to millions of people.

Hidden Costs?

The official cost of the project is $25 billion, but other sources give estimates of two to three times that amount, due to environmental costs. It is hard to assign an economic value to the loss of wildlife diversity in this area that previously supported many unique species. The true cost of the dam may never be known because corruption and inefficiency have plagued the project from the start. For example, money sent to compensate 13,000 people relocated near Gaoyang disappeared, and no people received payments. These negative effects of the Three Gorges Dam project will be difficult to remedy, but even more dams are planned for the Yangtze River.

When the dam waters rose, these ancient temples were flooded.

What Do You Think?

Based on the benefits received from the Three Gorges Dam, China is planning four new dams for the Yangtze River further upstream. The new dams will provide nearly double the electricity generated at Three Gorges, and would trap sediments before they reach the Three Gorges Dam reservoir. Now that the environmental consequences of large dams are known, do you think that China should reconsider additional, large hydroelectric projects?

SECTION 1 **Water Resources**

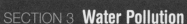

OBJECTIVES

- Only a small fraction of Earth's water supply is fresh water. The two main sources of fresh water are surface water and groundwater.

- River systems drain the land that makes up a watershed. The amount of water in a river system can vary in different seasons and from year to year.

- Groundwater accumulates in underground formations called *aquifers*. Surface water enters an aquifer through the aquifer's recharge zone.

- If the water in an aquifer is pumped out faster than it is replenished, the water table drops, which can affect humans and animals that depend on the groundwater.

KEY TERMS

surface water
river system
watershed
groundwater
aquifer
porosity
permeability
recharge zone

SECTION 2 **Water Use and Management**

OBJECTIVES

- There are three main types of water use: residential, industrial, and agricultural. Worldwide, most water use is agricultural.

- Dams and water diversion projects are built to manage surface-water resources. Damming and diverting rivers can have environmental and social consequences.

- Water conservation is necessary to maintain an adequate supply of fresh water. Desalination and transporting water are options to supplement local water supplies.

KEY TERMS

potable
pathogen
dam
reservoir
desalination

SECTION 3 **Water Pollution**

OBJECTIVES

- Water can become polluted by chemical, physical, or biological agents. Most water pollution in the United States is caused by nonpoint-source pollutants.

- Groundwater pollution is difficult to clean up because aquifers recharge slowly and because pollutants cling to the materials that make up an aquifer.

- Ocean pollution is mainly caused by coastal, nonpoint-source pollutants.

- Government legislation, such as the Clean Water Act of 1972, has succeeded in reducing surface-water pollution. Future challenges include reducing nonpoint-source pollution and groundwater pollution.

KEY TERMS

water pollution
point-source pollution
nonpoint-source pollution
wastewater
artificial eutrophication
thermal pollution
biomagnification

CHAPTER 11 Review

Reviewing Key Terms

Use each of the following terms in a separate sentence.

1. *aquifer*
2. *recharge zone*
3. *reservoir*
4. *wastewater*
5. *biomagnification*

For each pair of terms, explain how the meanings of the terms differ.

6. *surface water* and *groundwater*
7. *porosity* and *permeability*
8. *watershed* and *river system*
9. *point-source pollution* and *nonpoint-source pollution*
10. **Concept Map** Use the following terms to create a concept map: *Earth's surface, rivers, underground, fresh water, water table, 3 percent,* and *icecaps.*

Reviewing Main Ideas

11. Which of the following processes is *not* a part of the water cycle?
    a. evaporation
    b. condensation
    c. biomagnification
    d. precipitation

12. Most of the fresh water on Earth is
    a. located underground in aquifers.
    b. frozen in the polar icecaps.
    c. located in rivers, lakes, streams, and wetlands.
    d. found in Earth's atmosphere.

13. Which of the following processes is *not* used in a conventional method of water treatment?
    a. filtration
    b. coagulation
    c. aeration
    d. percolation

14. Which of the following is *not* an example of point-source pollution?
    a. oil that is escaping from a damaged tanker
    b. heavy metals that are leaching out of an underground mine
    c. water runoff from residential lawns
    d. untreated sewage that is accidentally released from a wastewater treatment plant

15. Which of the following pollutants causes artificial eutrophication?
    a. heavy metals from unlined landfills
    b. inorganic plant nutrients from wastewater and fertilizer runoff
    c. toxic chemicals from factories
    d. radioactive waste from nuclear power plants

16. Pumping large amounts of water from an aquifer may cause the
    a. water table to rise.
    b. recharge zone to shrink.
    c. wells in an area to run dry.
    d. percolation of groundwater to stop.

17. Oil pollution in the ocean is mostly caused by
    a. major oil spills, such as the 1989 *Exxon Valdez* oil spill.
    b. the cumulative effect of small oil spills and leaks on land.
    c. decomposed plastic materials.
    d. intentional dumping of excess oil.

18. Thermal pollution has a harmful effect on aquatic environments because
    a. water has been circulated around power-plant generators.
    b. it increases the number of disease-causing organisms in aquatic environments.
    c. it reduces the amount of dissolved oxygen in aquatic environments.
    d. it decreases the nutrient levels in aquatic environments.

Short Answer

19. What effect can buildings and parking lots have on an aquifer's recharge zone?

20. Why is the use of overhead sprinklers for irrigation inefficient? What is a more efficient method of irrigation?

21. List three advantages and three disadvantages of dams.

22. What is the process of eutrophication, and how do human activities accelerate it?

23. Describe the steps that are involved in the primary and secondary treatment of wastewater.

Interpreting Graphics

The graph below shows the annual flow, or discharge, of the Yakima River in Washington. Use the graph to answer questions 24–26.

24. **Determine** In which months is the river's discharge highest? What might explain these discharge rates?

25. **Compare** What might cause the peaks in river discharge between November and March?

26. **Predict** How might the data be different if the hydrograph readings were taken below a dam?

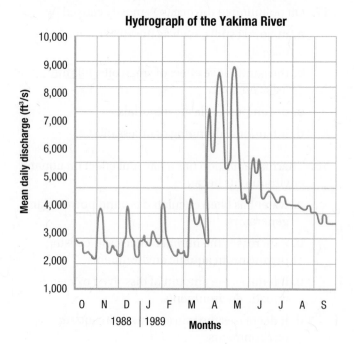

Hydrograph of the Yakima River

Critical Thinking

27. **Making Comparisons** Read the description of artificial eutrophication in this chapter. Do you think artificial eutrophication is more disturbing to the stability of a water ecosystem than natural eutrophication is?

28. **Analyzing Relationships** Water resources are often shared by several countries. A river, for example, might flow through five countries before it reaches an ocean. When water resources are shared, how should countries determine water rights and environmental responsibility?

29. **Making Inferences** Explain why it takes about 136 liters of water to produce a single serving of rice, but it takes more than 7,571 liters of water to produce a single serving of steak. What do you think the water is used for in each case?

30. **Making Inferences** Why is there so little fresh water in the world? Do you think that there would have been more fresh water at a different time in Earth's history?

31. **Social Studies** Find out how freshwater resources affected the development of one culture in history. Use at least five key terms from this chapter to write a two-paragraph description of how the availability of fresh water affected the culture you chose.

32. **Investigation** Find out about the source of the tap water in your home. Where does the tap water come from, and where does your wastewater go? Does the water complete a cycle? Make a poster to illustrate your findings. You may want to work with several classmates and visit the sites you discover.

Analyzing Data

The graph below illustrates the pumping rates for a set of wells that provide water to a small community. Use the graph to answer question 33.

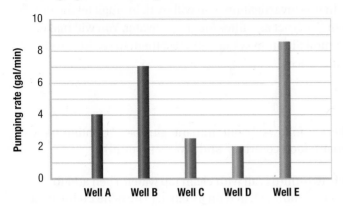

33. Analyzing Data How many gallons does Well B pump per day? What is the average pump rate for all of the wells? In one hour, how many more gallons of water will Well A pump than Well C?

34. Making Calculations If placing a container of water in your toilet tank reduces the amount of water per flush by 2 L, how much water would be saved each day if this were done in 80 million toilets? (Assume that each toilet is flushed five times per day.) Convert your answer into gallons (1 L = .26 Gal).

Making Connections

35. Communicating Main Ideas Why is water pollution a serious problem?

36. Writing Persuasively Write a letter to a senator in which you voice your support or criticism of a hypothetical water diversion project.

CASESTUDY

37. After reading the passage, explain why the Ogallala aquifer is so important.

38. How might global climate change affect the aquifer?

Why It Matters

39. How could towing icebergs to water-poor areas be made more economical?

STUDYSKILL

Root Words To practice vocabulary, write the key terms and definitions on a piece of paper and fold the paper lengthwise so that the definitions are covered. First, see how many definitions you already know. Then, write the definitions you do not know on another piece of paper, and practice until you know all of the terms.

Groundwater Filters

Objectives

Construct a model of Earth's natural groundwater filtering system.

Test the ability of your groundwater filters to filter contaminants out of different solutions.

Materials

beakers, 750 mL (5)

glucose solution

glucose test paper

graduated cylinder

gravel

metric ruler

soda bottles, 2 to 3 L (4)

red food coloring

sand

soil

stirring rod

wax pencil

optional contaminants: cooking oil, detergent, fertilizer, vinegar, soda

optional filter materials: alum, charcoal

As surface water travels downward through rock and soil, the water is filtered and purified. As a result, the water in aquifers is generally cleaner than surface water. In this investigation, you will work in small teams to explore how layers of Earth act as a filter for groundwater. You will make models of Earth's natural filtration system and test them to see how well they filter various substances.

Procedure

1. Label four beakers as follows: "Contaminant: glucose," "Contaminant: soil," "Contaminant: food coloring," and "Water (control)."

2. Fill these beakers two-thirds full with clean tap water. Then add to each beaker the contaminant listed on its label. (The table on the next page shows how much of each contaminant you should use.) Stir each mixture thoroughly.

3. Copy the data table into your notebook. Carefully observe each beaker, and record your observations. Use some of the glucose test paper to test the glucose level in the glucose beaker.

4. Make four separate filtration systems similar to the one shown below. Your teacher will provide you with bottle caps that have holes poked through them. Fasten each cap to a bottle. Cut the bottom off of each soda bottle, and fill each bottle with layers of gravel, sand, and soil. Consider using the optional filter materials, such as alum or charcoal, but be sure to make all four of your systems identical.

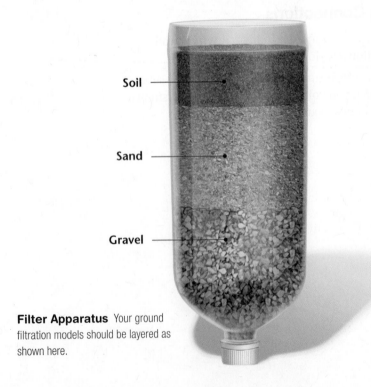

Filter Apparatus Your ground filtration models should be layered as shown here.

Soil

Sand

Gravel

OBSERVATIONS OF SUBSTANCES IN SURFACE WATER

Contaminant	Before filtration	After filtration
Glucose (15 mL)		
Soil (15 mL)		
Food coloring (15 drops)		
Water (control)		

5. You are now going to pour each mixture through a filtration system. But first predict how well the filters will clean each water sample. Write your predictions in your notebook.

6. Stir a contaminant mixture in its beaker, and immediately pour the mixture through a filtration system into a clean beaker. Observe the resulting "groundwater," and record your observations in the table you created. CAUTION: Do not taste any of the substances you are testing.

7. Repeat step 6 for each mixture. Clean and relabel the contaminant beakers as you go along.

Analysis

1. **Analyzing Results** Test the glucose-water mixture for the presence of glucose. Can you see the glucose?

2. **Analyzing Results** Was the soil removed from the water by filtering? Was the food coloring removed? How do you know?

Step 6 Pour each sample of contaminated surface water through a filter.

Conclusions

3. **Drawing Conclusions** How accurate were your predictions?

4. **Drawing Conclusions** What conclusions can you draw about the filtration model and the materials you used?

Extension

5. **Making Predictions** Choose a substance from the materials list that has not been tested. Predict what will happen if you mix this substance in the water supply.

6. **Evaluating Results** Now test your prediction. Use the filter that was the control in the earlier experiment. How did your results compare with your prediction?

7. **Analyzing Results** Compare your results with the results of other teams. What precautions do you recommend for keeping groundwater clean?

Chapter 12

Air

Section 1
What Causes Air Pollution?

Section 2
Air, Noise, and Light Pollution

Section 3
Acid Precipitation

Why It Matters

The Los Angeles, California, skyline at dusk reveals unhealthy levels of air pollution.

What are some approaches that urban areas can take to improve air quality?

CASESTUDY

Learn more about the effects of air pollution in the case study *The Health Effects of Ground-Level Ozone* on pages 310–311.

ONLINE ENVIRONMENTAL SCIENCE
HMDScience.com

Go online to access additional resources, including labs, worksheets, multimedia, and resources in Spanish.

©Deborah Davis/Getty Images

What Causes Air Pollution?

In most places in the United States, the air we breathe is fairly clean. In some places in the world, though, this is not the case. Areas of India and Bangladesh have air that is so polluted it harms people's health.

Clean air consists mostly of nitrogen and oxygen gas, as well as very small amounts of argon, carbon dioxide, and water vapor. When harmful substances build up in the air to unhealthy levels, the result is **air pollution.**

Much air pollution is the result of human activities, but pollutants can also come from natural sources. A volcano, for example, can spew clouds of particles and sulfur dioxide, SO_2, into the atmosphere. Natural pollutants also include dust, pollen, and spores.

Primary and Secondary Pollutants

A pollutant that is put directly into the air by human activity is called a **primary pollutant.** An example of a primary pollutant is soot from smoke. **Figure 1.1** shows some sources of primary air pollutants. **Secondary pollutants** form when primary pollutants react with other primary pollutants or with naturally occurring substances such as water vapor. An example of a secondary pollutant is ground-level ozone. Ground-level ozone forms when the ultraviolet rays of the sun cause emissions from cars, trucks, and other sources to react with oxygen in the atmosphere.

Objectives

▶ Name five primary air pollutants and give sources for each.

▶ Name the two major sources of air pollution in urban areas.

▶ Describe the way in which smog forms.

▶ Explain the way in which a thermal inversion traps air pollution.

Key Terms

air pollution
primary pollutant
secondary pollutant
smog
temperature inversion

✓ CHECK FOR UNDERSTANDING

Explain How is ground-level ozone an example of a secondary pollutant?

FIGURE 1.1

Primary Air Pollutants Each day in the United States, hundreds of thousands of tons of polluting emissions that result from human activity enter the air.

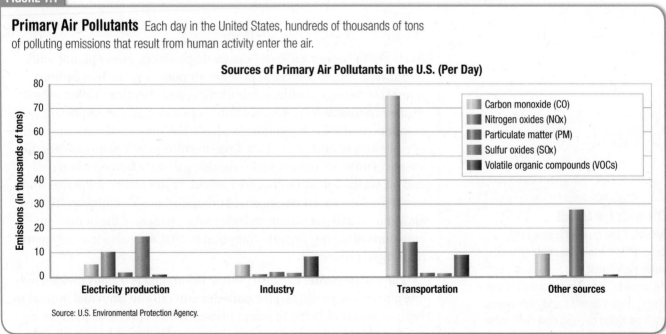

Sources of Primary Air Pollutants in the U.S. (Per Day)

Legend:
- Carbon monoxide (CO)
- Nitrogen oxides (NOx)
- Particulate matter (PM)
- Sulfur oxides (SOx)
- Volatile organic compounds (VOCs)

Y-axis: Emissions (in thousands of tons)

X-axis categories: Electricity production, Industry, Transportation, Other sources

Source: U.S. Environmental Protection Agency.

FIGURE 1.2

PRIMARY AIR POLLUTANTS

Pollutant	Description	Primary Sources	Effects
Carbon monoxide (CO)	CO is an odorless, colorless, poisonous gas. It is produced by the incomplete burning of fossil fuels.	Sources of CO are cars, trucks, buses, small engines, and some industrial processes.	CO interferes with the blood's ability to carry oxygen, slowing reflexes and causing drowsiness. In high concentrations, CO can cause death.
Nitrogen oxides (NO_x)	When combustion (burning) temperatures exceed 538°C, nitrogen and oxygen combine to form nitrogen oxides.	NO_x comes from burning fuels in vehicles, power plants, and industrial boilers.	NO_x can make the body vulnerable to respiratory infections, lung diseases, and cancer. NO_x contributes to the brownish haze seen over cities and to acid precipitation.
Sulfur dioxide (SO_2)	SO_2 is produced by chemical interactions between sulfur and oxygen.	SO_2 comes mostly from burning fossil fuels.	SO_2 contributes to acid precipitation as sulfuric acid. Secondary pollutants that result from reactions with SO_2 can harm plant life and irritate the respiratory systems of humans.
Volatile organic compounds (VOCs)	VOCs are organic chemicals that vaporize readily and form toxic fumes.	VOCs come from burning fuels. Vehicles are a major source of VOCs.	VOCs contribute to smog formation and can cause serious health problems, such as cancer. They may also harm plants.
Particulate matter (particulates or PM)	Particulates are tiny particles of liquid or solid matter.	Most particulates come from construction, agriculture, forestry, and fires. Vehicles and industrial processes also contribute particulates.	Particulates can form clouds that reduce visibility and cause a variety of respiratory problems. Particulates have also been linked to cancer. As well, they may corrode metals and erode buildings and sculptures.

Sources of Primary Air Pollutants

As shown in **Figure 1.2** above, household products, power plants, and motor vehicles are sources of primary air pollutants such as carbon monoxide, nitrogen oxide, sulfur dioxide, and chemicals called *volatile organic compounds* (VOCs). Carbon monoxide gas is an important component of the exhaust from vehicles. Vehicles are also a major source of emissions of nitrogen oxides. Coal-burning power plants are another source of nitrogen oxides. Sulfur dioxide gases are formed when coal and oil, which contain sulfur, are burned. Power plants, refineries, and metal smelters contribute much of the sulfur dioxide emissions to the air. Vehicles and gas station spillage make up most of the human-made emissions of volatile organic compounds. VOCs are also found in many household products.

Particulate matter can also pollute the air and is usually divided into fine and coarse particles. Fine particles enter the air from fuel burned by vehicles and coal-burning power plants. Sources of coarse particles are cement plants, mining operations, incinerators, wood-burning fireplaces, fields, and roads.

Connect to LAW

Off with His Head!

Around 1300 CE, King Edward I of England forbade the burning of coal while Parliament was in session. "Be it known to all within the sound of my voice," King Edward I said, "whosoever shall be found burning coal shall suffer the loss of his head."

The History of Air Pollution

Air pollution is not a new phenomenon. Whenever something burns, pollutants enter the air. Two thousand years ago, Seneca, a Roman philosopher and writer, complained about the foul air in Rome. In 1273, England's King Edward I ordered that burning a particularly dirty kind of coal called sea-coal was illegal. One man was even executed for disobeying this medieval "clean air act."

The world air-quality problem is much worse today because modern industrial societies burn large amounts of fossil fuels. As represented in **Figure 1.3**, most air pollution in industrialized countries comes from motor vehicles and industry.

Motor Vehicle Emissions

Almost one-third of our air pollution comes from gasoline burned by vehicles. According to the U.S. Department of Transportation, Americans drove their vehicles over three trillion miles in 2010. Roughly 90 percent of that mileage was from passenger and other light-duty vehicles. The rest was from trucks and buses.

Controlling Vehicle Emissions

The Clean Air Act, passed in 1970 and strengthened in 1990, gives the Environmental Protection Agency (EPA) the authority to regulate vehicle emissions in the United States. The EPA required the gradual elimination of lead in gasoline, and as a result, lead pollution has been reduced by more than 90 percent in the United States. In addition, catalytic converters, which are required in automobiles, clean exhaust gases of pollutants before the pollutants are able to exit the tailpipe. The EPA indicates that light-duty cars and trucks in 2010 burned fuel approximately 70 percent more efficiently and with about 40 percent fewer emissions of carbon dioxide than they did in 1975. In addition, cars and trucks produce approximately 95 percent fewer emissions of pollutants other than carbon dioxide than they did in the 1970s.

ECOFACT

Sea-Coal

In 12th-century London, wood was becoming too scarce and expensive to use as a fuel source. Large deposits of sea-coal, found off the northeast coast of England, provided a plentiful alternative. However, this soft coal did not burn efficiently. The sea-coal produced much smoke and not much heat. The smoke emanated from London homes and factories and combined with fog to produce smog.

FIGURE 1.3

Sources of Air Pollution The refinery shown in this photograph is a source of volatile organic compounds. The truck in the foreground is emitting nitrous oxide into the atmosphere.

Utility Incentives for Zero-emission Vehicles

The Los Angeles Department of Water and Power provides discounts of $0.025 per kilowatt hour (kWh) for electricity used to recharge electric vehicles. If the energy charge per kWh is $0.02949 and you use 150 kWh of electricity per month to recharge your vehicle, how much money would you save on your electric bill each month? each year? How much would you save if you had three electric cars?

California Zero-Emission Vehicle Program

A catalytic converter, as shown in **Figure 1.4**, is used to control emissions from most American vehicles. In California, motor vehicles account for more than half of the ozone and particulate matter that pollutes the air. To improve air quality, the state's Air Resources Board established the Zero-Emission Vehicle (ZEV) program in 1990 and has continued to update it to encourage the development of less-polluting vehicles. ZEV programs have also been adopted in Maine, Massachusetts, New York, and Vermont.

Zero-emission vehicles have no tailpipe emissions, no emissions from gasoline, and no emission-control systems, which deteriorate over time. Battery-powered electric vehicles are the only true ZEVs at the moment, but there are three types of partial ZEVs. One type is clean, fuel-efficient hybrid cars, which are powered by both batteries and gasoline engines. There are many models of hybrid cars, including models that are recharged by plugging in to a power source. Vehicles powered by hydrogen would emit only water vapor. As of 2011, such hydrogen-powered vehicles are still mostly in the prototype stage of development.

FIGURE 1.4

Car Emission The catalyst material in a catalytic converter (top) speeds up a chemical reaction that changes exhaust emissions to less harmful substances. The text below the images shows a car's contribution to air pollution.

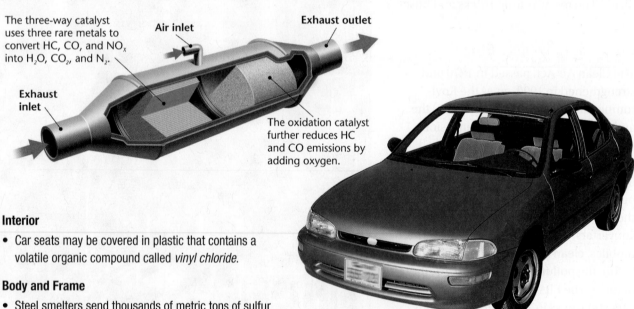

The three-way catalyst uses three rare metals to convert HC, CO, and NO_x into H_2O, CO_2, and N_2.

Air inlet

Exhaust outlet

Exhaust inlet

The oxidation catalyst further reduces HC and CO emissions by adding oxygen.

Interior

- Car seats may be covered in plastic that contains a volatile organic compound called *vinyl chloride*.

Body and Frame

- Steel smelters send thousands of metric tons of sulfur dioxide into the air each year.
- Many auto factories in Mexico, Eastern Europe, and some Asian countries lack pollution-control devices.

Fuel Tank

- When filling the car with gasoline, VOCs escape into the atmosphere.

Exhaust

- Car exhaust is a major source of nitrogen oxides, carbon monoxide, and hydrocarbons.
- In developing countries, car exhaust may contain over a thousand poisonous substances.

FIGURE 1.5

Industrial Pollution In 1996, the federal government established standards to reduce emissions of VOC-producing chemicals used in dry cleaning.

ECOFACT

Air Pollution's Impact on Birds
Scientists in Finland have documented the effects of harmful emissions from a copper smelter in Finland on two species of birds that live nearby. The two species of birds respond differently to the pollutants containing heavy metals and acidic substances. One species appears to suffer directly from the toxic effects of the pollutants. The other species suffers because the amount of insect food for its nestlings has been reduced. When heavy metal emissions from the smelter decreased, a rapid improvement in breeding success and a decrease in the heavy metal found in the bones of nestlings was observed.

Industrial Air Pollution

Many industries, as well as power plants that generate electricity, burn fuel to produce energy. They usually burn fossil fuels. Burning fossil fuels releases sulfur dioxide and nitrogen oxides into the air. Power plants that produce electricity emit at least two-thirds of all sulfur dioxide and more than one-third of all nitrogen oxides that pollute the air.

Some industries, such as the dry cleaning industry shown in **Figure 1.5**, also produce VOCs. VOCs are chemical compounds that form toxic fumes. Oil refineries, chemical manufacturing plants, furniture refinishers, and automobile repair shops also contribute to the VOCs in the air.

Regulating Air Pollution from Industry

The Clean Air Act requires many industries to use scrubbers or other pollution-control devices. Scrubbers remove some of the more harmful substances that would otherwise pollute the air. A *scrubber*, as shown in **Figure 1.6**, is a machine that moves gases through a spray of water that dissolves many pollutants.

Electrostatic precipitators are machines used in cement factories and coal-burning power plants to remove dust particles from smoke-stacks. In an electrostatic precipitator, gas containing dust particles is blown through a charged chamber. An electrical charge is transferred to the dust particles, which causes them to stick to one another and the sides of the chamber. The clean gas is released from the chamber, and the concentrated dust particles can then be collected and removed. Electrostatic precipitators remove more than 20 million tons of ash generated by coal-burning power plants from the air each year in the United States.

FIGURE 1.6

Scrubber Scrubbers work by spraying gases with water, which removes many pollutants.

Cleaned gas

Filter

Water

Dirty gas · Wet gas

Dirty water

✓ **CHECK FOR UNDERSTANDING**
Describe Name two pollution-control devices. State how they help to limit the amount of pollutants in air.

FIGURE 1.7

Smog The diagram below shows how smog is formed. Large cities with dry, sunny climates and millions of automobiles often suffer from smog.

❷ Ozone reacts with automobile exhaust to form smog.

Smog

Ozone

Automobile exhaust

❶ Automobile exhaust reacts with air and sunlight to form ozone.

Smog

When air pollution hangs over urban areas and reduces visibility, it is called **smog**. As you can see in **Figure 1.7**, smog results from chemical reactions that involve sunlight, air, automobile exhaust, and ozone. Pollutants released by vehicles and industries are the main causes of smog.

Temperature Inversions

The circulation of air in the atmosphere usually keeps air pollution from reaching dangerous levels. During the day, the sun heats the surface of Earth and the air near Earth. The warm air rises through the cooler air above and carries pollutants away from the ground and into the atmosphere.

Sometimes, however, pollution is trapped near the Earth's surface. Usually, air temperatures decrease with altitude, but sometimes a **temperature inversion** occurs when the air above is warmer than the air below. **Figure 1.8** shows how a temperature inversion traps pollutants near Earth's surface. The warmer air above keeps the cooler air at the surface from moving upward. Pollutants are trapped below with the cooler air. If a city is located in a valley, the city has a greater chance of experiencing temperature inversions. Los Angeles, which is surrounded on three sides by mountains, often has temperature inversions that trap smog in the city.

FIGURE 1.8

Air Circulation Normal air circulation is shown at left. A temperature inversion, in which pollutants are trapped near Earth's surface, is shown at right.

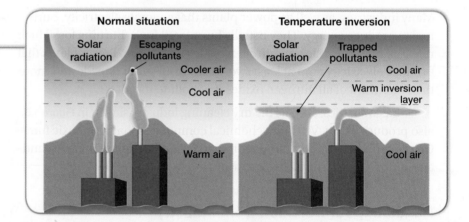

Normal situation

Solar radiation
Escaping pollutants
Cooler air
Cool air
Warm air

Temperature inversion

Solar radiation
Trapped pollutants
Cool air
Warm inversion layer
Cool air

✓ Section 1 **Formative Assessment**

▶ Reviewing Main Ideas

1. **Name** five primary air pollutants, and give important sources for each.

2. **Name** the two major sources of air pollution in urban areas.

3. **Describe** the way in which smog forms.

4. **Define** the term *temperature inversion*. Explain how temperature inversion traps pollutants near Earth's surface.

✔ Critical Thinking

5. **Making Decisions** Read the passage on the California Zero-Emission Vehicle Program. Should automobile makers be made to adhere to quotas of zero-emission vehicles set by states, even if it causes automakers to lose revenue?

6. **Analyzing Relationships** Can you think of any other possible type of pollution-control device that could be used to remove particulates from smokestacks in a manner similar to an electrostatic precipitator?

Air, Noise, and Light Pollution

SECTION 2

Objectives

▶ Describe three short-term effects and three long-term effects of air pollution on human health.

▶ Explain what causes indoor air pollution and how it can be prevented.

▶ Describe three human health problems caused by noise pollution.

▶ Describe solutions to energy waste caused by light pollution.

People who are very young or very old and people who have heart or lung problems are most affected by air pollutants. Decades of research have linked air pollution to disease. But because pollution adds to the effects of existing diseases, no death certificates list the cause of death as air pollution. Instead, diseases such as emphysema, heart disease, and lung cancer are cited as causes of death. The American Lung Association has estimated that Americans pay tens of billions of dollars a year in health costs to treat respiratory diseases caused by air pollution.

Short-Term Effects of Air Pollution on Health

Many of the effects of air pollution on people's health are short-term and are reversible if their exposure to air pollution decreases. The short-term effects of air pollution on people's health include headache; nausea; irritation to the eyes, nose, and throat; tightness in the chest; coughing; and upper respiratory infections, such as bronchitis and pneumonia. Pollution can also make the condition of individuals who suffer from asthma and emphysema worse.

Long-Term Health Effects of Air Pollution

Long-term effects on health that have been linked to air pollution include emphysema, lung cancer, and heart disease. Long-term exposure to air pollution may worsen medical conditions suffered by older people and may damage the lungs of children.

Key Terms

sick-building syndrome
asbestos
decibel (dB)

FIGURE 2.1

Air Pollution This police officer wears a smog mask as he directs traffic in Bangkok, Thailand.

©UNEP

Indoor Air Pollution

The quality of air inside a home or a building is sometimes worse than the quality of the air outside. Chemicals that are used to make carpets, building materials, paints, and furniture are major sources of pollutants in buildings. **Figure 2.2** shows examples of some indoor air pollutants.

Buildings that have very poor air quality have a condition called **sick-building syndrome.** Sick-building syndrome is most common in hot places where buildings are tightly sealed to keep out the heat. In Florida in the early 1990s, for example, a newly built, tightly sealed county courthouse had to be abandoned. Half of the people who worked there developed allergic reactions to fungi that were growing in the air-conditioning ducts, ceiling tiles, carpets, and furniture.

Identifying and removing the sources of indoor air pollution is the most effective way to maintain good indoor air quality. Ventilation, or mixing outdoor air with indoor air, is also necessary for good air quality. Activities such as renovation and painting, which produce indoor air pollution, require good ventilation.

CASESTUDY

The Health Effects of Ground-Level Ozone

You have learned that the ozone layer in the stratosphere shields Earth from the harmful effects of ultraviolet radiation from the sun. At the surface of the Earth, however, ozone is a human-made air pollutant that at certain concentrations damages human health.

Ozone forms from the reaction of volatile organic compounds (VOCs) and nitrogen oxides (NO_x) in the presence of heat and sunlight. High concentrations of ozone form in the atmosphere on sunny days that have high temperatures. The sources of VOCs and NO_x emissions are largely motor vehicles, power plants, gasoline vapors, and chemical solvents. Most ozone pollution forms in urban and suburban areas. However, ozone-producing chemicals may be transported hundreds of kilometers from their source.

As ozone concentrations in the atmosphere increase, greater numbers of people may experience harmful health effects of ozone on the lungs. Some of the short-term effects of ozone on health include irritation of the respiratory system, a reduction in lung function, the aggravation of asthma, and inflammation to the lining of the lungs. Scientists believe that ozone may have other damaging effects on human health. Lung diseases such as bronchitis and emphysema may be aggravated by ozone.

Children who engage in vigorous outdoor activities when pollutant concentrations are often high may have a greater risk of developing asthma or other respiratory illnesses.

©Neal Preston/Corbis

FIGURE 2.2

Indoor Pollutants Some indoor air pollutants and their sources are shown here.

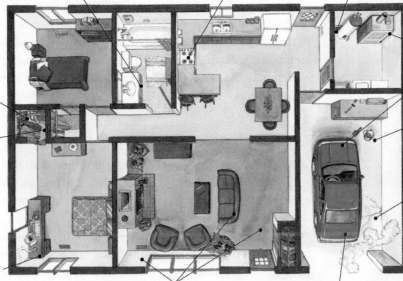

Bleach, sodium hydroxide, and hydrochloric acid from household cleaners

Nitrogen oxides from unvented gas stove, wood stove, or kerosene heater

Fungi and bacteria from dirty heating and air conditioning ducts

Tetrachloro-ethylene from dry-cleaning fluid

Carbon monoxide from faulty furnace and car left running

Methylene chloride from paint strippers and thinners

Paradichloro-benzene from moth-ball crystals and air fresheners

Radon-222 from uranium-containing rocks under the house

Tobacco smoke from cigarettes and pipes

Formaldehyde from furniture, carpeting, particleboard, and foam insulation

Gasoline from car and lawn mower

A therapist performs a lung-function test on a patient by using a machine that measures various aspects of lung function.

Scientists believe that permanent lung injury may result from repeated short-term exposure to ozone pollution. Children who are regularly exposed to high concentrations of ozone may have reduced lung function as adults. Exposure to ozone may also accelerate the natural decline in lung function that is part of the aging process.

Those who are most at risk from ozone include children, adults who exercise or work outdoors, older people, and people who suffer from respiratory diseases. In addition, there are some healthy individuals who have unusually high susceptibility to ozone.

Critical Thinking

1. **Making Decisions** Write a brief paragraph explaining whether or not lung-function tests should be mandatory for children who live in urban areas where high concentrations of ozone are frequent.

2. **Making Decisions** If lung-function tests become mandatory, who will pay for these tests, and who will provide the equipment? Should these tests be performed at school, in a doctor's office, or at a hospital?

FIGURE 2.3

Asbestos Asbestos forms in long, thin fibers. The worker is removing debris from a structure that was built with asbestos.

Radon Gas

Radon is a colorless, tasteless, odorless gas. It is also radioactive. *Radon* is produced by the decay of uranium, a radioactive element that occurs naturally in the Earth's crust. Radon can seep through cracks and holes in foundations into homes, offices, and schools, where it adheres to dust particles. When people inhale the dust, radon enters their lungs. In the lungs, radon can destroy the genetic material in cells that line the air passages. Such damage can lead to cancer, especially among people who smoke. Radon is the second-leading cause of lung cancer in the United States.

Asbestos

Several minerals that form in long, thin fibers and that are valued for their strength and resistance to heat are called **asbestos**. Asbestos is primarily used as an insulator and as a fire retardant, and it was used extensively in building materials. The U.S. government banned the use of most asbestos products in the early 1970s. Exposure to asbestos in the air is dangerous. Asbestos fibers that are inhaled can cut and scar the lungs, which causes the disease asbestosis. Victims of the disease have more and more difficulty breathing and may eventually die of heart failure. Schools in the United States have taken this threat seriously. Billions of dollars have been spent to remove asbestos from school buildings. **Figure 2.3** shows asbestos fibers and asbestos removal from a building.

FIGURE 2.4

INTENSITY OF COMMON NOISES

Noise	Intensity (dB)
Rocket engine	180
Jet engine	140
Rock concert	120
Car horn	110
Chainsaw	100
Portable CD player	90–120
Lawnmower	90
Conversation	60
Whisper	30
Faintest sound heard by the human ear	0

Noise Pollution

Unwanted sound is noise pollution, and it is one of the prices we pay for modern living. It is irritating, and it damages our hearing by destroying cells in our ears. Hearing loss has roughly doubled in the United States since the 1970s. About 14.9 percent of teens have permanent hearing loss, likely due to the prevalence of portable listening devices. One study found that people living in a quiet environment in Africa had better hearing at the age of 80 than most Americans do at 30. Noise can also have a negative impact on organisms on land and in the oceans. For example, loud sounds have caused whales and dolphins to strand on beaches.

The intensity of sound is measured in units called **decibels** (dB). **Figure 2.4** shows the intensity of some common noises. Each increase of 10 dB results in a 10-fold increase in sound intensity. For example, 20 dB is 10 times the intensity of 10 dB. A sound of 120 dB is at the threshold of pain. Noise pollution can be controlled by devices such as mufflers on vehicles and lawn mowers, and by insulation. In Europe, MP3 players must not produce more than 100 dB of noise. According to the National Institutes of Health, the safe threshold for personal listening devices is 85 dB for 8 hours. Personal listening devices are not regulated in the United States.

FIGURE 2.5

Light Pollution This view of Hong Kong shows how lighting in urban areas can cause skyglow, which is an effect of light that can dramatically reduce our view of the night sky.

Light Pollution

Research suggests that light pollution can increase headaches, fatigue, stress, and anxiety in humans. Also, light pollution in urban areas diminishes our view of the night sky, as shown in **Figure 2.5**, and can negatively affect our environment. Hatching baby sea turtles instinctively move towards light. They may move the wrong way towards street lights and may not survive. Some communities near sea turtle beaches turn off their lights at hatching time. Light can also cause problems for birds that migrate at night. In Chicago, lights of tall buildings are dimmed during the migration season, saving many birds.

Another important environmental concern of lighting is energy waste. One solution to energy waste includes shielding light so it is directed downward. Two other solutions are to use time controls so that light is used only when needed and to use low-pressure sodium sources—the most energy-efficient source of light—where possible.

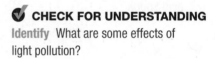

CHECK FOR UNDERSTANDING

Identify What are some effects of light pollution?

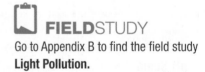

FIELDSTUDY

Go to Appendix B to find the field study **Light Pollution**.

©A Rroom with Views/Alamy Images

Section 2 **Formative Assessment**

▶ Reviewing Main Ideas

1. **Describe** the long-term effects and the short-term effects of air pollution on health.

2. **Describe** two ways in which indoor air pollution can be prevented.

3. **Describe** some of the human health problems caused by noise pollution.

4. **Describe** several solutions to the energy waste associated with light pollution.

✓ Critical Thinking

5. **Making Comparisons** Read the descriptions of noise and light pollution in this section. Explain ways in which noise pollution and light pollution are similar.

6. **Analyzing Relationships** Molds can grow in new, tightly sealed buildings where the humidity is high and the ventilation is poor. Explain how you would control the growth of mold in this type of environment.

▶ Explain the causes of
acid precipitation.

▶ Explain how acid precipitation
affects plants, soils, and
aquatic ecosystems.

▶ Describe three ways that acid
precipitation affects humans.

▶ Describe ways that countries
are working together
to solve the problem of
acid precipitation.

Key Terms

acid precipitation
pH
acid shock

Acid Precipitation

Imagine that you are hiking through the forests of the Adirondack Mountains in New York. You come to a lake and sit down to rest. You are amazed at how clear the water is; it is so clear that you can see the bottom of the lake. But after a few minutes you feel uneasy. Something is wrong. What is it? Suddenly, you realize that the lake has no fish.

What Causes Acid Precipitation?

The lake described in the introduction, and thousands of lakes throughout the world, are victims of acid precipitation, or acid rain. **Acid precipitation** is precipitation—rain, sleet, or snow—that contains a high concentration of acids. When fossil fuels are burned, they release oxides of sulfur and nitrogen. When the oxides combine with water in the atmosphere, they form sulfuric acid and nitric acid, which fall as acid precipitation. This acidic water flows over and through the ground, and into lakes, rivers, and streams. Acid precipitation can kill living things, and can result in the decline or loss of some local animal and plant populations.

A **pH** number is a measure of how acidic or basic a substance is. A pH scale is shown in **Figure 3.1**. As you can see from the scale, the lower the pH number is, the more acidic a substance is; the higher a pH number is, the more basic a substance is. Each whole number on the pH scale indicates a ten-fold change in acidity.

Pure water has a pH of 7.0. Normal precipitation is slightly acidic, because atmospheric carbon dioxide dissolves into the precipitation and forms carbonic acid. Normal precipitation has a pH of about 5.6. Acid precipitation has a pH of less than 5.0. **Figure 3.2** shows how acid precipitation forms.

FIGURE 3.1

pH Scale The pH scale measures how basic or how acidic a substance is. Below are the pH measurements of some common substances.

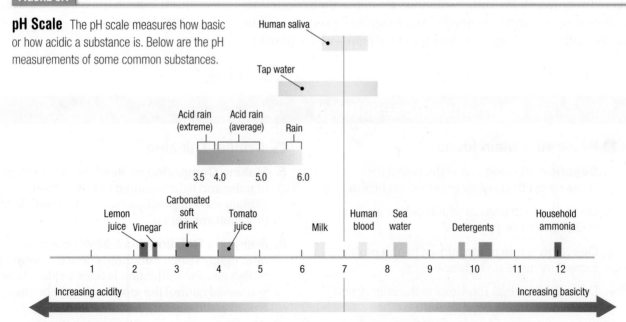

The pH of precipitation varies around the world and has changed through time. In North America, the pH of rain has been as low as 4.2 in some places. Since the problem of acid rain was identified, the EPA has worked with industries to cut emissions dramatically. Though much work remains, conditions are improving. In China and India, emissions of fossil fuels are increasing. There is growing concern that acid rain problems will increase in these areas.

How Acid Precipitation Affects Soils and Plants

Acid precipitation can lower the pH of soil and water. This increase in the concentration of acid is called *acidification*. Acidification changes the balance of a soil's chemistry in several ways. When the acidity of soil increases, some nutrients are dissolved and washed away by rainwater. Increased acidity causes aluminum and other toxic metals to be released and possibly absorbed by the roots of plants. Aluminum also causes root damage. Sulfur dioxide dissolved in water vapor clogs the openings on surfaces of plants. **Figure 3.3** shows the harmful effects of acid precipitation on trees over time.

©Simon Fraser/SPL/Photo Researchers, Inc.

FIGURE 3.2

Acid Precipitation Sulfur oxides and nitrogen oxides combine with water in the atmosphere to form sulfuric and nitric acids. Rainfall that contains these acids is called *acid precipitation.*

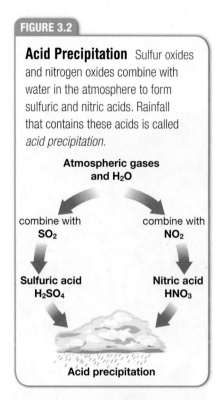

Atmospheric gases and H_2O

combine with SO_2

combine with NO_2

Sulfuric acid H_2SO_4

Nitric acid HNO_3

Acid precipitation

✔ **CHECK FOR UNDERSTANDING**

Compare How does the pH of pure water compare with that of acid precipitation?

FIGURE 3.3

Acid Precipitation The trees in this forest in Poland show the dramatic effect acid precipitation can have on plants.

Acid Precipitation and Aquatic Ecosystems

Aquatic animals are adapted to live in an environment with a particular pH range. If acid precipitation falls on a lake and changes the water's pH, acid can kill fish and other aquatic animals. The change in pH is not the only thing that kills fish. Acid precipitation causes aluminum to leach out of the soil surrounding a lake. The aluminum accumulates in the gills of fish and interferes with oxygen and salt exchange. As a result, fish are slowly suffocated.

The effects of acid precipitation are worst in the spring, when acidic snow that accumulated during the winter melts and rushes into lakes and other bodies of water. This sudden influx of acidic water that causes a rapid change in the water's pH is called **acid shock**. This phenomenon may kill large numbers of fish, as shown in **Figure 3.4**. Acid shock also affects the reproduction of fish and amphibians. They produce fewer eggs, and these eggs often do not hatch. The offspring that do survive often have birth defects and cannot reproduce.

Acid Precipitation and Humans

Acid precipitation can affect humans in a variety of ways. Toxic metals such as aluminum and mercury can be released into the environment when soil acidity increases. These toxic metals can find their way into crops, water, and fish. The toxins then poison the human body.

Acid precipitation can lead to other human health problems. Research has indicated that there may be a correlation between large amounts of acid precipitation received by a community and an increase in respiratory problems in the community's children.

The standard of living of some people is affected by acid precipitation. Decreases in numbers of fish caused by the acidification of lakes and streams can influence the livelihood of commercial fishers and people involved in the sportfishing industry. Forestry is also affected when trees are damaged by acid precipitation.

Acid precipitation can dissolve the calcium carbonate in common building materials, such as concrete, marble, and limestone. Some of the world's most important monuments are being dissolved by acid precipitation. These monuments include the Acropolis in Greece, the Taj Mahal in India, ancient temples and pyramids in Egypt and in the rain forests of Central America, and the Lincoln Memorial in Washington, DC.

International Conflict and Cooperation

One problem in controlling acid precipitation is that pollutants may be released in one area and fall to the ground hundreds of kilometers away. For example, some of the acid precipitation that falls in southeastern Canada results from pollution produced in the northeastern United States. **Figure 3.5** shows approximate areas of the world that produce pollutants and areas which are then affected by acid precipitation. Acid precipitation

FIGURE 3.4

Acid Shock Acid shock can cause the death of many fish.

QUICKLAB

Effects of Acid Precipitation

Procedure

1. Place a drop of mixed protozoan culture on a microscope slide and place a cover slip on top.
2. Observe the organisms under a microscope. Record your observations.
3. Use a pipette to place 2–3 drops of vinegar (which has a pH similar to that of acid precipitation) along one edge of the cover slip. Record your observations.

Analysis

1. Aquatic organisms are adapted to live within a specific range of pH. What did you observe when the protozoa came into contact with the vinegar?
2. What effects can acid precipitation have on aquatic ecosystems? on humans?

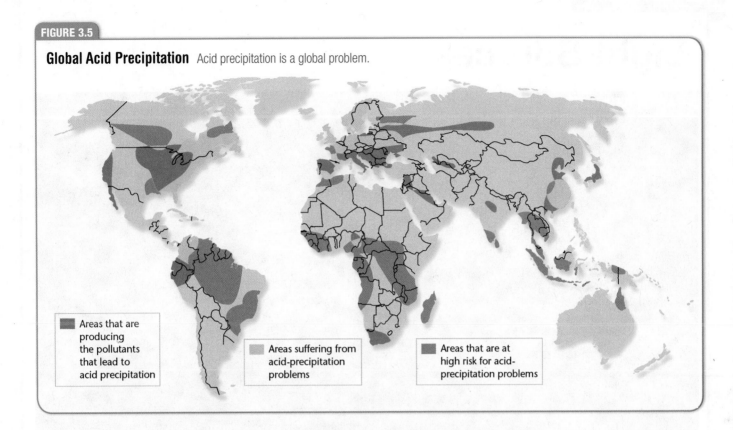

FIGURE 3.5

Global Acid Precipitation Acid precipitation is a global problem.

Areas that are
producing
the pollutants
that lead to
acid precipitation

Areas suffering from
acid-precipitation
problems

Areas that are at
high risk for acid-
precipitation problems

is an international problem. In the spirit of cooperation, Canada and the
United States signed the Canada–U.S. Air Quality Agreement in 1991.
Both countries agreed to reduce emissions that flow across the Canada–
U.S. boundary. As a result of this agreement, sulfur dioxide emissions
in the United States and Canada have been reduced dramatically since
the 1970s. In Europe, similar agreements reduced sulfur dioxide emissions by about 40 percent over the two decades after 1980, although
reductions in emissions of nitrogen oxides have been offset by vehicle
exhaust from increased road traffic. Meanwhile, China still burns large
amounts of high-sulfur coal without pollution controls. The polluted air
that results produces acid precipitation in other parts of Asia that are far
from the coal-burning plants in China.

✔ **CHECK FOR UNDERSTANDING**

Explain How can pollutants from the
United States produce acid precipitation
in Canada?

 Section 3 **Formative Assessment**

▶ **Reviewing Main Ideas**

1. **Explain** how acid precipitation forms.

2. **Describe** the harmful effects that acid
   precipitation can have on plants, soils, and
   aquatic ecosystems.

3. **Describe** three ways in which acid
   precipitation can affect humans.

4. **Describe** a way in which countries are
   working together to solve the problem of
   acid precipitation.

✔ **Critical Thinking**

5. **Inferring Relationships** In addition to
   negatively affecting forestry and the fishing
   industry, how might acid precipitation affect
   local economies?

6. **Analyzing Viewpoints** Write a short essay in
   which you discuss whether or not a country that
   releases significant amounts of pollutants into
   the air that fall as acid precipitation in another
   country should be expected to pay some of the
   costs of cleanup.

Light Sources

EARTH AT NIGHT

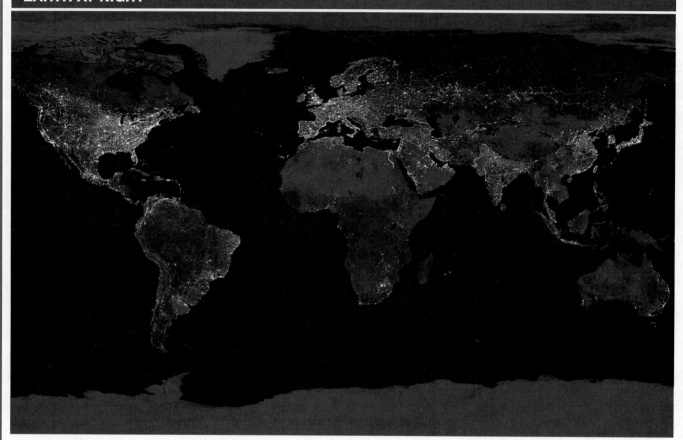

Map Skills

This satellite image of the Earth from space at night shows light sources that are human in origin. The map is a composite image made from hundreds of images taken by orbiting satellites. Use the map of light sources on Earth to answer the questions below.

1. **Inferring Relationships** Using the brightness of the light sources on the map as a key, can you estimate the locations of some of the most densely populated areas on Earth? Where are some of these areas?

2. **Inferring Relationships** Some climatic conditions on Earth, such as extreme cold, heat, wetness, or a thin atmosphere, make parts of our planet less habitable than others. Examples of areas on our planet that do not support large populations include deserts, high mountains, polar regions, and tropical rain forests. From the map, can you identify regions of the Earth where climatic conditions may not be able to support large human populations? What are some of these places?

3. **Finding Locations** Many large cities are seaports that are located along the coastlines of the world's oceans. From the map, can you pick out light sources along coastlines that might indicate the sites of large ports? Identify some of these cities by name.

4. **Inferring Relationships** From the differences in the density of the light sources, can you pick out any international borders?

ECOZine at HMDScience.com

Go online for the latest environmental science news and updates on all EcoZine articles.

Killer Smog

For the residents of the small Monongahela Valley town of Donora, Pennsylvania, living with the smoke that billowed from the local zinc smelter was an everyday occurrence—until October 26, 1948. On that night, a temperature inversion and an absence of wind began to trap a deadly mixture of sulfur dioxide, carbon monoxide, and metal dust that would hang in the valley air for five days. Over that period of time, 20 residents lost their lives and 7,000 other residents—about half of the town's population—suffered some form of respiratory problems.

The Weekend of the Killer Smog

By Saturday afternoon, October 29, 1948, the yellowish smog had become so thick that spectators in the stands at a local high school football game could not see the players on the field. Only the whistles of the referees could be heard. By nightfall, driving was unsafe. This proved to be catastrophic because doctors recommended that any residents who suffered from respiratory ailments be evacuated from town. In an attempt to alleviate the suffering of people who were struggling to breathe, several local firemen carried oxygen tanks through the streets to people's homes. Because of the low visibility, the firemen had to feel their way along buildings and fences. Because the supply of oxygen was limited, only a few breaths of oxygen could be given to each person. Eleven people died that night. A makeshift morgue was set up in the local community center.

This historical photo captures the town of Donora, Pennsylvania, as it is enveloped in smog at noon on Saturday, October 28, 1948.

Even as the killer smog choked the valley, the zinc smelter continued production throughout the night. The smelter continued sending more gases and dust into the air over Donora. The smelter was shut down only when the magnitude of the problem became apparent—at 6:00 a.m. on Sunday, October 30, 1948.

Later that day, a drizzling rain began to fall and washed the pollutants from the sky. By the time the rain fell, 20 people were dead. Thousands of other people were at home in bed or were filling the corridors and examining rooms of the two area hospitals. People who were less affected by the smog suffered from nausea and vomiting, headaches, and abdominal cramps. Some victims were choking or coughing up blood. The zinc smelter resumed operation on Monday morning, October 31.

The Aftermath

The smog of Donora was one of the United States' most serious environmental disasters. Shortly after the incident, the Pennsylvania Department of Health, the U.S. Public Health Service, and other agencies undertook investigations. This was the first organized attempt to document the effects of air pollution on health in the United States. The knowledge that air pollution could be linked directly to the deaths of individuals resulted in legislation at the local, regional, state, and federal levels. These laws were set to limit emissions of sulfur dioxide, carbon monoxide, particulate matter, and other pollutants. The greatest legacy of the Donora tragedy was passage of the Clean Air Act of 1970. According to a 2011 report, the direct benefits of amendments to the Clean Air Act of 1990 are estimated to be around $2 trillion and 230,000 fewer deaths by 2020! This is a staggering benefit for the $65 million direct cost of implementation.

What Do You Think?

Who do you think should be held responsible for the Donora, Pennsylvania, disaster? Explain your answer. Given what you know about the regulation of industrial pollutants under the Clean Air Act, do you think another incident such as the Donora killer smog could happen in the United States today?

SECTION 1 **What Causes Air Pollution?**

OBJECTIVES

- Primary pollutants are pollutants put directly in the air by human activity.
- Secondary pollutants are formed when a primary pollutant comes into contact with other primary pollutants or with naturally occurring substances and a chemical reaction takes place.
- Most air pollution comes from vehicles and industry.
- The air pollution that hangs over cities and reduces visibility is called smog.
- Pollution can be trapped near the surface of Earth by a temperature inversion.

KEY TERMS

air pollution

primary pollutant

secondary pollutant

smog

temperature inversion

SECTION 2 **Air, Noise, and Light Pollution**

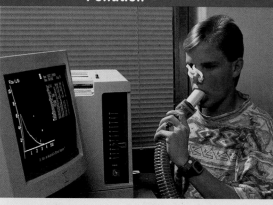

OBJECTIVES

- Air pollution may have both long- and short-term effects on human health.
- The air indoors may be more polluted than the air outside. Plastics, cleaning chemicals, and building materials are major sources of indoor air pollution.
- Noise is a pollutant that affects human health and the quality of life.
- Inefficient lighting diminishes our view of the night sky and wastes energy.

KEY TERMS

sick-building syndrome

asbestos

decibel (dB)

SECTION 3 **Acid Precipitation**

OBJECTIVES

- Acid precipitation is precipitation such as rain, sleet, or snow that contains a high concentration of acids.
- Acid shock occurs when a sudden influx of acidic water enters a lake or stream and causes a rapid change in pH that harms aquatic life.
- Pollutants released in one geographical area may fall to the ground hundreds of kilometers away as acid precipitation—sometimes in another country.

KEY TERMS

acid precipitation

pH

acid shock

CHAPTER 12 **Review**

Reviewing Key Terms

Use each of the following terms in a sentence.

1. *air pollution*
2. *smog*
3. *temperature inversion*
4. *sick-building syndrome*
5. *pH*

For each pair of terms, explain how the meanings of the terms differ.

6. *primary pollutant* and *secondary pollutant*
7. *asbestos* and *radon*
8. *pH* and *acid precipitation*
9. *acidification* and *acid shock*
10. **Concept Map** Use the following terms to create a concept map: *air pollution, primary pollutant, volatile organic compound, scrubber, secondary pollutant, smog,* and *temperature inversion.*

Reviewing Main Ideas

11. Which of the following air pollutants is *not* a primary pollutant?
    a. particulate matter
    b. ozone
    c. sulfur dioxide
    d. volatile organic compounds

12. A device used to clean exhaust gases before they exit an automobile's tailpipe is called a(n)
    a. electrostatic precipitator.
    b. catalytic converter.
    c. scrubber.
    d. None of the above

13. The majority of sulfur dioxide produced by industry comes from
    a. oil refineries.
    b. dry cleaners.
    c. chemical plants.
    d. coal-burning power plants.

14. Which of the following substances is *not* involved in the chemical reaction that produces smog?
    a. sunlight
    b. particulate matter
    c. automotive exhaust
    d. ozone

15. Which of the following respiratory diseases is considered a long-term effect of air pollution on human health?
    a. emphysema
    b. bronchitis
    c. pneumonia
    d. all of the above

16. Which of the following substances is a colorless, tasteless, and odorless radioactive gas?
    a. asbestos
    b. carbon monoxide
    c. radon
    d. ozone

17. A sound measuring 40 dB has how many times the intensity of a sound that measures 10 dB?
    a. 4 times
    b. 30 times
    c. 400 times
    d. 1,000 times

18. Which of the following choices is *not* an effective solution to the energy waste related to inefficient lighting?
    a. using low-pressure sodium lighting sources
    b. pointing lights on billboards and street signs upward
    c. placing light sources on time controls
    d. shielding light to direct it downward

19. Which of the following numbers on the pH scale would indicate that a substance is acidic?
    a. 5.0
    b. 7.0
    c. 9.0
    d. none of the above

20. Normal precipitation has a pH of
    a. 7.0.
    b. 5.6.
    c. 5.1.
    d. 4.5.

Short Answer

21. Define the term *zero-emission vehicle*. What types of vehicles qualify as zero-emission vehicles?

22. List five indoor air pollutants and examples of sources of each pollutant.

23. Explain the health hazards that radon gas poses for humans.

24. How does acid precipitation damage monuments such as the Acropolis, the Taj Mahal, and the Lincoln Memorial?

25. Explain why acid precipitation is a source of international conflict and why international cooperation is necessary to resolve the problem.

Interpreting Graphics

The map below shows the pH of precipitation measured at field stations in the northeastern United States in the year 2000. Use the map and legend to answer questions 26–27.

26. Which area(s) of the northeastern United States have the most-acidic precipitation?

27. Are the areas with the least acidic precipitation located close to or far from major cities?

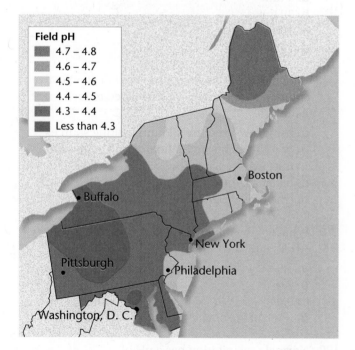

Field pH
- 4.7 – 4.8
- 4.6 – 4.7
- 4.5 – 4.6
- 4.4 – 4.5
- 4.3 – 4.4
- Less than 4.3

Boston
Buffalo
New York
Pittsburgh
Philadelphia
Washington, D. C.

Critical Thinking

28. **Making Decisions** Five states now have zero-emission vehicle programs in place that will help decrease some primary pollutants. What would be the advantages or disadvantages of a federal program that required automobile makers to produce a set number of ZEVs nationwide?

29. **Making Decisions** In some cities, noise-pollution laws, such as restrictions placed on the use of leaf blowers, have been put in place. Do you think the benefits of noise reduction outweigh the costs of enforcing the law?

30. **Inferring Relationships** As you read under the head "International Conflict and Cooperation," some of the acid precipitation that falls in southeastern Canada is produced by pollutants from the United States. How do the acid pollutants get from their sources to southeastern Canada?

31. **Health** Asbestos, lead paint, tobacco, and many other products have been linked to adverse effects on human health. Research one such case that has been brought into the courts. Describe the allegations and the outcome of the trial and write a paragraph that explains whether you agree or disagree with the decision.

32. **Make a Display** Create a display similar to the diagram that appears in Figure 2.2. This diagram may be of your home, your garage, a portion of your school, or a particular classroom in your school. Use the diagram to identify and label potential sources of indoor air pollutants. Photographs may be used to document these sources.

Analyzing Data

Use the graph below to answer questions 33 and 34.

33. Analyzing Data The graph below shows the estimated changes in air-pollution emissions in the United States between 1970 and 1997. Excluding NO_x, which type of emission experienced the greatest decrease over this period of time?

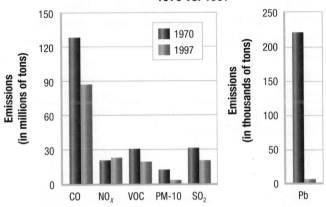

Air-Pollution Emissions in the U.S., 1970 vs. 1997

34. Interpreting Graphics Why is lead, Pb, shown separately from the other air pollutants?

Making Connections

35. Outlining Topics Outline the major sources of air pollution in the United States. Include information about pollution sources and pollution types.

36. Writing Persuasively Write a message to a legislator that expresses your concern about a particular aspect of air, noise, or light pollution that is important to you.

37. What are some sources of pollution that affect ground-level ozone? How do these pollutants lead to increased amounts of ground-level ozone?

38. Think about the effects of ground-level ozone on human health. What are some approaches that urban areas can take to combat increases in ground-level ozone and protect the health of their citizens?

Why It Matters

39. What role does temperature inversion play in the air quality of Los Angeles? What conditions cause temperature inversion to occur there? Research another urban area that experiences temperature inversion and describe why it occurs.

STUDYSKILL

Predicting Exam Questions Before you take a test, do you ever attempt to predict what the questions will be? For example, of the 10 multiple-choice questions that appear in this chapter review, how many would you have predicted to be asked in a review of this chapter? Before your next test, predict and answer possible exam questions.

The Acid Test

Objectives

Perform a chemical test that produces sulfur dioxide, a component of acid precipitation.

Hypothesize what the effects of acids that contain sulfur will be on plants.

Materials

beaker, 50 mL

clear plastic bags, large (2)

houseplants of the same type, potted (2)

sodium nitrite (2 g)

sulfuric acid, 1 M (2 mL)

twist tie or tape

Step 1 Place a plant and a beaker that contains sodium nitrite into a plastic bag. Do not seal the bag yet.

Acid precipitation is one of the effects of air pollution. When pollutants that contain nitrogen or sulfur react with water vapor in clouds, dilute acid forms. These acids fall to Earth as acid precipitation.

Often, acid precipitation does not occur in the same place where the pollutants are released. The acid precipitation usually falls some distance downwind—sometimes hundreds of kilometers away. Thus, the sites where pollutants that cause acid precipitation are released may not suffer the effects of acid precipitation.

Coal-burning power plants are one source of air pollution. These power plants release sulfur dioxide into the air. Sulfur dioxide reacts with the water vapor in air to produce acid that contains sulfur. This acid later falls to Earth as acid precipitation.

In this investigation, you will create a chemical reaction that produces sulfur dioxide. The same acids that result from coal-burning power plants will form as a result of the reaction. You will see the effects of acid precipitation on living things—in this case, plants.

Procedure

1. Place 2 g of sodium nitrite in a beaker. Place a plant and the beaker inside a plastic bag. Do not seal the bag yet. **CAUTION:** Steps 2–4 should be carried out *only* under a fume hood or outdoors.

2. Carefully add 2 mL of a 1 M solution of sulfuric acid to the beaker. Immediately seal the bag tightly, and secure the bag with a twist tie or tape. **CAUTION:** Because this reaction produces sulfur dioxide, a toxic gas, the bag should have no leaks. If a leak occurs, move away from the bag until the reaction is complete and the gas has dissipated.

3. Seal the same type of plant in an identical bag that does not contain sodium nitrite or sulfuric acid.

4. After 10 minutes, cut both bags open. Move to at least 5 m from the bags as the sulfur dioxide gas dissipates. Keep the plants and bags under the fume hood.

Day	Control Plant	Experimental Plant
1		
2		
3		

5. Predict the effects of the experiment on each plant over the next few days. Record your predictions.

6. Observe both plants over the next three days. Record your observations below.

Analysis

1. **Examining Data** How closely did your predictions about the effects of the experiment on each plant match your observations?

2. **Explaining Events** What does this experiment suggest about the effects of acid precipitation on plants?

Conclusions

3. **Drawing Conclusions** In what ways is this a realistic model of acid precipitation?

4. **Drawing Conclusions** In what ways is this experiment *not* a realistic simulation of acid precipitation?

Extension

5. **Analyzing Models** Would you expect to see similar effects occur as rapidly, more rapidly, or less rapidly in the environment? Explain your answer.

6. **Building Models** Acid precipitation is damaging to plants because it clogs the openings on the surfaces of plants and interferes with photosynthesis. What kind of a safe model would demonstrate the damaging effects of acid precipitation on plant photosynthesis? Would this model be a realistic simulation of acid precipitation?

Chapter 13

Why It Matters

Hurricanes need warm water and low atmospheric pressure to form and grow. These conditions are most often found in the low latitudes of the tropics. So hurricanes tend to form in the tropics near the equator.

An almanac is a type of calendar that includes weather forecasts for every day of the year. Why would this information be useful?

CASESTUDY

Learn how ice cores provide information about Earth's climate history in the case study Ice Cores: Reconstructing Past Climates on page 330.

 ONLINE ENVIRONMENTAL SCIENCE
HMDScience.com

Go online to access additional resources, including labs, worksheets, multimedia, and resources in Spanish.

Atmosphere and Climate Change

©NASA

Climate

Weather is the state of the atmosphere at a particular place at a particular moment. **Climate** is the long-term prevailing weather conditions at a particular place. In the U.S., local climate is the average of weather conditions over the past 30 years. To understand the difference between weather and climate, consider Seattle, Washington, and Phoenix, Arizona. These two cities may have the same weather on a particular day. For example, it may be raining, warm, or windy in both places. But their climates are quite different. Seattle's climate is cool and moist, whereas Phoenix's climate is hot and dry.

What Factors Determine Climate?

Climate is determined by a variety of factors. These factors include latitude, global air circulation patterns, oceanic circulation patterns, topography, solar activity, and volcanic activity. The most important of these factors is distance from the equator. For example, the two locations shown in **Figure 1.1** have different climates mostly because they are at different distances from the equator.

Objectives

- Explain the difference between weather and climate.
- Identify four factors that determine climate.
- Explain why different parts of Earth have different climates.
- Explain what causes the seasons.

Key Terms
climate
latitude
El Niño
La Niña

FIGURE 1.1

Climate Differences At left is Trunk Bay on the island of St. John in the U.S. Virgin Islands, which is located near the equator. At right is Paradise Bay on the Antarctic Peninsula.

(l) ©David Coleman/Alamy Images; (r) ©Krys Bailey/Alamy Images

Latitude

The distance from the equator measured in degrees north or south of the equator is called **latitude.** The equator is located at 0° latitude. The most northerly latitude is the North Pole, at 90° north, whereas the most southerly latitude is the South Pole, at 90° south.

Low Latitudes

Latitude influences climate because the amount of solar energy an area of Earth receives depends on its latitude. More solar energy falls on areas that are near the equator than on areas that are closer to the poles, as shown in **Figure 1.2**. The incoming solar energy is concentrated on a relatively small surface area at the equator.

In regions near the equator, night and day are both about 12 hours long throughout the year. In addition, temperatures are high year-round in areas close to sea level.

High Latitudes

The amount of energy arriving at the surface is lower in regions closer to the poles than it is near the equator. In the northern and southern latitudes, sunlight hits Earth at an oblique angle and spreads over a larger surface area than it does at the equator. Yearly average temperatures near the poles are therefore lower than they are at the equator. The hours of daylight also vary. At 45° north and south latitude, there is as much as 16 hours of daylight each day in summer and as little as 8 hours of sunlight each day in winter. Near the poles, the sun sets for only a few hours each day in summer and rises for only a few hours each day in winter.

FIGURE 1.2

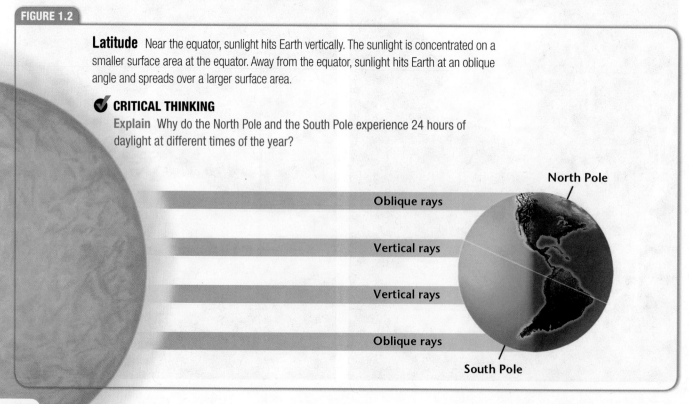

Latitude Near the equator, sunlight hits Earth vertically. The sunlight is concentrated on a smaller surface area at the equator. Away from the equator, sunlight hits Earth at an oblique angle and spreads over a larger surface area.

✔ **CRITICAL THINKING**

Explain Why do the North Pole and the South Pole experience 24 hours of daylight at different times of the year?

Oblique rays

Vertical rays

Vertical rays

Oblique rays

North Pole

South Pole

Global Air Circulation

Three important properties of air illustrate how air circulation affects climate. First, cold air sinks because it is denser than warm air. As cold air sinks, it compresses and warms. Second, warm air rises. It expands and cools at it rises. Third, warm air can hold more water vapor than cold air can. Therefore, when warm air cools, the water vapor it contains may condense into liquid water to form rain, snow, or fog.

Solar energy warms the ground, which warms the air above it. Cooler, denser air sinks and pushes the warm air up. The cold air increases the pressure on Earth's surface. Air moves from areas of high pressure to areas of low pressure. This movement of air is called *wind*. As Earth rotates, different latitudes receive different amounts of solar energy, which results in the pattern of global air circulation shown in **Figure 1.3**. This circulation pattern determines Earth's precipitation pattern. For example, the intense solar energy striking Earth's surface at the equator causes the surface as well as the air above the equator to become very warm. The warm air can hold large amounts of water that evaporate from the equatorial oceans and land. As the warm air rises, however, it cools, which reduces some of its ability to hold water. Thus, areas near the equator receive large amounts of rain.

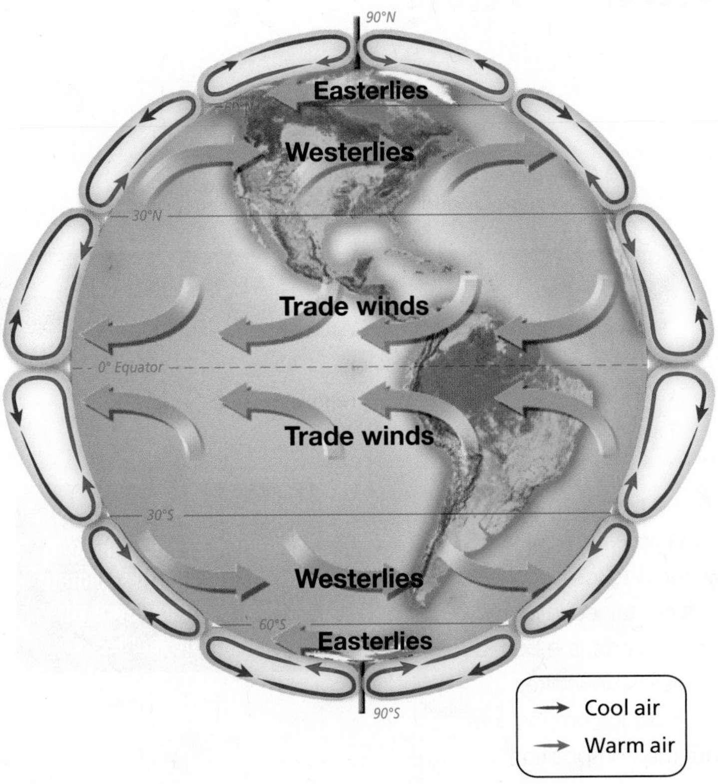

ECOFACT

Deserts

Air that is warmed at the equator rises and flows northward and southward to 30° north and south latitude, where it sinks. The sinking air is compressed and its temperature increases. As the temperature of the air increases, the air is able to hold a larger quantity of water vapor. Evaporation from the land surface is so great beneath these sinking warm air masses that little water returns to Earth in the form of precipitation. Thus, most of Earth's deserts lie at 30° north and south latitude.

Connect to METEOROLOGY

Tornadoes in the United States

Tornadoes occur almost exclusively in the United States and southern Canada. Cold, dry air from the north and warm, moist air from the south often collide on the flat region of the Great Plains. When this happens, a low pressure area is formed and air masses spiral around it, creating funnel clouds.

FIGURE 1.3

Global Air Circulation Three belts of prevailing winds occur in each hemisphere. The warming and cooling of air produces pressure belts every 30° of latitude.

90°N
Easterlies
Westerlies
30°N
Trade winds
0° Equator
Trade winds
30°S
Westerlies
60°S
Easterlies
90°S

→ Cool air
→ Warm air

Investigate Prevailing Winds

Procedure

1. Insert a push-pin through the center of a 10 in paper plate.

2. Push the pointed end of the pin into the eraser end of a pencil.

3. Spin the plate in a counterclockwise direction.

4. While the plate is spinning, try to draw a straight line from the center of the plate to the outer edge.

Analysis

Relate what you observed to the movement of winds and the rotation of Earth.

Areas of High and Low Pressures

Cool air normally sinks, creating areas of high pressure. Cool air over the equator cannot sink because hot air is rising below the cool air. As a result, warm, less-dense air at the equator forms an area of lower pressure. So, the cool air rises and is forced away from the equator toward the North and South Poles. At about 30° north latitude and 30° south latitude, some of this cool air sinks back down to Earth's surface. The air becomes warmer as it descends. The warm, dry air moves across the surface of Earth and causes water to evaporate from the land below, which creates dry conditions.

Air descending at 30° north latitude and 30° south latitude either moves toward the equator or toward the poles. Air moving toward the poles warms while it is near Earth's surface. At about 60° north latitude and 60° south latitude, this air collides with cold air traveling from the poles. The warm air is pushed up. When this rising air reaches the top of the troposphere, a small amount of the air returns back to the circulation pattern between 60° and 30° north latitude and 60° and 30° south latitude. However, most of this uplifted air is forced toward the poles. Cold, dry air descends at the poles, which are essentially very cold deserts.

CASESTUDY

Ice Cores: Reconstructing Past Climates

Imagine having at your fingertips a record of Earth's climate that extends back several thousand years. Today, ice cores are providing scientists an indirect glimpse of Earth's climate history. These ice cores have been drilled out of ice sheets thousands of meters thick in Canada, Greenland, and Antarctica.

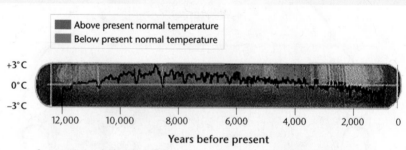

Source: National Glaciological Program.

How do scientists reconstruct the climate history of our planet from ice cores? As snow falls to Earth, the snow carries substances that are in the air at the time. If snow falls in a cold climate where it does not melt, the snow turns to ice because of the weight of the snow above it. The substances contained in snow, such as soot, dust, volcanic ash, and chemical compounds, are buried year after year, one layer on top of another. Air between snowflakes and grains becomes trapped in bubbles when the snow is compacted. These bubbles of air can provide information about the composition of the atmosphere over time.

With the help of ice cores, scientists are beginning to reconstruct Earth's climate history over hundreds of thousands of years.

Prevailing Winds

Winds that blow predominantly in one direction throughout the year are called *prevailing winds*. Because of the rotation of Earth, these winds do not blow directly northward or southward. Instead these winds are deflected to the right in the Northern Hemisphere. They are deflected to the left in the Southern Hemisphere.

Belts of prevailing winds blow most of the time in both hemispheres between 30° north and south latitudes and the equator. These belts of wind are called the *trade winds*. The trade winds blow from the northeast in the Northern Hemisphere and from the southeast in the Southern Hemisphere.

Prevailing winds known as the westerlies are produced between 30° and 60° north latitudes and 30° and 60° south latitudes. In the Northern Hemisphere, these westerlies are southwest winds. In the Southern Hemisphere, these westerlies are northwest winds, as shown in **Figure 1.4.** The polar easterlies blow from the poles to 60° north and south latitudes.

(tr) ©GSFC/NASA; (cr) ©Getty Images; (cl) ©SPL/Photo Researchers, Inc.

FIGURE 1.4

Prevailing Winds The red areas indicate fires around Sydney, Australia, at about 32° south. The smoke is blown by the prevailing westerly winds.

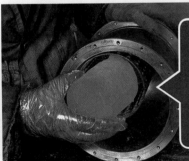

Whether scientists work on ice cores in the field or in the laboratory, all ice cores must be handled in such a way that the cores do not become contaminated by atmospheric pollutants.

Scientists can date ice cores based on differences that exist between snow layers that are deposited in the winter and in the summer. Knowing these differences allows scientists to count and place dates with the annual layers of ice.

Scientists can discover important events in Earth's climate history by studying ice cores. For example, volcanoes produce large quantities of dust, so a history of volcanic activity is preserved in ice cores. A record of concentrations of carbon dioxide, an important greenhouse gas, has also been preserved in air bubbles trapped in the ice. These ice cores provide evidence that greenhouse gas concentrations have changed in the past. Evidence of increases in global temperature of several Celsius degrees over several decades has been discovered in ice cores from thousands of years ago by analyzing isotopes in the ice.

Critical Thinking

1. **Evaluate Viewpoints** How might information about past carbon dioxide concentrations on Earth contribute to scientists' understanding of present carbon dioxide concentrations?

2. **Apply** What information, besides what is mentioned in this Case Study, might scientists learn about Earth's climatic history from ice cores?

FIGURE 1.5

El Niño Southern Oscillation The El Niño-Southern Oscillation (ENSO) is a periodic change in the location of warm and cold water masses in the Pacific Ocean. The phase of ENSO in which the eastern Pacific surface water is warm is called *El Niño*, and the phase in which it is cool is called *La Niña*.

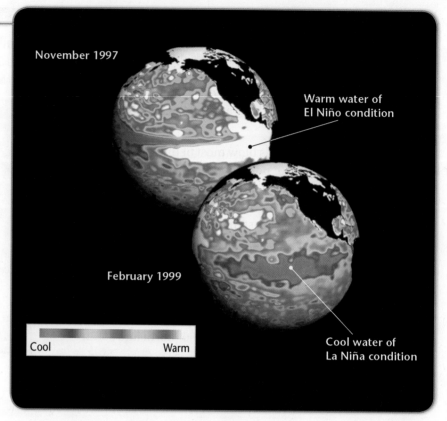

November 1997

Warm water of
El Niño condition

February 1999

Cool   Warm

Cool water of
La Niña condition

Oceanic Circulation Patterns

Ocean currents have a great effect on climate because water holds large amounts of energy as heat. The movement of surface ocean currents is caused mostly by winds and the rotation of Earth. These surface currents redistribute warm and cool masses of water around the planet. Some surface currents warm or cool coastal areas year-round. Surface currents affect the climate in many parts of the world. Here, we will only discuss surface currents that change their pattern of circulation over time.

El Niño—Southern Oscillation

El Niño (el NEEN yoh) refers to conditions where the waters near the equator in the Pacific Ocean are warmer than normal. During an El Niño, the strong winds that usually push warm water to the western Pacific Ocean and allow cool water to push up from below in the eastern Pacific Ocean weaken. This moves warm water into the equatorial Pacific. During El Niño, there is increased rainfall in the southern half of the United States and in equatorial South America. In 1982, up to 100 inches of rain fell during a six month period in Ecuador and northern Peru. What had been a coastal desert was transformed temporarily into a grassland. El Niño causes drought in Indonesia and Australia.

During **La Niña** (lah NEEN yah), the water in the eastern Pacific Ocean is cooler than usual. El Niño and La Niña are opposite phases of the *El Niño-Southern Oscillation* (ENSO) cycle. El Niño is the warm phase of the cycle, and La Niña is the cold phase, as illustrated in **Figure 1.5**.

ECOFACT

Temperature Inversions
The changes in ocean surface temperatures associated with El Niño and La Niña impact climate on a global scale. Shifts in temperature gradients can also be important on a local scale. For example, a temperature inversion exists when air temperature increases with height above Earth's surface. Inversions often form during the summer when large domes of high pressure tend to dominate weather conditions. Such inversions can cause long-lasting air pollution because they keep the air near the surface from rising and mixing with cleaner air above.

FIGURE 1.6

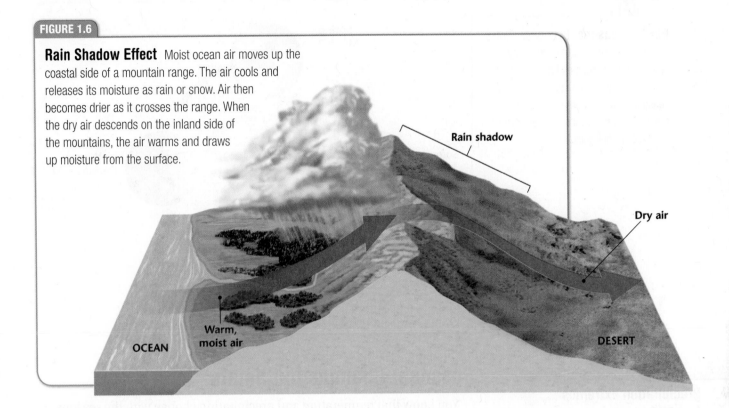

Rain Shadow Effect Moist ocean air moves up the coastal side of a mountain range. The air cools and releases its moisture as rain or snow. Air then becomes drier as it crosses the range. When the dry air descends on the inland side of the mountains, the air warms and draws up moisture from the surface.

Rain shadow

Dry air

Warm, moist air

OCEAN

DESERT

Topography

Mount Kilimanjaro, a 5,896 m extinct volcano in Tanzania, is about 3° south of the equator, but snow covers its peak year-round. Kilimanjaro illustrates the important effect of height above sea level (elevation) on climate. Temperatures fall by about 6°C (about 11°F) for every 1,000 m increase in elevation.

Mountains and mountain ranges also influence the distribution of precipitation. For example, consider the Sierra Nevada mountains of California. Warm air from the Pacific Ocean blows east, hits the mountains, and rises. As the air rises, it cools, which causes it to rain on the western side of the mountains. By the time the air reaches the eastern side of the mountains, it is dry. This effect is known as a rain shadow, as shown in **Figure 1.6**.

Other Influences on Earth's Climate

Both the sun and volcanic eruptions influence Earth's climate. At a *solar maximum*, shown in **Figure 1.7**, the sun emits an increased amount of ultraviolet (UV) radiation. UV radiation produces more ozone, warming the stratosphere. The increased radiation can also warm the lower atmosphere and surface of Earth a little.

In large-scale volcanic eruptions, sulfur dioxide gas can reach the upper atmosphere. The sulfur dioxide gas reacts with smaller amounts of water vapor and dust in the stratosphere. This reaction forms a bright layer of haze that reflects enough sunlight to cause the global temperature to decrease.

FIGURE 1.7

Sun Cycle The sun has an 11-year cycle in which it goes from a maximum of activity to a minimum and back to maximum.

✔ **CHECK FOR UNDERSTANDING**

Relate How do large-scale volcanic eruptions influence Earth's climate?

FIGURE 1.8

Earth's Seasons Because of Earth's tilt, the angle at which the sun's rays strike Earth changes as Earth orbits the sun. This change in angle accounts for seasonal climate differences around the world. The seasons for the Northern Hemisphere are shown here.

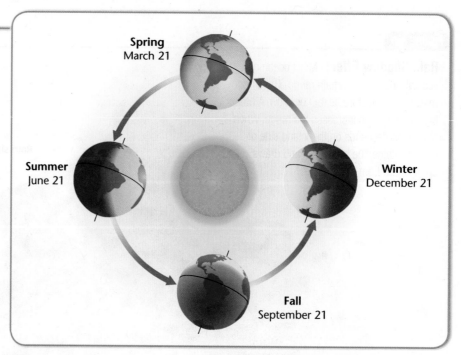

Spring
March 21

Summer
June 21

Winter
December 21

Fall
September 21

Precipitation Extremes on Earth

Cherrapunji, India, which is located in eastern India near the border of Bangladesh, is the wettest spot on Earth. Cherrapunji has an annual average precipitation of 1,065 cm. Arica, Chile, is located in extreme northern Chile near the Peruvian border. Arica is the driest spot on Earth and has an annual average precipitation of 0.8 mm. What is the difference in millimeters between the annual average precipitation in Cherrapunji and the annual average precipitation in Arica?

Seasonal Changes in Climate

You know that temperature and precipitation change with the seasons. But do you know what causes the seasons? As shown in **Figure 1.8**, the seasons result from the tilt of Earth's axis (about 23.5° relative to the plane of its orbit). Because of this tilt, the angle at which the sun's rays strike Earth changes as Earth moves around the sun.

During summer in the Northern Hemisphere, the Northern Hemisphere tilts toward the sun and receives direct sunlight. The number of hours of daylight is greatest in the summer. Therefore, the amount of time available for the sun to warm Earth becomes greater. During summer in the Northern Hemisphere, the Southern Hemisphere tilts away from the sun and receives less direct sunlight. During summer in the Southern Hemisphere, the situation is reversed. The Southern Hemisphere is tilted toward the sun, whereas the Northern Hemisphere is tilted away.

Section 1 Formative Assessment

▶ Reviewing Main Ideas

1. **Explain** the difference between weather and climate.

2. **Identify** four factors that determine climate.

3. **Explain** why different parts of Earth have different climates.

4. **Explain** what causes the seasons.

✔ Critical Thinking

5. **Relating Concepts** At the equator, there are no summers or winters, only wet and dry seasons. Write a paragraph that explains why this is the case.

6. **Analyzing Processes** If Earth were not tilted in its orbit, how would the climates and seasons be affected at the equator and between 30° north and south latitudes?

The Ozone Shield

SECTION 2

Objectives

▸ Explain how the ozone layer shields Earth from much of the sun's harmful radiation.

▸ Explain how chlorofluorocarbons damage the ozone layer.

▸ Explain the process by which the ozone hole forms.

▸ Describe the damaging effects of ultraviolet radiation.

▸ Explain why the threat to the ozone layer is still continuing today.

The **ozone layer** is an area in the stratosphere where ozone is highly concentrated. *Ozone* is a molecule made of three oxygen atoms. The ozone layer absorbs most of the ultraviolet (UV) light from the sun. Ultraviolet light is harmful to organisms because it can damage the genetic material in living cells. By shielding Earth's surface from most of the sun's ultraviolet light, the ozone in the stratosphere acts like a sunscreen for Earth's inhabitants.

Chemicals That Cause Ozone Depletion

During the 1970s, scientists recognized that a class of human-made chemicals called **chlorofluorocarbons (CFCs)** might be damaging the ozone layer. For many years CFCs were thought to be miracle chemicals. They are nonpoisonous and nonflammable, they do not corrode metals, and they are inexpensive to produce. CFCs quickly became popular as coolants in refrigerators and air conditioners. They were also used as a gassy "fizz" for making plastic foams and as a propellant in spray cans of everyday products such as deodorants, insecticides, and paint.

At Earth's surface, CFC molecules are chemically stable. But high in the stratosphere, where the powerful energy of the sun's UV radiation is absorbed, CFC molecules break apart. Once they break apart, chlorine atoms from the CFC molecules cause the breakdown of ozone. CFCs are one of several human-made compounds that deplete stratospheric ozone, called ozone-depleting substances (ODSs).

Over a period of 10 to 20 years, CFC molecules released at Earth's surface make their way into the stratosphere. **Figure 2.1** shows how the CFCs break down ozone in the stratosphere. Each CFC molecule contains from one to four chlorine atoms, and scientists have estimated that a single chlorine atom from CFC can break down 100,000 ozone molecules.

Key Terms

ozone layer
chlorofluorocarbons (CFCs)
ozone hole
polar stratospheric clouds

FIGURE 2.1

Breakdown of CFCs by UV light The CFC molecule in this illustration contains a single chlorine atom. This chlorine atom continues to enter the cycle and repeatedly destroys ozone molecules.

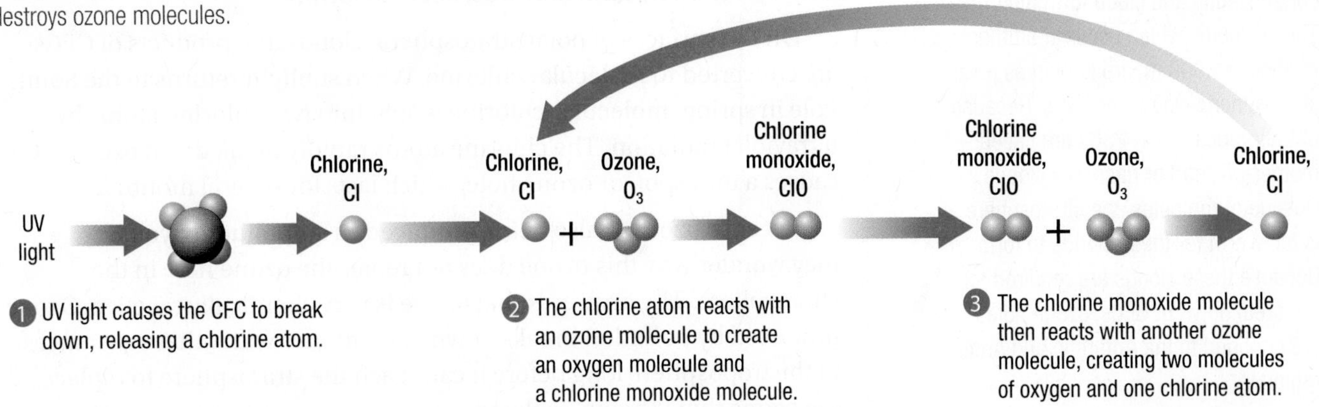

UV light

Chlorine, Cl

Chlorine, Cl   Ozone, O_3

Chlorine monoxide, ClO

Chlorine monoxide, ClO   Ozone, O_3

Chlorine, Cl

1. UV light causes the CFC to break down, releasing a chlorine atom.

2. The chlorine atom reacts with an ozone molecule to create an oxygen molecule and a chlorine monoxide molecule.

3. The chlorine monoxide molecule then reacts with another ozone molecule, creating two molecules of oxygen and one chlorine atom.

FIGURE 2.2

The Ozone Hole These satellite images show changes in the ozone hole between 1980 and 2012. The ozone hole, which appears purple here, grew until 2006 and has been gradually getting smaller since then.

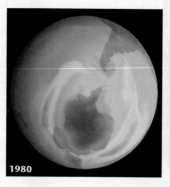
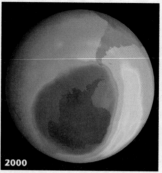
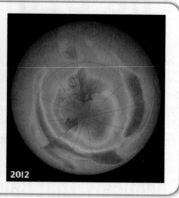

1980　　2000　　2012

The Ozone Hole

In 1985, a group of scientists working in Antarctica released data showing that the ozone layer above the South Pole had thinned by 50 to 98 percent. This was the first news of the **ozone hole,** a thinning of stratospheric ozone that occurs over the poles during the spring.

After the results were published, NASA scientists reviewed data that had been sent to Earth by the *Nimbus 7* weather satellite since the satellite's launch in 1978. They were able to see the first signs of ozone thinning in the data from 1979. Although the concentration of ozone fluctuates during the year, the data showed a growing ozone hole, as shown in **Figure 2.2.** Ozone levels over the Arctic have decreased as well.

Following the announcement in 1985, scientists and governments worldwide began working together with chemical companies to develop ways to prevent the ozone hole from growing. As a result, ozone in the stratosphere is no longer decreasing.

How Does the Ozone Hole Form?

During the dark polar winter, strong circulating winds over Antarctica, called the *polar vortex,* isolate cold air from surrounding warmer air. The air within the vortex grows extremely cold. When temperatures fall below about –80°C, high-altitude clouds made of water and nitric acid, called **polar stratospheric clouds,** begin to form.

On the surfaces of polar stratospheric clouds, the products of CFCs are converted to molecular chlorine. When sunlight returns to the South Pole in spring, molecular chlorine is split into two chlorine atoms by ultraviolet radiation. The chlorine atoms rapidly break down ozone. This causes a thin spot, or ozone hole, which lasts for several months.

Because ozone is also being produced as air pollution, you may wonder why this ozone does not repair the ozone hole in the stratosphere. The answer is that ozone is very chemically reactive. Ozone produced by pollution breaks down or combines with other substances in the troposphere long before it can reach the stratosphere to replace the ozone that is being depleted.

☑ **CHECK FOR UNDERSTANDING**

Identify What evidence showed that a hole had formed in the ozone layer?

Connect to METEOROLOGY

Polar Stratospheric Clouds
Because the stratosphere is extremely dry, clouds normally do not form in this layer of the atmosphere. However, during polar winters, temperatures become low enough to cause condensation and cloud formation. These clouds, which occur at altitudes of about 21,000 m, are known as polar stratospheric clouds, or PSCs. Because of their iridescence, PSCs are called mother-of-pearl or nacreous clouds. Outside of the poles, the stratosphere is too warm for these clouds to form. Because these clouds are required for the breakdown of CFCs, ozone holes are confined to the Antarctic and Arctic regions.

Effects of Ozone Thinning on Humans

As the amount of ozone in the stratosphere decreases, more ultraviolet light is able to pass through the atmosphere and reach Earth's surface, as shown in **Figure 2.3**. UV light is dangerous to living things because it damages DNA. DNA is the genetic material that contains the information that determines inherited characteristics. Exposure to UV light makes the body more susceptible to skin cancer, and may cause certain other damaging effects to the human body.

Effects of Ozone Thinning on Animals and Plants

High levels of UV light can kill *phytoplankton,* microscopic organisms that live near the surface of the ocean and are a basic food source in aquatic ecosystems. The loss of phytoplankton could disrupt ocean food chains and reduce fish harvests. In addition, a reduction in the number of phytoplankton would cause an increase in the amount of carbon dioxide (CO_2) in the atmosphere.

Some scientists think that increased UV light could be one of many factors contributing to global declines in amphibians, such as toads and salamanders. Increases in UV radiation could reduce the survival of amphibian eggs or may work with other stresses in the environment to harm various life stages.

UV light can damage plants by interfering with photosynthesis. This damage can result in lower crop yields. The damaging effects of UV light are summarized in **Figure 2.4**.

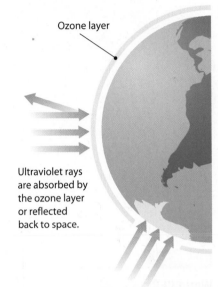

FIGURE 2.3

Ozone Depletion Depletion of the ozone layer allows more ultraviolet radiation to reach the surface of Earth.

Ozone layer

Ultraviolet rays are absorbed by the ozone layer or reflected back to space.

Ultraviolet rays penetrate to the Earth's surface through the ozone hole.

FIGURE 2.4	
DAMAGING EFFECTS OF UV LIGHT	
Humans	• increased incidence of skin cancer • premature aging of the skin • increased incidence of cataracts • weakened immune response
Amphibians	• reduced egg survival • genetic mutations among survivors • increased susceptibility to other stresses
Marine life	• death of phytoplankton in surface water • disruption of food chain • reduction in the number of photosynthesizers
Land plants	• interference with photosynthesis • reduced crop yields

Protecting the Ozone Layer

In 1987, a group of nations met in Canada and agreed to take action against ozone depletion. Under an agreement called the Montreal Protocol, these nations agreed to sharply limit their production of CFCs. Today the Montreal Protocol has been ratified by most of the world's nations with a long-term commitment to phase out all ozone-depleting substances.

According to the World Meteorological Organization's 2010 report on ozone depletion, many ODSs have been phased out. For example, aerosol cans no longer use CFCs as propellants, and air conditioners are CFC-free. Because many countries were involved and decided to control CFCs, many people consider ozone protection an international environmental success story. **Figure 2.5** illustrates the decline in world CFC production since the 1987 Montreal Protocol. Even with this success, scientists are still working to protect the ozone layer because CFC molecules remain active in the stratosphere for 60 to 120 years.

FIGURE 2.5

World CFC Production Chlorofluorocarbon production has declined greatly since developed countries agreed to ban CFCs in 1987.

CRITICAL THINKING

Relate How did the Montreal Protocol help to protect the ozone layer?

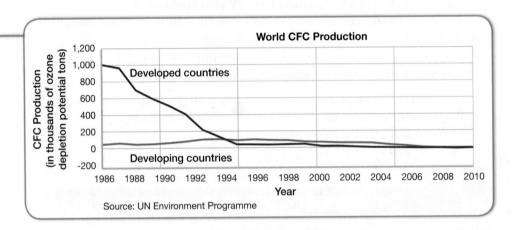

Source: UN Environment Programme

 Section 2 **Formative Assessment**

▶ Reviewing Main Ideas

1. **Describe** the process by which chlorofluorocarbons break down ozone molecules in the stratosphere.

2. **Describe** the process by which the ozone hole forms over Antarctica in spring.

3. **List** five harmful effects that UV radiation could have on plants or animals as a result of ozone thinning.

4. **Explain** why it will take years for the ozone layer to recover, even though the use of CFCs has declined significantly. Write a paragraph that explains your answer.

✔ Critical Thinking

5. **Making Decisions** If the ozone layer gets significantly thinner during your lifetime, what changes might you need to make in your lifestyle?

6. **Analyzing Relationships** CFCs were thought to be miracle chemicals when they were first introduced. What kinds of tests could be performed on any future miracle chemical to make sure serious environmental problems do not result from its use?

Climate Change

Have you ever gotten into a car that has been sitting in the sun with all its windows closed? Even if the day is cool, the air in the car is much warmer than the air outside. The reason warmth builds up inside a car is that the sun's light energy streams into the car through the clear glass windows. The carpets and upholstery in the car absorb the light and convert it into energy in the form of heat. This energy does not pass through glass as easily as light energy does. Sunlight continues to stream into the car through the glass, but the energy in the form of heat cannot get out. This energy continues to build up and is trapped inside the car. A greenhouse works the same way. By building a house of glass, gardeners trap the sun's light energy and grow delicate plants in the warm air inside the greenhouse even when there is snow on the ground outside.

SECTION 3

Objectives

▶ Explain why Earth's atmosphere is like the glass in a greenhouse.

▶ Explain why the carbon dioxide content of the atmosphere is increasing.

▶ Identify one possible explanation for the increase in average global temperature.

▶ Describe what a warmer Earth might be like.

The Greenhouse Effect

Earth is somewhat comparable to a greenhouse. Earth's atmosphere acts like the glass in a greenhouse. As shown in **Figure 3.1**, solar radiation enters the atmosphere as high-energy wavelengths of light that warm Earth's surface. This energy is absorbed and reradiated as infrared radiation from Earth's surface. Some of the energy escapes into space. The rest is absorbed by gases in the troposphere and warms the air. This process of warming Earth's surface and lower atmosphere is called the *greenhouse effect*.

Not every gas in our atmosphere absorbs and radiates the sun's energy in this way. Gases that do absorb and radiate infrared radiation from the sun are called **greenhouse gases.** The major greenhouse gases are water vapor, carbon dioxide, methane, and nitrous oxide. Of these, water vapor and carbon dioxide account for most of the absorption of energy that occurs in the atmosphere.

Key Terms

greenhouse gases

global warming

Kyoto Protocol

FIGURE 3.1

How the Greenhouse Effect Works

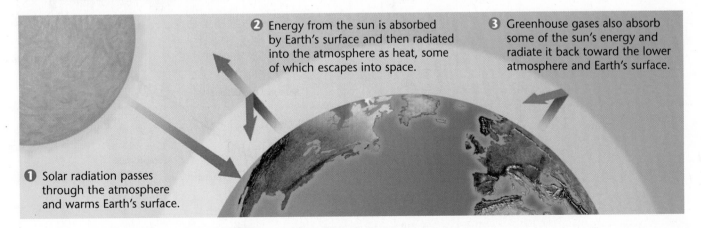

❷ Energy from the sun is absorbed by Earth's surface and then radiated into the atmosphere as heat, some of which escapes into space.

❸ Greenhouse gases also absorb some of the sun's energy and radiate it back toward the lower atmosphere and Earth's surface.

❶ Solar radiation passes through the atmosphere and warms Earth's surface.

Virtual INVESTIGATION
HMDScience.com

Carbon Dioxide and Global Warming

✓ **CHECK FOR UNDERSTANDING**

Identify What are two advantages of setting up instruments for measuring carbon dioxide on top of Mauna Loa?

FIELDSTUDY

Go to Appendix B to find the field study **Reducing Your Carbon Footprint.**

Measuring Carbon Dioxide in the Atmosphere

In 1958, a geochemist named Charles David Keeling installed an instrument at the top of a tall tower on the Mauna Loa observatory in Hawaii. Keeling wanted to measure the amount of CO_2 in the air, far from forests and cities where CO_2 levels vary every day. The winds that blow steadily over Mauna Loa have come thousands of miles across the Pacific Ocean, mixing as they traveled. Keeling reasoned that at Mauna Loa, the average CO_2 levels in the air could be measured for the entire Earth.

Much of the CO_2 that is released into the air dissolves in the ocean or is used by plants for photosynthesis. As a result, the levels of CO_2 in the air vary with the seasons. During the summer, growing plants use more CO_2 for photosynthesis than they release in respiration. This causes CO_2 levels in the air to decrease in the summer. In the winter, dying grasses and fallen leaves decay and release the carbon that was stored in them during the summer. As a result, CO_2 levels naturally rise.

Rising Carbon Dioxide Levels

After only a few years of measuring CO_2 levels, it became obvious that they were changing in ways other than just the seasonal fluctuations. These data in **Figure 3.2** show that CO_2 levels in the atmosphere have increased by over 20 percent in less than 50 years. This increase is due largely to the CO_2 released into the air when fossil fuels are burned. This data provide a record of changes in CO_2 levels since 1958. Levels of CO_2 in the atmosphere thousands of years ago can be determined by analyzing ice cores drilled from ice sheets. These measurements show that CO_2 levels in the atmosphere today are higher than they have been for the last 420,000 years, and probably for the last 20 million years.

FIGURE 3.2

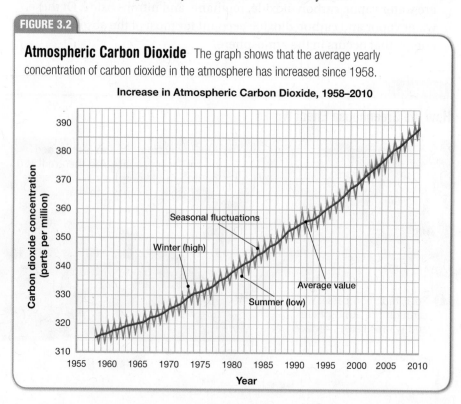

Atmospheric Carbon Dioxide The graph shows that the average yearly concentration of carbon dioxide in the atmosphere has increased since 1958.

Greenhouse Gases and Earth's Temperature

Most atmospheric scientists think that because greenhouse gases absorb and rerelease infrared radiation to Earth's surface, increased greenhouse gases in the atmosphere will result in an increase in global temperature. A comparison of CO_2 in the atmosphere and average global temperatures for the past 400,000 years supports this view.

Today, we are releasing more CO_2 than any other greenhouse gas into the atmosphere. Millions of tons of CO_2 are released into the atmosphere each year from power plants that burn coal or oil and from cars that burn gasoline. Millions of trees are burned in tropical rain forests to clear the land for farming. Thus, the amount of CO_2 and other greenhouse gases in the atmosphere is increasing. **Figure 3.3** shows the sources of some major greenhouse gases.

Global Climate Change

Figure 3.4 shows that the average temperature at Earth's surface increased during the twentieth century. This gradual increase is known as **global warming.** Because the rise in temperature correlates to the increase in greenhouse gases in the atmosphere, most scientists conclude that the increase in greenhouse gases, and other factors, have caused the increase in temperature. Thousands of experiments and computer models support this hypothesis. The increase in temperature is predicted to continue. This does not mean that temperatures are rising at a constant rate, or that they are rising in all parts of the world. As with changes in CO_2 levels, short-term variations in temperature are superimposed on larger trends. For example, the patterns of precipitation, frequency of fires, and extreme weather events are also predicted to change. So, most scientists use the term global climate change rather than global warming.

FIGURE 3.3

MAJOR GREENHOUSE GASES AND THEIR SOURCES

Carbon dioxide, CO_2: burning fossil fuels and deforestation

Methane, CH_4: animal waste, biomass burning, fossil fuels, landfills, livestock, rice paddies, sewage, and wetlands

Nitrous oxide, N_2O: biomass burning, deforestation, burning of fossil fuels, and microbial activity on fertilizers in the soil

Water vapor, H_2O: evaporation, plant transpiration

FIGURE 3.4

Global Surface Temperature This graph shows that the average surface temperature of Earth warmed during the 20th century. For example, the average global surface temperature in the year 2005 was 0.61°C above the 20th-century average temperature.

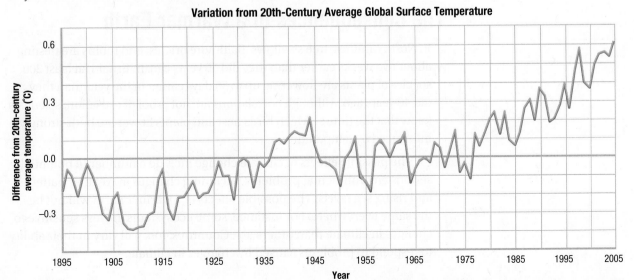

Variation from 20th-Century Average Global Surface Temperature

Source: National Climatic Data Center.

FIGURE 3.5

Modeling Climate Change These maps were developed from computer models. The map on the left shows the effect of greenhouse gases on Earth before sulfur pollution was added. The map on the right shows how the addition of the sulfur pollution variable causes a cooling effect.

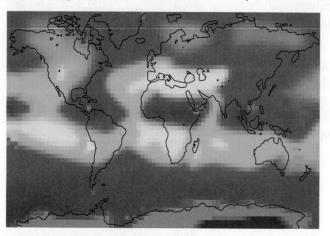

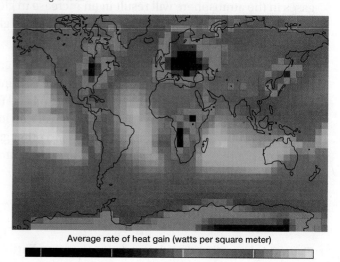

Average rate of heat gain (watts per square meter)

−1   0   1   2   3

Modeling Climate Change

Predictions about future changes in climate are based on computer models. Scientists use a growing body of research to find mathematical relationships among "drivers," such as solar input, wind patterns, and cloud cover and "response variables," such as troposphere temperature, sea surface temperature, ice cover, and sea level. These relationships are expressed as equations within complex models. The resulting models can be used to predict how factors such as temperature will be affected, as shown in **Figure 3.5**. Scientists validate the models by starting with historical conditions and then comparing model projections to known changes in climate. The models are constantly being updated with new information, but about a dozen different models show similar predictions. For example, all models predict widely increasing temperatures that are not simply driven by natural climate or solar variability. Humans are playing some role, though the exact human contribution is still uncertain.

The Consequences of a Warmer Earth

In North America, tree swallows, Baltimore orioles, and robins are nesting about two weeks earlier than they did 50 years ago. In Britain, at least 200 species of plants are flowering up to 55 days earlier in the year than they did 40 years ago. Although correlations are not proof of causation, scientists know that the time at which birds nest and plants flower are both strongly influenced by temperature.

The possible effects of climate change include a number of potentially serious environmental problems, including changes in weather patterns and rising sea levels. The possible effects of a warmer Earth will not be the same everywhere. For instance, some ecosystems are less sensitive to changes in climate than others are. Countries, too, will vary in their ability to respond to problems caused by changes in climate.

FIGURE 3.6

Melting Polar Ice This is a satellite image of an 11,000 km² iceberg—the size of Connecticut!—that split off from the Ross Ice Shelf in Antarctica in March of 2000.

Rising Sea Levels

Sea level has been measured in many locations over the past 100 years. Although there is some uncertainty about the total amount, sea levels are rising and will continue to rise. Sea level rises because as water warms, it expands. Also, ice that is currently over land is melting and the water is flowing into the ocean. Scientists are particularly concerned about melting of glaciers over land in Greenland and Antarctica. The rise in sea levels could flood coastal wetlands and other low-lying areas. Enormous numbers of people who live near coastlines could lose their homes and sources of income. Beaches could be extensively eroded. The salinity of bays and estuaries might increase, adversely affecting marine fisheries. Also, coastal freshwater aquifers could become too salty to be used as sources of fresh water.

Global Weather Patterns

If Earth warms up significantly, the surface of the oceans will absorb more energy in the form of heat, which may make hurricanes and typhoons more intense. Some scientists are concerned that climate change will also cause a change in ocean current patterns, such as a slowing of the Gulf Stream. Such a change could significantly affect the world's weather. For instance, some regions might have more rainfall than normal, whereas other regions might have less. Severe flooding could occur in some regions while droughts and fires devastate other regions.

Human Health Problems

Warmer average global temperatures pose potential threats to human health. Greater numbers of heat-related deaths could occur. Since trees and flowering plants, such as grasses, would flower earlier and for longer than they do now, people who are allergic to pollen would suffer from allergies for more of the year. Warmer temperatures could also enable mosquitoes—vectors of diseases such as malaria and Dengue Fever—to establish themselves in areas that are too cold for them currently.

Connect to BIOLOGY

Ocean Warming

Commercial fishing in the northern Atlantic Ocean depends heavily on a fish called a cod. In recent years, the number of cod in the North Atlantic has greatly decreased because of overfishing. In 2001 British scientists began a study to find out if there is also a link between the decline and the changing global climate. They sailed the ocean waters between Greenland and Iceland collecting samples of zooplankton. The scientists found that zooplankton levels have drastically decreased since 1963, the date of the last survey. The scientists believe that slowly warming ocean-water temperatures have in some way affected zooplankton in the North Atlantic Ocean, which has in turn impacted animals such as cod that rely on the zooplankton for food.

FIGURE 3.7

Effects of Drought These corn plants died from a lack of water.

✔ **CRITICAL THINKING**

Infer How could the impact of drought on crops affect the economy?

Agriculture

Agriculture would be severely impacted by climate change if extreme weather events, such as droughts, became more frequent. The effects of drought are shown in **Figure 3.7.** Higher temperatures could result in decreased crop yields. The demand for irrigation could increase, which would further deplete aquifers that have already been overused.

Effects on Plants and Animals

Climate change could alter both the range of plant species and the composition of plant communities. Trees could colonize cooler areas. Forests could shrink in the warmer part of their range and lose diversity. Increased frequency of fires may shift whole ecosystems.

Climate change may cause a shift in the geographical range of some animals. For example, birds in the Northern Hemisphere may not have to migrate as far south for winter. Warming in the surface waters of the ocean might cause a reduction of zooplankton, which many marine animals, such as the crabeater seal, shown in **Figure 3.8,** depend on for food. Warming in tropical waters may kill the algae that nourish corals, thus destroying coral reefs. As more CO_2 dissolves into oceans, the water could become more acidic, which could disrupt the ocean food webs.

Recent Findings

The Intergovernmental Panel on Climate Change (IPCC) is a network of approximately 2,500 of the world's leading climatologists from at least 70 countries. In 2007, the IPCC issued its Fourth Assessment Report (AR4). AR4 describes what is currently known about the global climate system and provides future estimates. Some of the findings of the IPCC state that since the third report in 2001, the average global surface temperature increased by 0.74°C, the temperature increase is both global and higher at northern latitudes, and the average global sea level continues to rise. The IPCC also reported that concentrations of atmospheric greenhouse gases have continued to increase as a result of human activities.

FIGURE 3.8

Climate Change Affects Organisms Despite its name, the crabeater seal actually feeds on zooplankton. This seal is a resident of Antarctica.

Reducing the Risk

The need to slow global climate change has been recognized by the global community. Some nations and organizations have engaged in reforestation projects to reduce CO_2, such as the project shown in **Figure 3.9**. However, the attempt to slow global climate change is made difficult by the economic, political, and social factors faced by different countries. Conflict has already arisen between developed and developing countries over future CO_2 emissions, the projections of which are shown in **Figure 3.10**.

The **Kyoto Protocol**, first negotiated in the 1990s, was an attempt to create a global treaty to reduce greenhouse gas emissions. Many countries have ratified the treaty, but not those responsible for the greatest greenhouse gas emissions, including the United States. Efforts to create a binding global agreement to reduce greenhouse gas emissions has remained a challenge. Many scientists, governments, organizations, businesses, and individuals are trying to find ways to reduce greenhouse gas emissions and address the effects of global climate change.

©Bruce Brander/Photo Researchers, Inc.

FIGURE 3.9

Reforestation Because plants take in carbon dioxide during photosynthesis, reforestation projects such as this project in Haiti help to offset a portion of global carbon dioxide emissions.

FIGURE 3.10

CO$_2$ Emissions Members of the Organization for Economic Cooperation and Development (OECD), most of which are developed countries, produced about 41 percent of global CO_2 emissions in 2010. By 2030, developing countries are projected to produce two-thirds of total CO_2 emissions. While U.S. emissions of CO_2 have generally been declining since 2007, global CO_2 emissions are projected to increase from about 31.3 billion metric tons in 2010 to about 40.6 billion metric tons by 2030.

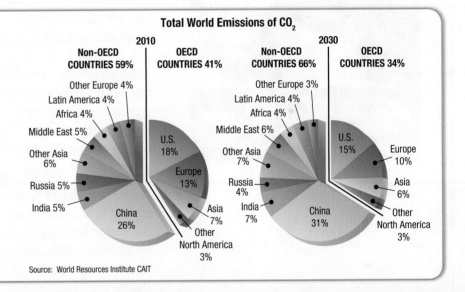

Total World Emissions of CO$_2$

Source: World Resources Institute CAIT

Section 3 Formative Assessment

▶ Reviewing Main Ideas

1. **Explain** why Earth's atmosphere is like the glass in a greenhouse.

2. **Explain** why carbon dioxide in the atmosphere is increasing.

3. **Describe** one explanation for why Earth's climate is becoming warmer.

4. **Analyze** the factors that have limited the effectiveness of the Kyoto Protocol.

✔ Critical Thinking

5. **Making Predictions** Read the text under the heading "Modeling Climate Change." What difficulties do scientists face when they attempt to construct models that accurately predict the rate of global warming?

6. **Analyzing Cause and Effect** How does pollution affect the greenhouse effect and global warming? How do these phenomena in turn affect the melting of glaciers and ice caps?

Climate Scientist

Susan Solomon will not soon forget crawling across the roof of an Antarctic field station in windchill temperatures of –62°C (–80°F), moving heavy equipment, and adjusting mirrors while the winds howled and whipped about her. Sounds like an adventure, right? It sure was! But it is just part of what Solomon has done to establish herself as one of the world's leading authorities on ozone destruction.

Q: What is the significance of discoveries regarding the ozone hole?

A: Before British scientists discovered the ozone hole in Antarctica, no one was sure about ozone changes in the atmosphere. The popular belief was that in 100 years there might be 5 percent less ozone. So there were questions about whether it was a serious environmental problem. But when the British researchers released data that showed 50 percent less ozone over Antarctica in 1985 than was present 20 years earlier, the research raised our awareness that the problem was far more serious than previously thought.

Q: How have you contributed to the study of ozone?

A: Well, when the British data was first released, no one had much of an explanation about what was causing the destruction of the ozone layer. I thought about the problem a lot. I got to thinking about types of clouds called *polar stratospheric clouds*. These are beautifully colored clouds that are known for their iridescence. While I was looking at these clouds, which are common in the Antarctic but rare elsewhere, it occurred to me that they may have something to do with ozone depletion. Perhaps they provide a surface for chemical reactions that activate reactive chlorine from CFCs (human-made chlorofluorocarbons). If so, once activated, the chlorine could contribute to reactions that destroy ozone.

Q: Did you get the chance to test your hypothesis?

A: Yes, the next year the National Science Foundation chose me to lead a group of 16 scientists for a nine-week expedition in Antarctica. We were the first team of scientists from the United States sent to the Antarctic to study the ozone hole. Within one month we could see that unnaturally high levels of chlorine dioxide did occur in the stratosphere during ozone depletion. This discovery was very exciting because it seemed that we were on the right track. We kept collecting data that year and collected more data during a second trip the next year. Pretty soon, the evidence seemed to support my hypothesis that CFCs and ozone depletion are linked.

Q: How has your research helped to make a difference in our world?

A: Since our findings and others were announced, the world's countries decided to stop making CFCs. As a result, the ozone hole will eventually go away, but it will take a very long time. So although we aren't adding CFCs to the atmosphere anymore, the CFCs from years past will still be hanging around in our atmosphere for the next 50 to 100 years. But I think our work has led in a small way to the realization that our actions do have consequences, and this realization should bring positive change.

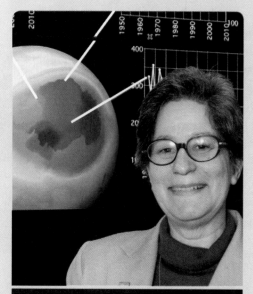

The ozone hole can be seen in this satellite image. The hole is the pale blue and black region immediately above Solomon's shoulder.

ECOZine at HMDScience.com

Go online for the latest environmental science news and updates on all EcoZine articles.

Dr. Solomon has received international recognition for her work on the ozone hole over the Antarctic. She is a member of the U.S. National Academy of Sciences, the European Academy of Sciences, the Académie des Sciences de France, and the Royal Society in the United Kingdom. In 2000, Dr. Solomon was awarded the National Medal of Science and the American Meteorological Society's Carl-Gustav Rossby Medal. She was co-chair of the science panel of the United Nations Intergovernmental Panel on Climate Change, which won the Nobel Peace Prize in 2007.

Q: What kinds of research projects are you working on today?

A: One of the main things I do is to study how a broad range of chemicals contributes to climate change—not just carbon dioxide, although carbon dioxide too, of course. To me it's one of the most interesting chemicals, but it's not the only one that is actually contributing to the way our climate is changing. So I'm doing work on everything from aerosol particles in the stratosphere to water vapor to different kinds of industrial chemicals like hydrofluorocarbons and perfluorocarbons. I'm a chemist by training and I'm absolutely fascinated by anything that affects the chemistry of our atmosphere or its climate. I'm also continuing to work on stratospheric ozone. There's a number of different issues there that from a scientific point of view remain tremendously fascinating and are still interesting questions for the community to address.

Q: Why would a young scientist want to study climate change?

A: Climate science is certainly one of the most important challenges that humanity has ever faced. Climate change, whichever way it comes out, whether it turns out to be something that we manage wisely or unwisely or whatever, I think it's quite clear that the planet in the next 20 to 40 years is going to change in ways that we haven't even really thought about. We're constantly turning the corner and being confronted with new ways in which climate change is manifesting itself, whether that's acidification of the ocean and what it may do to various different kinds of organisms or what it does to insects and the way that they interact with forests, things like the mountain pine beetle, which is ravaging the forests of the west and Canada, all those sorts of questions. How much are these things changing? How much of that change is human-induced? What is it going to do in the future? These are epic questions. I find it very exciting from a scientific point of view that we're standing on the threshold of a different planet. It's going to happen in our lifetime. So what better thing for a young scientist to pick than an area of science that is about to explode? It's just a great time to be doing climate science in my opinion.

Solomon has braved freezing polar temperatures to gather data about the ozone hole.

Polar stratospheric clouds like these led Solomon to make important discoveries about the cause of ozone depletion.

What Do You Think?

If Susan Solomon had not thought about polar stratospheric clouds and had not realized the role that these clouds play in ozone destruction, where do you think our current understanding of the ozone hole would be? How does this reinforce the idea that a single person can make a tremendous contribution to humankind?

SECTION 1 Climate

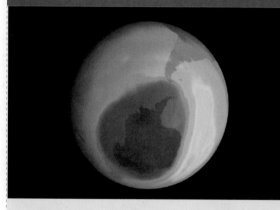

OBJECTIVES

- Climate is the long-term prevailing weather conditions at a particular place.

- Factors that determine climate include latitude, global atmospheric and oceanic circulation patterns, topography, and solar and volcanic activity. Latitude is the most important determining factor of climate.

- The angle at which the sun's rays strike Earth changes as Earth moves around the sun. This change in angle is what causes the seasons to change.

KEY TERMS

climate
latitude
El Niño
La Niña

SECTION 2 The Ozone Shield

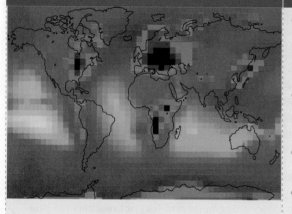

OBJECTIVES

- The ozone layer in Earth's stratosphere absorbs most of the ultraviolet (UV) light from the sun.

- Chlorofluorocarbons are human-made chemicals that break down ozone molecules and deplete the ozone layer.

- Ozone levels measured over the polar regions have been decreasing over the past several decades.

- Thinning of the ozone layer increases the amount of ultraviolet light that reaches Earth's surface.

KEY TERMS

ozone layer
chlorofluoro-
carbons (CFCs)
ozone hole
polar strato-
spheric clouds

SECTION 3 Climate Change

OBJECTIVES

- Gases that absorb and radiate infrared radiation from the sun are called *greenhouse gases*. The important greenhouse gases are water vapor, carbon dioxide, methane, and nitrous oxide.

- Global warming is the gradual increase in global temperature. This increase in temperature correlates to the increase in greenhouse gases in the atmosphere.

- Because climate patterns are complex, scientists use computer models to attempt to model climate change.

- Climate change could produce a number of potentially serious environmental problems.

- The Kyoto Protocol was first negotiated in the 1990s in order to create a global treaty to reduce greenhouse gas emissions.

KEY TERMS

greenhouse
gases
global warming
Kyoto Protocol

Reviewing Key Terms

Use each of the following terms in a separate sentence.

1. *latitude*
2. *El Niño*
3. *chlorofluorocarbons*
4. *polar stratospheric clouds*
5. *Kyoto Protocol*

For each pair of terms, explain how the meanings of the terms differ.

6. *weather* and *climate*
7. *El Niño* and *La Niña*
8. *ozone layer* and *ozone hole*
9. *greenhouse gases* and *global warming*
10. **Concept Map** Use the following terms to create a concept map: *ozone layer, ultraviolet (UV) light, chlorofluorocarbons, polar vortex, polar stratospheric clouds,* and *ozone hole.*

Reviewing Main Ideas

11. The belt of prevailing winds that is produced between 30° and 60° north latitudes and 30° and 60° south latitudes is called the
    a. doldrums.
    b. westerlies.
    c. polar easterlies.
    d. trade winds.

12. Which of the following statements about El Niño is true?
    a. El Niño is the cold phase of the El Niño–Southern Oscillation cycle.
    b. El Niño is a long-term change in the location of warm and cold water masses in the Pacific Ocean.
    c. El Niño produces storms in the northern Pacific Ocean.
    d. El Niño produces winds in the western Pacific Ocean that push warm water eastward.

13. Polar stratospheric clouds convert the products of CFCs into
    a. carbon dioxide.
    b. hydrochloric acid.
    c. nitric acid.
    d. molecular chlorine.

14. Which of the following is *not* an adverse effect of high levels of ultraviolet light?
    a. disruption of photosynthesis
    b. disruption of ocean food chains
    c. premature aging of the skin
    d. increased amount of carbon dioxide in the atmosphere

15. In which season (in the Northern Hemisphere) does carbon dioxide in the atmosphere decrease as a result of natural processes?
    a. fall
    b. winter
    c. summer
    d. spring

16. Which of the following gases is a greenhouse gas?
    a. carbon dioxide
    b. water vapor
    c. methane
    d. all of the above

17. The average global temperature increased by how many Celsius degrees during the 20th century?
    a. 0.4°C
    b. 0.7°C
    c. 0.6°C
    d. 1.0°C

18. Which of the following countries decided not to ratify the Kyoto Protocol?
    a. Russia
    b. United States
    c. Canada
    d. Finland

Short Answer

19. Name three properties of air that are important for understanding how air circulation affects global climate.

20. Explain how topography can influence the local pattern of precipitation.

21. Describe the properties chlorofluorocarbons possess that made them seem like miracle chemicals when they were discovered.

22. Explain why stratospheric ozone protection has been considered an environmental success story.

23. Explain the general process scientists use to make computer models of climate change.

24. Describe some of the environmental problems that rising sea level might cause.

25. Describe what is currently known about the state of the climate system as reported in the Fourth Assessment Report of the Intergovernmental Panel on Climate Change.

Interpreting Graphics

The graph below shows the average monthly temperature of two locations that are at the same latitude but are in different parts of the United States. Use the graph to answer questions 26–27.

26. Which location has the smallest temperature range between summer and winter?

27. What factors could cause the difference in climate between the two locations?

Critical Thinking

28. **Predicting Outcomes** Over a long period of time, how might living things adapt to increased carbon dioxide levels and climate change? Do you think most species will adapt, or are many species likely to go extinct? Write a short essay that explains your answers.

29. **Analyzing Information** In the stratosphere, ultraviolet radiation is part of the ozone-oxygen cycle. When UV light hits a molecule of oxygen (O_2), it splits it into two atoms of oxygen (O). When one of these atoms comes into contact with a molecule of oxygen, they combine to make ozone (O_3). When UV light hits an ozone molecule, it splits it into a molecule of oxygen and an atom of oxygen. Based on its role in this ozone-oxygen cycle, explain why ultraviolet radiation helps make life on Earth possible?

30. **Summarizing Information** Design a pamphlet that documents the harmful effects of ultraviolet light on living things. Figure 2.4 can be used as a source of information. You might also collect information by checking out the Web sites of the American Cancer Society and the Environmental Protection Agency. Distribute the pamphlet to your classmates.

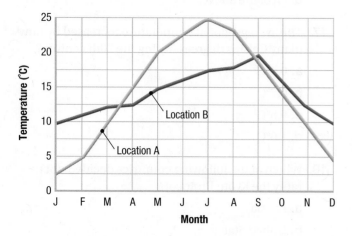

Analyzing Data

31. Making Calculations In 1958, the carbon dioxide level measured in Earth's atmosphere was approximately 315 parts per million (ppm). In 2000, the carbon dioxide level in the atmosphere had increased to approximately 368 ppm. What was the average annual increase in carbon dioxide in the atmosphere between 1958 and 2000 measured in ppm?

Making Connections

32. Communicating Main Ideas Imagine that you are a scientist who is studying the effects of chlorofluorocarbons on stratospheric ozone. Follow the path of a chlorine atom from the time it is released into the atmosphere from a CFC source through the time it has destroyed ozone molecules. Summarize your findings in a brief essay.

33. Writing Persuasively Imagine you are a scientist who has been studying the subject of climate change. You have been asked by the President of the United States to write a recommendation for his environmental policy on the subject. The President has asked you to provide important facts that can be used to promote the proposed policies. Summarize your recommendations in a brief letter.

34. Writing Persuasively You are the mayor of a low-lying coastal town. Write a plan of expansion for your town. The plan should take climate change into account. Report your plan of expansion in front of the class.

CASESTUDY

35. How will the computer models that are generated today to predict climate change be useful in the future?

36. Why might some countries be more reluctant than others to take measures to address human impact on climate change?

Why It Matters

37. Insurance companies set some of their rates by estimating the number of destructive natural events, such as hurricanes and floods, that will occur in the next 20 years. Explain why insurance companies would be interested in knowing scientists' predictions about climate change for the next two decades.

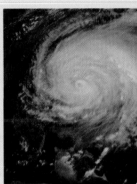

STUDYSKILL

Qualifiers When taking a test, locate qualifiers in the sentences. Qualifiers are words that modify or limit the meaning of another word or group of words. *Never, always, all, some, none, greatest,* and *least* are examples of qualifiers.

©NASA

S.T.E.M.

Build a Model of Global Air Movement

Objectives

Examine a model that shows how the movement of air creates a system of wind currents on Earth.

Hypothesize why the closed system of an aquarium is like the Earth and its atmosphere.

Materials

aquarium, 15 gal, glass, with cover

beaker, 500 mL

dry ice

electronic temperature probe

goose-neck lamp, adjustable, with a 100 W incandescent bulb

heating pad, wet/dry

hot and cold packs

ice cubes, large (24)

incense stick

masking tape

matches

thermometer, outdoor (2)

Warm air rises and cools, and cold air sinks and warms. This is true whether we are observing the temperature and air circulation in a room or around the globe. On Earth, this movement of air creates a system of wind currents as shown in the satellite image below. You will demonstrate this air movement by building a model. You will design and build a closed system that will simulate the movement of air between the polar regions and the equator. Remember that in the global circulation pattern, warm air moving toward the poles collides with cold air that is traveling from the poles. During this collision, which takes place at about 60° north latitude and 60° south latitude, the cold air sinks and causes the warm air to rise.

Procedure

1. Form a hypothesis about how winds move between cold polar regions and the equator.

2. Come up with a plan. Develop and conduct an experiment to determine how global air movement occurs. Limit the number of conditions you choose for your experiment to those that can be completed during the time your teacher has allotted for this lab. Consult with your teacher to make sure that the conditions you have chosen are appropriate.

3. Write out a procedure for your experiment. As you plan the procedure, make the following decisions:

   - Decide what methods and/or materials you will test.
   - Decide how you will measure or determine if a test is successful.
   - Select the materials and technology that you will need for your experiment from those that your teacher has provided.
   - Decide what your control(s) will be.
   - Decide what safety procedures are necessary.

Global Air Circulation

4. Have your teacher approve your plans.

5. Obtain your materials and set up any apparatus you will need.

6. Take appropriate safety precautions.

7. Make objective observations.

8. Collect data and organize them into appropriate tables and/or graphs. Be certain that the graphs and tables are properly constructed and labeled.

9. Create a labeled diagram of your prototype, including any measurements.

10. Share your results with other teams. Elicit their feedback on your design. If time permits, modify your design and repeat your tests.

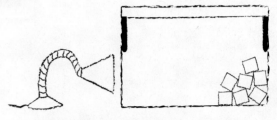

Diagramming Smoke Flow Make a simple diagram of your closed system showing the positions of the heat source and the cold source. Draw arrows to indicate the movement of the smoke in the system.

Analysis

1. **Summarizing Data** Summarize your findings and observations, including an analysis of any data tables or graphs that you created.

2. **Identifying Relationships** For each trial, describe how temperature differences between regions affected the flow of air.

Conclusions

3. **Evaluating Models** Was your design a good way to show the movement of air between regions of extreme temperature differences? Explain why or why not, and give examples of how your design could be improved.

4. **Making Predictions** Predict how air movement patterns will change if polar ice begins to thaw because of climate change.

Extension

5. **Analyzing Models** A closed system is a collection of elements that matter cannot escape from or enter. Your aquarium is an example of a closed system. Convection is the movement of warm air relative to cooler air. Discuss your observations of convection in the closed system of the aquarium. How can you apply this information to the movement of air over Earth?

6. **Analyzing Models** How is Earth and its atmosphere like a closed system? What factors that affect air movement, climate, and weather exist on Earth but not in your model?

Land

Why It Matters

Rapidly increasing human populations place severe stress on natural processes and nonrenewable resources.

How might new communities be developed such that fewer resources become depleted?

CASESTUDY

Learn more about how development planners are designing communities to be "twice green" in the case study Conservation Planning on page 366.

ONLINE ENVIRONMENTAL SCIENCE
HMDScience.com

Go online to access additional resources, including labs, worksheets, multimedia, and resources in Spanish.

©Jim Wark/AirPhoto

How We Use Land

SECTION 1

Objectives

▶ Distinguish between urban and rural land.

▶ Describe three major ways in which humans use land.

▶ Explain the concept of ecosystem services.

Some years ago, officials in California decided to find out how land was being used in the state. Measurements were made using maps, aerial photographs, field surveys, and a computerized mapping system. The results were startling. Between 1984 and 1992, nearly 84,000 hectares (about 210,000 acres) of farmland, rangeland, and woodland had been converted into suburbs and cities. This change is happening all over the world.

Land Use and Land Cover

We use land for many purposes, including farming, mining, recreation, and building cities and highways. Land cover is what you find on a patch of land, and it often depends on how the land is used. For example, land cover might be a forest, a field of grain, or a parking lot. There are different types of land cover and different human uses for each cover type, as shown in **Figure 1.1**.

Land that is covered mainly with buildings and roads is called **urban** land. The U.S. Census Bureau defines an urban cluster as an area that contains 2,500 or more people and usually has a governing body, such as a city council. Any area not classified as urban is considered rural. Land that contains relatively few people and large areas of open space is a **rural** area. The pie chart in **Figure 1.1** shows the relative proportion of each of the types of land cover defined in the table. As the table shows, most land provides one or more resources that humans consume. These resources include wood in forests, crops in farmland, and mineral resources.

Key Terms

urban

rural

ecosystem services

FIGURE 1.1

PRIMARY LAND-USE CATEGORIES

Land cover type	Human use of land
Rangeland	land used to graze livestock and wildlife
Forest land	land used for growing and harvesting wood, and harvesting wildlife, fish, nuts, and other resources
Farm or Cropland	land used to grow plants for food and fiber
Parks and preserves	land used for recreation, scenic enjoyment, and for preserving native animal and plant communities and ecosystems
Wetlands, mountains, deserts, and other	land that is difficult to adapt for human use
Urban land	land used for houses, businesses, industry, and roads

U.S. Land Cover The graph below shows the percentage of each land cover type in the United States.

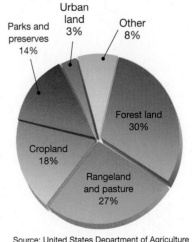

Source: United States Department of Agriculture

FIGURE 1.2

Changing Patterns The photo on the left, of New York City, shows a typical urban scene. The photo on the right, of the Connecticut River Valley, shows a typical rural scene.

Where We Live

Until about 1850, most people lived in rural areas. Many of them were farmers, who grew crops and raised livestock for food, clothing, and manufacturing. Other people managed the forests, worked in local mines or mills, or manufactured the necessities of life for a town.

The Industrial Revolution changed this pattern. Machinery was built that made it possible for fewer people to operate a farm or a grain mill. In addition, improved transportation allowed manufacturers to be located far from their customers. Thousands of jobs in rural areas were eliminated. Many people had to move to cities to find jobs **(Figure 1.2)**. As a result, urban areas grew rapidly during the 20th century and spread over more land. **Figure 1.3** shows that today, most people throughout the world live in urban areas. The movement of people from rural areas to urban areas happened rapidly in developed countries between about 1880 and 1950. Now, this movement is occurring rapidly in developing countries.

☑ **CHECK FOR UNDERSTANDING**

Identify What are two different types of land cover?

FIGURE 1.3

Urban Vs Rural This graph shows the proportion of people living in urban areas and rural areas in different parts of the world.

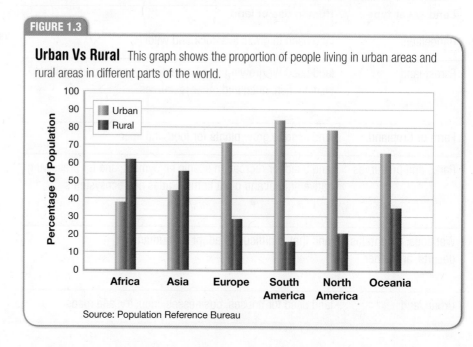

Source: Population Reference Bureau

The Urban-Rural Connection

Whether people live in cities or in the countryside, they are dependent on the resources produced in rural areas. These resources include clean drinking water, fertile soil and land for crops, trees for wood and paper, and much of the oxygen we breathe, which is produced by plants. The resources that are produced by natural and artificial ecosystems are called **ecosystem services**. Some examples of ecosystem services are listed in **Figure 1.4.**

Supporting Urban Areas

The area of rural land needed to support one person depends on many factors, such as the climate, the standard of living, and how efficiently resources are used. The average person in a developed country uses the ecosystem services provided by about 8 hectares of land and water. In the United States the average person uses the ecosystem services from more than 12 hectares, whereas the average person in Germany uses about 6 hectares' worth. People in some developing nations do not have access to all the resources for a healthy life. They may use ecosystem services from less than a hectare of land per person.

FIGURE 1.4

EXAMPLES OF ECOSYSTEM SERVICES
purification of air and water
preservation of soil and renewal of soil fertility
prevention of flood and drought
regulation of climate
maintenance of biodiversity
movement and cycling of nutrients
detoxification and decomposition of wastes
aesthetic beauty

Connect to MATH

Ecosystem Services

Earth contains about 12.4 billion hectares of productive land—cropland, grazing land, forest, fresh water, and fisheries. In 1996, the world population was about 5.7 billion people, for a mean of 2.18 hectares of productive land per person. The world population in 2011 surpassed 7 billion. On average, how much productive land per person was there when the population hit 7 billion?

CHECK FOR UNDERSTANDING

Compare How does each person's use of ecosystem services in the United States compare with each person's use in Germany?

Section 1 Formative Assessment

Reviewing Main Ideas

1. **Explain** how ecosystem services link rural lands with urban lands.
2. **Describe** three main ways in which humans use land. Write a paragraph to explain your answer.
3. **Distinguish** between rural lands and urban lands, and provide an example of each.

Critical Thinking

4. **Making Decisions** What could individuals do to reduce the loss of ecosystem services per person as the human population grows?
5. **Making Inferences** How does the movement of people from rural lands to urban lands affect people's relationship with natural resources?

- ▶ Describe the urban crisis, and explain what people are doing to deal with it.

- ▶ Explain how urban sprawl affects the environment.

- ▶ Explain how open spaces provide urban areas with environmental benefits.

- ▶ Explain the heat-island effect.

- ▶ Describe how people use a geographic information system as a tool for land-use planning.

Key Terms

urbanization

infrastructure

urban sprawl

heat island

land-use planning

geographic information system (GIS)

Urban Land Use

Historically, communities grew around good sources of water for drinking, agriculture, and transportation. Now, people tend to live where they can find the things that they need and want, such as jobs, schools, and recreational areas. For most people today, this means living in an urban area.

Urbanization

The movement of people from rural areas to cities is known as **urbanization**. People usually leave rural areas for more plentiful and better paying jobs in towns and cities. In developed countries, urbanization slowed in the second half of the 20th century. In 1960, 70 percent of the U.S. population was classified as urban. By 2011, this percentage had increased to slightly more than 79 percent. As urban populations have grown, many small towns have grown together and formed larger urban areas. The U.S. Census Bureau calls these complexes metropolitan areas. Some examples are Denver-Boulder in Colorado and Boston-Worcester-Lawrence in Massachusetts. **Figure 2.1** shows the expansion of the Washington, D.C.–Baltimore metropolitan area over the years. These maps were created using data from the U.S. Census Bureau.

Urban areas that have grown slowly or are carefully planned can be pleasant places to live. Roads and public transportation in these areas have been built to handle the growth, so that traffic flows freely. Buildings, roads, and parking lots are mixed in with green spaces and recreational areas. These green spaces may provide these urban areas with much needed ecosystem services such as moderation of temperature, infiltration of rainwater runoff, and aesthetic value.

FIGURE 2.1

Urbanization The Washington, D.C.–Baltimore area has grown larger and more densely populated over the years. Red areas indicate urban development.

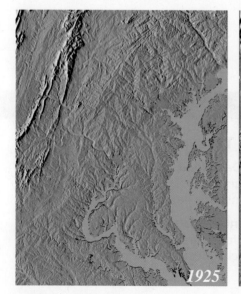
1925

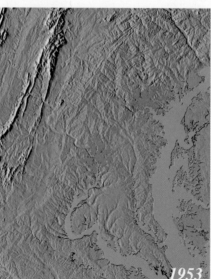
1953

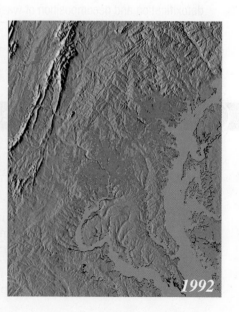
1992

The Urban Crisis

When urban areas grow rapidly, they often run into trouble. A rapidly growing population can overwhelm the infrastructure and lead to traffic jams, substandard housing, and polluted air and water. **Infrastructure** is all of the things that a society builds for public use. Infrastructure includes roads, sewers, railroads, bridges, canals, fire and police stations, schools, libraries, hospitals, water mains, and power lines. When more people live in a city than its infrastructure can support, the living conditions deteriorate. This growth problem has become so widespread throughout the world that the term *urban crisis* was coined to describe the problem. **Figure 2.2** shows an example of urban crisis in Hong Kong. The hillside is covered with substandard housing in an area that lacks the necessary infrastructure for people to live in healthy conditions.

Urban Sprawl

Rapid expansion of a city into the countryside around the city is called **urban sprawl**. Much of this expansion results from building suburbs or housing and associated commercial buildings on the boundary of a larger town. People living in the suburbs generally commute to work in the city by car. Many of these suburbs are built on land that was previously used for food production, as shown in **Figure 2.3**. In 2000, more Americans lived in suburbs than in cities and the countryside combined. Each year suburbs spread over another 1 million hectares (2.5 million acres) of land in the United States.

(tr) ©Brian Brake/Photo Researchers, Inc.; (b) ©Corbis RF/Alamy Images

FIGURE 2.2

Urban Growth Rapid urban growth has led to substandard housing on the hillsides above Hong Kong.

FIGURE 2.3

Urban Sprawl This photograph shows suburban development spreading out around farmland.

 **FIELD**STUDY

Go to Appendix B to find the field study **Land Use Planning.**

FIGURE 2.4

Marginal Lands The search for ocean views lead people to build these homes on the California coastline, which is giving way as a result of erosion.

FIGURE 2.5

Heat Islands The urban heat island over Atlanta is shown in this computer-enhanced satellite image. Areas with higher temperatures appear red.

✔ **CHECK FOR UNDERSTANDING**

Explain How do heat islands affect local rainfall?

Development on Marginal Lands

Many cities were first built where there was little room for expansion. As the cities grew, suburbs were often built on *marginal land*—land that is poorly suited for building. For example, Los Angeles and Mexico City are built in basins. These cities have expanded up into the surrounding mountains where the slopes are prone to landslides. The houses shown in **Figure 2.4** were built on land that is unsuitable for development because of the natural process of erosion along the coastline. Structures built on marginal land can become difficult or impossible to repair and can be expensive to insure.

Other Impacts of Urbanization

Environmental conditions in a city are different from those of the surrounding countryside. Cities both generate and trap more heat. Roads and buildings absorb more heat than vegetation does. They also retain heat longer. The increased temperature in a city is called a **heat island**. Atlanta, Georgia, is an example of a city that has a significant heat island, as shown in **Figure 2.5**.

Heat islands can affect local weather patterns. Hot air rises over a city, cooling as it rises, and eventually produces rain clouds. In Atlanta and many other cities, increased rainfall is a side effect of the heat island. The heat-island effect may be moderated by planting trees for shade and by installing rooftops that reflect rather than retain heat.

Urban Planning

Land-use planning is determining in advance how land will be used—where the best locations are for houses, businesses, and factories to be built, where land will be protected for recreation, and where infrastructure like sewers and electrical lines should be placed.

Making land-use plans is complex and often controversial. Federal, state, and local governments require developers to prepare detailed reports assessing the environmental impact of many projects. Developers, city governments, local businesses, and citizens often disagree about land-use plans. Projects that affect large or environmentally sensitive areas are often studied carefully and subject to heated debate.

Technological Tools

One important technological tool for land-use planning involves using a geographic information system.

A **geographic information system (GIS)** is a computerized system for storing, manipulating, and viewing geographic data. GIS software allows a user to enter different types of data about an area, such as the location of sewer lines, roads, and parks, and then create maps. **Figure 2.6** shows several images of Seattle, Washington, created from GIS data. Each image corresponds to a different combination of information. GIS allows users to display layers of information about an area and to overlay these layers, like overhead transparencies, on top of one another. It is used for environmental projects such as understanding habitat requirements of species, patterns of pollutant spread, and so on.

Connect to HISTORY

Ancient Urban Planning
People have practiced urban planning for thousands of years. The ancient Mexican city of Teotihuacan was a marvel of urban planning. The city had a grid plan oriented to 15 degrees, 25 minutes east of true north. It had two central avenues that divided the city into four quadrants. About 2,000 homes and apartment compounds lined the main avenue, which also had a channel running under it that gathered rainwater. Teotihuacan had all this—before 750 CE.

FIGURE 2.6

GIS Imaging The images below are of Seattle, Washington. Each image represents a different GIS layer, each with specific information.

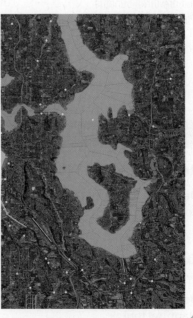

FIGURE 2.7

Mass Transit The BART transit system in California's San Francisco Bay Area moves thousands of people a day with much less environmental impact than if the people drove their own cars.

Transportation

Most cities in the United States are difficult to travel in without a car. Many U.S. cities were constructed after the invention of the automobile. In addition, availability of land was not a limiting issue, so many American cities sprawl over large areas. By contrast, most cities in Europe were built before cars, have narrow roads, and are compact.

In many cities, *mass transit systems* have been constructed to get people where they want to go. Mass transit systems, such as the one shown in **Figure 2.7**, use buses and trains to move many people at one time. Mass transit systems save energy, reduce highway congestion, reduce air pollution, and limit the loss of land to roadways and parking lots. Where the construction of mass transit systems is not reasonable, carpooling is an important alternative.

Open Space

Open space is land that is set aside for agriculture or scenic and recreational enjoyment. Open spaces within urban areas include parks, public gardens, and bicycle and hiking trails. Open spaces left in their natural condition are often called *greenbelts*. These greenbelts provide important ecological services.

Open spaces have numerous environmental benefits and provide valuable functions. The plants in open spaces absorb carbon dioxide, produce oxygen, and filter out pollutants from air and water. Plants even help keep a city cooler in the summer. Open spaces used for agriculture provide food resources. Some open spaces, especially those with vegetation, also reduce drainage problems by absorbing more of the rainwater runoff from building roofs, asphalt, and concrete. This ecological service results in less flooding after a heavy rain. Open spaces provide urban dwellers with much-needed places for exercise and relaxation.

✔ **CHECK FOR UNDERSTANDING**
Describe What are three benefits that are provided by open spaces in urban areas?

©Morton Beebe, S.F./Corbis

✔ Section 2 **Formative Assessment**

▶ Reviewing Main Ideas

1. **Describe** the term *urban crisis*, and explain how people are addressing it.

2. **Explain** how urban areas create heat islands.

3. **Explain** how open spaces provide environmental benefits to urban areas.

4. **Describe** how GIS can be used as a land-use planning tool.

✔ Critical Thinking

5. **Identifying Relationships** Write a short paragraph in which you describe the benefits of using a geographic information system for land-use planning.

6. **Making Decisions** Describe the environmental implications of urban sprawl.

Land Management and Conservation

SECTION 3
Objectives

▸ Explain the benefits of preserving farmland.

▸ Describe two ways that rangeland can be managed sustainably.

▸ Describe the environmental effects of deforestation.

▸ Explain the function of parks and of wilderness areas.

Key Terms

overgrazing
deforestation
reforestation
wilderness

As the human population grows, the resources of more rural land are needed to support the population. The main categories of rural land are farmland, rangeland, forest land, national and state parks, and wilderness. Throughout our history, we have sometimes managed these lands sustainably so that they will provide resources indefinitely. We have also sometimes reduced their productivity by overusing or polluting them. The condition of rural land is important because of the ecological services that it provides. These services are especially important for the urban areas that rely on the productivity of rural land.

Farmlands

Farmland, such as that shown in **Figure 3.1**, is land that is used to grow crops. The United States contains more than 100 million hectares of prime farmland. However, in some places, urban development threatens some of the most productive farmland. Examples of places where farmland is threatened are southern California, parts of North Carolina's Piedmont region, and the Twin Cities area of Minnesota. In 1996, the U.S. government established a national Farmland Protection Program to help state, county, and local governments protect farmland in danger of being paved over or otherwise developed. The program was renewed in 2008.

FIGURE 3.1

Threatened Farmlands This farmland next to the suburbs of Mililani, Hawaii, is used to grow a variety of crops.

©Douglas Peebles/Corbis

ECOFACT

Soil
Nothing can grow without soil. Soil used for agriculture should be sustainably managed. If not, then nutrients can be depleted or soil becomes so compacted that roots can't grow properly. Erosion can occur and healthy topsoil eroded away.

Rangelands

Land that supports different vegetation types like grasslands, shrublands, and deserts and that is not used for farming or timber production is called *rangeland*. Rangelands can be arid, like rangelands in the desert Southwest, or relatively wet, like the rangelands of Florida. The most common human use of rangeland is for the grazing of livestock, as shown in **Figure 3.2**. The most common livestock are cattle, sheep, and goats, which are valued for their meat, milk, wool, and hides. Native wildlife species also graze these lands. Like farmland, rangeland is essential for maintaining the world's food supply. World population growth may require a 40 percent increase in the food production of rangeland from 1977 to 2030.

Problems on the Range

Some rangelands in the United States have become degraded by poor land management strategies. Most damage to rangeland comes from **overgrazing**, or allowing more animals to graze in an area than the range can support. When animals overgraze, too many of the plants are eaten, and the land can become degraded. Overgrazing often results in changes in the plant community. Less desirable plant species may invade the area and replace more desirable plant species. In severe cases, all the vegetation is eaten. Once the plants are gone, there is nothing to keep the soil from eroding.

✔ **CHECK FOR UNDERSTANDING**

Explain How does rangeland become degraded?

FIGURE 3.2

Rangelands The photo below shows productive rangeland in the western United States.

Maintaining the Range

Much of the rangeland in the United States is public land managed by the federal government, which leases the rangeland to ranchers. Much of it is degraded. The Public Rangelands Improvement Act of 1978 was enacted to reverse this trend and improve land management practices.

Sustaining the productivity of rangeland generally means limiting herds to sizes that do not degrade the land. Rangeland may also be left unused for periods of time so that the vegetation can recover. Improving rangeland that has been degraded by overgrazing often includes methods such as killing invasive plants, planting native vegetation, and fencing areas to let them recover to the state they were in before they were overgrazed. Ranchers help control grazing by providing several small water sources so that livestock do not overgraze the vegetation around a single water source.

FIGURE 3.3

Harvesting Trees Methods for harvesting trees include clear-cutting (left) and selective cutting (right).

Forest Lands

Trees are harvested to provide products we use everyday, such as paper, furniture, and lumber and plywood for homes. In addition to wood and paper, we value forest products such as maple syrup and turpentine. There are many ecosystem services provided by forests; however, one of the most important is the removal of CO_2 from the air. This is known as *carbon sequestration*.

Harvesting Trees

People use enormous amounts of wood. The worldwide average is 1,800 cm³ of wood used per person each day. However, on average, each person in the United States uses about 3.5 times this amount. This is the equivalent of each person in the United States cutting down a tree that is 30 m tall every year. About 1.5 billion people in developing countries depend on firewood as their main source of fuel.

The timber industry classifies forest lands into three categories—virgin forest, which is forest that has never been cut; native forest, which is forest that is planted and managed; and tree farms, which are areas where trees are planted in rows and harvested like other crops. The two most widely used methods of harvesting trees are clear-cutting and selective cutting. These methods are shown in **Figure 3.3**. *Clear-cutting* is the process of removing all or most of the trees from an area of land. In some instances, a few "seed trees" or snags are left behind to help regrow the area or provide wildlife habitat. Standard clear-cutting can dramatically change or destroy established wildlife habitat and in some cases, cause soil erosion. Wood that is not commercially viable may be cut, but left behind to decay. The main alternative is selective cutting, which is usually practiced on smaller areas owned by individuals. *Selective cutting* is the process of cutting and removing only certain trees, leaving the rest. Selective cutting is more expensive than clear-cutting, but selective cutting is usually less destructive and can improve the health of the forest.

QUICKLAB

Measuring Soil Depth and Compaction

Procedure

1. Find a plot of undisturbed soil in a forest, meadow, park, or other undisturbed area near your school.

2. Press a 1 m wooden dowel down into the undisturbed soil as far as it will go. Measure (in centimeters) how deep the dowel went into the soil. Record the measurement, along with your observations on how soft the soil was and how easy it was to press the meterstick into the soil. Repeat this five times in the same plot of undisturbed soil.

3. Pour 1 L of water onto the undisturbed soil. Use a stopwatch to record how long it takes for the soil to fully absorb the water.

4. Repeat this procedure at a plot of disturbed soil in a path, dirt road, or other area where the soil is bare and vegetation has been cleared or trampled.

Analysis

1. How did the soil depth and hardness in the plot of undisturbed soil differ from that in the plot of disturbed soil?

2. Which plot absorbed water faster?

Deforestation

The clearing of trees from an area without replacing them is called **deforestation**. Most countries become severely deforested as populations expand and the demand for forest products increases. Forests are cleared to convert the land into farmland, or to make space for roads, homes, factories, and office buildings.

Deforestation reduces wildlife habitat, but it has other impacts, too. For example, without tree roots or a cover crop to hold the soil in place, soil is easily washed or blown into the valley below. In New York, forests on hillsides were cleared and plowed for farmland during the 19th century, and as much as 90 percent of the soil eroded. During the Great Depression, of the 1930s, hundreds of farmers in the area went bankrupt. The state bought many of the abandoned farms and let the forests regenerate. Today, many of the hillsides are covered with state forest, which is used for recreation.

The rate of deforestation is especially high in tropical rain forests, where the soil is relatively thin. Unless farming is done sustainably, clearing only small areas that will naturally regenerate, farmers must clear more forest every few years when the soil nutrients are used up. Whether forests are cleared for farming or wood, or commercial ranches or plantations, if trees are not replanted, natural resources are steadily depleted.

CASESTUDY

Conservation Planning

Undeveloped land is often sold to developers who have plans to build homes, or commercial properties, in that space. As more land is developed, green spaces can disappear – but now some urban planners are reversing this trend, trying to preserve ponds, forests, and grasslands as much as possible. These planners hope not only to conserve animal habitats and native plants, but also to improve the quality of life for people who do not want to live and work in a totally manmade landscape.

Traditionally, subdivision planners lay out streets for a development first, divide the remaining land into house lots of relatively equal size and shape, and then set aside certain lots to be used as public space. Conservation planning reverses this process, setting aside as much as 80 percent of a development to be common, or shared, green space, while putting new homes on much smaller lots. Planners like Randall Arendt pioneered the conservationist approach to planning. Arendt first goes out and physically walks around the space, finding out everything that he can about it. "If you don't like ticks or chiggers and are

Colored candies are used on top of land sketches to see how housing might be configured.

afraid of snakes," he warns student planners, "you need to get a different job." Arendt sketches the areas that will be protected natural habitat first, concentrating on preserving old growth forests, areas around rivers and streams, natural slopes and ridges in the land, arable land, and land that forms an important habitat for native plants and animals. After setting aside land to be protected, Arendt chooses locations for houses. Then he "connects the dots" to plan streets and walking trails, making sure streets curve around the natural lay of the land.

Reforestation

Clear-cut forest can be replanted or allowed to regrow naturally. **Reforestation** is the process by which trees are planted to re-establish trees that have been cut down in a forest land. In some places in the U.S., steep hillsides were deforested for farming or development and then abandoned when farming became less economical. The cost of deforestation, which caused soil erosion, landslides, and flooding, was too high. So forest has now been allowed to regenerate or has been replanted.

The area of east Texas known as the Big Thicket was heavily logged in the early 1900s. During the Depression, the federal government bought the land from timber companies in order to help them stay in business. Afterward the government kept the land and , in 1974, made it into the first National Preserve in the national park system.

Globally, more than 90 percent of timber comes from forests that are not sustainably managed, however, some governments require reforestation after timber has been harvested from public land. Many governments are currently working to improve reforestation efforts and promote less destructive logging methods, as seen in **Figure 3.4**. A number of private organizations have also established tree-planting programs.

FIGURE 3.4

Reforestation Tree seedlings have been planted to reforest this hillside as part of a reforestation project in the Fiji Islands.

Arendt typically takes planners out to walk around a site and make sketches. Later, they sit down and add details to their sketches. Arendt gives out handfuls of colored candies for planners to move around on top of their sketches to see how they might configure housing.

Many environmentalists are calling the work of conservation planners like Arendt "twice green," meaning the planning is environmentally green and financially prudent. Home buyers will pay more for smaller homes in conservation subdivisions, because the homes are in a more beautiful area and have yards that are more private. Preserving natural features means grading less land and moving less dirt, which saves developers money. In one Texas development, Arendt's plans saved developers approximately $250,000 – or 83% of the original planned grading costs. Conservation planning also saves money by not using traditional cement stormwater drainage and underground sewers, which are expensive to install. Instead of a fast flowing drainage system, planners reduce runoff by using rain gardens to hold stormwater as long as possible, letting stormwater gradually trickle first into fields, then wetlands, and then run off into rivers, ponds and streams.

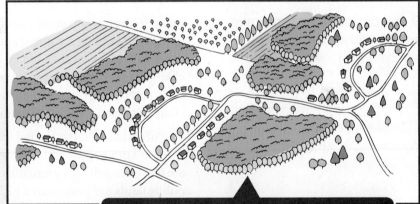

This diagram shows how green planning helps protect natural resources, while offering attractive and valuable building sites for development.

Critical Thinking

1. **Applying Ideas** Designer Andrea Tyson, a conservation planner from Naples, Florida, calls Arendt's approach "capitalism mated with conservation." Explain why you think she would use this term.

2. **Expressing Viewpoints** Some communities are enacting laws that require a certain percentage of land in new developments to be conserved. Do you think this is a good idea? Why or why not?

©Peter Arnold

FIGURE 3.5

U.S. National Parks National parks in the United States are concentrated in the West.

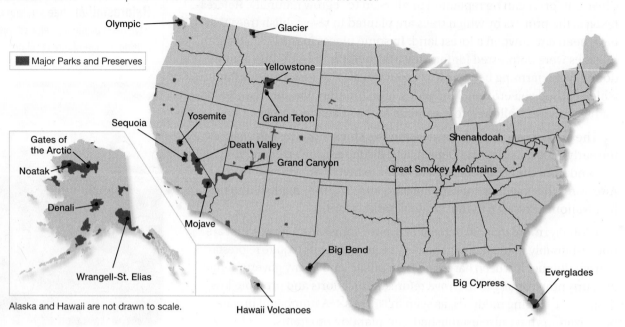

Major Parks and Preserves

Alaska and Hawaii are not drawn to scale.

Parks and Preserves

Describe What are three uses of public lands in the United States?

FIGURE 3.6

Biosphere Reserves Biosphere reserves are places where human populations and wildlife live side by side.

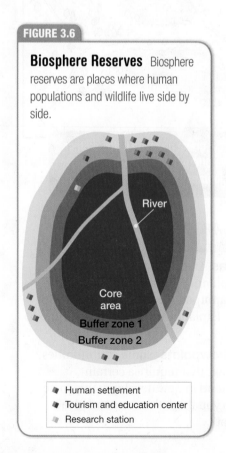

- ▰ Human settlement
- ▰ Tourism and education center
- ▰ Research station

In the 1870s, a group of explorers brought news to Congress of a magnificent expanse of land in Wyoming and Montana. The explorers expressed their concern that the land would be damaged by the development that had changed the northeastern United States. Congress agreed to protect the land, and the first national park—Yellowstone—was created. Today, the United States has about 50 national parks, as shown in **Figure 3.5**.

Public lands in the United States have many purposes. Most public lands are not as protected as the national parks are. Some public lands are leased to private companies for logging, mining, and ranching. Other public lands are maintained for hunting and fishing, as wildlife refuges, or for protecting endangered species.

International efforts include the United Nations' *Man and the Biosphere* Program. This program has set up several hundred preserves throughout the world since 1976. These preserves are called biosphere reserves and are unusual in that they include people in the management plan of the reserves, as shown in **Figure 3.6**.

Wilderness

The U.S. Wilderness Act, which was passed in 1964, designated certain lands as wilderness areas. **Wilderness** is an area in which the land and the ecosystems it supports are protected from all exploitation. So far, 474 regions covering almost 13 million hectares (32 million acres) have been designated as wilderness in the United States. **Figure 3.7** shows an example of a wilderness area. Wilderness areas are open to hiking, fishing, boating (without motors), and camping. Building roads or structures and using motorized equipment are not allowed in these areas.

Benefits of Protected Areas

Without protected areas and preserves around the world, many more species would be extinct and valuable ecosystem services lost. In a crowded world, these protected areas often provide the only place where unspoiled forests, deserts, or prairies remain. Without these areas, the plants and animals that can survive only in these ecosystems would disappear. These protected areas also provide recreation for people, and serve as outdoor classrooms and research laboratories where people can learn more about the natural world.

Threats to Protected Areas

Around the world, more people visit national parks and wilderness areas each year and leave their mark on the land. The same litter and traffic jams that have plagued our cities now plague many of our national parks. Rangelands, mining and logging sites, oil and gas drilling operations, factories, power plants, and urban areas are often close enough to the parks to affect their health. In addition, preserved areas are as affected by climate change and by air and water pollution as the rest of the world.

Private Conservation Efforts

Nongovernmental organizations and individuals also help protect natural and agricultural lands. Conservation organizations maintain preserves and individuals and communities, especially in tropical areas, protect local ecosystems to promote ecotourism. By 2011, over 1700 private land trusts protected more than 37 million acres of land in the U.S.

FIGURE 3.7

Protected Wilderness In the United States, wilderness areas, such as the High Uintas Wilderness area shown here, are supposed to be preserved untouched for our own and future generations.

✓ Section 3 **Formative Assessment**

▶ Reviewing Main Ideas

1. **Explain** what reforestation is and why it is important.

2. **List** and explain two methods of managing rangelands sustainably.

3. **Describe** the function of parks and of wilderness.

4. **Describe** the environmental effects of deforestation.

✔ Critical Thinking

5. **Recognizing Relationships** Read the first paragraph under the head "Threats to Protected Areas." Why do you suppose that some of our nation's national parks and wilderness areas are degraded?

6. **Recognizing Relationships** What are the benefits of preserving farmland?

Restoring The Range

When Ohioan J. David Bamberger first moved to San Antonio, Texas as a vacuum cleaner sales representative, he was charmed by the dry, grass-covered rangeland of the Texas Hill Country. But much of the land was degraded. It had been overgrazed by cattle and was left with thin soil and dried-up creeks.

Bamberger became intrigued by the idea of restoring some of the range to its original beauty. He was inspired by a book his mother gave him called Pleasant Valley, by Louis Bromfield. Long before it was popular, Bromfield had theories about how degraded habitats could be restored and how they could then be managed in a sustainable manner. Bamberger was intrigued by the idea of putting Bromfield's theories into action.

The Bamberger Ranch

In 1959, David Bamberger bought his first plot of land near Johnson City. Since then, David and Margaret Bamberger have expanded the ranch to nearly 2,300 hectares (5,500 acres). It is one of the largest habitat restoration projects in Texas, and shows the beauty of this area before it was damaged by human activities.

In its natural state, the ranch should have been grassland, with woody shrubs only near creeks. Instead, it had become overgrown with juniper shrubs and trees (often called cedar, *Juniperus ashei*), which can grow in poor soil and choke out other plants.

Bamberger read everything he could find on the degradation and restoration of rangeland. He found that two main things destroy the range: overgrazing and the suppression of wildfires. Overgrazing causes soil erosion. The lack of fires permits the growth of shrubs that shade out grasses and wildflowers.

The Bambergers set to work to restore the property. They cleared most of the junipers, which left more water in the soil. They planted native trees, wildflowers, and grasses, and they controlled the grazing.

David Bamberger, founder of the Bamberger Ranch Preserve.

ECOZine *at* HMDScience.com

Go online for the latest environmental science news and updates on all EcoZine articles.

Grazing is necessary for healthy grassland. The American prairies were home to huge herds of bison (buffalo), which cropped the grass and fertilized the soil with their droppings. The Bambergers combined the grazing they needed with the preservation of an endangered species. San Antonio Zoo asked the Bambergers if they could help preserve the endangered scimitar horned oryx, an antelope with thin, curved horns that is native to North Africa. Only a few small herds of this species remained, and the zoo feared that the oryx were becoming inbred, with too little genetic diversity. The Bambergers agreed, and the ranch is now home to a large herd of oryx.

The Effects of Restoration

The change in the ranch since Bamberger first bought it is most obvious at the fence line bordering the ranch. Beyond the fence there is a small forest of junipers and little other vegetation. On Bamberger's side, the main plants are grasses and wildflowers, with shrubs and trees in canyons and gullies beside the creeks. When the Bambergers first arrived, they counted only 48 species of birds on the ranch. Now, there are more than 219 species because plant diversity on the ranch has increased. In the early days, deer on the ranch weighed only about 20 kg. Now they weigh about 40 kg, thanks to the improved grazing.

In addition to deer and oryx, cattle and goats live on the ranch. Some of these are used for experiments on the effects of domestic animals on rangeland. Students and faculty from nearby universities are studying this question by using exclosures. These are fences that keep large animals out of an area. The vegetation inside an exclosure is invariably taller than that outside because grazing animals are excluded. But in addition, the plant mix inside the exclosure is different from that outside. This is because grazing mammals eat only a few nutritious species and leave the others.

The Distribution of Water

One important change in the ranch under the Bambergers' management has been the change in water distribution. Water is very important in rangeland, which naturally gets little rainfall. Many of the creeks dry up between rainy periods, but water remains in the soil and underground. Grasses have spreading root systems that absorb water from a wide area. Poor management changes this balance by allowing junipers to take over the land. A juniper can take up 10 L of water a day from the soil, leaving too little for nearby grasses and wildflowers to survive. Then, when it rains heavily, the junipers cannot absorb all the water and it runs off the land. With no grass roots to hold the soil in place, the soil erodes into the creeks. When the Bambergers arrived at the ranch, it was degraded rangeland. They drilled wells 150 meters deep (500 ft) and did not reach the water table. Now, with the restoration of grassland, soil erosion has been reduced and much more water remains in the soil. Creeks and lakes contain water for most of the year, and a dry spell is not a disaster. The water in the creeks and lakes is clear and full of fish, instead of muddy because it is full of soil.

Sustainability

The Bamberger Ranch is a working ranch, raising and selling livestock, but it is also home to dozens of other projects. Bamberger consultants advise others who are interested in managing rangeland in a sustainable fashion. Volunteers help by building and repairing nature trails and performing all kinds of maintenance work. The ranch hosts research on grasslands and range management, conferences on habitat restoration, and educational workshops.

At nearly 2,300 hectares, the Bamberger Ranch is one of the largest habitat restoration projects in Texas. This is a photo of a portion of the Bamberger Ranch used for sustainable ranching.

What Do You Think?

Habitat restoration shows us what the land was like before the settlers arrived. It also shows us how much the land has changed under human management. Can you think of any habitat in your area that could be restored? How would you go about trying to restore it? What do you think it would look like after restoration?

SECTION 1 **How We Use Land**

OBJECTIVES

- Land is covered with forest, cropland, pastures, roads, and towns.
- Urban areas are mostly covered with houses, roads, businesses, and industrial and municipal structures. Rural areas have less dense human populations and include forest land, cropland, rangeland, and other land cover types.
- Urban areas need very large areas of rural ecosystems to supply them with water, food, wood, and other ecosystem services.

KEY TERMS

urban

rural

ecosystem services

SECTION 2 **Urban Land Use**

OBJECTIVES

- Urbanization is the migration of people from rural to urban areas.
- When cities grow more rapidly than infrastructure can be built, they tend to suffer from substandard housing and traffic problems.
- Unplanned growth of a city results in urban sprawl, as low-density development spreads into the surrounding countryside.
- Land-use planning is essential if urban areas are to be pleasant places to live.

KEY TERMS

urbanization

infrastructure

urban sprawl

heat island

land-use planning

geographic information system (GIS)

SECTION 3 **Land Management and Conservation**

OBJECTIVES

- Farmland is used to raise crops and livestock.
- Rangeland is land used primarily for grazing livestock. Rangeland is easily degraded by overgrazing.
- Trees are harvested for many purposes. Deforestation can cause soil erosion and may threaten forest plants and animals with extinction.
- National lands are used for many purposes, including lumber, mining, and recreation. Wilderness is national land that is protected from all exploitation for the benefit of future generations.

KEY TERMS

overgrazing

deforestation

reforestation

wilderness

(t) ©Hanson Carroll; (c) ©Corbis RF/Alamy Images; (b) ©George & Monserrate Schwartz/Alamy Images

CHAPTER 14 Review

Reviewing Key Terms

Use each of the following terms in a separate sentence.

1. *rangeland*
2. *infrastructure*
3. *urbanization*
4. *ecosystem services*
5. *geographic information system*

For each pair of terms, explain how the meanings of the terms differ.

6. *heat island* and *urban sprawl*
7. *overgrazing* and *deforestation*
8. *urban* and *rural*
9. *selective cutting* and *clear-cutting*
10. **Concept Map** Use the following terms to create a concept map: *geographic information system, land-use planning, infrastructure, population,* and *urban area.*

Reviewing Main Ideas

11. Building a mass transit system is likely to have which of the following effects?
    a. increasing air pollution
    b. traffic congestion
    c. increasing the temperature of the urban heat island
    d. none of the above

12. National parks and wilderness areas are designed to do which of the following?
    a. provide recreation
    b. protect wildlife
    c. preserve natural areas
    d. all of the above

13. Which of the following is *not* an example of urbanization?
    a. Immigrants settle in New York City.
    b. A farmer who can no longer afford to lease farmland moves to a city.
    c. A drop in timber prices in Oregon causes a lumberjack to lose his job and he moves to Portland.
    d. An Indian family moves to the city of Calcutta after a landslide destroys their village.

14. Which of the following is *not* an example of infrastructure?
    a. a railroad
    b. a school
    c. a telephone line
    d. a dairy farm

15. Which of the following is a likely result of deforestation?
    a. The amount of carbon dioxide removed from the atmosphere is reduced.
    b. Wind blows soil away because the plant cover has been removed.
    c. Water runs off the land more rapidly and causes floods.
    d. all of the above

16. Which of the following is *not* likely to cause the degradation of rangeland?
    a. adding more animals to a herd grazing on rangeland
    b. a three year drought
    c. planting native grasses on the land
    d. driving a vehicle off-road

17. Which of the following is an example of reforestation?
    a. replanting forest land that has been clear-cut
    b. planting a cherry tree in your backyard
    c. planting oak trees in a city
    d. all of the above

18. Which of the following is *not* an ecosystem service provided by rural lands?
    a. oxygen in the air
    b. plastic for making bottles
    c. aesthetic beauty
    d. wood for making paper

Short Answer

19. Explain one way rangeland can be degraded.

20. Do national parks and forests in the United States protect ecosystems from human activities? Explain your answer.

21. What is the difference between a U.S. wilderness area and a national park?

22. Are national parks located only in the United States?

23. How can building a mass transit system improve living standards in an urban area?

Interpreting Graphics

The map below shows a typical UN Biosphere Reserve. Use the map to answer questions 24–26.

24. **Explain** Where is the reserve's research station located, and why has it been placed there rather than anywhere else in the reserve?

25. **Infer** What indicators can you see that this reserve might be an ecotourism destination?

26. **Examine** What does the map tell you about the function of buffer zone 2?

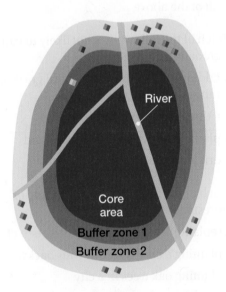

River

Core area

Buffer zone 1

Buffer zone 2

- Human settlement
- Tourism and education center
- Research station

Critical Thinking

27. **Recognizing Relationships** Read about clear-cutting under the head "Harvesting Trees." What effects does clear-cutting a hillside have on the environment?

28. **Drawing Inferences** If we see many invasive plant species and large areas of bare soil on rangeland, what conclusions can we draw about the land management practices on this rangeland? Explain your answer.

29. **Evaluating Assumptions** We tend to think that the main use of livestock is for meat. However, the Masai herders of Africa do not slaughter their cattle. They use the milk. They also bleed the cattle and use the blood to make a protein-rich sausage. What other uses for livestock can you think of that do not involve killing the animals?

30. **History** Find out how deforestation has affected a community. If you live in a forest biome, you can document the effects of deforestation on local rivers and farmland. If not, you will probably have to find an example on the Internet or in a magazine. Write a paragraph for your answer, using at least three key terms from this chapter.

31. **Research** Diagram the growth of your community over the last 100 years. Express this as a graph that shows the growth of the population and a map that shows the area of ground the community covers. There are various possible sources for the data you will need. If there is a local historical society, this is probably the best source. Otherwise, city hall or the local newspaper will probably have the information.

Analyzing Data

The graph below shows land cover in the United States in 1997. Use the graph below to answer questions 32–33.

Land Use in the United States

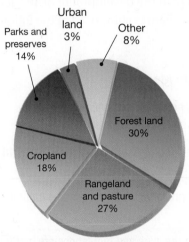

Urban land 3%
Other 8%
Parks and preserves 14%
Forest land 30%
Cropland 18%
Rangeland and pasture 27%

Source: United States Department of Agriculture

32. Analyzing Data If the percentage of cropland increased to 25 percent, and all other land cover categories except for rangeland and pasture remained the same, what percentage would rangeland and pasture be?

33. Making Calculations If 11 percent of cropland is idle (unplanted), what percentage of the United States is planted in crops at any one time?

Making Connections

34. Communicating Main Ideas In what ways does urban sprawl reduce the quality of life for people in the suburbs as well as in the town or city?

CASESTUDY

35. Describe how using conservation practices in land planning benefits both human societies and the environment.

36. Explain how the statement "Build up, not out," relates to land planning and urban sprawl.

Why It Matters

37. Describe how urban sprawl is affecting both humans and the environment.

STUDYSKILL

Flash Cards With a partner, make flash cards for the key words and most important ideas in the chapter. Take turns quizzing each other about the content of the course. Do another round, and this time the person being asked questions should try to use each key word and idea in a complete sentence.

Objectives

Create a simulated land-use model.

Recognize conflicts of interest that arise during a negotiation.

Analyze and draw conclusions about the effect of compromise on the desired outcome for each interested party in a land-use plan.

Materials

colored pencils

graph paper

pens

Laws

At least 10 percent of each type of habitat must be preserved.

Landfills must be at least 250 meters away from all housing, wetlands, and freshwater sites.

Roads and bridges may cross rivers and wetlands but they must go around large natural areas.

Roads must be connected to all developed areas of the city.

There must be no building over wetlands, slopes, or fresh water. Only parks may partially cover these habitats. Roads and bridges may cross them.

Creating a Land-use Model

Land-use plans are drawn up by planners, but they are created with the combined input of various members of a community. Along with three other people, you are meeting to plan the development of 400 acres of land for your growing city. Your team is composed of the following four members:

Team Members

The **Planner** is concerned with creating a plan that encourages the sort of growth that will attract businesses and new citizens to the area.

The **Developer** bought the land from the city and is interested in the right to build housing and a shopping center.

The **Conservationist** is interested in preserving open space and natural areas from further development.

The **Law Enforcer** ensures that all of the laws and regulations are met for any new development project.

Procedure

1. Have each team member select one of the four jobs above.

2. Use all or part of a large piece of graph paper as your map. Mark off an area that will represent 400 acres. Determine the approximate scale, and label the sides of your area accordingly.

3. The planner will color in the map as follows:
   a. 40 acres will be fresh water (rivers and/or lakes) and will be colored light blue.
   b. 80 acres will be wetlands that are right next to some of the fresh water and will be colored light purple or lavender.
   c. 40 acres will be land that is too sloped for building and will be colored tan.
   d. 240 acres is land that is good for development and will be colored light green.

4. Once the land is colored in, it cannot be altered. That will be the land you work with.

5. After the area is colored in, the group must discuss how and where to put the following items:
   a. 40 acres for a landfill.
   b. 20 acres for utilities such as power plants and water treatment facilities.

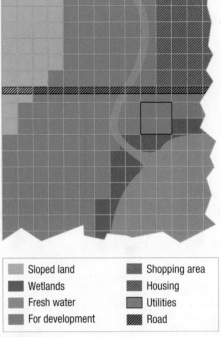

c. 40 acres for parks and wildlife.

d. 40 acres for housing. Try to put the houses near a beautiful area.

e. 40 acres for shopping.

f. 20 acres for anything that the group agrees to add. For example, you could add a few acres for community gardens or for sports and playing fields. The law enforcer cannot suggest anything, but if the group can't agree on what to add, the law enforcer may cast the deciding vote.

g. 40 acres of roads and bridges (you can divide an acre up so that you can build long, thin roads rather than create short, fat roads that are an entire acre thick). Make sure at least one road goes into and out of town.

6. The law enforcer should make sure that the plans abide by the planning regulations by checking the map for violations.

7. Use the key under the map to mark which areas are which. For example, an R denotes a road or bridge. Use a pencil and write in the things softly at first in case changes are to be made. You may need a second copy of the map in case you make mistakes the first time.

▨ Sloped land		▨ Shopping area	
▨ Wetlands		▨ Housing	
▨ Fresh water		▨ Utilities	
▨ For development		▨ Road	

Example Map This is an example of what your land-use model might look like.

Analysis

1. Describing Events Did everyone on your team agree on the plan, or were there conflicts of interest? Explain.

2. Describing Events Were you able to get everything your team wanted into the plan or did you face any problems? Describe what happened.

3. Identifying Patterns How did the features of the land constrain the plan that you made? Did you encounter any problems?

Conclusions

4. Evaluating Results Does the plan your group created meet the needs of all of the group members? Does it allow for development while preserving the environment?

5. Evaluating Models How do you think this land planning "simulation" compares to the real-life process of land-use planning?

Extension

6. Research and Communications Look in the newspaper or on the Internet for a story about a land-use controversy in your area. Identify the different members involved. Role-play with your team to see what forces will bear on this controversy.

Chapter 15

Section 1
Feeding the World

Section 2
Crops and Soil

Section 3
Animals and Agriculture

Food and Agriculture

Why It Matters

In order to survive, everybody needs to eat. Agriculture can be thought of as one of the most important relationships people have with the environment. As the world population grows, so too does the need for food.

How does the production of food affect the environment?

CASE STUDY

Learn about the importance of menhaden, a type of fish, to the commercial fishing industry in the case study Menhaden: The Fish Behind the Farm on pages 396–397.

ONLINE ENVIRONMENTAL SCIENCE
HMDScience.com

Go online to access additional resources, including labs, worksheets, multimedia, and resources in Spanish.

Image Credits: ©David R. Frazier Photolibrary, Inc./Alamy

Feeding the World

SECTION 1

Objectives

▶ Identify the major causes of malnutrition.

▶ Compare the environmental costs of producing different types of food.

▶ Explain how poverty is a major cause of malnutrition.

▶ Explain the importance of the green revolution.

In 2011, lack of rain, loss of soil, and war caused crops to fail in Somalia. This catastrophic combination resulted in **famine,** which is widespread starvation caused by a shortage of food. Events like the famine in Somalia present a frightening picture of the difficulty of feeding Earth's growing population. By 2050, the world's farmers will need to feed about 9 billion people. In this chapter, you will learn why feeding all the world's people a nutritious diet is difficult, and how food production can be increased without irreversibly damaging the environment.

Humans and Nutrition

The human body uses food both as a source of energy and as a source of materials for building and maintaining body tissues. The amount of energy that is available in food is expressed in *Calories*. One Calorie (Cal) is equal to 1,000 calories, or one kilocalorie. As shown in **Figure 1.1,** the major nutrients we get from food are carbohydrates, proteins, and lipids. Our bodies need smaller amounts of vitamins and minerals to stay healthy.

Malnutrition is a condition that occurs when people do not consume enough Calories or do not eat a sufficient variety of foods to fulfill all of the body's needs. There are many forms of malnutrition. For example, humans need to get eight essential amino acids from proteins. This is easily done if a variety of foods are eaten. However, in some parts of the world, the only sources of food may be corn or rice. Both corn and rice contain proteins, but they lack some essential amino acids, vitamins, and minerals. Protein-energy malnutrition results, affecting the normal physical and mental development of children.

Key Terms

famine
malnutrition
diet
yield

FIGURE 1.1

MAJOR NUTRIENTS IN HUMAN FOODS

Nutrient	Composition	Sources	Energy yield	Function
Carbohydrates	sugars	wheat, corn, and rice	4 Cal/g	is the main source of the body's energy
Lipids (oils and fats)	fatty acids and fatty alcohols	olives, nuts, and animal fats	9 Cal/g	helps form membranes and hormones
Proteins	amino acids	animal food and smaller amounts from plants	about 4 Cal/g	helps build and maintain all body structures

Connect to BIOLOGY

Essential Amino Acids

Animals make their own proteins from amino acids. Essential amino acids are those that must be supplied in the diet because the body needs them but cannot make them from other amino acids. A lack of essential amino acids in the diet can lead to the human diseases kwashiorkor and marasmus, which can cause brain damage in children.

FIGURE 1.2

World Food Production This bar graph shows that in 2009, more grains (wheat, corn, and rice) were produced than any other food. Wheat and corn are eaten by humans and are fed to farm animals.

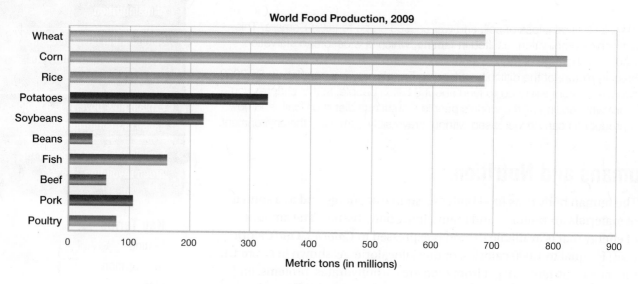

World Food Production, 2009

Metric tons (in millions)

Sources of Nutrition

A person's **diet** is the type and amount of food that he or she eats. A healthy diet is one that maintains a balance of the right amounts of nutrients, minerals, and vitamins. In most parts of the world, people eat large amounts of food that is high in carbohydrates, such as rice, potatoes, and bread. As shown in **Figure 1.2**, the foods produced in the greatest amounts worldwide are *grains*, which are plants of the grass family whose seeds are rich in carbohydrates. Besides eating grains, most people eat fruits, vegetables, and smaller amounts of meats, nuts, and other foods that are rich in fats and proteins.

Diets Around the World

People worldwide generally consume the same major nutrients and eat the same basic kinds of food. But diets vary by geographic region, as shown in **Figure 1.3**. People in more-developed countries tend to eat more food and a larger proportion of proteins and fats than people eat in less-developed countries. For example, in the United States, almost half of all Calories people consume come from meat, fish, and oil.

FIGURE 1.3

Total Calorie Supply People in developed countries generally eat more food and more proteins and fats than people in less developed countries eat.

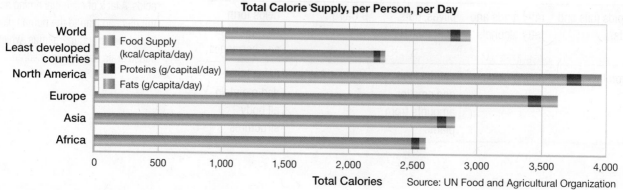

Total Calorie Supply, per Person, per Day

Total Calories   Source: UN Food and Agricultural Organization

The Ecology of Food

As the human population grows, farmland and suburbs replace forests and grasslands. Feeding everyone while maintaining natural ecosystems becomes more difficult. Different kinds of agriculture have different environmental impacts and different levels of efficiency.

Food Efficiency

The *efficiency* of a given type of agriculture is a measure of the quantity of food produced on a given area of land with limited inputs of energy and resources. An ideal food crop is one that efficiently produces a large amount of food with little negative impact on the environment.

On average, much more energy, water, and land are needed to produce a Calorie of food from animals than to produce a Calorie of food from plants. Animals that are raised for human use are usually fed plant matter. Because less energy is available at each higher level on a food chain, only about 10 percent of the energy from the plants gets stored in the animals. Thus, a given area of land can usually produce more food for humans when it is used to grow plants than when it is used to raise animals. The efficiency of raising plants for food is one reason why diets around the world are largely based on plants. However, meat generally provides more nutrients per gram than does most food from plants.

Old and New Foods

Researchers hope to improve the efficiency of food production by studying plants and other organisms that have high **yield**—the amount of food that can be produced in a given area. Researchers are interested in organisms that can thrive in various climates and that do not require large amounts of fertilizer, pesticides, or fresh water. Some organisms have been a source of food for centuries, while other sources are just being discovered, as shown in **Figure 1.4**.

Connect to MATH

Extra Calories

An active man who weighs 70 kg maintains his weight if he eats 2,700 Cal per day. Unused Calories are converted into stored fat at the rate of 1 kg of fat per 9,000 Cal that are unused. If this active man consumes 3,600 Cal per day, how much weight does he gain each year?

FIGURE 1.4

Food Sources Marine algae, or seaweeds, (left) have been harvested and eaten by humans for centuries. Glasswort (right) is a salad green that may become an important food source in the future because it can grow in salty soil.

(br) ©WILDLIFE GmbH/Alamy Images; (bl) ©Chris Hellier/Corbis

FIGURE 1.5

Lack of Resources Refugees in
Somalia wait in line for food assistance.

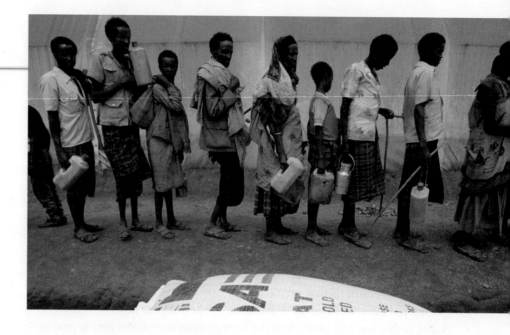

World Food Problems

The world's farmers produce enough grain to feed up to 10 billion people
an adequate vegetarian diet. However, no one is satisfied with eating just
the minimal amount of food needed for survival. And, many of us consume about a third of our Calories from animals, not grain.

Poverty and Violence

Malnutrition today is largely a result of poverty and violence, as indicated
in **Figure 1.5**. In 2010, the United Nations Food and Agriculture Organization (UNFAO) estimated that 925 million people around the world were
undernourished. Poverty affects both rural and urban people, especially
in the least developed regions. About 1.3 billion people live on less than
$1.25 per day, so they have few resources to purchase food. In addition,
diverting crops to use as biofuels raises food prices, which increases
malnutrition problems. *Subsistence agriculture*—farming to grow only
enough food for local use—is challenged by drought, degrading soil quality, high levels of conflict, and changing climate.

More Income and More Food

The number of people living in extreme poverty has declined by nearly
half a billion since 1980. This achievement is largely the result of rapid
economic development in East Asia, especially in China and India.
However, **Figure 1.6** shows that although the world's grain production has
increased for 50 years, it has not grown as fast as the world's population.
To feed the people of the world in 2050, we will need to produce more
food. As well, we will need to abolish poverty, among both rural and urban people. Increasing the productivity of the world's subsistence farmers
would help achieve both goals.

✔ **CHECK FOR UNDERSTANDING**

Summarize What could be done to
increase the productivity of the land
worked by subsistence farmers?

©Les Stone/Sygma/Corbis

FIGURE 1.6

Grain Production Worldwide grain production has increased steadily over time, but not as rapidly as the population has grown.

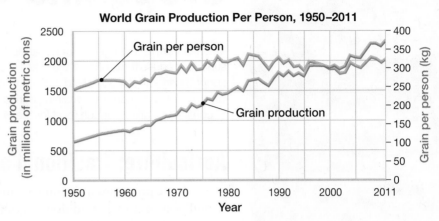

World Grain Production Per Person, 1950–2011

Source: U.S. Department of Agriculture

The Green Revolution

Between 1950 and 1970, Mexico increased its production of wheat eight-fold and India doubled its production of rice, without increasing the area of farmland used. These spectacular increases were called *the green revolution*. They resulted from new varieties of grain. The new varieties produce large yields if they are supplied with enough water, fertilizer, and pesticides. The green revolution reduced the price of food and improved the lives of millions of people.

The green revolution had limitations, however. Most of the increases that resulted from the green revolution came from large farms, which continue to increase their productivity. Because subsistence farmers often live in extreme poverty, they do not have the money to acquire the water and chemicals that the new crop varieties need.

In addition, subsistence farmers cannot use much machinery because their farms generally consist of less than two acres. Subsistence farmers need small-scale irrigation systems and high-value crops, such as vegetables and fruits, that they can sell. As shown in **Figure 1.7**, much research today is devoted to developing plant varieties that produce high yields of nutritious food on poor soil, using as little water and expensive chemicals as possible. Distributing the seeds and technology to scattered rural farms remains a problem to be solved.

FIGURE 1.7

Wheat Varieties This agricultural research scientist is checking the growth of wheat in an experimental plot.

✓ Section 1 Formative Assessment

▶ Reviewing Main Ideas

1. **Identify** the major causes of malnutrition.

2. **Compare** the environmental costs of producing different types of food.

3. **Explain** how malnutrition today is linked to poverty and violence.

4. **Describe** the importance and effects of the green revolution.

✔ Critical Thinking

5. **Identify Relationships** Study the graph in **Figure 1.6**. World grain production increased during the 1990s. Why did the amount of grain per person decline during that decade?

6. **Infer Relationships** Write a short paragraph that explains how a decrease in the production of grain worldwide could lead to a shortage of other food sources.

▶ Distinguish between traditional and modern agricultural techniques.

▶ Describe fertile soil.

▶ Describe the need for soil conservation.

▶ Explain the benefits and environmental impacts of pesticide use.

▶ Explain what is involved in integrated pest management.

▶ Explain how genetic engineering is used in agriculture.

Key Terms

topsoil
erosion
desertification
compost
salinization
pesticide
biological pest control
genetic engineering

Crops and Soil

Much of Earth's surface cannot be farmed. Only about 37 percent of Earth's land surface is agricultural, or land that can be used to grow crops. Urban areas occupy about 3 percent of Earth's land surface and are expanding, often into agricultural land. We need to use our remaining agricultural land as efficiently as possible for it to continue to grow enough food for the world while maintaining natural resources.

Agriculture: Traditional and Modern

The basic processes of farming include plowing, fertilization, irrigation, and pest control. In traditional agriculture, plows are pushed by the farmer or pulled by livestock. Plowing helps crops grow by mixing soil nutrients, loosening soil particles, and uprooting weeds. Organic fertilizers, such as manure, are used to enrich the soil so that plants grow strong and healthy. Fields are irrigated by water flowing through ditches. Weeds are removed by hand or machine. These traditional techniques have been used since the earliest days of farming, centuries before tractors and pesticides were invented.

In industrialized countries, the basic processes of farming are now carried out using modern agricultural methods. Machinery powered by fossil fuels is now used to plow the soil and harvest crops, as shown in **Figure 2.1.** Synthetic chemical fertilizers are now used instead of manure and plant wastes to fertilize soil. A variety of overhead sprinklers and drip systems may be used for irrigation. Synthetic chemicals are used to protect crops by killing pests.

FIGURE 2.1

Modern Agriculture In modern agriculture, machinery is used to do much of the work previously performed by humans and animals.

©Ron Chapple/Corbis

Fertile Soil: The Living Earth

Soil that can support the growth of healthy plants is called *fertile soil*. Plant roots grow in **topsoil,** the surface layer of soil, which is usually richer in organic matter than the subsoil is. Fertile topsoil is made up of living organisms, rocks, water, air, and organic matter, such as dead organisms.

Most soil starts to form when rock is broken down into smaller and smaller fragments by wind, water, and chemical weathering. *Chemical weathering* happens when the minerals in the rock react chemically with substances such as water to form new materials. Temperature changes and moisture cause rock to crack and break apart, which creates smaller particles on which the seeds of pioneer plants fall and take root. The dead material from plants and other organisms add to the soil. It can take hundreds or even thousands of years to form a few centimeters of soil.

Other processes also help to produce fertile topsoil. The rock particles supply mineral nutrients to the soil. Fungi and bacteria live in the soil. They decompose dead plants and organic debris, and add more nutrients to the soil. Earthworms, insects, and other small animals help plants grow by breaking up the soil and allowing air and water into it.

As you can see in **Figure 2.2**, several layers of soil lie under the topsoil. The bottom layer is bedrock, which is the solid rock from which most soil originally forms.

✓ **CHECK FOR UNDERSTANDING**
Identify Name two processes that help to make soil fertile.

FIGURE 2.2

Soil Profile Soil is made of rock particles, air, water, and dead and living organisms. The number and characteristics of the soil layers may be different in different types of soil.

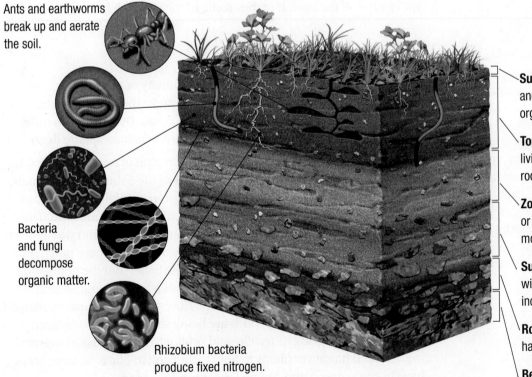

Ants and earthworms break up and aerate the soil.

Bacteria and fungi decompose organic matter.

Rhizobium bacteria produce fixed nitrogen.

Surface litter fallen leaves and partially decomposed organic matter

Topsoil organic matter, living organisms, and rock particles

Zone of leaching dissolved or suspended materials moving downward

Subsoil larger rock particles with organic matter, and inorganic compounds

Rock particles rock that has undergone weathering

Bedrock solid rock layer

FIGURE 2.3

Soil Erosion This map shows the vulnerability of soils worldwide to erosion by water.

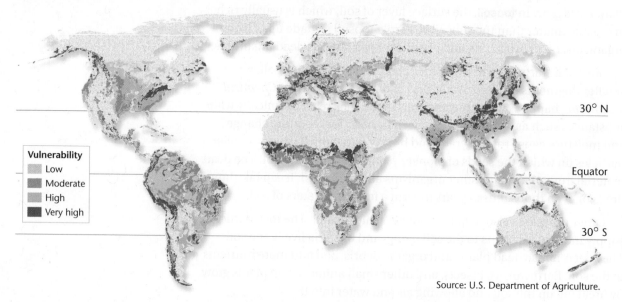

Source: U.S. Department of Agriculture.

Soil Erosion: A Global Problem

Erosion is the movement of rock, soil, and sand by wind and water. Eroded soil washes into nearby rivers or is blown away in clouds of dust. In the United States, about half of the original topsoil has been lost to erosion in the past 200 years. **Figure 2.3** shows potential soil erosion worldwide. Without topsoil, crops cannot grow.

Most farming methods increase the rate of soil erosion. Plowing loosens the soil and removes plants that hold the soil in place. When water runs off the land, it carries some of the soil with it.

Land Degradation

Land degradation happens when human activity or natural processes damage the land so that it can no longer support the local ecosystem. In areas with dry climates, desertification can result. **Desertification** is the process by which land in arid or semiarid areas becomes more desertlike.

Desertification is occurring in the Sahel region of northern Africa. In the past, people who lived in the drier parts of the Sahel grazed animals. People who lived in parts of the Sahel with more rainfall planted crops. The grazing animals were moved from place to place to find food. The cropland was planted for only a few years, and then the land was allowed to lie *fallow*, or to remain unplanted, for several years. These practices allowed the land to support the people in the Sahel. But the population in the region grew, and the land has since been farmed, grazed, and deforested faster than it can regenerate. Now, too many crops are planted too frequently, and fallow periods are being shortened or eliminated. As a result, the soil is losing its fertility and productivity. Because of overgrazing, the land has fewer plants to hold the topsoil in place. So large areas have become desert and can no longer produce food.

QUICKLAB

Preventing Soil Erosion
Procedure

1. Obtain three trays and fill one with sod, one with topsoil, and one with a layer of topsoil covered with a type of mulch, such as hay.
2. Raise one end of each tray by a minimum of 30 cm. Place the lower end of each tray into another, empty tray for which you have determined the mass.
3. Punch multiple holes in the bottom of a plastic coffee can.
4. Fill a plastic 2-L bottle with water.
5. Pour the water slowly through the holes in the plastic coffee can onto one tray to simulate heavy rainfall. Repeat for the remaining trays.
6. Use a balance to find the mass of each tray of runoff. Subtract the mass of the tray to find the mass of the soil and water eroded from each type of surface.

ANALYSIS

1. Which tray had the most soil erosion and water runoff? Which tray had the least? Why?

FIGURE 2.4

Soil Conservation Terracing (left) keeps soil in multiple, small, level fields. Contour plowing (right) follows the natural contours of the land. Both methods prevent soil erosion by keeping water from running directly downhill.

Soil Conservation

There are many ways of protecting and managing topsoil to reduce erosion. Soil usually erodes downhill, and many soil conservation methods are designed to prevent downhill erosion, as shown in **Figure 2.4**. Building soil-retaining terraces across a hillside may be cost-effective for producers of valuable crops, such as wine grapes and coffee. On gentler slopes, *contour plowing* is used. This method includes plowing across the slope of a hill instead of up and down the slope. An even more effective method of plowing is leaving strips of vegetation across the hillside instead of plowing the entire slope. These strips catch soil and water that run down the hill. Overhead irrigation tends to wash away soil. Soil (and water) can be conserved by using drip irrigation instead.

In traditional farming, plowing turns over soil to expose pests and to loosen soil for new seeds. In *no-till farming*, plowing is eliminated. Instead, the seeds of the next crop are planted among the remains of the previous crop, as shown in **Figure 2.5**. The remains of the first crop hold the soil in place while the new crop develops. No-till farming saves time compared with conventional methods. It can also reduce soil erosion to one-tenth of the erosion caused by traditional methods. However, no-till farming may not be suitable for some crops, especially where pests are poorly controlled by chemicals.

FIGURE 2.5

No-Till Farming A second crop is grown through the remains of the previous crop. This method helps prevent erosion.

FIGURE 2.6

World Fertilizer Use The use of inorganic fertilizers has increased dramatically worldwide since 1950.

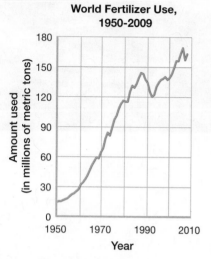

World Fertilizer Use, 1950-2009

Source: Earth Policy Institute

Enriching the Soil

In traditional farming, the soil is enriched by adding organic matter, such as manure and leaves, to the soil. As the organic matter decomposes, it adds nutrients to the soil and improves the texture of the soil. However, inorganic fertilizers that contain nitrogen, phosphorus, and potassium have changed farming methods. Without these fertilizers, world food production would be less than half of what it is today. Over the past 50 years, the use of such fertilizers has increased rapidly, as shown in **Figure 2.6.**

A modern method of enriching the soil is to use both organic and inorganic fertilizers by adding compost and chemical fertilizers to the soil. **Compost** is partly decomposed organic material. Compost comes from many sources. For example, you can buy composted cow manure in a garden store. Also, many cities and industries now compost yard waste and crop wastes. This compost is sold to farmers and gardeners, and the process is saving costly landfill space.

Salinization

The accumulation of salts in the soil is known as **salinization** (sal uh nie ZAY shuhn). Salinization is a major problem in places such as Australia, California, and Arizona, which have low rainfall and naturally salty soil. In these areas, irrigation water comes from rivers or groundwater, which is saltier than rainwater. When water evaporates from irrigated land, salts are left behind. Eventually, the soil may become so salty that plants cannot grow, as shown in **Figure 2.7**.

Irrigation can also cause salinization by raising the groundwater level temporarily. Once groundwater comes near the surface, the groundwater is drawn up through the soil like water is drawn up through a sponge. When the water reaches the surface, the water evaporates and leaves salts in the soil. Salinization can be slowed if irrigation canals are lined to prevent water from seeping into the soil, or if the soil is watered heavily to wash out salts.

FIGURE 2.7

Salinization This agricultural field is barren due to salinization.

©Kaj R. Svensson/Photo Researchers, Inc.

FIGURE 2.8

Crop Pests Examples of major crop pests include fungi (left), plant-eating insects (center), and weeds (right).

Pest Control

In North America, insects eat about 13 percent of all crops. Crops in tropical climates suffer even greater insect damage because the insects grow and reproduce faster in these climates. In Kenya, for example, insects destroy more than 25 percent of the nation's crops. Worldwide, pests destroy about 33 percent of the world's potential food harvest.

Different types of pests are shown in **Figure 2.8.** A *pest* is any organism that occurs where it is not wanted or that occurs in large enough numbers to cause economic damage. Humans try to control populations of different types of pests, including many plants, fungi, and microorganisms.

Wild plants often have more protection from pests than do crop plants. Wild plants grow throughout a landscape, so pests have a harder time finding and feeding on a specific plant. Crop plants, however, are usually grown together in large fields, which provides pests with a one-stop source of food. Wild plants are also protected from pests by a variety of pest predators that live on or near the plants. Some wild plants have even evolved defenses to many pests, such as poisonous chemicals that repel them.

Pesticides

Many farmers rely on pesticides to produce their crops. **Pesticides** are chemicals used to kill insects, weeds, and other crop pests. During the last 60 years, scientists invented many new pesticides. The pesticides were so effective that farmers began to rely on them almost completely to protect their crops from pests. However, pesticides can also harm beneficial plants and insects, wildlife, and even people.

ECOFACT

Crop Rotation
Farmers and gardeners have known for centuries that you get higher yields and less pest damage if you plant different crops each year on a piece of land. This method works because most pests are specialists and will only eat one or a few types of plants. The tomato hornworm is an example of one of these pests. If you plant tomatoes in one place every year, the hornworm population grows rapidly and will destroy the crop. If beans are planted in place of the tomatoes in alternate years, the hornworms cannot find food and will die.

FIGURE 2.9

Cropdusting A cropduster sprays pesticide on a field of pineapples in Hawaii. Cropdusting is an easy way to apply pesticide to a large area.

Pesticide Resistance

You might think that the most effective way to get rid of pests is to spray crops often with large amounts of pesticides, as shown in **Figure 2.9**. However, over time, this approach usually makes the pest problem worse. Pest populations can evolve *resistance,* which is the ability to survive exposure to a particular pesticide. More than 500 species of insects have developed resistance to pesticides, and this number grows annually.

Human Health Concerns

Pesticides are designed to kill organisms, so they may also be dangerous to humans. Problems may arise from toxicity or from the similarity of some chemicals to natural hormones. For example, cancer rates among children in areas of high pesticide applications are sometimes higher than the national average, and nervous system disorders may be common. Workers in pesticide factories or those who apply pesticides to crops may also become ill.

Pollution and Persistence

The problem of pesticides harming people and other organisms is especially serious with pesticides that are persistent. *Persistent* pesticides do not break down rapidly into harmless chemicals when they enter the environment. As a result, they accumulate in the water and soil. Some persistent pesticides have been banned in the United States, but many of them remain in the environment for many years. DDT, a persistent pesticide banned in the United States in the 1970s, can still be detected in the environment and has even been found in women's breast milk.

Connect to LAW

Pesticide Regulation

The only pesticides that are fully regulated in the United States are newly introduced pesticides designed for use on some food crops. Many older pesticides in use have not been adequately tested for toxicity and are not effectively regulated. According to the National Academy of Sciences, much of the cancer risk from pesticides in our diet comes from older pesticides used on foods such as tomatoes, potatoes, and oranges.

✔ CHECK FOR UNDERSTANDING

Explain Why can spraying pests with large amounts of pesticides become ineffective over time?

©John Zoiner

Biological Pest Control

Biological pest control is a form of *pest management* that uses living organisms to control pests. Every pest has enemies in the wild. These enemies can sometimes be used to control pest populations, as shown in **Figure 2.10.** Biological pest control may work well, but it can also have unintended negative consequences. The cane toad was introduced to Australia to control the damaging cane beetle. There is no evidence that the cane toad has reduced cane beetle populations, and the toads are spreading and negatively impacting native species.

Pathogens

Organisms that cause disease, called *pathogens* (PATH uh juhnz), can also be used to control pests. One of the most common pathogens used to control pests is the bacterium *Bacillus thuringiensis* (buh SIL uhs THUHR in JIEN sis), often abbreviated *Bt*. This bacterium can kill the caterpillars of moths and butterflies that are considered to be pests.

Plant Defenses

Scientists and farmers have bred plant varieties that have defenses against pests. For example, if you buy tomato plants or seeds, you may see that they are labeled "VNT" or "VFF." These labels mean they are resistant to certain fungi, worms, or viruses. Examples of plant defenses include chemical compounds that repel pests and physical barriers, such as tougher skin.

Chemicals from Plants

Another type of biological pest control also makes use of plants' defensive chemicals. For example, chemicals found in chrysanthemum plants are now sold as pesticides. Most insect sprays that contain these chemicals are designed for use in the home because they are less harmful to humans and pets. These products are biodegradable, which means that they are broken down by bacteria and other decomposers.

FIELDSTUDY

Go to Appendix B to find the field study **What A Pest!**

FIGURE 2.10

Biological Pest Control

A parasitic wasp injects its eggs into an aphid (left). A predatory mite attacks another mite species (right).

(bl) ©Holt Studios/Photo Researchers, Inc.; (r) ©Nigel Cattlin/Photo Researchers, Inc.

Organic Chemistry

All food contains organic chemicals, but the term *organic* is used differently in the field of chemistry than in agriculture. The term generally means "of or pertaining to living organisms." In chemistry, an *organic chemical* is any chemical compound that contains carbon. Most organic chemicals are derived from living organisms, but chemists can now synthesize organic chemicals—and even invent new ones—in the lab. In contrast, *organic agriculture* is the practice of raising crops or livestock without using synthetic chemicals. Foods labeled as *organic* in the grocery store have been raised using organic methods.

✔ **CHECK FOR UNDERSTANDING**

Describe What is one strategy that can be used to control insect pests?

Disrupting Insect Breeding

If you have a dog, you may feed it a pill once a month to keep it free of fleas. The pill likely contains a *growth regulator,* which is a chemical that interferes with some stage of a pest's life cycle. When a flea sucks the dog's blood, the flea ingests the growth regulator. The regulator stops the flea's eggs from developing into adult fleas.

Pheromones (FER uh mohnz), chemicals produced by one organism that affect the behavior of another organism, can also be used in pest control. For example, female moths release pheromones that attract males from miles away. By treating crops with pheromones, farmers can confuse the male moths and interfere with their mating behavior. Another way to prevent insects from reproducing is to make it physically impossible for the males to reproduce. For example, male insects are treated with X rays to make them sterile and then are released. When they mate with females, the females produce eggs that do not develop.

Integrated Pest Management

Integrated pest management is a modern method of controlling pests on crops. The steps involved in integrated pest management are shown in **Figure 2.11.** The goal of integrated pest management is to reduce pest damage to a level that causes minimal economic damage. A different management program is developed for each crop. The program can include a mix of farming methods, biological pest control, and chemical pest control. Each of these methods is used at the appropriate time in the growing season. Fields are monitored from the time the crops are planted. When significant pest damage is found, the pest is identified. Then a program to control the pest is created.

Biological methods are the first methods used to control a pest. Natural predators, pathogens, and parasites of the pest may be introduced to control it. Cultivation controls, such as vacuuming insects off the plants, can also be used. As a last resort, small amounts of insecticides may be used. The insecticides are changed over time to reduce the ability of pests to evolve resistance.

FIGURE 2.11

Integrated Pest Management This flow diagram shows the steps involved in integrated pest management.

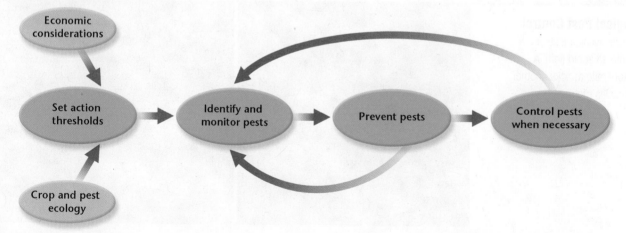

FIGURE 2.12

Genetic Engineering This diagram shows the main steps used to produce a genetically modified plant—in this case, corn that produces its own insecticide.

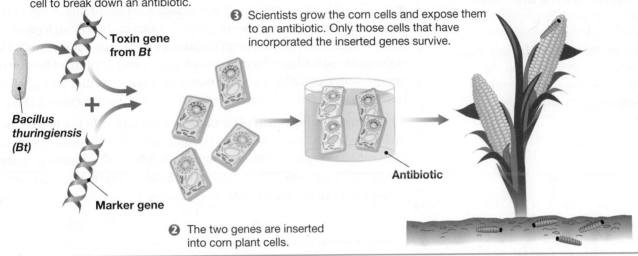

❶ Scientists isolate the gene from *Bt* that directs a cell to produce a toxin. The *Bt* gene is then joined to a "marker gene" that enables a cell to break down an antibiotic.

Toxin gene from *Bt*

Bacillus thuringiensis (Bt)

Marker gene

❷ The two genes are inserted into corn plant cells.

❸ Scientists grow the corn cells and expose them to an antibiotic. Only those cells that have incorporated the inserted genes survive.

Antibiotic

❹ The surviving cells grow into corn plants. These plants produce the *Bt* toxin, which kills caterpillars.

Engineering a Better Crop

Genetic engineering is a technique in which genetic material in a living cell is modified for medical or industrial use. Genetic engineering involves isolating genes from one organism and implanting them into another. Scientists may use genetic engineering to transfer desirable traits, such as resistance to certain pests. The plants that result from genetic engineering are called *genetically modified* (GM) plants.

Figure 2.12 shows an example of the steps used to produce a GM plant. In this case, the gene introduced into the plant is not a plant gene. It is an insecticide gene from *Bt*, a bacterium that produces a chemical that kills plant-eating caterpillars but does not harm other insects. Plants that have the *Bt* gene make this insecticide within their leaves. Hundreds of gene transfers have now been performed to create many other GM crops.

Implications of Genetic Engineering

In the United States, we now eat and use genetically engineered agricultural products every day. Many of these products have not been fully tested for their environmental impacts, and some scientists warn that these products will cause problems in the future.

For example, genes are sometimes transferred from one species to another in the wild. Suppose a corn plant that was genetically engineered to be resistant to a pesticide were to pass the resistance genes to a wild plant. That wild plant might be a pest that could then no longer be killed by that pesticide.

Connect to BOTANY

Artificial Selection

Plant breeding has been used since agriculture began. Farmers select seeds that have the tastiest tomatoes and the least pest damage. They save seeds from these plants to use in planting the next crop. The selected seeds are more likely to contain the genes for large, tasty fruits and for pest resistance than are seeds from other plants.

Nitrogen Fixation

One of the most valuable families of crop plants is the legumes (LEG yoomz), which include peas and beans. Legumes produce higher grade proteins than do most plants, so legumes are part of diets in many parts of the world. Planting legumes also improves the soil. Their roots have nodules containing bacteria that take nitrogen gas from the air and convert the nitrogen into a form other plants can use to build proteins.

Sustainable Agriculture

Large-scale modern farming has allowed production to grow tremendously. It has had some negative effects, too. In addition to the loss of topsoil, salinization, groundwater contamination, and nutrient pollution, it also has led to declines of family farms, poor conditions for many workers, and other social issues. Now, many people are working toward sustainable agriculture. Sustainable agriculture seeks to ensure environmental health, economic benefits, and social responsibility. A key part of sustainable agriculture is ensuring that farming can occur on a particular piece of land over the long-term without a loss of crop quality. To do this, sustainable agriculture maximizes soil quality and minimizes the use of energy, water, pesticides, and fertilizers. It also means that the right crops have to be selected for a particular location, as shown in **Figure 2.13**.

Organic farming is part of sustainable agriculture. In many countries, including the United States, specific rules have been set up for goods to be certified as organic. Although organic goods may cost more than those produced by other methods, many people are willing to pay this extra amount to help ensure sustainable practices.

FIGURE 2.13

Sustainable Agriculture At the Land Institute in Salina, Kansas, sustainable agriculture techniques are being used to increase seed quantity in wheatgrass (background) and to increase yield in young sunflowers (foreground).

©Patty Melander/The Land Institute

Section 2 **Formative Assessment**

▶ Reviewing Main Ideas

1. **Explain** the differences between traditional and modern farming methods.

2. **Explain** why soil conservation is an important agricultural practice.

3. **Compare** the benefits and environmental impacts of pesticide use.

✔ Critical Thinking

4. **Infer Relationships** Write a paragraph to explain the similarities and differences between traditional plant breeding and genetic engineering.

5. **Predict Consequences** Read the description of integrated pest control in this section. Why do you think this pest control technique is not practiced everywhere?

Animals and Agriculture

We have seen that an acre of land can grow more food from plants than from animals. However, most animal proteins contain more essential amino acids than do proteins found in plants, and most humans include some animal products in their diet. Food from animals has been the basis of life for some human populations for many thousands of years.

Our ancestors obtained animal proteins by hunting and fishing, but today most people get animal proteins from domesticated species. About 50 animal species have been **domesticated,** which means that they are bred and managed for human use. Domesticated animals include chicken, sheep, cattle, honey bees, silkworms, fish, and shellfish. In many parts of the world, goats, pigs, and water buffalo are also important domesticated animals.

Food from Water

Because fish are an important food source for humans, the harvesting of fish has become an important industry worldwide, as shown in **Figure 3.1**. However, as shown in **Figure 3.2**, when too many fish are harvested over a long period of time, ecological systems can be damaged.

Overharvesting

Catching or removing from a population more organisms than the population can replace is called **overharvesting.** Many governments are now trying to stop overharvesting. They have created no-fishing zones so that fish populations can recover. Research shows that fishing in areas surrounding no-fishing zones improves after no-fishing zones have existed for a few years. For the fishing industry to prosper in the future, better management is needed.

FIGURE 3.1

Fish Market Whole, fresh tuna are one of the many types of seafood for sale at the Tokyo fish market, the largest fish market in the world.

SECTION 3

Objectives

▶ Explain how overharvesting affects the supply of aquatic organisms used for food.

▶ Describe the current role of aquaculture in providing seafood.

▶ Describe the importance of livestock in providing food and other products.

Key Terms
domesticated
overharvesting
aquaculture
livestock
ruminant

FIGURE 3.2

Cod Fishery Collapse The North Atlantic cod fishery has collapsed because of overharvesting.

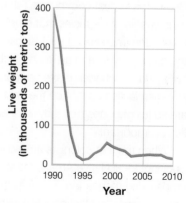

Source: Department of Fisheries and Oceans, Canada

FIGURE 3.3

Aquaculture This oyster farm in Washington shows how aquaculture concentrates seafood production.

Aquaculture

Fish and other aquatic organisms provide up to 20 percent of the animal protein consumed worldwide. To meet demand, there has been a rapid increase in **aquaculture** (AK wuh kuhl chuhr), the raising of aquatic organisms for human use or consumption. Aquaculture is not a new idea. This practice likely began in China about 4,000 years ago. Today, China leads the world in using aquaculture to produce freshwater fish.

Today, most of the catfish, oysters, salmon, crayfish, and rainbow trout eaten in the United States are the products of aquaculture. In the 1980s, domestic production of these species quadrupled, and imports of these species increased even faster. Worldwide, about 50 percent of seafood now comes from aquaculture.

There are a number of different methods of aquaculture. The oyster farm shown in **Figure 3.3** represents one such method. Fish farms are widely used for aquaculture, and there are several types. Open pens and cages allow fish to be farmed in lakes and coastal oceans. There are serious concerns about the use of these pens in many places, such as salmon farms in British Columbia, Canada. The large number of fish kept in one area discharges large amounts of waste and pollutes surrounding waters. Diseases and parasites that occur when fish are kept in high densities

CASESTUDY

Menhaden: The Fish Behind the Farm

One of the largest commercial fish catches in the United States each year is of a species that most people have never heard of—the menhaden (men HAYD 'n). Menhaden are small, silver, oily fish in the herring family and are found in the Atlantic Ocean from Maine to Florida. Menhaden make up more than one-third of the weight of commercial fish caught on the East Coast each year. But menhaden are so full of bones that they are inedible. So why are these small fish so important?

When the first colonists arrived in the area we now call New England, local Native Americans showed them how to fertilize their crops using menhaden. This was the origin of the belief that the best corn is grown by planting a fish with each seed. Later, menhaden oil was used in oil lamps, and ground menhaden was added to cattle feed.

Today, the menhaden catch is processed to produce fishmeal and fish oil. The oil is used in cooking oils and margarine. The fishmeal has a high protein content, and is added to the feed of pets, chickens, turkeys, hogs, cattle, and farm fish. Menhaden are

A menhaden catch is unloaded from purse seine nets in Chesapeake Bay, Virginia.

can affect wild populations. If farmed fish escape, they can also interfere with wild populations. In addition, some wild fish populations are being overharvested to provide food for farmed fish.

Many fish are raised in small ponds or in tanks where water is recirculated. Often, there are many individual ponds that each contain fish at a specific stage of development. Clean water is circulated through the ponds, bringing in oxygen while taking away carbon dioxide and fecal wastes. The fish grow to maturity in the ponds and then are harvested. Wastes can be treated before water is released back into natural bodies of water. These systems are less likely to have fish escape into wild populations. One important consideration for ponds and tanks is their location. If there are not adequate supplies of fresh water, local water supplies can be depleted. Also, aquaculture development in some areas has destroyed important ecosystems. For example, millions of acres of mangroves have been removed for shrimp aquaculture around the world.

Despite the associated environmental issues, aquaculture will continue to be an important source of protein for the human diet. Therefore, like sustainable agriculture, it is important that methods are developed that ensure that aquaculture is done in a way that minimizes environmental damage and can be sustained into the future.

also used by recreational fishers as bait for fish such as striped bass, shark, and tuna.

Menhaden spawn in the ocean. The eggs hatch into larvae, which are carried into estuaries where they spend their first year. After the menhaden mature, they return to the ocean and usually live within 50 km of the coast. The Chesapeake Bay is one of the most important nurseries for this species.

Menhaden live in large schools near the surface, so they are easily caught with *purse seine* nets, which are nets that hang down from the surface of the water. Boats towing the nets encircle the fish, which are captured when the lower margin of the net is pulled closed.

An adult menhaden is an important member of the marine ecosystem. Menhaden are filter feeders that scoop up large mouthfuls of water and filter out the plankton for food. An adult menhaden can filter a million gallons of water in six months.

The Chesapeake Bay Ecological Foundation estimates that the menhaden population removes up to one-fourth of the nitrogen pollutants dumped into the Chesapeake Bay each year. Because nitrogen runoff from lawns and farms is a major pollutant of the Chesapeake Bay, this function of the fish is important. Sport fishers also value menhaden as bait because they are the natural food of many sportfish.

Both environmentalists and the sport fishing industry were worried when the menhaden catch declined during the 1990s. The catch in 2000 was the second-lowest catch on record. Both groups believe that overharvesting by commercial fishing boats was the reason for the reduced catch. As a result, the Atlantic Menhaden Management Board, which manages the menhaden fishery, has been restructured to have fewer members who represent the commercial fisheries. Even with this change, according to the National Oceanic and Atmospheric Administration (NOAA), more menhaden were harvested than is sustainable in 2008.

Critical Thinking

1. **Apply Ideas** Many different groups have potentially conflicting interests in the future of the menhaden fishery. Write a paragraph that explains the opposing points of view of two of these groups.

2. **Express Viewpoints** If you were on the Atlantic Menhaden Management Board, what changes would you suggest to prevent the fishery from declining? Write a paragraph that explains these changes.

FIGURE 3.4

Livestock Operations Modern livestock operations, such as this pig farm, are large and efficient.

GLOBAL ESTIMATES OF ANIMAL POPULATIONS

	Global Livestock Populations		
Species	**1961**	**2009**	**Increase**
Chickens	3.9 billion	18.6 billion	377%
Sheep	1 billion	1.1 billion	10%
Cattle	942 million	1.4 billion	49%
Pigs	406 million	942 million	132%
Goats	349 million	880 million	152%
Horses, donkeys, and mules	110 million	113 million	2.7%

Source: UN Food and Agriculture Organization

Livestock

Domesticated animals that are raised to be used on a farm or ranch, or to be sold for profit, are called **livestock.** Large livestock operations, such as the pig farm shown in **Figure 3.4,** produce most of the meat that is consumed in developed countries. Meat production per person has increased worldwide since 1950, as shown in **Figure 3.5.** Livestock are also important in developing countries. In these countries, livestock provide leather, wool, eggs, and meat, and serve many other functions. Some are used as draft animals to pull carts and plows. Other livestock provide manure, which is used for fertilizer or as a heat source or as fuel for cooking. In arid ecosystems, livestock provide sustenance where crops could be grown only with expensive irrigation.

Ruminants

Cattle, sheep, and goats are **ruminants** (ROO muh nuhnts), which are cud-chewing mammals that have three- or four-chambered stomachs. *Cud* is the food that these animals regurgitate from the first chamber of their stomachs and chew again to aid digestion. Ruminants have microorganisms in their intestines, which allow the animals to digest plant materials that humans cannot digest. When we eat the meat of ruminants, we are using them to convert plant material, such as grass stems and woody shrubs, into food that we can digest.

Humans have created hundreds of breeds of cattle that are suited to life in different climates. Cattle are most common in North America, India, and Africa. But the cattle are not always slaughtered for meat. In Africa, for example, traditional Masai herders drink milk and blood from their cattle. India has almost one-fifth of the world's cattle. However, many of these cattle are not killed or eaten because cows are sacred to Hindus, who make up a large part of India's population. These cattle instead produce milk and dung, and are used as draft animals.

FIGURE 3.5

Meat Production Worldwide meat production per person has increased significantly since 1960.

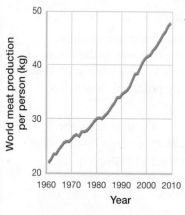

Source: Earth Policy Institute

©Daniel Pepper/Getty Images

Poultry

Since 1961, the population of chickens worldwide has increased by a greater percentage than the population of any other livestock. Chickens are a type of *poultry,* or domesticated birds raised for meat and eggs, which are good sources of essential amino acids. In more-developed countries, chickens and turkeys are usually raised in factory farms, as shown in **Figure 3.6.** This industry has been criticized because the animals typically live in cramped, artificial environments.

Fewer ducks and geese are raised worldwide than chickens, but in some areas ducks and geese are economically important. For example, the Chinese use ducks not only for meat, but also as part of an integrated system that produces several types of food at one time. The ducks' droppings are used to fertilize fields of rice called *rice paddies.* The rice paddies are flooded several times per year with water from nearby ponds. Mulberry trees, which feed silkworms, are also irrigated by the ponds. Plant materials and filtered sewage are dumped in the ponds and serve as food for carp and other fish. The integrated system uses little fresh water, recycles waste, and produces ducks, silk, rice, and fish.

FIGURE 3.6

Industrial Farms Modern chicken farms, such as this one, are often huge, industrial-scale operations.

Section 3 Formative Assessment

▶ Reviewing Main Ideas

1. **Explain** why the percentage of seafood produced by aquaculture is increasing so rapidly.

2. **Explain** how overharvesting affects the supply of fish such as salmon.

3. **Describe** the importance of livestock to cultures that consume no meat.

✔ Critical Thinking

4. **Infer Relationships** Read the description of poultry above and explain why chickens are an important source of food for many humans.

5. **Apply Ideas** Look at the graph in **Figure 3.5.** Write a short paragraph explaining why meat production has increased so rapidly.

Genetically Modified Foods

A scientist examines experimental samples of genetically modified fruit trees.

Genetically modified (GM) foods have been on sale in the world's supermarkets since 1994. We do not recognize them because the U.S. Food and Drug Administration (FDA) does not require that GM foods be labeled as such.

As the world's population rises, so does the need for food. Genetic engineering provides a way to increase food production. Biotechnologists can develop desirable characteristics in an organism by altering its genes or by inserting new genes into the organism's cells. For example, soybeans, corn, and other crop plants have been genetically modified to make proteins that protect them from the action of herbicides. Farmers who plant these GM crops can spray herbicides to control weeds without harming the crop.

GM foods are not limited to plant crops. GM animals have also been developed, including a strain of salmon that grows twice as fast as other salmon. The FDA has not yet cleared any GM animals for human consumption. But it has cleared many GM plant foods for sale. Not only is labeling of GM foods not required, it is actually unlawful to label foods that do not contain GM organisms. In 2011, consumer groups brought legal action against the U.S. government to force new labeling laws. Following are two points of view on GM foods.

Although these cans are labeled, genetically modified foods are not required to be labeled as such in the United States.

This farmer from Oaxaca, Mexico, holds up ears of traditional corn varieties. Some people fear that genes from genetically modified varieties could accidentally be introduced into native varieties.

The Benefits Outweigh the Risks

People who support development of GM plants and animals view the process as an extension of previous breeding techniques. Traditionally, farmers altered the genetic makeup of a species by crossbreeding different strains to combine their best traits into one strain. However, the direct manipulation of genes through genetic engineering makes it possible to control genetic changes more precisely and efficiently. It even makes it possible to insert genes from one species into another.

The potential to increase crop yields is one advantage of GM food plants. Some GM crops, including corn that contains *Bt* genes, produce their own insecticides. These GM crops not only have the potential for higher yields, but also can reduce the expense and toxic exposure associated with pesticide and herbicide use. Crops that have been genetically engineered to tolerate herbicides can reduce the cost and fuel emissions associated with using farm machinery to get rid of weeds.

Other beneficial characteristics of GM fruits and vegetables include development of produce that stays fresh longer or contains added nutrients. For example, inserting a gene that increases the amino acids in a plant food could give it more nutritional value. To combat world hunger, scientists might be able to develop seeds that grow well in areas with poor soil or little water.

The Risks Outweigh the Benefits

Critics of GM foods think that these products are significantly different from foods developed through traditional methods. Scientists can use genetic engineering to place genes from any species into another. Opponents are concerned about the safety of foods that contain these "foreign" genes.

One safety concern is the possibility of allergic reactions. Some foods, such as peanuts and shellfish, cause allergic reactions in many people. If genes from these foods are placed in entirely different products, people who eat these new products without knowing they contain the foreign genes may suffer allergic reactions.

Other critics object to GM foods for religious or ethical reasons. Certain religions prohibit eating pork and other foods. People may object to the insertion of genes from pigs or other prohibited foods into foods they normally eat. Similarly, vegetarians might object to eating foods that contain animal genes. Such insertions are particularly worrisome when the sources of modifications are not noted on packaging.

Another major concern is pesticide resistance. Insects can rapidly develop the ability to survive exposure to pesticides. When they do, farmers lose the ability to combat infestations and significant crop losses can result. Farmers who grow genetically engineered crops that make their own pesticides, such as *Bt* corn, must take special precautions against the development of pesticide resistance.

Some scientists are concerned that genetically engineered plant and animal species could accidentally be introduced into the wild. For example, fast-growing GM salmon that escape from aquaculture enclosures might thrive at the expense of wild species. Wild species could become extinct, thus reducing biodiversity and potentially affecting ecosystem stability.

These people in Montreal, Quebec, are protesting the importation of genetically modified organisms (GMOs). Many countries have not accepted genetically engineered crops as much as the United States has.

© Reuters New Media Inc./Corbis

What Do You Think?

Some people propose that genetically modified foods should have labels that identify them as such. Could such a measure decrease criticism about the safety of genetically modified foods? Based on what you have read, decide whether you would buy genetically modified foods at the grocery store. Explain your reasoning.

SECTION 1 **Feeding the World**

OBJECTIVES

- The foods produced in the greatest amounts worldwide are grains, the seeds of grass plants.

- Malnutrition is a condition that occurs when people do not consume enough Calories or do not eat a sufficient variety of foods to fulfill all of the body's needs.

- More food is needed each year to feed the world's growing population. Poverty and violence are the main reasons for hunger in the world today.

- The green revolution introduced new crop varieties with increased yields through the application of modern agricultural techniques.

KEY TERMS

famine

malnutrition

diet

yield

SECTION 2 **Crops and Soils**

OBJECTIVES

- The basic processes of farming are plowing, fertilization, irrigation, and pest control. Modern agricultural methods have replaced traditional methods in much of the world.

- Fertile soil is soil that can support the growth of healthy plants. Soil conservation methods are important for protecting and managing topsoil and reducing erosion.

- Pests cause considerable crop damage. The use of pesticides has both positive and negative effects on the environment. Integrated pest management can minimize the use of chemical pesticides.

- Genetic engineering is the process of transferring genes from one organism to another. Plants that result from genetic engineering are called genetically modified plants.

KEY TERMS

topsoil

erosion

desertification

compost

salinization

pesticide

biological pest control

genetic engineering

SECTION 3 **Animals and Agriculture**

OBJECTIVES

- Overharvesting has reduced the populations of many aquatic organisms worldwide.

- Aquaculture is the raising of aquatic animals, and shares many similarities to agriculture on land.

- Livestock are important for the production of food and other products. Worldwide meat production per person has increased greatly over the past several decades.

KEY TERMS

domesticated

overharvesting

aquaculture

livestock

ruminant

Reviewing Key Terms

Use each of the following terms in a separate sentence.

1. *overharvesting*
2. *erosion*
3. *livestock*
4. *yield*
5. *genetic engineering*

For each pair of terms, explain how the meanings of the terms differ.

6. *pesticide* and *biological pest control*
7. *compost* and *topsoil*
8. *livestock* and *ruminant*
9. *malnutrition* and *famine*
10. *salinization* and *desertification*
11. **Concept Map** Use the following terms to create a concept map: *contour plowing, no-till farming, organic farming, careful irrigation, soil erosion, nutrient depletion,* and *salinization.*

Reviewing Main Ideas

12. Malnutrition can be caused by
    a. a lack of enough Calories.
    b. a lack of carbohydrates.
    c. a lack of essential amino acids.
    d. all of the above

13. Humans need which of the following nutrients?
    a. carbohydrates and minerals
    b. lipids and vitamins
    c. proteins
    d. all of the above

14. Which of the following is *not* one the six most produced foods worldwide each year?
    a. potatoes
    b. beef
    c. rice
    d. wheat

15. Which of the following statements about human diets in all parts of the world is true?
    a. Most people eat pork.
    b. An adequate diet includes carbohydrates, proteins, and fats.
    c. Most people do not have protein in their diets.
    d. Most people are obese.

16. Malnutrition is largely a result of
    a. war.
    b. soil erosion.
    c. poverty.
    d. salinization.

17. Which of the following is *not* found in fertile soil?
    a. rock particles
    b. worms
    c. high concentrations of salts
    d. high concentrations of organic matter

18. Which of the following is *not* a soil conservation method?
    a. contour plowing
    b. salinization
    c. no-till farming
    d. terracing

19. Which of the following statements is a disadvantage of using chemical pesticides?
    a. Pesticides can pollute waterways.
    b. Pests evolve resistance to pesticides.
    c. Pesticides kill beneficial insects.
    d. All of the above.

20. How do pesticides that regulate growth work?
    a. They kill fleas.
    b. They disrupt the pest's life cycle.
    c. They attract predators of the pest.
    d. They prevent the pest from attacking the plant by poisoning its nervous system.

Short Answer

21. Why does it cost more to produce a kilogram of meat than to produce a kilogram of plants?

22. How does plowing soil increase soil erosion?

23. Why are biological controls for killing pests sometimes more effective than chemical pesticides are?

24. Why are ruminants valuable livestock?

25. Explain how soil degradation leads to loss of agricultural land.

Interpreting Graphics

Use the graph below to answer questions 26–28.

26. Analyzing Data In which year was the most corn planted? In which year was the least corn harvested?

27. Analyzing Data How many acres were planted with corn in 2007?

28. Draw Conclusions According to the graph, more acres of corn are planted than are harvested each year. Why?

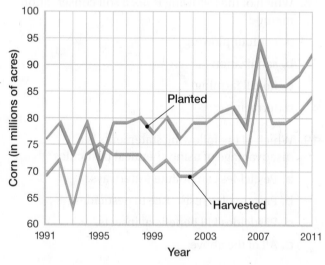

Source: U.S. Department of Agriculture

Critical Thinking

29. Make Predictions Reread the text under the heading "World Food Problems." Write a paragraph to predict how increasing the productivity of the world's subsistence farmers would affect poverty and food production.

30. Examine What incentives to conserve soil do farmers in developed nations have?

31. Infer Relationships Read the text in this chapter under the heading, "Disrupting Insect Breeding." Are pheromones a type of pesticide? Explain your reasoning.

32. Social Studies Thousands of tons of dead fish are shoveled back into the ocean each year from fishing vessels because the fish are species that consumers do not want to buy. Identify some ways that humans might be able to reuse this protein.

33. Economics Hundreds of thousands of people starve to death every year. How is this problem related to the problem of poverty? Explain your answer.

34. Prepare a Report Environmental degradation caused by farming is not a new problem. The Dust Bowl of the 1930s is an example of an environmental disaster caused by farming practices that we would now consider to be damaging. Investigate the Dust Bowl, and write a report about it. Include information about the farming practices, laws, and regulations that were introduced in the United States as a result of the lessons learned during the 1930s.

Analyzing Data

Use the table below to answer questions 35–38.

WORLD FOOD PRODUCTION (IN MILLIONS OF TONS)				
Food	1990	1995	1999	2009
Total Cereals	2000	2000	2000	2000
Wheat	590	540	590	690
Rice	520	550	610	690
Legumes	1000	1000	1000	1400
Poultry	41	54	65	92
Milk	542	540	570	702

35. Analyzing Data Compared to 1995, which foods had increased production in both 1999 and 2009?

36. Analyzing Data Which foods had lower production in 1995 than in 1990?

37. Analyzing Data Taking into account the 1999 data, can you think of any possible reasons for the answer to question 36?

38. Analyzing Data The human population of the world grew by 12 percent between 1990 and 2009. By what percentage did legumes production increase during this time?

Making Connections

39. Communicate Ideas Explain how insect reproduction enables insects to evolve pesticide resistance very rapidly.

40. Analyzing Information Explain why the pesticide DDT can still be detected in the environment even though its use was banned decades ago.

CASESTUDY

41. How is the menhaden fishing industry different from other fisheries?

42. Why are members of the sport fishing industry worried about the future of the menhaden catch?

Why It Matters

43. How has modern agriculture changed crop yield around the world?

44. What role might genetic engineering play in agriculture in the future?

STUDYSKILL

Making It a Habit Many people find that developing a routine helps them to study more effectively. Decide which time of day you feel most alert, and set it aside for studying. Make sure that any distractions around you will be minimal. When you regularly follow through with your study plan, you may find that you begin to learn more in less time.

Objectives

Hypothesize ways to reduce the amount of water a home garden needs.

Compare the amount of water different soil samples can hold.

Explain how adding materials to a soil sample can help increase the sample's ability to hold water.

Materials

beaker, 250 mL

compost, 5 g

crucible (or other heat-safe container)

dry chopped grass clippings, 5 g

eyedropper

filter paper

funnel

heat source (hot plate or oven)

metric balance

sawdust, 5 g

soil sample, 50 g

stirring rod

tongs

watch (or clock)

water

Procedure Step 4 Fold the moist filter paper into quarters, and then open it to form a cup that fits in a funnel.

Managing the Moisture in Garden Soil

You work as a soil specialist with the Smith County Soil Conservation District. You are trying to help Latisha Norton, a local resident, solve an agricultural problem. Latisha has found that she must water her vegetable garden very often to keep it healthy. As a result, her family's water bills have skyrocketed! Latisha and her family may have to give up their garden project because of the added expense.

You realize that the water is probably draining out of the garden soil too quickly. To solve this problem, you need to find out how much water the soil can hold. You visit her garden and collect several soil samples. (Your teacher will provide you with soil samples.)

Procedure

1. Dry your soil sample without burning any of the organic matter. To do this, place about 50 g of soil in a crucible or other heat-safe container. Using tongs, gently heat the sample over a hot plate or put the sample in an oven. Stir the sample occasionally with a stirring rod to ensure that the sample becomes completely dry.

2. After the sample is completely dry, weigh about 10 g of dry soil. Record the mass in a data table.

3. Dampen a circle of filter paper until it is thoroughly moist, but not dripping. Weigh the moist filter paper, and record its mass in a data table.

4. As shown below, fold the moist filter paper into quarters. Next, open the filter paper to form a cup that fits in a funnel. Place the cup-shaped filter paper in the funnel.

5. Place the dry soil sample on the filter paper in the funnel. Place the funnel in the beaker.

6. Add water to the soil sample one drop at a time until all of the soil is moist and water begins to drip out of the funnel. Stop adding water, and let the funnel sit for 5 min.

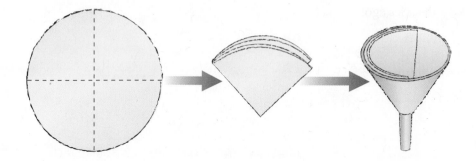

7. After 5 min, remove the filter paper and moist soil from the funnel, and weigh the paper and soil together. Record their mass in a data table.

8. Calculate the mass of the moistened soil sample by subtracting the mass of the damp filter paper from the mass of the completely moistened sample and the filter paper. Record the mass in a data table.

9. Calculate the amount of water that your soil sample can hold by subtracting the mass of the dry soil sample from the mass of the moistened soil sample. Record the result in a data table.

10. Calculate the percentage of water that your sample held. Divide the mass of water the soil held by the mass of the moistened soil sample, and multiply by 100. The higher the percentage is, the more water the soil can hold. Record the percentage in a data table.

11. Divide the remaining dry soil sample into three 5 g portions. To the first soil sample, add 5 g of dry compost. To the second soil sample, add 5 g of dry chopped grass clippings. To the third soil sample, add 5 g of dry sawdust. Weigh each mixed soil sample, and record the masses of the three samples in a data table.

12. Perform steps 3–10 for each of your mixed soil samples. Record your results in a data table.

Procedure Step 6 When adding water to the soil sample, add one drop at a time until all of the soil is moist and water begins to drip out of the funnel.

Analysis

1. **Organizing Data** Compare your results with the results of your classmates. Which soil samples held water the best? Why?

2. **Analyzing Data** Which of the additional materials improved the soil's ability to hold water?

Conclusions

3. **Evaluating Methods** Based on your results as well as your research, what could you recommend to Latisha to reduce the amount of water her garden needs?

Extension

4. **Designing Experiments** With the help of your teacher, choose one more material in addition to the three materials you used in step 11. Combine two of these materials, and mix them with a soil sample. Combine the remaining two materials with another soil sample. Perform steps 3–10 for these two mixed soil samples. Compare your results with the results you gathered earlier in the lab. Which combination of materials in the soil samples held water the best?

Mineral and Energy Resources

This pit in Brazil is one of the world's largest iron ore mines. Mineral and energy resources are essential to human societies, but extracting and using these resources has environmental consequences.

(b) ©Photoshot USA/Canada; (tcr) ©Rafael Macia/Photo Researchers, Inc.; (t) ©Dale O'Dell/Alamy Images; (tcr) ©Accent Alaska.com/Alamy Images

Chapter 16

Mining and Mineral Resources

Section 1
Minerals and Mineral Resources

Section 2
Mineral Exploration and Mining

Section 3
Mining Regulations and Mine Reclamation

Why It Matters

This open-pit copper mine in Arizona has changed the landscape dramatically.

When the mine is closed, how might the land be reclaimed to minimize environmental cost?

CASESTUDY

Learn more about how mining affects the environment in the case study Hydraulic Mining in the California Goldfields on pages 418–419.

ONLINE ENVIRONMENTAL SCIENCE
HMDScience.com

Go online to access additional resources, including labs, worksheets, multimedia, and resources in Spanish.

©Dale O'Dell/Alamy Images

Minerals and Mineral Resources

Take a look at the human-made objects that surround you. Almost every solid object you see is made from minerals. As shown in **Figure 1.1**, we depend on the use of mineral resources in almost every aspect of our daily lives. The current challenge is to obtain minerals at minimal cost to the environment. In this chapter, you will learn about minerals and the environmental effects of mining.

What Is a Mineral?

A **mineral** is a naturally occurring, usually inorganic solid that has a characteristic chemical composition, an orderly internal structure, and a characteristic set of physical properties. Minerals are made up of atoms of a single element, or of *compounds*—atoms of two or more elements chemically bonded together. The atoms that make up minerals are arranged in regular, repeating geometric patterns. The arrangement of the atoms, along with the strength of the chemical bonds between them, determine the physical properties of minerals.

The elements gold, silver, and copper are considered minerals. These types of minerals are called *native elements*. However, most minerals are compounds. For example, the mineral quartz is made up of silica, a compound consisting of one silicon atom and two oxygen atoms. When combined with other elements, silica forms most of the minerals that make up Earth's crust.

SECTION 1
Objectives

▶ Define the term *mineral*.

▶ Explain the difference between a metal and a nonmetal, and give two examples of each.

▶ Describe three processes by which ore minerals form.

Key Terms
mineral
ore mineral

✔ **CHECK FOR UNDERSTANDING**
Identify List three characteristics of all minerals.

📋 **FIELD**STUDY
Go to Appendix B to find the field study
Rock Ore Mineral?

FIGURE 1.1

Mineral Consumption Mineral consumption is greatest in developed countries, such as the United States. This graph shows the average amount of minerals a person in the United States will consume over his or her lifetime.

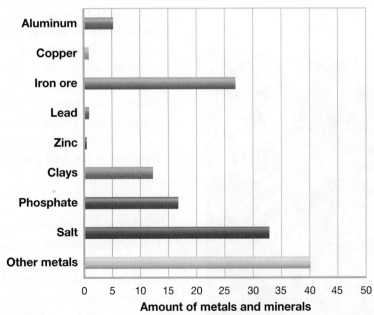

Amount of metals and minerals (in thousands of pounds)

Source: Mineral Information Institute.

FIGURE 1.2

Ore Minerals Certain minerals are mined because of the valuable metals they contain, as shown in the table. Wulfenite is a minor ore of lead. Nice specimens of wulfenite are also much sought after by mineral collectors.

SELECTED ELEMENTS AND THEIR ORE MINERALS

Element	Important ore minerals
Aluminum (Al)	gibbsite, boehmite, diaspore (bauxite)
Beryllium (Be)	beryl
Chromium (Cr)	chromite
Copper (Cu)	bornite, cuprite, chalcocite, chalcopyrite
Iron (Fe)	goethite, hematite, magnetite, siderite
Lead (Pb)	galena
Manganese (Mn)	psilomelane, pyrolusite
Mercury (Hg)	cinnabar
Molybdenum (Mo)	molybdenite
Nickel (Ni)	pentlandite
Silver (Ag)	acanthite
Tin (Sn)	cassiterite
Titanium (Ti)	ilmenite, rutile
Uranium (U)	carnotite, uraninite
Zinc (Zn)	sphalerite

FIGURE 1.3

Metallic Minerals Gold is one of the most economically important metallic minerals.

Ore Minerals

Minerals that are valuable and economical to extract are known as **ore minerals**. As shown in **Figure 1.2**, ore minerals contain elements, many of which are economically valuable. During the mining process, ore minerals, along with minerals that have no commercial value, or *gangue* (GANG) *minerals*, are extracted from the host rock. After extraction, mining companies use various methods to separate ore minerals from the gangue minerals. The ore minerals are then further refined to extract the valuable elements they contain. For mining to be profitable, the price of the final product must be greater than the costs of extraction and refining.

Metallic Minerals

Ore minerals are either metallic or nonmetallic. Metals conduct electricity, have shiny surfaces, and are opaque. Many valuable metallic minerals are native elements such as gold, shown in **Figure 1.3**. Silver and copper are also important native elements. Other important ore minerals are compounds in which metallic elements combine with nonmetallic elements, such as sulfur or oxygen.

Nonmetallic Minerals

Nonmetals tend to be good insulators, may have shiny or dull surfaces, and may allow light to pass through them. Nonmetallic minerals can also be native elements or compounds.

How Do Ore Minerals Form?

As shown in **Figure 1.4**, economically important ore deposits form in a variety of ways. The types of minerals that form depend on the environment in which they form. For example, metallic minerals form below ground when magma cools and hardens. The metallic minerals tend to form early in the cooling process and sink to the lower part of the magma body because they are denser. This process concentrates important ore minerals that can be extracted economically.

Hydrothermal Solutions

Hot, subsurface waters that contain dissolved minerals are called *hydrothermal solutions*. As hydrothermal solutions flow through cracks in rocks, they dissolve minerals they come in contact with. New minerals crystallize out of these solutions and then fill fractures to form ore deposits called *veins*.

CHECK FOR UNDERSTANDING
Explain How do evaporites form?

FIGURE 1.4

Mineral Environments Ore deposits form in different ways upon and beneath Earth's surface, and at the bottom of lakes and oceans.

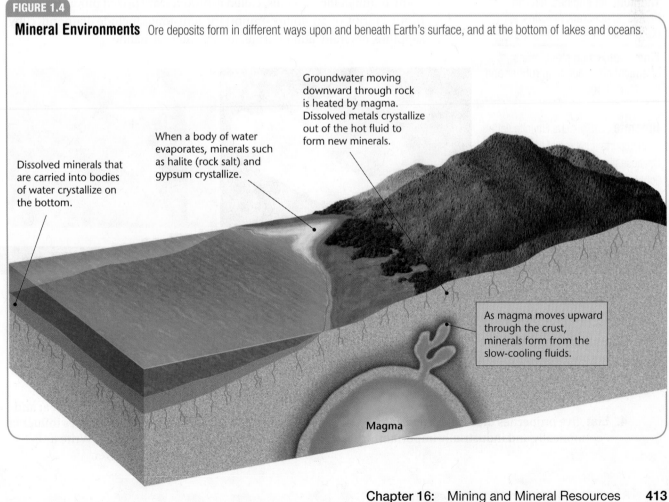

Groundwater moving downward through rock is heated by magma. Dissolved metals crystallize out of the hot fluid to form new minerals.

When a body of water evaporates, minerals such as halite (rock salt) and gypsum crystallize.

Dissolved minerals that are carried into bodies of water crystallize on the bottom.

As magma moves upward through the crust, minerals form from the slow-cooling fluids.

Magma

USES OF IMPORTANT METALLIC AND NONMETALLIC ELEMENTS

Aluminum: cans, foil; windows, doors, siding; appliances, cooking utensils; automobiles, aircraft

Copper: cables, wires; electrical and electronic products; plumbing, heating; alloys; coinage

Gold: computers; communications equipment; spacecraft; dentistry, medicine; jewelry

Iron: steel making

Lead: batteries; ammunition; glass; ceramics

Silicon: computer chips; glass; ceramics

Silver: photography; electrical and electronic products; mirrors; chemistry

Sulfur: sulfuric acid; gunpowder; rubber; fungicides

Titanium: jet engines, aircraft bodies, spacecraft, missiles; pigments

Zinc: coatings on steel; brass; chemical compounds in rubber and paints; coinage

Ilmenite The mineral ilmenite (left) is an important source of titanium. Because titanium is both strong and lightweight, it is used in aircraft such as this stealth fighter (right).

Evaporites

As rivers and streams wash over land surfaces, they dissolve salts and carry them into the sea or inland lakes. When the water in these seas or lakes evaporates, deposits of these salts, called *evaporites*, are left behind. Evaporites form in arid regions where rates of evaporation are high. Important evaporite minerals include halite (rock salt) and gypsum.

Mineral Resources and Their Uses

Certain metals are of major economic and industrial importance, as shown in **Figure 1.5**. Some metals can be pounded or pressed into various shapes or stretched very thinly without breaking. Other metals are good conductors of heat and electricity, or are prized for their durability and resistance to corrosion. Often, two or more metals are combined to form *alloys*. Alloys are important because they often combine the most desirable properties of the metals used to make them. Many new technologies depend on the mining of metallic minerals.

Nonmetals are among the most widely used minerals in the world. For example, gypsum has many applications in the construction industry. It is used to make drywall, or wallboard, for homes and commercial buildings. It is also a major component of concrete, which is used to build roads, buildings, and other structures. Industrial sand and gravel have uses that range from glassmaking to the manufacture of computer chips. Some nonmetallic minerals, called *gemstones*, are prized purely for their beauty, rarity, or durability. Important gemstones include diamond, ruby, sapphire, emerald, aquamarine, topaz, and tourmaline.

Section 1 **Formative Assessment**

▶ Reviewing Main Ideas

1. **Define** the term *mineral*.

2. **Explain** the difference between a metal and a nonmetal, and give examples of each.

3. **Describe** three processes by which minerals form.

4. **List** five properties that make metals economically and industrially important.

✔ Critical Thinking

5. **Analyzing Relationships** A mineral is a naturally occurring substance. Are synthetic minerals produced in laboratories minerals? Explain your answer.

6. **Making Comparisons** Unlike metals, nonmetals are not good conductors of heat and electricity. How might these properties influence the use of nonmetals in industry? Write a paragraph to explain your answer.

Placer Mining

When rock weathers and disintegrates, minerals within the rock are released. These minerals are concentrated by wind and water into surface deposits called **placer deposits**. The most important placer deposits are stream placers. Streams transport mineral grains to a point where they fall to the streambed and are concentrated. Concentration occurs at places where currents are weak and the dense mineral grains can no longer be carried in the water. These stream placers often occur at bends in rivers, where the current slows.

Placer deposits may form along coastlines from heavy minerals that wash down to the ocean in streams. These heavy minerals are concentrated by wave action.

Placer gold, diamonds, and other heavy minerals are mined by dredging. As shown in **Figure 2.7**, a dredge consists of a floating barge on which buckets fixed on a conveyor are used to excavate sediments in front of the dredge. Gold, diamonds, or heavy minerals are separated from the sediments within the dredge housing. The processed sediments are discharged via a conveyor that is located behind the dredge.

(tr) ©James L. Amos/Corbis; (bl) ©The Protected Art Archive/Alamy Images

FIGURE 2.7

Dredging This dredge is mining gold from placer deposits along a river on New Zealand's South Island.

Hydraulic mining in 1866, near French Corral, California.

Hydraulic mining proved to be an environmental disaster. Muddy water and sediments polluted rivers and caused them to fill with silt. The silt from the hydraulic mines traveled as far downstream as San Francisco and into the Pacific Ocean. As much as 1.4 to 3.6 million kilograms of mercury may have been released downstream, poisoning fish, amphibians, and invertebrates. Farmers in California's central valley sustained millions of dollars in damage as their fields were flooded when the sediment-choked Sacramento River overflowed its banks. But the farmers fought back. In January 1884, Judge Lorenzo Sawyer ruled that mine tailings could no longer be discharged into the rivers. The Sawyer decision was the first environmental ruling to be handed down in the United States. This ruling closed the door on hydraulic mining in the Sierra Nevada goldfields, where 2 billion cubic meters of soil and rocks had been carved from the mountainsides in just over 30 years.

Critical Thinking

1. **Making Inferences** What do you think were other environmental effects of hydraulic mining that were not mentioned in this article?

2. **Analyzing Relationships** Write a paragraph about how the mercury that was lost during hydraulic mining may still be affecting the environment today.

Surface Coal Mining
Procedure

1. Obtain a sample of some land (cream-filled cupcake).
2. Use a core sampler (toothpick) and carefully probe the surface to determine the depth and location of the coal seam.
3. Using your mining equipment (plastic spoon), carefully remove the topsoil (frosting) and overburden (cake above the filling); find and record the mass of each (in grams) and set them carefully aside.
4. Once you have reached the coal seam (cream-filled center), remove the coal (cream filling), find and record its mass and set it aside.
5. Restore the site by replacing the overburden and topsoil over the empty mine.

Analysis

1. Calculate the mass ratio of soil and overburden to coal.
2. How closely did the restored site resemble the land before it was mined?
3. What might need to be addressed to mine coal in a way that is environmentally sound?

FIGURE 2.8

Smelting At a smelter, ore is melted at high temperatures in a furnace to obtain a desired metal.

Smelting

In the process called **smelting**, crushed ore is melted at high temperatures in furnaces to separate impurities from molten metal. In the furnace, material called a *flux* bonds with impurities and separates them from the molten metal. The molten metal, which is desired, falls to the bottom of the furnace and is recovered. The flux and impurities, which are less dense, form a layer called *slag* on top of the molten metal. Gases such as sulfur dioxide form within the furnace and are captured, so they do not enter the environment. **Figure 2.8** shows a worker pouring molten aluminum from a ladle in a factory in China.

Undersea Mining

The ocean floor contains significant mineral resources, which include diamonds, precious metals such as gold and silver, mineral ores, and sand and gravel. Since the late 1950s, several attempts have been made to mine the ocean. These attempts met with varying degrees of success. Competition with land-based companies that can mine minerals more cheaply and the great water depths at which some mineral deposits are found are two of the reasons undersea mining has been largely unsuccessful to date.

Section 2 Formative Assessment

▶ Reviewing Main Ideas

1. **List** the steps in mineral exploration.
2. **Describe** three methods of subsurface mining.
3. **Describe** two methods of surface mining.
4. **Describe** the steps involved in smelting ore.
5. **Define** the term *placer deposit*, and explain how placer deposits form.

✔ Critical Thinking

6. **Making Comparisons** Read about surface and subsurface mining techniques. What are some of the advantages and disadvantages of each technique?

7. **Understanding Relationships** If a mining company were exploring a river for potential placer deposits, where are some likely places they would focus their exploration?

Mining Regulations and Mine Reclamation

SECTION 3

Objectives

▶ Describe seven important potential environmental consequences of mining.

▶ Name four federal laws that relate to mining and reclaiming mined land.

▶ Define the term *reclamation*.

▶ Describe two ways in which state governments regulate mining.

Key Terms

subsidence

reclamation

Growing world economies, new technologies, and increasing energy consumption fuel the need for raw materials. Increasing mining activity can alter enormous areas of land and water. This increases the potential for adverse environmental effects, even far from the location of mining.

Particularly in developed countries like the United States, mining operations are heavily regulated to reduce the negative environmental impacts, such as scars left on the landscape similar to those shown in **Figure 3.1**. For example, mining companies must develop a plan to reclaim the land before starting a mining operation. Most developing countries have more difficulty creating regulations or funding the enforcement of existing regulations. This results in considerable environmental and social harm. Even in developed countries, land altered by large-scale mining cannot be returned to its original condition, even with the best of intentions.

The Environmental Impacts of Mining

There are many environmental impacts of mining. In the United States, governments and mining companies are spending billions of dollars to clean up abandoned mines and to offset the negative effects of operating mines. In less-developed countries, mining that does not include environmental protection or restoration adversely affects human health and ecosystems.

FIGURE 3.1

Excavation At 215 m deep and 1.6 km in circumference, the "Big Hole" at the Kimberley Mine in South Africa is the largest hand-dug excavation in the world. By the time the mine closed in 1914, 22.5 million tons of rock had yielded almost 3,000 kg of diamonds.

©Phillip Richardson/Gallo Images/Corbis

Air and Noise Pollution

Smelting can release hazardous pollutants into the atmosphere. The smelting process involves high heat and the chemical reactions of substances that can be harmful to humans and other organisms. Metals, such as lead, mercury, and arsenic, can be toxic to plants and animals.

Surface mining can cause both air pollution and noise pollution. At surface coal mines, dust is produced by removing, loading, hauling, and dumping soil and overburden. Loading, hauling, and unloading rock all create dust emissions at open-pit mines. In addition, dust is created in open-pit mines when the ore-bearing rock is blasted apart.

Noise is created by the equipment that is used in a mine, as well as by blasting. Whereas equipment noise may be a nuisance, blasting can cause physical damage to nearby structures and organisms.

Water Contamination

Water resources can be negatively impacted by mining. Water that seeps into mines or through piles of excess rock can pick up or dissolve toxic substances like arsenic. These contaminants can wash into streams, where they can harm or kill aquatic life. Smelting also can add to water pollution.

Coal or minerals that contain sulfur can cause a similar problem. When these substances react with oxygen and water, they form dilute sulfuric acid. This acid can dissolve toxic minerals that remain in mines. The contaminated water that results from this process is known as *acid mine drainage,* or AMD. An example of AMD is shown in **Figure 3.2.** Mining regulation in the U.S. requires companies to dispose of acid-producing rock in such a way that water is not contaminated.

Displacement of Wildlife

Removing soil from a surface mine site strips away all plant life. With their natural habitat removed, animals will leave the area. In addition, when mining is completed and the soil is returned to the mine site, different plants and animals may establish themselves, which creates an entirely new ecosystem. These new ecosystems are often dominated by invasive rather than by native species.

Dredging can negatively affect aquatic ecosystems and physically change the bottoms of rivers. Dredging disturbs river bottoms and destroys aquatic plant life in the dredged portion of the river. The disturbance of a riverbed can cause sediments to contaminate a river for up to 10 km.

✔ **CHECK FOR UNDERSTANDING**

Explain Why does surface mining cause animals to leave an area?

FIGURE 3.2

Water Contamination Copper mines have polluted the Queen River in Tasmania with acid mine drainage. This photo shows the river flowing past residential housing.

Erosion and Sedimentation

Excess rock from mines is sometimes dumped into large piles called *dumps*. Running water erodes unprotected dumps and transports sediments into nearby streams. The sediments may harm water quality and aquatic life.

Soil Degradation

Soil at a mine site is removed from the uppermost layer downward. When this soil is stored for later reuse, care must be taken to ensure that the upper soil layers are not buried beneath soil layers that were originally below them. In this way, the soil layers that are richest in important nutrients are not covered. If soil is not removed and stored in separate layers, the soil may be nutrient poor when it is reclaimed.

Minerals that contain sulfur may be found in deeper soil layers. If these minerals are exposed to water and oxygen in the atmosphere, chemical reactions result in the release of acid, which then acidifies the soil. When the acidified soil is returned to the mine site, it may be difficult for plants to grow.

Subsidence

The sinking of regions of the ground with little or no horizontal movement is called **subsidence** (suhb SIED'ns). Subsidence occurs when pillars that have been left standing in mines collapse or the mine roof or floor fails.

Buildings, houses, roads, bridges, underground pipelines, and utilities that are built over abandoned mines could be damaged if the ground below them subsides. In November and December 2000, underground limestone mines that were several hundred years old collapsed in Edinburgh, Scotland. The collapse caused property damage and forced people to evacuate their homes. **Figure 3.3** shows the potential effects of mine subsidence.

Connect to MATH

Volume

Soil and overburden must be removed to reach a coal seam that is 10 m below Earth's surface. The exposed seam will be 1 km in length and 50 m wide. What is the total volume of soil and overburden that will have to be moved and stored? If the coal seam is 5 m thick, what is the volume of coal that will be removed? (Hint: The answers should be in m^3.) What is the ratio of overburden to coal?

✔ **CHECK FOR UNDERSTANDING**

Determine How might exposing deep soil layers to the atmosphere prevent plants from growing?

FIGURE 3.3

Subsidence A hole created by the subsidence of a gold mine swallowed this house in New Zealand.

©Dean Purcell/AP/Wide World Photos

FIGURE 3.4

Mine Fire This photo shows a coal seam that is on fire in a surface coal mine in China.

©Dr. Prakash/University of Arkansas, Geophysical Institute

ECOFACT

Bats and Mines

Over the past century, human disturbance of traditional bat roosting sites, such as caves and trees, has caused bats to move into abandoned mines. At present, 30 of the 45 species of bats in the United States live in mines. Some of the largest populations of endangered bat species now live in abandoned mines.

Underground Mine Fires

Fires that start in underground coal seams are one of the most serious environmental consequences of coal mining. Lightning, forest fires, and burning trash can all cause coal-seam fires. In addition, fires can start by themselves when minerals in the coal that contain sulfur are exposed to oxygen. These fires are hard to put out and are often left to burn themselves out, which may take decades or even centuries. For example, a fire that has been burning through an underground coal seam in an Australian mountain is estimated to be 2,000 years old! Underground fires that burn their way to the surface release smoke and gases that can cause respiratory problems. A fire in a coal seam is shown in **Figure 3.4.**

Mining Regulation and Reclamation

Mines on land in the United States are regulated by federal and state laws. To ensure that contaminants from mines do not threaten water quality, mining companies must comply with regulations of the Clean Water Act and the Safe Drinking Water Act. The release of hazardous substances into the air, soil, and water by mining is regulated by the Comprehensive Response Compensation and Liability Act. In addition, all mining operations must comply with the Endangered Species Act. This act ensures that mining activities will not affect threatened or endangered species and their habitats.

Reclamation

The process of returning land to its original or better condition after mining is completed is called **reclamation.** The Surface Mining Control and Reclamation Act of 1977 (SMCRA) created a program for the regulation of surface coal mining on public and private land. The act set standards that would minimize the surface effects of coal mining on the environment. SMCRA also established a fund that is administered by the federal government and is used to reclaim land and water resources that have been adversely affected by past coal-mining activities.

State Regulation of Mining

Within the United States, states have created programs to regulate mining on state and private lands. Mining companies must obtain permits from state environmental agencies before mining a site. These permits specify certain standards for mine design and reclamation. In addition, some states have bond forfeiture programs. In a bond forfeiture program, a mining company must post funds, called a *bond*, before a mining project begins. If the company does not mine and reclaim a site according to the standards required by its permits, the company must give these funds to the state. The state then uses the funds to reclaim the site. A surface mine in the process of reclamation is shown in **Figure 3.5**.

State agencies are also responsible for inspecting mines to ensure compliance with environmental regulations. Agencies issue violations to companies that do not comply with environmental regulations and assess fines for noncompliance. In addition, states such as Pennsylvania have begun large projects to reclaim abandoned mine lands. Acid mine drainage, mine fires, mine subsidence, and hazards related to open shafts and abandoned mining structures are all problems that these projects will attempt to correct.

FIGURE 3.5

Reclamation Reclamation often includes seeding, planting, and irrigating to return the land to its original state.

©Greenshoots Communication/Alamy Images

Section 3 Formative Assessment

Reviewing Main Ideas

1. **List** seven potential environmental impacts of mining.

2. **Name** four federal laws that regulate mining activities in the United States.

3. **Define** the term *reclamation*.

4. **Describe** two ways in which state governments regulate mining.

Critical Thinking

5. **Making Decisions** Give examples of environmental concerns that would be taken into account by a mining company when it created a reclamation plan for a mine site.

6. **Making Decisions** Read about how topsoil is removed and stored for later reclamation under the heading "Soil Degradation." How can this process be implemented to keep soils from degrading?

Mineral Production in the United States

TOP 10 MINERAL COMMODITIES PRODUCED IN THE UNITED STATES

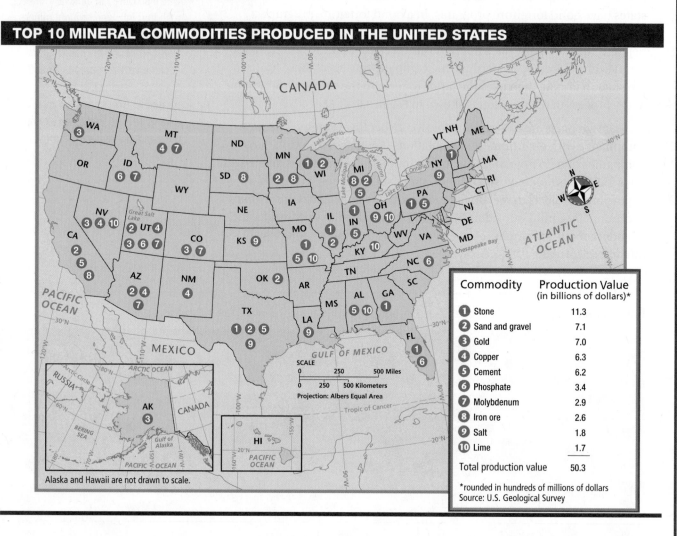

Alaska and Hawaii are not drawn to scale.

Commodity	Production Value (in billions of dollars)*
1 Stone	11.3
2 Sand and gravel	7.1
3 Gold	7.0
4 Copper	6.3
5 Cement	6.2
6 Phosphate	3.4
7 Molybdenum	2.9
8 Iron ore	2.6
9 Salt	1.8
10 Lime	1.7
Total production value	50.3

*rounded in hundreds of millions of dollars
Source: U.S. Geological Survey

MAP SKILLS

In 2009, the top 10 mineral commodities produced in the United States had a total value of about $50.3 billion. More than half of this production value came from the top three commodities: stone, sand and gravel, and gold. The map above shows the distribution of the production of these commodities by state. Use the map above to answer the following questions.

1. **Using a Key** Find your state on the map of mineral production. Which of the top 10 mineral commodities, if any, were produced in your state in 2009?

2. **Evaluating Data** Gold, copper, iron ore, and molybdenum are metals in the top 10 mineral commodities produced in 2009. What percentage of total 2009 production value do these metals represent? Which states were the principal producers of these metals in 2009?

3. **Evaluating Data** Stone, sand, and gravel are collectively known as *aggregates*. What percentage of total 2009 production value do aggregates represent? Which states were the major producers of aggregates in 2009?

4. **Using a Key** Which states produced salt in 2009?

Society and the Environment

ECOZine at HMDScience.com — Go online for the latest environmental science news and updates on all EcoZine articles.

Gold from Ghana

The world market price of gold rose from $260 to $1,730 per ounce between 2001 and 2012. Most people don't think about it, but the environmental and social consequences of this price increase have been substantial. This is especially true in countries where many people live in poverty. The situation in Ghana illustrates the complex interplay of societal and environmental processes that can lead to local crises or, alternatively, show cause for hope.

Ghana, which is located on the west coast of Africa, has an unusual geological history in which gold deposits were concentrated in several bands that cover about one-sixth of the country. Historical records show that gold began to be exported from Ghana starting in the 16th century, and now Ghana is Africa's second largest producer of gold. Much of the gold is in deposits suitable for large-scale mining operations, but a substantial amount is located in river deposits that can be mined in small operations with primitive equipment.

The government of Ghana is working diligently to overcome the economic challenges remaining from a history of colonial exploitation. Until recently, export earnings depended on just a few commodities. While Ghana's primary product for world trade used to be cocoa, gold is now the country's most important export. The literacy rate was 67% in 2009 (up from 58% in 2000), and about 28% of the population lives below the poverty level. In order to improve economic opportunity (and to recover some income), the Ghanaian government passed laws to regulate small-scale gold mining.

Underground mines in Ghana provide about 90% of exported gold. At least some of these large operations use environmentally friendly processes, such as bacterial oxidation instead of separating gold from other material with toxic mercury. Small-scale gold mining produces 10% of Ghana's gold. This segment of the industry is performed by people who lack the resources to apply modern gold-mining methods. In small-scale mining, gold is separated from alluvial sediments with environmentally harmful processes.

Using mercury is the most harmful process by which gold can be extracted from sediments. Mercury that enters the environment through water or air is toxic to humans and

Geologists and miners inspect core samples at an underground gold mine in Obuasi, Ghana.

ecological systems. Mercury-containing fumes are carried far from extraction sites, and mercury contaminates agricultural areas and drinking water. In addition, small-scale gold extraction can redirect rivers, increase erosion, and cause water pollution from acid-bearing rocks exposed by the mining. Contaminated and stagnant water increase diseases. These problems create major challenges to economic advancement for impoverished people.

While providing much-needed economic benefits for Ghana and many of its people, small-scale gold mining may be harming the long-term future of agriculture, including economically valuable cocoa and coffee plantations. Poisoning people and damaging subsistence agriculture add to the problems. The government is trying to address these issues, but people in poverty appear to have few options.

What Do You Think?

What are some strategies that you think would help reduce the environmental damage caused by gold extraction?

SECTION 1 Minerals and Mineral Resources

OBJECTIVES

- A mineral is a naturally occurring, usually inorganic solid that has a characteristic chemical composition, an orderly physical structure, and a characteristic set of physical properties.
- Minerals that are valuable and economical to extract are known as *ore minerals*.
- Ore minerals may form from the cooling of magma, the circulation of hot-water solutions through rocks, and the evaporation of water that contains salts.
- Metals are important economically because of their electrical and thermal conductivity, durability, and heat and corrosion resistance.

KEY TERMS

mineral
ore mineral

SECTION 2 Mineral Exploration and Mining

OBJECTIVES

- Mining companies conduct mineral exploration to identify areas where there is a high likelihood of finding valuable mineral resources in quantities worth mining.
- Room-and-pillar mining, longwall mining, and solution mining are subsurface mining methods.
- Open-pit mining, surface coal mining, quarrying, and solar evaporation are surface-mining methods.
- Minerals are concentrated by wind and water into surface deposits called *placer deposits*.
- Smelting is the process in which ore is melted at high temperatures to separate impurities from the molten metal.

KEY TERMS

subsurface mining
surface mining
placer deposit
smelting

SECTION 3 Mining Regulations and Mine Reclamation

OBJECTIVES

- Some of the environmental consequences of mining may include air and noise pollution, water contamination, displacement of wildlife, erosion and sedimentation, soil degradation, subsidence, and underground mine fires.
- The U.S. government has enacted legislation that regulates mining and attempts to minimize the impact of mining on the environment.
- Federal and state agencies issue permits to mining companies, issue violations and assess penalties when mining companies do not comply with standards set by their permits, and ensure that abandoned mine lands are reclaimed.

KEY TERMS

subsidence
reclamation

Reviewing Key Terms

Use each of the following terms in a separate sentence.

1. *mineral*
2. *placer deposit*
3. *smelting*
4. *subsidence*
5. *reclamation*

For each pair of terms, explain how the meanings of the terms differ.

6. *element* and *mineral*
7. *ore mineral* and *gangue mineral*
8. *placer deposit* and *dredging*
9. *subsurface mining* and *surface mining*
10. **Concept Map** Use the following terms to create a concept map: *subsurface mining, surface mining, room-and-pillar mining, longwall mining, solution mining, open-pit mining, surface coal mining,* and *quarrying.*

Reviewing Main Ideas

11. Which of the following statements does *not* correctly describe a mineral?
    a. A mineral is a naturally occurring substance.
    b. A mineral is an organic substance.
    c. A mineral is a solid substance.
    d. A mineral has a characteristic chemical composition.

12. Gold, silver, and copper are
    a. nonmetallic minerals.
    b. native elements.
    c. compounds.
    d. gangue minerals.

13. Ore deposits form from
    a. the cooling of magma.
    b. the evaporation of water that contains salts.
    c. the circulation of hot-water solutions in rocks.
    d. All of the above

14. Which of the following economically important elements is *not* a metal?
    a. zinc
    b. titanium
    c. copper
    d. sulfur

15. Which of the following methods is *not* a subsurface mining method?
    a. quarrying
    b. solution mining
    c. longwall mining
    d. room-and-pillar mining

16. Which of the following mining methods would most likely be used to mine salt?
    a. solution mining
    b. open-pit mining
    c. solar evaporation
    d. both (a) and (c)

17. Dredging would *not* be used to mine
    a. diamonds.
    b. salt.
    c. heavy minerals.
    d. gold.

18. Which of the following elements in minerals causes soil to become acidified?
    a. potassium
    b. calcium
    c. sulfur
    d. barium

19. Which of the following pieces of federal legislation established a program for regulating coal mining on public and private lands?
    a. the Comprehensive Response and Liability Act
    b. the Clean Air Act
    c. the Clean Water Act
    d. the Surface Mining Control and Reclamation Act of 1977

Short Answer

20. What is the difference between native elements and compounds?

21. Describe the solar evaporation process.

22. What are the surface and subsurface methods by which coal is commonly mined?

23. Explain why undersea mining has been largely unsuccessful to date.

24. Describe how reclaimed soil may become degraded.

25. Explain the purpose of a state bond forfeiture program.

Interpreting Graphics

The graph below shows total U.S. mineral production from 2006 to 2010. Use the graph to answer questions 26–27.

26. In 2006, metals accounted for $23 billion of the $39 billion total U.S. production of minerals. Metals accounted for what percentage of the total U.S. production of minerals?

27. In 2010, metals accounted for $29 billion of the $35 billion total U.S. production of minerals. Metals accounted for what percentage of the total U.S. production of minerals?

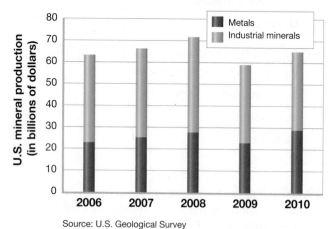

**Changes in U.S. Mineral Production
2006–2010**

Source: U.S. Geological Survey

Critical Thinking

28. Analyzing Relationships Read about the technological changes in the mining industry that are discussed in the introduction to Section 2. What method or methods of mining seem well suited for automation, particularly robotics?

29. Making Decisions Mining companies use computer models to show them where high- and low-grade ores are located in the deposit that they are mining. If the price of the ore mineral that a company is mining suddenly increases, how would computer modeling help the company economically exploit the mineral deposit to take advantage of the increase in price?

30. Social Studies Fifteen to 20 miles southwest of Santa Fe, New Mexico, are a series of low hills known as Los Cerrillos. Native Americans mined the blue-green gemstone turquoise from narrow veins in rock from these hills for more than 1,000 years, beginning in about the year 875. Research Native American mining at Los Cerrillos, New Mexico. Write a short report about your findings.

31. Debate A mining company has applied for permits to establish a surface mine on land that is located near a stretch of river in which an endangered species of fish lives. Assume that the ore to be mined is rare and has important new applications in cancer treatment. Weighing both sides of the argument, would you issue the permits? Make your case for or against issuing the mining permits in a debate with your classmates.

Analyzing Data

32. Making Calculations Some low-grade gold ores that have been mined economically average about 0.1 oz of gold per ton of ore. Five tons of rock must be removed to obtain one ton of ore. How many tons of rock must be mined to obtain 1 oz of gold? How many pounds of ore must be processed to obtain 1 oz of gold?

Making Connections

33. Communicating Main Ideas One of the main ideas of this chapter is that the human need for minerals requires mining companies to continually find new deposits of minerals that can be extracted inexpensively. Extraction must be done in such a way that the environment is not severely affected. Using surface coal mining or open-pit mining as an example, explain why it is difficult to mine large ore deposits without affecting the environment.

34. Writing Persuasively A mining company is applying for permits to establish an open-pit mine near your home. Do research to determine what impact, if any, the operation will have on your quality of life, the environment, and the economics of your community. Summarize your findings in a concise one-page paper.

35. Outlining Topics You are an exploration geologist who works for a mining company. You are searching for a new deposit of an ore mineral. Outline the steps you would take to find a deposit and to determine whether that deposit would be economical to mine.

CASESTUDY

36. How does hydraulic mining lead to flooding downstream from the mining site?

37. Besides the California gold rush, where else has hydraulic mining been used? Research at least one other type of hydraulic mining operation. How was the environment affected by the mining operation that you researched?

Why It Matters

38. This copper mine presents environmental challenges, but copper is a widely used, very important resource. Research and describe several uses of copper.

STUDYSKILL

Using Terms Work together with a study partner. Learn the definitions of both the boldfaced and italicized words that appear in this chapter. When both you and your partner feel confident in having learned the meanings of these terms, take out a piece of paper. On this paper, you and your partner will each write a one-page essay in which you use as many of these terms as possible. When you both are finished, exchange essays and review them for accuracy.

Extraction of Copper from Its Ore

Objectives

Extract copper from copper carbonate in much the same way that copper is extracted from malachite ore.

Hypothesize how this process can be applied to extract other metallic elements from ores.

Materials

Bunsen burner

copper (cupric) carbonate

funnel

iron filings

sulfuric acid, dilute

test-tube holder

test-tube rack

test tubes, 13 mm x 100 mm (2)

water

Most metals are combined with other elements in the Earth's crust. A material in the crust that is a profitable source of an element is called an *ore*. Malachite (MAL uh KIET) is the basic carbonate of copper. The green corrosion that forms on copper because of weathering has the same composition that malachite does. The reactions of malachite are similar to those of copper carbonate.

In this investigation, you will extract copper from copper carbonate using heat and dilute sulfuric acid. The process you will be using will be similar to the process in which copper is extracted from malachite ore.

Procedure

1. **CAUTION:** Wear your laboratory apron, gloves, and safety goggles throughout the investigation. Fill one of the test tubes about one-fourth full of copper carbonate. Record the color of the copper carbonate.

2. Light the Bunsen burner, and adjust the flame.

3. Heat the copper carbonate by holding the tube over the flame with a test-tube holder, as shown in the figure on the next page. **CAUTION:** When heating a test tube, point it away from yourself and other students. To prevent the test tube from breaking, heat it slowly by gently moving the test tube over the flame. As you heat the copper carbonate, observe any changes in color.

4. Continue heating the tube over the flame for 5 min.

5. Allow the test tube to cool. Observe any change in the volume of the material in the test tube. Then, place the test tube in the test-tube rack. Insert a funnel in the test tube, and add dilute sulfuric acid until the test tube is three-fourths full. **CAUTION:** Avoid touching the sides of the test tube, which may be hot. If any of the acid gets on your skin or clothing, rinse immediately with cool water and alert your teacher.

Copper Ore Malachite is a carbonate of copper that commonly forms in copper deposits. It is sometimes used as an ore of copper.

6. Allow the test tube to stand until some of the substance at the bottom of the test tube dissolves. After the sulfuric acid has dissolved some of the solid substance, note the color of the solution.

7. Use a second test tube to add more sulfuric acid to the first test tube until the first test tube is nearly full. Allow the first test tube to stand until more of the substance at the bottom of the test tube dissolves. Pour this solution (copper sulfate) into the second test tube.

8. Add a small number of iron filings to the second test tube. Observe what happens.

9. Clean all of the laboratory equipment, and dispose of the sulfuric acid as directed by your teacher.

Step 3 To heat the copper carbonate, hold the tube over the flame with a test-tube holder. Point the test tube away from yourself and other students.

Analysis

1. **Explaining Events** Disregarding any condensed water on the test-tube walls, what do you call the substance formed in the first test tube? Explain any change in the volume of the new substance relative to the volume of the copper carbonate.

2. **Explaining Events** When the iron filings were added to the second test tube, what indicated that a chemical reaction was taking place? Explain any change to the iron filings. Explain any change in the solution.

Conclusions

3. **Drawing Conclusions** Why was sulfuric acid used to extract copper from copper carbonate?

Extension

4. **Analyzing Data** Suppose that a certain deposit of copper ore contains a minimum of 1 percent copper by mass and that copper sells for $0.30 per kilogram. Approximately how much could you spend to mine and process the copper from 100 kg of copper ore and remain profitable?

5. **Making Comparisons** How is the process used in this experiment similar to the cyanide heap-leaching process used to extract gold from low-grade ore?

Chapter 17

Nonrenewable Energy

Section 1
Energy Resources and
Fossil Fuels

Section 2
Nuclear Energy

Why It Matters

The towers in this plant process
petroleum into its component
parts. What are a few different
products that are made
from petroleum?

CASESTUDY

Learn more about technologies
used to access natural gas in
the feature The "Gas" Rush—
Deep Hydraulic Fracturing on
pages 440–441.

**ONLINE
ENVIRONMENTAL SCIENCE**
HMDScience.com

Go online to access additional
resources, including labs,
worksheets, multimedia, and
resources in Spanish.

©Accent Alaska.com/Alamy Images

Energy Resources and Fossil Fuels

SECTION 1

Objectives

▸ List five factors that influence the value of a fuel.

▸ Explain how fuels are used to generate electricity in an electric power plant.

▸ Identify patterns of energy consumption and production in the world and in the United States.

▸ Explain how fossil fuels form and how they are used.

▸ Compare the advantages and disadvantages of fossil-fuel use.

▸ List three factors that influence predictions of fossil-fuel production.

How does a sunny day 200 million years ago relate to your life today? Chances are that if you traveled to school today or used a product made of plastic, you used some of the energy from sunlight that fell on Earth several hundred million years ago. Life as we know it would be very different without the fuels or products formed from plants and animals that lived even before the dinosaurs.

The fuels we use to run cars, ships, planes, and factories, and to produce electricity, are natural resources. Most of the energy we use comes from a group of natural resources called *fossil fuels*. **Fossil fuels** are the remains of ancient organisms that changed into coal, oil, or natural gas. Fossil fuels are central to life in modern societies, yet there are two main problems with fossil fuels. First, the supply of fossil fuels is limited. Second, obtaining and using them causes environmental problems. In the 21st century, societies will continue to explore alternatives to fossil fuels but will also focus on developing more-efficient ways to use these fuels.

Fuels for Different Uses

Fuels are used for five main purposes: cooking, transportation, manufacturing, heating and cooling buildings, and generating electricity to run machines and appliances. The suitability of a fuel for each application depends on the fuel's energy content, cost, availability, and safety, and the byproducts of the fuel's use. For example, it is hard to imagine an airplane, such as the one shown in **Figure 1.1**, running on coal. Although coal is readily available and inexpensive, to power an airplane using coal would require hundreds of tons of coal. Likewise, the people shown around the campfire are not warming themselves by burning airplane fuel, they are burning wood, which is a perfect fuel for their needs.

Key Terms

fossil fuels
electric generator
petroleum
oil reserves

FIGURE 1.1

Different Fuels, Different Purposes The airplane (left) is being refueled with a highly refined liquid fuel. Airplane fuel must have a high ratio of energy to weight. The campers (right) are keeping warm by burning wood in an open fire.

(br) ©Richard Hutchings/Photo Researchers, Inc.; (bl) ©Fstop/Alamy Images

Electricity—Power on Demand

The energy in fuels is often converted into electrical energy in order to power machines, because electricity is more convenient to use. Computers, for example, run on electricity rather than oil. Electricity can be transported quickly across great distances, such as an entire state, or across tiny distances, such as inside a computer chip. The electricity that powers the lights in your school was generated in a power plant and then carried to users through a distribution grid like the one shown in **Figure 1.2**. Two disadvantages of electricity are that it is difficult to store and other energy sources have to be used to generate it.

How Is Electricity Generated?

An **electric generator** is a machine that converts mechanical energy, or motion, into electrical energy. Generators produce electrical energy by moving an electrically conductive material within a magnetic field. Most commercial electric generators convert the movement of a turbine into electrical energy, as shown in **Figure 1.3**. A *turbine* is a wheel that changes the force of a moving gas or liquid into energy that can do work. In most power plants, water is boiled to produce the steam that turns the turbine. The water is heated by burning a fuel in coal-fired and gas-fired plants or from the fission of uranium in nuclear plants. The turbine spins a generator to produce electricity.

FIGURE 1.2

Electricity These pylons and wires are part of an electricity distribution grid in upstate New York.

FIGURE 1.3

How a Coal-Fired Power Plant Works

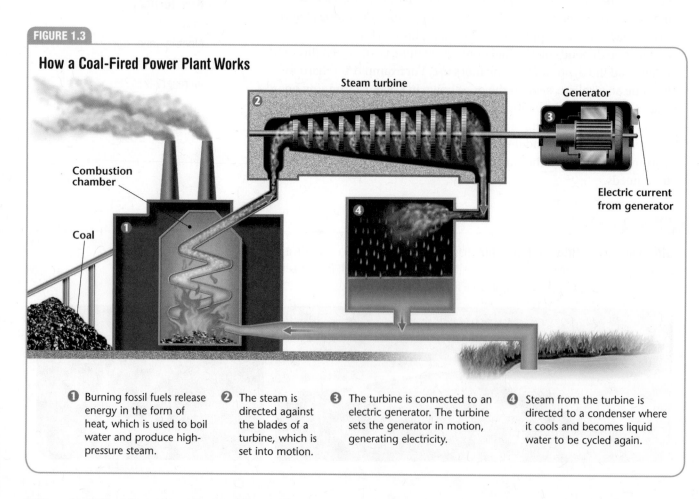

1 Burning fossil fuels release energy in the form of heat, which is used to boil water and produce high-pressure steam.

2 The steam is directed against the blades of a turbine, which is set into motion.

3 The turbine is connected to an electric generator. The turbine sets the generator in motion, generating electricity.

4 Steam from the turbine is directed to a condenser where it cools and becomes liquid water to be cycled again.

©Photoshot USA/Canada

FIGURE 1.4

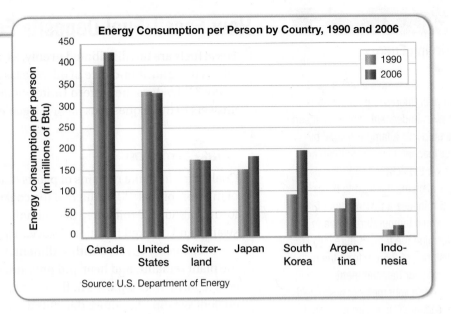

Energy Consumption During the period from 1990 through 2006, energy use per person stayed about the same in Switzerland and in the United States. Energy use per person in South Korea approximately doubled.

Energy Consumption per Person by Country, 1990 and 2006

Source: U.S. Department of Energy

Energy Use

Every product requires energy to produce. And the price of most products and services that you use reflects the cost of energy. Buying a plane ticket, for example, includes the cost of the fuel.

World Patterns

People in developed countries use much more energy than people in developing countries do. However, energy use in some developing countries is growing rapidly. Even within the developed world there are striking differences in energy use. For example, **Figure 1.4** shows that a person in Canada or the United States uses more than twice as much energy as a person in Japan or Switzerland does. Yet personal income in Japan and Switzerland is higher than personal income in Canada and the United States. One reason for this difference lies in how energy is generated and used in those countries.

Energy Use in the United States

Among the developed countries, the United States uses more energy per person than most other countries in the world. Part of the reason that the United States uses so much energy is that, as **Figure 1.5** shows, the United States uses more than 25 percent of its energy resources to transport goods and people, mainly by trucks and personal vehicles. In contrast, Japan and Switzerland have extensive rail systems and they are relatively small, compact countries. The availability and cost of fuels also influence fuel use. Residents of the United States and Canada enjoy some of the lowest gasoline taxes in the world. There is little incentive to conserve gasoline when its cost is so low.

FIGURE 1.5

U.S. Energy Use This graph shows the percentages of total energy use in the United States for different purposes.

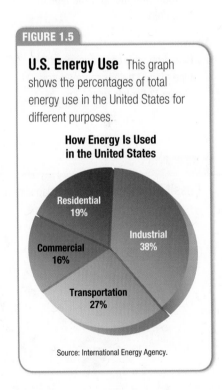

How Energy Is Used in the United States

Residential 19%

Commercial 16%

Industrial 38%

Transportation 27%

Source: International Energy Agency.

✔ **CHECK FOR UNDERSTANDING**

List Give two reasons why the United States uses more energy per person compared with most other countries.

How Fossil-Fuel Deposits Form

Fossil fuels are not distributed evenly, as shown in **Figure 1.6**. For example, why is there an abundance of oil in Texas and Alaska but very little in Maine? Why does the eastern United States produce so much coal? The answers to these questions lie in the geologic history of the areas.

Coal Formation

Coal forms from the remains of plants that lived in swamps hundreds of millions of years ago. Much of the coal in the eastern United States formed about 320 million to 300 million years ago, when vast areas of swampland covered this area. As ocean levels rose and fell, these swamps were repeatedly covered with sediment. Layers of sediment compressed the plant remains, and heat and pressure within the Earth's crust caused coal to form. Coal deposits in the western United States also formed from ancient swamps, but those deposits are much younger. The abundant coal deposits in states such as Wyoming formed between 100 million and 40 million years ago.

Oil and Natural Gas Formation

Oil and natural gas result from the decay of tiny marine organisms that accumulated on the bottom of the ocean millions of years ago. After these remains were buried by sediments, they were heated until they became complex, energy-rich molecules. Over time, the molecules migrated into the porous rocks that now contain them. Much of the oil and natural gas in the United States is located in Texas, North Dakota, California, Alaska, Oklahoma, and the Gulf of Mexico.

FIGURE 1.6

Fossil Fuel Deposits This map shows the approximate locations of coal, oil, and natural gas deposits in the United States.

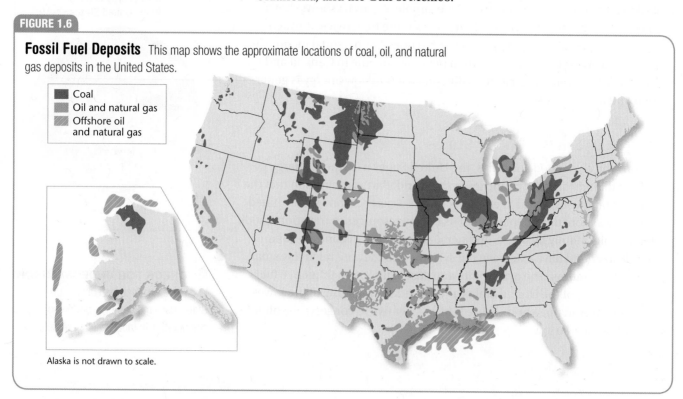

- Coal
- Oil and natural gas
- Offshore oil and natural gas

Alaska is not drawn to scale.

FIGURE 1.7

Energy Production The Middle East produces the largest share of the world's oil. Asia, however, produces the most coal.

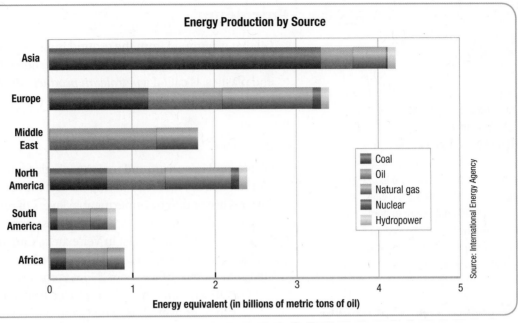

Energy Production by Source

Asia
Europe
Middle East
North America
South America
Africa

Legend:
- Coal
- Oil
- Natural gas
- Nuclear
- Hydropower

Source: International Energy Agency

Energy equivalent (in billions of metric tons of oil)

Coal

Most of the world's fossil-fuel reserves are made up of coal. Asia and North America are particularly rich in coal deposits, as shown in **Figure 1.7**. Two major advantages of coal are that it is relatively inexpensive and that it needs little refining after it has been mined. A little more than a third of the electricity generated in the United States comes from coal-fired power plants, as shown in **Figure 1.8**.

Coal Mining and the Environment

The environmental effects of coal mining vary. Underground mines can have a minimal effect on the environment at the surface. However, surface coal-mining operations sometimes remove the top of an entire mountain to reach the coal deposit. In addition, if waste rock from coal mines is not properly contained, toxic chemicals can leach into nearby streams. A lot of research focuses on developing better methods of locating the most productive, clean-burning coal deposits and developing less damaging methods of mining coal.

Air and Water Pollution

The quality of coal varies. Higher-grade coals, such as bituminous coal, produce more heat and less pollution than a lower-grade coal, such as lignite. Sulfur, which is found in all grades of coal, can be a major source of pollution when coal is burned. When high-sulfur, low-grade coal is burned, it releases much more pollution than a low-sulfur bituminous coal does. The air pollution and acid precipitation that result from burning high-sulfur coal without adequate pollution controls are serious problems in some countries. Ash from burning coal must be stored, and the toxic materials from coal ash can pollute both air and water. Carbon dioxide produced by burning coal contributes to climate change.

FIGURE 1.8

U.S. Electricity Generation

About one-third of the electricity generated in the U.S. comes from burning coal at power plants, such as the one pictured below.

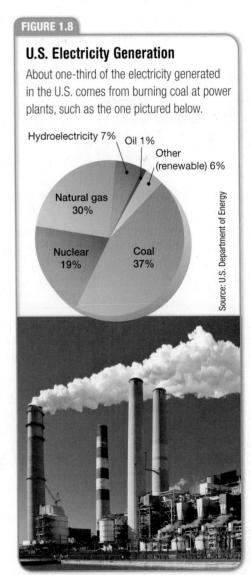

Hydroelectricity 7%
Oil 1%
Other (renewable) 6%
Natural gas 30%
Nuclear 19%
Coal 37%

Source: U.S. Department of Energy

©James Schwabel/Alamy Images

Catalytic Converters

Catalytic converters are one of the most important emission-control features on cars. These devices use two separate catalysts—a *reduction catalyst* and an *oxidation catalyst*. The reduction catalyst uses platinum and rhodium to separate nitrous oxides, forming nitrogen and oxygen molecules. The oxidation catalyst uses platinum and palladium to burn—or oxidize—hydrocarbons and carbon monoxide, forming carbon dioxide, which is less harmful.

✔ **CHECK FOR UNDERSTANDING**

Explain What is the purpose of drilling exploration wells for oil?

Petroleum

Oil that is pumped from the ground is also known as *crude oil*, or **petroleum**. Anything that is made from crude oil, such as fuels, chemicals, and plastics, is called a *petroleum product*. Much of the world's energy needs are met by petroleum products.

Locating Oil Deposits

Oil is found in and around major geologic features, such as folds, faults, and salt domes, that tend to trap oil as it moves in Earth's crust. These features are bound by impermeable layers of rock, which prevent the oil from escaping. The world's largest oil reserves are in the Middle East. Large oil deposits also exist in Venezuela, Canada, Russia, the United States, Libya, and Nigeria. The first oil well was 70 feet (21 m) deep in an area with many surface seeps. Now, some exploratory wells reach 35,000 feet (10,685 m). After the oil is removed from a well, it is transported to a refinery to be converted into fuels and other petroleum products.

The "Gas" Rush—Deep Hydraulic Fracturing

New technologies and innovative methods are needed to access unconventional sources of fossil fuels, such as the natural gas that is trapped in shales thousands of feet below Earth's surface. These technologies sometimes raise concerns about environmental consequences, but high levels of uncertainty about these consequences have led to ongoing political and scientific debates.

One example is hydraulic fracturing (*fracking*). Fracking is the use of fluid pressure to fracture rocks so that trapped oil or gas can flow to a well. The technique has been applied to extract oil and gas for decades. So what is new? Fracking is being done on a larger scale and now is combined with horizontal drilling. Fluids used in fracking include water and chemical additives to reduce friction, inhibit corrosion and bacterial growth, and reduce viscosity. Though many components are not toxic, some are problematic and many are kept secret. Fracking fluid—often millions of gallons per well—is injected under very high pressure. Once the pressure in the well is released, some fluid moves back to the well head (*flowback*). Fifteen to 80% of flowback is recovered for cleaning, reuse, or disposal.

Horizontal drilling increases the reach of a well four to five kilometers in several directions from the vertical bore. Because of favorable economic

Test drilling sites like the one pictured find gas contained within layers of shale rock. When found, gas is extracted using hydraulic fracturing.

The Environmental Effects of Using Oil

When petroleum fuels are burned, they release pollutants. Internal combustion engines in vehicles that burn gasoline and diesel pollute the air in many cities. These pollutants contribute to the formation of smog and cause health problems. Emissions regulations and technology such as catalytic converters have reduced air pollution in many areas. However, in developing countries, cars are generally older, and the gasoline that they burn contains significantly more sulfur, a pollutant that contributes to acid precipitation. In addition, the carbon dioxide released from burning petroleum fuels may contribute to climate change.

Oil spills, such as the one shown in **Figure 1.9**, are another potential environmental problem of oil use. Drilling in deep water or very cold ecosystems is increasing, and potential spills from the drilling process are problematic. Compared with surface wells, stopping leaks is very difficult when the wellhead is 5,000 feet under water. In arctic ecosystems, cold temperatures hinder clean-up efforts. Non-point pollution from everyday sources, such as leaking cars or improperly handled motor oil, adds more pollution to waterways but is less obvious to the public.

©Andy Levin/Photo Researchers, Inc.

FIGURE 1.9

Oil Spills These workers are cleaning up a Puerto Rico shoreline after an oil spill.

conditions, the amount of shale gas recovered using fracking and horizontal drilling doubled from 2009 to 2010, and the U.S. Energy Information Administration predicts another tripling of such shale gas extraction by 2035.

Benefits of the new technologies are potentially large. Increased access within the United States would allow 65 times the current annual use of natural gas and could also decrease oil imports by about one-third. Employment would be increased within the fossil fuel industry because new wells are needed to keep up production (recoverable gas depletes quickly for each well). Burning natural gas produces less pollution than oil or coal, and increased use of natural gas has helped reduce carbon dioxide emissions in the United States. Some scientists, though, worry about other pollution created during natural gas production.

What are the issues? Having more and bigger wells will increase the amount of wastes and potential contamination of the environment. For example, air or surface waters could be contaminated with methane that is released during fracking. While some studies found methane from fracking in surface water, others have found no links between fracking and methane contamination of waters.

Keeping fracking fluid and flowback out of drinking water and surface streams is another concern. Scientists experimentally added hydrofracturing fluids to a forested area; ground plants died within days, and half the trees died within two years. Supporters of hydraulic fracturing tend to point to the isolation of the shale layers from surface waters. Little exchange is expected between surface waters and the horizontal fractures that are separated by thousands of feet of rock. The most likely sources of contamination would be from leakage in the casing of the well, at the site of the well, or from transport and processing of flowback water.

The risk from a single well may be small, but the risk per well must be multiplied by the tens of thousands of wells that might be drilled and the millions of gallons of flowback water that must be processed.

How do we decide? What sources would you consider to be most reliable in evaluating risks and benefits? Can we wait until more information is available?

Critical Thinking

How would your perception of acceptable risk differ depending on if you were a business that produces natural gas, or a homeowner with a private water well near a hydraulic fracturing operation, or a person in a city who uses natural gas for heating and cooking?

FIGURE 1.10

Natural Gas Vehicle Except when it is refueling, a vehicle that runs on natural gas looks like one that runs on gasoline or diesel.

Natural Gas

About 20 percent of the world's nonrenewable energy comes from natural gas. Natural gas, or methane (CH_4), is a good example of how advances in technology can make a fuel more common. In the past, when natural gas was encountered in an oil well, it was burned off because it was considered a nuisance. As technology improved, transporting natural gas in pipelines and storing it compressed in tanks became more practical. Now, many more oil wells recover natural gas. Because burning natural gas produces fewer pollutants than burning other fossil fuels, vehicles or power plants that run on natural gas, such as the one in **Figure 1.10**, require fewer pollution controls. However, methane is a potent greenhouse gas, so new technologies will be needed to reduce methane emissions at wells.

Fossil Fuels and the Future

In 2011, fossil fuels supplied about 82 percent of the energy used worldwide. The U.S. Energy Information Administration projects that by 2040 world energy demand will have increased by 54%, mainly as a result of economic growth in developing countries. As the demand for energy resources increases, the cost of fossil fuels will likely increase enough to make other energy sources more attractive. Taxes or caps on emissions also may enhance the attractiveness of alternative energy sources. Planning now for the energy we will use in the future is important because it takes many years for a new source of energy to make a significant contribution to our energy supply.

Predicting Oil Production

Oil production is still increasing, but it is increasing more slowly than it has in the past. Many different factors must be considered when predicting oil production. **Oil reserves** are oil deposits that can be extracted profitably at current prices using current technology. Although some oil deposits are yet to be discovered, the oil industry does not expect to find major new reserves. However, deposits such as oil sands, once considered too difficult or not profitable enough to access, are beginning to be tapped as technology improves and prices increase.

Finally, all predictions of future oil production are guided by an important principle: the relative cost of obtaining fuels influences the amount of fossil fuels that we extract from Earth. For example, as the supply of readily available oil decreases, we may begin to rely less on oil reserves and focus on using oil more selectively. At that time, oil will begin to be used more for applications in which it is essential. Cars and power plants, which can be powered in many ways, will begin to rely on other energy sources.

FIELDSTUDY

Go to Appendix B to find the field study **Ride Along.**

Connect to MATH

World Energy Use

In 1980, worldwide production of petroleum was 59.6 million barrels per day. In 2012, petroleum production was 74.6 million barrels a day. Calculate the percent increase in oil production during this period.

FIGURE 1.11

Offshore Oil Extraction This offshore oil rig is extracting petroleum from beneath the ocean floor.

Future Oil Reserves

According to the World Energy Council, global oil reserves in 2013 were 25 percent higher than in 1993. Geologists disagree about how soon oil production from fields accessible from land will peak, with predictions of peak oil ranging from 2020 to after 2050. Additional oil reserves are under the ocean, but extracting oil from beneath the ocean floor is very expensive.

Section 1 **Formative Assessment**

▶ Reviewing Main Ideas

1. **Describe** five factors that influence the value of a fuel.

2. **Describe** how fossil fuels are used to produce electricity, and explain how an electric generator works.

3. **Describe** how coal, oil, and natural gas form, how these fuels are used, and how using each fuel affects the environment.

✔ Critical Thinking

4. **Analyzing Relationships** What is the relationship between natural gas and petroleum?

5. **Making Comparisons** Read the description of how fossil-fuel deposits form. Are fossil fuels produced today by the same geologic processes as in the past?

6. **Making Inferences** There was a dramatic increase in oil production worldwide after 1950. What do you think accounts for the increase?

Nuclear Energy

In the 1950s and 1960s, nuclear power plants were seen as the power source of the future because the fuel they use is clean and plentiful. It was predicted that a nationwide network of nuclear power plants would provide electricity that was "too cheap to meter." But in the 1970s and 1980s, almost 120 planned nuclear power plants were canceled, and about 40 partially constructed nuclear plants were abandoned. What happened? In this section, you will learn how nuclear power works and why about 14 percent of the world's electricity comes from nuclear power today.

Key Terms

nuclear energy
nuclear fission
nuclear fusion

Fission: Splitting Atoms

Nuclear power plants get their power from **nuclear energy**, the energy within the nucleus of an atom. The forces that hold together the nucleus of an atom are more than 1 million times stronger than the chemical bonds between atoms. In nuclear power plants, atoms of the element uranium are used as the fuel.

The nuclei of uranium atoms are bombarded with atomic particles called *neutrons*. These collisions cause the nuclei to split in a process called **nuclear fission**. A fission reaction is shown in **Figure 2.1**. Nuclear fission releases a tremendous amount of energy and more neutrons, which in turn collide with more uranium nuclei. If a fission reaction is allowed to continue, this chain reaction will escalate quickly. One example of an uncontrolled fission reaction is the explosion of an atomic bomb. In contrast, nuclear power stations are designed so that the chain reaction is controlled and produces a controllable level of energy.

FIGURE 2.1

Nuclear Fission Neutrons are released from the fission, or the splitting, of a uranium atom's nucleus. Some of these neutrons then cause other atoms to undergo nuclear fission in a process called a *chain reaction*.

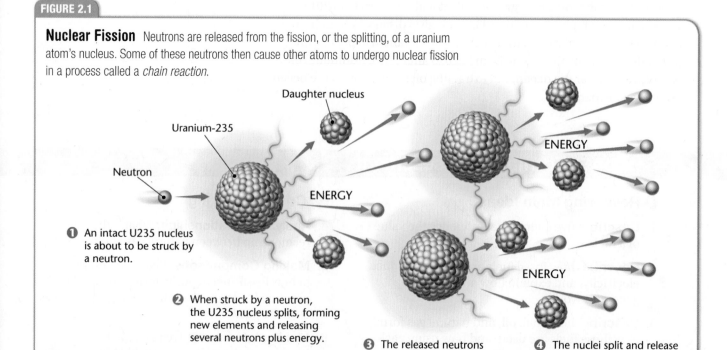

Daughter nucleus

Uranium-235

Neutron

ENERGY

ENERGY

ENERGY

❶ An intact U235 nucleus is about to be struck by a neutron.

❷ When struck by a neutron, the U235 nucleus splits, forming new elements and releasing several neutrons plus energy.

❸ The released neutrons strike other U235 nuclei.

❹ The nuclei split and release neutrons and energy.

How Nuclear Energy Works

A nuclear reactor is surrounded by a thick pressure vessel that is filled with a cooling fluid. The pressure vessel is designed to contain the fission products in case of an accident. Thick concrete walls also surround reactors, as shown in **Figure 2.2**.

Inside a reactor, shown in **Figure 2.3**, metal fuel rods that contain solid uranium pellets are bombarded with neutrons. The chain reaction that results releases energy and produces more neutrons. The reactor core contains control rods that control the rate of fission in the reactor. They do this by absorbing neutrons, which prevents the neutrons from causing fission reactions in the uranium fuel.

The heat released during nuclear reactions is used to generate electricity in the same way that power plants burn fossil fuels to generate electricity. In a nuclear power plant, energy released from the fission reactions heats a closed loop of water that heats another body of water. As the water boils, it produces steam that drives a steam turbine, which is used to generate electricity.

FIGURE 2.2

Nuclear Power Every year, the Diablo Canyon nuclear plant generates enough energy for 2 million Californian households—the energy equivalent of burning 20 million barrels of oil.

✔ **CHECK FOR UNDERSTANDING**

Explain What is the function of the pressure vessel of a nuclear reactor?

FIGURE 2.3

How a Typical Nuclear Power Plant Works

❷ The superheated water is pumped to a heat exchanger, which transfers the heat of the first circuit to the second circuit. Water in the second circuit flashes into high-pressure steam.

❸ Steam is directed against a turbine, setting it in motion. The turbine sets the generator in motion, generating electricity.

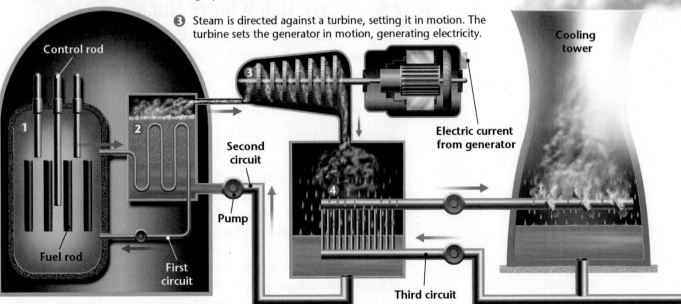

❶ Energy released by the nuclear reaction heats water in the pressurized first circuit to a very high temperature.

❹ A third circuit cools the steam from the turbine and the waste heat is released from the cooling tower in the form of steam.

Chapter 17: Nonrenewable Energy **445**

FIGURE 2.4

Uranium Uranium is a very compact fuel. A single uranium pellet (left) can generate as much energy as almost 1,800 pounds of coal.

(inset) ©RIA Novosti/Photo Researchers, Inc.; (tr) ©David R. Frazier Photolibrary, Inc./Alamy Images

The Advantages of Nuclear Energy

Nuclear energy has some advantages. Nuclear fuel is a very concentrated energy source, as shown in **Figure 2.4**. Furthermore, nuclear power plants do not produce greenhouse gases. When operated properly, nuclear plants release less radioactivity than coal-fired power plants do. Many countries with limited fossil-fuel reserves rely heavily on nuclear plants to supply electricity. France, for example, generates about three-fourths of its electricity from nuclear power. France produces less than one-fifth of the air pollutants per person than does the United States, which relies on fossil fuels for almost 75 percent of its electricity needs.

Why Aren't We Using More Nuclear Energy?

Building and maintaining a safe reactor is very expensive. The last 20 nuclear reactors built in the United States cost more than $3,000 per kilowatt of electrical capacity. In contrast, wind power is being installed at less than $1,000 per kilowatt. This cost will decrease as construction costs decrease.

Storing or Processing Waste

The difficulty of finding a safe place to store nuclear wastes is one of the greatest disadvantages of nuclear power. The fuel cycle of uranium produces fission products that remain dangerously radioactive for thousands of years. Uranium mining and fuel development produce radioactive wastes. In addition, the used fuel, liquids, and equipment from a reactor core are also considered hazardous wastes. Storage sites for nuclear wastes must be located in areas that are geologically stable for tens of thousands of years. The United States has spent decades unsuccessfully trying to develop a storage site. Scientists are also researching ways to recycle the radioactive elements in nuclear fuel. One political problem is that nuclear power can create materials for weapons.

CHECK FOR UNDERSTANDING

Explain Why is it so difficult to find a place that can be used to store nuclear waste safely?

Safety Concerns

In a poorly designed nuclear plant, the fission process can potentially get out of control. This is what happened during the world's worst nuclear reactor accident, which occurred due to poor design and human error at Chernobyl in the Ukraine in 1986. In 2011, an unusually large earthquake and tsunami overwhelmed the safety technologies of a nuclear power plant in Fukushima, Japan. Reactor meltdowns expelled radioactive materials into the air and ocean. The amounts of radiation released were about 10% of the levels from Chernobyl. The accident stimulated a reevaluation of nuclear technologies and policies in many countries.

The most serious nuclear accident in the United States occurred in 1979 at the Three Mile Island nuclear power plant in Pennsylvania. Human error, along with blocked valves and broken pumps, caused the accident. Fortunately, only a small amount of radioactive gas escaped. Since this accident, the U.S. Nuclear Regulatory Commission has required numerous safety improvements to nuclear power plants.

Connect to HISTORY

Three Mile Island
The Three Mile Island accident was a wake-up call for the nuclear industry. Many reforms and safety measures were instituted throughout the industry after the accident occurred. In 1989, 10 years after the accident, the nuclear plant at Three Mile Island received the best INPO rating in the world. The rating was based on a measure of reliability, efficiency, and safety. In 1999, the plant set a world record after running continuously for 688 days.

The Future of Nuclear Power

One possible future energy source is nuclear fusion. **Nuclear fusion** occurs when lightweight atomic nuclei combine to form a heavier nucleus and release huge amounts of energy. **Figure 2.5** illustrates the process of nuclear fusion. Nuclear fusion occurs in all stars, including our sun. Fusion is potentially a safer energy source than nuclear fission because it creates less dangerous radioactive byproducts. However, the technical problems are so complex that building a nuclear fusion plant may take decades or may never happen. The future of fission nuclear power will be influenced by new technologies that reduce the capital required to build plants. Possibilities include *light water reactors* or *high temperature gas reactors.* Researchers also are exploring technologies to use nuclear power to generate hydrogen, which can be used as a non-polluting fuel for transportation.

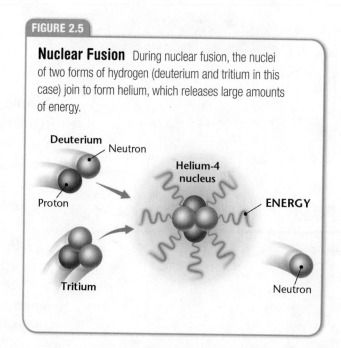

FIGURE 2.5

Nuclear Fusion During nuclear fusion, the nuclei of two forms of hydrogen (deuterium and tritium in this case) join to form helium, which releases large amounts of energy.

Deuterium
Neutron
Proton
Helium-4 nucleus
ENERGY
Tritium
Neutron

Section 2 **Formative Assessment**

▶ Reviewing Main Ideas

1. **Compare** a power plant that burns fossil fuels with a nuclear power plant.

2. **Describe** two advantages and two disadvantages of nuclear power plants.

3. **Explain** the difference between nuclear fission and nuclear fusion.

✔ Critical Thinking

4. **Applying Ideas** Read about the advantages of nuclear energy. Explain why countries such as France and Japan rely heavily on nuclear power.

5. **Making Decisions** Which poses more of an environmental threat: transporting spent nuclear fuel or transporting toxic chemicals? Write your opinion in the form of a short essay.

Pipelines and Oil Sands

Oil sands are mixtures of oil, clay, sand, and water. Many large deposits of oil sands are located in Canada.

The world needs oil. Oil is best known for its use as a fuel, but it also is used to make plastics, lubricants, and many chemicals. For decades, oil has been inexpensive and has been treated as an almost inexhaustible resource.

In the past decade, people have become more aware of the limited supplies of easily obtainable oil. Also, conflicts in oil-producing areas have limited supplies. Oil prices have skyrocketed. The price and new technologies have made it economically worthwhile to extract oil from places where it was once too expensive or too difficult to access.

Tar sands, which are also called oil sands, are one example of hard-to-get oil that is now being extracted. The oil from tar sands cannot be pumped out of the ground in the same way as in drilling operations. This is because the oil is very viscous and is mixed with clay, sand, and water. To access some oil sand deposits, huge mines must be dug that remove all of soils above the deposits. Then the oil and sediment mixture is extracted before the oil is separated. About two tons of sand are needed to produce one barrel of oil. This type of mining is very expensive and environmentally destructive, compared with other methods of extracting oil. New technologies are allowing oil to be extracted from deeper deposits.

There currently is debate about whether oil sands should be mined at all. The debate became even more intense in 2011 and 2012 because of a proposed pipeline—the Keystone XL pipeline—that would link the oil sands of Alberta, Canada to refineries in Texas. The Obama administration denied the permit to build the pipeline in 2012, but there are plans to submit a proposal for a similar pipeline that will take a different route.

The Case for the Pipeline

Supporters of the pipeline argue that the environmental impacts are outweighed by the creation of jobs and the enhancement of national security. Canada and the United States have been close trading partners and have been on good terms for decades. The same cannot be said of oil producers in the Middle East that supply much of the oil used in the United States. Also, political instability in the Middle East could compromise U.S. access to adequate oil supplies.

The refineries in Texas where the pipeline would terminate are built to refine oil from low-quality starting products, such as the oil sands. Although these refineries are already near capacity, a pipeline would bring a reliable supply of oil to them, and they would not have to import oil via tanker ships from other parts of the world.

The other argument for the pipeline is that it would create many jobs, both in Canada and the United States. Although there is disagreement over the numbers, there could be thousands to tens of thousands of jobs created to manufacture parts for and build the pipeline.

Finally, supporters of the pipeline suggest that the oil sands will be developed, regardless of what happens with the pipeline, because of increasing global demand for energy. Not building the pipeline will only deny jobs in the United States, supporters argue. Supporters also indicate that there are continuing efforts to make oil extraction from the Alberta oil sands more environmentally friendly.

Workers clean up along the Kalamazoo river in Michigan after a pipeline oil spill.

The Case Against the Pipeline

Arguments against the pipeline fall into two major categories: concerns over using the oil sands at all and concerns about the pipeline's route through environmentally sensitive areas.

Many scientists and environmentalists are very concerned that the development and use of the oil sands will have dire consequences for climate change. One climate scientist from NASA has stated that making full use of the oil sands would make it impossible to avoid significant and very damaging climate change, because of the huge amount of oil in the oil sands. Others claim that having this additional oil available would keep fuel prices low, which would slow efforts to switch to clean energy sources, such as solar and wind power. Most of the climate impact comes from the burning of oil. However, the production of liquid fuels from oil sands produces more greenhouse gases than production from standard oil.

The second major worry is about the pipeline itself. Oil spills happen along pipelines and have the potential to contaminate important habitats, including rivers and underground water supplies (aquifers). Along an existing pipeline from Canada to the Midwest of the United States there have been 14 spills, including one in 2011. Also in 2011, there were oil spills from oil sands pipelines into the Yellowstone River in Montana and the Kalamazoo River in Michigan.

The Keystone XL pipeline was proposed to cross a portion of Nebraska above the Ogallala Aquifer. This 174,000-mi^2 aquifer provides drinking and irrigation water for portions of many western states. Studies suggest that a spill could contaminate huge areas of the aquifer and disrupt drinking water supplies. This concern was largely responsible for the Obama administration's rejection of the pipeline permit.

Finally, opponents to the pipeline question the number of jobs that might be created. In addition, some labor groups in Canada oppose the pipeline because they think the majority of environmental damage may be done in Canada, while the majority of jobs created will be in the United States.

What Do You Think?

The debate over pipelines and the use of oil sands is far from over. There is likely to be another application for a pipeline to bring oil from Alberta to Texas or a proposal to pipe oil across Canada to ships that could take it to refineries in Asia. What do you think should be done?

SECTION 1 **Energy Resources and Fossil Fuels**

OBJECTIVES

- Most of the world's energy needs are met by fossil fuels, which are nonrenewable resources.

- Coal is abundant in North America and Asia. In the United States, coal is used primarily to produce electricity.

- Petroleum can be refined into fuels to power vehicles and machines. Petroleum can also be used to manufacture many other products.

- Natural gas is often found above oil deposits. In general, burning natural gas releases fewer pollutants than burning coal or oil.

- The extraction, transportation, and use of fossil fuels cause many environmental problems, including air and water pollution and habitat destruction.

- Calculations of fossil-fuel reserves predict that oil production will peak and then decline in the early 21st century.

KEY TERMS

fossil fuel
electric generator
petroleum
oil reserves

SECTION 2 **Nuclear Energy**

OBJECTIVES

- Nuclear energy is energy that exists within the nucleus of an atom. When uranium nuclei are bombarded with neutrons, they undergo fission and release large amounts of energy.

- In a nuclear power station, the heat generated by fission is used to heat water to form steam. The steam drives turbines that generate electricity.

- The main advantages of nuclear power are that the fuel is compact and the power stations generally do not pollute. The main disadvantage is that nuclear power produces radioactive waste, which will be dangerous for centuries.

KEY TERMS

nuclear energy
nuclear fission
nuclear fusion

Reviewing Key Terms

Use each of the following terms in a separate sentence.

1. *fossil fuel*
2. *petroleum*
3. *oil reserves*
4. *nuclear fission*
5. *nuclear fusion*

For each pair of terms, explain how the meanings of the terms differ.

6. *petroleum* and *oil reserve*
7. *turbine* and *electric generator*
8. *nuclear fission* and *nuclear fusion*
9. **Concept Map** Use the following terms to create a concept map: *oil well, petroleum, refinery, gasoline, natural gas, plastics,* and *oil reserve.*

Reviewing Main Ideas

10. Which of the following statements provides a reason for the widespread use of fossil fuels?
    a. Fossil fuels are a renewable source of energy.
    b. Fossil fuels are readily available and inexpensive.
    c. Fossil fuels are not harmful to the environment.
    d. all of the above

11. Which of the following pairs are design features that nuclear power plants and coal-fired power plants share?
    a. fuel rods and containment buildings
    b. turbines and generators
    c. combustion chamber and reactor cores
    d. none of the above

12. The main reason for the worldwide slowdown in the construction of nuclear power plants is that
    a. we have run out of uranium fuel.
    b. the electricity from nuclear power is generally more expensive to produce than electricity from other sources.
    c. nuclear reactors are inherently unsafe.
    d. nuclear reactors release large quantities of greenhouse gases.

13. Which is an example of the direct use of fossil fuels?
    a. a nuclear reactor
    b. an oil-fired furnace
    c. a wind generator
    d. a wood-burning stove

14. Which of the following statements describes the process by which modern nuclear power plants use nuclear energy?
    a. Power plants use nuclear fusion to split uranium atoms and release nuclear energy.
    b. Power plants use nuclear fusion to combine atomic nuclei and release nuclear energy.
    c. Power plants use nuclear fission to split uranium atoms and release nuclear energy.
    d. Power plants use nuclear fission to combine atomic nuclei and release nuclear energy.

15. If fossil fuels are still forming today, why are they considered nonrenewable resources?
    a. Fossil fuels are broken down by natural processes faster than they form.
    b. We are depleting fossil fuels much faster than they form.
    c. The fossil fuels being formed today are deep under the ocean, where they cannot be reached.
    d. The only fossil fuels being produced are methane hydrates, which we cannot use yet.

16. Which of the following is *not* a disadvantage of nuclear energy?
    a. the difficulty of safe storage of nuclear waste
    b. the high levels of air pollution produced
    c. the high cost of construction and maintenance of a nuclear power plant
    d. the possibility that a nuclear chain reaction can get out of control

Short Answer

17. Why have fossil fuels become our primary energy resource?

18. How did the Three Mile Island accident affect nuclear safety in the United States?

19. What factors make nuclear power expensive?

20. What is the difference between oil reserves and oil deposits?

Interpreting Graphics

The graph below shows the different contributions of various fuels to the U.S. energy supply since 1850. Use the graph to answer questions 21–25.

21. When did oil first become a more important energy source than coal?

22. Why do you think the use of coal increased so rapidly between 1850 and 1920?

23. The data for oil and natural gas are nearly parallel—they rise and fall together. Why do you think this pattern exists?

24. Why do you think the use of coal is on the rise after having fallen in the 1950s?

25. Why do you think that the use of wood as a fuel has not significantly increased or decreased since about 1850?

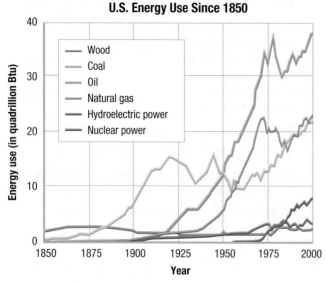

U.S. Energy Use Since 1850

Legend:
— Wood
— Coal
— Oil
— Natural gas
— Hydroelectric power
— Nuclear power

Y-axis: Energy use (in quadrillion Btu)
X-axis: Year

Source: U.S. Department of Energy.

Critical Thinking

26. Demonstrating Reasoned Judgment The invention of plastics had a damaging effect on the environment because most plastics break down very slowly, so they remain in landfills and are dangerous to wildlife. However, the invention of plastics also affected the environment in many positive ways. List as many positive effects as you can.

27. Analyzing Relationships Read the description of how fossil-fuel deposits form. Explain why fossil fuels are a form of stored solar energy.

28. Analyzing Relationships The United States currently imports about half of all the crude oil it uses. Why might this be a problem? Write a paragraph that describes the recommendations that you would make to U.S. lawmakers, manufacturers, and consumers to reduce the country's dependence on foreign oil.

29. Economics What incentives could encourage automobile manufacturers in the United States to produce more fuel-efficient cars? The U.S. government could increase the requirements for fuel efficiency. However, at least two other strong forces are likely to change the types of vehicles that manufacturers produce. What do you think these forces are?

30. Prepare a Display Find out how petroleum, natural gas, coal, or uranium are extracted. For example, engineers have developed methods to drill sideways to reach oil deposits thousands of feet underground. Research one method and prepare a model or a posterboard display that communicates your findings. Be sure to include information about the environmental effects of the method you studied.

Analyzing Data

The graph below compares the contribution of each world region to world oil production. Use the graph to answer question 31.

31. Analyzing Data If the total sales of oil in 2002 were $500 billion, what is the value of the oil produced by each region?

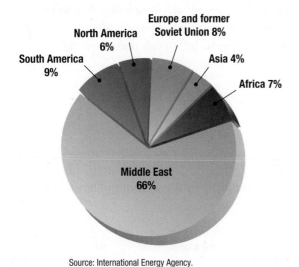

North America 6%

South America 9%

Europe and former Soviet Union 8%

Asia 4%

Africa 7%

Middle East 66%

Source: International Energy Agency.

Making Connections

32. Communicating Main Ideas How would our lives change if oil reserves became so depleted that gasoline was very expensive?

33. Recognizing Relationships Outline the major forms of environmental change that have resulted from fossil-fuel use. Include your thoughts on subjects such as habitat loss, pollution, and our use of land. Remember to include positive environmental changes.

34. Describe how hydraulic fracturing, sometimes called *fracking,* is used to extract natural gas.

35. What are some of the risks associated with hydraulic fracturing?

36. What are some of the uses of natural gas? What are some of the benefits of using natural gas, compared with other energy sources?

Why It Matters

37. Even though petroleum is a naturally occuring substance, it is a nonrenewable source of energy. Research and briefly describe the process by which petroleum is formed. Why is it considered to be nonrenewable?

STUDYSKILL

Get Organized Being organized can help make studying more efficient and less confusing. Start by reducing clutter and consolidating loose papers. Arrange your items by subject, and be sure to label your books, notebooks, and dividers. A planner, or agenda book, can help you balance schoolwork with other activities. It also can serve as reminder of upcoming deadlines and help you to prioritize multiple tasks.

Objectives

Identify the ways in which electricity is consumed in your household.

Compute the energy consumption of your household.

Interpret an electric utility bill and an electric meter.

Materials

calculator

electric bill

notebook

pen or pencil

Your Household Energy Consumption

We use electricity for many activities at home, such as drying clothes, cooking food, and heating and cooling. The total amount of energy that we use depends both on how much energy each individual appliance consumes and on how long we use the appliance each day. In this lab, you will survey your household to determine how much electricity you consume and you will analyze an electric bill to calculate how much you pay for your electricity.

Procedure

1. Create a table similar to the one shown below. To determine daily energy consumption in kilowatt-hours, divide the wattage of an appliance by 1,000 and then multiply by the number of hours the item is used per day.

Appliance	Energy consumed in 1 hour (watts)	Hours used (per day)	Daily energy consumption (Kwh)

2. Walk through your home, and identify all appliances and devices that use electricity. List each item in your table.

3. Fill in each column in your table. Determine the wattage of each item by referring to the table on the next page.

4. Find the electric meter. It may be on an outside wall of your house or apartment building. Record the current reading on the meter. The reading may change as you watch it. If so, electricity is currently being consumed in your household. If the reading is changing, write down an estimate of the current reading.

Keeping Track of Energy Use An electric meter (below) records the amount of electricity that a household uses. A utility bill (right) calculates the cost of the electricity used.

Electric Service	Meter#	Read Date		Reading
	141707	04/05/2002		87671.00
		03/07/2002		87503.00
		Read Difference		168.00
		Total Consumption in KWH		168
	Billing Rate: Residential Service Winter			
	Customer Charge..			$6.00
	Energy Charge		168.00 @ $ .0355000 per KWH.........................	$5.96
	Fuel Charge		168.00 @ $ .0177400 per KWH.........................	$2.98

©KAKIMAGE/Alamy Images

Analysis

1. **Organizing Data** Add up the energy consumption per day for all items. This number is the total energy consumed by your household in one day.

2. **Organizing Data** On your electric bill, find the total number of kilowatt-hours consumed during this time period. An electric bill usually lists a meter reading for the beginning of the time period and for the end of the time period. The difference is the energy consumption in kilowatt-hours.

3. **Analyzing Data** Divide the number of kilowatt-hours from your electric bill by the number of days in the time period. This number reflects the average daily energy consumption for this time period.

4. **Analyzing Results** Compare the daily energy consumption that you calculated from your home survey with the average calculated from your electric bill. Is there a difference? If so, what could explain the difference?

5. **Analyzing Data** Find the cost of electricity per kilowatt-hour on your electric bill. How much does washing your clothes in a washing machine cost?

Conclusions

6. **Drawing Conclusions** What can you conclude about energy consumption in your home? What activities consume the most energy? How could you reduce the energy consumption in your home?

7. **Evaluating Methods** How could the energy survey be refined to estimate more accurately your daily energy consumption?

Extension

8. **Communicating Ideas** Even when an appliance is turned off, it can still consume electricity. This type of electricity consumption is called a *phantom load*. Find out about phantom loads and prepare a booklet that shows how people can reduce this type of energy use.

ENERGY CONSUMPTION FOR COMMON HOUSEHOLD APPLIANCES

Appliance	Energy consumed in 1 hour (watts)
Ceiling fan	120
Clock radio	10
Clothes dryer (electric)	3,400
Clothes washer	425
Coffee maker	1,050
Dishwasher	1,800
Hair dryer	1,500
Heater (portable)	1,100
Iron	1,400
Light bulbs	60, 75, 100
Microwave oven	900
Personal computer	270
Refrigerator (frost free, 16 ft^3)	725
Stereo	400
Television (color)	130
Toaster	1,100
Toaster oven	1,225
Vacuum cleaner	1,200
VCR/DVD	19/22
Water heater (40 gal)	5,000
Water pump (deep well)	650
Window fan	150

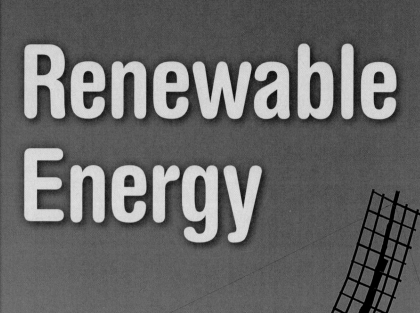

Chapter 18

Renewable Energy

Section 1
Renewable Energy Today

Section 2
Developing Energy Technologies

Why It Matters

The power of the wind is one of the oldest energy sources used by humans. These Spanish windmills were built to grind grain hundreds of years ago. Today, wind energy is a rapidly growing industry.

Why is the development of renewable and alternative energy sources important?

CASESTUDY

Learn about the energy efficient tiny house movement in the case study A Super-Efficient Home on pages 482–483.

ONLINE ENVIRONMENTAL SCIENCE
HMDScience.com

Go online to access additional resources, including labs, worksheets, multimedia, and resources in Spanish.

Renewable Energy Today

When someone mentions renewable energy, you may think of high-tech solar-powered cars, but life on Earth has always been powered by energy from the sun. **Renewable energy** is energy from a source that is replenished quickly enough that it will not be used up faster than it can be produced. In addition to solar energy, renewable energy sources include wind energy, moving water, and heat produced by natural processes within Earth.

Many governments plan to increase their use of renewable energy sources. For example, the European Union plans to produce 20 percent of their energy from renewable sources by 2020. Such a change will reduce the environmental and economic problems caused by the use of nonrenewable energy. However, the use of all sources of energy, including renewable sources, affect the environment.

Solar Energy—Power from the Sun

What does the space station shown in **Figure 1.1** have in common with a plant? Both are powered by energy from the sun. The sun is a medium-sized star that radiates energy from nuclear fusion reactions in its core. Only a small fraction of the sun's energy reaches Earth. However, this energy is enough to power the wind, the growth of plants, and the water cycle. Nearly all renewable energy comes directly or indirectly from the sun. You use direct solar energy every day. When the sun shines on a window and heats a room, the room is being heated by energy from the sun. Solar energy can also be used indirectly to generate electricity in solar cells.

SECTION 1

Objectives

- List six forms of renewable energy, and compare their advantages and disadvantages.

- Describe the differences between passive solar heating, active solar heating, and photovoltaic energy.

- Describe the current state of wind energy technology.

- Explain the differences in biomass fuel use between developed and developing nations.

- Describe how hydroelectric energy, geothermal energy, and geothermal heat pumps work.

Key Terms

renewable energy
passive solar heating
active solar heating
biomass fuel
hydroelectric energy
geothermal energy

FIGURE 1.1

Solar Energy What does the plant have in common with a space station's solar panels? Both use energy from the sun.

(br) ©Gunter Ziesler/Peter Arnold, Inc./Getty Images; (bl) ©JPL/NASA

FIGURE 1.2

Passive Solar Heat Seven hundred years ago, the Ancestral Puebloans, also called the Anasazi, lived in passive solar heated cliff dwellings in Mesa Verde, Colorado.

Passive Solar Heating

The cliff dwellings shown in **Figure 1.2** used passive solar heating, the simplest form of solar energy. **Passive solar heating** uses the sun's energy to heat something directly. In the Northern Hemisphere, south-facing windows receive the most solar energy, so passive solar buildings have large windows that face south. Solar energy enters the windows and warms the house. At night, the heat is released slowly to help keep the house warm. Passive solar buildings must be well insulated with thick walls, ceilings, and floors in order to prevent heat loss.

Passive solar buildings are oriented according to the yearly movement of the sun. In summer, the sun's path is high in the sky and the overhang of the roof shades the building and keeps it cool. In winter, the sun's path is lower in the sky, so sunlight shines into the house and warms it. If there is reliable winter sunlight, an extremely efficient passive solar heating system can heat a house even in very cold weather without using any other source of energy. However, an average household could reduce its energy bills by using any of the passive solar features shown in **Figure 1.3**.

CASESTUDY

A Super-Efficient Home

"The sure thing you can do to be sustainable as you are building a new house is just to build it small," says California architect Jay Shafer. Recent Northwestern University engineering graduate Kaycee Overcash agrees. "The greenest square foot is the one you don't build," she says.

Pioneers in the tiny house movement, Shafer and Overcash are dedicated to finding ever more efficient ways to live well in less space—often less than 150 square feet. The average tiny house is barely bigger than a typical walk-in closet.

What makes a tiny house more energy efficient than a large mansion? The resources needed to heat, cool, or provide electricity for a tiny house can be equally small in scale. Some tiny houses need such little energy that they can easily be maintained "off grid," which means that they do not need to be connected to a city's utility system. Instead, these houses have features that can generate heat and electricity, and may manage to provide heated water as well. For example, the house Overcash helped to design and build uses a rainwater collection system.

The Simpler Life

What can you fit inside a tiny house? Shafer, who founded the Tumbleweed Tiny House Company, specializes in finding clever ways to do more with less. He installs tiny appliances, utilizes every space for several purposes, and makes use of spaces that often go unused.

Sustainable living, energy efficiency, and self sufficiency are just a few of the tenets of the tiny house movement.

FIGURE 1.3

Passive Solar House A passive solar house is designed to reduce heating and cooling expenses.

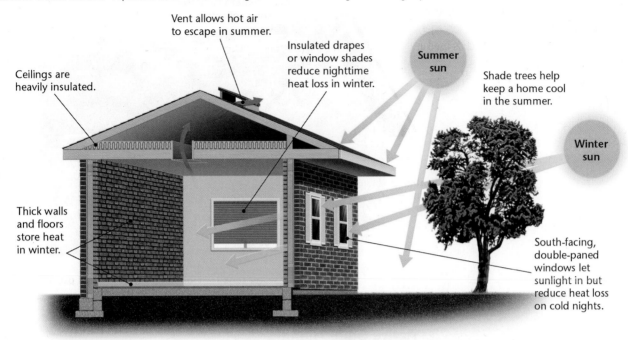

Vent allows hot air to escape in summer.

Insulated drapes or window shades reduce nighttime heat loss in winter.

Summer sun

Shade trees help keep a home cool in the summer.

Winter sun

Ceilings are heavily insulated.

Thick walls and floors store heat in winter.

South-facing, double-paned windows let sunlight in but reduce heat loss on cold nights.

For example, one of Shafer's first homes, at 89 square feet, included a "full" kitchen with downsized appliances such as a two-burner stove, a dorm-sized refrigerator, and a toaster oven. A bathroom the size of a toilet stall doubled as a shower stall when waterproof sliding doors were pulled shut. A house this small can easily be heated with a tiny stove, and Shafer's living room included one built right into his tiny living room wall. Shafer's bedroom, a sleeping loft, could be turned into a wind tunnel for cooling by opening windows at both ends.

"We just looked at sailboats and how they manage their interiors," says Finnish architect Jussi Palva of the 150 square-foot home that he and his wife created for weekend getaways. The Palvas' house features an elevated living room—so shoes and firewood can be stored under the floor—and a rope ladder to a loft bed.

Variations on a Theme

Depending on what one is willing to give up—privacy, for example, or indoor plumbing—it is possible to make a tiny house even tinier, or to make it more spacious by reducing its features. The Palvas, for example, made more space in their weekend house by using the public bathrooms at the beach—their house does not have a bathroom. Colorado theater set designer Glenn Grassi took a different approach,

hiding bathroom appliances cleverly inside the living room of the 84 square-foot house he built. Grassi's house uses an antique parlor chair as the seat for a composting toilet concealed under it (located near a wood stove so he can toss ashes into the toilet to improve decomposition rates), and has a half-sized tiled shower stall hidden under a platform bed. A bag of water for a five-minute shower is warmed by a solar water heater.

"On stage," Grassi explains, "you learn that everything you build affects something else, and everything has to have multiple purposes."

Critical Thinking

1. **Inferring Relationships** Some tiny house advocates are using what they have learned from the tiny house movement to create tiny apartments in big cities. What ideas from the tiny house movement do you think could also be applied to living in a small apartment?

2. **Applying Ideas** Do you think that you and/ or your family could live in a house that had under 100 square feet of living space? What do you think would be the advantages and disadvantages of such a living arrangement?

FIGURE 1.4

Active Solar Heating In a solar water heating system, a liquid is pumped through solar collectors. The heated liquid flows through a heat exchanger that transfers the energy to water, which is used in a household.

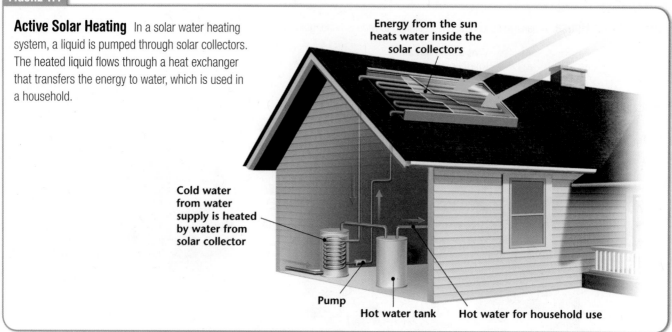

Energy from the sun heats water inside the solar collectors

Cold water from water supply is heated by water from solar collector

Pump

Hot water tank

Hot water for household use

Active Solar Heating

Energy from the sun can be gathered by collectors and used to heat water or to heat a building. This technology is known as **active solar heating**. More than 1.5 million homes in the United States use active solar energy to heat water. Solar collectors, usually mounted on a roof, capture the sun's energy, as shown in **Figure 1.4**. A liquid is heated by the sun as it flows through the solar collectors. The hot liquid is then pumped through a heat exchanger, which heats water for the building. About 8 percent of the energy used in the United States is used to heat water; therefore, active solar technology could save a lot of energy.

Photovoltaic Cells

Solar cells, also called *photovoltaic* (FOHT oh vahl TAY ik) *cells*, convert the sun's energy into electricity, as shown in **Figure 1.5**. Solar cells have no moving parts, and they run on nonpolluting power from the sun. So why don't solar cells meet all of our energy needs? A solar cell produces a very small electrical current. Meeting the electricity needs of a small city would require covering hundreds of acres of land with solar panels. Solar cells also require extended periods of sunshine to produce electricity. This energy is stored in batteries, which supply electricity when the sun is not shining.

Despite these limitations, the demand for electricity from solar energy has grown about 30 percent per year over the past 20 years. Solar cells are becoming increasingly efficient and less expensive. Solar cells have great potential for use in developing countries, where energy consumption is minimal and electricity distribution networks are limited. Currently, solar cells provide energy for more than 3 million households in the developing world.

FIGURE 1.5

Solar Cell Sunlight falls on a semiconductor, causing it to release electrons. The electrons flow through a circuit that is completed when another semiconductor in the solar cell absorbs electrons and passes them on to the first semiconductor.

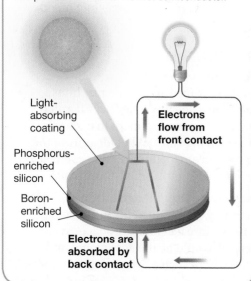

Light-absorbing coating

Phosphorus-enriched silicon

Boron-enriched silicon

Electrons flow from front contact

Electrons are absorbed by back contact

FIGURE 1.6

Wind Power Cost and Efficiency The cost of wind power has been falling steadily as wind turbines have become more efficient.

✔ **CRITICAL THINKING**

Analyze In what year did wind power production begin to experience a significant spike in growth?

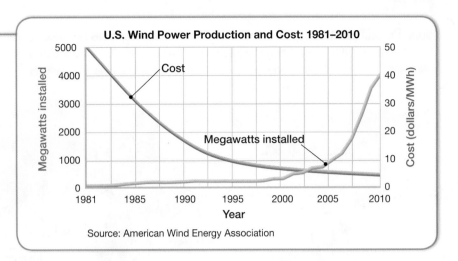

U.S. Wind Power Production and Cost: 1981–2010

Source: American Wind Energy Association

Wind Power—Cheap and Abundant

Energy from the sun warms Earth's surface unevenly, which causes air masses to flow in the atmosphere. We experience these air mass movements as wind. Wind power, which converts wind movement into electric energy, is the fastest-growing energy source in the world. New wind turbines are cost effective and can be built in just a few months. As a result, the cost of wind power has declined dramatically, as shown in **Figure 1.6**.

Wind Farms

Large arrays of wind turbines, such as the one shown in **Figure 1.7**, are called *wind farms*. In California, large wind farms supply electricity to 530,000 homes. In windy rural areas, small wind farms with 20 or fewer turbines are also becoming common. Because wind turbines take up relatively little space, some farmers can add wind turbines to their property and still use the land for other purposes. Farmers can then sell the electricity the turbines generate back to the local utility.

An Underdeveloped Resource

Scientists estimate that the windiest spots on Earth could generate more than ten times the energy used worldwide. Today, all of the large energy companies are developing plans to use more wind power. Wind experts foresee a time when prospectors will travel the world looking for potential wind-farm sites, just as geologists prospect for oil reserves today. However, one of the problems of wind energy is transporting electricity from rural areas where it is generated to urban centers where it is needed. In the future, the electricity may be used on the wind farm to produce hydrogen from water. The hydrogen could then be trucked or piped to cities for use as a fuel.

FIGURE 1.7

Wind Farms California wind farms, such as this one in Altamont Pass, generate more than enough electricity to light a city the size of San Francisco.

FIGURE 1.8

Wood Consumption The consumption of wood as an energy source has increased by nearly 80 percent since 1960. In developing countries such as Nepal, Burma, Guatemala, Congo (DRC), and Kenya, the use of fuelwood places an enormous burden on local environments.

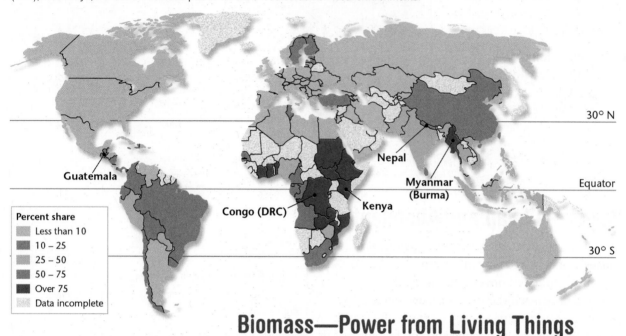

Percent share
- Less than 10
- 10 – 25
- 25 – 50
- 50 – 75
- Over 75
- Data incomplete

FIELDSTUDY
Go to Appendix B to find the field study
Biomass Survey.

Biomass—Power from Living Things

Plant material, manure, and any other organic matter that is used as an energy source is called a **biomass fuel.** While fossil fuels are organic and can be thought of as biomass energy sources, fossil fuels are nonrenewable. Renewable biomass fuels, such as wood and dung, are major sources of energy in developing countries, as shown in **Figure 1.8**. More than half of all wood cut in the world is used as fuel for heating and cooking. Wood can become a nonrenewable resource if trees are cut down faster than they grow. Major habitat loss, deforestation, and soil erosion can result. In addition, harmful air pollution may result from burning wood and dung.

Methane

When bacteria decompose organic wastes, one byproduct is methane gas. Methane can be burned to generate heat or electricity. In China, more than 30 million households use biogas digesters to ferment manure and produce gas used for heating and cooking. In the developed world, biomass that was once thought of as waste is being used for energy. For example, some landfills in the United States generate electricity by using the methane from the decomposition of trash.

Alcohol

Liquid fuels can also be derived from biomass. For example, ethanol, an alcohol, can be made by fermenting fruit or agricultural waste. Many companies are trying to develop commercial-grade ethanol using algae. Vehicles can run on ethanol or *gasohol*, a blend of gasoline and ethanol. Gasohol produces less air pollution than do fossil fuels. Some U.S. states require the use of gasohol in vehicles as a way to reduce air pollution.

FIGURE 1.9

Hydroelectric Energy Hydroelectric dams convert the *potential energy*, or stored energy, of a reservoir of water into the *kinetic energy*, or moving energy, of a spinning turbine. The movement of the turbine is then used to generate electricity.

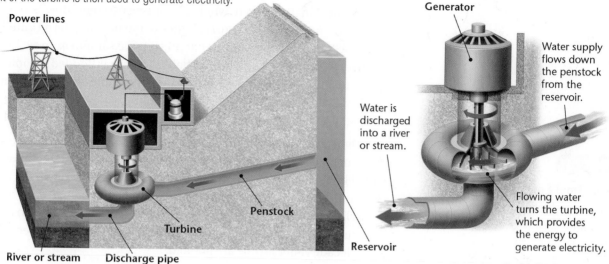

Hydroelectricity—Power from Moving Water

Energy from the sun causes water to evaporate, condense in the atmosphere, and fall back to Earth's surface as rain. As water flows across the land, the energy in its movement can be used to generate electricity. **Hydroelectric energy**, which is energy produced from moving water, is a renewable resource that accounts for about 20 percent of the world's electricity. The countries that lead the world in hydroelectric energy generation are, in decreasing order, China, Canada, Brazil, the United States, and Russia.

Figure 1.9 shows how a hydroelectric power plant works. Large hydroelectric power plants have a dam that is built across a river to hold back a reservoir of water. The water in the reservoir is released to turn a turbine, which generates electricity. The energy of this water is evident in **Figure 1.10**, which shows the spillway of Itaipu Dam in Paraguay.

The Benefits of Hydroelectric Energy

Although hydroelectric dams are expensive to build, they are relatively inexpensive to operate. Unlike fossil fuel plants, hydroelectric dams do not release air pollutants that cause acid precipitation. In addition, hydroelectric dams tend to last much longer than fossil fuel-powered plants. Dams also provide other benefits such as flood control and water for drinking, agriculture, industry, and recreation.

FIGURE 1.10

Itaipu Dam Paraguay's Itaipu Dam supplies about 75 percent of the electricity used by Paraguay and 25 percent of the electricity used by Brazil.

Disadvantages of Hydroelectric Energy

A dam changes a river's flow, which can have far-reaching consequences. A reservoir floods large areas of habitat above the dam. The water flow below the dam is reduced, which disrupts ecosystems downstream. For example, many of the salmon fisheries of the northwestern United States have been destroyed by dams that prevent the salmon from swimming upriver to spawn. When the land behind a dam is flooded, people are often displaced. Between 40 and 80 million people around the world have been displaced by dam projects. Dam failure can be another problem— if a dam bursts, people living in areas below the dam can be killed.

Dams can also affect the land below them. As a river slows down, the river deposits some of the sediment it carries. This fertile sediment builds up behind a dam instead of enriching the land farther down the river. As a result, farmland below a dam can become less productive. Recent research has also shown that the decay of plant matter trapped in reservoirs can release relatively large amounts of greenhouse gases, especially in the first decades after forests are flooded.

Modern Trends

In the United States, the era of large dam construction is probably over. But in developing countries, such as Brazil, India, and China, the construction of large dams continues. However, a modern trend is *micro-hydropower*, which is electricity produced in a small stream without having to build a big dam. The turbine may even float in the water, therefore not disturbing the flow. Micro-hydropower is much cheaper than large hydroelectric dam projects, and it permits energy to be generated from small streams in remote areas.

Geothermal Energy—Power from within Earth

In some areas of the world, underground reservoirs of water in Earth's crust are heated by energy within Earth. Such places are sources of **geothermal energy**—the energy generated from heat within Earth. As **Figure 1.11** shows, this heat can be used to generate electricity. Geothermal power plants pump heated water or steam from geothermal reservoirs and use the water or steam to power a turbine that generates electricity. Usually the water is returned to Earth's crust where it is heated and used again.

The United States is the world's largest producer of geothermal energy. The world's largest geothermal power plant is The Geysers in California, which produces electricity for about 725,000 households. Other countries that produce geothermal energy include the Philippines, Iceland, Japan, Mexico, Italy, and New Zealand. Although geothermal energy is considered a renewable resource, the water in geothermal reservoirs must be managed carefully so that it is not depleted.

FIGURE 1.11

Geothermal Energy Geothermal power plants generate electricity using the following steps: ❶ steam rises through a well; ❷ steam drives turbines, which generate electricity; ❸ leftover liquid water is pumped back into the hot rock.

Hot rock

Heated water

FIGURE 1.12

Geothermal Heat Pump In winter (left), the ground is warmer than the air. A fluid is circulated underground to warm a house. In summer (right), the ground is cooler than the air, and the fluid is used to cool a house.

The ground is warmer than the air in winter.

The ground is cooler than the air in summer.

Heat is transferred from the ground to warm the house.

Heat is transferred from the house to the ground to cool the house.

Geothermal Heat Pumps: Energy for Homes

More than 600,000 homes in the United States are heated and cooled using geothermal heat pumps such as the one shown in **Figure 1.12.** Because the temperature of the ground is nearly constant year-round, a *geothermal heat pump* uses stable underground temperatures to warm and cool homes. A heat pump is simply a loop of piping that circulates a fluid underground. In warm summer months, the ground is cooler than the air, and the fluid is used to cool a home. In cooler winter months, the ground is warmer than the air, and the fluid is used to warm the home.

✓ Section 1 Formative Assessment

▶ Reviewing Main Ideas

1. **List** six forms of renewable energy, and compare the advantages and disadvantages of each.

2. **Describe** the differences between passive solar heating, active solar heating, and photovoltaic energy.

3. **Describe** how hydroelectric energy, geothermal energy, and geothermal heat pumps work.

4. **Explain** whether all renewable energy sources have their origin in energy from the sun.

✓ Critical Thinking

5. **Making Decisions** Which renewable energy source would be best suited to your region? Write a paragraph that explains your reasoning.

6. **Identifying Trends** Identify a modern trend in hydroelectric power and in wind energy.

7. **Analyzing Relationships** Write a short essay that explains the differences in biomass fuel use between developed and developing countries.

SECTION 2

Objectives

- Describe three alternative energy technologies.

- Identify two ways that hydrogen could be used as a fuel source in the future.

- Explain the difference between energy efficiency and energy conservation.

- Describe two forms of energy-efficient transportation.

- Identify three ways that you can conserve energy in your daily life.

Key Terms

alternative energy
ocean thermal energy
  conversion (OTEC)
fuel cell
energy efficiency
energy conservation

Developing Energy Technologies

To achieve a future where energy use is sustainable, we must make the most of the energy sources we already have and develop new sources of energy. **Alternative energy** describes energy sources that are still in development. Renewable alternatives to fossil fuels, also called alternative fuels, are critical for a sustainable economy. For an alternative energy source to become a viable option for the future, the source must be proven to be cost effective. Also, the environmental effects of using the energy source must be acceptable. Government investment is often the only way to research some of these future energy possibilities.

Tidal Power

Tides are the movement of water in the oceans and seas caused by gravitational attraction between the sun, Earth, and the moon. The tides, which happen once or twice each day, are marked by the rising and falling of the sea level. The energy of the tides was used nearly a thousand years ago to power mills in France and Britain. Today, tidal power is used to generate electricity in countries such as France, Russia, and Canada.

As **Figure 2.1** shows, a tidal power plant works much like a hydroelectric dam. As the tide rises, water flows behind a dam; when the sea level falls, the water is trapped behind the dam. When the water in the reservoir is released, it turns a turbine that generates electricity. Although tidal energy is renewable and nonpolluting, there remain major technological challenges to make it economically viable on a larger scale.

FIGURE 2.1

Tidal Power Plant As the tide rises, water enters a bay behind a dam. The gate then closes at high tide. At low tide, the gate opens and the water in the bay rushes through, spinning a turbine that generates electricity.

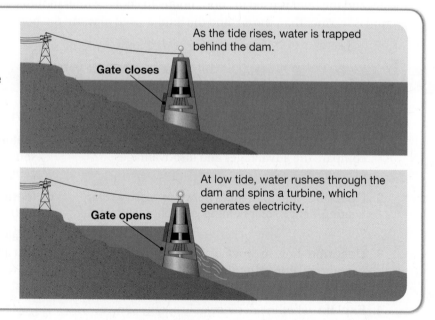

Gate closes

As the tide rises, water is trapped behind the dam.

Gate opens

At low tide, water rushes through the dam and spins a turbine, which generates electricity.

Ocean Thermal Energy Conversion

In the tropics, the temperature difference between the surface of the ocean, which is warmed by solar energy, and deep ocean waters can be as much as 24°C (43°F). An experimental power station off the shores of Hawaii uses this temperature difference to generate electricity. This technology, which is shown in **Figure 2.2**, is called **ocean thermal energy conversion (OTEC)**. In this system, a vacuum is used to boil sea water. This is possible because water boils at low temperatures when it is at low pressure in a vacuum chamber. The boiling water turns into steam, which spins a turbine. The turbine runs an electric generator. Cold water from the deep ocean cools the steam, turning the steam into water that can be used again.

Japan has also experimented with OTEC power, but so far, no project has been able to generate electricity cost-effectively. One problem with OTEC is that the power needed to pump cold water up from the deep ocean uses about one-third of the electricity the plant produces. The environmental effects of pumping large amounts of cold water to the surface are also unknown.

Hydrogen—A Future Fuel?

Hydrogen is the most abundant element in the universe. Hydrogen gas, or H_2, can be burned as a fuel. Hydrogen gas does not exist naturally on Earth, but it can be extracted from compounds such as water (H_2O) and natural gas (CH_4). This extraction requires a source of energy, such as electricity, to split the molecules apart. Hydrogen can be renewable or not depending on where the energy comes from to obtain it. In the future, we may also be able to grow plants to produce hydrogen cost-effectively, as shown in **Figure 2.3**.

FIGURE 2.2

Ocean Thermal Energy Conversion In an open cycle OTEC plant, warm surface water is brought to a boil in a vacuum chamber. The boiling water produces steam to drive a turbine that generates electricity. Cold deep-ocean water is pumped in to condense the steam. Fresh water is a byproduct of this type of OTEC plant.

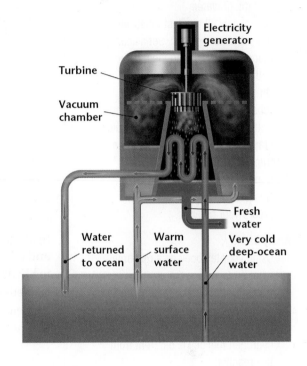

Electricity generator

Turbine

Vacuum chamber

Fresh water

Water returned to ocean

Warm surface water

Very cold deep-ocean water

✔ **CHECK FOR UNDERSTANDING**

Identify What are two advantages of using hydrogen as a fuel?

FIGURE 2.3

Hydrogen Fuel from Plants Hydrogen fuel can be made from any material that contains a lot of hydrogen, including the experimental plot of switchgrass shown here.

Hydrolysis
PROCEDURE

1. Coat a 9 V cell with petroleum jelly. Be careful not to get any jelly on the terminals.
2. In a beaker, dissolve 15 g of NaCl in 600 mL of water.
3. Completely fill two test tubes with the saltwater solution. Set aside.
4. Place the 9 V cell into the beaker with the remaining salt solution.
5. Quickly invert one of the test tubes of salt water over one of the battery terminals, so that the liquid stays within the tube and no air is trapped inside. Hold it in place.
6. Repeat for the second test tube.
7. Observe for several minutes and record your findings.

Analysis

1. Using your textbook as a resource, what happened at the positive terminal? What happened at the negative terminal?
2. Explain how the function of a hydrogen fuel cell is different from this reaction.
3. What are the reasons why hydrogen fuel cells are not currently in wide use?

FIGURE 2.4

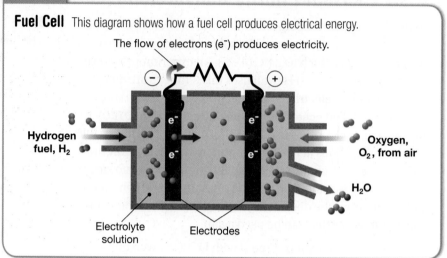

Fuel Cell This diagram shows how a fuel cell produces electrical energy.

The Challenge of Hydrogen Fuel

Why is hydrogen the fuel of the future and not of today? There are two main problems. First, the current methods that are used to produce hydrogen are not very efficient. They require a lot of energy, are expensive, and cause pollution. In the future, this problem may be solved by producing hydrogen from water using solar power. Second, a lot of hydrogen is needed to produce the same amount of energy as a tank of gasoline. Therefore, the hydrogen must be compressed to fit into a vehicle. Tanks that hold hydrogen safely at high pressure are still being developed.

Fuel Cells

Fuel cells, such as the one shown in **Figure 2.4**, may be the engines of the future. Like a battery, a **fuel cell** produces electricity chemically, by combining hydrogen fuel with oxygen from the air. When hydrogen and oxygen are combined, electrical energy is produced and water is the only byproduct. Fuel cells today mostly use hydrogen but they can be fueled by anything that contains plenty of hydrogen, including natural gas, alcohol, or even gasoline. Using fossil fuels, however, undermines the goal of finding alternative fuels.

Energy Efficiency

Energy efficiency is the percentage of energy put into a system that does useful work. Energy efficiency can be determined using this simple equation: energy efficiency (in %) = useful energy out/energy in × 100. Thus, the energy efficiency of a light bulb is the proportion of electrical energy that reaches the bulb and is converted into light energy rather than into heat. The relationship between the transfer of energy to the work done and the heat transferred is known as the *first law of thermodynamics*. This law explains that the energy going in must equal the energy coming out of a system. Therefore any heat transfer reduces the energy available for work, thus affecting efficiency.

This relationship holds true for biological systems as well as physical systems. Most of our devices are fairly inefficient. More than 40 percent of all commercial energy used in the United States is wasted. Most of it is lost from inefficient vehicles, furnaces, and appliances and from leaky, poorly insulated buildings. We could save enormous amounts of energy by using fuel cells instead of internal combustion engines in cars, and by changing from incandescent to fluorescent light bulbs, as shown in **Figure 2.5**. However, many increases in efficiency involve sacrifices or investments in new technology.

Efficient Transportation

Nothing would increase the energy efficiency of American life more than developing efficient engines to power vehicles and increasing the use of public transportation systems. The internal combustion engines that power most vehicles use fuel inefficiently and produce air pollution. The design of these engines has hardly changed since 1900, but they may change radically in the next 50 years. As gasoline prices increase, so too will the demand for fuel-efficient vehicles.

Hybrid Cars

Hybrid cars, such as the one shown in **Figure 2.6**, are examples of energy-efficient vehicles. Hybrid cars use a small, efficient gasoline engine most of the time, but they also use an electric motor when extra power is needed. Hybrid cars feature other efficient technologies. They convert some of the energy of braking into electricity and they store this energy in the battery. To save fuel, hybrid cars sometimes shut off the gasoline engine, such as when the car is idling. Hybrid cars are also designed to be aerodynamic, and they are made of lightweight materials so they need less energy to accelerate. Hybrid cars cost less to refuel than conventional vehicles, and they produce less harmful emissions. These benefits have led auto makers to design many hybrid car models, including hybrid trucks and sport utility vehicles (SUVs).

FIGURE 2.5

ENERGY EFFICIENCY OF COMMON CONVERSION DEVICES

Device	Efficiency
Incandescent light bulb	5%
Fluorescent light bulb	22%
Internal combustion engine (gasoline)	10%–15%
Human body	20%–25%
Steam turbine	45%
Fuel cell	60%

✔ **CHECK FOR UNDERSTANDING**

Identify Name three ways that hybrid cars are energy-efficient.

FIGURE 2.6

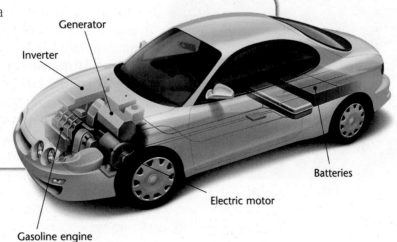

Hybrid Car A hybrid car has a gasoline engine and an electric motor. The batteries that power hybrid cars are expensive to replace, and new technologies will be needed to recycle used batteries effectively.

Generator

Inverter

Batteries

Electric motor

Gasoline engine

Cogeneration

One way to use fuel more efficiently is *cogeneration*, the production of two useful forms of energy from the same fuel source. For example, the wasted heat from an industrial furnace can power a steam turbine that produces electricity. The industry may use the electricity or sell it to a utility company. Small cogeneration systems have been used for years to supply heat and electricity to multiple buildings at specific sites. Small units suitable for single buildings are now available in the United States.

Energy Conservation

Energy conservation means saving energy. It can occur in many ways, including using energy-efficient devices and wasting less energy. The cyclist in **Figure 2.7** is conserving energy by bicycling instead of driving. Many U.S. cities, including Minneapolis, Minnesota; Denver, Colorado; and Washington, D.C., have instituted bike-sharing programs.

Cities and Towns Saving Energy

The town of Osage, Iowa, numbers around 3,400 people. You might not think a town this small could make much of a difference in energy conservation. Yet the town adopted an energy conservation plan that saves more than $1 million each year. The residents plugged the leaks around windows and doors where much of the heat escapes from a house. They also replaced inefficient furnaces and insulated their hot water heaters. Businesses in Osage found ways to conserve energy, too. In addition to saving energy, the town has greatly improved its economy through energy conservation. Businesses have relocated to the area in order to take advantage of low energy costs. Unemployment rates have also declined. This small town in Iowa is just one example of the dramatic benefits of energy conservation.

Conservation Around the Home

The average household in the United States spends more than $1,500 on energy bills each year. Unfortunately, much of that energy is wasted. Most of the energy lost from homes is lost through poorly insulated windows, doors, walls, and roof. So a good way to increase energy efficiency is to add to the insulation of a home. Replacing old windows with new high-efficiency windows can reduce your energy bill by 15 percent. Two of the best places to look for ways to conserve energy are doors and windows.

FIGURE 2.7

Energy Conservation In Copenhagen, Denmark, companies provide free bicycles in exchange for publicity. Anyone wishing to use a bike is free to borrow one after paying a refundable deposit. The program helps cut down on pollution and auto traffic.

©Dean Pictures/The Image Works

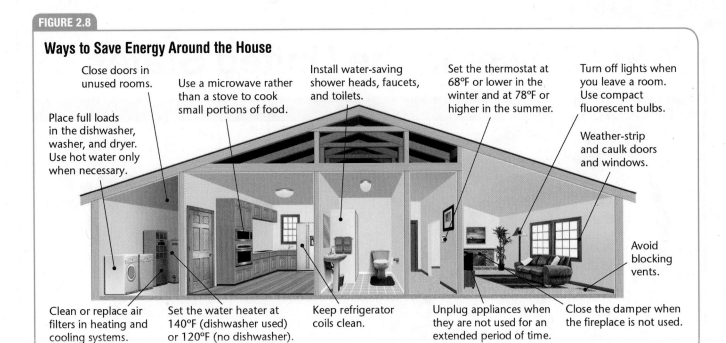

FIGURE 2.8

Ways to Save Energy Around the House

Close doors in unused rooms.

Use a microwave rather than a stove to cook small portions of food.

Install water-saving shower heads, faucets, and toilets.

Set the thermostat at 68°F or lower in the winter and at 78°F or higher in the summer.

Turn off lights when you leave a room. Use compact fluorescent bulbs.

Place full loads in the dishwasher, washer, and dryer. Use hot water only when necessary.

Weather-strip and caulk doors and windows.

Avoid blocking vents.

Clean or replace air filters in heating and cooling systems.

Set the water heater at 140°F (dishwasher used) or 120°F (no dishwasher).

Keep refrigerator coils clean.

Unplug appliances when they are not used for an extended period of time.

Close the damper when the fireplace is not used.

Much of the energy lost from a house escapes as hot air in winter or cold air in summer passes through gaps around doors and windows. Hold a ribbon up to the edges of doors and windows. If it flutters, you've found a leak. Sealing these leaks with caulk or weather stripping will help conserve energy. There are dozens of other ways to reduce energy use around the home. Some of these are shown in **Figure 2.8**.

Conservation in Daily Life

There are many simple lifestyle changes that can help save energy. First, remember that using less of any resource usually translates into saving energy. For example, washing your clothes in cold water uses only 25 percent of the energy needed to wash your clothes in warm water. **Figure 2.9** lists a few ways that you can conserve energy every day. Can you think of other ways?

FIGURE 2.9

ENERGY CONSERVATION TIPS

Walk or ride a bicycle for short trips.

Carpool or use public transportation whenever possible.

Drive a fuel-efficient automobile.

Choose ENERGY STAR® products.

Recycle and reuse products whenever possible.

Set computers to "sleep" mode when they are not in use.

 Section 2 Formative Assessment

⏵ Reviewing Main Ideas

1. **Describe** three alternative energy technologies, and identify two ways that hydrogen gas could be used as a fuel in the future.

2. **List** as many ways as you can for individuals and communities to conserve energy.

3. **Describe** the difference between energy conservation and energy efficiency.

✔ Critical Thinking

4. **Making Inferences** What factors influence a person's choice to conserve energy?

5. **Making Comparisons** Read the description of hydrogen fuel cells and explain why hydrolysis (splitting water molecules with electricity to produce hydrogen and oxygen) is the opposite of the reaction that occurs in a hydrogen fuel cell.

Wind Power in the United States

U.S. WIND POWER PROJECTS

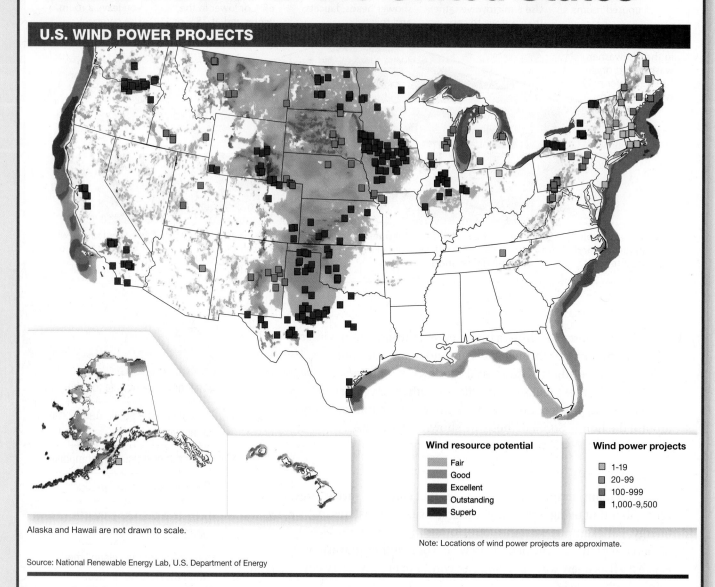

Alaska and Hawaii are not drawn to scale.

Wind resource potential
- Fair
- Good
- Excellent
- Outstanding
- Superb

Wind power projects
- 1–19
- 20–99
- 100–999
- 1,000–9,500

Note: Locations of wind power projects are approximate.

Source: National Renewable Energy Lab, U.S. Department of Energy

Map Skills

1. **Analyzing Data** Why are most of the wind farms located in the western and central United States and not in the eastern United States?

2. **Understanding Topography** Examine Idaho, Wyoming, Montana, and Colorado. What landscape feature might account for the strong winds in those western states?

3. **Using the Key** Use the wind power key to locate where you would plan five wind power projects that are larger than 50 MW.

4. **Using the Key** The Great Plains states have been called the "Saudi Arabia of wind energy." Use the key to explain what this statement means.

5. **Finding Locations** The first offshore wind farm in the United States is proposed off the East Coast. Find where the proposed wind farm will be located, and describe the wind conditions in that area.

6. **Using the Key** Use the map to determine which state has the greatest unused potential for wind energy. Explain your reasoning.

ECOZine at HMDScience.com

Go online for the latest environmental science news and updates on all EcoZine articles.

Solar Living

What is it like to live in a house powered entirely by the sun's energy? You might expect the house to lack some modern comforts—perhaps it would be cramped, unattractive, too cold during the winter, too hot during the summer, or dimly lit at night. And it's sure to be expensive, right? These things are not always true, and none of these issues are the case if the house is a successful entry in the Solar Decathlon.

Judging the Entries

The Solar Decathlon competition, sponsored by the United States Department of Energy (DOE), gives teams of college students a chance to design, build, and run a solar-powered house. Each entry is evaluated on the following 10 qualities:

Architecture	Comfort Zone
Market Appeal	Hot Water
Engineering	Appliances
Communications	Home Entertainment
Affordability	Energy Balance

Meeting the Requirements

A house that earns a high score in architecture is comfortable to live in and compatible with its surroundings, and the overall design pleases and inspires visitors. Market appeal is judged on practical livability; engineering on functionality and efficiency; affordability on cost; and so on.

Each of the measurable requirements is specific: for example, the house must be able to deliver 15 gallons of hot water (110°F) in 10 minutes or less, efficiently run appliances to heat and cool food, and wash and dry laundry. To demonstrate home entertainment, the teams must, among other things, give two dinner parties and host a movie night.

Winning the Competition

The 2011 Solar Decathlon included 20 teams from around the U.S. and the world. The winning house, which was built by a team from the University of Maryland, received a score of 951 out of 1000. After the competition, some houses are sold, while many are used for research and placed on display for the public at the universities where they were designed.

The solar panels on each house use energy from the sun to produce electricity that is used to power appliances, lights, mechanical systems, and electronics.

More About the Competition

The Solar Decathlon began in 2002. Starting in 2005, the competition has been held every two years. In addition to providing practical instruction for those who take part in the competition, the Solar Decathlon also allows the general public to learn more about solar-powered homes through activities such as house tours and workshops. The Solar Decathlon also occurs internationally with competitions held in Europe and China.

What Do You Think?

What features can you see in the house that might produce or conserve energy? Would you be interested in taking part in a competition like the Solar Decathlon?

SECTION 1 Renewable Energy Today

OBJECTIVES

- Renewable energy is energy from a source that replenishes itself quickly enough so that it will not be used faster than it can be produced.

- Solar energy can be used to heat a house directly or to heat another material, such as water, which can then be used to heat a house. Solar cells can also be used to generate electricity.

- Wind power is the fastest growing source of energy in the world.

- Many people in developing countries get most of their energy from biomass such as fuelwood or manure. Biomass is increasingly used in developed countries to generate electricity.

- Hydroelectric energy is electricity generated by the energy of moving water.

- Geothermal energy comes from heat generated within Earth and can be used to generate electricity.

KEY TERMS

renewable energy

passive solar heating

active solar heating

biomass fuel

hydroelectric energy

geothermal energy

SECTION 2 Developing Energy Technologies

OBJECTIVES

- Alternative energy sources are energy sources that are still in development.

- Ocean thermal energy conversion (OTEC) uses the temperature difference between layers of ocean water to generate electricity.

- Hydrogen gas may be one of the fuels of the future. It can be made by combining energy with a compound that contains hydrogen and produces only water as a waste product when burned.

- Hydrogen fuel cells may be the engines of the future. Many experiments with them are now underway.

- Energy efficiency is the percentage of energy put into a system that does useful work. Energy conservation means saving energy.

KEY TERMS

alternative energy

ocean thermal energy conversion (OTEC)

fuel cell

energy efficiency

energy conservation

CHAPTER 18 **Review**

Reviewing Key Terms

Use the correct key term to complete each of the following sentences.

1. Much of the energy needs of the developing world are met by _____, such as fuelwood.

2. A _____ converts the potential energy of moving water into the kinetic energy of a spinning turbine.

3. Turning off the lights when you leave a room is an example of _____.

Use each of the following terms in a separate sentence.

4. *renewable energy*

5. *geothermal energy*

6. *alternative energy*

7. *energy conservation*

8. Concept Map Use the following terms to create a concept map: *sun, hydroelectric energy, solar energy, passive solar heating, active solar heating, water cycle, biomass fuel, wind energy, photovoltaic cell,* and *electric current.*

Reviewing Main Ideas

9. Which of the following forms of renewable energy uses the sun's energy most directly?
   a. biomass fuel
   b. passive solar heating
   c. geothermal energy
   d. a hydrogen fuel cell

10. Which of the following energy sources is useful in most parts of the world?
    a. tidal power
    b. OTEC
    c. geothermal energy
    d. active solar energy

11. A house that uses passive solar heating in the Northern Hemisphere will
    a. have large south-facing windows.
    b. have little insulation.
    c. have large north-facing windows.
    d. lack a vent in the roof.

12. A passive solar house in the Southern Hemisphere will face
    a. north.
    b. south.
    c. east.
    d. west.

13. Photovoltaic cells convert the sun's energy into
    a. heat.
    b. fuel.
    c. electricity.
    d. light.

14. In a developing country, you are most likely to find biomass used
    a. to generate electricity.
    b. for manufacturing.
    c. for heating and cooking.
    d. as a source of hydropower.

15. Which of the following is *not* true of fuel cells?
    a. They produce electricity.
    b. They will work with many different fuels.
    c. They are more energy efficient than most engines used today.
    d. They cannot be fueled by hydrogen gas.

16. Which renewable energy source is the fastest growing energy source in the world?
    a. oil
    b. wind
    c. biomass
    d. photovoltaic cells

17. Which statement describes why geothermal heat pumps work?
    a. They are located in areas with abundant geothermal energy.
    b. The ground is warmer than the air in summer and colder than the air in winter.
    c. The ground is colder than the air in summer and warmer than the air in winter.
    d. They run on hydrogen fuel cells.

Short Answer

18. Rivers are recharged by the water cycle, so what is the original source of hydroelectric energy?

19. Salt water breaks down metals rapidly. What effect is this likely to have on the cost of electricity produced from tidal power?

20. Why is it likely that hydroelectric energy will be generated increasingly by micro-hydropower plants rather than by large hydroelectric dams?

Interpreting Graphics

Use the information in the figure below to answer questions 21–23.

21. **Determine** Describe the path of the water in the loop during winter. Where is the water warmed? Where is the water cooled?

22. **Determine** Describe the path of the water in the loop during summer. Where is the water warmed? Where is the water cooled?

23. **Compare** What is the difference in the temperature between the house, the closed loop, and the air in the summer? What is the temperature difference in the winter?

Critical Thinking

24. **Making Comparisons** Read the description of energy efficiency and energy conservation in this chapter. How are the two concepts related? Give several examples.

25. **Analyzing Ideas** Does the energy used by fuel cells come from the sun? Explain your answer.

26. **Analyzing Ideas** Explain whether you think the most important advances of the 21st century will be new sources of energy or more efficient use of sources that already exist.

27. **Drawing Inferences** Don Huberts of Shell Hydrogen said, "The Stone Age didn't end because the world ran out of stones." He was talking about the future of fossil fuels. Write a short essay that explains what he meant.

28. **Geography** Create a world map that shows at least 10 renewable energy or alternative energy projects currently in operation. Annotate your map with details and photographs of each project.

29. **Making Comparisons** Each of the following pairs includes one renewable and one nonrenewable form of energy. Compare the advantages and disadvantages of the two sources of energy in each pair: (a) nuclear power and solar power (photovoltaic cells) and (b) fossil fuels and hydrogen fuel.

Analyzing Data

The circle graph below shows electric generating capacity from renewable sources in the United States in 2009. Use the data to answer questions 30–31.

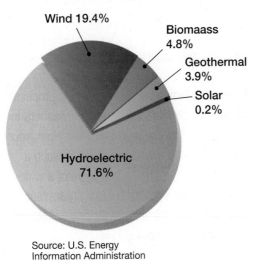

Wind 19.4%

Biomaass 4.8%

Geothermal 3.9%

Solar 0.2%

Hydroelectric 71.6%

Source: U.S. Energy Information Administration

30. Making Calculations How much generating capacity came from biomass, geothermal, wind, and solar combined?

31. Making Calculations In 2009, the United States had a total of 127,070 MW of electric generating capacity from renewable energy. How much of that capacity came from biomass? How much came from wind power?

Making Connections

32. Communicating Main Ideas Explain why scientists are working to reduce the use of the two main sources of energy people use today—fossil fuels and biomass.

33. Writing Persuasively Write a guide that encourages people to conserve energy and offers practical tips to show them how.

CASESTUDY

34. Why is a tiny house more energy efficient than a normal-size house?

35. In what ways could you increase the energy efficiency in the place where you live?

Why It Matters

36. What types of renewable energy could be used in the area where you live? Explain your answer.

STUDYSKILL

Get Some Exercise Ride a bike, go for a walk, or play a game of basketball. Try to get at least a half hour of exercise before you begin studying. Then when you study you will be more relaxed and you will be able to focus on the subject you want to learn. As you study, take a moment to notice if the exercise helped. Research has shown that regular physical exercise helps fight memory loss.

Blowing in the Wind

Objectives

Prepare a detailed sketch of your solution to the design problem.

Design and build a functional windmill that lifts a specific weight as quickly as possible.

Materials

blow-dryer, 1,500 W

dowel or smooth rod

foam board

glue, white

paper clips, large (30)

paper cup, small (1)

spools of thread, empty (2)

string, 50 cm

optional materials for windmill blades: foam board, paper plates, paper cups, or any other lightweight materials

MEMO

To: Division of Research and Developers

Quixote Alternative Energy Systems is accepting design proposals to develop a windmill that can be used to lift window washers to the tops of buildings. As part of the design engineering team, your division has been asked to develop a working model of such a windmill. Your task is to design and build a prototype of a windmill that can capture energy from a 1,500 W blow-dryer. Your model must lift 30 large paper clips a vertical distance of 50 cm (approximately 2 ft) as quickly as possible.

Procedure

1. Build the base for your windmill (shown below). Begin by attaching the two spools to the foam board using the glue. Make sure the spools are parallel before you glue them.

2. Pass a dowel or a smooth rod through the center of the spools. The dowel should rotate freely. Attach one end of the string securely to the dowel between the two spools.

3. Poke a hole through the middle of the foam board to allow the string to pass through.

4. Attach the cup to the end of the string. You will use the cup to lift the paper clips.

5. Place your windmill base between two lab tables or in any other area that will allow the string to hang freely.

Procedure Step 1 Your windmill base should allow the dowel to spin as freely as possible. The pinwheel shown at the end of the dowel is a suggested design for your windmill blades.

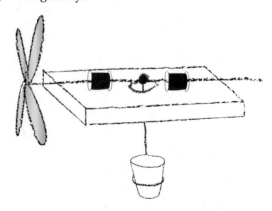

6. Prepare a sketch of your prototype windmill blades based on the objectives for this lab. Include a list of the materials that you will use and safety precautions (if necessary).

7. Have your teacher approve your design before you begin construction.

8. Construct a working prototype of your windmill blades. Test your model several times to collect data on the speed at which it lifts the paper clips. Record your data for each trial.

9. Vary the type of material used for construction of your windmill blades. Test the various blades to determine whether they improve the original plan.

10. Vary the number and size of the blades on your windmill. Test each design to determine whether the change improves the original plan.

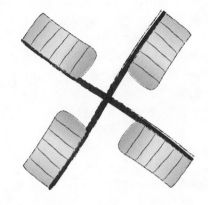

Analysis

1. **Summarizing Results** Create a data table that lists the speed for each lift for several trials. Include an average speed.

2. **Graphing Data** Prepare a bar graph that shows your results for each blade design.

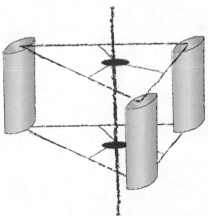

Conclusions

3. **Evaluating Methods** After you observe all of the designs, decide which ones you think best solve the problem and explain why.

4. **Evaluating Models** Which change improved your windmill the most—varying the materials for the blades, varying the number of blades, or varying the size of the blades? Would you change your design further? If so, how?

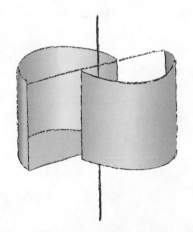

Extension

5. **Researching** Windmills have been used for more than 2,000 years. Research the three basic types of vertical-axis machines and the applications in which they are used. Prepare a report of your findings.

6. **Making Models** Adapt your design to make a water wheel. You'll find that water wheels can pull much more weight than a windmill can. Find designs on the Internet for micro-hydropower water wheels such as the Pelton wheel, and use the designs as inspiration for your models. You can even design your own dam and reservoir.

Procedure Step 6 Make a sketch of your windmill blade designs before constructing them.

Chapter 19

Waste

Why It Matters

The United States Environmental Protection Agency estimates that the capacity of the remaining active landfills will be reached in the next 20 years. Many communities are unwilling to have new landfills constructed.

What can be done to decrease or eliminate the need for landfills?

CASESTUDY

Expand your knowledge about the steps pharmaceutical manufacturers are taking to make their processes "greener" in the case study Green Chemistry on page 496.

ONLINE ENVIRONMENTAL SCIENCE
HMDScience.com

Go online to access additional resources, including labs, worksheets, multimedia, and resources in Spanish.

©Photoshot USA/Canada

Solid Waste

▶ Name one characteristic that makes a material biodegradable.

▶ Identify two types of solid waste.

▶ Describe how a modern landfill works.

▶ Name two environmental problems caused by landfills.

It is lunchtime. You stop at a fast-food restaurant and buy a burger, fries, and a soda. Within minutes, the food is gone, and you toss your trash into the nearest wastebasket. **Figure 1.1** shows items that might be in your trash. Once you throw away your trash, you probably do not give it a second thought. But where does the trash go?

The trash from the wastebasket probably will be picked up by a collection service and taken to a landfill. There the trash will be dumped with thousands of tons of other trash and covered with a layer of soil. A landfill provides a place to store trash, but the trash does not simply disappear. Where will your trash go when the landfill fills up? What would happen if rainwater ran down into the landfill and leached a harmful chemical, such as paint thinner, and it seeped into the groundwater? Suddenly, the trash that was not bothering anyone is causing an environmental problem.

Key Terms
solid waste
biodegradable
municipal solid waste
landfill
leachate

The Generation of Waste

Imagine multiplying the waste disposal problems that come with your lunch by the number of things that you and everyone else throw away each day. Every year, the United States generates more than 10 billion metric tons of solid waste. **Solid waste** is any discarded solid material. Solid waste includes everything from junk mail to coffee grounds to cars. Many products that we buy today are used once and then thrown away. As a result, the amount of solid waste Americans produce every year has almost tripled since the 1960s. Of this amount, about a third is recycled, and approximately 55 percent is deposited in landfills.

FIGURE 1.1

Out of Sight—Out of Mind Where does your trash go when you throw it away?

©Michelle Bridwell/Frontera Fotos

FIGURE 1.2

No Place to Go The barge *Mobro* (right) from Islip, New York, sailed up and down the East Coast and to the Gulf of Mexico for five months looking for a place to dump its load of garbage. The map below shows its route.

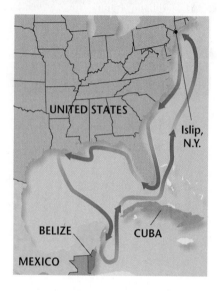

Space and Waste

Today, many towns are running out of space needed to dispose of the amounts of waste that people produce. For example, in 1987, the barge shown in **Figure 1.2** was loaded with 3,200 tons of garbage and left the town of Islip, New York, in search of a place to unload its waste. The barge sailed along the Atlantic coast to the Gulf of Mexico for more than five months in search of a state that would be willing to dispose of the waste. When no one would accept the garbage, it was finally burned in New York, and the 430 tons of ash were sent to Islip to be buried.

Population and Waste

While Earth's human population and the amount of waste we produce grow larger, the amount of land available for waste disposal becomes smaller. In pre-industrial times, the human population was smaller and more of their wastes degraded naturally. This made disposing of the waste much easier. However, today, the average person living in the United States produces 4.4 pounds of solid waste per day, as shown in **Figure 1.3**. With higher densities of people, more land is needed for agriculture, industry, and housing, which reduces the land available for waste disposal. Because the human population and the amount of waste we create are increasing and the amount of available land is decreasing, it is becoming much harder to dispose of the waste we create.

FIGURE 1.3

Municipal Solid Waste The total amount of municipal solid waste generated in the United States has increased by 60% in the past 30 years.

✔ **CRITICAL THINKING**

   Describe What is meant by "solid waste recovery?"

Source: U.S. Environmental Protection Agency

©Rick Maiman/Sygma/Corbis

Not All Wastes Are Equal

Problems are caused not only by the amount of solid waste but also by the type of solid waste. There are two main types of solid waste: biodegradable and nonbiodegradable. A material is **biodegradable** if it can be broken down by biological processes. Plant and animal matter are examples of biodegradable materials. Products made from natural materials are usually biodegradable. Examples of biodegradable products include newspapers, paper bags, cotton fibers, and leather.

Many products made from synthetic materials are not biodegradable. A *nonbiodegradable material* cannot be broken down by biological processes. Synthetic materials are made by combining chemicals to form compounds that do not form naturally. Polyester, plastic, and parts of electronics, such as those shown in **Figure 1.4**, are examples of synthetic materials.

Plastic Problems

Plastics illustrate how nonbiodegradable materials can cause problems. Plastics are made from petroleum or natural gas. Petroleum and natural gas consist mostly of carbon and hydrogen, which are the same elements that make up most molecules found in living things. But in plastics, these elements are put together in molecular chains that are not found in nature. Over millions of years, microorganisms have evolved the ability to break down nearly all biological molecules. However, microorganisms have not yet evolved ways to break down the molecular structures of most plastics. Therefore, some plastics that we throw away may accumulate and last for hundreds or even thousands of years. When these do break down, the small particles can get into the water. There, they are ingested by filter-feeding marine animals. Biotoxins that are in the particles are then passed up the food chain.

✔ **CHECK FOR UNDERSTANDING**

Determine Is a product made of polyester biodegradable or nonbiodegradable?

FIGURE 1.4

Electronic Trash These discarded computers have been exported from the United States and disposed of overseas. Unwanted computers, televisions, audio equipment, and printers are types of electronic waste.

©Universal Images Group/Getty Images

FIGURE 1.5

Papering America Paper makes up most of the municipal solid waste in the United States. How much of the waste shown in this graph could be recycled?

United States Municipal Solid Waste (Percentage by Weight)

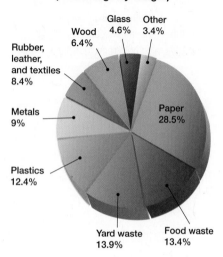

- Wood 6.4%
- Glass 4.6%
- Other 3.4%
- Rubber, leather, and textiles 8.4%
- Metals 9%
- Plastics 12.4%
- Paper 28.5%
- Yard waste 13.9%
- Food waste 13.4%

Source: U.S. Environmental Protection Agency

Connect to MATH

Municipal Solid Waste
The United States generated approximately 236 million tons of municipal solid waste in 2003. In 1998, the United States generated approximately 223 million tons of municipal solid waste. What was the percent increase in municipal solid waste generation from 1998 to 2003?

FIGURE 1.6

Lined Landfills Modern landfills are lined with clay and plastic, and have a system for collecting and treating liquid that passes through the compacted solid waste.

Types of Solid Waste

Most of what we throw out on a day-to-day basis is called municipal solid waste. Manufacturing waste, such as the computers shown in **Figure 1.4**, and mining waste make up about 70 percent of the other types of solid waste produced in the United States.

Municipal Solid Waste

About 2 percent of the total solid waste in the United States is made up of **municipal solid waste**, which is the waste produced by households and businesses. **Figure 1.5** shows the composition of municipal solid waste in the United States. Although municipal solid waste makes up only 2 percent of the total solid waste in the United States, this amounts to about 250 million tons each year. That is enough waste to fill a convoy of garbage trucks that would stretch around Earth about six times. However, recent data show that waste generation in the U.S. may be slowing.

Manufacturing, Mining, and Agriculture

Solid waste from manufacturing, mining, and agriculture makes up most of the rest of the total solid waste produced in the United States. This waste includes items such as scrap metal, plastics, paper, sludge, and ash. Consumers do not directly produce waste from manufacturing, but they indirectly create it by purchasing products that have been manufactured.

Waste from mining consists of rock and minerals that are left over from excavation and processing. In the past, these mine tailings were left exposed in large heaps and runoff from them contaminated nearby water sources. Now, tailings are disposed of by refilling and landscaping abandoned mines. Agricultural waste includes crop wastes and manure, which are biodegradable and can be broken down and returned to the soil. However, the increasing use of fertilizers and pesticides may mean that if this waste is returned to the soil, it could harm plants and animals. It could also contaminate groundwater in the area.

©Ray Pfortner

Solid Waste Management

Around half of municipal waste in the United States is sent to landfills such as the one shown in **Figure 1.6**. However, some waste is incinerated, and more than 30 percent is recycled, as shown in **Figure 1.7**. By comparison, in 1970, we recycled only 6.6 percent of our waste.

Landfills

A **landfill** is a permanent waste-disposal facility where wastes are put in the ground and covered each day with a layer of soil, plastic, or both. A modern landfill is shown in **Figure 1.8**. The most important function of a landfill is to contain waste so that it does not leach toxins into the surrounding soil and groundwater.

Problems with Landfills

One problem with landfills is **leachate**, a liquid that forms when water seeps down through a landfill and collects dissolved chemicals from decomposing garbage. Landfills typically have monitoring wells and storage tanks to measure and store leachate, which can then be treated as wastewater. However, if not monitored properly, leachate can contaminate groundwater supplies.

Another problem with landfills is that decomposing organic waste may produce highly flammable methane gas. The gas can be pumped out of landfills and used as fuel. However, if not monitored safely, methane can seep into nearby basements and cause dangerous explosions.

FIGURE 1.7

WHERE MUNICIPAL SOLID WASTE IN THE UNITED STATES GOES

Waste-disposal method	Percentage of waste by weight
Stored in landfills	55
Recycled	30
Incinerated	15

✔ **CHECK FOR UNDERSTANDING**

Interpret How can leachate in a landfill affect drinking water in nearby wells?

FIGURE 1.8

Landfill Structure This landfill generates electricity by burning methane gas produced by decomposing garbage.

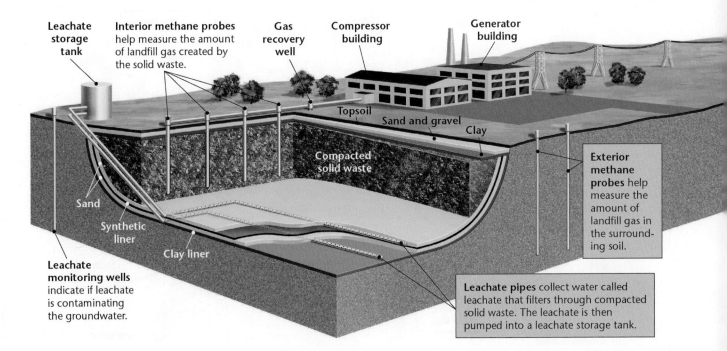

Leachate storage tank

Interior methane probes help measure the amount of landfill gas created by the solid waste.

Gas recovery well

Compressor building

Generator building

Topsoil

Sand and gravel

Clay

Compacted solid waste

Exterior methane probes help measure the amount of landfill gas in the surrounding soil.

Sand

Synthetic liner

Clay liner

Leachate monitoring wells indicate if leachate is contaminating the groundwater.

Leachate pipes collect water called leachate that filters through compacted solid waste. The leachate is then pumped into a leachate storage tank.

FIGURE 1.9

Safeguards Before laws were passed making safeguards mandatory for new landfills, leachate could seep out, contaminating the surrounding soil and water.

Safeguarding Landfills

As part of efforts by Congress to reduce landfill pollution problems, as shown in **Figure 1.9,** laws governing solid waste disposal require that new landfills be built with certain safeguards in place. New landfills must be lined with clay and a plastic liner and must have systems for collecting and treating leachate. Vent pipes must be installed to carry methane out of the landfill, to be released into the air or burned to produce energy.

Adding these safeguards to landfills increases the cost of building them. Also, finding acceptable places to build landfills is difficult. The landfills must be close to the city producing the waste but must be far enough from residents who object to having a landfill near their homes. This community reluctance is sometimes referred to by the acronym, *NIMBY*, which stands for "Not In My Back Yard." Solutions to landfill issues are likely to be expensive, either because of the legal fees a city must pay to fight residents' objections or because of the cost of transporting garbage to a more distant site.

Building More Landfills

The total number of active municipal-solid-waste landfills in the United States in 1988 was about 8,000. By 2008 the total number of active landfills had declined to about 1,900, but the overall landfill capacity had actually increased. These changes reflect the fact that as old landfills were filled up, waste-management companies built fewer but much larger landfills. The map in **Figure 1.10** shows regional differences in the number of landfills as well as in the percentage of municipal solid waste that is sent to landfills.

FIGURE 1.10

Landfill Capacity The map below shows the number of landfills in each region and the percentage of that region's municipal solid waste (MSW) sent to landfills in 2008.

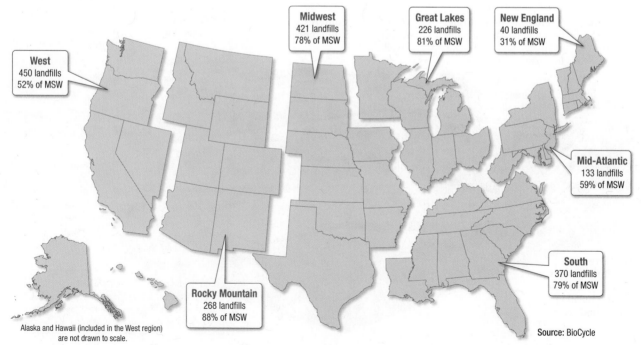

West
450 landfills
52% of MSW

Midwest
421 landfills
78% of MSW

Great Lakes
226 landfills
81% of MSW

New England
40 landfills
31% of MSW

Mid-Atlantic
133 landfills
59% of MSW

Rocky Mountain
268 landfills
88% of MSW

South
370 landfills
79% of MSW

Alaska and Hawaii (included in the West region) are not drawn to scale.

Source: BioCycle

©Universal Images Group/Getty Images

Incinerators

One option for sending less waste to landfills is to burn it in incinerators, as shown in **Figure 1.11**. In 2008, the United States had 115 operational incinerators that were capable of burning in excess of 94,000 metric tons of municipal solid waste per day. However, the waste that is burned does not disappear. Although incinerators can reduce the weight of solid waste by 75 percent, they cannot separate materials that should not be incinerated before burning the waste. So, some materials that should not be burned, such as cleansers, batteries, and paints, end up in the air as polluting gases. The rest of the solid waste is converted into ash that must be disposed of in a landfill.

Incinerated material takes up less space in landfills, but the material can be more toxic than it was before being incinerated. Even incinerators that have special air pollution control devices release small amounts of poisonous gases and particles of toxic heavy metals into the air.

FIGURE 1.11

Incineration A solid-waste incinerator reduces the amount of trash that goes to landfills and can be used to generate electricity. However, the material that is created by the incinerator can be toxic.

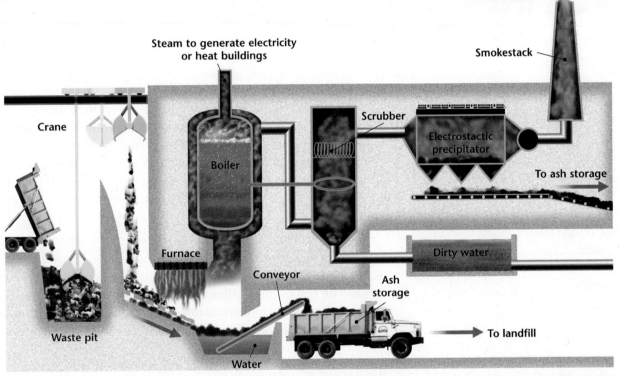

Steam to generate electricity or heat buildings

Smokestack

Crane

Scrubber

Electrostactic precipitator

Boiler

To ash storage

Dirty water

Furnace

Conveyor

Ash storage

Waste pit

To landfill

Water

Section 1 Formative Assessment

▶ Reviewing Main Ideas

1. **Explain** what makes a material biodegradable.

2. **Describe** how a modern landfill works. List two environmental problems that can be caused by landfills. Explain your answer.

3. **Describe** one advantage and one disadvantage of incinerating solid waste.

✔ Critical Thinking

4. **Identifying Relationships** Name two nonbiodegradable products that you use. What makes them nonbiodegradable? Name biodegradable products that you can use instead.

5. **Identifying Alternatives** Explain what you can do to help reduce the amount of solid waste that you throw away and to reduce what is thrown away in your community.

Objectives

- Identify three ways you can produce less waste.

- Describe how you can use your consumer buying power to reduce solid waste.

- List the steps that an item must go through to be recycled.

- List two benefits of composting.

- Name one advantage and one disadvantage to producing degradable plastic.

Key Terms

source reduction
recycling
compost

FIGURE 2.1

Reuse and Reduce Using dish towels instead of paper towels is one way to reduce solid waste.

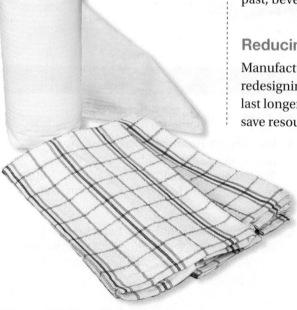

Reducing Solid Waste

If landfills and incinerators can pollute the environment and are expensive to operate, what else can we do to safely reduce solid waste? This section examines ways to reduce solid waste through producing less waste, recycling, and changing the materials and products we use. All of these techniques help reduce waste before it is delivered to landfills or incinerators. This method of reducing solid waste is known as source reduction. **Source reduction** is any change in design, manufacture, purchase, or use of materials or products to reduce their amount or toxicity before they become municipal solid waste.

Consumer Power

If we produce less waste, we will reduce the expense and difficulty of collecting and disposing of it. Many ideas for reducing waste are common sense, such as using both sides of a sheet of paper and not using unneeded bags, napkins, or utensils at stores and restaurants.

Reusing Materials

As a consumer, you can influence manufacturers to reduce solid waste. If you buy products that have less packaging, products that last longer, or reusable products, you will encourage manufacturers to produce more of those products. For example, you can buy products such as dish towels instead of paper towels, as shown in **Figure 2.1**. You can also buy rechargeable batteries instead of regular batteries to help reduce solid waste.

Until about 1965, nearly all beverages were sold in bottles that were designed to be returned to stores when empty. The empty bottles were then collected, washed, and refilled at bottling plants. Today, there is a demand for disposable bottles rather than for refillable bottles. If consumers began to use more refillable bottles similar to those used in the past, beverage manufacturers would begin producing them again.

Reducing Waste

Manufacturers could also reduce waste and conserve resources by redesigning products to use less material. A return to products that last longer and that are designed to be easily repaired would both save resources and reduce waste disposal problems.

Recovering Resources

In addition to reducing waste, we need to find ways to make the best use of all the materials we throw away. **Recycling** is the process of reusing materials or recovering valuable materials from waste or scrap. Making products from recycled materials usually saves energy, water, and other resources. For example, 95 percent less energy is needed to produce aluminum from recycled aluminum than from ore. About 70 percent less energy is needed to make paper from recycled paper than from trees.

Recycling: A Series of Steps

When most people think about recycling, they probably think about only the first step—putting their bottles, cans, and newspapers into a recycling bin. However, as shown in **Figure 2.2**, there are a series of steps needed for recycling to work.

First, the discarded materials must be collected from users and taken to a facility where they can be sorted by type. Next, each type of material must be cleaned and made ready to be used again. For example, glass is sorted by color and is crushed, and paper is sorted by type and made into a pulp with water. Then the materials are used to manufacture new products. Finally, the new products, ranging from newspapers to playground equipment, are sold to consumers. If more people buy products made from recycled materials, the increased demand encourages manufacturers to supply recycled products. When manufacturers build facilities to make recycled products, it becomes easier for communities to sell the materials they collect from residents for recycling.

FIELDSTUDY
Go to Appendix B to find the field study
Recycling

✔ **CHECK FOR UNDERSTANDING**
Infer How can consumer demand influence the packaging of bottled beverages?

FIGURE 2.2

The Steps of Recycling include ❶ collecting and sorting discarded materials by type, ❷ taking the materials to a recycling facility, ❸ cleaning the discarded materials so that they can be shredded or crushed, and ❹ reusing the shredded or crushed materials to manufacture new products.

FIGURE 2.3

BENEFITS OF COMPOSTING

keeps organic wastes out of landfills

provides nutrients to the soil

increases beneficial soil organisms, such as worms and centipedes

suppresses some plant diseases

reduces the need for fertilizers and pesticides

✓ **CHECK FOR UNDERSTANDING**

Explain What conditions help biodegradable material break down rapidly?

Composting

Yard waste often makes up as much as 14 percent of a community's solid waste. None of this waste has to go to a landfill. Because yard waste is biodegradable, it will decompose in a compost pile. Fruit and vegetable trimmings and table scraps will also decompose in a compost pile. Adding meat scraps and animal wastes to compost is not recommended, though, as they can attract pests and carry disease. The more oxygen and moisture there are in a compost pile, the more rapidly microorganisms will break down the biodegradable waste. Eventually the material becomes **compost**, a dark brown, crumbly material that is spread on gardens and fields to enrich the soil. Compost is rich in the nutrients that help plants grow. More benefits of composting are listed in **Figure 2.3**.

Grass clippings can be composted or left on the lawn to add nutrients back into the soil as they decompose. Sweeping the clippings into storm drains is against the law in some places, because they can block the drains and contribute to flooding after heavy rainfall. Some cities collect yard waste from homes and compost it at a central facility. Composting can also be an effective way of handling waste from food-processing plants and restaurants. If all biodegradable wastes were composted, the amount of solid waste going to landfills would be reduced.

CASESTUDY

Paper or Plastic?

"Do you want paper or plastic, or did you bring your own, reusable bags?" Many grocery stores offer a choice between either paper or plastic bags for sacking grocery items, or have reusable bags for purchase. Many people make their choice based on convenience. But what is the best choice for someone who is concerned about the environment?

On the surface, it may seem that paper is the better choice. Paper comes from a renewable resource—trees—and is biodegradable. Plastic, on the other hand, comes from petroleum or natural gas, which are usually considered nonrenewable resources. In addition, the plastic bags available in most stores are not biodegradable.

Upon closer examination, however, the decision may not be as simple as it seems. Plastic bags take up less room in a landfill, and removing large numbers of trees from forests to manufacture paper can disrupt woodland ecosystems. Plus, a tremendous amount of energy is required to convert trees into pulp and then manufacture paper from the pulp. Concern has also arisen about reusable bags fostering bacterial growth, and high lead content has been found in some reusable polypropylene bags.

Making an educated decision at the grocery store will help reduce solid waste.

To make the best decision about which product is better for the environment, the following questions should be considered:

- How much raw material, energy, and water is needed to manufacture each bag?

- What waste products will result from the manufacture of each bag, and what effect will those wastes have on water, the atmosphere, and the land?

- Can recycled materials be used in the manufacture of the bag? If so, to what degree will the use of recycled materials reduce the amount of raw materials, energy,

Changing the Materials We Use

Simply changing the materials we use could eliminate much of the solid waste we produce. For example, single-serving drink boxes are made of a combination of foil, cardboard, and plastic. The drink boxes are hard to recycle because there is no easy way to separate the three components. More of our waste could be recycled if such products were no longer made and if all drinks came in recyclable glass, cardboard, or aluminum containers.

Recycling other common household products into new, useable products could also help eliminate solid waste. For example, newspapers can be recycled to make cardboard, egg cartons, and building materials. Telephone books, magazines, and catalogs can also be recycled to make building materials. Used aluminum beverage cans can be recycled to make new beverage cans, lawn chairs, aluminum siding for houses, and cookware. Used glass jars and bottles can be recycled to make new glass jars and bottles. Finally, plastic beverage containers can be recycled to make nonfood containers, insulation, carpet yarn, textiles, fiberfill, scouring pads, toys, plastic lumber, and crates.

and water used and wastes produced in making the bag?

- How will the bag decompose, and what will the environmental impact be if it is incorrectly disposed of?

Although several studies have analyzed these questions, most have been conducted by parties with a vested interest, such as plastic or paper manufacturing companies. Often, the researchers fail to study all of the important factors listed above.

But the debate has caused industries to improve the way their products affect the environment. Previously, paper bags were considered best, but new technology has allowed the plastics industry to gain a larger market share. By incorporating recycled plastic into the bags and making plastic bags from degradable plant materials, manufacturers improved the image of plastic bags.

Therefore, the debate continues and environmentally conscious people are still wondering which is better. Right now there seems to be no right answer. However, the following are environmentally sound options.

- Carry your groceries in bags brought from home (paper, plastic, or canvas bags).

- Choose the bag you are most likely to reuse in the future.

- If you have only a few small items, do not use a bag.

A reusable canvas shopping bag may be the best response to the paper-or-plastic question.

Critical Thinking

1. **Identifying Relationships** Explain how environmentally conscious shoppers have helped improve paper and plastic bag manufacturing in this country.

2. **Understanding Concepts** Why should a person care which bag he or she is given at the grocery store?

FIGURE 2.4

Biodegradable Plastic Green plastics made from living things are biodegradable.

100% NATURAL FIBRES
100% BIODEGRADABLE
2-3 YEAR LIFE
BREAKS DOWN IN ACTIVE
COMPOST WITHIN
6 MONTHS

Degradable Plastics

As you read earlier, most plastics are not biodegradable. To make plastic products more appealing to people who are concerned about the environment, several companies have developed new kinds of plastics that they say are degradable. One type, called *photodegradable plastic*, is made so that when it is left in the sun for many weeks, it becomes weak and brittle and eventually breaks into pieces.

Another type of degradable plastic, called *green plastic*, is made by blending the sugars in plants with a special chemical agent to make plastic. Green plastics are labeled as "green" because they are made from living things and are considered to be more environmentally friendly than other plastics. The production of green plastics requires 20 to 50 percent less fossil fuel than the production of regular plastics does. A number of items like the flowerpots in **Figure 2.4** are now made of green plastic. This plastic has been engineered to degrade within a short period of time after being thrown away. When this plastic is buried, the bacteria in the soil eat the sugars and leave the plastic weakened and full of microscopic holes. The chemical agent then gradually causes the long plastic molecules to break into shorter molecules. These two effects combine to cause the plastic to eventually fall apart into small pieces.

Problems with Degradable Plastics

The main problem with these so-called degradable plastics is that although they do break apart and the organic parts can degrade, the plastic parts are only reduced to smaller pieces. This type of plastic can help reduce the harmful effects that plastic litter has on animals in the environment, because the plastic pieces will be too small to get caught in their throats or around their necks. However, the small pieces of plastic will not disappear completely. Instead, the pieces of plastic will be spread around and may affect smaller organisms. So, these biodegradable plastics can remain in landfills for many years, just as regular plastics can.

Section 2 Formative Assessment

▶ Reviewing Main Ideas

1. **Name** three things you could do each day to produce less waste.

2. **Explain** how buying certain products can help reduce solid waste.

3. **Describe** the steps it takes to recycle a piece of plastic.

4. **List** two benefits of composting.

✔ Critical Thinking

5. **Analyzing Methods** What are the advantages and disadvantages to producing degradable plastics?

6. **Applying Ideas** Read the Case Study in this section and decide which type of bag you would choose the next time you go shopping. Explain why you made this choice. What are other uses of the bag you chose?

Hazardous Waste

SECTION 3

Objectives

- Name two characteristics of hazardous waste.
- Describe one law that governs hazardous waste.
- Describe two ways to treat hazardous waste safely.

Many of the products we use today, from laundry soap to computers, are produced in modern factories that use thousands of chemicals. Some of these chemicals make up parts of the products, while other chemicals are used as cleaners. Large quantities of the chemicals used are often left over as waste. Many of these chemicals are classified as **hazardous waste**, which is any waste that is a risk to the health of humans or other living things.

Types of Hazardous Waste

Hazardous wastes may be solids, liquids, or gases and contain toxic, corrosive, or explosive materials. Hazardous wastes include substances such as paints, batteries, or biomedical materials. More examples of hazardous wastes are listed in **Figure 3.1**.

Disposal of hazardous wastes often is not as carefully planned as the manufacturing processes that produced them. One case with horrifying results occurred at Love Canal, in Niagara Falls, New York. Begun in the late 1800s as an ideal community, the land was eventually sold. By 1920, it had become a dumping site for toxic materials. Eventually, it was bought by the Niagara Falls School Board for a dollar, even though the board knew of the toxins buried there. Schools and low-income housing were built on the site. In the late 1970s, corroded barrels began popping up in yards, and an abnormal number of health problems and birth defects were reported for the area.

The events at Love Canal shocked people into paying more attention to how hazardous wastes were being managed. As a result of Love Canal and other hazardous waste incidents in the U.S., Federal laws were passed to clean up old waste sites and regulate future waste disposal.

Key Terms

hazardous waste
deep-well injection
surface impoundment

FIGURE 3.1

TYPES OF HAZARDOUS WASTE

dyes, cleansers, and solvents
PCBs (polychlorinated biphenyls) from older electrical equipment, such as heating systems and television sets
solvents, lubricants, and sealants
toxic heavy metals, such as lead, mercury, cadmium, and zinc
pesticides
radioactive wastes from spent fuel that was used to generate electricity

Hazardous Waste Dumping An improperly maintained hazardous waste site can leak toxic wastes into the air, soil, and groundwater.

©Shepard Sherbell/Corbis Saba

Resource Conservation and Recovery Act

The Resource Conservation and Recovery Act (RCRA) was passed by Congress in 1976 and amended in 1984. The RCRA created the first significant role for federal government in waste management. The act was established to regulate solid and hazardous waste disposal and to protect humans and the environment from waste contamination.

The primary goals of the RCRA include protecting human health from the hazards of waste disposal, conserving energy and natural resources by recycling and recovering, reducing or eliminating waste, and cleaning up waste, which may have spilled, leaked, or been improperly disposed of.

Resource Conservation and Recovery Act

The Resource Conservation and Recovery Act (RCRA), which governs municipal solid waste disposal, also requires producers of hazardous waste to keep records of how their wastes are handled from the time the wastes are made to the time the wastes are placed in an approved disposal facility. If the wastes cause a problem in the future, the producer is legally responsible for the problem. RCRA also requires all hazardous waste treatment and disposal facilities to be built and operated according to standards that are designed to prevent the facilities from polluting the environment.

The Superfund Act

Because the safe disposal of hazardous wastes is expensive, companies or individuals that produce hazardous wastes may be tempted to dump them illegally to save money. Congress passed the Comprehensive Environmental Response, Compensation, and Liability Act (CERCLA), more commonly known as the Superfund Act, in 1980 and reauthorized it again in 1986. The Superfund Act gives the U.S. Environmental Protection Agency (EPA) the right to sue the owners of hazardous waste sites who illegally dumped waste. The law also gave the EPA the right to force site owners to pay for the cleanup and created a fund to pay for cleaning up abandoned hazardous waste sites when owners couldn't be identified.

Cleaning up improperly discarded waste is difficult and extremely expensive. Underfunded by the government, CERCLA often depends upon heavy fines to force responsible parties to pay for the cleanup. At Love Canal alone, $275 million was spent to put a clay cap on the site, to install a drainage system and treatment plant for leaking wastes, and to relocate residents. Many Superfund sites still need to be cleaned up, as shown in **Figure 3.2**. As of 2008, cleanup had been completed at only 341 of the roughly 1,620 approved or proposed Superfund sites.

FIGURE 3.2

Superfund Sites This map shows the number of approved and proposed Superfund sites as of 2001. These sites are some of the most hazardous areas in the United States.

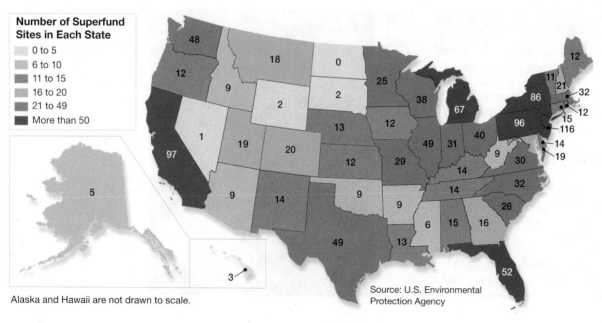

Number of Superfund Sites in Each State
- 0 to 5
- 6 to 10
- 11 to 15
- 16 to 20
- 21 to 49
- More than 50

Alaska and Hawaii are not drawn to scale.

Source: U.S. Environmental Protection Agency

FIGURE 3.3

Transporting Hazardous Waste Safely transporting hazardous waste is an important part of hazardous waste management.

✔ **CRITICAL THINKING**

Describe What security measures must be taken by transportation companies to prevent tampering with hazardous waste shipments?

Hazardous Waste Management

Each year, the United States produces about 252 million metric tons of hazardous waste, and this amount is growing. It is difficult to guarantee that the transport (**Figure 3.3**) and disposal techniques used today will not eventually pollute our air, food, or water.

Preventing Hazardous Waste

One way to prevent hazardous waste is to produce less of it. In recent years, many manufacturers have discovered that they can redesign manufacturing methods to produce less or no hazardous waste. For example, some manufacturers that used chemicals to clean metal parts of machines have discovered that they can use tiny plastic beads instead. The beads act like a sandblaster to clean the parts, can be reused several times, and are not hazardous when disposed of. Often, such techniques save the manufacturers money by cutting the cost of materials as well as by cutting the cost of waste disposal.

Another way to deal with hazardous waste is to find a way to recycle or reuse it. Companies sometimes work together to reduce waste. For example, a company that once would have thrown a cleaning solvent away after one use may instead sell it to another company that has a use for it.

Conversion into Nonhazardous Substances

Some types of wastes can be treated with chemicals to make the wastes less hazardous. For example, lime, which is a base, can be added to acids to neutralize them. Also, cyanides, which are extremely poisonous compounds, can be combined with oxygen to form carbon dioxide and nitrogen. In other cases, wastes can be treated using *bioremediation*. Sludge from petroleum refineries or wastewater treatment facilities, for example, may be converted by bacteria into less harmful substances.

✔ **CHECK FOR UNDERSTANDING**

Explain How can cleaning machinery with plastic beads rather than solvents help to reduce hazardous waste?

Hazardous Chemical Reactions

After a material is thrown away, it may become more hazardous as a result of a chemical reaction with other discarded wastes. For example, metallic mercury is considered to be toxic. Metallic mercury is often used in thermometers and computers. If it is buried in a landfill, the bacteria in a landfill can cause it to react with methane to form methyl mercury. Methyl mercury, which is more toxic than metallic mercury, can cause severe nerve damage.

Land Disposal

Most of the hazardous waste produced in the United States is disposed of on land. One land disposal facility, illustrated in **Figure 3.4**, is called deep-well injection. During **deep-well injection**, wastes are pumped deep into the ground, where they are absorbed into a dry layer of rock below the level of groundwater. After the wastes are buried below the level of groundwater, the wastes are covered with cement to prevent contamination of the groundwater. Another common land disposal facility is a **surface impoundment**, which is basically a pond that has a sealed bottom. The wastes accumulate and settle to the bottom of the pond, while water evaporates from the pond and leaves room to add more wastes.

Hazardous wastes in concentrated or solid form are often put in barrels, transported to another location and either stored or buried in landfills. Hazardous waste landfills are similar to those used for ordinary solid waste, but these landfills have extra safety precautions to prevent leakage.

In theory, if all of these facilities are properly designed and built, they should provide safe ways to dispose of hazardous wastes. However, if they are not properly maintained, they can develop leaks that may result in contamination of the air, soil, or groundwater.

CASESTUDY

Green Chemistry

Walk into any pharmacy, and you will see a wide range of headache tablets for sale. Several popular brands contain ibuprofen as the active ingredient. But the production of ibuprofen used to create a headache itself.

When first developed and patented in the 1960s, the six-step process to make ibuprofen produced large quantities of unwanted byproducts. In fact, more waste was made than useful product. In the 1990s, a new three-step process was developed. This process uses millions of metric tons fewer chemicals as raw materials and prevents the formation of millions of metric tons of waste. Fewer chemicals used and less waste produced adds up to a process that is better for the environment and less expensive for the manufacturer. This is an example of green chemistry in action.

A set of principles guide green chemists. The first principle of the ACS Green Chemistry Institute is "Prevention: It is better to prevent waste than to treat or clean up waste after it has been created." Ideally, raw materials should be renewable, and the product should biodegrade into harmless substances when it is no longer

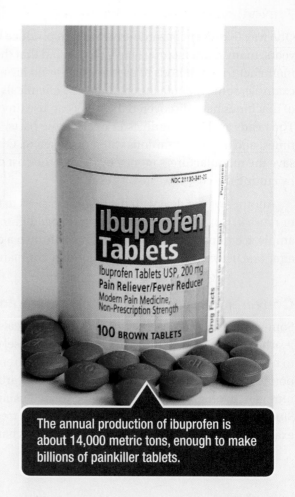

The annual production of ibuprofen is about 14,000 metric tons, enough to make billions of painkiller tablets.

FIGURE 3.4

Deep-Well Injection One way to dispose of hazardous waste is through deep-well injection, in which hazardous wastes are pumped deep into the ground.

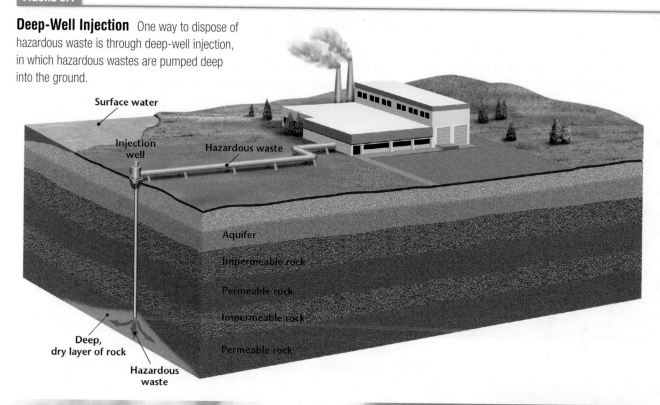

Surface water

Injection well

Hazardous waste

Aquifer

Impermeable rock

Permeable rock

Impermeable rock

Permeable rock

Deep, dry layer of rock

Hazardous waste

needed. The ideal process would use little energy and convert all the raw materials into final product. Chemists are not usually able to develop processes that meet all of these guidelines. The closer they can get to an ideal process, however, the better it is for the environment.

For example, the old process for the manufacture of ibuprofen used a substance called aluminum trichloride to increase the speed of one of the reactions. Unfortunately, aluminum trichloride decayed during the reaction. It ended up as a waste product that usually went into landfills. In the new process, a different substance is used to speed up the reaction. This substance does not break down. It is the gas hydrogen fluoride, which is easily separated from the reactant mixture and reused.

In addition, the original process converted only 40 percent of the weight of the raw materials used into ibuprofen. The new process raises this conversion to around 99 percent, including the useful byproduct, acetic acid (the acid in vinegar).

In 1992, a plant for the manufacture of ibuprofen, using the principles of green chemistry, opened in Bishop, Texas. The largest of its kind, the facility is still in use and is capable of producing about 6 billion tablets every year—about a quarter of the world's demand for ibuprofen. The company that developed the green process was rewarded with a Presidential Green Chemistry Challenge Award.

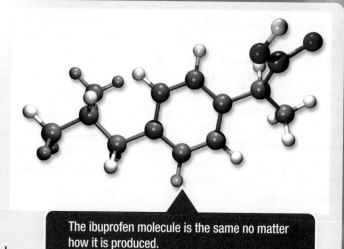

The ibuprofen molecule is the same no matter how it is produced.

Critical Thinking

1. **Making Decisions** Think of a chemistry experiment you have done. Write a paragraph to explain how the experiment could have been "greener."

2. **Evaluate Viewpoints** Should subsidies be given to companies to encourage them to develop and put into practice greener processes?

FIGURE 3.5

Remediation Chemicals can be used to clean up hazardous wastes. This tractor is applying chemicals to an oil spill to help absorb the oil.

ECOFACT

Biomining

Bacteria are not only used to break down hazardous wastes, but they are also used to extract copper and gold from ore. This technique is called *biomining*. Currently, 25 percent of the world's copper is produced through biomining. Today, scientists are attempting to bioengineer bacterial strains that can mine poisonous heavy metals such as arsenic, cadmium, and mercury from ore.

✓ **CHECK FOR UNDERSTANDING**

Describe What are two problems associated with using incinerators to dispose of hazardous waste?

Remediation

Some hazardous wastes can be cleaned up, absorbed, or broken down, or their toxicity can be reduced by treatment with biological and chemical agents. This process is known as environmental *remediation*.

Biologically Treating Hazardous Waste

Certain bacteria can be used to clean up an area in the environment that has been contaminated with hazardous substances, such as crude oil, PCBs, and cyanide. Plants that absorb heavy metals can also be planted in contaminated areas. As shown in **Figure 3.5**, chemicals are used to neutralize and absorb hazardous wastes.

Incinerating Hazardous Waste

Some hazardous wastes are disposed of in specially designed incinerators. Incinerators can be a safe form of disposal, but they have several problems. Incineration is generally the most expensive form of waste disposal because it requires a lot of energy. Incinerators also need pollution-control devices and must be carefully monitored so that hazardous gases and particles are not released into the air. After hazardous waste is incinerated, the leftover ash usually needs to be buried in a hazardous waste landfill.

When we put hazardous waste into disposal facilities for long-term storage, they must be closely monitored. For example, the only way to make radioactive wastes nonhazardous is to let them sit for thousands of years until the radioactivity decreases to safe levels. Therefore, engineers and geologists search for disposal sites that probably will not be damaged by movements of Earth for thousands of years.

Exporting Hazardous Waste

Until recently, only local laws regulated waste disposal in the United States. Companies would often get rid of hazardous wastes by sending them to landfills in other states, especially the less populated southern states. In the 1980s, as southern populations grew, these states began to refuse hazardous wastes from other states.

Hazardous wastes are also exported through international trade agreements. Some hazardous wastes are exported to other countries because there may be a facility in another country that specializes in treating, disposing of, or recycling a particular hazardous waste.

Hazardous Wastes at Home

You may think of hazardous waste management as a problem that only big industries face. Chemicals, including house paint, pesticides, and batteries, all create hazardous waste and are used in homes, schools, and businesses ,as shown in **Figure 3.6**. Hazardous materials poured down the drain or put in the trash end up in solid-waste landfills. These should instead be disposed of in a specially designed hazardous waste landfill.

Disposing of Household Hazardous Waste

To make sure that household hazardous waste is disposed of properly, cities around the country have begun to provide collection of household hazardous waste. Some cities collect materials only once or twice a year, while other cities have permanent facilities where residents can drop off hazardous waste. Trained workers sort the hazardous materials and send some materials for recycling and pack other materials into barrels for disposal. Used batteries and motor oil are recycled. Paint may be blended and used for city park maintenance or to clean up graffiti.

Motor Oil

If you have ever changed the oil in your car yourself, you have probably wondered what to do with the old, dirty oil. It is illegal to pour it on the ground or throw it in the trash, because even a single can of oil can contaminate as much as 3.8 million liters (1 million gallons) of water. You may be surprised, however, to find out that people in the United States illegally throw away about 700 million liters (185 million gallons) of used motor oil every year. This amount does not include the oil disposed of by service stations and automobile repair shops.

So what can people do with the oil? One option is to take it to an automobile service station, where it will be turned in for recycling. Some cities have designated oil-collection receptacles, as shown in **Figure 3.7**. These cities recycle the used oil turned in by citizens. If you do not know what services your community provides, you can call your local city government and find out.

©Mark Williamson/Oxford Scientific/Getty Images

FIGURE 3.6

COMMON HAZARDOUS HOUSEHOLD PRODUCTS

motor oil	pesticides
paints	fertilizers
batteries	cleaners
computers	antifreeze
mobile phones	

FIGURE 3.7

Motor Oil Used motor oil should be disposed of at an automobile service station or in an oil-collection receptacle.

✔ Section 3 Formative Assessment

▶ Reviewing Main Ideas

1. **Identify** one law that governs hazardous waste.

2. **Describe** two common ways to dispose of hazardous waste in the United States. What is one advantage and one disadvantage of one of these methods?

3. **Describe** how bacteria could be used to degrade hazardous wastes. Write a short paragraph to explain your answer.

✔ Critical Thinking

4. **Evaluating Ideas** Suppose that a surface impoundment site for hazardous waste is planned for your community. Would you oppose locating the site in your community? Explain your answer.

5. **Applying Ideas** Suppose someone dumped leftover motor oil on a driveway. Could this disposal method contaminate the air, water, or soil? Explain your answer.

How Should Nuclear Waste Be Stored?

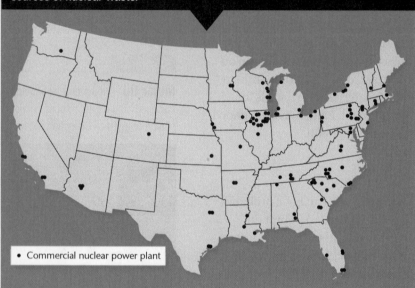

This map shows nuclear power plants around the United States, all of which are sources of nuclear waste.

• Commercial nuclear power plant

Nuclear fuel is used to generate electricity at power plants. When nuclear fuel rods can no longer serve this function, they are classified as high level radioactive waste. High-level radioactive waste includes solids, liquids, and gases containing a high concentration of radioactive isotopes that take approximately 100,000 years to decay. While nuclear energy is clean energy that can easily provide power for large cities without producing any air pollution, nuclear waste poses a major disposal problem.

Forever Storage

One option for disposing of nuclear waste is to take what scientists call a geologic approach, storing the waste in an underground location, protected by mountain bedrock or desert salt flats, that is not prone to earthquakes and does not have water flowing through it.

Finland expects to complete such a facility in 2020. It is called Onkalo, which means "hidden." Onkalo consists of spiraling steel and concrete tunnels bored into a mountain of bedrock. Spent fuel rods will be stored in copper canisters deposited in beds of bentonite clay. Once Onkalo is full, sometime in the 2100s, Finland plans to backfill it. "It was important that we found a solution," says Timo Seppala, who works for the contractor constructing the site, "that would require no surveillance or management by future generations." Sweden is planning a similar facility, expected to be operational in 2020.

In 1987, Congress chose Yucca Mountain to be the location for the first U.S. permanent storage site for waste produced by nuclear power plants. But Nevadans and activists lobbied hard to stop the project. Opponents argued that in 100,000 years, climate changes might increase precipitation in the area. Then Yucca Mountain's underground water table might rise high enough to come into contact with the stored nuclear waste—and wash radioactive particles into the water supply. Although the waste is sealed in waterproof canisters, activists point out that no canister can be expected to last for 100,000 years. Current technology can only provide canisters to last for 500 to 1,000 years.

In 2010, President Barack Obama directed the U.S. Department of Energy to drop its plans for the site.

©David Howells/Corbis

Temporary Storage

Meanwhile, U.S. nuclear waste is being held on site at the nuclear power plants that produced it. More than 65,000 tons of nuclear waste is being held at about 75 different nuclear reactors around the country (some of these reactors have since been shut down, but they continue to be staffed for the sake of protecting the waste that is stored there). Used nuclear fuel rods are stored in canisters that are held in pools of water, for cooling, or in solid concrete casks. Many of these storage sites, though, have been used for so many decades that they are approaching their maximum capacity.

Recycling Nuclear Waste

"Spent" nuclear fuel is made up of about 95.6 percent unused uranium. It is possible to reprocess nuclear waste, remove the unused uranium, and use it for fuel. Doing so greatly reduces the amount of nuclear waste that is produced by nuclear power plants. In fact, France has recycled its nuclear waste since the very first years of its nuclear industry. In France, producing enough electricity to provide power to a family of four for 20 years produces a quantity of nuclear waste about the size of a pack of gum.

However, reprocessing nuclear waste means separating uranium from plutonium. Plutonium is left over as a byproduct of nuclear recycling. Since plutonium can be used to make nuclear weapons, recycling nuclear waste has proven to be politically controversial in some countries, including the U.S.

Rows of metal drums store nuclear waste from Rhode Island in a facility near Oak Ridge, Tennessee.

What Do You Think?

Do research and find the locations for nuclear power plants in the U.S. that currently store nuclear waste onsite in pools and casks. Plot the locations on a map. Which option do you think is safer: transporting nuclear waste to a facility such as the now-cancelled Yucca Mountain facility, leaving the waste onsite at power plants, or finding a way to recycle it?

SECTION 1 **Solid Waste**

OBJECTIVES

- Every year, people in the United States generate more than 10 billion metric tons of solid waste.

- Materials that are biodegradable, such as newspapers and cotton fibers, can be broken down by biological processes. Materials that are not biodegradable such as plastics, are a major cause of disposal problems.

- Municipal solid waste makes up only a small fraction of the total solid waste generated, but it still amounts to over 236 million tons per year.

- Landfills and incinerators are two facilities used for disposing solid waste.

KEY TERMS

solid waste

biodegradable

municipal solid waste

landfill

leachate

SECTION 2 **Reducing Solid Waste**

OBJECTIVES

- Source reduction is a method by which we can produce less waste, recycle, and reuse materials.

- Recycling is the process of reusing materials or recovering valuable materials from waste or scrap.

- A compost pile made from plant and animal matter can be spread on gardens and fields to enrich the soil.

- Degradable plastic is a type of plastic that is partially made from living things.

KEY TERMS

source reduction

recycling

compost

SECTION 3 **Hazardous Waste**

OBJECTIVES

- Hazardous waste is any waste that is a risk to the health of humans or other living things.

- The Resource Conservation and Recovery Act (RCRA) and the Superfund Act were established to regulate solid and hazardous waste disposal and to protect humans and the environment from waste contamination.

- Activities at home can create hazardous waste. Household hazardous wastes should be properly disposed of at designated collection sites.

KEY TERMS

hazardous waste

deep-well injection

surface impoundment

CHAPTER 19 Review

Reviewing Key Terms

Use each of the following terms in a separate sentence.

1. *source reduction*
2. *leachate*
3. *municipal solid waste*
4. *biodegradable*
5. *recycling*

Use the correct key term to complete each of the following sentences.

6. _____ is any waste that is a risk to the health of humans or other living things.

7. A dark brown, crumbly material made from decomposed matter is called _____.

8. A _____ is a waste disposal facility where wastes are put in the ground and covered each day with a layer of dirt, plastic, or both.

9. **Concept Map** Use the following terms to create a concept map: *solid waste, hazardous waste, landfills, types of waste, surface impoundment, methods of waste disposal, incineration,* and *deep-well injection.*

Reviewing Main Ideas

10. Solid waste includes all of the following *except*
    a. newspaper and soda bottles.
    b. food scraps and yard clippings.
    c. ozone and carbon dioxide.
    d. junk mail and milk cartons.

11. If your shirt is partly cotton and partly polyester, what part is biodegradable?
    a. cotton.
    b. polyester.
    c. both (a) and (b).
    d. none of the above.

12. Microorganisms are unable to break down plastics because plastics
    a. are made from oil.
    b. are too abundant.
    c. are made of unknown elements.
    d. do not occur in nature.

13. Municipal solid waste is approximately what percentage of all solid waste?
    a. 2 percent
    b. 20 percent
    c. 60 percent
    d. 90 percent

14. Leachate is a substance that
    a. is produced in a compost pile.
    b. is a byproduct of bacterial digestion.
    c. is produced by incinerators.
    d. contains dissolved toxic chemicals.

15. Which of the following is not a benefit of incinerating waste?
    a. It reduces the material sent to landfills.
    b. It produces energy in the form of heat.
    c. It can be used to produce electricity.
    d. It neutralizes all of the toxic materials.

16. Manufacturers could reduce waste and conserve resources by making products that
    a. use more materials.
    b. are more durable.
    c. are difficult to repair.
    d. are disposable.

17. Which of the following is one way to reduce an over-supply of recyclable materials?
    a. build more recycling plants
    b. increase the types of recyclable materials
    c. increase the demand for products made from recycled materials
    d. put the excess materials in landfills

18. Most of the municipal solid waste in the United States is
    a. stored in landfills.
    b. recycled.
    c. incinerated.
    d. None of the above

Short Answer

19. Do you think incineration is an efficient disposal method for glass and metal wastes? Write a short paragraph that explains why or why not.

20. How do plastic liners and layers of clay help protect the environment around a landfill?

21. What are the materials that make up compost? List at least three benefits of composting.

22. How does the Superfund Act allow the federal government to ensure proper disposal of hazardous waste?

Interpreting Graphics

The graph below shows the number of active landfills in the United States from the year 1988 to the year 1998. Use the graph to answer questions 23–25.

23. **Determine** Approximately how many active landfills existed in 1988? in 1998?

24. **Explain** During the span of 10 years, did the overall number of active landfills increase or did the number decrease? What may have caused this change? Explain your answer.

25. **Predict** If this trend continues, what might the graph look like for the year 2028?

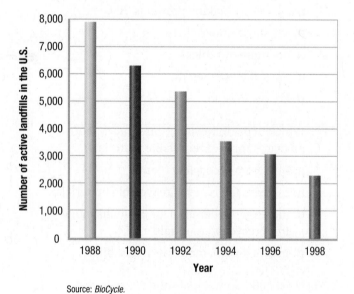

Source: *BioCycle.*

Critical Thinking

26. **Understanding Concepts** During the 1970s, the production of municipal solid waste decreased. An economic recession was also occurring. How might the reduction in waste have been related to the recession?

27. **Making Comparisons** Read the description of recycling in this chapter and compare the benefits of buying a product that has been recycled to the benefits of buying a brand new product. Which product would you prefer to buy? Explain your answer.

28. **Evaluating Information** How would a ban on the production of plastics affect both the environment and society?

29. **Identifying Relationships** When we purchase hazardous household products, such as motor oil, bleach, and pesticides, what happens to the containers when they are empty? What happens to the hazardous waste that these products create?

30. **Predicting Consequences** How might a person's current shopping habits affect the quality of the environment 100 years in the future?

31. **Social Studies** Use an almanac to determine which five states have the greatest number of hazardous waste sites. What factors do you think might account for the number of hazardous waste sites located in a state?

32. **Make a Display** Do a special project about recycling in your community. Determine what types of materials are collected, where they are taken for processing, how they are recycled, and what products are made from them. Display your findings on a poster.

Analyzing Data

Use the table below to answer questions 33–35.

PAPER PRODUCTS IN MUNICIPAL SOLID WASTE		
Product	Generation (tons)	Percentage recycled
Newspapers	13,620	56.4
Books	1,140	14.0
Magazines	2,260	20.8
Office papers	7,040	50.4

33. **Evaluating Data** How many tons of paper products were generated according to the table?

34. **Making Calculations** How many tons of newspapers were recycled? How many tons of newspapers were not recycled?

35. **Making Calculations** How many tons of office papers were recycled? How many tons of office papers were not recycled?

Making Connections

36. **Writing Persuasively** Pretend that you work for a company that sells degradable plastics. Write an advertising campaign that would persuade consumers to buy materials made from your company's brand of degradable plastic.

37. **Outlining Topics** Describe the various ways in which hazardous waste can be disposed of. List the advantages and disadvantages of each way.

CASESTUDY

38. As a consumer, how can you influence manufacturers to utilize green chemistry?

39. How can using green chemistry help reduce the amount of hazardous wastes produced?

Why It Matters

40. How does the United States compare with other developed countries in terms of solid waste produced per person, per year?

STUDYSKILL

Increase Your Vocabulary To learn and remember vocabulary words, use a dictionary for words you do not understand and become familiar with the glossaries of your textbooks.

Out of Sight—Out of Mind

Objectives

Recognize various categories and amounts of solid waste produced.

Compute percentages of waste, by category, produced per person in a single day.

Generalize data from a small sample for a large population using calculations.

Infer from small data samples the impact that waste production has on a large population.

Evaluate how waste data can be used to communicate results and offer solutions.

Materials

balance, triple beam, or electronic

calculator

paper towels

plastic bags

ruler

Do you have any idea what happens to the things you throw away every day? The items that we can't reuse or recycle end up in a landfill somewhere. Various government and private agencies study the amount and types of waste we produce and are continuously working to solve the problems of waste disposal. In this lab activity, you will determine how much solid waste you produce during a typical day. You will also predict through calculations how much solid waste your population produces each day.

Procedure

1. On the day before the lab activity, collect all the items you would normally throw away. Put all of your waste in a plastic bag, including wrappers, napkins, straws, unopened containers of condiments, and disposable trays, notebook or printer paper, drink cans and bottles, etc. You should not include uneaten food of any kind.

2. The day of the lab, each group member should place his or her plastic bag of waste on the worktable. Each member should separate his or her waste on a paper towel into the following categories: paper and cardboard, plastic, metal, glass, wood, and food.

3. For each category of waste, determine the mass of waste produced by each person in the group. Create a data table similar to the one shown below and record the masses.

4. Determine the total mass for each category for the lab group. Then, determine the average mass of solid waste per student for each category. Finally, determine the overall total amount of solid waste produced for each student.

Waste category	Student 1	Student 2	Student 3	Total mass of lab group	Average mass/student
Paper and cardboard					
Plastic					
Metal					
Glass					
Wood					
Food					
Total					

Analysis

1. **Organizing Data** Use the equation below to determine the percentages for the waste categories that make up your total waste as an individual. Add another column to your data table to record this value.

$$\frac{\text{Mass (in grams) of waste category}}{\text{Mass (in grams) of total waste}} \times 100 = \text{waste category's percentage of total waste}$$

2. **Organizing Data** Use the equation above to determine the percentages for the waste categories that make up the total waste for your lab group. Divide the total waste for each category from the table on the previous page by the grand total and multiply by 100. Add another column to your data table to record these values.

Step 4 Determine the mass of the waste produced in grams for each category of waste.

3. **Examining Data** Compare your averages for the different categories and your total with other groups in the class. How and why are the data different or similar?

4. **Examining Data** Which category of waste makes up the greatest percentage of the total waste? Explain your answer.

Conclusions

5. **Making Predictions** How can you calculate the lunch waste produced in each category and overall by your entire school's student body in a day? Use your equation to make this calculation.

6. **Applying Conclusions** How can you use the knowledge you have acquired by doing this calculation exercise to reduce the amount of waste you produce?

Extension

7. **Research and Communications** Write a letter to the editor of your school newspaper, the editor of the local newspaper, or your school principal or cafeteria manager sharing the data your class has gathered and calculated. Offer creative solutions to eliminate and reduce some of the waste.

ECOZINE
HMDScience.com

Go online for more information about
these feature articles in the unit:

Our Health and Our Future

The casuarina tree is native to Australia and is one of the few pine trees that grow in nutrient-poor, sandy areas. This casuarina plantation on the coast of South Africa was established to hold sand dunes in place and to serve as a local source for wood fuel.

(t) ©Michel Gounot/Godong/Corbis; (b) ©Alex Webb/Magnum Photos

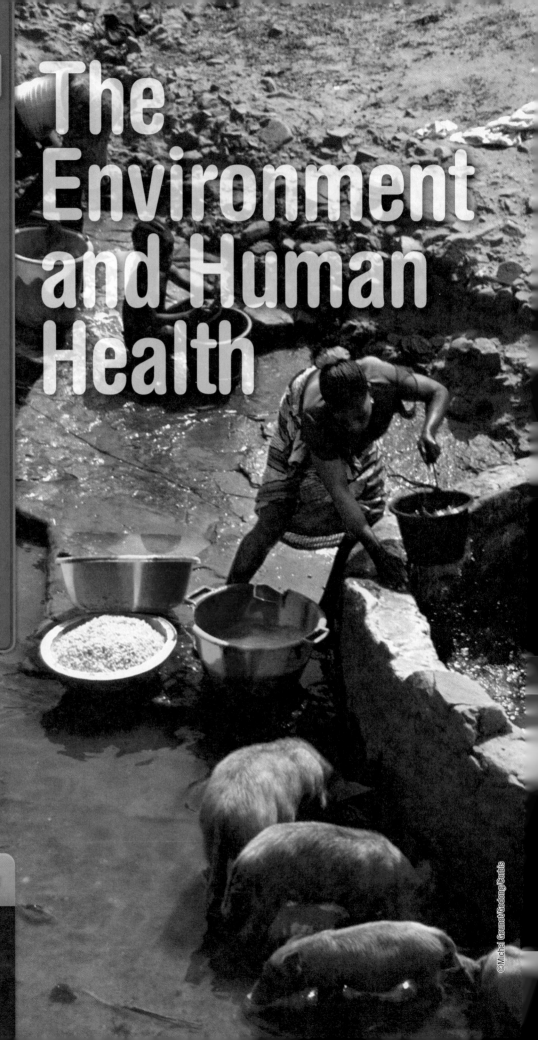

CHAPTER 20

The Environment and Human Health

Section 1
Pollution and Human Health

Section 2
Biological Hazards

Why It Matters

Sanitation, the practice of treating water, wastewater, and trash, can reduce the incidence of infectious diseases spread through polluted water. However, safe and reliable community water supply systems are expensive to build and maintain. In some countries, common water sources are used for drinking, bathing, washing dishes and clothes, and food preparation.

How can water be made safer for human consumption and take into account different cultural practices?

CASESTUDY

Learn about pollutants that affect fertility in humans and other animals in the case study Chemicals that Disrupt Hormones on page 516.

ONLINE ENVIRONMENTAL SCIENCE
HMDScience.com

Go online to access additional resources, including labs, worksheets, multimedia, and resources in Spanish.

©Michel Gounot/Godong/Corbis

Pollution and Human Health

If you have ever coughed from breathing car exhaust, you have experienced a mild health effect of air pollution. Pollution of air, water, and soil is frequently in the news. Because people in the United States are concerned about pollution, our country enjoys a relatively clean environment. But this situation is also due to the efforts of scientists who have studied the relationship between pollution and human health. Scientists are also beginning to understand the broader relationships between health and the environment.

Environmental Effects on Health

Pollution causes illnesses in two main ways. First, pollution may cause illnesses directly by poisoning, as in the cases of lead poisoning and lung cancer. Second, pollution may cause illnesses indirectly by infectious diseases that are spread in polluted environments. Examples of these diseases include cholera and river blindness, which are caused by organisms that inhabit polluted water.

The World Health Organization (WHO) has begun to collect data on how the environment affects human health. **Figure 1.1** shows the WHO's estimate of poor health by world region as a graph. Poor health is represented by the estimated number of days of healthy life that are lost to death and disease. The graph shows that, in general, people in developed countries suffer less from environmental causes of poor health. In developing countries, environmental causes of poor health are largely due to parasites and bacteria in polluted water and insect-borne diseases, such as malaria.

SECTION 1

Objectives

> List five pollutants, their sources, and their possible effects on human health.

> Explain how scientists use toxicology and epidemiology.

> Explain how pollution can come from both natural sources and human activities.

> Describe the relationship between waste, pollution, and human health.

Key Terms
toxicology
dose
dose-response curve
epidemiology
risk assessment
particulates

FIGURE 1.1

Environmental Pollution and World Health

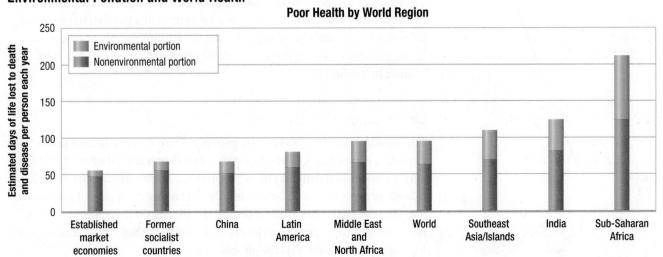

Poor Health by World Region

Estimated days of life lost to death and disease per person each year

- Environmental portion
- Nonenvironmental portion

Established market economies · Former socialist countries · China · Latin America · Middle East and North Africa · World · Southeast Asia/Islands · India · Sub-Saharan Africa

Source: *Epidemiology.*

FIGURE 1.2

TYPES AND EFFECTS OF POLLUTANTS

Pollutant	Source	Possible Effects
Pesticides	agriculture and landscaping	nerve damage, birth defects, and cancer
Lead	lead paint and gasoline	brain damage and learning problems
Particulate matter	vehicle exhaust, burning waste, fires, and tobacco smoke	respiratory damage (asthma, bronchitis, cancer)
Coal dust	coal mining	black lung disease
Bacteria in food	poor sanitation and poor food handling	gastrointestinal infections

Toxicology

The word *toxic* means poisonous. **Toxicology** is the study of toxic substances, including their nature, effects, detection, methods of treatment, and exposure control. **Figure 1.2** lists some important pollutants and their toxic effects.

Toxicity: How Dangerous Is It?

We are exposed to small amounts of chemicals every day in food, in the air we breathe, and sometimes in the water we drink. Almost any chemical can be harmful if large enough amounts are taken in. The question is whether the concentration of any particular chemical in the environment is high enough to be harmful.

To determine the effect of a pollutant on health, we need to know how much of the pollutant is in the environment and how much gets into the body. Then we need to determine what concentration of the toxin damages the body. The amount of a harmful chemical to which a person is exposed is called the **dose** of that chemical. The damage to health that results from exposure to a given dose is called the *response*. Whether a chemical has a toxic effect depends in part on the dose. The response also depends on the number of times a person is exposed, the person's size, and how well the person's body breaks down the chemical.

A *persistent chemical* is a chemical that breaks down slowly in the environment. The pesticide DDT is an example of a persistent chemical. Persistent chemicals are dangerous because more people are likely to come into contact with them, and these chemicals are more likely to remain in the body.

Dose-Response Curves

The toxicity of a chemical can be expressed as a **dose-response curve**, as shown in **Figure 1.3**. A dose-response curve shows the relative effect of various doses of a drug or chemical on one or more organisms as determined by experiments. Sometimes, there is a *threshold dose*. Exposure to any amount of the chemical less than the threshold dose has no adverse effect on health. Exposure to levels above the threshold dose usually leads to more or increased adverse effects.

FIGURE 1.3

Dose-Response Curve A dose-response curve shows the response of an organism to different concentrations of a substance.

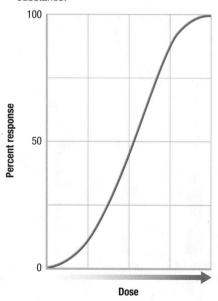

FIGURE 1.4

Epidemiologic Data This map shows the location of cases of mercury poisoning in Virginia. Patterns point scientists toward areas of mercury pollution.

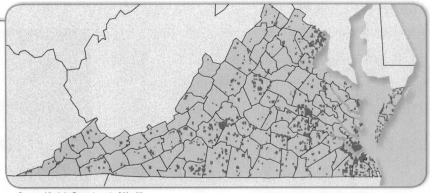

Source: Virginia Department of Health

Epidemiology

When an epidemic occurs, such as a widespread flu infection, health officials use their knowledge of epidemiology to take action. **Epidemiology** (EP uh DEE mee AHL uh jee) is the study of the spread of diseases. Epidemiologists collect data from health workers on when and where cases of a disease have occurred. This information can be used to produce a map like the one in **Figure 1.4.**

Then scientists trace the disease to try to find its origin and how to prevent it from spreading. For example, in a case of mercury poisoning, health officials may ask questions such as: What did the people with mercury poisoning have in common? Were they all exposed to the same chemicals? How widespread is the disease?

Risk Assessment

In order to safeguard the public, health officials determine the risk posed by specific hazards. Risk is the probability of a negative outcome. In the case of human health, risk is the probability of suffering a disease, injury, or death.

Scientists and health officials work together on risk assessments for pollutants. A **risk assessment** is an estimate of the risk posed by a specific substance. During a risk assessment, scientists first compile and evaluate existing information on the substance. Second, they determine how people might be exposed to it. **Figure 1.5** shows a diagram from a computer model of how air pollutants might travel through a city area. The third step is determining the toxicity of the substance. Finally, scientists characterize the risk that the substance poses to the public. Risk assessments may lead to government regulations on how and where the substance can be used. In the United States, the Environmental Protection Agency (EPA) formulates these regulations.

FIGURE 1.5

Epidemiologic Modeling Air flow models like this one help scientists predict the path that air pollutants may follow through a city. The bright orange areas are receiving the most pollutants.

FIGURE 1.6

Natural Causes of Particle Pollution

Dust A dust storm descends upon Marrakesh, Morocco, in the photo above. Dust is perhaps the most common natural pollutant.

Volcanic Ash A town is coated with ash after the 1991 eruption of Mount Pinatubo, in the Philippines.

Pollution from Natural Sources

You may think of pollution as being entirely caused by people, but some pollutants occur naturally in the environment. Naturally occurring pollutants usually become hazardous to health when they are concentrated above their normal levels in the environment. One example is the radioactive gas radon. In some areas, radon from granite bedrock may seep into buildings, where it becomes concentrated. Because it is an odorless gas, people may unknowingly breathe it in. Radon causes an estimated 15,000 to 22,000 cancer deaths every year in the United States.

Particulates

The most common pollutants from natural sources are dust, soot, and other particulates. **Particulates** (pahr TIK yoo lits) are particles in the air that are small enough to breathe into the lungs. These particles become trapped in the tiny air sacs in our lungs and cause irritation. This irritation can make lung conditions, such as chronic bronchitis and emphysema, worse. **Figure 1.6** shows particle pollution from a dust storm, and pollution from a volcanic eruption. Wildfires also produce large amounts of particulates.

Heavy Metals

Another type of pollution from natural sources is caused by *heavy metals*. Dangerous heavy metals include the elements arsenic, cadmium, lead, and mercury. These metals occur naturally in rocks and soil. Most of these elements cause nerve damage when they are ingested beyond their threshold dose. Selenium, also found naturally in many soils, is actually a beneficial element when taken in very small quantities. But larger doses cause birth defects in birds.

Pollution from Human Activities

Human activities release thousands of types of chemicals into the environment, but we know surprisingly little about the health effects of most of them. Only about 10 percent of commercial chemicals have been tested for their toxicity, and about 1,000 new chemicals are introduced every year. **Figure 1.7** shows the introduction of pollutants into the environment by human activities.

Recent Improvements

In the United States, regulations have helped reduce our exposure to pollutants. Most vehicles and factories now have pollution-control devices. As a result, people living in the United States contain lower levels of some toxic chemicals in their bodies, on average, than they did in the recent past. In 2001, 2003, and 2005, the U.S. Centers for Disease Control and Prevention (CDC) released studies on chemical residues in the U.S. population. Levels of nicotine (from smoking), mercury, and several other toxic chemicals were considerably lower in these peoples' tissues than they had been in 1991. Because we know so little about the effects of chemicals on our health, new health risks are discovered frequently. For example, scientists now think that chemical pollution may be at least part of the cause of Parkinson's disease and Alzheimer's disease.

Burning Fuels

Despite advances in public health resulting from pollution control, air pollution is still a major health problem. Burning fuels in vehicles, home furnaces, power plants, and factories introduces enormous amounts of pollutants into the air. These pollutants include the gas carbon monoxide and particulates. Gasoline and coal burning contribute to many premature deaths each year from asthma, heart disease, and lung disorders. A recent study found that long-term exposure to air contaminated with soot particles raises a person's risk of dying from lung and heart diseases.

FIELDSTUDY

Go to Appendix B to find the field study **Sources of Pollution.**

✔ **CHECK FOR UNDERSTANDING**

Identify Name three potential effects on human health from burning gasoline and coal.

FIGURE 1.7

Human Causes of Water and Air Pollution

Paper mills contribute pollutants to rivers.

Vehicle emissions cloud the air in urban areas worldwide.

(bl) ©Peter Turnley/Corbis; (br) ©Still Pictures

Concentration

Concentrations of chemicals in the environment are often expressed in parts per million (ppm) or parts per billion (ppb). One teaspoon of salt in two gallons of water produces a salt concentration of 1,000 ppm. What salt concentration, in ppm, would result from dissolving one teaspoon of salt in five gallons of water?

Pesticides

Pesticides are chemicals designed to kill unwanted organisms such as insects, fungi, or weeds. Pesticides are beneficial in that they allow us to grow more food by reducing pest damage. Many of the increases in food production in the past 60 years are partly due to the development and use of more effective pesticides. But because pesticides are designed to kill organisms, they are often dangerous to humans in large enough doses. Although we are exposed to pesticide residues on fruits and vegetables, the amounts consumed by most people pose little danger.

Most modern pesticides, such as most of those used in the United States, break down quickly in the environment into harmless substances. Widely used *organophosphate* pesticides have replaced more persistent pesticides, such as DDT. But organophosphates are very toxic, causing nerve damage and perhaps cancer. In 2004, U.S. poison centers reported nearly 7,200 cases of organophosphate poisoning. Most cases of pesticide poisoning affect the people applying the chemicals.

Persistent chemicals are still used in many developing countries. Such pesticides pose the greatest risk to children, whose internal organs are still developing and who eat and drink more in relation to their body weight than adults do.

CASESTUDY

Chemicals that Disrupt Hormones

One important field of environmental science is *ecotoxicology*, the study of the effects of pollutants on organisms. Studies may investigate genetic, cellular, or reproductive changes in organisms exposed to specific pollutants in the environment. Laboratory experiments are conducted to determine the threshold dose of the pollutant in the organism.

Scientists have collected evidence that many pollutants disrupt the endocrine system. In humans and other organisms, the glands that make up the endocrine system produce *hormones*. Hormones are chemicals that circulate in the bloodstream and control most life processes, including the development of muscles and sex organs. Some pollutants, called *hormone mimics*, behave like natural hormones. Others, called *hormone disrupters*, prevent natural hormones from functioning normally. Even low levels of these pollutants can affect developing embryos and infants.

Researchers first discovered hormone mimics in male trout and eels that contained egg-yolk proteins usually produced only by females. These fish were downstream from sewage treatment plants. Lab experiments showed that the water contained estrogen-like chemicals and that these chemicals induced the male fish to make female proteins. The chemicals are thought to have come from detergents and from the urine of women taking contraceptive pills.

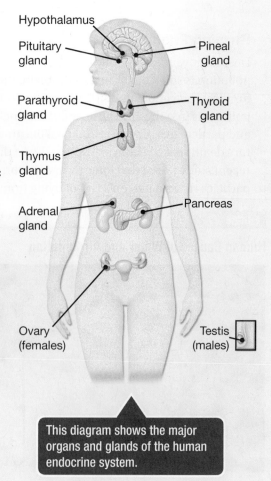

Hypothalamus
Pituitary gland
Pineal gland
Parathyroid gland
Thyroid gland
Thymus gland
Adrenal gland
Pancreas
Ovary (females)
Testis (males)

This diagram shows the major organs and glands of the human endocrine system.

Industrial Chemicals

We are exposed to low levels of industrial chemicals every day, particularly inside new buildings that have new furnishings. Toxic chemicals are used to make building materials, carpets, cleaning fluids, and furniture. Older buildings, like the one shown in **Figure 1.8**, were often painted using lead-based paint. Lead is directly linked to brain damage and learning disabilities. Children under age six are most at risk for lead poisoning.

Often, industrial chemicals are not known to be toxic until they have been used for many years. For example, polychlorinated biphenyls (PCBs) are oily fluids that have been used for years as insulation in electrical transformers. PCBs break down very slowly in the environment. In 1996, studies showed that children exposed to PCBs in the womb can develop learning problems and IQ deficits. The waters of the Great Lakes are polluted by PCBs, and doctors warn pregnant women not to eat certain fish from these lakes. Studies have shown that adults with high concentrations of PCBs in their tissues have more memory problems than adults who do not.

FIGURE 1.8

Industrial Pollutants Lead poisoning in children is most often due to direct exposure to lead-based paint.

The fertility of American alligators, such as this one, has been reduced by their exposure to hormone-disrupting pollutants.

Most hormone disrupters interfere with the sex hormones. They prevent normal production of testosterone in males or increase the chances of sexual abnormality in females. Some hormone disrupters include phthalates, which are used in cosmetics like hair dyes and fingernail polish. Polychlorinated biphenyls (PCBs), some pesticides, lead, and mercury may also act as hormone disrupters.

Many cases of pollution by hormone disrupters have been documented. Alligators in a polluted Florida lake had such abnormally small penises and low testosterone levels that they could not reproduce. In 2002, scientists reported that even small amounts of the widely used herbicide atrazine disrupt the sexual development of frogs. Killer whales of the Pacific Northwest and beluga whales in the St. Lawrence Estuary have high levels of hormone disrupting chemicals in their bodies. Their populations display reproductive problems, tumors, and sexual abnormalities, possibly caused by hormone disrupters. Hormone disrupters in the environment may also affect humans. In the past 50 years, there has been a large increase in cancers of the prostate, testicles, ovaries, and breasts in most industrialized countries. All of these forms of cancer can be accelerated by abnormal levels of sex hormones.

Experimentation related to hormone disrupters is difficult and can be ethically challenging. Scientists must rely on many lines of evidence to determine chemical toxicity, such as documented abnormalities and comparative studies of the impact of the same chemicals on other species.

Critical Thinking

1. If humans are increasingly exposed to water pollutants, what are some possible results?

2. Name some possible ethical challenges related to hormone-disruptor experimentation?

FIGURE 1.9

Solid Waste Pollution Waste that is not disposed of properly can pollute beaches, where it can pose a threat to swimmers and sunbathers.

✔ **CRITICAL THINKING**

Apply What are two examples in the image of pollution related to inadequate waste disposal?

©UNEP

Waste Disposal

Much of the pollution in our environment is a by-product of inadequate waste disposal. **Figure 1.9** shows the pollution of a beach with solid waste. Wastewater from cities can carry oil and dozens of toxic chemicals into our waterways. Waste incineration plants can emit toxic products into the air, and mining can release toxic contaminants into streams and rivers.

Methods of disposing of waste have improved. However, problems remain. Many old landfills are leaking. And many communities still have sewage treatment plants that release raw sewage into a river or the ocean after heavy rains. In addition, laws regulating waste disposal are not always enforced.

The United States government has not decided how it will dispose of radioactive waste from nuclear power plants. Meanwhile, the waste remains at or near the plants, and small quantities of radioactive iodine, cesium, and other elements leak into nearby waterways.

✔ SECTION 1 **Formative Assessment**

▶ **Reviewing Main Ideas**

1. **List** five pollutants, their sources, and their possible effects on human health.

2. **Explain** how pollution can arise from both natural sources and from human activities.

3. **Describe** the relationship between waste, pollution, and human health.

✔ **Critical Thinking**

4. **Making Comparisons** Write a short paragraph that explains the relationship between toxicology and epidemiology.

5. **Analyzing Relationships** In what ways do human activities increase the health risks from natural pollutants?

Biological Hazards

Objectives

▶ Explain why the environment is an important factor in the spread of some diseases.

▶ List two changes to the environment that can lead to the spread of infectious diseases.

▶ Explain what scientists mean when they say that certain viruses are emerging.

Some of the damage to human health in which the environment plays a role is not caused by toxic chemicals but by organisms that carry disease. Today, we have outbreaks of diseases that did not exist or that few people had heard of 100 years ago, such as AIDS, Ebola, West Nile virus, hantavirus, and mad cow disease. In addition, diseases that have killed people for centuries, such as malaria, tuberculosis, yellow fever, and hookworm, kill many more people today than they did 50 years ago. All these diseases are caused by organisms. One of the reasons these diseases are now widespread is that we have altered our environment in ways that encourage them to spread.

The Environment's Role in Disease

Infectious diseases are caused by **pathogens,** organisms or viruses that cause disease. Some of these diseases, such as tuberculosis and whooping cough, are spread from person to person through the air. Other diseases are spread by drinking water that contains the pathogen. Still other diseases are transmitted by a secondary host, such as a mosquito. A **host** is an organism in which a pathogen lives all or part of its life. **Figure 2.1** lists the most deadly infectious diseases worldwide.

Key Terms

pathogen
host
vector

FIGURE 2.1

DEATHS FROM DISEASES IN 2004, *Estimated by the World Health Organization*		
Disease and examples	**Cause**	**Estimated deaths per year (in millions)**
Total infectious and parasitic diseases	bacteria, viruses, and parasites	9.5
Respiratory infections (pneumonia, influenza, and whooping cough)	bacteria, viruses	4.3
AIDS	virus	2.0
Diarrheal diseases (cholera, typhus, typhoid, and dysentery)	bacteria, viruses, parasites	2.2
Tuberculosis	bacteria	1.5
Childhood diseases (measles and diphtheria)	virus	0.8
Malaria	parasitic protist	0.9
Tetanus	bacteria	0.2
Tropical diseases (trypanosomiasis, Chagas' disease, schistosomiasis, and leishmaniasis)	bacteria, viruses, and parasites	0.2

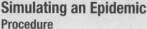

QUICKLAB

Simulating an Epidemic
Procedure

1. Using a computer with Internet service, open the simulation at http://www.personal.kent.edu/~mdball/infectious_Disease_Model.htm
2. Using the slider, change the number of initial-healthy to 50.
3. Push the Setup button, then click Go.
4. Run the simulation until there are no more color changes of the "people" in the simulation window.
5. Record your observations.

Analysis

1. What did you observe about the spread of disease when the population was small?
2. Explain the effect the increase in population had on the way the epidemic spread.

✔ **CHECK FOR UNDERSTANDING**

Identify Why are local water supplies in developing countries often polluted?

FIGURE 2.2

Treatment for Dehydration This child is undergoing rehydration therapy during a cholera epidemic in South Africa.

Infectious Disease

Most infectious diseases are transmitted through water. In developing countries, where there is not enough water for basic needs, the local water supply is often used for drinking, washing, and sewage disposal. So, the water is often polluted and is a good breeding ground for pathogens. The pathogens breed in water and transfer diseases directly to humans through water, or organisms that carry the pathogens transfer them to humans through the water. An organism, such as a mosquito, that transmits a pathogen or parasite to another organism is called a **vector.** The construction of irrigation canals and dams, particularly in the tropics, has increased the habitat for vectors. For example, the Three Gorges Dam in China has created a huge freshwater lake. This lake is the habitat of the snail vector in which the parasitic worm that causes schistosomiasis lives.

Cholera

The deadliest waterborne diseases come from drinking water polluted by human feces. Pathogens, such as those that cause *cholera* and *dysentery,* enter the water in human feces. These diseases cause the body to lose water by diarrhea and vomiting. **Figure 2.2** shows a child being treated for dehydration. Cholera and dysentery cause most infant deaths around the world. Up to 80 percent of cases can be successfully treated by rehydration.

Malaria

The disease *malaria* was once the world's leading cause of death. Today it remains in the top five causes of death from infectious diseases worldwide. Malaria is caused by parasitic protists and is transmitted by a bite from infected females of certain species of mosquitoes. The mosquito vector lays her eggs in stagnant fresh water, which is where the mosquito larva develops. No effective vaccine exists, but simple measures like the use of inexpensive sleeping nets can greatly reduce deaths due to malaria.

©Jean-Marc Bouju/AP/Wide World Photos

FIGURE 2.3

Soil Erosion Soil erosion in Nepal leads to the spread of parasites such as the hookworm, which often enters the body through bare feet.

Environmental Change and Disease

Many ways in which we alter the environment make the environment more suitable for pathogens to live and reproduce. For example, soil is often polluted with chemicals and pathogens. When soil erodes, these pollutants blow away and wash away with the soil and may contaminate areas thousands of miles away. Many parasites are spread through soil that is contaminated with feces. Hookworm, which causes acute exhaustion, was once common in the United States. People are infected by walking barefoot on soil that contains human and animal feces or by consuming contaminated food or water. **Figure 2.3** shows soil erosion in Nepal. Roughly 60 percent of the population in Nepal is infected by parasitic worms, with much higher incidence in rural areas. The high number of infections is most likely due to increased contaminated soil exposure caused by widespread erosion.

Antibiotic Resistance

Our actions cause pathogens to evolve resistance to antibiotics that are used to kill them. For example, in the United States, large quantities of antibiotics are fed to livestock each year to speed their growth. As a result, *Salmonella, Escherichia coli (E. coli)*, and other bacteria that live in livestock evolve resistance to antibiotics. These bacteria make thousands of people in the U.S. sick each year when they eat contaminated meat that has been improperly refrigerated or undercooked.

We also use enormous amounts of antibiotics to treat human illnesses. In 1979, 6 percent of European strains of pneumonia bacteria were resistant to antibiotics. Ten years later, 44 percent of the strains were resistant. Tuberculosis (TB) is another illness treated with antibiotics. The spread of TB in recent years is mostly due to the evolution of antibiotic resistance in the bacterium that causes TB.

ECOFACT

Suburbs Spread Lyme Disease
Lyme disease is the most widespread vector-borne disease in the United States. It is caused by a bacterium similar to the one that causes the sexually transmitted disease syphilis. The vector is a tick found on white-tailed deer. The suburbs are a suitable place for deer to grow and reproduce, and their populations have exploded as suburbs have expanded. Lyme disease infects more than 20,000 people a year in the United States.

l(inset) ©Sebastian Kaulitzki/Alamy Images; (t) ©Chloe Hall/Alamy Images

FIGURE 2.4

Spread of Disease

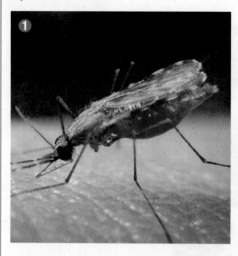
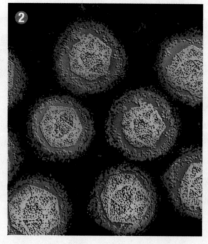
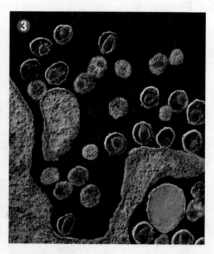

Diseases can be spread by vectors ❶ such as the *Anopheles* mosquito, which transmits *Plasmodium*, the parasite that causes malaria. ❷ The dengue virus is transmitted by the *Aedes* mosquito, and ❸ HIV is spread directly from one person to another.

✔ **CRITICAL THINKING**

Relate How could changes in the environment influence diseases like malaria and Dengue Fever?

✔ **CHECK FOR UNDERSTANDING**

Identify Why was it necessary to develop new methods for controlling mosquitoes that transmit malaria?

Connect to BIOLOGY

The Viral Advantage

Antibiotics kill bacteria but not viruses, such as those that cause colds and flu. Antibiotics kill bacteria by interfering with their cellular mechanisms. Viruses do not have cellular mechanisms. Many antibiotics destroy the system a bacterium uses to make proteins. Viruses do not make their own proteins. Instead, they take over the cellular machinery of the cells they invade and use the cells to make proteins.

Vector-Borne Diseases

Malaria was common in much of the United States and Europe before the days of mosquito control. Historically, malaria was controlled by draining marshes and rice paddies where the mosquitoes breed and by spraying with pesticides. The *Anopheles* mosquito, shown in **Figure 2.4,** breeds in water and is the secondary host that transmits malaria. However, mosquitoes have evolved resistance to most pesticides. Newer methods for controlling mosquitoes involve spreading growth regulators that prevent mosquito larvae from maturing into adults or that sterilize the female mosquitoes. Malaria is common in tropical countries where mosquito control is still limited. Also, some epidemiologists think that climate changes may increase the areas where diseases like malaria and Dengue Fever occur, including areas of Central America, South America, Africa, and Asia.

Emerging Viruses

In recent years, scientists have been focusing on so-called emerging viruses that were unknown 100 years ago. One example is AIDS (acquired immune deficiency syndrome), which is caused by HIV (human immune deficiency virus), shown in **Figure 2.4**. Most viral diseases spread directly from one person to another. Often, the virus invades the body through a cut or through mucus membranes. Dengue infection is a leading cause of illness and death in the tropics and subtropics. Dengue Fever, is caused by the dengue virus, shown in **Figure 2.4,** which is transmitted by the *Aedes* mosquito. Our main defense against viral diseases is vaccination. The problem with vaccines is that they are very specific. When a new strain of a viral pathogen evolves, a new vaccine must be developed.

Cross-Species Transfers

In recent years, scientists have discovered an increasing number of pathogens that have made a *cross-species transfer,* or have moved from one species to another. For example, HIV and West Nile virus fall into this category. The pathogens that cause these diseases have lived for centuries in some species of wild animals and have done little damage. When the pathogens invade humans, the pathogens cause serious diseases. Some ecologists think that the ways in which we are altering the environment and destroying habitats ensure that diseases like these will become more common in the future.

Examples of Cross-Species Transfers

One example of pathogens that made a cross-species transfer occurred in Argentina. Herbicides were sprayed on crops in Argentina. The herbicide killed the native grasses and allowed other plants to invade the farmland. These new plants attracted a species of rodent that feeds on them. The rodents were carrying viruses for a hemorrhagic fever, which infected many of the agricultural workers. Hemorrhagic fevers cause hemorrhages, or internal bleeding, by breaking blood vessels. Hantavirus is an example of a virus that causes hemorrhagic fever.

Influenza, or flu, is highly contagious. The flu virus passes from humans to animals (particularly birds) and back to humans again. Hong Kong flu gets its name from the fact that the virus was transmitted to humans from ducks bred in Hong Kong for food. **Figure 2.5** shows a poultry market, where the Hong Kong flu virus probably transferred from birds to people. Because flu is so easily spread from one person to another, epidemiologists predict that the greatest threat to human health may be the outbreak of a new, very virulent strain of influenza virus, which would spread rapidly through crowded urban populations.

FIGURE 2.5

Cross-Species Transfer Poultry markets, such as this one in Hong Kong, can contribute to the cross-species transfer of viruses from birds to humans.

SECTION 2 Formative Assessment

▶ Reviewing Main Ideas

1. **List** two changes to the environment that can lead to the spread of infectious diseases.

2. **Explain** why some diseases are likely to spread as a result of climate change.

3. **Describe** why the environment is an important factor in the spread of cholera.

4. **Explain** the term emerging virus.

✔ Critical Thinking

5. **Understanding Concepts** Read the information under the heading "Antibiotic Resistance." How is the use of antibiotics by humans increasing antibiotic resistance in pathogens?

6. **Analyzing Relationships** How do human activities cause pathogens to move from one species to another? Give examples of cross-species transfer to help explain your answer.

Lyme Disease Risk

LYME DISEASE RISK IN THE UNITED STATES

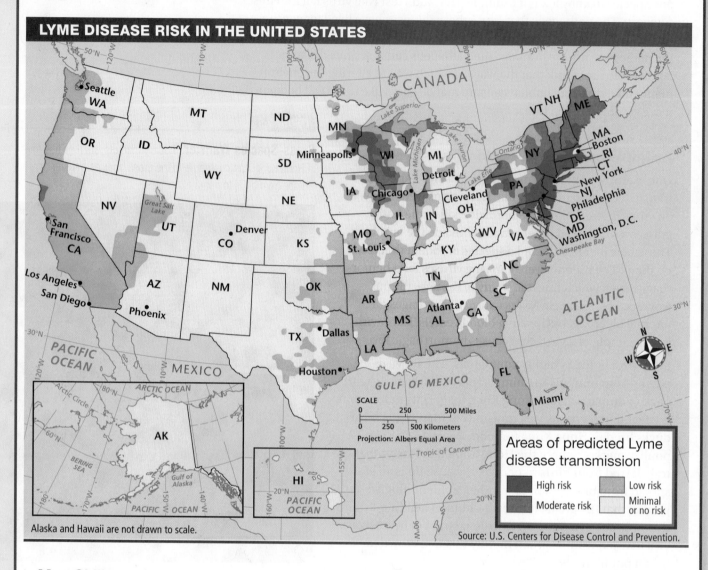

Alaska and Hawaii are not drawn to scale.

Source: U.S. Centers for Disease Control and Prevention.

Map Skills

Use the Lyme disease risk map for the United States to answer the questions below.

1. **Interpreting Graphics** Using the map above, determine the risk of contracting Lyme disease in your city or town.

2. **Interpreting Graphics** In what general region of the United States is the risk of contracting Lyme disease greatest?

3. **Recognize Relationships** Can you determine the relationship between the risk of contracting Lyme disease

and the concentration of ticks that act as vectors for the disease? Explain your answer.

4. **Analyzing Data** What is the difference between the risk of contracting Lyme disease in rural Massachussetts and the risk of contracting Lyme disease in rural Nevada?

5. **Inferring Conclusions** What factors might account for the relatively high risk of contracting Lyme disease in the Northeast?

ECOZINE *at* HMDScience.com

Go online for the latest environmental science news and updates on all EcoZine articles.

Water Challenges

In the United States and other developed countries it is easy to get clean water. These countries have systems to deliver water to distant places. They also have effective laws and management to preserve the water supply and have good waste collection and treatment systems. In much of the world, this is not the case. Access to clean water is one of the world's biggest health challenges. For example, in many African countries, there is not enough water. In places where there is plenty of water, it often is contaminated with human wastes or pollutants. Thousands of people die every day from diarrhea caused by drinking unsafe water.

Making a Difference

For the last several decades, many organizations have been cooperating to bring clean water to people around the world. One of these programs is the Global Water for Sustainability Program (GLOWS). GLOWS is a team of organizations, led by Florida International University, funded by the United States Agency for International Development. By working with governments of developing countries and local communities, they increase social, economic, and environmental benefits of clean water. They do this by helping countries develop management plans for water use and creating infrastructure to deliver and purify water. This ensures that there is enough clean water available and that people don't have to travel too far to get water. GLOWS trains members of local communities in waste and water management to maintain water resources into the future. Although there is still much to do, international programs including GLOWS have improved water access and sanitation for more than a billion people already.

Water in a Changing World

The challenges of ensuring adequate water resources for people are complicated by environmental changes. Drought, sea level rise, floods, and other factors associated with climate change threaten water supplies. Drought and salt water moving into freshwater supplies can reduce the amount of water available to people. Floods can make waters unsafe to drink if pollutants enter the water supply. Understanding the impacts of climate change and natural disasters is a critical part of GLOWS's work.

Safe water is a basic human necessity for cleaning, cooking, and drinking. At least one in eight people worldwide do not have access to a safe and reliable water supply.

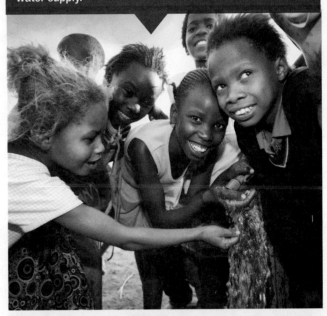

What Do You Think?

It is important to invest resources to improve access to water wisely. How would you concentrate your money if you were going to try to improve conditions for the largest number of people in an area?

(t) ©Paul Hackett/In Pictures/Corbis; (b) ©Anjum Naveed/AP Images

SECTION 1 **Pollution and Human Health**

OBJECTIVES

- Toxic chemicals from both natural sources and human activities that pollute air, soil, water, and food may damage human health.

- Toxicology is used to determine how poisonous a substance is.

- After an outbreak of illness occurs, epidemiologists attempt to find its origin and try to find ways to prevent future epidemics.

- Most pollutants come from human activities, but some pollutants occur naturally.

- Improperly disposed of wastes may leak hazardous pollutants into the environment.

KEY TERMS

toxicology

dose

dose-response curve

epidemiology

risk assessment

particulates

SECTION 2 **Biological Hazards**

OBJECTIVES

- Most human diseases that have an environmental component are caused by pathogens.

- The environment provides breeding grounds for pathogens and for their secondary hosts and vectors.

- The transmission of many diseases involves water. We increase the areas where organisms that carry these diseases can reproduce when we create irrigation canals and inadequate sewage systems.

- Environmental changes that help spread infectious diseases include climate change and expanding suburbs and farmland.

- Many emerging diseases are caused by pathogens that have made cross-species transfers from animals to humans.

KEY TERMS

pathogen

host

vector

Reviewing Key Terms

Use each of the following terms in a separate sentence.

1. *dose*
2. *vector*
3. *risk assessment*
4. *particulates*
5. *epidemiology*

For each pair of terms, explain how the meanings of the terms differ.

6. *pathogen* and *host*
7. *response* and *dose*
8. *toxicology* and *epidemiology*
9. **Concept Map** Use the following terms to create a concept map: *habitat destruction, pathogen, animal, vector, and human disease.*

Reviewing Main Ideas

10. Which of the following is not a true statement about the effects of pollution on health?

    a. It is difficult to determine how pollution affects health because many factors often contribute to a disease.

    b. The toxic effects of a pollutant depend upon the dose to which you are exposed.

    c. Many pollutants cause chronic diseases that result from exposure to the pollutant over the course of many years.

    d. Persistent chemicals are less toxic than chemicals that break down rapidly.

11. Which of the following is not a disease?

    a. malaria

    b. dengue fever

    c. human imunodeficiency virus (HIV)

    d. schistosomiasis

12. Cholera is usually transmitted from person to person by water because

    a. it is caused by a snail that breeds in water.

    b. it is usually contracted by someone drinking water polluted with human feces that contain the cholera pathogen.

    c. it is transmitted by mosquitoes.

    d. it is caused by a virus.

13. Tuberculosis (TB), which was once almost eradicated, is becoming more common, even in developed countries, because

    a. new varieties of the tuberculosis pathogen have evolved in rodents.

    b. livestock are given antibiotics.

    c. the pathogen that causes TB breeds in polluted water.

    d. some strains of the pathogen that causes TB are resistant to antibiotics.

14. Which of the following statements about environmental pollutants is true?

    a. Our environment contains fewer toxic chemicals than it did 50 years ago.

    b. Hormone mimics in our water supply pose no danger to humans.

    c. There is no health risk from pollutants in indoor air.

    d. People who live in the United States contain lower levels of some toxic chemicals in their bodies than they did 20 years ago.

15. Which of the following actions is most likely to prevent yellow fever, which is transmitted by mosquitoes, from becoming epidemic?

    a. preventing dehydration in patients by treating them with oral rehydration therapy

    b. taking antibiotics

    c. encouraging people to empty water out of old cans, tires, plant saucers, and other areas that contain standing water

    d. spraying the area repeatedly with pesticides

Short Answer

16. How do scientists determine the toxicity of a chemical?

17. How can land use change contribute to the spread of infectious disease?

18. What role does the environment play in the transmission of infectious diseases?

19. Why would lung disease be more common in a large urban area than in a remote rural area?

Interpreting Graphics

The graph below shows the dose-response curves for two chemicals. Use the graph to answer questions 20–22.

20. Which chemical is more toxic at a lower dose?

21. Which chemical is more toxic at a very large dose?

22. Can you tell from the graph which chemical is more likely to be a problem if it persists in the environment?

Dose-Response Curve

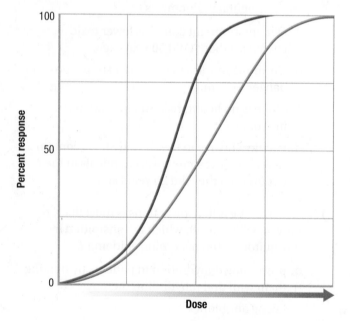

Critical Thinking

23. **Compare and Contrast** In what ways does a disease such as lung cancer, which is caused by breathing pollutants over a long period of time, differ from a disease such as malaria, which is caused by a pathogen?

24. **Analyzing Information** In 1775, Percival Pott noted that chimney sweeps had a high rate of cancer of the scrotum. What further investigations might be performed to find out what occupational hazard might be causing the cancer? How many of these would have been possible at the time, and how many require modern technology?

25. **Evaluate Viewpoints** Write a proposal to reduce the mosquito population of an area. How might you encourage the public to assist in this effort?

26. **Form a Model** Read about mosquitoes under the heading "Malaria." How would you design an irrigation system to minimize the chances that mosquitoes would breed in it?

27. **Summarizing Information**   Collect half a dozen pesticide containers that still have their labels. Make a table that has three columns. List the names of the pesticides in one column. Then read the label on each container. Use this information to decide which pesticide is the most dangerous and which pesticide is the least dangerous. In the second column, label the pesticides as most to least dangerous. In the third column, list the most important safety precautions required of anyone who uses the pesticides. **CAUTION:** Do not get pesticides on your face, and wash your hands thoroughly after handling the pesticide cans.

Analyzing Data

The table below shows four diseases and the number of cases of each disease that were reported to the United States Centers for Disease Control in 1990 and 1998. Use the table below to answer questions 28–29.

Disease	1990	1998
Cryptosporidiosis	2	3,793
Lyme disease	7,943	16,801
Malaria	1,292	1,611
Typhoid fever	552	375

28. Analyzing Data Malaria cases increased between 1990 and 1998. What other facts would you want to know before deciding that the United States has a growing malaria problem?

29. Making Calculations By what percentage did the number of typhoid fever cases decline between 1990 and 1998?

Making Connections

30. Communicating Main Ideas Why do sewage systems that overflow when it rains need to be replaced with modern systems that do not overflow?

31. Writing Persuasively Write a letter to a newspaper. In the letter, argue either for or against homeowners' use of pesticides on their lawns and gardens.

CASESTUDY

32. What types of human activities contribute to chemical pollution in the environment?

33. Explain the relationship between the health of an organism and its environment.

Why It Matters

34. Why is safe and clean water important for human health?

STUDYSKILL

Vocabulary Practice To practice vocabulary, write the terms and definitions on a piece of paper and fold the paper lengthwise so that the definitions are covered. First, see how many definitions you already know. Then, write the definitions you don't know on another piece of paper, and practice again until you know all of them.

Lead Poisoning and Mental Ability

Objectives

Analyze the relationship between lead poisoning and children's IQ.

Graph experimental data.

Interpret graphical data.

People are usually exposed to lead in old buildings that were painted with lead paint. The lead can enter the body in dust that is breathed in and can permanently damage the brain and nervous system. Lead poisoning can cause aggressive behavior, hyperactivity, headaches, and hearing loss. At high levels, it can cause seizures, coma, and even death. The Centers for Disease Control and Prevention (CDC) state that a lead level of 10 micrograms per deciliter in the blood can be harmful. (A microgram is one-millionth of a gram, and a deciliter is one-tenth of a liter.) Recent studies suggest even levels below 10 micrograms can be harmful, especially for children. In this lab, you will explore the effect of lead poisoning on the mental ability of children. The children all grew up near a lead smelter, a factory where raw lead ore is processed. Scientists measured the concentration of lead in the children's blood over time. Psychologists also performed tests on the children to determine their IQ. You will analyze the data to see if you can find a pattern.

Effects of Lead Lead smelters, such as the one shown here in Romania, can cause air pollution and lead poisoning.

Procedure

1. Design a hypothesis for the relationship between the lead concentration in the blood, the IQs, and the ages of the children. As the blood-lead concentration increases, how would you expect the person's IQ to change? How do you think this relationship would change as the children grow older?

2. The table on the next page lists the blood-lead concentration and IQ data for a group of 494 children. The children were measured five times between the ages of six months old and seven years old. The children were divided into four groups according to the amount of lead in their blood. Group 1 had the lowest concentration of lead, and group 4 had the highest concentration of lead. Prepare a graph for the data in the table. Plot the blood-lead concentration on the x-axis and IQ on the y-axis. Label each axis with the correct units. Choose an appropriate scale for each axis so that the entire range of data in the table will fit on the graph.

3. Plot the data from the table on your graph, using a different color for each age group. Then connect all the data points for each age group in the color chosen for that group. You should have five lines of data on your graph.

Group of children	Average blood-lead concentration *(micrograms per deciliter)*	Average IQ score
6 mo	8.3	109.4
	12.6	104.7
	16.8	102.9
	24.2	100.0
15 mo	11.8	109.3
	18.6	106.5
	24.4	102.9
	34.4	101.3
3 yr	11.6	110.2
	17.4	106.5
	22.4	102.2
	30.2	100.0
5 yr	8.3	109.3
	12.6	106.1
	17.2	104.1
	24.2	98.8
7 yr	6.6	109.6
	10.1	107.7
	13.7	102.7
	20.0	98.7

(Group numbers 1, 2, 3, 4 for each age group)

Lead Paint Dust from lead paint peelings can cause lead poisoning.

Analysis

1. **Analyzing Data** For a single age group, how does IQ vary with lead concentration? Is this true for all age groups?

2. **Analyzing Data** How does the relationship between lead concentration and IQ change as a child grows older?

Conclusions

3. **Draw Conclusions** What conclusions can you draw from your analysis about the effect of lead on IQ?

4. **Inferring Conclusions** Based on your conclusions, what long-term effects might lead poisoning have on a community?

Extension

5. **Analyzing Conclusions** Based on the data presented in this lab, do you think the CDC's limit of 10 micrograms per deciliter is reasonable? Explain your answer.

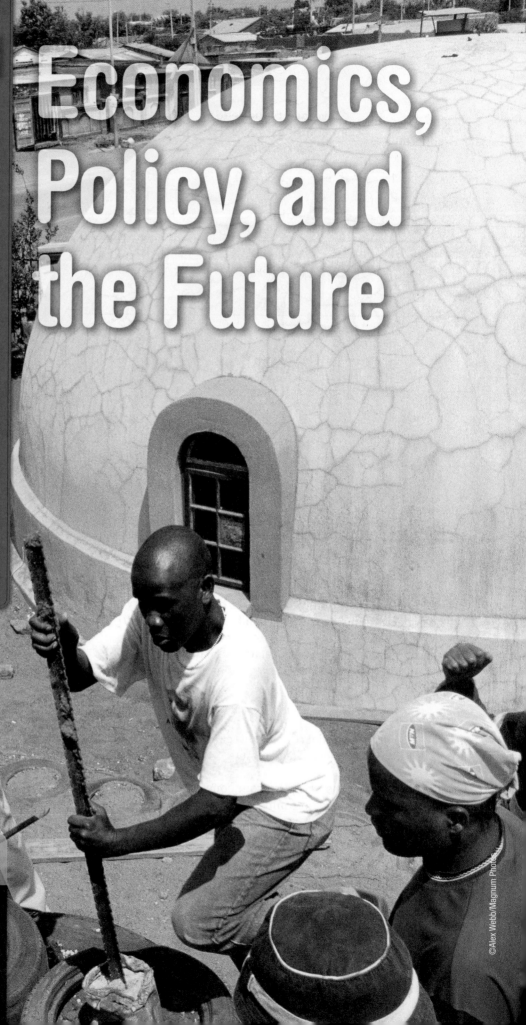

Chapter 21

Section 1
Economics and International Cooperation

Section 2
Environmental Policies in the United States

Section 3
The Importance of the Individual

Why It Matters

These people are using old tires to insulate a community center in Ivory Park, South Africa. Community members created a sustainable eco-village here through cooperation with local and international governments and organizations.

Why is working together an important aspect of solving environmental problems?

CASESTUDY

Learn about the conflict between international agreements and the open oceans fishing industry in the case study Saving Species in the Open Ocean on pages 536–537.

Economics, Policy, and the Future

ONLINE ENVIRONMENTAL SCIENCE
HMDScience.com

Go online to access additional resources, including labs, worksheets, multimedia, and resources in Spanish.

Economics and International Cooperation

Over seven billion people live on Earth. They are supported by unprecedented levels of human resource use, productivity, and scientific knowledge. On average, people live longer and are more educated than they were 50 years ago. They are also less likely to live in acute poverty. But Earth still faces many problems. Our goal must be to live in a sustainable way worldwide. **Sustainability** is the condition in which human society can go on indefinitely and future generations can have a standard of living as high as our own.

To live in a sustainable way, we need to look for new ways to solve problems. For example, cheap fuels to produce energy are becoming scarce and many of them negatively affect the climate. We need to develop sustainable solutions. We need to develop cheap, renewable, and minimally-polluting sources of energy. Many scientists are working on this problem to help people continue to live at a high standard of living for generations to come.

International Development and Cooperation

We live in a time of *globalization*. Environmental and economic conditions are linked across political borders around the world. People cross these borders in search of economic opportunities and a better quality of life. Increasingly, governments, organizations, and businesses around the world must work together. Despite having different opinions, world leaders, researchers, and other stakeholders meet to identify common goals and to address worldwide issues, as shown in **Figure 1.1**.

SECTION 1

Objectives

▸ Describe some of the challenges to achieving sustainability.

▸ Describe several agreements relating to the environment.

▸ Explain how economics and environmental science are related.

▸ Compare two ways that governments influence economics.

▸ Give an example of a private effort to address environmental problems.

Key Terms
sustainability
economics

✔ **CHECK FOR UNDERSTANDING**
Summarize What does it mean to live in a sustainable way?

FIGURE 1.1

Cooperation Researchers from around the world meet to collaborate at an environmental economics conference.

©PhotoStock-Israel/Alamy Images

Sustainable Development

Many meetings and agreements among international governments have dealt with environmental concerns along with economic and political concerns. For example, the first Earth Summit was held in 1992 in Rio de Janeiro, Brazil. It was a sign of new levels of international environmental awareness and cooperation. Representatives from around the world drew up several agreements. One of these agreements was Agenda 21, which was a general plan to address a range of environmental problems while allowing continued economic development.

Climate and Atmosphere

One important treaty about the atmosphere was the Montreal Protocol, which was adopted in 1987. It successfully reduced the amount of ozone-destroying chemicals in the atmosphere. However, not all agreements are successful. Any country may choose not to sign, enforce, or provide funding to implement an agreement, which may lead to the ultimate failure of the agreement.

For example, the Kyoto Protocol, adopted in 1997, attempted to avoid or slow down global warming by reducing greenhouse-gas emissions around the world. Most of the developed countries promised to reduce their emissions by about 5 percent by 2012. However, some countries argued against the Kyoto Protocol, saying that it would be too costly to implement. In contrast, most climate scientists did not think it did enough to stabilize the climate. The United States did not sign the treaty. As of 2012, post-Kyoto efforts for binding agreements to reduce greenhouse-gas emissions have failed. Environmental organizations, business leaders, and governments are trying to find other ways to combat climate change.

Other Agreements

Hundreds of other international agreements have been made as new environmental issues have emerged. One important agreement is CITES (the Convention on International Trade in Endangered Species of Wild Fauna and Flora). CITES was formed to help save species from extinction by controlling international trade. Under CITES, international trade is not permitted for almost 1,000 species of endangered plants and animals, including the Bengal tiger, shown in **Figure 1.2**. Thousands more species are protected by restrictions on trade.

The Role of Non-Governmental Organizations (NGOs)

Many people think of governments, ambassadors, and politicians when they hear about international agreements. They hear about industries that lobby on behalf of business interests. Non-governmental organizations (NGOs) also play an important role in international agreements. NGOs are legally formed groups that are not part of a government or for-profit business. Many NGOs advocate on behalf of environmental issues at international meetings, while others advocate on behalf of local or regional issues.

FIGURE 1.2

International Trade Restrictions The Bengal tiger is one species that has benefited from international trade restrictions.

For example, The Nature Conservancy is a nonprofit organization that uses a simple economic strategy to preserve ecosystems. This organization collects donations of money and land. If the donated land is not targeted for preservation, the organization trades or sells the land. Large preserves are put together by a combination of donations, exchanges, and purchases of land. The organization has created preserves in all 50 states and in more than 30 countries.

Economics and the Environment

Economics is the study of the choices people make as they use and distribute limited resources. In traditional economics, *markets* are seen as self-contained economic systems, in which money and products flow in cycles. People within a market will decide the *value* of something by comparing the costs and benefits from their own perspective. For example, people decide how much they will pay for a product or how much they must be paid to do a certain job. These values change over time as people see changes in the costs or benefits of their actions.

Economists say that an economic system is successful when it maximizes societal benefit. Often, that benefit is measured as economic growth, which is an increase in the flow of money and products within a market. However, economic systems attempt to account for external factors that do not have a direct economic value, such as air, wildlife, or human health. They also attempt to account for economic transactions that affect other people and ecosystems indirectly. As the fields of economics and various sciences share knowledge, economists are able to develop more complex and realistic models of resource use. The resource use model illustrated in **Figure 1.3** shows that economic systems are both contained within and dependent upon the environment.

Economists see environmental problems as *market failures*. The market has failed if the price of something does not reflect its true cost. For example, the price of gasoline does not reflect the other expenses caused by vehicle emissions. Illnesses caused by air pollution cost society billions of dollars a year. In a balanced economic system, the price of gasoline should reflect these costs. One difficulty in pricing is that sometimes we do not know the environmental costs. An economic system can include only those costs that are understood at the time when people make decisions.

FIGURE 1.3

Resource Use Model A complete economic model shows that economic systems operate within natural systems.

Ecosystem Value

Many economists believe that if we can place a proper value on ecosystems, then we can incorporate true costs into products. Doing so should let markets do the work of environmental protection. If materials or actions are too costly to the environment, people will not be willing to pay for them. One way economists put value on ecosystems is by asking how much money people would be willing to pay to have the ecosystem in its natural form. Another method is to estimate the replacement value of ecosystem services that are provided. *Ecosystem services* can include such things as purifying water, pulling carbon dioxide out of the atmosphere, or protecting coasts from storms. By quantifying ecosystem services we can determine the cost of environmental damages.

Assessing the value of environmental resources also makes it possible to understand trade-offs. Few environmental issues are easy to solve. What is good, or needed, for one group may not be good for the environment or another group of people. Research conducted by environmental scientists and the work done by environmental economists makes it possible to formulate well-informed decisions about actions that individuals, companies, or governments should take.

CASESTUDY

Saving Species in the Open Ocean

To a person standing on the shore, the ocean appears limitless. However, within those waters, many ocean fish and mammal populations have declined, some to near extinction. Overharvesting created most of these declines, which continue today. Because no country controls the open ocean, the ocean was treated for many years as if the resources it contained were free for anyone to take. Another problem in managing the oceans is that many species travel huge distances and move from one country's waters to another's. International cooperation is needed to ensure that marine fisheries are rebuilt to ensure healthy ecosystems and economic prosperity. This cooperation takes many forms and involves many types of organizations, but requires sound science to work.

One of the most well-known international organizations that manages marine species is the International Whaling Commission (IWC). The IWC was formed because most large whale species were endangered after many years of overharvesting. For decades, the IWC tried to limit the number of whales killed with different strategies, but these strategies did not work well. Finally, the IWC called for a total ban on whaling beginning in 1984. Although populations of a few whale species have recovered since whaling was restricted, other populations of whale species have not. One problem is that some countries have violated quotas or claimed that they need to kill whales for scientific research. Most scientists do not think this "whaling for research," which results in the meat being sold, is needed because there are other ways to gather the data. Even in 2012, there is still "scientific whaling" occurring in the whale sanctuary around Antarctica.

Regional Fisheries Management Organizations (RFMOs) are organizations created by countries with a fishing interest in an area. RFMOs manage fish populations of the open oceans. They also manage populations of fish that migrate through the waters of multiple countries and work to prevent the unintentional catch (also called bycatch) of species such as albatrosses, sea turtles, and

Regulation and Economic Incentives

Governments influence economic systems. They do this by making regulations and creating punishments. Governments also create *economic incentives* by paying out money for actions that benefit society or charging taxes on actions that have a social cost. For example, some governments offer rebates to people who purchase energy-saving appliances.

Governments have tried many ways to regulate environmental damage such as pollution. However, regulations are criticized when they are difficult to enforce, do not distribute costs evenly, or do not control environmental damage. One newer approach is to combine regulation with economic markets by creating markets for pollutants. These are called *cap-and-trade strategies*. For example, governments can set an upper limit for industrial emissions of sulfur dioxides, but let companies freely trade permits for releasing parts of the total pollution allowed. This strategy encourages innovation by rewarding those that pollute the least.

The hardest resources to manage are those that are not easily controlled. Problems with such open-access resources are called the *tragedy of the commons*. Without cooperation, individuals try to get as much as they can, and the resources are depleted. In the end, everyone loses.

This Japanese whaling ship is harvesting Antarctic minke whales in the Southern Ocean for alleged scientific purposes.

dolphins. RFMOs try to set fishing levels that will prevent fish populations from crashing, encourage the use of fishing practices that reduce bycatch, and reduce illegal fishing.

RFMOs have had limited successes and face major challenges. The organizations often lack the legal power to enforce catch limits. The countries fishing in an area may differ greatly in their commitment to fishing sustainably, the economic challenges they face, or opinions on how catches should be divided among countries. Another problem is the presence of illegal, unregulated, and unreported (IUU) fishing within the areas RFMOs are trying to manage. This fishing makes it almost impossible to effectively manage

fisheries. RFMOs have tried to combat IUU fishing by not allowing IUU vessels to use the services in their ports. A study in 2010 found that even with RFMOs, two-thirds of the high seas fisheries are depleted or overexploited.

Critical Thinking

1. **Expressing Opinions** Write a paragraph describing why you think that it is so hard for RFMOs to manage fisheries on the high seas.

2. **Predicting Outcomes** If whale populations increase, should countries be allowed to hunt them again? Explain your answer.

Conservation Group Assets
In 2010, a conservation group owned land worth a total of $1.3 billion. In 2011, it gained ownership of additional land worth $322 million. In the same year, it also sold land worth $88 million and gave away land worth $12 million to governments and other groups. What was the value of land held by the conservation group at the beginning of 2012?

Private Efforts

Businesses and private organizations also play a role in addressing environmental problems. Many businesses have found that recycling their wastes saves money and improves their public image. Saving energy makes business sense and also helps reduce emissions of greenhouse gases that contribute to climate change.

Cooperation among private organizations and with governments may include conducting research or creating plans for environmental management. **Figure 1.4** shows an area of Africa that several governments and private organizations are working together to manage. Local residents are also included in the process of planning for the area.

FIGURE 1.4

Collaboration The area around Mount Kilimanjaro in Tanzania is an important home to wildlife such as elephants and giraffes. Several governments and organizations are working with local residents to manage the area for both wildlife preservation and sustainable economic development.

©Gunter Ziesler/Peter Arnold, Inc./Getty Images

Section 1 Formative Assessment

Reviewing Main Ideas

1. **Describe** some of the challenges to achieving sustainability.

2. **Compare** two ways that governments influence economics.

3. **Give an example** of a private effort to address environmental problems.

Critical Thinking

4. **Analyzing Processes** Write a paragraph that explains why a local government might use tax money to purchase park lands.

5. **Applying Ideas** Read about interactions of economics and the environment. List some ways that both governments and organizations could encourage people to conserve resources.

Environmental Policies in the United States

Objectives

▶ Describe two major developments in U.S. environmental history.

▶ Give examples of three federal agencies that have environmental responsibilities.

▶ Explain the purpose of Environmental Impact Statements.

▶ Give an example of how citizens can affect environmental policy at each level of government—local, state, and national.

▶ Evaluate the media as a source of information about the environment.

Many people in the United States have demonstrated a concern about environmental problems. In both local and national elections in the United States, candidates often talk about environmental issues in their campaigns. Each year, millions of dollars are donated to environmental causes by U.S. citizens and businesses, and billions of federal tax dollars are spent to uphold environmental policies and to manage resources. In recent decades, the United States has reduced many types of pollution and improved water quality in many places. But the United States is still struggling to use its resources in a sustainable way, preserve its unique ecosystems, and reduce its impact on the global environment.

History of U.S. Environmental Policy

During the 1800s, people in the United States made use of the country's vast resources. Prairies were turned into cropland, ancient forests were cut down to construct buildings, and several species of animals were hunted to extinction. By the 1900s, people began to realize the consequences of these actions. Their attitudes started to change. Leaders such as President Theodore Roosevelt and conservationist John Muir, shown in **Figure 2.1**, called for increased protection and management of the nation's resources. Many national forests and parks, and agencies to manage them, were established around the early 1900s.

Key Terms

Environmental Impact Statement

lobbying

FIGURE 2.1

Conservation Leaders In the late 1800s and early 1900s, President Theodore Roosevelt (on left) and naturalist John Muir (on right) were leaders in the conservation of natural areas. They are shown here at Glacier Point in Yosemite National Park, one of the first U.S. national parks.

©Bettmann/Corbis

Inherited Laws

In parts of the United States that were previously under the control of European countries, some of the old laws regarding property and land use are still in effect. In Texas and California, many provisions of Spanish land law still apply to the states' water sources. Most rivers and creeks in these states are public property. Also, Texas has ownership of coastal areas stretching 10.4 mi from its shores. This gives Texas the ownership of many offshore oil deposits. Other coastal states own only 3 mi, as established by English common law in those states.

Environmental Agencies and Laws

Throughout the 1900s, U.S. citizens became more aware of environmental problems. Widespread crop disasters in the 1930s showed the country that poor farming practices were causing soil erosion and poverty. Policies to encourage soil conservation were adopted. People objected to living near smelly garbage dumps, so research on better methods of waste disposal began. The public began to complain about pollution. The first Earth Day, celebrated around the world in 1970, was a sign of widespread environmental awareness. In that same year, the U.S. Environmental Protection Agency (EPA) was established.

U.S. lawmakers have created many policies and federal agencies to manage environmental affairs, as shown in **Figure 2.2**. For example, the EPA enforces the Clean Air Act and the Clean Water Act. These acts set standards for acceptable levels of pollutants in air and water. The EPA uses regulations and economic incentives to encourage individuals and businesses to meet these standards. Environmental laws change as we learn more and draw different conclusions about how much to spend on preserving the environment. Deciding when to spend money to preserve the environment is equally important. Usually, anticipating and solving a possible problem before it occurs costs less than solving the problem after.

FIGURE 2.2

U.S. FEDERAL AGENCIES AND THEIR ENVIRONMENTAL RESPONSIBILITIES

Department or Agency	Responsibilities
Environmental Protection Agency	enforces National Environmental Policy Act; Clean Water Act; Clean Air Act; Solid Waste Disposal Act; Superfund; Federal Insecticide, Fungicide, and Rodenticide Control Act; Waste Reduction Act; Toxic Substances Control Act; Resource Conservation and Recovery Act; Energy Policy Act
Department of the Interior	enforces Wild and Scenic Rivers Act (managed across several agencies)
U.S. Fish and Wildlife Service	enforces Endangered Species Act, National Wildlife Refuge System Act, Alaska National Interest Lands Conservation Act, Species Conservation Act, Fish and Wildlife Improvement Act, Fish and Wildlife Conservation Act
Bureau of Land Management	enforces Federal Land Policy and Management Act, Taylor Grazing Act
National Parks Service	manages national parks
Office of Surface Mining Reclamation and Enforcement	enforces Surface Mining Control and Reclamation Act
Department of Agriculture	enforces Soil and Water Conservation Act, National Forests Management Act
Department of Commerce	monitors the nation's resources to support both environmental and economic health
National Oceanic and Atmospheric Administration	monitors international atmosphere, climate, and oceans
National Marine Fisheries Service	manages living marine resources and their habitat
Nuclear Regulatory Commission	regulates nuclear power stations and nuclear waste
Department of Energy	enforces National Energy Act, Public Utility Regulatory Policies Act

FIGURE 2.3

Mitigating Environmental Damage The Grand Canyon ecosystem was changed when the Glen Canyon Dam was built upstream in 1962. An Environmental Impact Statement in the 1980s evaluated alternative ways to operate the dam.

Environmental Impact Statements

Most government agencies are required to file an Environmental Impact Statement (EIS) for any proposed project or policy that would have a significant effect on the environment. An **Environmental Impact Statement** states the need for a project, the project's impact on the environment, and how any negative impact can be minimized. Proposals for the construction of dams, highways, airports, and other projects that the federal government controls or funds must be evaluated with an EIS.

The public can comment on an EIS. For example, if a new dam is proposed, scientists and citizens may comment on any problems they foresee. Although public comment on an EIS rarely stops a project, the feedback may cause changes in the project's plans.

Federal agencies may also conduct an EIS when they plan changes in the regulation of public resources. Usually, several alternative actions are evaluated. For example, an EIS was conducted in the 1980s to evaluate alternative ways to release water from Glen Canyon Dam. Federal agencies were looking for ways to restore natural conditions downstream in the Grand Canyon, shown in **Figure 2.3.**

Unfunded Mandates and Economic Impacts

Some limits have been placed on the federal government's power to pass environmental laws. In 1995, Congress passed a law to prevent *unfunded mandates,* which are federal regulations that do not provide funds for state or local governments to implement the regulations. The federal government must now provide funding for any new laws that will cost more than $50 million to implement. Congress can no longer pass laws such as the Clean Water Act, which requires local communities to conduct their own tests of public water supplies. Another limit being placed on many federal agencies requires the agencies to evaluate both the economic and environmental impacts of their policies.

ECOFACT

U.S. Public Lands

Twenty-eight percent of the area of the United States is publicly owned. This means that local, state, or federal governments hold the land in the public interest. Most of this public land is federally controlled and is found in western states. Eighty percent of Nevada is publicly owned, and more than 60 percent of Alaska, Utah, and Idaho is publicly owned land.

©Helene Simonin/Alamy Images

FIELDSTUDY

Go to Appendix B to find the field study
Local Politics

Influencing Environmental Policy

You can influence environmental policy. For example, as a citizen, you can contact your elected representatives to tell them your opinion on issues. There are also many other ways that consumers, businesses, the media, and organizations can influence policy at all levels of government.

Many laws related to the environment are created at the national level. However, there are also many state and local laws that affect the environment. It is easier for an individual to influence policy at the local level than at the national level. It is also usually easier for citizens to organize and contact their representatives at the local level.

Local Governments

Local governments make many decisions for their communities. City councils and governmental agencies hold public meetings, such as the meeting shown in **Figure 2.4**. Local governments can decide how land may be used and developed, and where businesses and housing may be located. Local governments and agencies also create plans for public facilities, for waste disposal and recycling, and for many other facets of local life.

One problem with local environmental planning is that communities often do not coordinate their plans. For example, your community may plan for clean air or water, but a neighboring community may allow development that pollutes your area. On the other hand, sometimes local communities do work together. For example, towns along the Hudson River in New York are cooperating to provide a "greenway" of natural areas for public use that stretches hundreds of miles along the river.

✔ **CHECK FOR UNDERSTANDING**

Identify What is one way that people can influence environmental policy at the local level?

FIGURE 2.4

Decision Making Many environmental decisions are made at the local level. Citizens can participate in local government at public meetings (left). Some communities set aside local wildlife habitat and green spaces, such as the Barton Creek Greenbelt in Austin, Texas (right).

State Governments

Environmental policy is also strongly influenced at the state level. The federal government passes laws that set environmental standards, but often these laws are minimum standards. Individual states may create laws that set higher standards. California's vehicle emission standards are higher than the federal standards because that state wants to control its problems with air pollution caused by traffic. States also have a lot of independent control over how to implement laws and manage public resources. For example, Ohio's Department of Natural Resources has used the state's endangered plant law to acquire habitats and to educate the public about the state's 350 endangered plant species.

Lobbying

Lawmakers are heavily influenced by lobbying on many sides of issues. **Lobbying** is an organized attempt to influence the decisions of lawmakers. Both environmental and industry groups hire lobbyists to provide information to lawmakers and urge them to vote a certain way. One way to influence policy is to support an organization that lobbies for the policies that you agree with.

The Media and Sources of Information

Electronic media, such as television news, as shown in **Figure 2.5,** is the main source of information about environmental topics for most of us. Popular websites, blogs, TV, and radio tell us, for example, when Congress is debating about oil drilling in the Arctic National Wildlife Refuge or when our local government is planning to build a new sewage plant. However, media reports are usually brief and may leave out information.

If you want to fully understand environmental problems, you will want to find information from sources other than popular media. Many other sources are available, and you should evaluate all sources for bias and accuracy. Scientists and others who are familiar with environmental issues produce reports, peer-reviewed articles, magazines, and websites that contain in-depth information. Local organizations hold public meetings and produce newsletters. And through the Internet, you can get first-hand information from people all over the world.

FIGURE 2.5

News Sources A news broadcast may be the only way that many people learn about an environmental problem.

☑ **CRITICAL THINKING**

Identify From what other sources can people get information?

☑ **CHECK FOR UNDERSTANDING**

Explain Why should you look for information about environmental topics in sources other than the popular media?

 Section 2 **Formative Assessment**

▶ Reviewing Main Ideas

1. **Describe** two major developments in U.S. environmental history from each of the past two centuries.

2. **Give examples** of at least three federal agencies with environmental responsibilities.

3. **Explain** the purpose of Environmental Impact Statements. In what ways are citizens allowed to respond to an Environmental Impact Statement?

☑ Critical Thinking

4. **Relating Concepts** Describe three environmental issues that are important to your community.

5. **Expressing Viewpoints** Read about the ways of influencing environmental policy. Explain which of these ways you think is most effective.

6. **Evaluating Information** Write a paragraph that evaluates an environmental news story from a website, newspaper, or TV program.

► Give examples of individuals who have influenced environmental history.

► Identify ways in which the choices that you make as an individual may affect the environment.

The Importance of the Individual

It is easy to feel that one person does not make much difference to the environment, but we all affect the environment with our daily actions. By learning about environmental problems and solutions, we are able to make responsible decisions and help others make similar choices. History has shown that one individual can have an influence on many others.

FIGURE 3.1

PEOPLE WHO HAVE INFLUENCED ENVIRONMENTAL THINKING

Henry David Thoreau (1817–1862) was a conservationist and writer who is best known for his essays about his stay in a cabin at Walden Pond in Massachusetts.	David Attenborough (1926–) is a British broadcaster and naturalist most well-known for his ground-breaking documentary series "Planet Earth."
John Muir (1838–1914) was a Scottish-born naturalist and writer who founded the Sierra Club, explored the American West, and was an advocate for preserving western lands as wilderness.	Marion Stoddart (1928–) led efforts to save the Nashua River in Massachusetts from pollution and development. *A River Ran Wild* is a book about her efforts. She is still active in protecting the Nashua River.
Theodore "Teddy" Roosevelt (1858–1919) was the first American president to strongly support conservation. He founded the Forest Service and created the first National Monuments.	Paul Ehrlich (1932–) is a Stanford ecologist who warned of the dangers of rapid population growth with his 1968 book, *The Population Bomb*.
Alice Hamilton (1869–1970) was the first American expert on diseases caused by working with chemicals. In the early 1900s, she warned workers about exposure hazards and opposed the addition of lead to gasoline.	Jane Goodall (1934–) studied chimpanzees in Tanzania's Gombe Stream National Park. Her books raised awareness of the plight of several endangered species and prompted new thinking about primate behavior.
Aldo Leopold (1887–1948) was an ecologist and forester who wrote about the land ethic in his book *A Sand County Almanac,* published in 1949.	Sylvia Earl (1935–) is an American oceanographer. She is an explorer-in-residence with the National Geographic Society. A winner of the 2009 TED Prize, she is an advocate for the establishment of marine protected areas around the world.
Rachel Carson (1907–1964) was a biologist with the U.S. Fish & Wildlife Service, who raised awareness of toxic pesticides with her 1962 book, *Silent Spring.*	Wangari Maathai (1940–2011) was the founder of the Green Belt Movement, a grassroots environmental nonprofit based in Kenya. She won the 2004 Nobel Peace Prize "for her contribution to sustainable development, democracy, and peace."
Garrett Hardin (1915–2003) was a distinguishing professor of human ecology who is best known for his 1968 essay "The Tragedy of the Commons."	John Cronin (1950–) is known internationally for his work as an advocate for New York's Hudson River. He was named a "Hero for the Planet" by *Time* magazine.

Influential Individuals

Some individuals who have influenced thinking about the environment are listed in **Figure 3.1**. These people are famous because they brought attention to problems or convinced many people to think about new ideas. Many of these individuals wrote best-selling books about the subjects they knew well. These books were easy to understand and inspired people to think about environmental problems in a new way.

The 1960s Decade

During the 1960s, environmental issues became widely known. It was then that biologists such as Paul Ehrlich, Rachel Carson, and Garrett Hardin drew public attention to environmental problems such as pollution, rapid population growth, and resource depletion.

In *Silent Spring,* Rachel Carson, shown in **Figure 3.2,** argued that many public lands and resources were not adequately protected. She argued that resources such as water had to be protected and kept in natural, unpolluted conditions. Partly as a result of Carson's book, Congress passed the Wilderness Act in 1964. This let the government set aside some federal lands as wilderness areas. These areas may only be used for low-impact recreation such as hiking and camping, and visitor numbers are limited.

Rising Awareness

Also in the 1960s, several environmental disasters made headlines. Air pollution in New York City was blamed for hundreds of deaths. The bald eagle became endangered as a result of the widespread use of the pesticide DDT. There was a massive oil spill near Santa Barbara, California. Lake Erie became so polluted that many of its beaches had to be closed. Eventually, pressure from the public led to new laws and efforts to reduce environmental damage. The first Earth Day, held in 1970, was a historic demonstration of public concern for environmental issues.

Connect to HISTORY

Historical Writers

Americans have been influenced by descriptions of America written by early explorers. An example is this passage written in 1805 by Meriwether Lewis, from his journal of the famous Lewis and Clark expedition:

"I beheld the Rocky Mountains for the first time . . . these points of the Rocky Mountains were covered with snow and the sun shone on it in such manner as to give me the most plain and satisfactory view. While I viewed these mountains I felt a secret pleasure in finding myself so near the head of the heretofore conceived boundless Missouri."

FIGURE 3.2

Influential Individuals Examples of individuals who have brought attention to environmental issues: ❶ David Attenborough, ❷ Rachel Carson, and ❸ Wangari Maathai.

QUICKLAB

Think Globally, Act Locally
Procedure

1. Using a computer with an Internet connection, perform a search using the key terms, "ecological footprint calculator."
2. Enter your environmental data into the calculator to determine how much land it takes to support your personal lifestyle.
3. Construct a data table in your science journal and record each category, along with your data.

Analysis

1. Does your footprint indicate that you are currently living an ecologically sustainable lifestyle? Explain your answer.
2. Compare your results with your classmates. Brainstorm ways that you can make your lifestyle more ecologically sustainable.

Applying Your Knowledge

What will you be in the future? At the very least, you can expect to be a citizen who has the right to vote, a consumer who has choices of how to spend your money, and a member of the human race who has a role in the global environment. To make the decisions you will face, you can draw on your knowledge of environmental science.

Voting

One of the most important decisions you may make is in the act of voting, as shown in **Figure 3.3.** The people we elect will make decisions that affect our environmental future. You have the right to support the candidates and laws that you think are best in both local and national elections. You can easily find out what a candidate thinks about environmental issues before an election. You can find information about candidates through the media, voter organizations, and websites.

One way to take action on environmental problems is as part of a group of people who share your concerns and interests. You can find many groups in your community asking for volunteers for activities such as planting trees, picking up trash, or maintaining trails. Many large nonprofit organizations hold meetings, educational activities, and trips to natural areas all over the country.

Weighing the Evidence

A popular environmental slogan is to "think globally, act locally." This slogan reminds us that our everyday actions have broader effects. Being aware of the effects of our actions is an important step in making decisions that affect the environment. What choices of action could you make today that will affect your environment?

Each of us has the responsibility to educate ourselves as we make the decisions that affect the world around us. There is a wealth of information about environmental issues on the Internet, in libraries, and in the media. When you research a topic, use reliable sources for statistics and information. Do not be misled by information that may look convincing but that has no supporting evidence.

FIGURE 3.3

Exercise Your Right to Vote Voting is an opportunity to make a decision that affects the environment.

©Fred Prouser/Reuters/Corbis

Consumer Choices

Another environmental slogan you may have heard is "reduce, reuse, recycle." As consumers, we can reduce the amount of things we buy and use, we can reuse things that are often used only once, and we can recycle many materials. How many ways can you think of to apply these ideas in your everyday life?

As a consumer, you may choose to buy products that are produced sustainably or that do less damage to the environment. As shown in **Figure 3.4**, it is not always easy to tell which products meet this standard. But as you learn more about environmental science, you'll be prepared to make decisions that guarantee that your impact on the environment will be a positive one.

Daily Living

As you have learned, the choices you make every day can have an impact on the environment. Though a decision to turn off the water while you brush your teeth or to toss a plastic bottle into a recycling bin rather than in the trash may seem small, each eco-friendly decision you make adds up. The choices you make can influence the behavior of others, too.

✔ **CHECK FOR UNDERSTANDING**
Summarize What is an example of a consumer choice that benefits the environment?

FIGURE 3.4

Consumer Choice As consumers, we make many choices that affect the environment.

✔ **CRITICAL THINKING**
Describe What choices could you make today that will affect your environment?

✔ Section 3 **Formative Assessment**

▶ **Reviewing Main Ideas**

1. **Give examples** of at least three individuals in history who have had an impact on environmental thinking. What traits do they have in common?

2. **Identify** at least three ways individual citizens can influence their environment.

3. **List** five choices that you could make today that would have some kind of effect on the environment.

✔ **Critical Thinking**

4. **Identifying Relationships** Think of one activity that you do often. Write a paragraph explaining all the environmental effects, positive and negative, that this activity might have over time.

5. **Predicting Consequences** Choose one environmental issue that you have learned about in this book and describe all the ways that you could make a difference on this issue.

Get Involved with the Environment

Southwest Conservation Corps crew members help to build a mountain bike trail in Salida, Colorado.

You can only learn so much environmental science indoors. Sometimes, you just have to go out and get mud on your boots. Luckily many nonprofit environmental groups offer programs in which you can do just that—and make a difference while doing it.

Environmental organizations across the country offer students the opportunity to learn in living ecosystems. Time commitments and program formats vary widely—from field trips and weekend workshops to long-term internships and school partnerships that continue for years.

Center for Land-Based Learning

An organization called the Center for Land-Based Learning, based in northern California, focuses its work on farmland, ranchland, and other areas where human activities and environmental needs must be kept in balance. One of its programs, called Student and Landowner Education and Watershed Stewardship (SLEWS), teaches habitat preservation and restoration. This program includes many activities, such as the restoration of a hedgerow habitat between farm fields for the benefit of local plants and animals.

Another of their programs, called Project GROW (Gathering to Restore Oak Woodlands), is restoring an oak woodland that was disturbed during highway construction. By the third year of the project, students had helped to gather and plant 400 acorns, plant 1,000 native grass plugs, map the area in geographic information systems (GIS), build and install irrigation systems, as well as build 15 nest boxes.

Youth Conservation Corps

The Youth Conservation Corps (YCC) program was founded in 1971. On the national level, the YCC is a partnership between the Department of the Interior and the U.S. Department of Agriculture. The YCC offers paid opportunities for students between the ages of 15 and 18. YCC projects, which typically last from 8 to 10 weeks during the summer, include conservation work projects such as trail construction, habitat preservation, and assistance with wildlife research. Most projects take place with federal agencies such as the National Park Service (NPS), U.S. Forest Service, U.S. Fish & Wildlife Service, and Bureau of Land Management. Though most programs are non-residential, students who participate in YCC projects in Yosemite or Yellowstone National Parks live on-site for the duration of the program.

ECOZine at HMDScience.com

Go online for the latest environmental science news and updates on all EcoZine articles.

Many states also offer YCC programs. These programs have varying age requirements. State YCC projects are similar to those at the national level, and typically include conservation projects in state parks.

The Student Conservation Association

The Student Conservation Association (SCA), founded in 1957, is one of the oldest organizations in resource conservation. The SCA offers programs in all 50 states, and has more than 50,000 alumni. As a participant in an SCA program, you might travel to another region for a project, or you could find one close to home. Many students enter an SCA program during or after college, but there are also options for high school students beginning at age 15.

Opportunities for high school students include volunteer positions with Conservation Crews and Community Conservation programs. Conservation Crews are for students between the ages of 15 and 19. Crews consist of six to eight students who work under the supervision of a trained crew leader on month-long projects in the frontcountry or backcountry. Typical Conservation Crew activities include trail building and habitat restoration projects. Community Conservation programs include year-round Community Conservation Leadership Corps positions and Summer Community Crews. These community programs offer students real-world training and service opportunities in the field of conservation, often in an urban setting.

Participation in an SCA program gives students the chance to serve the land while also gaining practical skills that will last a lifetime. In addition, many participants in SCA programs end up pursuing a career in the field of conservation. In fact, over 60 percent of SCA alumni become conservation professionals, and 12 percent of National Park Service employees came to the NPS initially through an SCA program.

If you are interested in making a longer commitment to the SCA, you might choose to participate in a Conservation Internship, which is available to those 18 and older. An SCA internship is an excellent way to test your interest in a variety of environmental careers by offering you the chance to work alongside established professionals in the field. These internships typically last between 12 weeks and 12 months. Examples of Conservation Internships include work as a biology technician at Carlsbad Caverns National Park in New Mexico;, as a fisheries intern in Alaska, or as a backcountry park ranger in the Red River Gorge in Kentucky. Many of these internships

Summer community crew positions with the SCA offer practical experience in the field of conservation.

offer stipends for travel to and from the internship site, free housing, a weekly living allowance, and an education award at the completion of the internship, which can be used to pay for future educational expenses or to pay off a portion of student loans.

The Benefits to You

Volunteer and paid opportunities obviously benefit the local ecosystems, but what do you get from it, in addition to dirt under your fingernails? The following is a short list of just some of the benefits:

- Learn a new skill, such as how to build and install an irrigation system, take a tree inventory, or build a box for a nesting owl.
- Improve your science classwork by learning the science behind what you see in a living ecosystem.
- Work side-by-side with professional scientists, collecting data or samples for ongoing investigations.
- Become aware of the career possibilities related to working in the outdoors.
- Make lasting friendships, working closely with others who share your interests.

What Do You Think?

Are you interested in pursuing a career in the field of conservation or environmental science? What volunteer opportunities exist where you live?

© Jim West/Alamy Images

SECTION 1 Economics and International Cooperation

OBJECTIVES

- Achieving sustainability will require cooperation and communication at many levels of society.

- Some goals of international agreements on the environment have been achieved and successfully implemented. Other goals have been set but not yet achieved.

- Economic systems operate within the environment by using resources and by returning both desired and undesired results. Economic systems sometimes fail to balance all the costs and benefits of people's actions.

KEY TERMS

sustainability

economics

SECTION 2 Environmental Policies in the United States

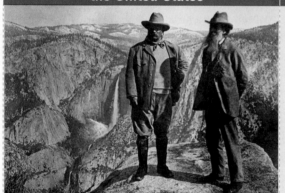

OBJECTIVES

- Since the early 1900s, the U.S. government has developed policies to address environmental problems and has established agencies to implement those policies.

- Citizens can influence policy at all levels of government but especially at the local level.

- Lobbying and the media also influence policy and public opinion.

KEY TERMS

Environmental Impact Statement

lobbying

SECTION 3 The Importance of the Individual

OBJECTIVES

- Individuals can have an effect on environmental interactions through leadership and education. Many environmental problems were brought to the public's attention by a few individuals.

- You make important decisions about the environment every day. How you choose to spend money, vote, and use resources will have an impact on the environment.

- You can apply scientific thinking and knowledge to any decisions that you may face.

CHAPTER 21 **Review**

Reviewing Key Terms

Use each of the following terms in a separate sentence.

1. *sustainability*

2. *economics*

Use the correct key term to complete each of the following sentences.

3. Every federal project must complete a(n) _____.

4. Many groups try to influence government policies through _____.

5. Concept Map Use the following terms to create a concept map: *groups, individuals, lobbying, state laws, federal laws,* and *voting.*

Reviewing Main Ideas

6. Which of the following trends is *not* a challenge to achieving sustainability?

a. the increasing human population

b. the decreasing supply of fresh water in the world

c. disagreement among governments

d. advancement of scientific understanding

7. At the 1992 Earth Summit, representatives from around the world

a. created the Kyoto Protocol.

b. tried to balance economic development with environmental sustainability.

c. could not reach agreement on anything important.

d. talked about environmental problems for the first time ever.

8. International environmental agreements include

a. the Montreal Protocol.

b. Earth Day.

c. the World Trade Organization.

d. the Wilderness Act of 1964.

9. Economic systems

a. do not depend on limited natural resources.

b. rarely balance the costs and benefits of every action.

c. should not include the costs of pollution with the costs of an action.

d. must operate within the environment.

10. Which of the following statements about U.S. environmental policy is *not* true?

a. During most of the 19th century, most Americans were not concerned about environmental consequences.

b. During the 1960s, several individuals had strong effects on public thinking about environmental issues.

c. Before Earth Day 1970, no one in the United States cared about the environment.

d. The Environmental Protection Agency was established at a time of increasing public awareness of environmental problems.

11. State and local environmental regulations

a. cannot be influenced by individuals.

b. simply enforce federal standards.

c. do not have to follow federal standards.

d. are often more strict than federal standards.

12. The main function of an Environmental Impact Statement is

a. to predict the effect a federal project might have on the environment.

b. to produce a record of environmental change throughout history.

c. to satisfy the requirements of international agreements.

d. to limit real estate development and the activities of businesses.

13. Local governments do not regulate

a. recycling.

b. sewage treatment.

c. garbage disposal.

d. Environmental Impact Statements.

Short Answer

14. What do world leaders do at gatherings such as the Earth Summit?

15. Why are some treaties not successful?

16. In what ways do state or local regulations differ from federal regulations?

17. Describe several ways that citizens can influence environmental policy.

18. How can a consumer affect the environment?

Interpreting Graphics

The figures below show a type of label that is required by law to be placed on all new appliances. Use the figures to answer questions 19–22.

19. Compare What is the most likely reason that the tag on the right has an "energy star" symbol?

20. Evaluate Which quantity on the tags is the most important piece of information about these appliances?

21. Analyze Why do you think the government has required such labels to be placed on all new appliances?

22. Justify There are two types of refrigerators represented on these labels: top-freezer and side-by-side. Which type is generally more efficient? How can you tell?

Critical Thinking

23. Expressing a Viewpoint Read the section about influential individuals in this chapter. Describe at least one effect that one of these individuals may have had on your life.

24. Making Predictions What might the effects be if the United States doubled the tax on gasoline over the next 10 years?

25. History Some people argue that developing nations should be allowed to create polluting industries in order to develop economically, just as the developed nations did in the past. Explain your opinion of this argument.

26. An International Treaty Write a proposal for a new international treaty that would address a pressing environmental problem and that you think could be agreed upon by many nations.

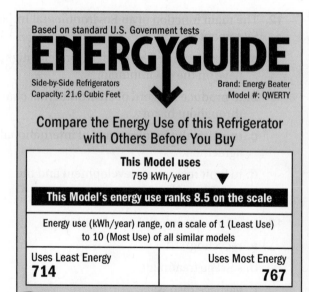

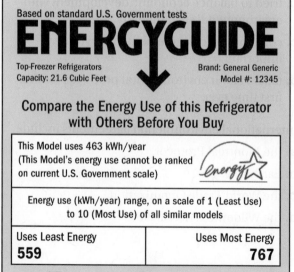

Analyzing Data

27. Making Calculations The average amount of water used to take a shower is 11.7 gallons. If a person takes a shower every day, how much water do they use every year in showers alone? An energy-efficient shower head reduces the amount of water used to 8.8 gallons. How many gallons of water would you save each year if you installed an energy-efficient shower head?

Making Connections

28. Communicating Main Ideas Describe some signs that the world may be progressing toward a sustainable future. What are some likely challenges ahead?

29. Expressing Original Ideas Describe your vision of a sustainable future. Consider lifestyles, technology, forms of government, economic systems, and social organizations.

CASESTUDY

30. Why is it difficult to manage environmental issues that affect the world's oceans?

31. What might be a way to entice countries that opt out of international agreements to change their decision?

Why It Matters

32. How can decisions that you make impact the environment in a positive way?

STUDYSKILL

Preparing for a Debate Participating in a debate can help you analyze an issue. To support a point of view, you must also understand opposing views. For practice, choose an issue discussed in this chapter or elsewhere in this book. At the top of a sheet of paper, state the basic problem. Draw two or more columns, and summarize different points of view at the top of each column. Then list the arguments in favor of each view. Try to find arguments that can be made against each point of view on similar points.

Organizing a Sustainable Product Guide

Objectives

Collect Data on the sustainability of common household products.

Prepare and present the sustainability of common household products.

Summarize your research in a guide to sustainable products.

Materials

Internet access, if available

magazines and newspapers with product advertisements

Sustainability is defined as the condition in which human needs are met in such a way that a human population can survive indefinitely. The goal of sustainability is to improve the quality of life in our communities without depleting the many resources on which life on Earth depends.

Sustainable products are those products providing environmental, social, and economic benefits, while protecting public health, welfare, and the environment. To be classified as sustainable, a product must accomplish these goals over its full life cycle, from the gathering of raw materials, manufacturing the raw materials into a product, shipping it to the consumer, its use by the consumer, to final disposal. A product is not sustainable if it meets these goals in some portions of its life cycle, while failing to meet them in others.

One function of government is to manage the production sustainability of the country, since this is key to the economic and environmental welfare of that country's population. Although governments manage production sustainability, many people think it is up to the consumer to be a force to drive manufacturers toward producing sustainable products. According to this theory, if many consumers stop purchasing non-sustainable products, manufacturers will stop making them.

Three simple criteria may be used to determine sustainability.

Cyclic The product is made from compostable (vegetative) or recyclable (such as paper, metals, plastics, or glass) materials. Not all materials are manufactured into a form favorable for recycling.

Renewable The manufacture of the product uses forms of renewable energy that are cyclic and safe (such as solar, wind, geothermal, or natural gas from decomposing waste).

Safe The product does not use materials that can be toxic during use or after disposal.

In this lab, you will learn about materials used to make various products. You will then use this information to classify consumer products as sustainable or non-sustainable, using the three criteria above. Finally, you will prepare a consumer guide to sustainable products.

Procedure

1. Devise a scale that rates the sustainability of products. Find advertisements in newspapers and magazines for ten products people commonly use, or examine ten actual products.

2. Find information about each product's ingredients or the materials used to manufacture it. Include the packing materials in your research. Consider the product's expected lifespan and methods of disposal for the product.

3. Prepare an index card for each product. You can cut out a picture of the product from the advertisement or draw a picture of the product. Each card should show the product information you researched. Each card should also indicate a sustainability rating that you assign to each product.

Sustainable Products Examples of sustainable products include cleaners made from non-toxic ingredients and paper towels made from recycled paper products.

Analysis

1. **Classifying** Gather the index cards from all lab team members. Devise a way to organize the information. You might sort by product type, by rating, or by any other category that seems logical.

2. **Organizing Data** Use the index cards to prepare a guide about sustainable products as a lab team. Your team also might include guidelines for choosing products, and information about agencies and organizations that provide information on sustainable products. The guide can be delivered in any form, such as a website, computer presentation, or a pamphlet.

Conclusions

3. **Evaluating Methods** Compare the presentations of each of the lab teams. In your opinion, which group's presentation did the best job of providing information to consumers on sustainable products. Why?

Extension

4. **Research and Communications** Locate information on the production sustainability track record (mining/growing, manufacturing, and shipping) of the companies that make the products that you identified as sustainable. Prepare a chart comparing each product's consumer sustainability and a production sustainability track record of the manufacturer. Present your information to the class.

Student Resources

Lab Safety

General Guidelines for Laboratory Safety

In the laboratory, you can engage in hands-on explorations, test your scientific hypotheses, and build practical laboratory skills. However, while working in the laboratory or in the field, it is your responsibility to protect yourself and other students by conducting yourself in a safe manner. You will avoid accidents in the laboratory by following directions, handling materials carefully, and taking your work seriously. Read the following general safety guidelines and review the descriptions of the safety symbols on pp. xxiv–xxv before working in the laboratory.

SafeEyeProtect　　SafeClothing　　SafeCaustic　　SafeChemical

SafeAnimal　　SafePlants　　SafeElectric　　SafeHeating

SafeSharp　　SafeHandGlove　　SafeFire　　Gas Safety

SafeGlassware　　SafeDisposal　　Hygienic Care/ Clean Hands

Before You Begin...

- Be prepared. Study assigned experiments before class. Resolve any questions about procedures before starting work.

- Keep your work area uncluttered. Store books, backpacks, jackets, or other items you do not need out of the way.

- Arrange the materials you are using for an experiment in an orderly fashion on your work surface. Keep laboratory materials away from the edge of the work surface.

- Tie back long hair and remove dangling jewelry. Roll up sleeves and secure loose clothing.

- Do not wear contact lenses in the laboratory. Chemicals could get between the contact lenses and your eyes and cause irreparable eye damage. If your doctor requires that you wear contact lenses instead of glasses, then you should wear eyecup safety goggles— similar to goggles that are worn for underwater swimming—in the laboratory.

- Do not wear open-toed shoes, sandals, or canvas shoes in the laboratory because they will not protect your feet if any chemical, glassware, or other object is dropped on them.

- Know the location of the nearest phone. Find out where emergency telephone numbers, such as the number for the nearest poison control center, can be found.

- Know the location of safety equipment such as eyewash stations and fire extinguishers. Know how to operate this equipment.

- Know the fire evacuation routes established by your school.

- Before you begin the experiment, review the supplies you will be using and the safety issues you should be concerned about. Be on the alert for the safety symbols shown on this page and those that appear in your experiment.

While You Are Working...

- Do not play in the lab. Take your lab work seriously, and behave appropriately in the laboratory. Be aware of your classmates' safety as well as your own at all times.

- Never perform an experiment not authorized by your teacher.

- Never work alone in the laboratory.

- Always wear safety goggles and a lab apron when you are working in the lab. Laboratories contain chemicals that can damage your clothing, skin, and eyes.

- Wear protective gloves when working with an open flame, chemicals, solutions, wild or unknown plants, or other items as directed by your teacher.

- Never look directly at the sun through any optical device or use direct sunlight to illuminate a microscope. The focused light can seriously damage your eyes.

- When heating substances in a test tube, always point the test tube away from yourself and others.

- Keep your hands away from the sharp or pointed ends of scalpels, scissors, and other sharp instruments.

- Observe all of the safety symbols that accompany the procedural steps of the experiment. Be sure to follow the safety practices that are called for in the experiment.

- Never put anything in your mouth, and never touch or taste substances in the laboratory unless your teacher instructs you to do so.

- If your teacher instructs you to smell a chemical in the laboratory, follow the correct procedure. The correct method is to fan your hand gently over the substance, waving its vapors toward your nose. Do not put your nose directly over the substance.

- Never eat, drink, chew gum, or apply cosmetics in the laboratory. Do not store food or beverages in the lab area.

- Report any accident, chemical spill, or unsafe incident to your teacher immediately.

- Check labels on containers of chemicals to be certain you are using the right material.

- When diluting an acid or base with water, always add the acid or base to water. Do NOT add water to the acid or base.

- Dispose of chemicals according to your teacher's instructions.

- Never return unused chemicals to the containers from which you obtained them. Do not put any object into a bottle containing a laboratory chemical.

Emergency Procedures

Don't panic. In the event of a laboratory emergency, follow these instructions.

- In the event of a fire, alert the teacher and leave the laboratory immediately.

- If your clothes catch fire, STOP, DROP, and ROLL! The quickest way to smother a fire is to drop to the floor and roll.

- If your lab partner's clothes or hair catches fire, grab the nearest fire blanket and use it to extinguish the flames. Inform your teacher immediately.

- If a chemical spills on your skin or clothing, wash it off immediately with plenty of water and notify your teacher.

- If a chemical gets into your eyes or on your face, go to an eyewash station immediately and flush your eyes (including under the eyelids) with running water for at least 15 minutes. Hold your eyelids open with your thumb and fingers, and roll your eyeball around. While doing this, have another student notify your teacher.

- If a chemical spills on the floor, do not clean it up yourself. Keep your classmates away from the area and alert your teacher immediately.

- If you receive a cut, even if it is just a small one, notify your teacher.

Safety with Animals in the Laboratory

Observing and experimenting with animals can enrich your understanding of environmental science. However, you must use extreme caution to assure your own safety as well as the safety and comfort of the animals. When working with animals in the laboratory, be sure to follow these guidelines.

- Do not touch or approach any animal unless your teacher specifically gives you permission.

- Handle animals only as your teacher directs. Mishandling or abusing any animal will not be tolerated.

- Do not bring any animal into the laboratory without your teacher's permission.

- Wear gloves or other appropriate protective gear when working with animals.

- Wash your hands after touching any animal.

- Inform your teacher immediately if you are scratched, bitten, stung, or otherwise harmed by an animal.

- Always follow your teacher's instructions regarding the care of laboratory animals. Ask questions if you do not clearly understand what you are supposed to do.

- Keep each laboratory animal in a suitable, escape-proof container in a location where the animal will not be frequently disturbed. Animal containers should provide adequate ventilation, warmth, and light.

- Keep each laboratory animal's container clean. Clean cages of small birds and mammals daily.

- Provide each laboratory animal with water at all times.

- Feed animals regularly, according to their individual needs.

- If you are responsible for the care or feeding of animals, arrange for necessary care on weekends and holidays and during vacations.

- No study that involves inflicting pain on a vertebrate animal should ever be conducted.

- Vertebrate animals must not be exposed to excessive noise, exhausting exercise, overcrowding, or other distressing stimuli.

- When an animal must be removed from the laboratory, your teacher will provide a suitable method.

Safety with Plants in the Laboratory

Some plants or plant parts are poisonous to the point of fatality, depending on the weight of the person and the amount of plant material ingested. Therefore, many plants or plant parts can present a safety hazard to you. When working with plants in the laboratory be sure to follow these guidelines.

- Never place any part of any plant in your mouth unless instructed to do so by your teacher. Seeds obtained from commercial growers can be particularly dangerous because such seeds may be coated with hormones, fungicides, or insecticides.

- Do not rub sap or juice of fruits on your skin or into an open wound.

- Never inhale or expose your skin or eyes to the smoke of any burning plant or plant parts.

- Do not bring unknown wild or cultivated plants into the laboratory.

- Do not eat, drink, or apply cosmetics after handling plants without first washing your hands.

- Provide adequate light and water and appropriate soil and temperature for plants growing in the laboratory.

- If you are responsible for plants, make necessary arrangements for their care on weekends and holidays and during vacations.

Finishing Up in the Laboratory...

- Broken glass, chemicals, and other laboratory waste products should be disposed of in separate special containers. Dispose of waste materials as directed by your teacher.

- Clean tables and sinks as directed by your teacher.

- Make sure all water faucets, gas jets, burners, and electrical appliances are turned off.

- Return all laboratory materials and equipment to their proper places.

- Wash your hands thoroughly with soap and water after completing each experiment.

Safe and Successful Fieldwork

Environmental scientists conduct much of their research in the field. For environmental scientists—and environmental science students such as you—there are three important issues to consider when working in the field. One issue is your personal safety. Another issue is the successful completion of the scientific work you set out to do. The third consideration is protection of the environment you have come to study. The following guidelines will help you address these three issues.

- Dress in a manner that will keep you comfortable, warm, and dry. Wear long pants rather than shorts or a skirt. Wear sturdy shoes that have closed toes. Do not wear sandals or heels. Wear waterproof shoes if you will be working in wetlands.

- Bring rain gear if there is any possibility of rain.

- Bring sunglasses, sunscreen, and insect repellent as needed.

- Do not go alone beyond where you can be seen or heard; travel with a partner at all times.

- Do not approach wild mammals, snakes, snapping turtles, or other animals that may sting, bite, scratch, or otherwise cause injury.

- Do not touch any animal in the wild without specific permission from your teacher.

- Find out whether poisonous plants or dangerous animals are likely to be where you will be going. Learn how to identify any hazardous species.

- Do not pick wildflowers or touch plants or plant parts unless your teacher gives you permission. Do not eat wild plants.

- Immediately report any hazard or injury to your teacher.

- Be sure you understand the purpose of your field trip and any assignments you have been given. Bring all needed school supplies and keep them organized in a binder, backpack, or other container.

- Be aware of the impact you are having on the environments you visit. Just walking over fragile areas can harm them, so stay on trails unless your teacher gives you permission to do otherwise.

- Sketching, photographing, and writing field notes are generally more appropriate than collecting specimens for observation. Collecting from a field site may be permitted in certain cases, but always obtain your teacher's permission first.

- Do not leave garbage at the field site. Strive to leave natural areas just as you found them.

APPENDIX B
Field Studies

Taking Notes in the Field

It is essential for someone studying the environment to keep a journal with field notes. Field notes provide a crucial record of observations and activities that can be used later to verify facts and track important ecological changes. Keeping a journal that incorporates these observations, along with your thoughts and ideas, can provide valuable insight into what is going on in the environment you are investigating.

To be useful, field notes must be kept up to date and written in a consistent format. Options for keeping your journal might include purchasing an inexpensive, waterproof field notebook or a carbonless-copy lab notebook from various online vendors. A less expensive option is to use a hardbound composition book that can be purchased anywhere that sells school supplies.

If your teacher requires that you keep a journal that is separate from your field notes, you can make a light, easy-to-carry clipboard by cutting out a 9" x 12" piece of heavy cardboard or foamboard. Slip a sturdy rubber band around the board to hold sheets of paper and a pencil. This will give you a surface to write on when you are out in the field and will keep your notes and pencil from getting lost. Later, you can insert the loose note pages into a binder, arranged in chronological order.

Use pencil instead of ink when making field notes. That way, if the pages should become damp for any reason, your writing will not be lost.

Science Journal

- Begin your journal with a cover page, giving your name and the year.
- Decide which sections your journal will need to be divided into (this may be determined by your teacher), such as warm-up exercises, field notes, and species counts.
- After the cover page (do NOT write on the back of the cover page), title the next page *Table of Contents*. Skip a line and write the name of the first section. Turn the page and write the title of the second section at the top of the right-hand page. Do this for each section.
- Starting on the first right-hand page after the Table of Contents pages, number all of the right-hand pages in the journal in the bottom right-hand corner. Do NOT number the backs of the pages.
- Your journal should contain all of the data and observations collected in your field notes (if keeping them both in one notebook, page numbers can be given).
- If you have been observing or doing population counts for a particular species or group of species, each day's observations should be recorded in its own section, headed by the name of the species or community being studied (for example, wildflower meadow community, monarch butterflies, pine-bore beetles).
- Use your field notes, along with field guides and other references, to identify any unknown species found during your excursion.
- Don't hesitate to record your personal thoughts and experiences that occurred in the field (for example, "accidentally stepped into fire-ant hill but managed to brush most of them off without getting bitten"). These can help you remember more details later.

Field Notes

Always begin each day's field notes on a new page, with the date and location listed at the top of the page. If you have been given a specific task to accomplish while out in the field, write a brief description of your instructions.

You might include the following data in your field notes.

- Current weather conditions — You can use an armored thermometer to check air temperature or, if available, an electronic weather probe that provides additional data, such as humidity, barometric pressure, and altitude. If you have a smartphone, there are applications you can download that provide the ambient temperature,

GPS coordinates for each data-collection site, and local weather data. You can also jot down your personal observations of the weather.

- Note any recent events or disturbances in the area you are observing, such as storms, droughts, fires, construction, plowing or cultivation, and tree or brush removal.

- Give a brief description of the topography and vegetation for the area you are observing. These include hills, plains, beach, dunes, forest, marsh, meadow, desert, stream, riverbank, and general types of plant species (pine trees, shrubs, grasses, reeds). Simple sketches can also be of great value.

- If you are changing positions during your field-work, make note of the route you take so that each place you collect data can be located again. Use a compass to aid you in this process.

- Each time you stop to collect data, make brief notes of the time, location, and surroundings where you made your observations. Collect as much specific information about the area as time and availability of equipment allow.

  For example, if you are observing an aquatic ecosystem, collect information on water temperature; dissolved oxygen levels; turbidity levels; depth of water; composition of bank and bottom substrate; direction of flow (if any); color of water; presence of algae, scum, foam, or oily films on water surface; and odor. Observations of soil might include color, estimated particle size, sandy, clay, rocky, shells, pH.

- Describe the methods you use to collect your data (for example, quadrat, transect, capture-mark-release).

- For each type of observation or data collection you do, list the materials and equipment you used (for example, leaf hopper collected in insect net and preserved in plastic vial with alcohol).

- Include any quantitative data you collect, such as estimates of species numbers, sizes of plants or animals observed, behavior of organisms (along with how frequently the behavior occurs), and measurements of the area or conditions.

- Make note of anything you collect, including specimens, photographs, and video. If collecting specimens, note the methods you used to collect and keep the specimens. If possible, return any specimens to the same location where you collected them when you are through with them.

- Write down any questions, ideas, predictions, or other inspirations that come to you while you are in the field.

- Keep all your observations brief, but be sure you can remember the meaning of any symbols or abbreviations you use when you see them later.

- If you are not collecting physical specimens and cannot immediately identify a species while in the field and do not have a field guide with you, assign it a number and general designation (for example, insect #12); make detailed notes of color, shape, and other characteristics. Make a simple sketch or take a photograph.

- If you keep a separate journal, you can expand on your thoughts when you record your field notes. If you keep only one combined field notebook/journal, then sit down and write your expanded observations at the end of the field experience, while your thoughts and impressions are fresh in your mind.

Field Study Activities

There is one Field Study per chapter in this textbook.

CHAPTER 1, PAGE 10
Measure Up

Measure As you begin to study the environment around you, one of the skills you will need is making accurate and precise measurements. Select an area outside your school where you will collect data. In a group of 2–3 students, select the appropriate data-collection tools provided by your teacher. Construct a data table in your science journal to record your data.

1. Determine the following measurements:
   - the circumference of a tree, in meters
   - the temperature of the air in the shade and in the sunlight, in °C
   - the mass of a rock, in grams
   - the length of a blade of grass, in millimeters
   - the volume of a small rock or pebble, in cubic centimeters
   - the area of your observation site, in square meters

2. Record your raw data and any calculations you make in finding your final measurements.

CHAPTER 2, PAGE 43
Organizing Data

Conceptual Model Select an area to observe near your home or school. Choose the type of data you would like to collect from a short list provided by your teacher. For example, you might choose to identify organisms that are part of the same food chain in that area. Use your textbook as a reference to construct a conceptual model in your science journal that organizes your data and shows how the pieces of information are related.

CHAPTER 3, PAGE 72
Detecting CO$_2$
Investigate

1. Label two test tubes *Control* and *Exhaust* and place them in a test-tube rack. Into each, add 10 mL of water and 20 drops of bromothymol blue indicator.

2. Attach the open end of a small balloon to the bottom of a glass or metal funnel with rubber tubing.

3. Go outside, where your teacher will start the test vehicle. *Caution*: Avoid breathing in the exhaust fumes or touching the exhaust pipe, which can become extremely hot.

4. Place the open end of the funnel over the opening on the vehicle's exhaust pipe. Allow the exhaust to fill the balloon to a diameter of about 10 cm. Detach the rubber tubing, pinch the balloon closed, and return to the classroom.

5. Stretch the balloon over the top of the Exhaust test tube. Tip the balloon and test tube back and forth 10 times.

6. Construct a data table in your science journal. Use colored pencils to record the color of the liquid in both tubes.

7. Compare the color of the control liquid with that of the liquid mixed with the exhaust fumes. Record your observations.

CHAPTER 4, PAGE 100
Coevolution

Identify Flowering plants evolved simultaneously with the organisms that pollinate them. The most common plant pollinators are insects. Walk around your school or neighborhood, or if it is wintertime, a local store that sells plants and flowers. In your science journal, sketch the structure of several different types of flowers. Identify and record characteristics of the flowers that are adaptations meant to attract pollinators.

CHAPTER 5, PAGE 132
Investigating Succession

Survey Explore two or three blocks in your neighborhood, and find evidence of succession. Make notes in your science journal about the location and the evidence of succession that you observe. Pay attention to sidewalks, curbs, streets, vacant lots, and buildings, as well as parks, gardens, fields, and other open areas. Create a map from your data that identifies where succession is taking place in your neighborhood.

CHAPTER 6, PAGE 160
Xeriscaping

Identify To conserve water or live more sustainably, many people have started xeriscaping their yards. Xeriscaping involves planting hardy, native plants that thrive with little water. Survey your community and identify a yard or public area that has been xeriscaped. Use field guides to identify the plants and record their common and scientific names in your science journal. Use colored pencils to draw a map of the area you observed, labeling the plants you identified.

CHAPTER 7, PAGE 184
Once Upon a Time

Explore Most people don't realize that hundreds of millions of years ago, North America was mostly underwater. In every state, there are places where evidence of ancient oceans and the organisms that lived in them can still be found. With your class, explore an area in your community identified by your teacher and look for fossils of ancient aquatic life. In your science journal, draw a simple map of the search area and use your map to record where fossils are found. Make simple sketches or photographs of anything you find, to identify later. Record all your observations.

CHAPTER 8, PAGE 204
Observing Competition

Investigate You can study competition among bird species at home or at school. Build a bird feeder using a plastic milk jug, a metal pie pan, or another inexpensive material. Fill the feeder with unsalted bread crumbs, sunflower seeds, or commercial birdseed.

Observe the birds that visit the feeder. Sit quietly in the same spot, and make observations at the same time each day for several days in a row.

In your science journal, record your observations, including data about the kinds of birds that use the feeder, the kinds of seeds the birds prefer, the factors that affect how much the birds eat, and the kinds of birds that are better competitors for the birdseed. Add drawings or photos of the birds you see and then use a field guide to identify them.

CHAPTER 9, PAGE 227
Population Issues

Observe Is your community experiencing rapid growth, or is the population in decline? Both of these situations can lead to population-related problems.

Take a walk or drive around your community and record your observations in your science journal. Try to answer the following questions and any others that you may think of:

- Are more people moving into your community or moving away?
- Are there frequent traffic jams on major roads in your area?
- Does your community have its own public services (law enforcement, fire department, hospital, and so on), or do you depend on a nearby community?
- Are schools in your area overcrowded?
- Are houses and other buildings spaced close together?
- Do most people in your community use public water supplies, or do they depend on private wells?
- Are there any other environmental issues, such as water quality or loss of wildlife habitat, that are associated with the number of people who live in your community?
- Is your community doing anything to address the issues you have cited? Explain.

Hold a class discussion about what you and other students observed.

CHAPTER 10, PAGE 257
Simple Biodiversity Assessment

Identify Discover the diversity of weeds and other plants in a small area. Yards, gardens, and vacant lots are good places to conduct such a study. Mark off a 0.5 m^2 section. Use a field guide to identify every plant species that you can. Be specific—don't just record *grass* or *weeds*.

Identify how many different types of plants there are. You may want to sketch or photograph some of the plants. Then count the number of each type of plant you identified. Record your results in your science journal.

CHAPTER 11, PAGE 284
Sources of Water Pollution

Identify Walk around your neighborhood, and record potential sources of point or nonpoint water pollution, such as runoff from parking lots, motor oil being poured into storm drains, and lawn fertilizer being used. Suggest ways in which the amount of pollution from each source might be reduced. Record your observations, suggestions, and any evidence that supports your analysis in your science journal.

CHAPTER 12, PAGE 313
Light Pollution

Observe Walk outside your home at night and look up at the sky. Can you see any stars? If you see very few or none, then your community may be experiencing light pollution. Along some coastlines where sea turtles lay their eggs, too much light at night can confuse the hatching babies, causing them to move away from the ocean. How might light pollution affect wildlife or plants in your community? Record your observations in your science journal.

CHAPTER 13, PAGE 340
Reducing Your Carbon Footprint

Calculate Use an online carbon-footprint calculator to determine your personal level of carbon emissions and then do a walk around the inside and outside of your school. In your science journal, make a three-column chart with the headings *Pros, Cons,* and

Solutions. List all the ways your school is reducing carbon emissions under *Pros.* List all the things the school could be doing better under *Cons.* In the third column, list the ways your school could improve its overall carbon footprint. Compare your findings with those of your classmates and make a master chart. Brainstorm ideas of what you could reasonably do to help your school become "greener."

CHAPTER 14, PAGE 359
Land-Use Planning

Survey No community stays the same forever. Whether you live in a city, a suburb, a small town, or a rural area, you may see old buildings being torn down, signs announcing new buildings, evidence of new road construction, or land being cleared for a new housing subdivision or shopping center. Most communities have a Planning Commission that has to approve these sorts of changes. If there is a major change proposed, public hearings may be held to give citizens a chance to voice their opinions.

In your science journal, construct a three-column data table. Label the first column *Change,* the second column *Pros,* and the third one *Cons.*

Walk, ride, or drive around your community and keep a record of any changes to your area. In the second column, record ways in which you feel the change will have a beneficial impact. In the last column, note any negative side effects of the change. Compare your data with those of your classmates.

CHAPTER 15, PAGE 391
What a Pest!

Identify Walk through the neighborhood around your school or home. In your science journal, keep a record of the pest organisms that you find. These might include plants, insects, or other animals that are harmful to other organisms or to their surroundings, such as poison ivy, mosquitoes, or fire ants. Do some research to find out what measures, if any, are being taken to deal with pests and record these in your journal. As you work your way through this study, try to determine if the pests are being dealt with in a way that is safe for people and the environment or if abatement efforts create a different sort of hazard.

CHAPTER 16, PAGE 411
Rock Ore Mineral?

Classify Minerals may be composed of one or more elements but are usually compounds. Rocks, on the other hand, are made up of multiple minerals. When a mineral is economically valuable, it is known as an ore.

Do an Internet search for information on the key phrase "common minerals and their uses." In your science journal, make a list of 10 different minerals. Record what they are used for and whether or not they are scarce or expensive to use.

Walk around your neighborhood, home, and school and record ways in which you see these minerals being used in everyday life. For any of the minerals that are difficult or expensive to obtain, make note of any alternative materials or ways in which existing minerals might be reused or recycled.

CHAPTER 17, PAGE 442
Ride Along

Determine Who is the person in your family who runs the most errands in the community? Make arrangements with that person to run errands on a day when you can go along. (*Note:* If you normally use GPS, turn it off for this activity.)

Obtain a street or road map of the area in which you will be traveling. Before setting out from home, record the time in your science journal and make a mark on the map to indicate the location of your home. If your vehicle has a trip odometer, you may want to start it at zero or make a note of the starting mileage of the vehicle. At the location for each errand, record the address, the time you arrive, and the time you leave again, and mark the location on the map. When you have finished all of the errands, record the time when you return home.

Use your collected data or trip odometer reading to find out the total distance covered from the time you left home until you returned. Then, using either your map, a GPS device, or an Internet map website, determine if the routes you took from place to place were the shortest, most efficient methods of getting from one place to another.

Examine your results and determine if there is a more time- and fuel-efficient route to use when running your family's regular errands.

CHAPTER 18, PAGE 462
Biomass Survey

Survey Plant material, decomposing manure, and any other renewable organic matter that is used as an energy source is called a **biomass fuel.** Walk around your neighborhood and list as many sources of biomass fuel as you can find, such as a pile of firewood or plant stalks left after harvesting a crop. What do you think the advantages and disadvantages of using biomass as a fuel in your area would be? Record your observations.

CHAPTER 19, PAGE 489
Recycling

Observe Recycling is the process of reusing or recovering valuable materials from waste or scrap. Making new products from used cans, bottles, paper, and wood generally saves energy, water, and other resources. Make observations of the area in which you live and document ways in which scrap or waste materials are being recycled or have been used to make new products such as park benches made from recycled plastic bottles.

CHAPTER 20, PAGE 515
Sources of Pollution

Identify Human activities produce many types of pollution that can be hazardous to the health of humans and other organisms. Look around your community and record potential sources of air, water, solid-waste, light, and noise pollution. Identify what type each source is, where it is located, and list suggestions for ways in which the amount of pollution from each source might be reduced. Be sure to support your analysis by listing the evidence you used to identify each source.

CHAPTER 21, PAGE 542
Local Policies

Identify As a citizen of your community, you can influence local environmental policies. Identify an environmental issue in your area, such as people dumping used motor oil into storm drains. Find out what, if anything, is being done to correct the problem. Then design and implement a plan to help your community become more aware of the issue and what they can do to improve or correct it. Be sure to have your teacher approve your plan before you implement it.

Note-Taking and Study Skills

Graphic organizers are tools to help you take notes. Some graphic organizers are best used as you read to help you understand concepts. Others are best used to summarize or review information. Using a variety of graphic organizers will help you to understand and remember what you have learned.

During Reading

Use these graphic organizers while you are reading. They help you organize ideas in paragraphs and sections as you read them.

PROCESS DIAGRAM

What is it? A process is a series of steps that produces a result. Process diagrams show these steps.

How do you make it? Start with the first step and then write or draw each step, one after the other, and connect them with arrows.

CYCLE DIAGRAM

What is it? A cycle, such as the cell cycle, is a repeating series of events that happen one after another. Cycles do not have a beginning or an end. Cycle diagrams identify the steps in a cycle or process that repeat regularly.

How do you make it? Draw a cycle diagram to show processes that repeat without a beginning or ending. Use the arrows between the boxed steps to show the direction or order in which the cycle happens.

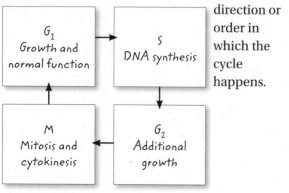

SUPPORTING MAIN IDEAS NOTES

What is it? A main idea graphic helps separate and organize reading material into important concepts and related details of support. You can choose the main idea graphic that best fits the material. The first strategy is useful when details follow some type of order.

How do you make it? First, find the main idea. The main idea may be the title of the section, it may be labeled "main idea" or "key concept" in your book, or it may be the topic sentence in a paragraph. Write the main idea in the top box. Next, summarize or paraphrase details that help explain that idea in the boxes that follow.

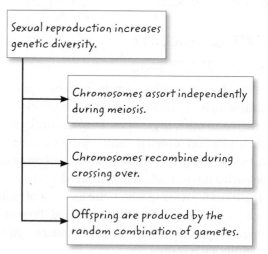

MAIN IDEA WEB

Another way you can take notes on main ideas is to draw a web. Write the main idea in the center and the details in the web around it. This is useful when the details do not occur in any particular order.

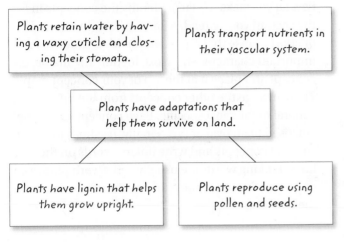

Plants retain water by having a waxy cuticle and closing their stomata.

Plants transport nutrients in their vascular system.

Plants have adaptations that help them survive on land.

Plants have lignin that helps them grow upright.

Plants reproduce using pollen and seeds.

TWO-COLUMN NOTES

What is it? Two-column notes is a strategy for taking notes to show

- vocabulary and their definitions
- processes or cycles and their steps
- main ideas and supporting details
- questions and possible answers
- causes and effects
- comparisons and contrasts

How do you make it? List processes, concepts, main ideas, or vocabulary in the left column of a two-column table. Write the description or explanation of the words or concepts in the right-hand column across from the words in the left column. You can also draw pictures in the right-hand column.

Leave enough space between words or concepts in the left-hand column so that you can write notes in the right column.

To study for quizzes and tests, fold your two-column notes in half vertically so you can see only the left column. Ask yourself to describe and explain the word in the left column.

Cellular Respiration	produces ATP occurs in mitochondria $C_6H_{12}O_6 + 6O_2 \rightarrow 6CO_2 + 6H_2O$
Photosynthesis	absorbs sunlight occurs in chloroplasts $6CO_2 + 6H_2O \rightarrow C_6H_{12}O_6 + 6O_2$

After Reading

Use these graphic organizers after you have read material and have taken notes on it. These organizers help you summarize the most important concepts and relate them to each other.

CAUSE-AND-EFFECT DIAGRAM

What is it? This strategy shows cause-and-effect relationships. In the diagram below, several effects result from a single cause. Those effects can cause more effects. A cause-and-effect diagram can also be drawn to show how multiple causes can produce a single effect.

How do you make it? Write the cause in the first box and write the effects in the boxes connected to the cause. Then think about what effects can result from the first effects. Connect them.

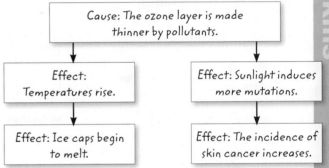

Cause: The ozone layer is made thinner by pollutants.

Effect: Temperatures rise.

Effect: Sunlight induces more mutations.

Effect: Ice caps begin to melt.

Effect: The incidence of skin cancer increases.

CONTENT FRAME

What is it? A content frame is a table that helps you organize and condense large amounts of information.

How do you make it? To make a content frame, make a table. Label the rows along the side with characteristics. Label the columns with the topics or categories. You can also include a column for drawings or sketches.

Biome	Tropical	Temperate	Tundra
Climate	Warm and rainy	Hot summers, cold winters	Cold and dry
Vegetation	Lush, thick forests	Broadleaf forests	Mosses and similar
Example	Manaus, Brazil	Burlington, Vermont	Barrow, Alaska

VENN DIAGRAM

What is it? A Venn diagram helps you show how two processes, ideas, or things are alike and different.

How do you make it? Draw two circles that overlap, like the ones below. Write one of the words or processes that you are going to compare in each circle. For example, the word *arteries* is written in the left circle and the word *veins* is written in the right circle. Under *arteries,* list characteristics or traits that only arteries possess. Under *veins,* list characteristics or traits that only veins possess. In the intersection of the two circles, list the traits that both arteries and veins share.

When you finish the diagram, write a sentence to summarize the similarities and differences: "Both veins and arteries have three-tissue layers and are each part of the closed circulatory system, but arteries are thicker and more muscular, and veins are thinner and have valves."

CONCEPT MAP

What is it? A concept map is a diagram that shows the main concepts from a passage you've read as well as the relationships between those concepts. Concept maps are useful tools for organizing and reviewing information.

How do you make it? First, identify the concepts in the section you've read. A concept is a single word or short phrase that represents an idea, process, or important characteristic. Next, identify the major concept and place it at the top of your concept map. Then arrange the other concepts from the most general to the most specific. Each concept should be enclosed in an oval or box. Finally, use lines to connect concepts and write linking words on the lines. Linking words are usually verbs, verb phrases, or prepositions that show the relationship between the concepts.

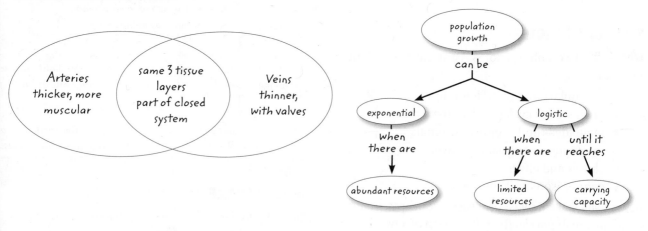

Y DIAGRAM

What is it? A Y diagram can be used instead of a Venn diagram to show how two processes, ideas, or things are alike and different.

How do you make it? On the top parts of the Y, list the characteristics of each topic separately. Then find the characteristics that are the same in both halves. Write them at the bottom part of the Y and cross them out from the top half. When you finish, the top limbs of the Y show differences, and the bottom part shows similarities between the two topics.

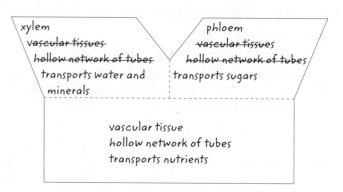

FoldNotes

FoldNotes are a useful study tool that you can use to organize concepts. One FoldNote focuses on a few main concepts. By using a FoldNote, you can learn how concepts fit together. FoldNotes are designed to make studying concepts easier, so you can remember ideas for tests.

Go to **HMDScience.com** for step-by-step animated instructions for how to make these FoldNotes

TRI-FOLD

A tri-fold is a useful tool that helps you track your progress. By organizing the chapter topic into what you know, what you want to know, and what you learn, you can see how much you have learned after reading a chapter.

PYRAMID

A pyramid provides a unique way for taking notes. The three sides of the pyramid can summarize information into three categories. Use the pyramid as a tool for studying information in a chapter.

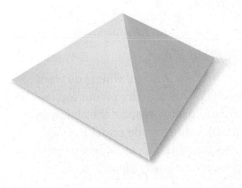

BOOKLET

A booklet is a useful tool for taking notes as you read a chapter. Each page of the booklet can contain a main topic from the chapter. Write details of each main topic on the appropriate page to create an outline of the chapter.

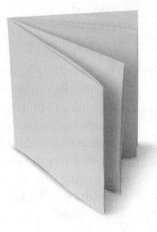

LAYERED BOOK

A layered book is a useful tool for taking notes as you read a chapter. The four flaps of the layered book can summarize information into four categories. Write details of each category on the appropriate flap to create a summary of the chapter.

DOUBLE-DOOR FOLD

A double-door fold is useful when you want to compare the characteristics of two topics. The double-door fold can organize characteristics of the two topics side by side under the flaps. Similarities and differences between the two topics can then be easily identified.

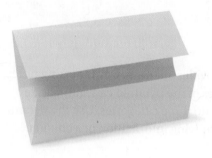

FOUR-CORNER FOLD

A four-corner fold is useful when you want to compare the characteristics of four topics. The four-corner fold can organize the characteristics of the four topics side by side under the flaps. Similarities and differences between the four topics can then be easily identified.

TABLE FOLD

A table fold is a useful tool for comparing the characteristics of two or three topics. In a table fold, all topics are described in terms of the same characteristics so that you can easily make a thorough comparison.

TWO-PANEL FLIP CHART

A two-panel flip chart is useful when you want to compare the characteristics of two topics. The two-panel flip chart can organize the characteristics of the two topics side by side under the flaps. Similarities and differences between the two topics can then be easily identified.

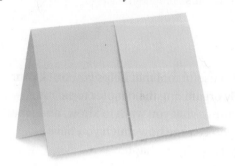

THREE-PANEL FLIP CHART

A three-panel flip chart is useful when you want to compare the characteristics of three topics. The three-panel flip chart can organize the characteristics of the three topics side by side under the flaps. Similarities and differences among the three topics can then be easily identified.

KEY-TERM FOLD

A key-term fold is useful for studying definitions of key terms in a chapter. Each tab can contain a key term on one side and its definition on the other. Use the key-term fold to quiz yourself on the definitions of the key terms in a chapter.

Analyzing Science Terms

You can often unlock the meaning of an unfamiliar science term by analyzing its word parts. Many parts of scientific words carry a meaning that derives from Latin or Greek. The parts of words listed below provide clues to the meanings of many science terms.

Word part	Meaning	Example
a-	not, without	abiotic
acr-, agr-	field	agriculture, acre
amphi-	both	amphibian
anti-	against	antibiotic
atmos-	vapor	atmosphere
auto-	self, same	autotrophic
benth-	depth	benthic, benthos
bio-	life	biology, biosphere, biotic
chloro-	green	chlorophyll
-cide	kill	insecticide, fungicide
co-, con-	with, together	coevolution, cooperation, commensalism
dem-, demo-	people	demography, epidemic
-duct-	to lead, draw	reproduction
e-, ec-, ex-	out, away from, outside	extinction, experiment
eco-	home, environment	ecology, ecosystem, economics
eu-	good, well	eutrophic
evolu-	to unroll	evolution
gen-	to give birth, produce	genetic, generation, genus
geo-	earth	geology, geosphere
hetero-	different	heterotroph
hydro-	water	hydrosphere, hydroelectric
im-, in-, ir-	not, without or in, into	invertebrate, immigration, irrigation
-ion	the act of	pollution, destruction
lith-	stone	lithosphere
-log-	to study	ecology, geology
-lu-, -lue-	dirt, impurity	pollution
mar-	sea	marine
micro-	small	microscopic, microorganisms
nutri-	food, nourishment	nutrient
organ-	tool, instrument	organic, organism
per-	through	permeable
photo-	light	photosynthesis
phyto-, -phyte	plant	phytoplankton, epiphyte
pre-	before, in front of	predator, prey, precipitation
pro-	forward	reproduction
re-	back, again	recycle, reproduce
spec-	appearance or shape	species, spectrum
-sphere	ball, globe	geosphere, ecosphere
stat-	position, standing	statistics, status
strati-, strato-	spread, layer	stratosphere
temper-	to measure or regulate	temperate, temperature
terra-, terre-	earth, land	terrain, terrestrial
thermo-	heat	thermosphere, thermal
-troph-	to feed, gather	eutrophic, autotroph

Math Skills Refresher

Geometry

A useful way to model the objects and substances studied in science is to consider them in terms of their shapes. For example, many of the properties of a wheel can be understood by pretending that the wheel is a perfect circle.

When using shapes as models, your ability to calculate the area or volume of shapes is a useful skill. The table below provides equations for the area and volume of several geometric shapes.

GEOMETRIC AREAS AND VOLUMES

Geometric Shape	Useful Equations
Rectangle	Area $= lw$
Circle	Area $= \pi r^2$ Circumference $= 2\pi r$
Triangle	Area $= \frac{1}{2} bh$
Sphere	Surface area $= 4\pi r^2$ Volume $= \frac{4}{3} \pi r^3$
Cylinder	Volume $= \pi r^2 h$
Rectangular box	Surface area $= 2(lh + lw + hw)$ Volume $= lwh$

PRACTICE

1. Calculate the area of a triangle that has a base of 900.0 m and a height of 500.0 m.

2. What is the volume of a cylinder that has a diameter of 14 cm and a height of 8 cm?

3. Calculate the surface area of a 4 cm cube.

Exponents

An exponent is a number that is superscripted to the right of another number. The best way to explain how an exponent works is with an example. In the value 5^4, the 4 is the exponent of the 5. The number with its exponent means that 5 is multiplied by itself 4 times:

$$5^4 = 5 \times 5 \times 5 \times 5 = 625$$

You will frequently hear exponents referred to as *powers*. Using this terminology, you can read the above equation as "five to the fourth power equals 625" or "five to the power of four equals 625." Keep in mind that any number raised to the power of 0 is equal to 1: $5^0 = 1$. Also, any number raised to the power of 1 is equal to itself: $5^1 = 5$.

A scientific calculator is a must for solving most problems involving exponents. Many calculators have dedicated keys for squares and square roots, but scientific calculators usually have a special key shaped like a caret, ^, for entering exponents. If you type in "5^4" and then hit the "=" key or the "Enter" key, the calculator will determine that 5^4 = 625 and display that answer.

EXPONENTS

	Rule	Example
Zero power	$x^0 = 1$	$7^0 = 1$
First power	$x^1 = x$	$6^1 = 6$
Multiplication	$(x^n)(x^m) = (x^{n+m})$	$(x^2)(x^4) = x^{(2+4)} = x^6$
Division	$\frac{x^n}{x^m} = x^{(n-m)}$	$\frac{x^8}{x^2} = x^{(8-2)}$ $= x^6$
Exponents raised to a power	$(x^n)^m = x^{nm}$	$(5^2)^3 = 5^6 = 15{,}625$

Order of Operations

Use this phrase to remember the correct order for long mathematical problems: "Please Excuse My Dear Aunt Sally" (some people just remember the acronym "PEMDAS"). This acronym stands for "parentheses, exponents, multiplication, division, addition, and subtraction." This is the correct order in which to complete operations. These rules are summarized in the table below.

ORDER OF OPERATIONS

1. Simplify groups inside parentheses. Start with the innermost group and work outward.
2. Simplify all exponents.
3. Perform multiplication and division in order from left to right.
4. Perform addition and subtraction in order from left to right.

Look at the following example.

$$4^3 + 2 \times \left[8 - (3 - 1)\right] = ?$$

First, simplify the operations inside parentheses. Begin with the innermost parentheses:

$$(3 - 1) = 2$$
$$4^3 + 2 \times [8 - 2] = ?$$

Then, move on to the next-outer parentheses:

$$[8 - 2] = 6$$
$$4^3 + 2 \times 6 = ?$$

Now, simplify all exponents:

$$4^3 = 64$$
$$64 + 2 \times 6 = ?$$

Next, perform the remaining multiplication:

$$2 \times 6 = 12$$
$$64 + 12 = ?$$

Finally, perform the addition:

$$64 + 12 = 76$$

Algebraic Rearrangements

Algebraic equations contain *constants* and *variables*. Constants are simply numbers, such as 2, 5, and 7. Variables are represented by letters such as x, y, z, a, b, and c. Variables are unspecified quantities and are also called the *unknowns*. Often, you will need to determine the value of a variable in an equation that contains algebraic expressions.

An algebraic expression contains one or more of the four basic mathematical operations: addition, subtraction, multiplication, and division. Constants, variables, or terms made up of both constants and variables can be involved in the basic operations.

The key to finding the value of a variable in an algebraic equation is that the total quantity on one side of the equals sign is equal to the quantity on the other side. If you do the same operation on either side of the equation, the results will still be equal. To determine the value of a variable in an algebraic expression, you try to reduce the equation into a simple one that tells you exactly what x (or some other variable) equals.

Look at the simple problem below.

$$8x = 32$$

If we wish to solve for x, we can multiply or divide each side of the equation by the same factor. You can perform any operation on one side of an equation as long as you do the same thing to the other side of the equation. In this example, if we divide both sides of the equation by 8, we have:

$$\frac{8x}{8} = \frac{32}{8}$$

The 8s on the left side of the equation cancel each other out, and the fraction $\frac{32}{8}$ can be reduced to give the whole number 4. Therefore, $x = 4$.

Next, consider the following equation.

$$2x + 4 = 16$$

If we divide each side by 2, we are left with $x + 2$ on the left and 8 on the right:

$$x + 2 = 8$$

Now, we can subtract 2 from each side of the equation to find that $x = 6$. In all cases, whatever operation is performed on the left side of the equals sign must also be performed on the right side.

PRACTICE

Rearrange each of the following equations to give the value of the variable indicated with a letter.

1. $8x - 32 = 128$

2. $6 - 5(4a + 3) = 26$

3. $-3(y - 2) + 4 = 29$

4. $-2(3m + 5) = 14$

5. $\left[8 \frac{(8 + 2z)}{3z}\right] + 2 = 5$

6. $\frac{(6b + 3)}{3} - 9 = 2$

Scientific Notation

Many quantities that scientists deal with are very large or very small values. For example, light travels at about 300,000,000 meters per second, and an electron has a mass of about 0.000 000 000 000 000 000 000 000 000 9 g. Obviously, it is difficult to read, write, and keep track of numbers like these. We avoid this problem by using a method dealing with powers of the number 10.

Study the positive powers of 10 shown in the following table. You should be able to check these numbers using what you know about exponents. The number of zeros in the equivalent number corresponds to the exponent of the 10, or the power to which the 10 is raised. The equivalent of 10^4 is 10,000, so the number has four zeros.

But how can we use the powers of 10 to simplify large numbers such as the speed of light? The speed of light is equal to $3 \times 100,000,000$ m/s. The factor of 10 in this number has 8 zeros, so it can be rewritten as 10^8. So, 300,000,000 can be expressed as 3×10^8.

Negative exponents can be used to simplify numbers that are less than 1. Study the negative powers of 10 in the table. In these cases, the exponent of 10 equals the number of decimal places you must move the decimal point to the right so that there is one digit just to the left of the decimal point. In the case of the mass of an electron, the decimal point has to be moved 28 decimal places to the right for the numeral 9 to be just to the left of the decimal point. The mass of the electron, about 0.000 000 000 000 000 000 000 000 000 000 9 g, can be rewritten as about 9×10^{-28} g.

POWERS OF 10	
Power of 10	Decimal Equivalent
10^4	10,000
10^3	1,000
10^2	100
10^1	10
10^0	1
10^{-1}	0.1
10^{-2}	0.01
10^{-3}	0.001

Scientific notation is a way to express numbers as a power of 10 multiplied by another number that has only one digit to the left of the decimal point. For example, 5,943,000,000 is 5.943×10^9 when expressed in scientific notation. The number 0.000 083 2 is 8.32×10^{-5} when expressed in scientific notation.

PRACTICE

Rewrite the following values using scientific notation.

1. 12,300,000 m/s

2. 0.000 000 000 004 5 kg

3. 0.000 065 3 m

4. 55,432,000,000,000 s

5. 273.15 K

6. 0.000 627 14 kg

Significant Digits

The following list can be used to review how to determine the number of *significant digits* (also called *significant figures*) in a given value or measurement.

Rules for Significant Digits:

1. All nonzero digits are significant. For example, 1,246 has four significant digits (shown in red).

2. Any zeros between significant digits are also significant. For example, 1,206 has four significant digits.

3. If the value does not contain a decimal point, any zeros to the right of a nonzero digit are not significant. For example, 1,200 has only two significant digits.

4. Any zeros to the right of a significant digit and to the left of a decimal point are significant. For example, 1,200. has four significant digits.

5. If a value has no significant digits to the left of a decimal point, any zeros to the right of the decimal point and also to the left of a significant digit are not significant. For example, 0.0012 has only two significant digits.

6. If a value ends with zeros to the right of a decimal point, those zeros are significant. For example, 0.1200 has four significant digits.

After you have reviewed the rules, use the following table to check your understanding of the rules. Cover up the second column of the table and try to determine how many significant digits each number in the first column has. If you get confused, refer to the rule given.

SIGNIFICANT DIGITS

Measurement	Number of significant digits	Rule
12,345	5	1
2,400 cm	2	3
305 kg	3	2
2,350. cm	4	4
234.005 K	6	2
12.340	5	6
0.001	1	5
0.002 450	4	5 and 6

When performing mathematical operations with measurements, you must remember to keep track of significant digits. If you are adding or subtracting two measurements, your answer can only have as many decimal positions as the value that has the fewest number of decimal places. When multiplying or dividing measurements, your answer can only have as many significant digits as the value with the fewest number of significant digits.

PRACTICE

1. Determine the number of significant digits in each of the following measurements:

   a. 65.04 mL   **c.** 0.007 504 kg
   b. 564.00 m   **d.** 1,210 K

2. Perform each of the following calculations, and report your answer with the correct number of significant digits and units:

   a. 0.004 dm + 0.12508 dm
   b. 340 m ÷ 0.1257 s
   c. 40.1 m × 0.2453 m
   d. 1.03 g − 0.0456 g

Graphing Skills

Line Graphs

In laboratory experiments, you will usually be controlling one variable and seeing how it affects another variable. Line graphs can show these relations clearly. For example, you might perform an experiment in which you measure the growth of a plant over time to determine the rate of the plant's growth. In this experiment, you are controlling the time intervals at which the plant height is measured. Therefore, time is the independent variable. The height of the plant is the dependent variable. The table on the next page gives some sample data for an experiment that measures the rate of plant growth.

The independent variable is plotted on the x-axis. This axis will be labeled "Time (days)" and will have a range from 0 to 35 days. Be sure to properly label each axis, including the units.

The dependent variable is plotted on the y-axis. This axis will be labeled "Plant Height (cm)" and will have a range from 0 to 5 cm.

EXPERIMENTAL DATA FOR PLANT GROWTH VS. TIME

Time (days)	Plant height (cm)
0	1.43
7	2.16
14	2.67
21	3.25
28	4.04
35	4.67

Think of your graph as a grid with lines running horizontally from the *y*-axis and vertically from the *x*-axis. To plot a point, find the *x* value on the *x*-axis. For the example above, plot each value for time on the *x*-axis. Follow the vertical line from the *x*-axis until it intersects the horizontal line from the *y*-axis at the corresponding *y* value. For the example, each time value has a corresponding height value. Place your point at the intersection of these two lines.

The line graph below shows how the data in the table might be graphed.

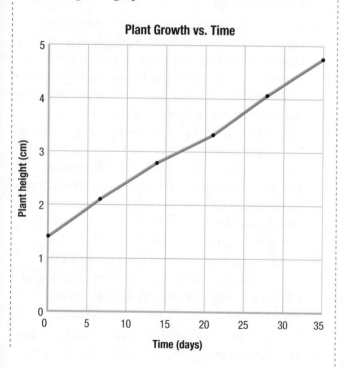

Bar Graphs

Bar graphs are useful for comparing data values. If you wanted to compare the area or depth of the major oceans, you might use a bar graph. The table below gives the data for each of these quantities.

DEPTH OF THE MAJOR OCEANS

Ocean	Depth (m)
Pacific Ocean	4,028
Atlantic Ocean	3,926
Indian Ocean	3,963
Arctic Ocean	1,205

To create a bar graph from the data in the table, begin on the *x*-axis by labeling four bar positions with the names of the four oceans. Label the *y*-axis "Depth (m)." Be sure the range on your *y*-axis encompasses 1,205 m and 4,028 m. Then draw the bars to represent the area of each ocean, with a bar height on the *y*-axis that matches each ocean's area value, as shown in the bar graph below.

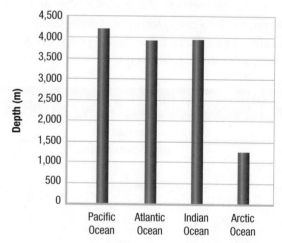

Circle Graphs

Circle graphs are an easy way to visualize how many parts make up a whole. Frequently, Circle graphs are made from percentage data. For example, you could create a circle graph showing percentage of different materials that make up the waste generated in cities of the United States. Study the example data in the table on the next page.

UNITED STATES MUNICIPAL SOLID WASTE

Material	Percentage of total waste
Paper	28.5%
Food waste	13.4%
Yard waste	13.9%
Plastics	12.4%
Metals	9.0%
Rubber, leather, and textiles	8.4%
Wood	6.4%
Glass	4.6%
Other	3.4%

To create a circle graph from the data in the table, begin by drawing a circle to represent the whole, or total. Then imagine dividing the circle into 100 equal sections to represent 100 percent. Shade in 28 consecutive sections and label that area "Paper." Continue to shade sections with other colors until the entire circle graph has been filled in and until each type of waste has a corresponding area in the circle, as shown in the graph below.

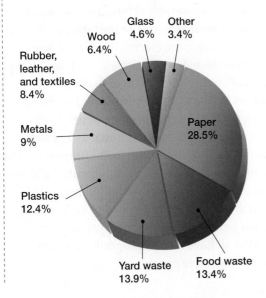

United States Municipal Solid Waste
(Percentage by Weight)

Source: U.S. Environmental Protection Agency

Answers

Geometry

1. $225{,}000 \text{ m}^2$

2. $1{,}230 \text{ cm}^3$ (rounded to three significant figures)

3. 96 cm^2

Exponents

1. 9

2. 14,348,907

3. 537,824

4. 1

Order of Operations

1. 24

2. 7

Algebraic Rearrangements

1. $x = 20$

2. $a = -1.75$

3. $y = -6.3$

4. $m = -4$

5. $z = 2$

6. $b = 5$

Scientific Notation

1. $1.23 \times 10^7 \text{ m/s}$

2. $4.5 \times 10^{-12} \text{ kg}$

3. $6.53 \times 10^{-5} \text{ m}$

4. $5.5432 \times 10^{13} \text{ s}$

5. $2.7315 \times 10^2 \text{ K}$

6. $6.2714 \times 10^{-4} \text{ kg}$

Significant Digits

1. a. 4

 b. 5

 c. 4

 d. 3

2. a. 0.129 dm

 b. 2700 m/s

 c. 9.84 m^2

 d. 0.98 g

Chemistry Refresher

Atoms and Elements

Every object in the universe is made up of particles of matter. Matter is anything that has mass and takes up space. An element is a substance that cannot be separated into simpler substances by chemical means. Elements cannot be separated in this way because each element consists of only one kind of atom. An atom is the smallest unit of an element that maintains the properties of that element.

ATOMIC STRUCTURE

Atoms are made up of small particles called *subatomic particles*. The three major types of subatomic particles are **electrons**, **protons**, and **neutrons**. Electrons have a negative electrical charge, protons have a positive charge, and neutrons have no electrical charge. The protons and neutrons are packed close to one another and form the **nucleus**. The protons give the nucleus a positive charge. The electrons of an atom are located in a region around the nucleus known as an **electron cloud**. The negatively charged electrons are attracted to the positively charged nucleus. An atom may have several energy levels in which electrons are located.

ATOMIC NUMBER

To help in the identification of elements, scientists have assigned an **atomic number** to each kind of atom. The atomic number is equal to the number of protons in the atom. Atoms with the same number of protons are all of the same element. In an uncharged, or electrically neutral, atom there are an equal number of protons and electrons. Therefore, the atomic number also equals the number of electrons in an uncharged atom. The number of neutrons, however, can vary for a given element. Atoms that have different numbers of neutrons but are of the same element are called **isotopes**.

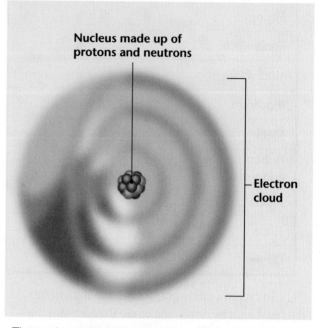

Nucleus made up of protons and neutrons

Electron cloud

The nucleus of the atom contains the protons and neutrons. The protons give the nucleus a positive charge. The negatively charged electrons are in the electron cloud surrounding the nucleus.

PERIODIC TABLE OF THE ELEMENTS

A periodic table of the elements is shown on the next page. In a periodic table, the elements are arranged in order of increasing atomic number. Each element in the table is found in a separate box. In each horizontal row of the table, each element has one more electron and one more proton than the element to its left. Each row of the table is called a period. Changes in chemical properties across a period correspond to changes in the elements' electron arrangements. Each vertical column of the table, known as a **group**, contains elements that have similar properties. The elements in a group have similar chemical properties because they have the same number of electrons in their outer energy level. For example, the elements helium, neon, argon, krypton, xenon, and radon all have similar properties and are known as the noble gases.

MOLECULES AND COMPOUNDS

When the atoms of two or more elements are joined chemically, the resulting substance is called a **compound**. A compound is a new substance with properties different from those of the elements that compose it. For example, water (H_2O) is a compound formed when atoms of hydrogen (H) and oxygen (O) combine. The smallest complete unit of a compound that has all of the properties of that compound is called a **molecule**.

CHEMICAL FORMULAS

A chemical formula indicates what elements a compound consists of. It also indicates the relative number of atoms of each element present. The chemical formula for water is H_2O, which indicates that each water molecule consists of two atoms of hydrogen and one atom of oxygen.

CHEMICAL EQUATIONS

A chemical reaction occurs when a chemical change takes place. (In a chemical change, new substances with new properties are formed.) A chemical equation is a useful way of describing a chemical reaction by means of chemical formulas. The equation indicates what substances react and what the products are. For example, when carbon and oxygen combine, they can form carbon dioxide. The equation for this reaction is $C + O_2 \rightarrow CO_2$.

ACIDS, BASES, AND PH

An ion is an atom or group of atoms that has an electrical charge because it has lost or gained one or more electrons. When an acid, such as hydrochloric acid (HCl), is mixed with water, it separates into ions. An **acid** is a compound that produces hydrogen ions (H^+) in water. The hydrogen ions then combine with a water molecule to form a hydronium ion (H_3O^+). A solution that contains hydronium ions is an acidic solution. A **base**, on the other hand, is a substance that produces hydroxide ions (OH^-) in water.

To determine whether a solution is acidic or basic, scientists measure pH. **pH** is a measure of how many hydronium ions are in solution. The pH scale ranges from 0 to 14. The middle point, pH = 7, is neutral, neither acidic nor basic. Acids have a pH of less than 7; bases have a pH of more than 7. The lower the number, the stronger the acid. The higher the number, the stronger the base. A pH scale is shown in Chapter 12.

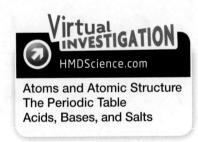

Virtual **INVESTIGATION**

HMDScience.com

Atoms and Atomic Structure
The Periodic Table
Acids, Bases, and Salts

Periodic Table

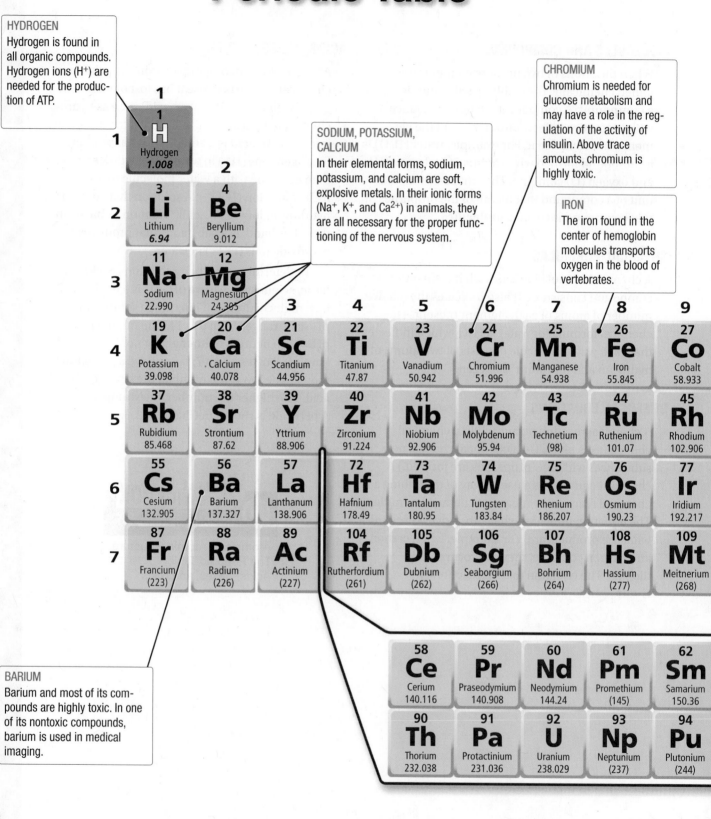

HYDROGEN
Hydrogen is found in all organic compounds. Hydrogen ions (H^+) are needed for the production of ATP.

SODIUM, POTASSIUM, CALCIUM
In their elemental forms, sodium, potassium, and calcium are soft, explosive metals. In their ionic forms (Na^+, K^+, and Ca^{2+}) in animals, they are all necessary for the proper functioning of the nervous system.

CHROMIUM
Chromium is needed for glucose metabolism and may have a role in the regulation of the activity of insulin. Above trace amounts, chromium is highly toxic.

IRON
The iron found in the center of hemoglobin molecules transports oxygen in the blood of vertebrates.

BARIUM
Barium and most of its compounds are highly toxic. In one of its nontoxic compounds, barium is used in medical imaging.

| Metal | Metalloid | Nonmetal | **Fe** Solid | **Hg** Liquid | ◯ Gas |

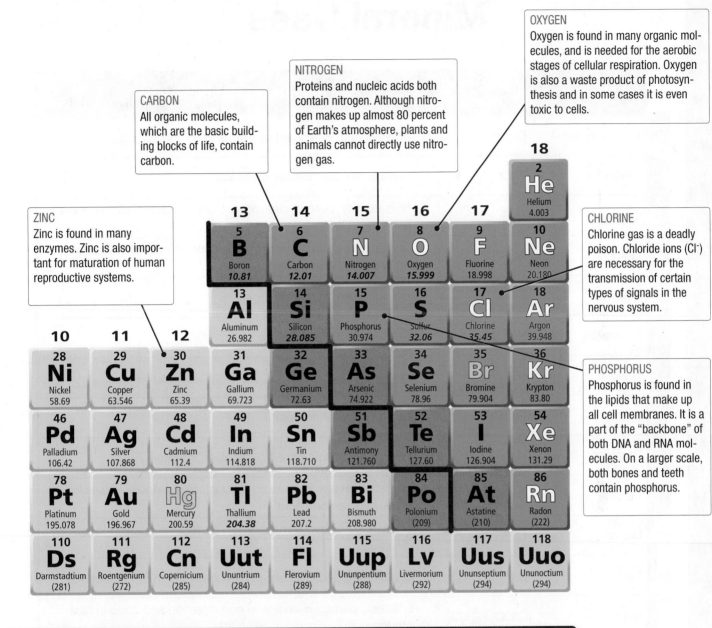

OXYGEN
Oxygen is found in many organic molecules, and is needed for the aerobic stages of cellular respiration. Oxygen is also a waste product of photosynthesis and in some cases it is even toxic to cells.

NITROGEN
Proteins and nucleic acids both contain nitrogen. Although nitrogen makes up almost 80 percent of Earth's atmosphere, plants and animals cannot directly use nitrogen gas.

CARBON
All organic molecules, which are the basic building blocks of life, contain carbon.

ZINC
Zinc is found in many enzymes. Zinc is also important for maturation of human reproductive systems.

CHLORINE
Chlorine gas is a deadly poison. Chloride ions (Cl⁻) are necessary for the transmission of certain types of signals in the nervous system.

PHOSPHORUS
Phosphorus is found in the lipids that make up all cell membranes. It is a part of the "backbone" of both DNA and RNA molecules. On a larger scale, both bones and teeth contain phosphorus.

Atomic number
Number of protons in the nucleus of the element

Name

Symbol
Each element has a symbol. The symbol's color represents the element's state at room temperature.

Atomic mass
This value is the average atomic mass of isotopes of this element. Each element for which this value is bolded and italicized has an atomic mass that is officially expressed as a range of values. In nature, the average atomic mass often varies depending on the properties of the material in which the element is found.

Mineral Uses

	Mineral	Chemical Formula	Identifying Characteristics
Metallic Minerals	Chalcopyrite	$CuFeS_2$	brassy color; iridescent tarnish; soft for metal; brittle
	Chromite	$FeCr_2O_4$	iron-black color; weakly magnetic
	Galena	PbS	high density; perfect cleavage in four directions, which forms a cube; low hardness
	Gold	Au	golden color; low hardness; high density; malleable (can be pressed into various forms)
	Ilmenite	$FeTiO_3$	tabular crystals; no cleavage
	Magnetite	Fe_3O_4	8-sided crystals; magnetic
	Uraninite	UO_2	black to steel black color; dull luster; radioactive
Nonmetallic Minerals	Barite	$BaSO_4$	high density for nonmetal
	Borax	$Na_2B_4O_7 \cdot 10H_2O$	low hardness; low density; dissolves in water
	Calcite	$CaCO_3$	perfect cleavage in three directions; low hardness; fizzes in dilute hydrochloric acid
	Diamond	C	extreme hardness; transparency; perfect cleavage in four directions
	Fluorite	CaF_2	cubic or 8-sided crystals; perfect cleavage in four directions
	Gypsum	$CaSO_4 \cdot 2H_2O$	softness; perfect cleavage in one direction and good in two others
	Halite	$NaCl$	low hardness; perfect cleavage in three directions, which forms cubes; salty taste
	Sulfur	S	yellow color; low hardness; poor conductor of heat; odor
	Kaolinite	$Al_2Si_2O_5(OH)_4$	low hardness; white color; noncrystalline
	Quartz	SiO_2	hardness; conchoidal fracture; crystals form six-sided prisms
	Talc	$Mg_3Si_4O_{10}(OH)_2$	very low hardness; massive; perfect cleavage, which forms thin, flexible flakes; soapy or greasy feel

Explanation of Terms

cleavage: the splitting of a mineral along smooth, flat surfaces

fracture: the tendency of a mineral to break along curved or irregular surfaces; conchoidal fracture is a smooth, curved fracture

hardness: a measure of a mineral to resist scratching

luster: the way the surface of a mineral reflects light

Economically Important Deposits	Important Uses
Chile, USA, Indonesia	power transmission, electrical and electronic products, building wiring, telecommunications equipment, industrial machinery and equipment
South Africa, Kazahkstan, India	production of stainless steel, alloys, metal plating
Australia, China, USA	batteries, ammunition, glass and ceramics, x-ray shielding
South Africa, USA, Australia	computers, communications equipment, spacecraft, jet engines, dentistry, jewelry, coins
Australia, South Africa, Canada	jet engines; missile components; white pigment in paints, toothpaste, and candy
China, Brazil, Australia	steelmaking
Canada, Australia	fuel in nuclear power reactors, manufacture of radioisotopes
China, India, USA	weighting agent in oil well drilling fluids, automobile paint primer, x-ray diagnostic work
Turkey, USA, Russia	glass, soaps and detergents, agriculture, fire retardants, plastics and polymer additives
China, USA, Russia	cement, lime production, crushed stone, glassmaking, chemicals, optics
Australia, Democratic Republic of the Congo, Russia	jewelry, cutting tools, drill bits, computer chip production
China, Mexico, South Africa	hydrofluoric acid, steelmaking, water fluoridation, solvents, glass manufacture, enamels
USA, Iran, Canada	wallboard, building plasters, manufacture of cement
USA, China, Germany	chemical production, human and animal nutrition, highway de-icer, water softener
Canada, USA, Russia	sulfuric acid, fertilizers, gunpowder, tires
USA, Uzbekistan, Czech Republic	glossy paper, whitener and abrasive in toothpaste
USA, Germany, France	glass, computer chips, ceramics, abrasives, water filtration
China, USA, Republic of Korea	ceramics, plastics, paint, paper, rubber, cosmetics

Economics Concepts

You may think that economics is about the complicated numbers of stock markets and interest rates, but the field of economics is based on simple concepts. *Economics* is the study of how people make decisions about the production, distribution, and consumption of limited resources as they attempt to fulfill their needs and wants. While economics can be a complex subject to study, it is a key part of understanding the relationship of humans and their environment. Here we will present some of the most basic concepts of economics.

Resources and Value

Resources that people use to create useful and desirable products are called *economic resources* or *capital*. Products and capital may exist in the form of *goods* or *services*. There are three general types of capital: natural, manufactured, and human. *Natural resources*, sometimes called *earth capital*, are resources such as land, fertile soil, air and water, oceans, wildlife, and minerals. *Manufactured capital* includes tools, machines, buildings, and other things that are made from natural resources and that are used to produce goods and services. *Human capital* includes the mental and physical abilities for which people may be paid wages or salaries.

A given resource or product has a specific *value* to a given group of people at a particular time. Generally, the *value* of something is the amount of money most people are willing to pay for it. For example, if many people are willing to pay $10 for a music download, the value of that download is $10. But value is not always the same as price. Some e-stores might sell the same music download for $5. If the download's price were lower than its value, an economist would say the download is *undervalued*.

Economic activities that produce goods and services are called *industries*. A basic industry involves people using natural resources directly. The highest level of industry involves people working mostly with information instead of goods. The degree to which a single business or economic system has activities at multiple levels of industry is called *economic diversity*. For example, the United States has a high degree of economic diversity, but a small island that subsists on fishing and tourism has low economic diversity.

Economic Systems and Governments

Most societies use some type of *economic system* to decide what to produce, how to produce, and for whom to produce. The main difference between economic systems is in how much the government regulates the activities of businesses or controls access to resources.

In a *market economy* (also called a *capitalist, free-market,* or *free-enterprise system*), people own businesses and make their own decisions about what to make, sell, or buy. The theory of a market economy is that competition in open markets will result in the highest-quality goods being produced in the most efficient way and for the lowest price. In market theory, individuals acting in self-interest will efficiently decide what goods and services to buy or sell, so supply will be balanced with demand.

In a *command economy*, or a *centrally planned economy*, the government controls production and determines the amount and price of goods and services produced. Command economies are typically practiced by communist governments. A few countries and cultural groups still practice a *traditional economy*, which means they make economic decisions based on local customs or traditions.

However, economic systems are rarely practiced exactly according to theory. Most countries have a *mixed economy* in which a combination of government control and free markets exist. Governments may produce goods and services or may try to influence the flow of goods and services by charging taxes, paying out subsidies, or making regulations.

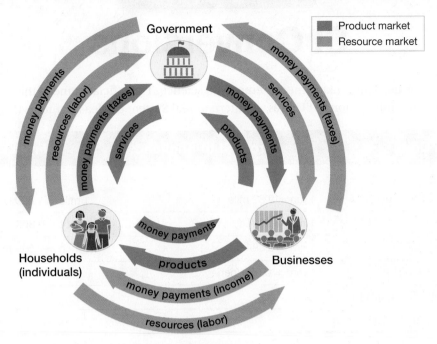

| Product market |
| Resource market |

An Economic System Model This *circular-flow model* illustrates the exchange of resources, products, and money payments in the economic system of nations such as the United States.

Economic Growth and Development

The economic growth within a country is usually measured by looking at the country's *gross domestic product* (GDP), or by looking at the *gross national product* (GNP). A country's GDP is the total value of all goods and services produced within the country in a year. The GNP is like the GDP, but the GNP includes income from outside of the country generated by individuals or companies based within the country. To represent each person's part in the economy, economists calculate the GNP or GDP *per capita*, which means the average GNP or GDP per person in the country.

Economists and social scientists often categorize countries based on indicators of their economic and social development. Countries that have high average incomes, slow population growth, diverse economies, and strong social support systems are considered to be *more developed*. Countries that have low average incomes, simple economies, and rapid population growth are considered to be *less developed*. However, these categories are difficult to apply because countries may develop in different ways and because the economies of different countries are interconnected as people and goods move between countries.

The economies of the world are now so interconnected that economists often refer to the *global economy*. In the 20th century, most countries became more developed and tended toward market system economies. Also, international trade continued to increase. Many countries now work together to help manage the global economy. International organizations such as the World Bank, the World Trade Organization, and the European Union have become as influential as national governments.

SI Conversions

The metric system is used for making measurements in science. The official name of this system is the Système International d'Unités, or International System of Measurements (SI).

SI Units	From SI to English	From English to SI
Length		
kilometer (km) = 1,000 m	1 km = 0.62 mile	1 mile = 1.609 km
meter (m) = 100 cm	1 m = 3.28 feet	1 foot = 0.305 m
centimeter (cm) = 0.01 m	1 cm = 0.394 inch	1 inch = 2.54 cm
millimeter (mm) = 0.001 m	1 mm = 0.039 inch	
micrometer (µm) = 0.000 001 m		
nanometer (nm) = 0.000 000 001 m		
Area		
square kilometer (km^2) = 100 hectares	1 km^2 = 0.386 square mile	1 square mile = 2.590 km^2
hectare (ha) = 10,000 m^2	1 ha = 2.471 acres	1 acre = 0.405 ha
square meter (m^2) = 10,000 cm^2	1 m^2 = 10.765 square feet	1 square foot = 0.093 m^2
square centimeter (cm^2) = 100 mm^2	1 cm^2 = 0.155 square inch	1 square inch = 6.452 cm^2
Volume		
liter (L) = 1,000 mL = 1 dm^3	1 L = 1.06 fluid quarts	1 fluid quart = 0.946 L
milliliter (mL) = 0.001 L = 1 cm^3	1 mL = 0.034 fluid ounce	1 fluid ounce = 29.577 mL
microliter (µL) = 0.000 001 L		
Mass		
kilogram (kg) = 1,000 g	1 kg = 2.205 pounds	1 pound = 0.454 kg
gram (g) = 1,000 mg	1 g = 0.035 ounce	1 ounce = 28.35 g
milligram (mg) = 0.001 g		
microgram (µg) = 0.000 001 g		
Energy		
British Thermal Units (BTU)	1 BTU = 1,055.056 joules	1 joule = 0.00095 BTU
Temperature		

°F 0 20 40 60 80 100 120 140 160 180 200 220

°C −20 −10 0 10 20 30 40 50 60 70 80 90 100

Freezing point of water

Room temperature

Normal human body temperature

Conversion of Fahrenheit to Celsius:

$$°C = \frac{5}{9}(°F - 32)$$

Conversion of Celsius to Fahrenheit:

$$°F = \frac{9}{5}(°C) + 32$$

Environmental Careers

ENVIRONMENTAL EDUCATOR

As a child who watched *The Underwater World of Jacques Cousteau* on public television every chance she had, **Niki Espy** dreamed of one day studying aquatic mammals for a living. She went to college with the intent of continuing on to graduate school to focus on behavioral studies in marine biology. But while pursuing a bachelor's degree in biology, she interned as a naturalist. Today, Espy works for the Milwaukee Public Museum. She provides educational programs for children, adults, and families and is responsible for developing and implementing school programs that focus on cultural and natural history. Espy also facilitates training for educators, including teachers, student teachers, museum volunteers, and museum docents.

> If we look at humans as a separate component of the world, we will not be able to truly reach sustainability.

Q: How does your current job relate to environmental education?

Espy: I use the principles of environmental education to teach about natural and cultural history. The basics of awareness, appreciation, knowledge, and action assist me daily in my educational endeavors. I believe that if we don't have an understanding of the world, we can't begin to value or protect our resources. The museum's educational programs lead students to question, explore, analyze, evaluate, and discuss how the introductions of exotic plants and animals and the urbanization of the Milwaukee area have affected biodiversity. While interpreting the plant and animal changes, we don't forget the people and how indigenous groups used the land.

Q: What is the importance of including people in a discussion on biodiversity and environmental impact?

Espy: If we look at humans as a separate component of the world, we will not be able to truly reach sustainability. By placing people in the equation, we can look at our behaviors and our impact on local and global ecoregions, economies, and social systems and can obtain the answers we need to create a sustainable future.

MORE ON THIS CAREER

Many museums have volunteer programs in which volunteers work directly with the public or in different administrative or scientific departments. For example, volunteers at the Milwaukee Public Museum may provide assistance at the information desk, give tours to the public through the exhibit galleries, demonstrate objects visitors can touch, help educate visitors about special exhibits, and work at special events. In addition, volunteers may work "behind the scenes" in research areas such as anthropology, archeology, botany, geology, paleontology, and zoology. For more information on volunteer programs, contact a museum near you.

One of Niki Espy's goals as an environmental educator is to increase awareness and knowledge of the natural world.

ENVIRONMENTAL ENGINEER

John Roll began college studying chemistry and biology. Halfway through his undergraduate degree, he switched to agricultural engineering with a focus on water-quality issues. Roll completed his master's degree in agricultural engineering and expanded his environmental background to include livestock waste management. He spent the first three years after graduation on a project involving treated solids from a municipal wastewater treatment facility. For the next 14 years, Roll was manager of land reclamation and environmental permits for a surface coal mining company in Illinois. In 1990, Roll entered Oklahoma State University, where he studied groundwater transport of contaminants and received a doctorate in Biosystems Engineering.

Q: *What does an environmental engineer study in college?*

Roll: First and foremost, a student must obtain an engineering degree. The individual must have a desire to study hard, and it helps to possess an aptitude for the math and hard-science courses (physics, chemistry, and mechanics) required by engineering programs. An environmental engineer can come from different engineering study areas, but all individuals should share a common desire to apply engineering principles to an aspect of the environment that is interesting to them. Agricultural engineering, chemical engineering, civil engineering, general engineering, geological engineering, and mechanical engineering programs routinely graduate individuals who work on environmental issues specific to their discipline.

Q: *What kind of jobs does an environmental engineer do?*

Roll: The range of jobs performed by an environmental engineer is extremely varied. A chemical engineer may develop new manufacturing methods that remove toxic contaminants from a product. A civil engineer may be involved in the design of water and wastewater treatment plants, the development of better methods to treat wastes, the development of road-building processes that are more environmentally friendly, and the design of groundwater treatment schemes. Mechanical and general engi-

I have found out through firsthand experience that environmental issues require very careful communication skills.

John Roll is shown conducting a survey of plant cover on reclaimed mined land.

neering graduates may work on controlling air pollution from factories and producing changes in manufacturing methods to create less waste. Agricultural engineers often work on environmental issues involving livestock waste, runoff-water quality, erosion control, and application methods to lower the quantity of fertilizer, herbicides, and insecticides used to grow crops.

Q: *What is the most important skill an environmental engineer should possess?*

Roll: An environmental engineer must be skilled in the application of science and engineering principles to help solve a problem. Using a team approach to an environmental problem will yield a broader view on the issue. Team members usually have expertise in different environmental disciplines, and this results in multiple views on how to solve the problem at hand. Therefore, probably the least expected but the most important skill for an environmental engineer is the ability to communicate clearly through written and spoken words.

Q: *Do you feel that environmental issues are often misunderstood?*

Roll: I have found out through firsthand experience that environmental issues require very careful communication skills. Environmental issues are often controversial. However, open communication between all interested parties, including those individuals who are against a project, can prevent misunderstanding. For example, the plans for the Industry Coal Mine were finalized after discussions with governmental agencies, local citizens, and authorities. The planning and public meetings lasted almost three years, and during this time everyone had a chance to question the coal company about its plans and to express their views. The public opinion ranged from very favorable to a few individuals who were totally against the project. By addressing the issues with good faith, a reclamation plan was developed that was ultimately approved by all state and federal agencies, local county officials, and zoning boards.

Q: *What is the future need for environmental engineers?*

Roll: My feeling is that the future will be a good one for environmental engineers. Since 1970, the environment has been an important focus for many people. Congress passed new laws and created new agencies such as the Environmental Protection Agency (EPA) to specifically address environmental problems. The agencies wrote regulations based on laws passed by Congress and approved by the President, and this resulted in new or additional permits, approvals, and public comment requirements for activities that might harm the environment. In order to enforce the regulations, new agencies were created in the states as well as the federal government. Industry and government currently hire many environmental engineers to meet regulatory requirements.

MORE ON THIS CAREER

For more information on environmental engineering as a career, contact the American Academy of Environmental Engineers.

John Roll managed the reclamation of this surface coal mine in Illinois. Land that has been reclaimed is seen to the right of the cut that is being mined.

ENVIRONMENTAL ARCHITECT

To **Michael Reynolds**, a house is not just a home, and old tires and empty soda cans are not just trash. For almost 30 years, this Taos, New Mexico, architect has been designing and building energy-efficient houses out of automobile tires, cans, and other discarded items. These houses, which Reynolds now calls "Earthships," not only provide a comfortable, affordable place for people to live but also contribute to a sustainable future for our planet.

The Origin of the Earthship Design

In 1970, a TV report about the growing number of beverage cans littering the streets and fields of the United States started Reynolds thinking about ways in which trash could be used to build houses. Through many years of experimentation, he found that sturdy walls could be built by packing soil into old tires, stacking the tires like bricks, and covering them with cement or adobe, a heavy clay often used in buildings in the Southwest. Reynolds had this design tested by structural engineers to ensure that the walls would meet or surpass any existing building code requirements. One engineer even commented that the design could be used to construct dams!

Building an Earthship

The tire-stack design is used for three of the outside walls of an Earthship. These walls are approximately 1 m (3 ft) thick, and this large mass causes the walls to act as a battery, storing energy from the sun and releasing the energy when needed. The base of the Earthship is built below the frost line (the deepest level to which the ground freezes). Below this line, the ground maintains a constant temperature— around 15°C (59°F)—and walls anchored below the frost line usually stay at that temperature too. The fourth wall, which faces south, is constructed completely of glass to capture as much sunlight as possible. In the winter, the tire-stack walls hold in the sun's warmth. In the summer, cool air enters through windows in the front while warm air escapes through a skylight in the back.

To Reynolds, an Earthship is not just a home—it's a lifestyle.

Earthships, above, often look more like natural land formations than like houses. Michael Reynolds, left, uses discarded materials, such as used soda cans, to construct environmentally friendly houses.

A greenhouse, built along the Earthship's southern glass wall, can provide residents with a sustainable food source.

Even the soil that is excavated for the site of the house is used to build the house. Some of the soil is pounded into the tires to construct the walls, and the remaining soil is piled against the outside of these walls and on top of the roof (constructed of beams) for further insulation. The most suitable location for this design is a south-facing slope of a hill, where the Earthship can simply be built into the hill. Often, Earthships look more like natural formations of land than houses.

Inside the house, walls between rooms are constructed by embedding empty beverage cans into mortar or mud. When these walls are covered with cement and then painted with latex paint or some other durable finish, they look just like walls constructed with conventional materials. Other inside surfaces, including stairs and even bathtubs, can be built using the beverage-can technique. Because the cans are so lightweight, this method can even be used to create dramatic interior structures such as arches and domes.

The Environmental Impact of the Earthship Design

Earthships are typically built to obtain electricity from photovoltaic cells that convert sunlight to electricity. All household water is supplied by rainwater that is collected on the roof. Wastewater from sinks, tubs, and the laundry room is recycled to nourish plants in the greenhouse, which can provide a sustainable source of food. With these features, people who live in Earthships use fewer of the Earth's resources and often have no utility bills.

Because Earthships are environmentally friendly and inexpensive to buy and maintain, more and more people are choosing them instead of conventional homes. Earthships now exist in almost every state and in many countries around the world, including Canada, Mexico, Bolivia, and Japan. Wetter environments simply require that the house is built entirely above the ground and uses more cans and tires.

More tires in the design certainly wouldn't be a problem. According to the Environmental Protection Agency, more than 250 million tires are discarded in the United States every year. But most landfills do not accept tires because of their tendency to rise to the surface even when the landfill is covered over. Tire dealers usually pay to have used tires hauled away to stockpile areas, where they sit indefinitely. Earthships provide one way to diminish the stockpiles.

Michael enthusiastically shares his Earthship concept with others. To Michael, an Earthship is not just a home—it's a lifestyle. His dedication to designing Earth-friendly homes is a result of his commitment to "reducing the stress involved in living on the Earth, for both humans and the planet."

The tire-stack design of the outer walls accounts for much of the Earthship's energy efficiency. These tire stacks will be covered with cement or adobe for a finished exterior.

MORE ON THIS CAREER

For more information on environmentally friendly, energy-efficient housing, use the Internet to locate government and nonprofit organizations that are involved in "green" building projects.

ENVIRONMENTAL FILMMAKER

Haroldo Castro considers himself a "citizen of the planet." It's easy to see why: he was born in Italy to a Brazilian father and a French mother, he was educated in France, he speaks five languages, and he has visited more than 80 countries. Furthermore, Castro has devoted his life to improving the planet's well-being. He has accomplished this by taking photographs, writing books and articles, and producing award-winning video documentaries. Castro works for Conservation International (CI), an environmental organization that establishes partnerships with countries all over the world to develop and implement ecosystem conservation projects.

Q: *What do you do at CI?*

Castro: I am the International Communications Project Director. What I do is make documentaries and take photographs of CI's conservation projects. These videos and photos are designed to teach people how to better interact with their local environment. Most of our work is done in countries that have tropical rain forests, such as those in Latin America, Asia, and Africa.

Q: *Can you describe one of your documentaries?*

Castro: Sure. We made a documentary in Guatemala about products that local people can sustainably harvest from the northern tropical forests.

After one year of production, we completed a half-hour documentary called *Between Two Futures*. CI then distributed the video to government officials, environmental organizations, university professors, and teachers. We also encouraged its broadcast on TV channels in Guatemala and other Latin American countries.

The film has been a real success story. I think our ability to be culturally sensitive to the Guatemalan people contributed in large part to the film's success. Each of us who worked on the project had a Latin American background. We worked closely with the Guatemalan people, we had a Guatemalan narrator, and we used only Guatemalan music. If you are trying to deliver an important message to people of a different culture, it's important to step into their shoes and deliver it from their point of view.

Q: *What is your educational background and experience?*

Castro: Although I do have a degree in economics, my best education and training has definitely come from traveling and other real-life experiences. I learn by studying the diverse cultures around the world.

Once I spent two years traveling around Latin America by van; another time I drove from Europe to India in six months. These experiences are my education. When my friends say that it is necessary to have a master's degree or doctorate to gain respect, I respond by saying that I have a PhD in "Travelology." That's a degree I think my real-world experience on the road has earned me.

Haroldo Castro, below left, is shown directing a video crew in Rio de Janeiro, Brazil.

If you are trying to deliver an important message to people of a different culture, it's important to step into their shoes and deliver it from their point of view.

Q: *Do you ever have to deal with crisis situations?*

Castro: [laughter] If there is not a crisis when I'm traveling, I'm worried—it usually means there will be a disaster later! Anyone who travels a lot has to deal with crises, such as getting sick on local food or getting robbed. I've had equipment stolen from Lebanon to Peru!

I would like to tell you a story. Several years ago we were working in a remote rain-forest region of Mexico for 10 days. When we were ready to leave, we boarded a small plane and set out for the nearest commercial airport, only to learn that it had been closed. We were forced to go to a nearby military airport instead.

When we landed and began to unload our large boxes of equipment, the military personnel got very nervous. We looked pretty grungy and unshaven and covered with mud. It was obvious that we'd been in the rain forest awhile. They thought we were terrorist guerrillas and surrounded us with machine guns. For three hours we pleaded our case, and finally they let us go. I think you might call that a crisis situation!

Q: *If a high school student were to ask you what he or she could do to help the environment, what would your answer be?*

Castro: I would say . . . Learn all you can, appreciate the world around you, and follow your passion. If you like photography, go out and take pictures of things that leave you with good and bad

Haroldo Castro is filming slash-and-burn agriculture.

impressions. If you like gardening, start experimenting with seedlings. Whatever your interest, my advice is just go for it!

MORE ON THIS CAREER

Many government offices, publishers, and environmental organizations have in-house communications departments for producing films or photographs. Have a librarian help you make a list of such places, and then call these places for more information and for possible volunteer or internship ideas.

While you're at the library, look through *The Guide to International Film and Video Festivals* for any mention of environmental film festivals in your area. Castro recommends attending a film festival if at all possible. "Doing so," he said, "would give you the invaluable opportunity to see some of the best films produced and to talk to the people who made them." If you can't find the guide or would like further information, contact the **Association of Independent Video & Filmmakers**.

For Castro, capturing images on film—such as this Guatemalan girl holding a hummingbird—allows him to recall rich travel experiences.

CLIMATE RESEARCHER

One summer when **Dr. Richard Somerville** was just a child, he built a weather station in his family's backyard. His creation grew out of a fascination for the great power of weather—a phenomenon that affects all of us every day. Using instruments made out of coffee cans, balloons, and rubber bands, young Richard began keeping track of daily weather conditions and questioning how the world's weather systems worked. As time went on, he began to question more than just the weather—he looked at clouds, oceans, and the world of living things as well. These pursuits led Somerville to the prestigious Scripps Institution of Oceanography. Today he is a professor of meteorology at the Scripps Institution, which is part of the University of California at San Diego in La Jolla, California.

Q: *What exactly is meteorology?*

Somerville: Simply put, it is the science of the atmosphere—especially the study of weather and weather forecasting.

There are two general classes of technology that are most important to my work: satellites and computers.

Richard Somerville records observations while standing on a bridge in San Diego, California.

Q: *What most appeals to you about your job?*

Somerville: Probably the most exciting aspect of any scientist's work involves those few, rare "Eureka!" moments when you realize that you've discovered something that no one else on Earth knows about. That's quite a feeling. It's also rewarding to know that you're adding to the knowledge of others, transferring important pieces of information to important people who can use that information to improve this world.

Q: *What does your research involve?*

Somerville: Well, I do research on the greenhouse effect, on climate changes in general, and on the effects of long-range climate changes. I also study El Niño events and Indian monsoons. I see how these events and phenomena affect people—such as people involved in agriculture. The climate really affects the way people live!

I'm also researching whether the activities of humans are affecting the atmosphere. For example, each year, the world's growing population uses more and more energy by burning coal, oil, natural gas, and wood. When all of these substances are burned, they add carbon dioxide to the atmosphere. So I study the atmosphere to see how much the added carbon dioxide is intensifying the greenhouse effect. Then I try to determine how those changes will affect humans. You see, the more we know about the atmosphere, the better we can predict what will happen next.

Q: *How are your research data used?*

Somerville: Many of my findings can affect public policy. For instance, how should the energy of the world be generated? I can help policymakers explore this question by providing them with data about the effects of fuels such as coal, oil, and gas on the atmosphere. Then I can recommend that they establish policies to reduce human reliance on those

This scientist uses state-of-the-art equipment to gather information about changes in ocean temperatures over time.

fuel sources. I can also encourage the use of resources such as solar, wind, and hydroelectric power.

Q: What tools do you use to obtain your data?

Somerville: There are two general classes of technology that are most important to my work: satellites and computers. Together these two items have virtually revolutionized this field by hugely expanding what we've been able to observe and understand. Satellites, for example, can provide us with a whole different perspective of our world. The photographs generated by a satellite allow us to look at global temperatures as well as specific weather and sea conditions. Data are also collected on clouds, soil, and vegetation. By analyzing these observations, we can monitor changing conditions and identify possible problem areas.

Computers help us make sense of the data. Computer equipment in the satellites helps to answer our questions and helps us better visualize the data. Personal computers help us record and summarize our findings. Then we have "super computers," which can simulate the motions of the atmosphere and the ocean, and thereby help us answer questions and make predictions.

We also have access to ships and airplanes that are loaded with highly specialized equipment. These research platforms can be sent to specific areas of the world to gather more information about a situation or condition.

Q: What are the most frustrating aspects of your job?

Somerville: Other demands that limit the time I spend doing research. There's a large fraction of time and energy that must be spent making research possible—you have to find money, so you spend lots of time writing proposals and doing other administrative work.

Q: What school subjects turned out to be the most important for your career?

Somerville: You might be surprised. Math and science classes are essential, but in retrospect I value my English courses the most. Scientists are writers—the final products of their research are shown in published papers.

Q: What personal qualities do you think are most essential for a successful person in your field?

Somerville: There are an enormous variety of scientists—some are sloppy, some are organized, some like to work alone, and some in teams. One thing all good scientists have in common, though, is dedication—they all want to do science above anything else. I think Thomas Edison's famous quotation "Genius is 1 percent inspiration and 99 percent perspiration" is really on the mark. Not everyone can be born a genius, but anyone who is really dedicated can have a good career in science.

MORE ON THIS CAREER

If you are interested in learning more about a career in meteorology, contact the **American Meteorological Society**.

RESEARCH WILDLIFE BIOLOGIST

Many people imagine wildlife biologists wrestling large game animals to the ground, slapping radio collars around their necks, and then creeping through the forest for weeks on end to study the creatures. According to **Mariko Yamasaki,** research wildlife biologist for the U.S. Department of Agriculture, Forest Service, there is a lot more to wildlife biology than that. To her, "Nature is fascinating on many, many levels, from the tiniest ant all the way up to charismatic animals such as bears and wolves. We have to get away from the notion that animals with feathers or fur and big brown eyes are more important than slimy, scaly creatures with beady eyes. All organisms have a role—we must be sure that their contribution to the big picture is recognized."

Q: *What is your educational background and experience?*

Yamasaki: My background is basically a long and colorful stringing together of different experiences. I have bachelor's degrees in anthropology and zoology and a master's degree in natural resources (specific to wildlife). By the time I got out of school in the late 1970s, I came up against a surprising attitude—people in my home state really couldn't conceive of having female biologists supervising in the field. So I looked outside my home state. I ended up studying bald eagles for the Bureau of Land Management out West. This sort of snowballed into a permanent appointment in Washington as a wildlife biologist for the Bureau of Land Management. Today I work at the Northeastern Forest Experiment Station, where I do research in forested lands that cover a 200-mile radius, including parts of Maine and New Hampshire.

To Mariko Yamasaki, every creature, no matter how small or seemingly insignificant, has an important role in this biosphere. She is shown here searching for salamanders in the wild.

Q: *What organisms are you studying in the field right now?*

Yamasaki: I'm studying small mammals, such as mice, shrews, voles, and squirrels. My colleagues and I also study insectivorous bats, migratory birds, and terrestrial salamanders. These are animals that we know something about, such as their basic biology, but we don't know how they respond to forest management. We're looking at these critters to get a sense of how they fit into the bigger picture.

Q: *What types of questions are you trying to answer about these animals?*

Yamasaki: One question my colleagues and I are trying to answer right now is how terrestrial salamanders respond to "even-aged management" of northern hardwoods. Even-aged management involves harvesting a large area of trees whose ages are within 20 years of each other.

We have to get away from the notion that animals with feathers or fur and big brown eyes are more important than slimy, scaly creatures with beady eyes.

©Ken Dudzik/U. S. Department of Agriculture

Yamasaki wants to know if the way trees are harvested from forested areas like this one affects the survival of terrestrial salamanders.

Foresters often use even-aged management because it is an efficient means of harvesting large amounts of timber at one time. My hypothesis is that when a large area of trees has been harvested, the ground temperature might change because the area is suddenly exposed to direct sunlight. This might affect the population and distribution of terrestrial salamanders in a negative way. I use the data I gather to make recommendations to forest managers about how they can manage tracts of forest to best support the needs of salamanders and other wildlife.

Q: *Do you work with other people a lot?*

Yamasaki: There's an old stereotype that a wildlife biologist leads a solitary life studying nature. This simply isn't true—it's important to know how to work with people and how to understand and deal with a variety of viewpoints. There is rarely a day that I sit alone in my office. But I will say that a wildlife biologist does have some control over the matter—generally, you can work with people as much or as little as you want.

Q: *Do you ever have to deal with crisis situations?*

Yamasaki: Not really, but I do see a lot of controversy, particularly related to wildlife and the use of natural resources. My work has often become the object of heated debate. Some people will support my findings wholeheartedly, while others call them worthless. There are any number of ways of dealing with this kind of pressure. I've found that it's real important to get my information together and

analyze it as thoroughly as possible so that I can stand behind what I'm saying. It's also important to realize that everyone is entitled to an opinion.

Q: *What are the most interesting or exciting aspects of your work?*

Yamasaki: Oh, heavens! Being out and observing the natural world. Being able to test hypotheses. Being up real early on a bird survey. It's never the same twice. I also enjoy discovering something new—there's nothing any more special than that. There's a lot out there! The scale of things to observe and study is mind-boggling.

Q: *What advice might you give to someone who is searching for a career?*

Yamasaki: I think it's important to do something you are really interested in. My career, just like anybody else's, is not always a bed of roses. But if you really care about what you do, you can get beyond the problems and complications inherent to any job. It's also important to think that you've got something to contribute. I think that I can help contribute to the way people view wildlife, and that's important to me.

This group of community leaders, politicians, and scientists is discussing how best to use the natural resources of a forested region in Maine.

MORE ON THIS CAREER

If you are interested in learning more about a career in wildlife biology, contact **The Wildlife Society** or the **American Institute of Biological Sciences**.

ANY JOB CAN BE ENVIRONMENTAL

You don't have to be in an environmental career to make a positive impact on the environment. **Gun Denhart** is an excellent example of how you can make a difference through your career, even if your career doesn't directly involve the environment.

Hanna Andersson

Gun Denhart is the cofounder of Hanna Andersson in Portland, Oregon. Hanna Andersson is a company that specializes in selling baby clothing and children's clothing through a mail-order catalog service. The company began in 1983 as an in-home enterprise, in which a spare room was used as the company office and the garage served as the warehouse. One-inch-square fabric samples were cut and pasted into each of the 75,000 catalogs that were mailed that first year. Hanna Andersson has grown enormously since 1983. An adult line of clothes was added, several retail stores were opened, and a Web site was established.

The Used Clothing Recycling Program

As a parent, Gun Denhart realized that children outgrow their clothing very quickly and that clothing purchased at Hanna Andersson will last for more than a single child. Rather than waste clothing, she reasoned, why not pass these clothes on to children in need? So Denhart instituted a program called Hannadowns®. The purpose of the program is to encourage the purchasers of Hanna Andersson clothing to recycle their used clothes. Denhart says, "You can make a critical difference. Most often, my clothes last for more than one child's use, and it's a great feeling to pass them on to younger children in your family, to your friends, or to charitable organizations. It is heartbreaking to realize how many children live at risk—an unbelievable 22 percent of children live below the poverty level in America. Providing them with nourishing food and warm clothing is a never-ending job. Fortunately, there are organizations that offer clothing and supportive services. To help them make a critical difference in children's lives, please send your outgrown children's clothes in good condition to these organizations."

In the first 16 years of the company's existence, Hanna Andersson customers donated over one million pieces of recycled clothes to children in need. These clothes could have ended up in landfills but have instead clothed kids all over the world.

In the first 16 years of the company's existence, Hanna Andersson customers donated over one million pieces of recycled clothes to children in need.

This clothing will be recycled because of an innovative program designed by Gun Denhart.

Ecoskills

BOOSTING YOUR HOME'S ENERGY EFFICIENCY

Many people don't realize the impact that energy production has on the environment. No matter what kind of energy plant serves your area, the production of that energy carries with it certain environmental risks. For example, when we burn coal to create electricity, many pollutants are released into the air. These pollutants may cause environmental problems such as global warming and acid rain. The more energy each of us uses, the more we contribute to these problems. So it makes environmental sense to conserve energy. Conservation is also a good way to save money—just a few energy-saving measures can substantially lower an energy bill.

Could the energy efficiency of your home be improved? Perform the following energy audit to find out.

The Wind Test

One day when it's windy outside, fasten a sheet of tissue paper onto a hanger with a piece of tape, as shown below. Next, hold the hanger in front of a window at the point where the window meets the

This simple device could help you improve the energy efficiency of your home.

wall. Hold the hanger still. If the paper moves, you've found a draft. Note the location of the draft in your science journal. Check all around the window, making comments about the drafts you find. Then examine all the other windows, doors, electrical outlets, plumbing pipes, and baseboards that are on the outer walls of your home. Note every place where the tissue moves.

These drafts of air that you've discovered can add 20 to 35 percent to your heating and cooling bills. Fortunately, you can seal these air leaks with weatherstripping and caulk. Weatherstripping is for moving parts, such as doors and window frames. Caulk is for sealing cracks along joints and edges. These materials are relatively inexpensive, can be found at any hardware store, and can save 7 to 20 percent on your heating and cooling bills.

FOR MORE INFORMATION

Your local electric company can probably send you a packet of energy- and cost-saving ideas. In addition, your city may sponsor thorough in-house energy audits as well as rebates and loans for improving the energy efficiency of your home. Contact your city's electric utilities conservation department for more information.

Consult your library or bookstore for books on improving your home's energy efficiency. You might find these books helpful.

Consumer Guide to Home Energy Savings, 9th ed., by Jennifer Thorne Amann, Alex Wilson, and Katie Ackerly, American Council for an Energy-Efficient Economy. Gabriola Island, BC, Canada: New Society Publishers, 2007.

The Homeowner's Handbook to Energy Efficiency, by John Krigger and Chris Dorsi. Helena, Montana: Saturn Resource Management, Inc., 2008.

ELIMINATING PESTS NATURALLY

A huge cockroach is crawling across your floor. How will you get rid of it? Don't reach for an expensive store-bought chemical that could possibly contaminate the local water supply or even harm someone in your household. Instead, try a natural remedy!

Cockroaches

Make a roach trap by putting honey in the bottom of a jar and setting it upright where the pests are most likely to visit. The sweet smell of the honey will lure roaches into the jar, but the stickiness of the substance will make it impossible for them to escape. You could also line the cracks where you think roaches are entering your home with bay leaves. The smell of bay leaves repels roaches. Prevent roaches from entering your home by keeping all food covered and stored and by cleaning dirty dishes. Seal cracks in walls, baseboards, and ducts with caulk so that roaches and other pests can't get in.

Ants

Sealing cracks with caulk will also help keep ants out of your home. In the meantime, squeeze fresh lemon or lime juice into the holes or cracks. Then leave the peels where you've seen ants. Scatter mint around your shelves and cabinets, or pour a line of cream of tartar, red chili pepper, salt, paprika, dried peppermint, or talcum powder where ants enter your home. These substances either repel or kill the pests. Another effective remedy for ridding your home of ants or cockroaches is to sprinkle a mixture of equal parts of boric acid and confectioners' sugar in dry areas where ants and cockroaches are found. The pests will eat the sugar and then die from the effects of the boric acid. Caution: If ingested, boric acid is acutely toxic to pets and small children. Use boric acid only in areas that are out of reach of kids and pets.

Ticks and Fleas

If your pet has a problem with ticks or fleas, try feeding the animal brewer's yeast or vitamin B. Also wash your pet regularly with soap and water, then dry the animal and spray an herbal mixture of rosemary and water onto its coat. (You can make the mixture by steeping ½ cup of fresh or dried rosemary in one quart of boiling water. Let the liquid cool, pour it into a pump bottle, and then spray it onto your animal's coat.)

You can help reduce the number of ticks and fleas that bother your pet by bathing it frequently and spraying an herbal mixture on its coat.

You can control the ticks and fleas in your yard by sprinkling the grass with diatomaceous earth, which is available at many nurseries. Diatomaceous earth consists of tiny glasslike skeletons of diatoms (a type of single-celled algae). These skeletons scratch the outer layer of an insect's body as it crawls along the ground. The insect eventually dies of dehydration. Bacteria can also enter the insect's body through the open wounds, exposing the insect to disease. Caution: Diatomaceous earth can be harmful to your lungs if inhaled. Wear a protective mask when spreading the substance.

FOR MORE INFORMATION

Your city's environmental and conservation services department (if there is one) may have other remedies for pests and recipes for nontoxic household cleaners. Check your local bookstore or library for books on natural pesticides, organic gardening, and chemical-free homes. You might find these books helpful.

The Organic Gardener's Handbook of Natural Pest and Disease Control, by Fern Marshall Bradley, Barbara W. Ellis, and Deborah L. Martin. New York, New York: Rodale Inc., 2009.

Natural Pest Control Alternatives to Chemicals for the Home and Garden, by A. Lopez. Malibu, CA: Invisible Gardener, 2004.

ENVIRONMENTAL SHOPPING

Try to count how many products you've used today. It's probably not as easy as you think. In the first few minutes of your day, you may have used a dozen products.

All of those products and their packaging are made from valuable resources. More often than not, once those resources are used, they're tossed in a trash can and eventually hauled to the local landfill.

You can cut back on the amount of waste you send to the landfill and conserve resources in the process. On your next few shopping trips, think about the products you choose. If you're like most Americans, you'll probably be amazed at how many wasteful shopping habits you have. But after a while you'll begin to know instinctively which products are best for you and the environment.

On your next few shopping trips, think about the products you choose. If you're like most Americans, you'll probably be amazed at how many wasteful shopping habits you have.

Your Personal Shopping Guide

Read the information on the following page, and think of a way to reproduce it so that you (and other members of your household) have it handy when you set out on a shopping trip. For example, you may want to copy the questions and answers on the side of a brown paper bag. That way you'll have a shopper's guide and you'll need one less sack at the checkout stand. Another option is to write your guidelines on the back of an old grocery receipt and then adhere the receipt to the refrigerator with a magnet so that it will be handy for the other shoppers in your household. The options are limitless, so be creative. Try to incorporate recycled items into your design!

Before you create your personal shopping guide, you may want to review Chapter 19 Section 2, "Reducing Solid Waste."

FOR MORE INFORMATION

Consult your local library or a bookstore to find references that will help you with your environmental shopping. You might find one of the following books helpful.

The Rough Guide to Shopping with a Conscience, by Duncan Clark and Richie Unterberger. New York, New York: Duncan Clark and Richie Unterberger, 2007.

The Better World Shopping Guide, by Ellis Jones. British Columbia, Canada: Ellis Jones, 2010.

An Environmental Shopper's Guide

Do I really need this product? Can I use something I already have?	Borrow or rent products you don't use often.
Is this a "throwaway" item that is designed to be used once or twice and then thrown away?	Avoid using disposable products whenever possible. Nondisposable alternatives may be more expensive initially, but in the long run they often save you money.
Does this product have more packaging than it really needs?	Look for alternatives with less packaging or wrapping. Purchase products in bulk or in a larger size so that in the long run you use less packaging (and save money!). Buy fresh vegetables and fruit instead of frozen or canned products.
Was this product's container or packaging made with recycled materials?	Choose products that have recycled paper, aluminum, glass, plastic, or other recycled materials in their packaging.
Is this product's container or packaging made from cardboard, aluminum, glass, or another material that I can easily recycle?	Find out which materials you can conveniently recycle, and then buy those sorts of containers. Also, think of ways to reuse old containers rather than throwing them out.
Does this product have bleaches, dyes, or fragrances added to it? Does it contain phosphates? Is it made from a petroleum-based synthetic fabric, such as polyester?	Phosphates and many other chemicals can pollute water sources. Look for natural, organic, and phosphate-free alternatives. When purchasing clothing, choose cotton or wool over synthetic fabrics.
Does the company that makes this product have a good environmental record?	You may have to do a little research to answer this one. Try the references listed on the facing page.
Although this product has a "green" label, is it really good for me and the environment?	Don't be deceived by advertising and product labeling; carefully examine the contents of a product before you purchase it.
Do I really need a shopping bag to carry home the items I'm purchasing? If so, will I be more likely to recycle or reuse a plastic shopping bag or a paper one?	If you purchase just one or two items, tell the grocer that you don't need a bag to carry them. For more items, bring old paper or plastic sacks with you when you go to the store, or use a canvas bag, which will last through many trips.
How much energy do I spend getting to the store?	If possible, ride your bike or walk to the store. If not, condense several short trips into one longer trip for a bigger supply of items.

MAKING YOUR OWN COMPOST HEAP

Why on Earth would you want to pile a bunch of garbage in your yard and let it rot? Crazy as the idea may sound, it's actually a very good one—copied straight from nature itself.

Compost is the natural product of Earth's organic decaying process. When a dead organism decomposes, nutrients are returned to the soil. A compost heap is a collection of organic materials such as leaves, grass, and fruit peelings that will decompose over time to create rich, fertile soil. By making your own compost heap, you can reduce the amount of waste you send to the local landfill and create an excellent natural fertilizer for your garden.

There are many opinions on how to construct the best compost heap—it can be as basic or as fancy as you like. Either way, composting is easy, and it's almost impossible to foul up the process.

A compost heap can be placed just about anywhere in the yard. Either a sunny or a shady spot will be fine. You will want to keep it out of the way of normal activity, however.

Many people choose a spot on a concrete slab or a grassy area and then simply pile their materials there. This method is easy and effective.

A compost heap contains a mishmash of many different organic materials. Most of your heap will probably consist of grass clippings and leaves. You can also add raw vegetables, other uncooked food scraps, coffee grounds, tea bags, cotton, dust, discarded plants, and weeds. Avoid adding pet manure, cooked foods, and meat of any kind. If you add raw food wastes, cover them with leaves to keep away flies and to prevent an unpleasant odor.

Your heap will begin to decompose through the action of microorganisms. It's a good idea to shovel a couple of scoops of soil from your yard into the heap. The microorganisms in the soil will immediately begin decomposing the items in the heap.

By making your own compost heap, you can reduce the amount of waste you send to the local landfill and create an excellent natural fertilizer for your garden.

You may choose to keep your compost pile in a ready-made container similar to this one.

Anatomy of a Compost Heap

Leaves and grass clippings

Garden and kitchen wastes

Soil from your garden

Leaves and grass clippings

Small tree branches and twigs

Turn the heap at least once a month to keep it well aerated and active. After the organic matter has broken down to the point that no single item is recognizable, it's ready to work into your garden's soil. The entire process can take anywhere from two months to one year, depending on the kinds of materials being decomposed and how often the heap is turned. Composting is more of an art than a science, so be prepared to experiment!

Compost Heap Container

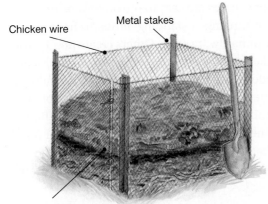

Chicken wire

Metal stakes

Loose wire can be twisted around two sections of chicken wire to create a "door" for easy turning.

You can build this container for your compost heap with a few materials from your local hardware store.

Compost Container

If you choose to contain your compost pile, you will be able to add more materials to a smaller area. You can buy a ready-made container from a hardware store or you can build one yourself.

If you decide to build one, you may wish to use metal stakes and chicken wire to create a container like the one shown at left. Keep in mind, however, that as long as the container allows air to get in and out, the type of container you choose is limited only by your imagination!

FOR MORE INFORMATION

Consult your library for a manual on composting. You might find one of these helpful.

The Complete Compost Gardening Guide, by Barbara Pleasant and Deborah L. Martin. North Adams, Massachusetts: Barbara Pleasant and Deborah L. Martin, 2008.

Learn to Compost: 30 Easy Tips to Turn You into the Master Composter, by Alex Masters. Alex Masters, 2012.

CREATING A WILDLIFE GARDEN

Manicured lawns and non-native vegetation are not part of a natural ecosystem. Although these have been standard in urban and suburban neighborhoods for years, they usually require pesticides, fertilizers, water, and attention just to survive. In addition, they often exclude wildlife by removing some of their natural sources of food, water, and shelter.

To attract wildlife to your home, you simply need to provide native plants and the sorts of water sources and shelters naturally available to the wildlife in your area.

Plants

Plants are probably the most crucial element of your wildlife garden. Whether you have a lot of space for planting a wildflower meadow, a balcony on which you can create a container garden full of native plants, or a few windows to which you can attach boxes full of bright and cheerful wildflowers, you will need a variety of native plants. Check with a local nursery, library, or bookstore for recommendations.

> To attract wildlife to your home, you simply need to provide native plants and the sorts of water sources and shelters naturally available to the wildlife in your area.

Water

People often overlook the need all animals have for water. Although some animals obtain enough water from the foods they eat, most require additional water for drinking and bathing.

Water sources are easy to provide. Many people purchase hanging or standing birdbaths from a nursery or hardware store. Others create ponds. You can make a simple pond by setting an old trash-can lid upside down in a corner of your yard and filling it with water. Surround your water source with plants, rocks, and other items so that the wildlife can find cover if necessary. In addition, make sure your pond or birdbath is at least partially shallow so that no animal is in danger of drowning, and keep the water clean.

Food and Shelter

Many different kinds of birdhouses and feeders are available at nature stores, hardware shops, and nurseries. Most of these can be hung on a balcony, and some can even be adhered to a window. You could also make your own birdhouse or feeder. A milk jug with a large hole cut in its side that is filled with seed and hung from a tree or balcony is an excellent way to feed many birds. If you would like to attract bats to your yard, use the Internet to find out how to make (or purchase) a bat house.

Woodpiles, rock piles, and brush piles are valuable sources of shelter for wildlife such as lizards and toads that might not otherwise frequent your backyard habitat. The most successful pile is one that incorporates different-sized spaces among the various components. You can make your pile attractive by planting vines in and around it.

Caution: *A shelter like the one described above may also attract poisonous snakes. Find out if any live in your area; if so, you may want to refrain from making a shelter pile.*

FOR MORE INFORMATION

Consult your library or bookstore for books on gardening with plants native to your area, gardening for the wildlife in your area, and xeriscape techniques. You might find these books helpful.

The Wildlife Gardener's Guide, by Brooklyn Botanic Garden All-Region Guides. Brooklyn, New York: Brooklyn Botanic Garden, 2008.

Welcoming Wildlife to the Garden, by Catherine J. Johnson, Susan M. McDiarmid, and Edward R. Turner. British Columbia, Canada: Edward R. Turner, 2002.

FLUSHING LESS WATER

A typical American uses over 100 gallons of water before he or she even leaves for work or school in the morning, and much of that water is wasted. You may wish to review Figure 2.3 in Chapter 11, which shows daily water use in the United States per person.

Many Americans are beginning to change their wasteful practices, however. One simple and inexpensive way you can waste less water is by making a water-displacement device for your toilet's tank. This device takes up space in the tank so that less water is required to fill the tank with every flush. It takes only about 10 minutes to make, and with it you can save 1–2 gallons of water every time you flush. This may not sound like much, but it adds up quickly. Most toilets use 5–7 gallons of water with every flush. If a toilet is flushed an average of eight times per day, it uses around 52 gallons of water per day, or 18,980 gallons per year. If you can save 11–12 gallons of water with every flush, you'll save 4,380 gallons of water each year. If just 250 other people take similar measures, over 1 million gallons of water could be saved each year.

Making a Quick and Easy Water Displacer

1. Remove the label from a plastic container. (Milk jugs, juice bottles, and dishwashing soap bottles work well. Be prepared to experiment with different-sized containers.) Drop a few rocks into the container to weigh it down, fill the container with water, and put the lid back on.

2. Place the container in the toilet tank, as shown at left.

3. Be certain that the container doesn't interfere with the flushing mechanism inside the tank.

4. Experiment with different containers. Your goal is to use the largest container that the tank will hold while still maintaining an effective flush.

ONE FINAL IMPORTANT NOTE

The more water you save, the less you pay for. No matter which water-saving device you install, your water bill should be noticeably lower.

Maps

World Physical Relief

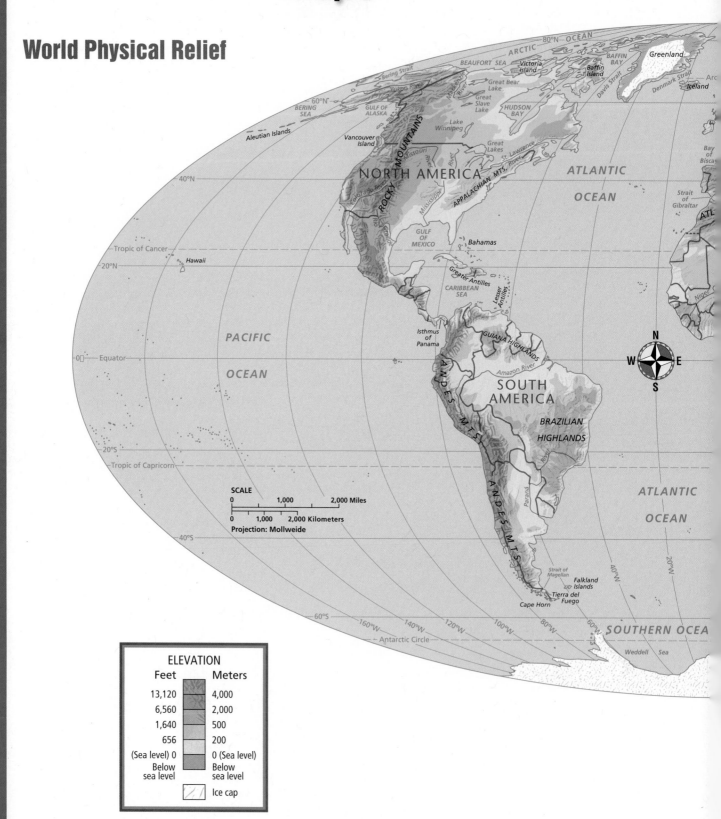

SCALE

0   1,000   2,000 Miles

0   1,000   2,000 Kilometers

Projection: Mollweide

ELEVATION

Feet		Meters
13,120		4,000
6,560		2,000
1,640		500
656		200
(Sea level) 0		0 (Sea level)
Below sea level		Below sea level
	Ice cap	

ARCTIC 80°N OCEAN
North BARENTS KARA LAPTEV EAST SIBERIAN
Cape SEA SEA SEA SEA
BALTIC
SEA
URAL MOUNTAINS Yenisey Lena River Kolyma R.
Ob River
Volga River 60°N SEA OF KAMCHATKA
EUROPE OKHOTSK PENINSULA
ARAL Lake Altai Mts. Amur River Sakhalin
BLACK SEA SEA Balkhash
CASPIAN SEA TIAN SHAN GOBI Hokkaidō
MEDITERRANEAN SEA ASIA (Yellow River) 40°N
Tigris Euphrates River Persian Gulf HIMALAYAS SEA OF Honshū
JAPAN JAPAN
Nile River RED SEA THAR Ganges River EAST Shikoku
SAHARA ARABIAN DESERT (Yangtze) River CHINA Kyūshū
PENINSULA SEA
AFRICA ARABIAN Bay SOUTH Taiwan Tropic of Cancer
SEA of CHINA 20°N
Bengal Mekong River SEA Philippine PACIFIC
Sri Islands
Lanka Strait
Congo River of MALAY OCEAN
Lake Malacca PENINSULA
Lake Tanganyika Victoria Singapore Borneo Equator 0°
Sumatra New
Sulawesi Guinea Solomon
(Celebes) Islands
Java East Timor
INDIAN OCEAN CORAL
Madagascar SEA
Mozambique Channel GREAT SANDY New
DESERT Caledonia
KALAHARI AUSTRALIA Tropic of Capricorn
DESERT GREAT
Cape of VICTORIA Darling River North
Good Hope DESERT GREAT DIVIDING RANGE Island
TASMAN New
SEA NEW Zealand
ANTARCTICA Tasmania South ZEALAND
Island
20°E 40°E 60°E 80°E 100°E 120°E 140°E 160°E 60°S

20°E 30°E 40°E 50°E 60°E 80°E
North KARA
Denmark Strait Cape SEA
Kjølen Mts. BARENTS
Iceland SEA
SCALE
N 0 250 500 750 Miles
W E URAL MTS.
60°N S 0 250 500 750 Kilometers
Projection: Mollweide
NORTH Volga
British SEA River
Isles BALTIC
SEA EUROPE
50°N
ATLANTIC Rhine River
OCEAN ALPS
Bay Danube River BLACK SEA
of
Biscay
40°N
MEDITERRANEAN SEA
Strait of Crete
Gibraltar

World Climate Regions

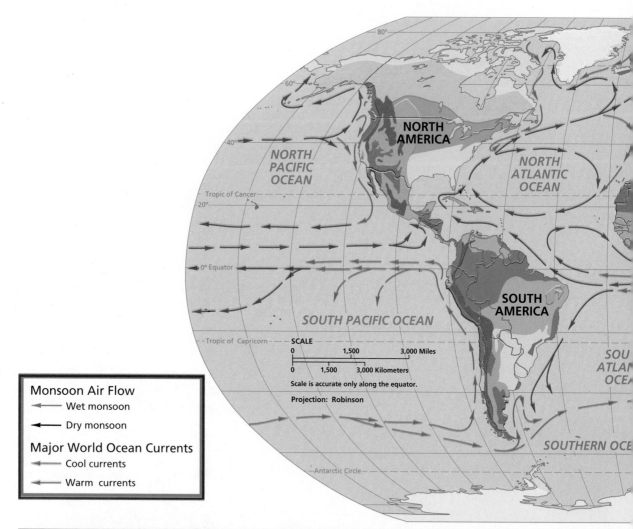

Monsoon Air Flow
- ← Wet monsoon
- ← Dry monsoon

Major World Ocean Currents
- ← Cool currents
- ← Warm currents

NORTH AMERICA

NORTH PACIFIC OCEAN

NORTH ATLANTIC OCEAN

Tropic of Cancer

0° Equator

SOUTH PACIFIC OCEAN

SOUTH AMERICA

SOU ATLAN OCEA

Tropic of Capricorn

SCALE

0   1,500   3,000 Miles

0   1,500   3,000 Kilometers

Scale is accurate only along the equator.

Projection: Robinson

SOUTHERN OCE

Antarctic Circle

	Climate	Geographic Distribution	Major Weather Patterns	Vegetation
Tropical	**TROPICAL HUMID**	along equator; particularly equatorial South America, Congo Basin in Africa, Southeast Asia	warm and rainy year-round, with rain totaling anywhere from 65 to more than 450 in. (165–1,143 cm) annually; typical temperatures are 90°–95°F (32°–35°C) during the day and 65°–70°F (18°–21°C) at night	tropical rain forest
	TROPICAL WET AND DRY	between humid tropics and deserts; tropical regions of Africa, South and Central America, South and Southeast Asia, Australia	warm all year; distinct rainy and dry seasons; precipitation during the summer of at least 20 in. (51 cm); monsoon influences in some areas, such as South and Southeast Asia; summer temperatures average 90°F (32°C) during the day and 70°F (21°C) at night; typical winter temperatures are 75°–80°F (24°–27°C) during the day and 55°–60°F (13°–16°C) at night	tropical grassland with scattered trees
Dry	**ARID**	centered along 30° latitude; some middle-latitude deserts in interior of large continents and along western coasts; particularly Saharan Africa, Southwest Asia, central and western Australia, southwestern North America	arid; precipitation of less than 10 in. (25 cm) annually; sunny and hot in the tropics and sunny with great temperature ranges in middle latitudes; typical summer temperatures for lower-latitude deserts are 110°–115°F (43°–46°C) during the day and 60°–65°F (16°–18°C) at night, while winter temperatures average 80°F (27°C) during the day and 45°F (7°C) at night; in middle latitudes the hottest month averages 70°F (21°C)	sparse drought-resistant plants; many barren, rocky, or sandy areas
	SEMIARID	generally bordering deserts and interiors of large continents; particularly northern and southern Africa, interior western North America, central and interior Asia and Australia, southern South America	semiarid; about 10–20 in. (25–51 cm) of precipitation annually; hot summers and cooler winters with wide temperature ranges similar to desert temperatures	grassland; few trees
Middle Latitudes	**MEDITERRANEAN**	west coasts in middle latitudes near cool ocean currents; particularly southern Europe, part of Southwest Asia, northwestern Africa, California, southwestern Australia, central Chile, south-western South Africa	dry sunny warm summers and mild wetter winters; precipitation averages 14–35 in. (35–90 cm) annually; typical temperatures are 75°–80°F (24°–27°C) on summer days; the average winter temperature is 50°F (10°C)	scrub woodland and grassland
	HUMID SUBTROPICAL	east coasts in middle latitudes; particularly southeastern United States, eastern Asia, central southern Europe, southeastern parts of South America, South Africa, and Australia	hot humid summers and mild humid winters; precipitation year-round; coastal areas are in the paths of hurricanes and typhoons; precipitation averages 40 in. (102 cm) annually; typical temperatures are 75°–90°F (24°–32°C) in summer and 45°–50°F (7°–10°C) in winter	mixed forest

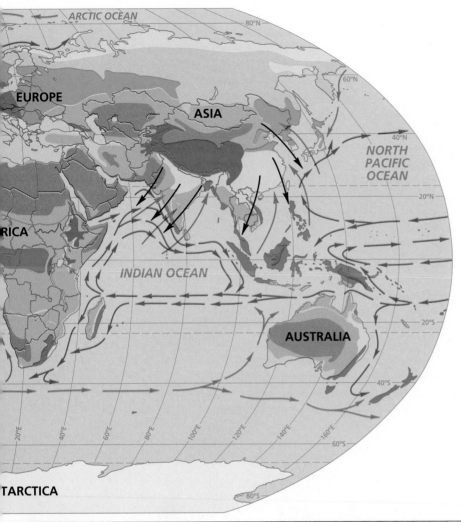

	Climate	Geographic Distribution	Major Weather Patterns	Vegetation
Middle Latitudes	**MARINE WEST COAST**	west coasts in upper-middle latitudes; particularly northwestern Europe and North America, southwestern South America, central southern South Africa, southeastern Australia, New Zealand	cloudy mild summers and cool rainy winters; strong ocean influence; precipitation averages 20–98 in. (51–250 cm) annually; westerlies bring storms and rain; average temperature in hottest month is usually between 60°F and 70°F (16°–21°C); average temperature in coolest month usually is above 32°F (0°C)	temperate evergreen forest
	HUMID CONTINENTAL	east coasts and interiors of upper-middle latitude continents; particularly northeastern North America, northern and eastern Europe, northeastern Asia	four distinct seasons; long cold winters and short warm summers; precipitation amounts vary, usually 20–50 in. (51–127 cm) or more annually; average summer temperature is 75°F (24°C); average winter temperature is below freezing	mixed forest
High Latitudes	**SUBARCTIC**	higher latitudes of interior and east coasts of continents; particularly northern parts of North America, Europe, and Asia	extremes of temperature; long cold winters and short mild summers; low precipitation amounts all year; precipitation averages 5–15 in. (13–38 cm) in summer; temperatures in warmest month average 60°F (16°C) but can warm to 77°F (25°C); winter temperatures average below 0°F (–18°C)	northern evergreen forest
	TUNDRA	high-latitude coasts; particularly far northern parts of North America, Europe, and Asia, Antarctic Peninsula, subantarctic islands	cold all year; very long cold winters and very short cool summers; low precipitation amounts; precipitation average is 5–15 in. (13–38 cm) annually; warmest month averages less than 50°F (10°C); coolest month averages a little below 0°F (–18°C)	moss, lichens, low shrubs; permafrost bogs in summer
	ICECAP	polar regions; particularly Antarctica, Greenland, Arctic Basin islands	freezing cold; snow and ice year-round; precipitation averages less than 10 in. (25 cm) annually; average temperatures in warmest month do not reach higher than freezing	no vegetation
	HIGHLAND	high mountain regions, particularly western parts of North and South America, eastern parts of Asia and Africa, southern and central Europe and Asia	greatly varied temperatures and precipitation amounts over short distances as elevation changes; prevailing wind patterns can affect rainfall on windward and leeward sides of highland areas	forest to tundra vegetation, depending on elevation

World Political Regions

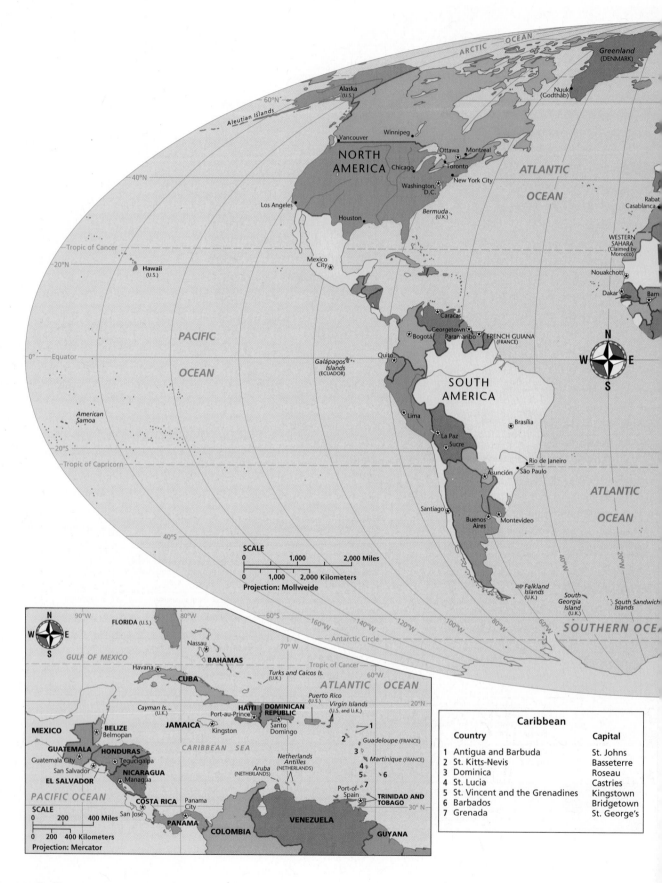

SCALE
0   1,000   2,000 Miles
0   1,000   2,000 Kilometers
Projection: Mollweide

SCALE
0   200   400 Miles
0   200   400 Kilometers
Projection: Mercator

Caribbean	
Country	**Capital**
1 Antigua and Barbuda	St. Johns
2 St. Kitts-Nevis	Basseterre
3 Dominica	Roseau
4 St. Lucia	Castries
5 St. Vincent and the Grenadines	Kingstown
6 Barbados	Bridgetown
7 Grenada	St. George's

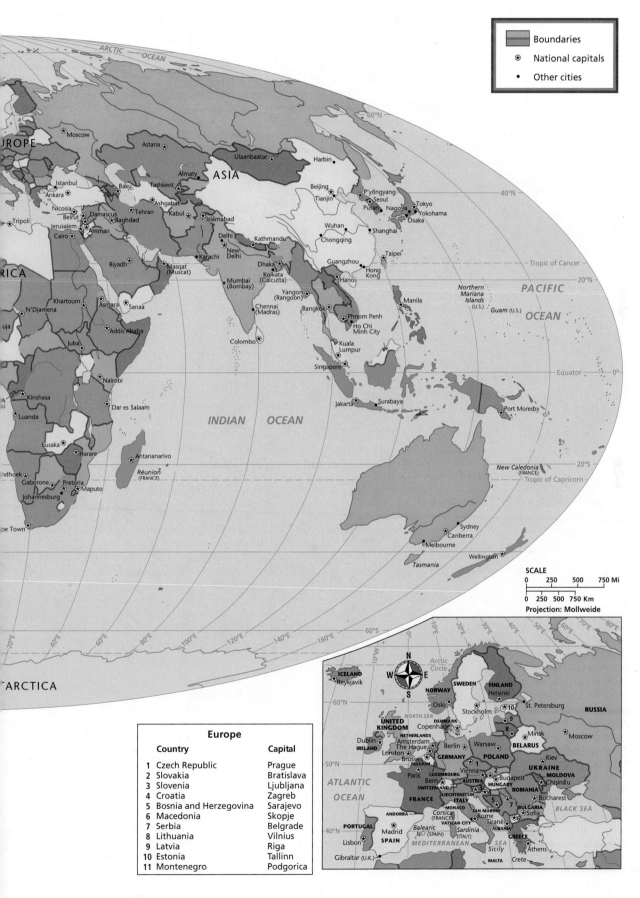

| Boundaries |
|⊛ National capitals |
|• Other cities |

ARCTIC OCEAN

60°N

EUROPE

Moscow

Astana

Ulaanbaatar

Harbin

ASIA

Istanbul

Almaty

Ankara

Baku

Tashkent

40°N

Beijing

P'yŏngyang
Seoul

Tokyo
Yokohama

Nicosia

Ashgabat

Tehran

Kabul

Tianjin

Pusan
Nagoya
Osaka

Beirut
Damascus
Baghdad

Islamabad

Jerusalem
Amman

Wuhan

Shanghai

Tripoli

Cairo

Delhi
New
Delhi

Kathmandu

Chongqing

AFRICA

Riyadh

Karachi

Dhaka

Guangzhou

Taipei

Tropic of Cancer

Masqat
(Muscat)

Kolkata
(Calcutta)

Hanoi

Hong
Kong

Khartoum

N'Djamena

Asmara
Sanaa

Mumbai
(Bombay)

Yangon
(Rangoon)

Northern
Mariana
Islands
(U.S.)

Guam (U.S.)

20°N

PACIFIC

Abuja

Chennai
(Madras)

Bangkok

Phnom Penh

Manila

OCEAN

Addis Ababa

Ho Chi
Minh City

Juba

Colombo

Kuala
Lumpur

Nairobi

Kinshasa

Dar es Salaam

Singapore

Equator

0°

Luanda

INDIAN   OCEAN

Jakarta

Surabaya

Port Moresby

Lusaka

Harare

Antananarivo

New Caledonia
(FRANCE)

20°S

Windhoek

Gaborone
Johannesburg

Pretoria
Maputo

Réunion
(FRANCE)

Tropic of Capricorn

Cape Town

Sydney
Canberra

Melbourne

Wellington

Tasmania

20°E 40°E 60°E 80°E 100°E 120°E 140°E 160°E 60°S

ANTARCTICA

SCALE

| 0 | 250 | 500 | 750 Mi |
| 0 | 250 500 750 Km |

Projection: Mollweide

Europe	
Country	**Capital**
1 Czech Republic	Prague
2 Slovakia	Bratislava
3 Slovenia	Ljubljana
4 Croatia	Zagreb
5 Bosnia and Herzegovina	Sarajevo
6 Macedonia	Skopje
7 Serbia	Belgrade
8 Lithuania	Vilnius
9 Latvia	Riga
10 Estonia	Tallinn
11 Montenegro	Podgorica

N
W   E
S

Arctic
Circle

ICELAND
Reykjavik

SWEDEN
FINLAND

NORWAY
Helsinki

60°N

Oslo

Stockholm

10

St. Petersburg

RUSSIA

NORTH SEA

9

UNITED
KINGDOM

DENMARK
Copenhagen

8

Minsk

Moscow

Dublin

Amsterdam
The Hague

Berlin

Warsaw

BELARUS

IRELAND

NETHERLANDS

London

Brussels

GERMANY

POLAND

Kiev

BELGIUM

50°N

LUXEMBOURG

1

UKRAINE

Paris

Bern

Vienna

Budapest

MOLDOVA
Chişinău

SWITZERLAND

AUSTRIA

HUNGARY

ATLANTIC

LIECHTENSTEIN

ITALY

2

ROMANIA

OCEAN

FRANCE

3

4

7

Bucharest

MONACO

SAN MARINO

BULGARIA

BLACK SEA

ANDORRA

Corsica
(FRANCE)

VATICAN CITY

Rome

5

Sofia

PORTUGAL

Madrid

Balearic
Is. (SPAIN)

Sardinia
(ITALY)

11

6

Tirane

ALBANIA

Lisbon

SPAIN

GREECE

40°N

Sicily

Athens

Gibraltar (U.K.)

MEDITERRANEAN   SEA

MALTA

Crete

World Population Density

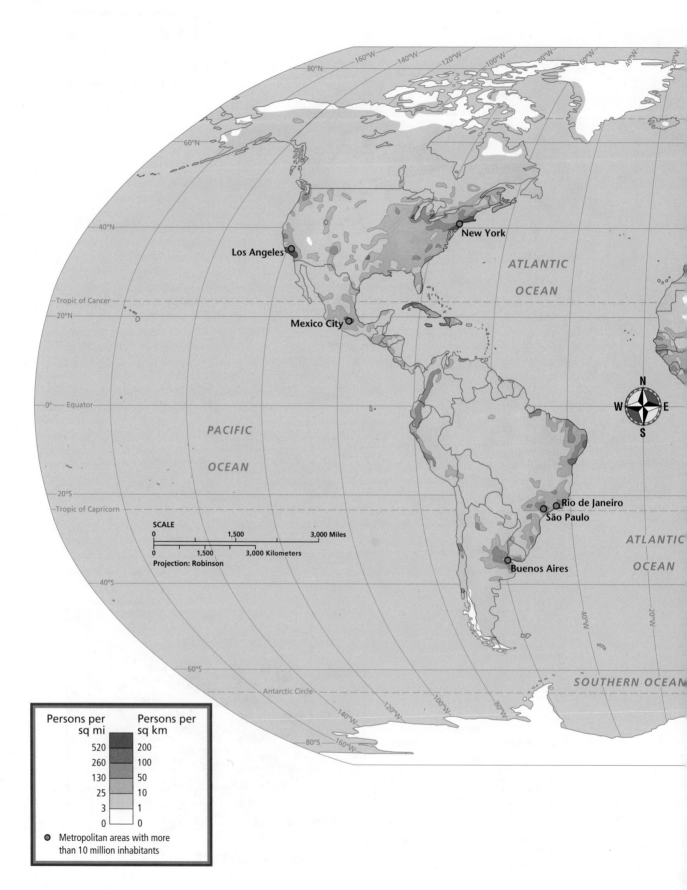

SCALE

0   1,500   3,000 Miles

0   1,500   3,000 Kilometers

Projection: Robinson

Persons per sq mi	Persons per sq km
520	200
260	100
130	50
25	10
3	1
0	0

● Metropolitan areas with more than 10 million inhabitants

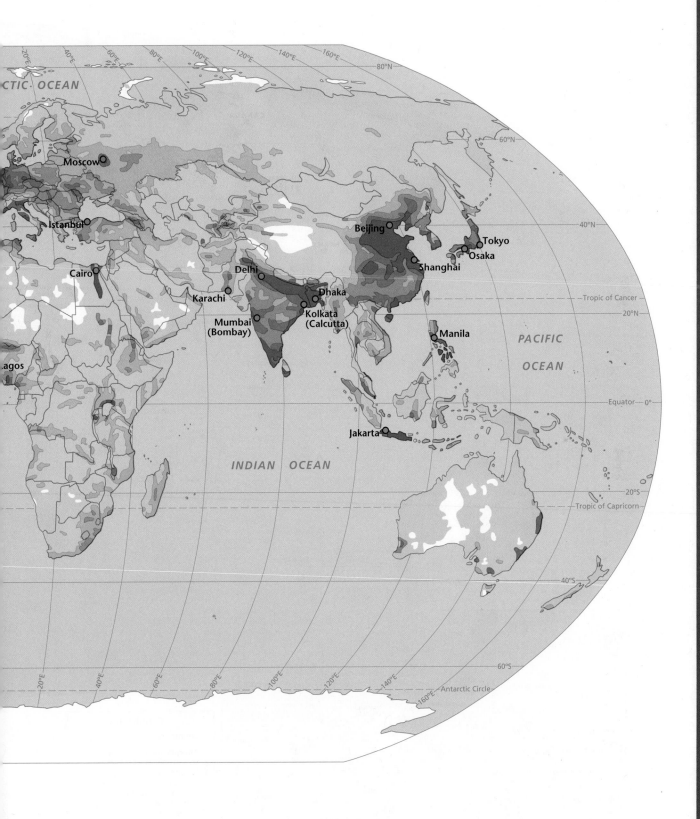

ᴄᴛɪᴄ OCEAN

Moscow

Istanbul

Cairo

.agos

Karachi

Delhi

Mumbai
(Bombay)

Dhaka

Kolkata
(Calcutta)

Beijing

Shanghai

Tokyo

Osaka

Manila

PACIFIC

OCEAN

INDIAN OCEAN

Jakarta

80°N

60°N

40°N

Tropic of Cancer

20°N

Equator — 0°

20°S

Tropic of Capricorn

40°S

60°S

Antarctic Circle

20°E
40°E
60°E
80°E
100°E
120°E
140°E
160°E
80°N

20°E
40°E
60°E
80°E
100°E
120°E
140°E
160°E

World Carbon Dioxide Emissions Per Person

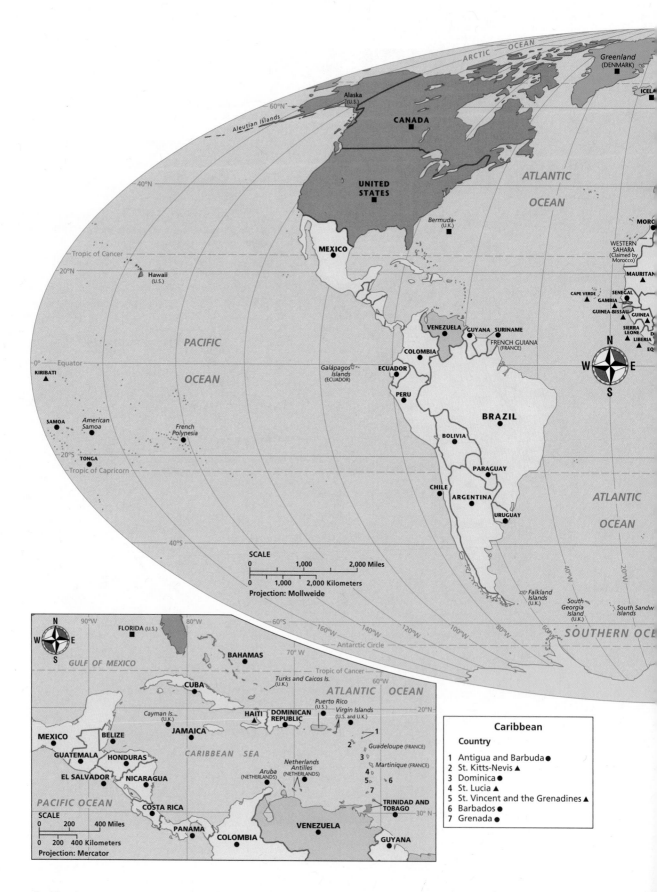

SCALE
0   1,000   2,000 Miles
0   1,000   2,000 Kilometers
Projection: Mollweide

SCALE
0   200   400 Miles
0   200   400 Kilometers
Projection: Mercator

Caribbean
Country

1 Antigua and Barbuda ●
2 St. Kitts-Nevis ▲
3 Dominica ●
4 St. Lucia ▲
5 St. Vincent and the Grenadines ▲
6 Barbados ●
7 Grenada ●

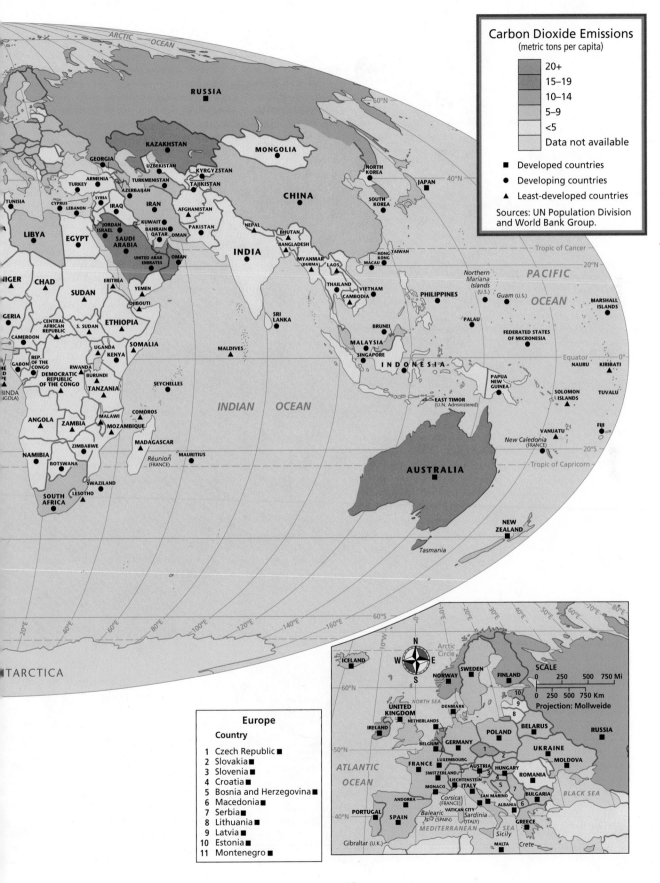

Carbon Dioxide Emissions
(metric tons per capita)

- 20+
- 15–19
- 10–14
- 5–9
- <5
- Data not available

- ■ Developed countries
- ● Developing countries
- ▲ Least-developed countries

Sources: UN Population Division and World Bank Group.

Europe

Country

1 Czech Republic ■
2 Slovakia ■
3 Slovenia ■
4 Croatia ■
5 Bosnia and Herzegovina ■
6 Macedonia ■
7 Serbia ■
8 Lithuania ■
9 Latvia ■
10 Estonia ■
11 Montenegro ■

SCALE

0   250   500   750 Mi

0   250   500   750 Km

Projection: Mollweide

U.S. Physical Relief

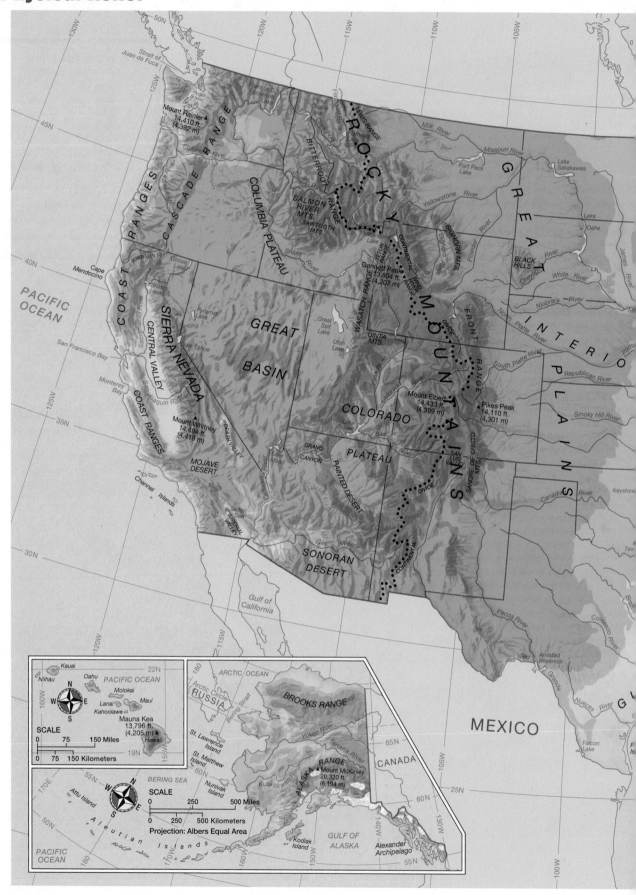

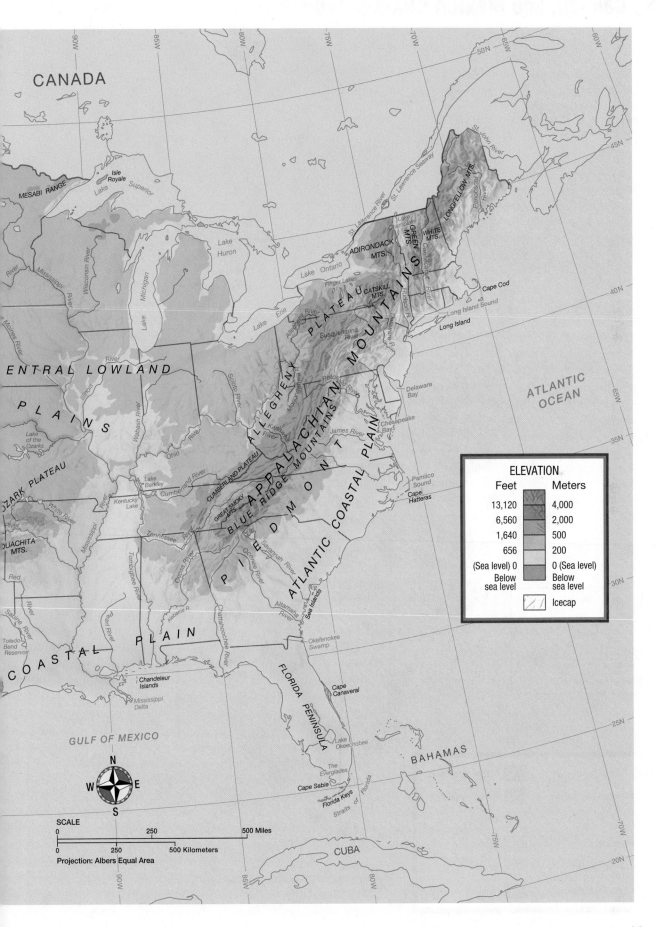

CANADA

MESABI RANGE

Isle
Royale

Lake Superior

Lake Huron

Lake Michigan

CENTRAL LOWLAND

PLAINS

Lake of the Ozarks

OZARK PLATEAU

OUACHITA MTS.

COASTAL PLAIN

Toledo Bend Reservoir

Chandeleur Islands

Mississippi Delta

GULF OF MEXICO

Mississippi River
Wisconsin River
Des Moines River
Illinois River
Wabash River
Scioto River
Ohio River
White River
Mississippi River
Red River
Sabine River
Pearl River
Tombigbee River
Alabama R.
Coosa River
Tennessee River
Cumberland River
Kentucky River
Lake Barkley
Lake Michigan
Kanawha River
Allegheny River
Monongahela River
Chattahoochee River
Oconee River
Altamaha River
Savannah River
Okefenokee Swamp

FLORIDA PENINSULA

Cape Canaveral

Lake Okeechobee

The Everglades

Cape Sable

Florida Keys

Straits of Florida

CUBA

BAHAMAS

Lake Ontario

Lake Erie

Finger Lakes

ADIRONDACK MTS.

CATSKILL MTS.

PLATEAU

ALLEGHENY

APPALACHIAN MOUNTAINS

BLUE RIDGE MOUNTAINS

PIEDMONT

CUMBERLAND PLATEAU

GREAT SMOKY MTS.

ATLANTIC COASTAL PLAIN

Susquehanna River

Potomac River

James River

St. Lawrence River

St. Lawrence Seaway

Lake Champlain

GREEN MTS.

WHITE MTS.

LONGFELLOW MTS.

St. John River

Penobscot River

Connecticut River

Hudson R.

Cape Cod

Long Island Sound

Long Island

Delaware Bay

Chesapeake Bay

ATLANTIC OCEAN

Pamlico Sound

Cape Hatteras

Sea Islands

ELEVATION

Feet		Meters
13,120		4,000
6,560		2,000
1,640		500
656		200
(Sea level) 0		0 (Sea level)
Below sea level		Below sea level
	Icecap	

SCALE

0   250   500 Miles

0   250   500 Kilometers

Projection: Albers Equal Area

N
W   E
S

Maps

U.S., Canada, and Mexico Climate Regions

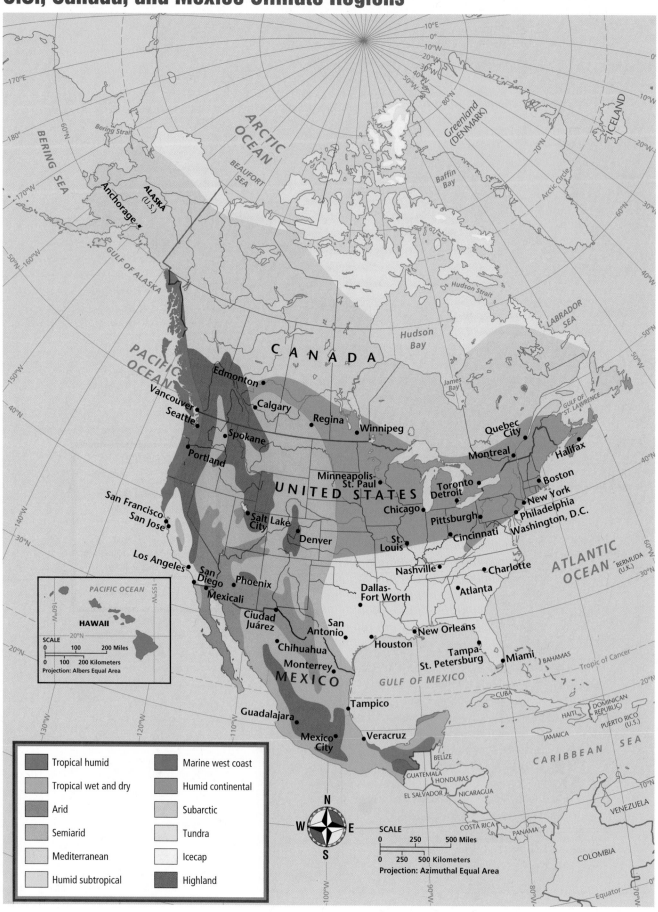

Legend:

- Tropical humid
- Tropical wet and dry
- Arid
- Semiarid
- Mediterranean
- Humid subtropical
- Marine west coast
- Humid continental
- Subarctic
- Tundra
- Icecap
- Highland

U.S., Canada, and Mexico Fossil Fuel Deposits

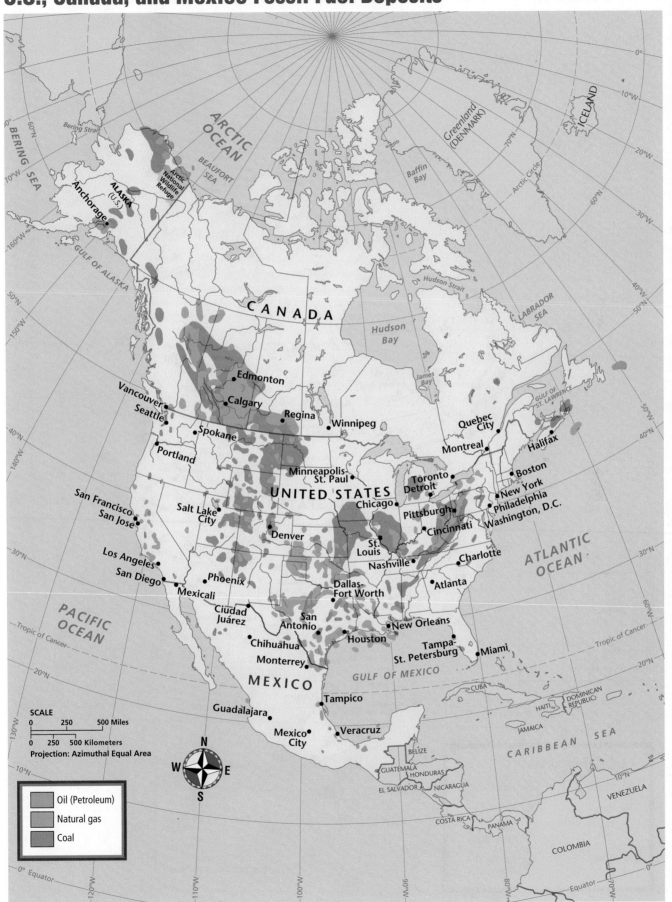

SCALE
0   250   500 Miles
0   250   500 Kilometers
Projection: Azimuthal Equal Area

Oil (Petroleum)
Natural gas
Coal

U.S., Canada, and Mexico Mineral and Energy Resources

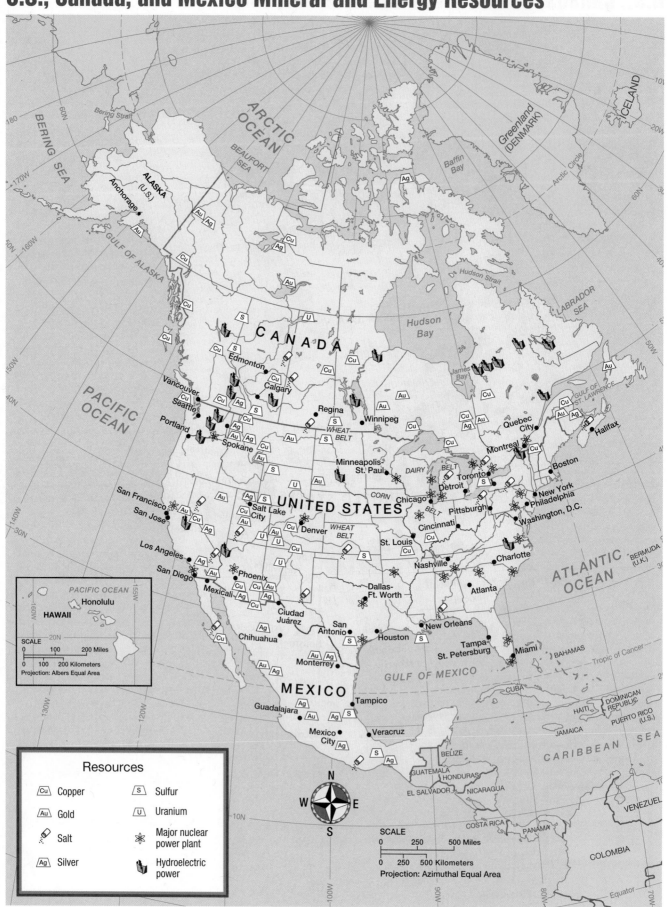

Resources

Cu Copper
Au Gold
Salt
Ag Silver
S Sulfur
U Uranium
✳ Major nuclear power plant
Hydroelectric power

HAWAII
PACIFIC OCEAN
Honolulu
SCALE
0   100   200 Miles
0   100   200 Kilometers
Projection: Albers Equal Area

SCALE
0   250   500 Miles
0   250   500 Kilometers
Projection: Azimuthal Equal Area

U.S., Canada, and Mexico Land Use

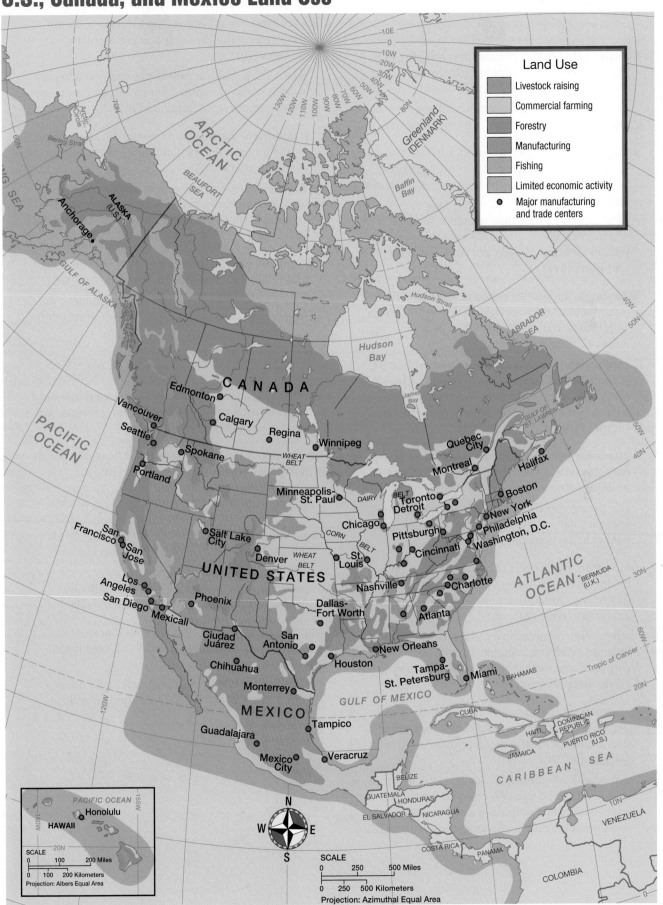

Land Use
- Livestock raising
- Commercial farming
- Forestry
- Manufacturing
- Fishing
- Limited economic activity
- Major manufacturing and trade centers

ARCTIC OCEAN

BEAUFORT SEA

BERING SEA

Bering Strait

Arctic Circle

ALASKA (U.S.)

Anchorage

GULF OF ALASKA

PACIFIC OCEAN

Greenland (DENMARK)

Baffin Bay

Hudson Strait

Hudson Bay

James Bay

LABRADOR SEA

GULF OF ST. LAWRENCE

CANADA

Edmonton
Vancouver
Calgary
Seattle
Regina
Spokane
Winnipeg
Portland
WHEAT BELT
Quebec City
Montreal
Halifax
Minneapolis-St. Paul
DAIRY
Toronto
BELT
Boston
Detroit
New York
San Francisco
San Jose
Salt Lake City
Chicago
Pittsburgh
Philadelphia
Washington, D.C.
CORN
Denver
WHEAT BELT
St. Louis
BELT
Cincinnati
UNITED STATES
Los Angeles
Phoenix
Nashville
Charlotte
ATLANTIC OCEAN
BERMUDA (U.K.)
San Diego
Mexicali
Dallas-Fort Worth
Atlanta
Ciudad Juárez
San Antonio
New Orleans
Chihuahua
Houston
Tampa-St. Petersburg
Miami
BAHAMAS
Tropic of Cancer
Monterrey
GULF OF MEXICO
MEXICO
Tampico
CUBA
Guadalajara
DOMINICAN REPUBLIC
HAITI
PUERTO RICO (U.S.)
Mexico City
Veracruz
JAMAICA
CARIBBEAN SEA
BELIZE
GUATEMALA
HONDURAS
EL SALVADOR
NICARAGUA
VENEZUELA
COSTA RICA
PANAMA
COLOMBIA

N W E S

SCALE
0   250   500 Miles
0   250   500 Kilometers
Projection: Azimuthal Equal Area

PACIFIC OCEAN
Honolulu
HAWAII

SCALE
0   100   200 Miles
0   100   200 Kilometers
Projection: Albers Equal Area

A

abiotic (ay bie AHT ik) **factor** describes the non-living part of the environment, including water, rocks, light, and temperature (94)

factor abiótic un factor ambiental que no está asociado con las actividades de los seres vivos (94)

acid precipitation precipitation, such as rain, sleet, or snow, that contains a high concentration of acids, often because of the pollution of the atmosphere (314)

precipitación ácida precipitación tal como lluvia, aguanieve o nieve, que contiene una alta concentración de ácidos debido a la contaminación de la atmósfera (314)

acid shock the sudden runoff of large amounts of highly acidic water into lakes and streams when snow melts in the spring or when heavy rains follow a drought (316)

cambio brusco de la acidez entrada súbita de grandes cantidades de agua muy ácida a los lagos y arroyos cuando la nieve se derrite en la primavera o cuando llueve en abundancia después de una sequía (316)

active solar heating the gathering of solar energy by collectors that are used to heat water or heat a building (460)

calentamiento solar activo la recopilación de energía solar por medio de colectores que se usan para calentar agua o un edificio (460)

adaptation the process of becoming adapted to an environment; an anatomical, physiological, or behavioral change that improves a population's ability to survive (99)

adaptación el proceso de adaptarse a un ambiente; un cambio anatómico, fisiológico o en la conducta que mejora la capacidad de supervivencia de una población (99)

age structure the classification of members of a population into groups according to age or the distribution of members of a population in terms of age groups (220)

estructura de edades la clasificación en grupos de los miembros de una población en función de su edad, o bien, la distribución de los miembros de una población en función de grupos de edad (220)

agriculture the raising of crops and livestock for food or for other products that are useful to humans (10)

agricultura cultivar cosechas y criar ganado para usarlos como alimento o para producir productos útiles para los seres humanos (10)

air pollution the contamination of the atmosphere by the introduction of pollutants from human and natural sources (303)

contaminación del aire la contaminación de la atmósfera debido a la introducción de contaminantes provenientes de fuentes humanas y naturals (303)

alternative energy energy that does not come from fossil fuels and that is still in development (466)

energía alternativa energía que no proviene de los combustibles fósiles y que todavía se encuentra en desarrollo (466)

altitude the height of an object above a reference point, such as sea level or the Earth's surface (145)

altitud la altura de un objeto sobre un punto de referencia, tal como el nivel del mar o la superficie de la Tierra (145)

angiosperm (AN jee oh spuhrm) a flowering plant that produces seeds within a fruit (105)

angiosperma una planta que da flores y que produce semillas dentro de la fruta (105)

aquaculture (AK wuh kuhl chuhr) the raising of aquatic plants and animals for human use or consumption (396)

acuacultura el cultivo de plantas y animales acuáticos para uso o consumo humano (396)

aquifer a body of rock or sediment that stores groundwater and allows the flow of groundwater (273)

acuífero un cuerpo rocoso o sedimento que almacena agua subterránea y permite que fluya (273)

archaea prokaryotes (most of which are known to live in extreme environments) that are distiguished from other prokaryotes by differences in their genetics and in the makeup of their cell wall; members of the domain Archaea (singular, archaeon) (102)

arqueas procariotes (la mayoría de los cuales viven en ambientes extremos) que se distinguen de otros procariotes por diferencias genéticas y por la diferente composición de su pared celular; miembros del dominio Archaea (102)

artificial eutrophication a process that increases the amount of nutrients in a body of water through human activities, such as waste disposal and land drainage (288)

eutrificación artificial un proceso que aumenta la cantidad de nutrientes en una masa de agua debido a actividades humanas, tales como el desecho de residuos y el drenaje de la tierra (288)

artificial selection the selective breeding of organisms (by humans) for specific desirable characteristics (100)

selección artificial la reproducción selectiva de organismos (por los seres humanos) para obtener características específicas deseeables (100)

asbestos any of six silicate minerals that form bundles of minute fibers that are heat resistant, flexible, and durable (312)

asbesto cualquiera de seis minerales de silicato que forman montones de fibras diminutas que son resistentes al calor, flexibles y resistentes (312)

asthenosphere the solid, plastic layer of the mantle beneath the lithosphere; made of mantle rock that flows very slowly, which allows tectonic plates to move on top of it (61)

astenosfera la capa sólida y plástica del manto, que se encuentra debajo de la litosfera; está formada por roca del manto que fluye muy lentamente, lo cual permite que las placas tectónicas se muevan en su superficie (61)

atmosphere a mixture of gases that surrounds a planet, such as Earth (67)

atmósfera una mezcla de gases que rodea un planeta, tal como la Tierra (67)

B

bacteria extremely small, single-celled organisms that usually have a cell wall and reproduce by cell division (singular, *bacterium*) (102)

bacterias organismos extremadamente pequeños, unicelulares, que normalmente tienen pared celular y se reproducen por división celular (102)

barrier island a long ridge of sand or narrow island that lies parallel to the shore (182)

isla barrera un largo arrecife de arena o una isla angosta ubicada paralela a la costa (182)

benthic zone the bottom region of oceans and bodies of fresh water (174)

zona bentónica la región del fondo de los océanos y de las masas de agua dulce (174)

benthos organisms that live at the bottom of oceans or bodies of fresh water (173)

benthos organismos que viven en el fondo de los océanos o de las masas de agua dulce (173)

biodegradable capable of being broken down by biological processes, such as the action of bacteria (483)

biodegradable algo que puede ser descompuesto por medio de procesos biológicos, tales como la acción de las bacterias (483)

biodiversity the variety of organisms in a given area, the genetic variation within a population, the variety of species in a community, or the variety of communities in an ecosystem (15, 241)

biodiversidad la variedad de organismos que se encuentran en un área determinada, la variación genética dentro de una población, la variedad de especies en una comunidad o la variedad de comunidades en un ecosistema (15, 241)

Biodiversity Treaty an international agreement aimed at strengthening national control and preservation of biological resources; associated with the UN Conference on Environment and Development (UNCED or Earth summit) in 1992 (257)

Tratado de la Biodiversidad un acuerdo internacional cuyo objetivo es fortalecer el control y conservación nacional de los recursos biológicos; asociado con la Conferencia de las Naciones Unidas sobre el Medio Ambiente y el Desarrollo (UNCED o Cumbre de la Tierra) en 1992 (257)

biological pest control the use of certain organisms by humans to eliminate or control pests (391)

control biológico de plagas el uso de ciertos organismos por parte de los seres humanos para eliminar o controlar plagas (391)

biomagnification the accumulation of pollutants at successive levels of the food chain (292)

bioaumento la acumulación de contaminantes en niveles sucesivos de la cadena alimenticia (292)

biomass fuel plant material, manure, or any other organic matter that is used as an energy source (462)

combustible de biomasa material vegetal, abono o cualquier otra materia orgánica que se use como fuente de energía (462)

biome a large region characterized by a specific type of climate and certain types of plant and animal communities (143)

bioma una región extensa caracterizada por un tipo de clima específico y ciertos tipos de comunidades de plantas y animales (143)

biosphere the part of Earth where life exists (80)

biosfera la parte de la Tierra donde existe la vida (80)

biotic factor an environmental factor that is associated with or results from the activities of living organisms (94)

factor biótico un factor ambiental que está asociado con las actividades de los seres vivos o que resulta de ellas (94)

canopy the layers of treetops that shade the forest floor (148)

dosel vegetal las capas de las copas de los árboles que dan sombra al suelo del bosque (148)

carbon cycle the movement of carbon from the nonliving environment into living things and back (124)

ciclo del carbono el movimiento del carbono del ambiente sin vida a los seres vivos y de los seres vivos al ambiente (124)

carrying capacity the largest population that an environment can support at any given time (200)

capacidad de carga la población más grande que un ambiente puede sostener en cualquier momento dado (200)

cellular respiration the process by which cells produce energy from carbohydrates; atmospheric oxygen combines with glucose to form water and carbon dioxide (120)

respiración celular el proceso por medio del cual las células producen energía a partir de los carbohidratos; el oxígeno atmosférico se combina con la glucosa para formar agua y dióxido de carbono (120)

chaparral a type of vegetation that includes broad-leafed evergreen shrubs and that is located in areas with hot, dry summers and mild, wet winters (158)

chaparral un tipo de vegetación que incluye arbustos de hoja perenne y ancha, y que se ubica en áreas donde los veranos son calientes y secos y los inviernos son templados y húmedos (158)

chemical weathering the process by which rocks break down as a result of chemical reactions (66)

desgaste químico el proceso por medio del cual las rocas se fragmentan como resultado de reacciones químicas (66)

chlorofluorocarbons hydrocarbons in which some or all of the hydrogen atoms are replaced by chlorine and fluorine; used in coolants for refrigerators and air conditioners and in cleaning solvents; their use is restricted because they destroy ozone molecules in the stratosphere (abbreviation, CFCs) (335)

clorofluorocarbonos hidrocarburos en los que algunos o todos los átomos de hidrógeno son reemplazados por cloro y flúor; se usan en líquidos refrigerantes para refrigeradores y aires acondicionados y en solventes para limpieza; su uso está restringido porque destruyen las moléculas de ozono de la estratosfera (abreviatura: CFCs) (335)

climate the average weather conditions in an area over a long period of time (144, 327)

clima las condiciones promedio del tiempo en un área durante un largo período de tiempo (144, 327)

climax community a final, stable community in equilibrium with the environment (132)

comunidad clímax una comunidad final y estable, que está en equilibrio con el ambiente (132)

commensalism a relationship between two organisms in which one organism benefits and the other is unaffected (209)

comensalismo una relación entre dos organismos en la que uno se beneficia y el otro no es afectado (209)

community a group of various species that live in the same habitat and interact with each other (96)

comunidad un grupo de varias especies que viven en el mismo hábitat e interactúan unas con otras (96)

competition the relationship between two species (or individuals) in which both species (or individuals) attempt to use the same limited resource such that both are negatively affected by the relationship (204)

competencia la relación entre dos especies (o individuos) en la que ambas especies (o individuos) intentan usar el mismo recurso limitado, de modo que ambas resultan afectadas negativamente por la relación (204)

compost a mixture of decomposing organic matter, such as manure and rotting plants, that is used as fertilizer and soil conditioner (388, 490)

composta una mezcla de materia orgánica en descomposición, como por ejemplo, estiércol y plantas en estado de putrefacción, que se usa como fertilizante y acondicionador del suelo (388, 490)

conceptual model a verbal or graphical explanation for how a system works or is organized (43)

modelo conceptual una explicación verbal o gráfica acerca de cómo funciona o está organizado un sistema (43)

condensation the change of state from a gas to a liquid (73)

condensación el cambio de estado de gas a líquido (73)

conduction the transfer of energy as heat through a material (70)

conducción la transferencia de energía en forma de calor a través de un material (70)

consumer an organism that eats other organisms or organic matter instead of producing its own nutrients or obtaining nutrients from inorganic sources (118)

consumidor un organismo que se alimenta de otros organismos o de materia orgánica, en lugar de producir sus propios nutrientes o de obtenerlos de fuentes inorgánicas (118)

control group in an experiment, a group that serves as a standard of comparison with another group to which the control group is identical except for one factor (33)

grupo de control en un experimento, un grupo que sirve como estándar de comparación con otro grupo, al cual el grupo de control es idéntico excepto por un factor (33)

convection the movement of matter due to differences in density that are caused by temperature variations; can result in the transfer of energy as heat (70)

convección el movimiento de la materia debido a diferencias en la densidad que se producen por variaciones en la temperatura; puede resultar en la transferencia de energía en forma de calor (70)

coral reef a limestone ridge found in tropical climates and composed of coral fragments that are deposited around organic remains (183)

arrecife de coral una cumbre de piedra caliza ubicada en climas tropicales, formada por fragmentos de coral depositados alrededor de restos orgánicos (183)

core the central part of the Earth below the mantle; also the center of the sun (61)

núcleo la parte central de la Tierra, debajo del manto; *también,* el centro del Sol (61)

correlation the linear dependence between two variables (35)

correlación la dependencia linear entre dos variables (35)

crust the thin and solid outermost layer of the Earth above the mantle (60)

corteza la capa externa, delgada y sólida de la Tierra, que se encuentra sobre el manto (60)

dam a structure that is built across a river to control a river's flow (280)

presa una estructura que se construye a través de un río para controlar el flujo del río (280)

data any pieces of information acquired through observation or experimentation (34)

datos cualquier parte de la información que se adquiere por medio de la observación o experimentación (34)

decibel the most common unit used to measure loudness (abbreviation, dB) (312)

decibel la unidad más común que se usa para medir el volumen del sonido (abreviatura: dB) (312)

decision-making model a conceptual model that provides a systematic process for making decisions (45)

modelo de toma de decisiones un modelo conceptual que brinda un proceso sistemático para tomar decisiones (45)

decomposer an organism that feeds by breaking down organic matter from dead organisms; examples include bacteria and fungi (119)

descomponedor un organismo que desintegra la materia orgánica de organismos muertos y se alimenta de ella; entre los ejemplos se encuentran las bacterias y los hongos (119)

deep-well injection deep-well disposal of hazardous waste (496)

inyección a pozo profundo método de desecho de residuos peligrosos por inyección a pozo (496)

deforestation the process of clearing forests (366)

deforestación el proceso de talar bosques (366)

demographic transition the general pattern of demographic change from high birth and death rates to low birth and death rates, as observed in the history of more-developed countries (223)

transición demográfica el patrón general de cambio demográfico de tasas de nacimiento y mortalidad altas a tasas de nacimiento y mortalidad bajas, tal como se observa en la historia de los países más desarrollados (223)

demography the study of the characteristics of populations, especially human populations (219)

demografía el estudio de las características de las poblaciones, sobre todo las poblaciones humanas (219)

density the number of individuals of the same species that live in a given unit of area (198)

densidad el número de individuos de la misma especie que viven en una unidad superficial determinada (198)

desalination (DEE SAL uh NAY shuhn) a process of removing salt from ocean water (283)

desalación (o desalinización) un proceso de remoción de sal del agua del océano (283)

desert a region that has little or no vegetation, long periods without rain, and extreme temperatures; usually found in warm climates (160)

desierto una región con poca vegetación o sin vegetación, largos períodos sin lluvia y temperaturas extremas; generalmente se ubica en climas calientes (160)

desertification the process by which human activities or climatic changes make arid or semiarid areas more desertlike (386)

desertificación el proceso por medio del cual las actividades humanas o los cambios climáticos hacen que un área árida o semiárida se vuelva más parecida a un desierto (386)

diet the type and amount of food that a person eats (380)

dieta el tipo y cantidad de alimento que come una persona (380)

dispersion in ecology, the pattern of distribution of organisms in a population (198)

dispersión en ecología, el patrón de distribución de organismos en una población (198)

distribution the relative arrangement of the members of a statistical population; usually shown in a graph (39)

distribución la organización relativa de los miembros de una población estadística; normalmente se muestra en una gráfica (39)

domesticated describes organisms that have been bred and managed for human use (395)

domesticado término que describe a organismos que han sido reproducidos y criados para uso humano (395)

dose the amount of a harmful substance to which a person is exposed; the quantity of medicine that needs to be taken over a period of time (512)

dosis la cantidad de medicina que se necesita tomar durante un período de tiempo; *también*, la cantidad de una sustancia dañina a la que está expuesta una persona (512)

dose-response curve a graph that shows the relative effect of various doses of a drug or chemical on an organism or organisms (512)

curva de dosis-respuesta una gráfica que muestra el efecto relativo de varias dosis de un medicamento o substancia química en un organismo u organismos (512)

ecological footprint a calculation that shows the productive area of Earth needed to support one person in a particular country (19)

huella ecológica un cálculo que muestra el área productiva de la Tierra que se requiere para mantener a una persona en un cierto país (19)

ecological succession a gradual process of change and replacement in a community (129)

sucesión ecológica un proceso gradual de cambio y sustitución en una comunidad (129)

ecology the study of the interactions of living organisms with one another and with their environment (6)

ecología el estudio de las interacciones de los seres vivos entre sí mismos y entre sí mismos y su ambiente (6)

economics the study of how individuals and groups make decisions about the production, distribution, and consumption of limited resources as the individuals or groups attempt to fulfill their needs and wants (535)

economía el estudio de cómo los individuos y grupos toman decisiones acerca de la producción, distribución y consumo de recursos limitados, al mismo tiempo que estos individuos o grupos intentan satisfacer sus necesidades y deseos (535)

ecosystem a community of organisms and their abiotic environment (93)

ecosistema una comunidad de organismos y su ambiente abiótico (93)

ecosystem services the role that organisms play in creating a healthful environment for humans (357)

servicios del ecosistema el papel que juegan los organismos en la creación de un ambiente saludable para los seres humanos (357)

ecotourism a form of tourism that supports the conservation and sustainable development of ecologically unique areas (244)

ecoturismo una forma de turismo que apoya la conservación y desarrollo sustentable de áreas ecológicamente únicas (244)

electric generator a device that converts mechanical energy into electrical energy (436)

descarga eléctrica la liberación de electricidad almacenada en una fuente (436)

El Niño (el NEEN yoh) the warm phase of the El Niño–Southern Oscillation; a periodic occurrence in the eastern Pacific Ocean in which the surface-water temperature becomes unusually warm (332)

El Niño la fase caliente de la Oscilación Sureña "El Niño"; un fenómeno periódico que ocurre en el océano Pacífico oriental en el que la temperatura del agua superficial se vuelve más caliente que de costumbre (332)

emergent layer the top foliage layer in a forest where the trees extend above surrounding trees (148)

capa emergente la capa superior de follaje en un bosque, en la que los árboles se extienden sobre los árboles circundantes (148)

endangered species a species that has been identified to be in danger of extinction throughout all or a significant part of its range, and that is thus under protection by regulations or conservation measures (245)

especie en peligro de extinción una especie que se ha identificado como en peligro de extinción en toda su zona de distribución o en una parte importante de ella, y que, por lo tanto, se encuentra protegida por normas y medidas de conservación (245)

Endangered Species Act an act that the U.S. Congress passed in 1973 to protect any plant or animal species in danger of extinction (255)

Ley de Especies en Peligro de Extinción una ley que el Congreso de los Estados Unidos emitió en 1973 cuyo fin es proteger las especies de animales o plantas que están en peligro de extinguirse (255)

endemic species a species that is native to a particular place and that is found only there (248)

especie endémica una especie que es nativa de un lugar particular y que únicamente se encuentra allí (248)

energy conservation the process of saving energy by reducing energy use and waste (470)

conservación de energía el proceso de ahorrar energía al reducir el uso y el gasto inútil de energía (470)

energy efficiency the percentage of energy put into a system that does useful work (468)

eficiencia energética el porcentaje de energía que se pone en un sistema que realiza un trabajo útil (468)

Environmental Impact Statement an assessment of the effect of a proposed project or law on the environment (541)

Evaluación del Impacto Ambiental una evaluación del efecto que una propuesta de proyecto o ley tendrá en el ambiente (541)

environmental science the study of the air, water, and land surrounding an organism or a community, which ranges from a small area to Earth's entire biosphere; it includes the study of the impact of humans on the environment (5)

ciencias ambientales el estudio del aire, agua y tierra circundantes en relación con un organismo o comunidad, desde un área pequeña de la Tierra hasta la biosfera completa; incluye el estudio del impacto que los seres humanos tienen en el ambiente (5)

epidemiology (EP uh DEE me AHL uh jee) the study of the distribution of diseases in populations and the study of factors that influence the occurrence and spread of disease (513)

epidemiología el estudio de la distribución de las enfermedades en poblaciones y el estudio de los factores que influyen en la incidencia y propagación de las enfermedades (513)

epiphyte a plant that uses another plant for support, but not for nourishment (148)

epifita una planta que utiliza otra planta para sostenerse pero no para alimentarse (148)

erosion a process in which the materials of Earth's surface are loosened, dissolved, or worn away and transported from one place to another by a natural agent, such as wind, water, ice, or gravity (66, 386)

erosión un proceso por medio del cual los materiales de la superficie de la Tierra se aflojan, disuelven o desgastan y son transportados de un lugar a otro por un agente natural, como el viento, el agua, el hielo o la gravedad (66, 386)

estuary an area where fresh water from rivers mixes with salt water from the ocean; the part of a river where the tides meet the river current (179)

estuario un área donde el agua dulce de los ríos se mezcla con el agua salada del océano; la parte de un río donde las mareas se encuentran con la corriente del río (179)

eutrophication an increase in the amount of nutrients, such as nitrates, in a marine or aquatic ecosystem (175)

eutrofización un aumento en la cantidad de nutrientes, tales como nitratos, en un ecosistema marino o acuático (175)

evaporation the change of state from a liquid to a gas (73)

evaporación el cambio de estado de líquido a gas (73)

evolution a heritable change in the characteristics within a population from one generation to the next; the development of new types of organisms from preexisting types of organisms over time (97)

evolución un cambio hereditario en las características de una población que se produce de una generación a la siguiente; el desarrollo de nuevos tipos de organismos a partir de organismos preexistentes a lo largo del tiempo (97)

exotic species a species that is not native to a particular region (247)

especie exótica una especie que no es originaria de una región en particular (247)

experiment a procedure that is carried out under controlled conditions to discover, demonstrate, or test a fact, theory, or general truth (33)

experimento un procedimiento que se lleva a cabo bajo condiciones controladas para descubrir, demostrar o probar un hecho, teoría o verdad general (33)

experimental group in an experiment, a group that is identical to a control group except for one factor and that is compared with the control group (33)

grupo experimental en un experimento, un grupo que es idéntico al grupo de control, excepto por un factor, y que es comparado con el grupo de control (33)

exponential growth logarithmic growth, or growth in which numbers increase by a certain factor in each successive time period (199)

crecimiento exponencial crecimiento logarítmico o crecimiento en el que los números aumentan en función de un cierto factor en cada período de tiempo sucesivo (199)

famine widespread malnutrition and starvation in an area due to a shortage of food, usually caused by a catastrophic event (379)

hambruna desnutrición e inanición generalizadas en un área debido a una escasez de alimento, normalmente causada por un suceso catastrófico (379)

fertility rate the average number of children a woman of childbearing years would have in her lifetime, if she had children at the current rate for her country (221)

tasa de fertilidad el número promedio de hijos que una mujer en edad fértil tendría durante su vida si tuviese hijos de acuerdo con el índice vigente para su país (221)

food chain the pathway of energy transfer through various stages as a result of the feeding patterns of a series of organisms (122)

cadena alimenticia la vía de transferencia de energía través de varias etapas, que ocurre como resultado de los patrones de alimentación de una serie de organismos (122)

food web a diagram that shows the feeding relationships between organisms in an ecosystem (122)

red alimenticia un diagrama que muestra las relaciones de alimentación entre los organismos de un ecosistema (122)

fossil fuel a nonrenewable energy resource formed from the remains of organisms that lived long ago; examples include oil, coal, and natural gas (435)

combustible fósil un recurso energético no renovable formado a partir de los restos de organismos que vivieron hace mucho tiempo; algunos ejemplos incluyen el petróleo, el carbón y el gas natural (435)

fresh water water that contains insignificant amounts of salts, as in rivers and lakes (79)

agua dulce agua que contiene una cantidad insignificante de sales, como el agua de los ríos y lagos (79)

fuel cell a device that produces electricity chemically by combining hydrogen fuel with oxygen from the air (468)

pila de combustible un aparato que produce electricidad químicamente al combinar combustible de hidrógeno con oxígeno del aire (468)

fungus an organism whose cells have nuclei, rigid cell walls, and no chlorophyll and that belongs to the kingdom Fungi (103)

hongo un organismo que tiene células con núcleos y pared celular rígida, pero carece de clorofila, perteneciente al reino Fungi (103)

gene a segment of DNA that is located in a chromosome and that codes for a specific hereditary trait (242)

gene un segmento de ADN ubicado en un cromosoma, que codifica para un carácter hereditario específico (242)

genetic engineering a technology in which the genome of a living cell is modified for medical or industrial use (393)

ingeniería genética una tecnología en la que el genoma de una célula viva se modifica con fines médicos o industriales (393)

geographic information system an automated system for capturing, storing, retrieving, analyzing, manipulating, and displaying geographic data (abbreviation, GIS) (351)

sistema de información geográfica un sistema automatizado que sirve para capturar, almacenar, obtener, analizar, manipular y mostrar datos geográficos (abreviatura: SIG) (351)

geosphere the mostly solid, rocky part of Earth; extends from the center of the core to the surface of the crust (59)

geosfera la capa de la Tierra que es principalmente sólida y rocosa; se extiende desde el centro del núcleo hasta la superficie de la corteza terrestre (59)

geothermal energy the energy produced by heat within Earth (464)

energía geotérmica la energía producida por el calor del interior de la Tierra (464)

germ plasm hereditary material (chromosomes and genes) that is usually contained in the protoplasm of germ cells (253)

plasma germinal material hereditario (cromosomas y genes) que normalmente se encuentra contenido en el protoplasma de las células germinales (253)

global warming a gradual increase in average global temperature (341)

calentamiento global un aumento gradual de la temperatura global promedio (341)

greenhouse effect the warming of the surface and lower atmosphere of Earth that occurs when carbon dioxide, water vapor, and other gases in the air absorb and reradiate infrared radiation (72)

efecto de invernadero el calentamiento de la superficie terrestre y de la parte más baja de la atmósfera, el cual se produce cuando el dióxido de carbono, el vapor de agua y otros gases del aire absorben radiación infrarroja y la vuelven a irradiar (72)

greenhouse gas a gas composed of molecules that absorb and radiate infrared radiation from the sun (339)

gas de invernadero un gas compuesto de moléculas que absorben radiación infrarroja del Sol y la vuelven a irradiar (339)

groundwater the water that is beneath the Earth's surface (272)

agua subterránea el agua que está debajo de la superficie de la Tierra (272)

growth rate an expression of the increase in the size of an organism or population over a given period of time (198)

tasa de crecimiento una expresión del aumento en el tamaño de un organismo o población a lo largo de un cierto período de tiempo (198)

gymnosperm (JIM noh SPUHRM) a woody vascular seed plant whose seeds are not enclosed by an ovary or fruit (105)

gimnosperma una planta leñosa y vascular, la cual produce semillas que no están contenidas en un ovario o fruto (105)

habitat the place where an organism usually lives (96)

hábitat el lugar donde un organismo vive normalmente (96)

habitat conservation plan a land-use plan that attempts to protect threatened or endangered species across a given area by allowing some tradeoffs between harm to the species and additional conservation commitments among cooperating parties (255)

plan de conservación del hábitat un plan de uso de la tierra que tiene como objetivo proteger a las especies amenazadas o en peligro de extinción en un área determinada, permitiendo algunas compensaciones entre el daño a las especies y compromisos adicionales de conservación entre las partes en cooperación (255)

hazardous wastes wastes that are a risk to the health of humans or other living organisms (493)

residuos peligrosos residuos que son un riesgo para la salud de los seres humano y otros seres vivos (493)

heat island an area in which the air temperature is generally higher than the temperature of surrounding rural areas (360)

isla de calor un área en la que la temperatura del aire es generalmente más alta que la temperatura de las áreas rurales circundantes (360)

host an organism from which a parasite takes food or shelter (519)

huésped el organismo del cual un parásito obtiene alimento y refugio (519)

hydroelectric energy electrical energy produced by the flow of water (463)

energía hidroeléctrica energía eléctrica producida por el flujo del agua (463)

hydrosphere the portion of Earth that is water (59)

hidrosfera la porción de la Tierra que es agua (59)

hypothesis (hie PATH uh sis) a testable idea or explanation that leads to scientific investigation (32)

hipótesis una idea o explicación que conlleva a la investigación científica y que se puede probar (32)

infrastructure the basic facilities of a country or region, such as roads, bridges, and sewers (225, 359)

infraestructura los servicios básicos de un país o región, tales como caminos, puentes y drenaje (225, 359)

invertebrate (in VUHR tuh brit) an animal that does not have a backbone (106)

invertebrado un animal que no tiene columna vertebral (106)

keystone species a species that is critical to the functioning of the ecosystem in which it lives because it affects the survival and abundance of many other species in its community (242)

especie clave una especie que es crítica para el funcionamiento del ecosistema en el que vive porque afecta la supervivencia y abundancia de muchas otras especies en su comunidad (242)

Kyoto Protocol an international treaty according to which developed countries that signed the treaty agree to reduce their emissions of carbon dioxide and other gases that may contribute to global warming by 2012 (345)

Protocolo de Kyoto un tratado internacional en función del cual los países desarrollados que lo firmaron acceden a reducir sus emisiones de dióxido de carbono y otros gases que pueden contribuir al calentamiento global para el año 2012 (345)

landfill an area of land or an excavation where wastes are placed for permanent disposal (485)

entierro de residuos un área de terreno o una excavación donde se colocan los residuos para deshacerse de ellos permanentemente (485)

land-use planning a set of policies and activities related to potential uses of land that is put in place before an area is developed (361)

planeación del uso de tierras un conjunto de políticas y actividades relacionadas con los usos potenciales de la tierra, que se establecen antes de desarrollar un área (361)

La Niña (lah NEEN yah) the cool phase of the El Niño–Southern Oscillation; a periodic occurrence in the eastern Pacific Ocean in which the surface-water temperature becomes unusually cool (332)

La Niña la fase fría de la Oscilación Sureña "El Niño"; un fenómeno periódico que ocurre en el océano Pacífico oriental en el que la temperatura del agua superficial se vuelve más fría que de costumbre (332)

latitude the distance north or south from the equator; expressed in degrees (145, 328)

latitud la distancia hacia el norte o hacia el sur del ecuador; se expresa en grados (145, 328)

law of supply and demand a law of economics that states that as the demand for a good or service increases, the value of the good or service also increases (17)

ley de la oferta y la demanda una ley de economía que establece que al aumentar la demanda de un bien o servicio, el valor del bien o servicio también aumenta (17)

leachate a liquid that has passed through solid waste and has extracted dissolved or suspended materials from that waste, such as pesticides in the soil (485)

lechado un líquido que ha pasado a través de desechos sólidos y ha extraído materiales disueltos o suspendidos de los desechos, como por ejemplo, pesticidas en el suelo (485)

least developed countries countries that have been identified by the United Nations as showing the fewest signs of development in terms of income, human resources, and economic diversification (228)

países menos desarrollados países que la Organización de las Naciones Unidas ha identificado como los que muestran las menores señales de desarrollo en términos de ingresos, recursos humanos y diversificación económica (228)

life expectancy the average length of time that an individual is expected to live (222)

esperanza de vida la longitud promedio de tiempo que se espera que un individuo viva (222)

lithosphere the solid, outer layer of the Earth that consists of the crust and the rigid upper part of the mantle (61)

litosfera la capa externa y sólida de la Tierra que está formada por la corteza y la parte superior y rígida del manto (61)

littoral zone a shallow zone in a freshwater habitat where light reaches the bottom and nurtures plants (174)

zona litoral una zona poco profunda del hábitat de agua dulce donde la luz llega al fondo y nutre a las plantas (174)

livestock domesticated animals that are raised to be used on a farm or ranch or to be sold for profit (398)

animales de cría animales domesticados que se crían para usarse en una granja o rancho o para ser vendidos con el fin de obtener una ganancia (398)

lobbying an attempt to influence the decisions of lawmakers (543)

cabildeo un intento de ejercer una influencia en las decisiones de los legisladores (543)

malnutrition a disorder of nutrition that results when a person does not consume enough of each of the nutrients that are needed by the human body (379)

desnutrición un trastorno de nutrición que resulta cuando una persona no consume una cantidad suficiente de cada nutriente que el cuerpo humano necesita (379)

mangrove swamp a tropical or subtropical marine swamp that is characterized by the abundance of low to tall trees, especially mangrove trees (182)

manglar un pantano marino tropical o subtropical que se caracteriza por la abundancia de árboles bajos a altos, especialmente árboles de mangle (182)

mantle in Earth science, the layer of rock between the Earth's crust and core (61)

manto en las ciencias de la Tierra, la capa de roca que se encuentra entre la corteza terrestre y el núcleo (61)

mathematical model one or more equations that represent the way a system or process works (44)

modelo matemático una o más ecuaciones que representan la forma en que funciona un sistema o proceso (44)

mean the number obtained by adding up the data for a given characteristic and dividing this sum by the number of individuals (39)

media el número que se obtiene al sumar los datos de una característica determinada y dividir esta suma entre el número de individuos (39)

migration in general, any movement of individuals or populations from one location to another; specifically, a periodic group movement that is characteristic of a given population or species (221)

migración en general, cualquier movimiento de individuos o poblaciones de un lugar a otro; específicamente, un movimiento periódico en grupo que es característico de una población o especie determinada (221)

mineral a natural, usually inorganic solid that has a characteristic chemical composition, an orderly internal structure, and a characteristic set of physical properties (411)

mineral un sólido natural, normalmente inorgánico, que tiene una composición química característica, una estructura interna ordenada y propiedades físicas y químicas características (411)

model a pattern, plan, representation, or description designed to show the structure or workings of an object, system, or concept (42)

modelo un diseño, plan, representación o descripción cuyo objetivo es mostrar la estructura o funcionamiento de un objeto, sistema o concepto (42)

municipal solid waste waste produced by households and businesses (484)

desechos sólidos municipales desechos producidos por las casas y negocios (484)

mutualism a relationship between two species in which both species benefit (208)

mutualismo una relación entre dos especies en la que ambas se benefician (208)

natural resource any natural material that is used by humans, such as water, petroleum, minerals, forests, and animals (14)

recurso natural cualquier material natural que es utilizado por los seres humanos, como agua, petróleo, minerales, bosques y animales (14)

natural selection the process by which individuals that are better adapted to their environment survive and reproduce more successfully than less well adapted individuals do; a theory to explain the mechanism of evolution (97)

selección natural el proceso por medio del cual los individuos que están mejor adaptados a su ambiente sobreviven y se reproducen con más éxito que los individuos menos adaptados; una teoría que explica el mecanismo de la evolución (97)

nekton all organisms that swim actively in open water, independent of currents (173)

necton todos los organismos que nadan activamente en las aguas abiertas, de manera independiente de las corrientes (173)

niche (NICH) the unique position occupied by a species, both in terms of its physical use of its habitat and its function within an ecological community (203)

nicho la posición única que ocupa una especie, tanto en lo que se refiere al uso de su hábitat como en cuanto a su función dentro de una comunidad ecológica (203)

nitrogen cycle the process in which nitrogen circulates among the air, soil, water, plants, and animals in an ecosystem (126)

ciclo del nitrógeno el proceso por medio del cual el nitrógeno circula en el aire, suelo, agua, plantas y animales de un ecosistema (126)

nitrogen-fixing bacteria bacteria that convert atmospheric nitrogen into ammonia (126)

bacterias fijadoras de nitrógeno bacterias que transforman el nitrógeno atmosférico en amoniaco (126)

nonpoint-source pollution pollution that comes from many sources rather than from a single specific site; an example is pollution that reaches a body of water from streets and storm sewers (285)

contaminación no puntual contaminación que proviene de muchas fuentes, en lugar de provenir de un solo sitio específico; un ejemplo es la contaminación que llega a una masa de agua a partir de las calles y los drenajes (285)

nuclear energy the energy released by a fission or fusion reaction; the binding energy of the atomic nucleus (444)

energía nuclear la energía liberada por una reacción de fisión o fusión; la energía de enlace del núcleo atómico (444)

nuclear fission the process by which the nucleus of a heavy atom splits into two or more fragments; the process releases neutrons and energy (444)

fisión nuclear el proceso por medio del cual el núcleo de un átomo pesado se divide en dos o más fragmentos; el proceso libera neutrones y energía (444)

nuclear fusion the process by which nuclei of small atoms combine to form a new, more massive nucleus; the process releases energy (447)

fusión nuclear el proceso por medio del cual los núcleos de átomos pequeños se combinan y forman un núcleo nuevo con mayor masa; el proceso libera energía (447)

observation the process of obtaining information by using the senses; the information obtained by using the senses (31)

observación el proceso de obtener información por medio de los sentidos; la información que se obtiene al usar los sentidos (31)

ocean thermal energy conversion the use of temperature differences in ocean water to produce electricity (abbreviation, OTEC) (467)

conversión de la energía térmica del océano el uso de diferencias en la temperatura del agua del océano para producir electricidad (abreviatura: OTEC, por sus siglas en inglés) (467)

oil reserves oil deposits that are discovered and are in commercial production (442)

reservas de petróleo depósitos de petróleo que son descubiertos y se encuentran en producción comercial (442)

ore mineral a mineral that contains one or more elements of economic value (412)

mineral metalífero un mineral que contiene uno o más elementos de valor económico (412)

organism a living thing; anything that can carry out life processes independently (95)

organismo un ser vivo; cualquier cosa que pueda llevar a cabo procesos vitales independientemente (95)

overgrazing the depletion of vegetation due to the continuous feeding of too many animals (364)

sobrepastoreo el agotamiento de la vegetación debido a la alimentación continua de demasiados animales (364)

overharvesting catching or removing from a population more organisms than the population can replace (395)

sobrecosechar capturar o sustraer de una población más organismos de los que la población puede reemplazar (395)

ozone a gas molecule that is made up of three oxygen atoms (69)

ozono una molécula de gas que está formada por tres átomos de oxígeno (69)

ozone hole a thinning of stratospheric ozone that occurs over the poles during the spring (336)

agujero en la capa de ozono un adelgazamiento del ozono estratosférico, el cual occure encima de los Polos durante la primavera (336)

ozone layer the layer of the atmosphere at an altitude of 15 to 40 km in which ozone absorbs ultraviolet solar radiation (335)

capa de ozono la capa de la atmó-sfera ubicada a una altitud de 15 a 40 km, en la cual el ozono absorbe la radiación solar (335)

parasitism a relationship between two species in which one species, the parasite, benefits from the other species, the host, which is harmed (208)

parasitismo una relación entre dos especies en la que una, el parásito, se beneficia de la otra, el huésped, que resulta perjudicada (208)

particulates (pahr TIHK yoo lihts) fine particles that are suspended in the atmosphere and that are associated with air pollution (514)

materia particulada partículas finas que se encuentran suspendidas en la atmósfera y que están relacionadas con la contaminación del aire (514)

passive solar heating the use of sunlight to heat buildings directly (458)

calentamiento solar pasivo el uso de la luz solar para calentar edificios directamente (458)

pathogen a microorganism, another organism, a virus, or a protein that causes disease; an infectious agent (277, 519)

patógeno un microorganismo, otro organismo, un virus o una proteína que causa enfermedades; un agente infeccioso (277, 519)

permafrost in arctic regions, the permanently frozen layer of soil or subsoil (162)

permafrost en las regiones árticas, la capa de suelo o subsuelo que se encuentra congelada permanentemente (162)

permeability the ability of a rock or sediment to let fluids pass through its open spaces or pores (273)

permeabilidad la capacidad de una roca o sedimento de permitir que los fluidos pasen a través de sus espacios abiertos o poros (273)

pesticide a poison used to destroy pests, such as insects, rodents, or weeds; examples include insecticides, rodenticides, and herbicides (389)

pesticida un veneno que se usa para destruir plagas, tales como insectos, roedores o maleza; entre los ejemplos se encuentran los insecticidas, rodenticidas y herbicidas (389)

petroleum a liquid mixture of complex hydrocarbon compounds; used widely as a fuel source (440)

petróleo una mezcla líquida de compuestos hidrocarburos complejos; se usa ampliamente como una fuente de combustible (440)

pH a value that is used to express the acidity or alkalinity (basicity) of a system; each whole number on the scale indicates a tenfold change in acidity; a pH of 7 is neutral, a pH of less than 7 is acidic, and a pH of greater than 7 is basic (314)

pH un valor que expresa la acidez o la alcalinidad (basicidad) de un sistema; cada número entero de la escala indica un cambio de 10 veces en la acidez; un pH de 7 es neutro, un pH de menos de 7 es ácido y un pH de más de 7 es básico (314)

phosphorus cycle the cyclic movement of phosphorus in different chemical forms from the environment to organisms and then back to the environment (127)

ciclo del fósforo el movimiento cíclico del fósforo en diferentes formas químicas del ambiente a los organismos y de regreso al ambiente (127)

photosynthesis the process by which plants, algae, and some bacteria use sunlight, carbon dioxide, and water to produce carbohydrates and oxygen (117)

fotosíntesis el proceso por medio del cual las plantas, algas y algunas bacterias utilizan la luz solar, dióxido de carbono y agua para producir carbohidratos y oxígeno (117)

pioneer species a species that colonizes an uninhabited area and that starts an ecological cycle in which many other species become established (130)

especie pionera una especie que coloniza un área deshabitada y empieza un ciclo ecológico en el cual se establecen muchas otras especies (130)

placer deposit a deposit that contains a valuable mineral that has been concentrated by mechanical action (419)

yacimiento de aluvión un yacimiento que contiene un mineral valioso que se ha concentrado debido a la acción mecánica (419)

plankton the mass of mostly microscopic organisms that float or drift freely in the waters of aquatic (freshwater and marine) environments (173)

plancton la masa de organismos casi microscópicos que flotan o se encuentran a la deriva en aguas (dulces y marinas) de ambientes acuáticos (173)

poaching the illegal harvesting of fish, game, or other species (247)

caza furtiva la cosecha ilegal de peces, presas u otras especies (247)

point-source pollution pollution that comes from a specific site (284)

contaminación puntual contaminación que proviene de un lugar específico (284)

polar stratospheric cloud a cloud that forms at altitudes of about 21,000 m during the Arctic and Antarctic winter or early spring, when air temperatures drop below −80°C (336)

nube polar estrato-sférica una nube que se forma en altitudes de aproximadamente 21,000 m durante el invierno ártico y antártico o al principio de la primavera, cuando la temperatura del aire disminuye a menos de −80°C (336)

pollution an undesirable change in the natural environment that is caused by the introduction of substances that are harmful to living organisms or by excessive wastes, heat, noise, or radiation (14)

contaminación un cambio indeseable en el ambiente natural, producido por la introducción de substancias que son dañinas para los organismos vivos o por desechos, calor, ruido o radiación excesivos (14)

population a group of organisms of the same species that live in a specific geographical area and interbreed (95, 197)

población un grupo de organismos de la misma especie que viven en un área geográfica específica y se reproducen entre sí (95, 197)

porosity the percentage of the total volume of a rock or sediment that consists of open spaces (273)

porosidad el porcentaje del volumen total de una roca o sedimento que está formado por espacios abiertos (273)

potable suitable for drinking (277)

potable que puede beberse (277)

precipitation any form of water that falls to the Earth's surface from the clouds; includes rain, snow, sleet, and hail (73)

precipitación cualquier forma de agua que cae de las nubes a la superficie de la Tierra; incluye a la lluvia, nieve, aguanieve y granizo (73)

predation an interaction between two organisms in which one organism, the predator, kills and feeds on the other organism, the prey (206)

depredación la interacción entre dos organismos en la que un organismo, el depredador, mata a otro organismo, la presa, y se alimenta de él (206)

prediction a statement made in advance that expresses the results that will be obtained from testing a hypothesis if the hypothesis is supported; the expected outcome if a hypothesis is accurate (32)

predicción una afirmación que se hace por anticipado, la cual expresa los resultados que se obtendrán al poner a prueba una hipótesis si ésta es corroborada; el resultado esperado si la hipótesis es correcta (32)

primary pollutant a pollutant that is put directly into the atmosphere by human or natural activity (303)

contaminante primario un contaminante que es colocado directamente en la atmósfera por las actividades humanas o naturales (303)

primary succession succession that begins in an area that previously did not support life (129)

sucesión primaria sucesión que comienza en un área donde previamente no podía existir la vida (129)

probability the likelihood that a possible future event will occur in any given instance of the event; the mathematical ratio of the number of times one outcome of any event is likely to occur to the number of possible outcomes of the event (40)

probabilidad termino que describe qué tan probable es que ocurra un posible evento futuro en un caso dado del evento; la proporción matemática del número de veces que es posible que ocurra un resultado de cualquier evento respecto al número de resultados posibles del evento (40)

producer an organism that can make organic molecules from inorganic molecules; a photosynthetic or chemosynthetic autotroph that serves as the basic food source in an ecosystem (118)

productor un organismo que elabora moléculas orgánicas a partir de moléculas inorgánicas; un autótrofo fotosintético o quimiosintético que funciona como la fuente fundamental de alimento en un ecosistema (118)

protist an organism that belongs to the kingdom Protista (104)

protista un organismo que pertenece al reino Protista (104)

radiation the energy that is transferred as electromagnetic waves, such as visible light and infrared waves (70)

radiación la energía que se transfiere en forma de ondas electromagnéticas, tales como las ondas de luz y las infrarrojas (70)

recharge zone an area in which water travels downward to become part of an aquifer (274)

zona de recarga un área en la que el agua se desplaza hacia abajo para convertirse en parte de un acuífero (274)

reclamation the process of returning land to its original condition after mining is completed (424)

restauración el proceso de hacer que la tierra vuelva a su condición original después de que se terminan las actividades de explotación minera (424)

recycling the process of recovering valuable or useful materials from waste or scrap; the process of reusing some items (489)

reciclar el proceso de recuperar materiales valiosos o útiles de los desechos o de la basura; el proceso de reutilizar algunas cosas (489)

reforestation the reestablishment and development of trees in a forest land (367)

reforestación el restablecimiento y desarrollo de los árboles en un bosque (367)

renewable energy energy from sources that are constantly being formed (457)

energía renovable energía que proviene de fuentes que se están formando constantemente (457)

reproductive potential the maximum number of offspring that a given organism can produce (199)

potencial reproductivo el número máximo de crías que puede producir un determinado organismo (199)

reservoir an artificial body of water that usually forms behind a dam (280)

represa una masa artificial de agua que normalmente se forma detrás de una presa (280)

resistance in biology, the ability of an organism to tolerate a chemical or disease-causing agent (101)

resistencia en biología, la capacidad de un organismo de tolerar a un agente químico o causante de enfermedades (101)

risk the probability of an unwanted outcome (41)

riesgo la probabilidad de que se produzca un resultado no deseado (41)

risk assessment the scientific assessment, study, and management of risk; a scientific estimation of the likelihood of negative effects that may result from exposure to a specific hazard (513)

evaluación de riesgos la evaluación, estudio y administración del riesgo por medios científicos; un cálculo científico de la probabilidad de que ocurran efectos negativos debido a la exposición a un peligro específico (513)

river system a flowing network of rivers and streams draining a river basin (271)

sistema fluvial una red de ríos y arroyos en flujo que drenan una cuenca fluvial (271)

ruminant (ROO muh nuhnt) a cud-chewing mammal that has a three- or four-chambered stomach; examples include sheep, goats, and cattle (398)

rumiante un mamífero que mastica los alimentos dos veces, el cual tiene un estómago con tres o cuatro cámaras; entre los ejemplos se encuentran los borregos, cabras y ganado (398)

rural describes an area of open land that is often used for farming (355)

rural término que describe un área de tierra abierta que a menudo se usa para la labranza (355)

salinity a measure of the amount of dissolved salts in a given amount of liquid (76)

salinidad una medida de la cantidad de sales disueltas en una cantidad determinada de líquido (76)

salinization (SAL uh nie ZAY shuhn) the accumulation of salts in soil (388)

salinización la acumulación de sales en el suelo (388)

salt marsh a maritime habitat characterized by grasses, sedges, and other plants that have adapted to continual, periodic flooding; salt marshes are found primarily throughout the temperate and subarctic regions (182)

marisma un hábitat marino que se caracteriza por tener pasto, juncias y otras plantas que se han adaptado a la inundación continua y periódica; las marismas se encuentran principalmente en las regiones templadas y subárticas (182)

sample the group of individuals or events selected to represent a statistical population (40)

muestra el grupo de individuos o sucesos que se seleccionan para representar a una población estadística (40)

savanna a plain full of grasses and scattered trees and shrubs; found in tropical and subtropical habitats and mainly in regions with a dry climate, such as East Africa (155)

sabana una planicie llena de pastizales y árboles y arbustos dispersos; se encuentra en los hábitats tropicales y subtropicales y, sobre todo, en regiones con un clima seco, como en el este de África (155)

secondary pollutant a pollutant that forms in the atmosphere by chemical reaction with primary air pollutants, natural components in the air, or both (303)

contaminante secundario un contaminante que se forma en la atmósfera por medio de una reacción química con contaminantes primarios del aire, componentes naturales del aire o ambos (303)

secondary succession the process by which one community replaces another community that has been partially or totally destroyed (129)

sucesión secundaria el proceso por medio del cual una comunidad reemplaza a otra, la cual ha sido parcial o totalmente destruida (129)

sick-building syndrome a set of symptoms, such as headache, fatigue, eye irritation, and dizziness, that may affect workers in modern, airtight office buildings; believed to be caused by indoor pollutants (310)

síndrome del edificio enfermo un conjunto de síntomas, como dolor de cabeza, fatiga, irritación de los ojos y mareo, que puede afectar a las personas que trabajan en edificios modernos que cuentan con ventanas selladas; se cree que es producido por los contaminantes del interior del edificio (310)

smelting the melting or fusing of ore in order to separate impurities from pure metal (420)

fundir derretir una mena con el fin de separar las impurezas del metal puro (420)

smog urban air pollution composed of a mixture of smoke and fog produced from industrial pollutants and burning fuels (308)

esmog contaminación urbana del aire, compuesta por una mezcla de humo y niebla producida por contaminantes industriales y combustibles (308)

solid waste a discarded solid material, such as garbage, refuse, or sludges (481)

desechos sólidos un material sólido desechado, como por ejemplo, basura, residuos o sedimentos (481)

source reduction any change in the design, manufacture, purchase, or use of materials or products to reduce their amount or toxicity before they become municipal solid waste; also the reuse of products or materials (488)

reducción de la fuente cualquier cambio en el diseño, manufactura, compra o uso de materiales o productos para reducir su cantidad o toxicidad antes de que se conviertan en desechos sólidos municipales; también, la reutilización de productos o materiales (488)

species a group of organisms that are closely related and can mate to produce fertile offspring; also the level of classification below genus and above subspecies (95)

especie un grupo de organismos que tienen un parentesco cercano y que pueden aparearse para producir descendencia fértil; *también,* el nivel de clasificación debajo de género y arriba de subespecie (95)

statistics the collection and classification of data that are in the form of numbers (38)

estadística la recolección y clasificación de datos que encuentran en forma de números (38)

stratosphere the layer of the atmosphere that lies between the troposphere and the mesosphere and in which temperature increases as altitude increases; contains the ozone layer (69)

estratosfera la capa de la atmósfera que se encuentra entre la troposfera y la mesosfera y en la cual la temperatura aumenta al aumentar la altitud; contiene la capa de ozono (69)

subsidence the sinking of regions of the ground surface with little or no horizontal movement (423)

hundimiento del terreno el hundimiento de regiones de la superficie del suelo con muy poco o sin ningún movimiento horizontal (423)

subsurface mining a mining method in which ore is extracted from beneath the ground surface (416)

minería subsuperficial un método de explotación de minas en el que la mena se extrae de la parte inferior de la superficie del suelo (416)

surface impoundment a natural depression or a human-made excavation that serves as a disposal facility that holds an accumulation of wastes (496)

separación superficial una depresión natural o una excavación hecha por el hombre que sirve como vertedero de basura para acumular desechos (496)

surface mining a mining method in which soil and rocks are removed to reach underlying coal or minerals (417)

minería superficial un método de explotación de minas en el que se remueven el suelo y las rocas para llegar al carbón o minerales subyacentes (417)

surface water all the bodies of fresh water, salt water, ice, and snow that are found above the ground (270)

  agua superficial todas las masas de agua dulce, agua salada, hielo y nieve que se encuentran arriba del suelo (270)

survivorship the percentage of newborn individuals in a population that can be expected to survive to a given age (220)

  supervivencia el porcentaje de individuos recién nacidos de una población que se espera que sobrevivan hasta una edad determinada (220)

sustainability the condition in which human needs are met in such a way that a human population can survive indefinitely (21, 533)

  sustentabilidad la condición en la que se cumple con las necesidades humanas de una forma tal que una población humana pueda sobrevivir indefinidamente (21, 533)

symbiosis a relationship in which two different organisms live in close association with each other (209)

  simbiosis una relación en la que dos organismos diferentes viven estrechamente asociados uno con el otro (209)

taiga a region of evergreen, coniferous forest below the arctic and subarctic tundra regions (153)

  taiga una región de bosques siempreverdes de coníferas, ubicado debajo de las regiones árticas y subárticas de tundra (153)

tectonic plate a block of lithosphere that consists of the crust and the rigid, outermost part of the mantle; also called lithospheric plate (62)

  placa tectónica un bloque de litosfera formado por la corteza y la parte rígida y más externa del manto; también se llama placa litosférica (62)

temperate deciduous forest a forest (or biome) that is characterized by trees that shed their leaves in the fall (152)

  bosque caducifolio templado un bosque (o bioma) que se caracteriza por árboles a los que se les caen las hojas en el otoño (152)

temperate grassland a community (or biome) that is dominated by grasses, has few trees, and is characterized by cold winters and rainfall that is intermediate between that of a forest and a desert (156)

  pradera templada una comunidad (o bioma) que está dominada por pastos, tiene pocos árboles y se caracteriza por inviernos fríos y precipitación pluvial que es intermedia entre la de un bosque y la de un desierto (156)

temperate rain forest a forest community (or biome), characterized by cool, humid weather and abundant rainfall, where tree branches are draped with mosses, tree trunks are covered with lichens, and the forest floor is covered with ferns (151)

  selva tropical templada una comunidad de bosque (o bioma) caracterizada por tiempo frío y húmedo y lluvia en abundancia, en la cual las ramas de los árboles están cubiertas por moho, los troncos de los árboles están cubiertos por líquenes y el suelo del bosque está cubierto por helechos (151)

temperature inversion the atmospheric condition in which warm air traps cooler air near Earth's surface (308)

  inversión de la temperatura la condición atmosférica en la que el aire caliente retiene al aire frío cerca de la superficie terrestre (308)

thermal pollution a temperature increase in a body of water that is caused by human activity and that has a harmful effect on water quality and on the ability of that body of water to support life (289)

contaminación térmica un aumento en la temperatura de una masa de agua, producido por las actividades humanas y que tiene un efecto dañino en la calidad del agua y en la capacidad de esa masa de agua para permitir que se desarrolle la vida (289)

threatened species a species that has been identified to be likely to become endangered in the foreseeable future (245)

especie amenazada una especie que se ha identificado como candidata para estar en peligro de extinción en el futuro inmediato (245)

topsoil the surface layer of the soil, which is usually richer in organic matter than the subsoil is (385)

capa superior del suelo la capa superficial del suelo, la cual normalmente es más rica en materia orgánica que el subsuelo (385)

toxicology the study of toxic substances, including their nature, effects, detection, methods of treatment, and exposure control (512)

toxicología el estudio de las substancias tóxicas, incluyendo su naturaleza, efectos, detección, métodos de tratamiento y control de exposición (512)

trophic level one of the steps in a food chain or food pyramid; examples include producers and primary, secondary, and tertiary consumers (122)

nivel trófico uno de los pasos de la cadena alimenticia o de la pirámide alimenticia; entre los ejemplos se encuentran los productores y los consumidores primarios, secundarios y terciarios (122)

tropical rain forest a forest or jungle near the equator that is characterized by large amounts of rain and little variation in temperature and that contains the greatest known diversity of organisms on Earth (146)

selva tropical un bosque o jungla que se encuentra cerca del ecuador y se caracteriza por una gran cantidad de lluvia y poca variación en la temperatura, y que contiene la mayor diversidad de organismos que se conoce en la Tierra (146)

troposphere the lowest layer of the atmosphere, in which temperature drops at a constant rate as altitude increases; the part of the atmosphere where weather conditions exist (68)

troposfera la capa inferior de la atmósfera, en la que la temperatura disminuye a una tasa constante a medida que la altitud aumenta; la parte de la atmósfera donde se dan las condiciones del tiempo (68)

tundra a treeless plain that is located in the Arctic or Antarctic and that is characterized by very low winter temperatures; short, cool summers; and vegetation that consists of grasses, lichens, and perennial herbs (162)

tundra un llano sin árboles que se ubica en la región ártica o antártica y se caracteriza por temperaturas muy bajas en el invierno, veranos cortos y frescos y vegetación que consiste en pasto, líquenes y hierbas perennes (162)

U

understory a foliage layer that is beneath and shaded by the main canopy of a forest (148)

capa sumergida una capa de follaje que se encuentra debajo de la bóveda principal de un bosque y está cubierta por ella (148)

urban describes an area that contains a city (355)

urbana término que describe a un área que contiene una ciudad (355)

urbanization an increase in the ratio or density of people living in urban areas rather than in rural areas (227, 358)

urbanización un aumento en la razón o densidad de las personas que viven en áreas urbanas en lugar de en áreas rurales (227, 358)

urban sprawl the rapid spread of a city into adjoining suburbs and rural areas (359)

derrame urbano la rápida propagación de una ciudad hacia los suburbios adjuntos y áreas rurales (359)

value a principle or standard that an individual considers to be important (45)

valor un principio o norma que un individuo considera importante (45)

variable (VER ee uh buhl) a factor that changes in an experiment in order to test a hypothesis (33)

variable un factor que se modifica en un experimento con el fin de probar una hipótesis (33)

vector in biology, any agent, such as a plasmid or a virus, that can incorporate foreign DNA and transfer that DNA from one organism to another; an intermediate host that transfers a pathogen or a parasite to another organism (520)

vector en biología, cualquier agente, como por ejemplo un plásmido o un virus, que tiene la capacidad de incorporar ADN extraño y de transferir ese ADN de un organismo a otro; un huésped intermediario que transfiere un organismo patógeno o un parásito a otro organismo (520)

vertebrate an animal that has a backbone; includes mammals, birds, reptiles, amphibians, and fish (107)

vertebrado un animal que tiene columna vertebral; incluye a los mamíferos, aves, reptiles, anfibios y peces (107)

wastewater water that contains wastes from homes or industry (286)

agua de desecho agua que contiene desechos de los hogares o la industria (286)

water cycle the continuous movement of water between the atmosphere, the land, and the oceans (73)

ciclo del agua el movimiento continuo del agua entre la atmósfera, la tierra y los océanos (73)

water pollution contamination of water by waste matter or other material that is harmful to organisms that are exposed to the water (284)

contaminación del agua contaminación del agua con materiales de desecho u otros materiales que dañan a los organismos que están expuestos al agua (284)

watershed the area of land that is drained by a water system (271)

cuenca hidrográfica el área del terreno que es drenada por un sistema de agua (271)

wetland an area of land that is periodically underwater or whose soil contains a great deal of moisture (173)

pantano un área de tierra que está periódicamente bajo el agua o cuyo suelo contiene una gran cantidad de humedad (173)

wilderness a region that is not cultivated and that is not inhabited by humans (368)

área silvestre una región que no ha sido cultivada ni está habitada por seres humanos (368)

yield the amount of crops produced per unit area (381)

rendimiento la cantidad de cosechas producidas por unidad de área (381)

Note: Page references followed by *f* refer to figures.

A

abiotic factors, 94, 94*f*

acid, R25

acidification, 315, 347

acid mine drainage (AMD), 422, 422*f*

acid precipitation, 314–317
aquatic ecosystems and, 316, 316*f*
causes of, 314–315, 314*f*, 315*f*, 324–325, 439
human health and, 316
international effects of, 316–317, 317*f*
soil and plant impacts, 315, 315*f*

acid shock, 316

acquired immune deficiency syndrome (AIDS), 519, 522

active solar heating, 460, 460*f. See also* **solar energy**

activism, 257, 257*f*

adaptation
in aquatic ecosystems, 174
to competition, 205
natural selection and, 97, 99–100, 99*f*, 100*f*, 105, 107
predator-prey, 206–207, 206*f*, 207*f*

aerosols, 67
aerosol cans, 338, aerosol particles, 347

Africa
cattle in, 398
desertification in, 386
diamonds in, 421*f*
fertility rates in, 232*f*
gold in, 427, 427*f*
insect damage in, 389
malaria in, 520*f*
predators in, 22–23, 22*f*

Agenda 21, 534

age structure, 220, 220*f*, 238–239, 238*f*

aggregate, 417

agricultural revolution, 10, 10*f*

agriculture. *See also* **fish; food**
aquaculture, 396–397, 396*f*
biodiversity and, 243–244
climate change, 344, 344*f*
crop origins, 224, 224*f*
desertification, 386
efficiency of, 381
farmland management, 363, 363*f*

genetic engineering, 393–394, 393*f*, 400–401
green revolution, 383
habitat preservation and, 254, 254*f*
irrigation, 276, 278–279, 281, 281*f*, 387–388
land shortages, 227, 227*f*
livestock, 398–399, 398*f*, 399*f*
organic, 392
pest control, 389–392, 391*f*, 392*f*
rangelands, 364, 364*f*, 370–371
resistance in, 101, 101*f*
salinization, 388
soil conservation, 387, 387*f*
soil erosion, 386, 386*f*
soil fertility, 385, 385*f*, 388, 388*f*
solid waste from, 484
subsistence, 382
sustainable, 394, 394*f*
traditional *vs.* modern, 384, 388
water use in, 276, 278–279, 279*f*

AIDS (acquired immune deficiency syndrome), 519, 522

air pollution
acid precipitation, 128, 314–317, 324–325
from coal burning, 439, 439*f*
health effects of, 307–311
history of, 304, 305
indoor, 310–312, 311*f*
industrial, 307–308, 307*f*, 319, 319*f*
from mining, 422
motor vehicle emissions, 305–306, 306*f*, 308*f*, 440
primary and secondary pollutants, 303–304, 303*f*, 304*f*
smog, 308, 308*f*, 319, 319*f*
sources of, 304–308
temperature inversions, 308, 308*f*

air pressure, 68, 68*f*, 330

Alaska, 41, 291, 291*f*

alcohol fuel, 462

algal bloom
eutrophication, 175, 175*f*
fertilizers and, 128, 128*f*, 288, 288*f*

algebraic rearrangement, R19–R20

Allen, Charles, 164–165, 164*f*, 165*f*

allergic reaction, 401

alloy, 414

Alonso, Alfonso, 108–109, 108*f*

alternative energy, 466. *See also* **renewable energy**

altitude, 140, 141, 145, 145*f*

AMD (acid mine drainage), 422, 422*f*

amino acids, 379

amphibians
near lakes and ponds, 174, 174*f*
UV light and, 337, 337*f*
vertebrates, 107
worldwide decline in, 247

Anasazi, 233, 233*f*

angiosperm, 105, 105*f*

animal. *See also* **birds; fish; habitat; livestock;** *specific biomes*
characteristics of, 102*f*, 106–107, 106*f*, 107*f*
climate change and, 344, 344*f*
domesticated, 395
in estuaries, 180
genetically engineered, 400
invertebrates, 106, 106*f*
livestock, 398–399, 398*f*, 399*f*
mining and, 422
raptor rehabilitation, 548–549, 548*f*, 549*f*
vertebrates, 107, 107*f*

Antarctic Bottom Water, 78

Antarctic ecosystem, 185. *See also* **polar region**

antibiotic resistance, 101, 521

ants, 258–259

apatite, 127

aquaculture, 396–397, 396*f*

aquatic ecosystem, 173–178. *See also* **coastal wetland; marine ecosystem; ocean**
acid precipitation and, 316, 316*f*
algal blooms in, 128, 128*f*, 175, 175*f*, 288
characteristics of, 173
food chains and webs in, 120–121, 122, 122*f*
freshwater wetlands, 175–177, 175*f*, 176*f*, 177*f*
lakes and ponds, 174–175, 174*f*, 175*f*
rivers, 178, 178*f*

aqueduct, 279–280, 279*f*

aquifer. *See also* **groundwater**
anatomy of, 274*f*–275*f*
contamination of, 289–290, 290*f*
effects of climate change on, 343–344
location of, U.S., 79*f*, 272*f*
Ogallala, 272–273, 272*f*

porosity and permeability of, 273, 274*f*–275*f*
recharge zones, 79, 274, 275*f*

archaea, 102, 102*f*

architect, environmental, R36–R37

Arctic. *See* **polar region**

Arctic Ocean, 75, 75*f*, 185

Arendt, Randall, 366–367

Argentina, 523

arsenic, 514

artificial eutrophication, 288, 288*f*

artificial selection, 100, 100*f*

asbestos, 312, 312*f*

asthenosphere, 61, 61*f*

Atlantic Ocean, 75, 75*f*

atmosphere, 67–72. *See also* **air pollution; climate**
air movement in, 352–353
air pressure, 68, 68*f*, 330
carbon dioxide in, 125, 340, 340*f*
composition of, 67–68, 67*f*
in Earth system, 59, 59*f*
global air circulation, 252–253, 329–331, 329*f*, 331*f*
greenhouse effect, 72, 72*f*, 339–341, 339*f*, 340*f*
heating of, 70–71, 70*f*–71*f*
layers of, 67*f*, 68–69, 68*f*
temperature inversions, 308, 308*f*

atomic number, R24

atomic structure, R24

Attenborough, David, 544*f*, 545*f*

aurora borealis, 68*f*, 69

Australia, 200, 200*f*

automobile
carbon dioxide from, R8
emissions from, 305–306, 306*f*, 308*f*, 440
fuel cells in, 306, 468, 468*f*
hybrid, 306, 469, 469*f*
pollution regulation, 306, 306*f*, 440
urban sprawl, 359, 359*f*
zero-emission, 306

autotrophs, 118, 118*f*

averages, 39

B

baby boom, 221*f*

Bacillus thuringiensis (Bt), 391, 393, 393*f*

CITES (Convention on International Trade in Endangered Species), 256, 256f, 534

Clean Air Act (1970), 305, 307

Clean Water Act (1972), 292–293, 293t, 305, 424

climate, 327–334
altitude and, 145, 145f
biomes and, 144–145, 144f, 145f
climate regions, North America, R60f–R61f, R70f
deforestation and, 150
global air circulation, 252–253, 329–331, 329f, 331f
greenhouse effect and, 72, 72f, 339–341, 339f, 340f
latitude and, 327, 328, 328f
ocean circulation patterns, 332, 332f
seasons and, 334
sun cycle and, 333, 333f
topography and, 327, 333, 333f
volcanic eruptions and, 65, 333
weather vs., 327

climate change, 339–345
attempts to slow, 345, 345f, 534
consequences of, 342–344, 343f
global warming, 341–342, 341f, 342f, 522f
greenhouse effect, 72, 72f, 339–341, 339f, 340f
ice core data on, 330–331, 330f, 331f, 340
modeling, 341–342, 342f
recent findings on, 35, 344, 347

climate scientist, 346–347, 346f, R40–R41

climatogram, 170–171, 170f

climax community, 132

closed system, 12, 81, 81f, 352–353, 353f

cloud, polar stratospheric, 336, 346, 346f

coal
electricity from, 304, 324, 436, 439, 439f
formation of, 438
mining, 417, 420, 424, 424f
pollution from, 341, 422
sea coal, 305

coal-burning power plant, 304, 324, 341, 436, 436f

coastal wetland, 179–182
barrier islands, 182, 182f, 187
biodiversity in, 249

coral reefs, 92f, 93, 183, 183f, 249
estuaries, 179–181, 179f
mangrove swamps, 182, 182f
rising sea levels and, 343
salt marshes, 182
storm surge and, 74–75, 75f

cod fish, 343

coevolution, 100, 100f, 209, R8

cogeneration, 470

Colorado River, 280

coloration, warning, 206

commensalism, 204f, 209, 209f

community, 96, 130

competition, 201, 204–205, 204f, 205f, R9

compost, 388, 490, R52–R53

compound, R25

Comprehensive Response, Compensation, and Liability Act (CERCLA), 293f, 424, 494

computer model, 342

concept mapping, R14

conceptual model, 43, 43f

condensation, 73, 73f, 269, 269f

condor, 252, 252f

conduction, 70, 70f

conifer, 105, 105f, 154, 154f

conservation. See also renewable energy
of aquifers, 272–273
of energy, 470–471, 470f, 471f
energy efficiency, 468–470, 469f, R47
of habitats and ecosystems, 108–109, 109f, 254–257, 254f, 255f
in planning, 366–367, 367f, 542
private efforts in, 538
recycling, 489–490, 489f, 491, 499, R46
of soil, 387, 387f
student conservation clubs, 548–549, 548f, 549f
of water, 281–282, 281f, 282f, R8, R56

consumer, 118, 118f

consumer choice, 18–19, 18f, 547, R50–R51

content frame, R13

contour plowing, 387, 387f

control group, 33

convection, 70, 71f

Convention on International Trade in Endangered Species (CITES), 256, 256f, 534

copper mining, 14, 14f, 422f, 432–433

coral bleaching, 183

coral polyp, 183, 183f

coral reef
critical biodiversity in, 249
as ecosystems, 92f, 93, 183, 183f
latitude and, 328
threat to, 183

core, 61, 61f

correlations, 35, 35f, 37

cost-benefit analysis, 17

coyotes, 205

critical biodiversity areas, 248–249, 248f, 249f. See also biodiversity

Cronin, John, 544f

crop origin, 224, 224f. See also agriculture

crop rotation, 389

cross-species transfer, 523

cruise ship discharge, 291

crust, 60, 61f

Cryptosporidium, 286

Cuyahoga River, 292, 292f

cyanide heap leaching, 417, 417f

cycle diagrams, R12

D

dam removal, 12–13, 13f

dams, 280–281, 280f, 463–464, 463f, 541

Darwin, Charles, 97–98, 98f, 197. See also evolution

data, 34, 34f

DDT
in aquatic food chains, 120–121, 120f, 121f
biological magnification of, 120–121, 292, 292f
endangered species and, 247, 545
persistence of, 390

decibel (dB), 312, 312f

decision making, 45–49, 45f, 46f, 47f, 48f

decomposer
in the benthic zone, 173–174, 174f
in ecosystems, 119, 119f

in the nitrogen cycle, 126–127
in tropical rain forests, 147

deep-well injection, 496, 497f

deforestation, 9, 150–151, 150f, 151f, 366

demographic transition, 223–224, 223f, 224f

demography, 219–221. See also population (human)

density, 198, 198f

density-dependent regulation, 202, 202f

desalination, 283, 283f

desert biome, 160–161, 160f, 161f

desertification, 386

deserts, latitude and, 329

developed vs. developing countries, 18–19, 18f, 19f, 228–229, 229f

diagrams, 32f, 43, 43f, R12–R14

diatoms, 104

diet, 380, 380f. See also food

disease. See also human health; specific diseases
cross-species transfers, 523
deaths from, 519f
environment and, 519, 519f, 521–523, 522f
global warming and, 343
infectious, 519, 519f, 522
pollution and, 226–227, 226f, 510f, 511
vector-borne, 522, 522f
waterborne, 520

dispersion, 198, 198f

dissolved oxygen, 288, 289

dissolved solids, 76, 76f

distributions, 39, 39f

diversity, levels of, 242. See also biodiversity

DNA, 42, 42f, 337

domain, 102, 102f

domesticated animal, 395. See also animals; livestock

Doppler radar, 134f

dose, 512

dose-response curve, 512, 512f

dredging, 419, 419f, 422

drinking water, 276–277, 276f

drip irrigation, 281, 281f, 387

drought, 35, 35f, 344, 344f

dust storm, 514, 514f

dwarf wedge mussel, 5f, 31–33, 32f, 38–39, 38f

species
counting, 264–265
definition of, 95
endangered or threatened, 245–246, 246*f*, 255, 255*f*
endemic, 248
estimating loss of, 248
exotic, 247, 247*f*
extinct, 246*f*
genetic diversity, 242, 243, 243*f*
keystone, 242, 242*f*
legal protection, 255–257
number of, 241, 241*f*
preserving, 252–253, 252*f*, 253*f*
recovery plans, 255
tropical rain forests, 149, 149*f*

species interaction
commensalism, 204*f*, 209, 209*f*
competition, 201, 204–205, 204*f*, 205*f*, R9
mutualism, 204*f*, 208, 208*f*
parasitism, 204*f*, 208, 208*f*
predation, 204*f*, 206–207, 206*f*, 207*f*

species recovery plan, 255

spot map, 37*f*

state government, 543

statistical population, 38, 38*f*, 40

statistics, 38–41, 38*f*, 39*f*, 41*f*

steppes, 156, 156*f*, 157*f*

St. Helens, Mount, 65, 65*f*, 130, 130*f*, 131*f*

Stoddart, Marion, 544*f*

storm surge, 74

stratosphere, 68*f*, 69, 333, 335–338, 346–347

Student Conservation Association (SCA), 549

submarine volcano, 74

subsidence, 423, 423*f*

subsistence farmer, 382

subsurface mining, 416, 416*f*

suburban sprawl, 227, 227*f*

succession. *See* **ecological succession**

succulents, 161, 161*f*

sulfur dioxide, 304*f*, 315, 319, 324

sulfur oxide
acid precipitation from, 315, 315*f*, 324
climate change and, 342*f*
in U.S. air pollution, 303*f*, 304*f*, 319

sun. *See* **solar energy**

sun cycle, 333, 333*f*

Superfund (CERCLA), 293*f*, 424, 494

supply and demand, 17, 17*f*

surface impoundment, 496

surface mining, 417–418, 417*f*

Surface Mining Control and Reclamation Act of 1977 (SMCRA), 424

surface water, 270

survivorship, 220, 220*f*

sustainability, 21, 394, 394*f*, 533–534

swamp, 175, 177, 177*f*, 182, 182*f*

symbiosis, 209

taiga biome, 153–154, 153*f*, 154*f*

Tasmanian tiger, 15, 15*f*

tectonic plates, 62, 62*f*, 63*f*

temperate deciduous forest, 152–153, 152*f*

temperate grassland, 156–158, 157*f*, 158*f*, 159*f*

temperate rain forest, 151, 151*f*

temperature
atmospheric, 68–69, 68*f*
biomes and, 144, 144*f*
in cities, 360, 360*f*
global surface, 341, 341*f*
ice core data on, 330–331, 330*f*
oceanic, 76–77, 76*f*

temperature inversion, 308, 308*f*

Teotihuacan, 361

terracing, 387*f*

territories, 201

Thailand, 228–229, 228*f*

thermal pollution, 289, 289*f*

thermal radiation, 70–71, 70*f*–71*f*

thermocline, 76, 76*f*

thermosphere, 69

threatened species, 245–246, 246*f*, 255

Three Gorges Dam, 294–295, 294*f*, 295*f*, 520

Three Mile Island, 447

threshold dose, 512

tidal power, 466, 466*f*

titanium, 414*f*

topographic map, 50, 50*f*, R58*f*–R59*f*, R68*f*–R69*f*

topography, climate and, 333, 333*f*

topsoil, 385, 385*f*

toxicology, 512, 512*f*

trade winds, 329*f*, 331

Tragedy of the Commons, 16–17, 16*f*, 537

transpiration, 150

transportation, 283, 362, 362*f*

trash. *See* **solid waste**

tree ring data, 35, 35*f*

tributary, 79, 79*f*

trophic level, 122–123, 122*f*

tropical rain forest, 146–150
biodiversity in, 149, 149*f*, 248–249, 248*f*, 249*f*
climate in, 146
layers of, 148, 148*f*
location of, 146, 147*f*

tropical seasonal forest, 155

tropopause, 67*f*

troposphere, 68, 68*f*, 71

Troy, fall of, 9

tsunamis, 74

tuberculosis (TB), 521

tube worm, 118, 118*f*

tundra biome, 144*f*, 162–163, 162*f*, 163*f*

turbine, 436, 436*f*, 445*f*

two-column notes, R13

ultraviolet (UV) **radiation**
chlorofluorocarbons and, 335, 335*f*
human health and, 337, 337*f*
ozone and, 69, 335, 335*f*
plant and animal impacts of, 337, 337*f*
sun cycle and, 333

underground storage tank, 289–290

understory vegetation, 108–109, 148, 148*f*

unfunded mandate, 541

unit conversions, R32

United Nations (UN), 228, 230

United States. *See also* **regulations**
acid precipitation, 316–317, 317*f*
aquifers, 79*f*

biodiversity, 251, 251*f*
climate regions, R68*f*
diet, 380
ecological footprint, 19, 19*f*, R10
ecosystem services, 357
electricity, 439*f*
energy use, 437, 437*f*, 439*f*
environmental policies, 539–543, 540*f*
fertility rate, 221, 221*f*
fossil fuel deposits, 438, 438*f*, R69*f*
geothermal power, 464
hazardous waste, 494, 494*f*
irrigation, 279
landfill capacity, 486*f*
land use map, R71*f*
mineral and energy resources, R70*f*
national parks, 368, 368*f*
nuclear waste, 500–501
population growth, 221, 221*f*
relief map, R66*f*–R67*f*
species protection, 255, 255*f*
urbanization, 358–359, 358*f*
water quality, 292–293, 293*f*
water use, 276–277, 277*f*
wetlands, 176*f*, 186*f*

uranium, 444, 444*f*, 446*f*

urban, 355

urban crisis, 359, 359*f*

urbanization, 227, 358–360
conservation planning in, 366–367, 367*f*
heat islands, 360, 360*f*
land-use planning, 361–362, 361*f*, 542
marginal lands, 360, 360*f*
metropolitan areas, 358, 358*f*
urban crisis, 359, 359*f*
urban sprawl, 359, 359*f*

urban land, 355, 355*f*, 357, 357*f*

urban planning, 361–362, 361*f*, 542

urban sprawl, 359, 359*f*

UV radiation. *See* **ultraviolet** (UV) **radiation**

values, 45, 45*f*, 48–49, 48*f*

variable, 33

vectors, 520, 522, 522*f*

vegetation. *See* **plant**

Venn diagram, R14

vertebrates, 107, 107*f*

viruses, 522